HISTORICAL MEMORANDA
CONCERNING
PERSONS AND PLACES IN OLD DOVER NEW HAMPSHIRE

Collected by
Rev. Dr. Alonzo Hall Quint, and Others, and Published
in the *Dover Enquirer* From 1850 to 1888

Republished, in Part, in the *Dover Enquirer* From
December 10, 1897 to January 5, 1900

Edited by
John Scales, A. B., A. M.
of Dover, N.H.

Avi memorantur avorrum.

Volume One

HERITAGE BOOKS
2007

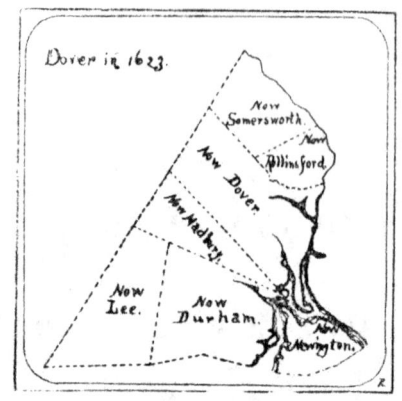

TOWNS WHICH CONSTITUTE OLD DOVER.

The above cut represents the territory of Old Dover as it was till 1713, when Newington was cut off; a few years later Durham was separated from the old town; then Somersworth and finally Madbury and Lee, a few years before the Revolution.

HERITAGE BOOKS
AN IMPRINT OF HERITAGE BOOKS, INC.

Books, CDs, and more—Worldwide

For our listing of thousands of titles see our website
at
www.HeritageBooks.com

A Facsimile Reprint
Published 2006 by
HERITAGE BOOKS, INC.
Publishing Division
65 East Main Street, Westminster, Maryland 21157-5026

Originally published
DOVER, N.H.
MARCH 1900

— Publisher's Notice —
In reprints such as this, it is often not possible to remove blemishes from the original. We feel the contents of this book warrant its reissue despite these blemishes and hope you will agree and read it with pleasure.

International Standard Book Number: 978-0-7884-4382-8

PREFACE.

In December 1897 was commenced the republication of the Historical Memoranda in the DOVER ENQUIRER that began to appear in that paper in 1850; this work was begun at the earnest request of Librarians of many public libraries, and others, who wished to get access to this valuable material which the late Rev. Dr Alonzo Hall Quint had collected during nearly forty years.

As the matter was printed from week to week in the ENQUIRER, the same type was used to print four pages of the book week by week, and the result is the book you have in hand. The ENQUIRER was sold to Cooke & Stone in May 1899, and they continued the publication weekly till late in October, copy being furnished them by the writer of this preface; from that time till their failure in January, 1900, when the ENQUIRER passed into new hands, the Memoranda was published at irregular periods finally reaching ninety-seven numbers.

The Editor then took the matter in hand and had printed forty pages additional in book form, which brings forth to the public the larger part of the most valuable of the Memoranda.

The Editor has bestowed much labor and has had no little anxiety, to accomplish what has been done, and yet there is one half as much left, not touched, as is included in this book, In order to make this remaining part accessible, in some small degree, the Editor gives below a list of the unpublished numbers, their subject matter, and the dates of the old ENQUIRERS in which they appeared, all of which are on file in the Public Library, Dover, N. H,

132   Pitman family March 28, 1854.

133, 146, 212, 242, 249, 254, 258; Tuttle family April 4, Nov. 28, 1854; July 5, 1860; March 16, 1865; Nov. 8, 1866; April 16, and Nov. 5, 1868.

143.   Barrington Settlement of, Oct. 3, 1854.

146½, 147, 147½   Foss family, Dec. 5, and 19, 1854; Jan. 4, 1855.

150, 151.   Clements family April 26, May 3, 1855.

152.   Province fortifications, May 17, 1855.

164   Items from records of First Church in Boston and Plymouth, Oct. 2, 1856.

165.   Items from Somersworth Church Jan. 1, 1857.

II

166—169. Wingate family Jan. 8, 15, 29, Feb. 12 and Nov. 26, 1857.
192. Austin family, May 19, 1859.
197—200. Dover under Massachusetts government, July 7, 14, 28, Aug. 4, 1859.
201. Ham family in Portsmouth, Sept 22, 1859.
202—204. Randall family, Sept. 29, Oct. 6 and 13, 1859.
205. Atkinson Silver waiter, list of names on it, Dec. 1, 1859.
206. Biographical sketch of Peter Levius, Dec. 29, 1859.
207—209. Biographical sketch of Rev. William Waldron of Boston, May 3, 10, and 17, 1860
211. Items of Dover news in the N. H. Gazette, of 1756—1760, with biographical sketch of Capt. Robert Oram, June 7, 1860.
214—219. Extracts from the first newspaper published in Dover, 1790-1800; Jan. 31, Feb. 21, May 9, and 30, July 18, Sept. 12, 1861.
222. Concerning the hanging of Elisha Thomas for murder, in 1788, the first man who was hung in Dover, May 8, 1862.
223. Items of Dover News in Salem Mercury, 1788; May 22, 1862.
224. Spinney family, Feb 19, 1863.
231. Gage family, Nov. 26, 1863.
233—238. Concerning the Factory Square, with biographical sketches of men who were engaged in business there; March 24, May 5, June 2, July 7, Sept. 1, 1864.
239, 240. Edgerly family, Dec. 8, 22, 1864.
245. Concerning American Barouets, April 19, 1866.

246, 248. Extracts from N. H. Council records from 1692 to 1705, concerning Dover officers and soldiers during the Indian troubles, July 19, and Aug. 30, 1866.
250, 251 Wallingford family, Feb. 21, Aug. 21, 1867.
253. Meserve family, Dec. 19, 1867.
255. Nute family, April 30, 1868.
256. Dore family, June 4, 1868.
257. Merrow family, July 2 and 9, 1868.
261. Wiggin family, April 8, 15, 22, 29, 1869.
262. Biographical sketch of Col. Nathaniel Meserve, June 10, 1869.
263. Biographical sketch of Capt. Thomas Wiggin, July 1, and of Job Clements, Esq., July 15, 1869.
264. Biographical sketches of Capt. Samuel Tibbetts and, Capt. Philip Cromwell, Nov. 11, 1864.
265. Cloutman family, Nov. 18, 1869
266. Early judiciary of Dover, Feb. 9, 1871.
268, 269. Concerning Rev. George Burdett and Archibishop Laud, Nov. 11 and 18, 1875
273 Fresh Creek land grants, Dec. 23, 1875
274. Land grant along the Newichawannock river, Dec. 30, 1875.
275. Wentworth land grants in Rollinsford, Jan 6, 1876.
276. Near the Wentworth grants, Jan. 13, 1876.
277, 278. Hayes family, Jan. 20 and 27, 1876
279. Hanson family in England, Feb. 3, 1876.
280 281. Henry Mellin's "Bache-

III

lors of Dover," Feb. 10, 17, 1876.

282—288. C ncerning the old Dover Hotel and its owners, Hanson, Titcomb, Sever, Gage, Hodgdon, Wyatt, March and Wrisley, Feb. 24 March 2, 16 and 30, April 13, May 4 and 11, 1876

289—295. Ricker family, Dec. 7, 21 and 28, 1876, Jan. 25, Feb. 1 and 8, 1877.

292. Rev. George Burdett before emigration, Jan. 18, 1877.

296—303. Second edition of Hall genealogy, March 22, to May 10, 1877.

307. Downs family, Aug. 2, 1877.

314 Roll of Dover soldiers at Louisburg in 1745, Jan. 31, 1878.

327—330. Town Records of various dates in Enquirers between Nov 28 1878 and February 1879.

331—332. Heard family, March 1879

333—336 Town Records, April and May 1879

337—338. Church family, May and June 1879.

339—351. Town Records, June and July 1879.

352—355. These numbers are a revised edition of Nos. 184-5 concerning John Waldron of Dover, N. H, who is said to have been kidnapped by Capt. John Heard of Dover, a shipmaster who found him in the streets of an English seaport; July and August, 1879

356—360. Town Records from fragments of papers for the years 1675—1677, August 1879.

361—366. Concerning mill privileges from 1647 to 1669, Sept. 1879

367—368 A Dover Tax list for 1664

—1665, October 1879.

369. Concerning ancient school masters in Dover, beginning with Rev. Hanserd Knollys, 1638; Rev. Daniel Maud, 1642; Mr. Charles Buckner, 1658; Rev. John Reyner, 1660; John Sullivan, 1723; he was father of Gen. John Sullivan; Major Samuel Hale, 1745; Dr. Samuel Wigglesworth, 1752; Rev. Dr. Jesse Appleton, 1792, who was later President of Bowdoin college; Rev. Robert Gray, 1800; 25 Dec. 1879.

370. Is a copy of the letter from Boston in June 1689, sent by the Council to warn Major Walderne of the impending danger from an attack by the Indians; the letter arrived a day too late to save the village from destruction Jan 1, 1880.

371. Dover tax list for 1666, Feb. 19 1880.

372 A list of taverns on the various stage routes in New Hampshire in 1772, Feb. 26, 1880.

373—374. Dover Tax lists for 1666 and 1677, March 18 and 25, 1880.

375. Col. Amos Cogswell, one of Dover's Revolutionary soldiers, and his descendants in South Dakota, April 1880.

376—380, 389—404. History of the Old Nail Factory at Cochecho, and biographical sketches of men who were connected with it. Published at various dates between May 27 and July 23 1880; and Sept. 18. 25 1885.

381 Extracts from the New Hampshire Annual Register for 1772, showing list of the officers of the Provincial government Nov. 25, 1880

382—387. Kimball family, Augus

1880

388. Contributed by Benjamin Titcomb Whitehouse, being extracts from notes made in ancient almanacs by Mr. Samuel Emerson. Jan. 23, 1885.

405—407 Protestant Episcopal Church in Dover, by Herman W. Stevens beginning Oct. 2, 1885.

409—414. Concerning Durham after its separation from Dover, beginning Nov. 20, 1885.

415—421. Town Records of various dates from 1674 to 1717, December 1885, Jan. 1886.

422. Concerning the capture of Fort William and Mary in December 1774; by Miss Mary P. Thompson, July 16, 1886.

423. Rev. Dr. Quint's criticism of Miss Thompson's article on the capture of Fort William and Mary, Sept. 17 1886.

424 Miss Thompson's reply to Dr. Quint's criticism of her article on the capture of the fort, Oct. 1, 1886.

425. Dr. Quint's rejoinder to Memoranda No. 424

426—429, 433, 434. Concerning the Burnham Garrison in Durham, by Miss Mary P. Thompson, April and May 1888

430—432, 435, 436. Durham Meeting Houses; these numbers are by Dr. Quint and Miss Thompson, who have a lively discussion regarding the locations, etc., April and May 1888.

437. Concerning Francis Mathews, by Miss Thompson, June 1888

438--440. Edward Leathers of Dover and his descendants, September 1888

This was the last Memoranda contributed by Rev. Dr. Quint; his first number was published thirty-eight years before that. Lucien Thompson, Esq, contributed several numbers on the Congregational Church in Durham beginning Feb. 17, 1896 and closing June 9 of that year The last Memoranda published was Nov. 9, 1896 being an article by Mr. Thompson on the Woodman garrison, which was destroyed by fire Nov. 8, of that year. Thus the DOVER ENQUIRER during a half century gave to the public a series of historical articles, whose value far surpasses all that has appeared in other papers of the State during that period. I was Editor of the ENQUIRER from May 1883 to May 1899.

JOHN SCALES

Dover, N H., March 1900.

DOVER HISTORICAL MEMORANDA.

Republished From the Dover Enquirer, Beginning July 30, 1850.

At the urgent request from various sources we commence today the republication of the Dover Historical Memoranda that have appeared in the Dover Enquirer from time to time since 1850. The first number was published July 30, 1850; the first nine numbers relate to the town officers and were arranged by George Wadleigh, Esq., then editor and publisher of the Enquirer. His introduction was as follows:

John Scales.
Dover, N. H., Dec. 3, 1897.

The oldest record extant of any Public Town Meeting in Dover, is found in a book entitled "No. 7 old Book of Records."—a fact which indicates that several volumes of the early records are lost. The meeting was held for the choice of Recorder, or Town Clerk, on the 1st day of October, 1647, and Wm. Pomfrett was chosen. The records show that he continued to serve in that capacity until 1683, and probably till 1689, in which year John Tuttle was chosen his successor. The next meeting of which there is any record was for the choice of "Townsmen for the prudential affairs of the Town," and was holden the 27th day of September 1648. Ambrose Gibbons, Richard Waldron, Thomas Layton, Anthony Emery and Wm. Pomfrett were chosen.

The first Moderator of a Town Meeting whose name is recorded is that of "Elder Wentworth," under date of 1661.

The first Representative chosen to the General Court from this town, it appears by Belknap's History, was Edward Starbuck, who was elected in 1643. William Hilton was chosen in 1644; William Heath in 1645, William Waldron and Edward Starbuck in 1646. In 1647-8-9 no Representatives appear to have been chosen, or if there was the record is lost. The following are the names of the Town Clerks, Representatives, and Townsmen, or Selectmen, chosen from 1650 to 1659. The probabilities are that officers once chosen continued to serve until their successors were elected.

Instead of giving the first nine numbers in the form in which they originally were arranged by Mr. Wadleigh, we give the revised and corrected list as made by Rev. Dr. A. H. Quint, in 1891, for the City Government, which omits nothing that the first had and adds much to it.

J. S.

TOWN CLERKS.

The list of clerks is doubtless complete, but early dates are scarce.

1. William Walderne. Perhaps from 1635; certainly from Dec. 1641, until his death, Sept. 1646.

2. George Smith. Appointed by Massachusetts in Nov. 1646, and served one year.

3. William Pomfrett. Chosen by the town Nov. 1647; served certainly into 1665, and perhaps to 1670. In his writing is our oldest extant volume of our records, and it is marked "No. 7" on its parchment cover.

4. Deacon John Hall. Certainly in 1670, perhaps earlier; served into 1679, doubtless later, and perhaps to 1685. He had been chosen clerk by the town 6 June 1659, but the Court refused to swear him into office.

5. John Evans. Probably chosen early in 1686. A vote of 13 Sept. 1686, fixed his pay, and vote of Oct. 1686 orders that all town books and papers be brought to the selectmen, to be by them delivered to "John Evans the towne clerke." He probably served until his murder by the Indians, 28 June 1689.

6. John Ham. He signed the record of the election of his successor, 12 March 1693-4.

7. John Tuttle. Chosen unanimously, 12 March 1693-4; was in office in 1719, and probably until his death, which took place in 1719 or 1720.

8. Thomas Tebbetts. Chosen 25 April 1720, and may have been a little earlier; was in office 8 Sept. 1727.

9. Paul Gerrish. From 15 March 1727-8 until his death 6 June 1743.

10. Joseph Hanson. From 27 June 1743 until into 1758, and apparently until his death, 5 Sept. 1758.

11. Ephraim Hanson, son of the last preceding. From 18 Sept. 1758 until 1772, and apparently until his death, 24 March 1772.

12. Thomas Westbrook Waldron. From 30 March 1772 until his death, 3 April 1785.

13. John Burnham Hanson, brother of Ephraim above. From 25 April 1785 until his death, 17 Dec. 1788.

14. Nathaniel Cooper. From 29 Dec. 1788 until his death, March 1795.

15. Walter Cooper, son of the last preceding. From 30 March 1795 until his resignation, which took effect 4 Nov. 1799.

16. Dominicus Hanson, grandson of Joseph above. From 4 Nov. 1799 until his resignation, 29 Oct. 1816.

17. Andrew Pierce. From 4 Nov. 1816 until election of successor.

18. James Richardson. From 14 March 1820 until election of successor.

19. Charles Young. From 11 March 1836 until election of successor.

20. George Piper. From 15 March 1838 until election of successor.

21. Thomas Stackpole. From 18 March 1843 until election of successor.

22. George Thomas Wentworth. From 13 March 1845 until election of successor.

23. Charles Emery Soule. From 14 March 1850; resigned 31 Dec. 1852.

24. Charles Augustus Tufts, great-great-grandson of Joseph Hanson above. Appointed by the selectmen 5 January 1853; served until election of successor.

25. Amasa Roberts. From 12 March 1853 until the organization of the city government 25 March 1856.

SELECTMEN.

1647, Nov.—Ambrose Gibbons, William Pomfrett, Anthony Emery, Richard Walderne, Thomas Layton.

1648, Nov. 27. Ambrose Gibbons, Richard Walderne, Thomas Layton, Anthony Emery, William Pomfrett.

1649, 1650. No record.

1651, Dec. 8. Capt. Richard Walderne, Mr. Valentine Hill, Henry Lankstaff, William Wentworth, William Furber.

1652-54 No record.

1655. Hatevil Nutter, John Bickfo·d, Henry Lankster, Job Clements, and probably one more.

1656. No record.

1657, March 30. Valentine Hill, Elder William Wentworth, Ralph Hall, William Furber.

1658, April 19. Capt. Ralph Hall, Thomas Layton, Thomas Canney, Thomas Footman, Robert Burnum.

1659, June 6. Lieut. Ralph Hall, James Nute, Richard Otis, Robert Burnum, Henry Lankster.

1660, June 13. Elder William Wentworth, Peter Coffin, Deacon John Hall, William Beard, Robert Burnum.

1661, June 5. Elder Hatevil Nutter, Ralph Hall, William Furber, John Goddard, Thomas Beard.

1662, June 15. William Pomfrett, William Beard, John Woodman, Richard Walderne, Ralph Hall.

1663, April 20. Capt. Richard Walderne, Ralph Hall, Ens. John Davis, Henry Lankster, John Bickford, sen.

1664, April 28. Capt. Richard Walderne, Henry Lankster, Sarg. John Roberts, Ens. John Davis, Elder William Wentworth.

1665. The same.

1666, April 2. Capt. Richard Walderne, Anthony Nutter, Robert Burnum, John Martin, Job Clements.

1667, April 8. Capt. Richard Walderne, Job Clements, Sarg. William Furber, Ens. John Davis, Corporal Anthony Nutter.

1668, April 20. Capt. Richard Walderne, Elder William Wentworth, Robert Burnum, Lieut. Peter Coffin, Sarg. John Roberts.

1669, May 3. Capt. Richard Walderne, Henry Lankster, Lieut. Peter Coffin, Job Clements, Robert Burnum.

1670, March 7. William Furber, William Wentworth, Philip Cromwell, Thomas Roberts, Jr., John Woodman.

1671, March 13. Capt. Richard Walderne, Philip Cromwell, Thos. Roberts, Jr., Wm. Furber, Ens. John Davis.

1672, March 4. Capt. Richard Walderne, Lieut. Peter Coffin, Henry Lankster, Robert Burnum, Anthony Nutter.

1673. Month lost. Capt. Richard Walderne, Arthony Nutter, John Roberts, Robert Burnum, John Gerrish.

1674, March 2. Capt. Richard Walderne, John Roberts, Anthony Nutter, John Wingett, John Gerrish, Robert Burnum, John Woodman.

1675. Capt. Richard Walderne, Job Clements, Peter Coffin, Anthony Nutter, John Woodman.

1676. John Clements, Philip Cromwell, Anthony Nutter, and doubtless two others.

1677, March 5. Capt. Richard Walderne, Job Clements, Lieut. Anthony Nutter, Ens. John Davis, Sarg. John Roberts.

1678—1685—No record.

1686. John Woodman, Thomas Edgerly, Nicholas Harrison, John Winget, John Tuttle.

1687, Aug. 10. John Winget, John Tuttle, William Furber, Thomas Chesley, sen., John Woodman.

1688, May 21. John Tuttle, Thomas Chesley, William Furbur, Tristram Coffin, Thomas Edgerly, James Huckins.

1689—1693. No record.

1694, April 16. Corporal Thomas Roberts, Samuel Heard, John Bickford, Jeremiah Burnum. Capt. John Woodman.

1695, April 22. Capt. John Gerrish, Zacharias Field, Nathaniel Hill, Thomas Chesley, sen.. Joseph Meader,

1696, April 27. Capt. John Gerrish, Lieut. William Furber, Corporal Thomas Tebbets, Ens. Stephen Jones, Sarg. Thomas Downs, Thomas Bickford.

1697. No record.

1698. James Davis, Ezekiel Wentworth, Nathaniel Hill, and doubtless two others.

1699, May 30. Ens. Thomas Tebbets, Nathaniel Heard, Joseph Hill, Joseph Smith, Thomas Edgerly.

1700, 1701. Not certain. A very imperfect record probably belongs to one of these years, which gives John Drew [Tristram] Heard,....[Sm]ith, sen.,—Davis.—[B]ickford.

1702, April 6. Samuel Tebbetts, John Meader, Jr., Joseph Jones, Ezekiel Wentworth, John Downing.

1703, April 5. Thomas Roberts, sen., Tobias Hanson, Joseph Jones, Frances Mathes, John Dam. Jones and Mathes refused to serve, and Samuel Chesley and Robert Huckins were chosen April 17.

1704, April 25. Sarg. Thomas Roberts William Frost, Francis Mathes, Capt. Samuel Chesley, John Dam.

1705, April 7. Samuel Emerson, Richard Waldron, Esq., Capt. John Knight, Joseph Meader, Jonathan Woodman.

1706, April 22. Thomas Roberts, sen., Richard Waldron, Joseph Jones, Capt. John Knight, Capt. Samuel Chesley.

From this time the elections were in May, until 1717, and perhaps later.

1707, 1708, 1709, 1710. Thomas Roberts, sen., Richard Waldron, Capt. John Knight, Joseph Jones, Sarg. Francis Mathes.

1711. Sarg. Joseph Roberts, Richard Waldron, John Smith, sen., Sarg. Joseph Meader, Capt. John Knight.

1712. Joseph Roberts, Richard Waldron, John Smith, Joseph Meader, sen., John Smith, sen. Lieut. John Downing.

1713. Lieut. Joseph Roberts, Col. Richard Waldron, Sarg. Joseph Meader, sen., John Smith, sen. Lieut. John Downing.

Newington, separated from Dover held its first meeting 6 Aug. 1713.

1714. Lieut. Joseph Roberts, Col. Richard Waldron, Mr. Joseph Jones, Ens. Francis Mathes, Lieut. John Downing.

1715. Capt. Thomas Tebbets, Tobias Hanson, Joseph Meader, John Amblar, Sarg. Thomas Roberts.

1716. Capt. Thomas Tebbets, Col. Richard Waldron, Ens. Paul Wentworth, Sarg. Joseph Meader, Mr. John Amblar.

1717. Capt. Thomas Tebbets, Col. Richard Waldron, Ens. Paul Wentworth, Lieut. Joseph Jones, Mr. Philip Chesley.

1718, 1719. No record.

1720, May 26. Thomas Tebbets, Thomas Roberts, Tobias Hanson, John Smith, Francis Mathes.

1721. Joseph Roberts, Tobias Hanson, Timothy Robinson, and doubtless two others.

1722, 1723. No record.

1724. Stephen Jones, John Smith, Benjamin Wentworth, Nicholas Hartford, and probably one other.

1725. Francis Mathes, James Nute, John Smith and doubtless two others.

1726. Nicholas Hartford, James Nute, Francis Mathes and doubtless two others.

1727 May 5. Paul Wentworth, Nicholas Hartford, Samuel Smith, James Nute, Francis Mathes.

From this time (and perhaps earlier) the elections were invariably in March.

1728. Nicholas Hartford, Thomas Hanson, James Nute, Capt. Francis Mathes, Samuel Smith.

1729. John Canney, Capt. Paul Wentworth, Capt. Stephen Jones, Jonathan Thomson, John Winget.

1730. Nicholas Hartford, Lieut. John Wingett, Capt. Stephen Jones, Capt. Paul Wentworth, Jonathan Thompson.

1731. Paul Wentworth, Nicholas Hartford, Lieut. John Wingett, Capt. Francis Mathes, Lieut. Samuel Smith.

1732. Capt. Thomas Millet, Lieut. John Wingett, Paul Wentworth, Capt. Francis Mathes, Lieut. Samuel Smith.

Durham was separated from Dover 15 May 1732.

1733. Nicholas Hartford, Tobias Hanson, Lieut. James Davis, Paul Wentworth, Capt. Thomas Wallingford.

1734, 1735. Capt. Thomas Millet, Lieut. John Winget, Paul Wentworth; under vote to have but three.

1736, 1737, 1738. Capt. Thomas Millet, Lieut. John Winget, Capt. Paul Wentworth, Eli Demeritt, jr., Capt. Tristram Coffin.

1739. Joseph Austin, John Gage, Capt. Thomas Wallingford, Lieut. Thomas Davis, Joseph Hanson, jr.

1740. Capt. Thomas Millet, John Winget, Capt. Paul Wentworth, Eli Demeritt, jr., John Wood.

1741. Capt. Thomas Millet, Lieut. John Winget, Capt. Thomas Wallingford, Eli Demeritt, jr., Joseph Hanson, jr.

1742, 1743. Capt. Thomas Millet, Lieut. John Winget, Joseph Roberts, Capt. Thomas Wallingford, Eli Demeritt, jr.

1744, 1745. Thomas Millet, Lieut. John Winget, Eli Demeritt, jr., Thomas Wallingford, Ephraim Ham.

1746. Thomas Millet, Capt. Joseph Hanson, Thomas Wallingford, Major Thomas Davis, Capt. John Winget.

1747. Thomas Millet, Capt. John Winget, Eli Demeritt, Capt. John Wentworth, Ephraim Ham.

1748. Thomas Millet, Capt. Joseph Hanson, Major Thomas Davis, Col. Thomas Wallingford, John Gage.

1749, 1750. Thomas Millet, Ephraim Ham, Eli Demeritt, Capt. John Wentworth, Capt. John Winget.

1751. (Thomas Millet chosen but declined to serve.) Lieut. Stephen Roberts, Capt. Thomas Westbrook Waldron, Shadrach Hodgdon, Dr. Moses Carr, Joseph Hanson, jr.

1752. Thomas Millet, Capt. John Winget, Eli Demeritt, Capt. John Wentworth, Joseph Hanson, jr.

1753. Capt. Thomas W. Waldron, Thomas Millet, Lieut. Solomon Emerson, Capt. John Wentworth, Joseph Hanson, jr.

1754. Thomas Millet, Capt. Thomas W. Waldron, Capt. John Wentworth, Lieut. Solomon Emerson, Joseph Hanson, jr.

Somersworth was separated from Dover 22 April 1754.

1755. Thomas Millet, Joseph Hanson, jr., James Young.

1756. Samuel Emerson, Joseph Hanson, jr., Ebenezer Demeritt, Capt. Thomas

W. Waldron, James Young.
1757. Samuel Emerson, Joseph Hanson, jr., Ebenezer Demeritt, John Gage, jr., James Young.
1758. Capt. Howard Henderson, Joseph Hanson, jr., Ebenezer Demeritt, Capt. Thomas W. Waldron, James Young.
1759, 1760, 1761. Capt. Howard Henderson, Joseph Hanson, Ebenezer Demeritt, James Young, Capt. Thomas W. Waldron.
1762. Thomas Tuttle, Ephraim Hanson, John Winget, Nathaniel Horn, Ens. Joseph Roberts.
1763. Thomas Tuttle, Ephraim Hanson, John Winget, jr., Nathaniel Horn, Ens. Joseph Roberts.
1764. Elijah Estes, Otis Baker, John Tasker, Jacob Sawyer, Lieut. Joshua Wingate.
1765. Elijah Estes, Otis Baker, John Tasker, Jacob Sawyer, Lieut. Joshua Wingate.
1766. Clement Meserve, Solomon Hanson, Daniel Hayes, Nathaniel Horn, Capt. Dudley Watson.
1767. Lieut. Clement Meserve, Capt. John Gage, Daniel Hayes, Nathaniel Horn, Ephriam Ham.
1768. Capt. Caleb Hodgdon, Capt. John Gage, Nathaniel Horn.
1769. Lieut. William Hanson, Ephraim Hanson, Ezekiel Varney.
1770. Capt. Caleb Hodgdon, John Waldron, 3d, John Kielle.
1771, 1772, 1773. Capt. Caleb Hodgdon, Capt. Stephen Evans, Lieut. John Wingate.
1774, 1775. Capt. Caleb Hodgdon, John Kielle, Samuel Heard.
1776. Benjamin Pierce, John Waldron, 3d, John Gage.
1777. Ephraim Ham, Col. John Waldron, Andrew Torr.
1778. Col. John Waldron, Andrew Torr, Ephraim Ham.
1779. Col. Joshua Wingate, John Burnham Hanson, Capt. John Gage.
1780. Joshua Wingate, John Gage, Andrew Torr.
1781. Major Caleb Hodgdon, Col. John Waldron, Major Benjamin Titcomb.
1782. Ens. Andrew Torr, Capt. John Gage, Col. Joshua Wingate.
1783. John Kielle, Ens. Andrew Torr, Col. John Waldron.
1784, 1785. Andrew Torr, Col. John Waldron, John Kielle.
1786. John Kielle, John Waldron, Andrew Torr.
1787, 1788, 1789. Andrew Torr, John Waldron, John Kielle.
1790. Joseph Drew, Stephen Sawyer, John Kielle.
1791, 1792. Andrew Torr, John Waldron, Ephraim Ham.
1793, 1794, 1795, 1796, 1797. Capt. Moses Wingate, Stephen Sawyer, Aaron Roberts.
1798, 1799. Deacon Benjamin Pierce, Col. John Waldron, Andrew Torr.
1800. Deacon Benjamin Pierce, Stephen Sawyer, Moses Wingate.
1801. Col. John Waldron, Capt. Moses Wingate, Dea. Benjamin Pierce.
1802. Stephen Sawyer, Tobias Tuttle, Daniel Henderson.
1803. Stephen Sawyer, Daniel Henderson, Samuel Wentworth.
1804.. Tobias Tuttle, Mark Walker, Samuel Kimball.
1805. Tobias Tuttle, Stephen Sawyer, Samuel Kimball.
1806, 1807. Tobias Tuttle, Samuel Kim-

ball, Ephraim Ham, 3d.
1808, 1809, 1810. Tobias Tuttle, Stephen Patten, jr., Jonathan Hanson, jr.
1811, 1812. John Waldron, Nicholas Peaslee, Capt. Andrew Peirce.
1813, 1814. Tobias Tuttle, Andrew Peirce, Nicholas Peaslee, Samuel Kimball.
1815. Andrew Peirce, Nicholas Peaslee, Samuel Kimball.
1816. Andrew Peirce, Nicholas Peaslee, Stephen Patten, jr.
1817. Nicholas Peaslee, Samuel Kimball, Stephen Patten, jr.
1818. Samuel Kimball, Nicholas Peaslee, Jonathan Locke.
1819. Samuel Kimball, John Kittredge, Nicholas Peaslee.
1820. John Kittredge, Samuel Kimball, Nicholas Peaslee.
1821, 1822. John Kittredge, Samuel Kimball, Joseph Tuttle.
1823. Samuel Kimball, Thomas W. Kittredge, Joseph Tuttle.
1824, 1825. Samuel Kimball, Thomas W. Kittredge, Andrew Varney.
1826, 1827. Thomas W. Kittredge, Andrew Varney, Eri Perkins.
1828. Thomas W. Kittredge, Andrew Varney, Walter Sawyer.
1829. Thomas W. Kittredge, Andrew Varney, Daniel Osborne.
1830. Thomas W. Kittredge, Andrew Varney, Walter Sawyer.
1831. James B. Varney, Ebenezer Hanson, Alonzo Roberts.
1832. Ezekiel Hurd, James B. Varney, Ebenezer Hanson.
1833, 1834. Ezekiel Hurd, Andrew Pierce, jr., Alonzo Roberts.
1835. John Riley, William Hale, jr., Ezekiel Hurd.
1836. Ezekiel Hurd, John Riley, David Peirce.
1837. Ezekiel Hurd, David Peirce, James Tuttle, jr.
1838. John Riley, Sharonton Baker, Andrew Varney.
1839. Sharonton Baker, Andrew Varney, Thomas E. Sawyer.
1840. John Riley, Sharonton Baker, Stephen Toppan.
1841. John Riley, Stephen Toppan, Samuel Howard.
1842. Samuel Howard, Joshua Banfield, Solomon Jenness.
1843. Nathaniel Wiggin, Daniel Pinkham, Ezekiel Hurd.
1844. Ezekiel Hurd, Nathaniel Wiggin, John H. White.
1845. John Tredick, Samuel Dunn, jr., William B. Wiggin.
1846. Samuel Dunn, jr., William B. Wiggin, Andrew Varney.
1847. Samuel Dunn, jr., Andrew Varney, Oliver S. Horn.
1848. Thomas E. Sawyer, Oliver S. Horn, Elijah Wadleigh.
1849. Samuel Dunn, jr., Ezekiel Hurd, Leonard S. Rand.
1850. Sharonton Baker, Samuel Dunn, Andrew Varney.
1851. Edmund J. Lane, Samuel S. Clark, Andrew Varney.
1852. Samuel S. Clark, Edmund J. Lane, Moses Gage.
1853. Jonas D. Townsend, John Clements, Samuel Dunn.
1854. Jonas D. Townsend, John Clements, Nathaniel Paul.
1855. Charles Clements, Daniel Hussey, David Steele.

The last Board.

REPRESENTATIVES.

1650, 1651. John Baker.
1652, 1653. Valentine Hill.
1654. Richard Walderne and Valentine Hill.
1655. Valentine Hill.
1656. Richard Walderne.
1657, 1658. None recorded.
1659. Richard Walderne.
1660, 1661, 1662, 1663, 1664, 1665, 1666, 1667, 1668, 1669. Richard Walderne.
1670, 1671. Richard Walderne and Richard Cooke.
1672, 1673. Richard Walderne and Peter Coffin.
1674, 1675. Richard Walderne and Anthony Nutter.
1676. Anthony Nutter.
1677, 1678. Richard Walderne.
1679. Richard Walderne and Peter Coffin.
1680, 1681, 1682, 1683. Peter Coffin. Anthony Nutter, Richard Walderne, Jr.
1684, 1685, 1686, 1687, 1688, 1689, 1690, 1691, 1692, 1693, 1694. John Gerrish, John Woodman and Anthony Nutter.
1695, 1696 1697. Capt. John Woodman, En. William Furber, John Hall.
1698, 1699. Capt. John Tuttle, Lt. James Davis, Lt. William Furber.
1700, 1701, 1702, 1703, 1704, 1705, 1706. Richard Waldron and John Tuttle.
1707. John Tuttle.
1708, 1709, 1710, 1711, 1712, 1713. Capt. Tebbetts, Samuel Emerson.
1714, 1715. Capt. Timothy Gerrish, En. Stephen Jones, Capt. John Downing.
1716. Samuel Tebbetts, Capt. James Davis.
1717, 1718, 1719. Sarg. Samuel Tebbetts, Capt. James Davis.
1720, 1721, 1722, 1723, 1724, 1725, 1726,
1727. None recorded.
1728. Capt. Samuel Tebbets, Capt. Francis Mathes, Paul Gerrish.
1729, 1730. None recorded.
1731. Paul Gerrish, Francis Mathes, Thomas Millet.
1732. Nicholas Harford, William Dam, Paul Wentworth.
1733, 1734, 1735, 1736, 1737. Thomas Millet, Paul Gerrish.
1738. None recorded.
1739. Thomas Millet, Paul Gerrish, Thomas Wallingford.
1740. Lt. James Davis, John Gage, Capt. Thomas Wallingford.
1741. Thomas Davis, John Gage Thomas Wallingford.
1742. John Canney, John Gage, Thomas Wallingford.
1743. No record.
1744. Thomas Millet, John Winget, Thomas Wallingford.
1745. Maj. Thomas Davis, John Gage, Thomas Wallingford.
1746, 1747, 1748. No record.
1749. John Wentworth, Thomas Millet, Thomas Davis.
1750, 1751. No record.
1752. John Wentworth, Thomas Davis, Thomas Millet.
1753, 1754. No record.
1755. Thomas Millet, T. W. Waldron.
1756. T. W. Waldron, Howard Henderson.
1757. 1758, 1759, 1760, 1761. No record.
1762, 1763, 1764, 1765. Howard Henderson, Thos. W. Waldron.
1766, 1767. No record.
1768. Thomas W. Waldron, Otis Baker.
1769, 1770. No record.
1771. John Gage, Otis Baker.
1772, 1773. No record.

1774. John Gage, Caleb Hodgdon. (Mr. Gage died after his election and John Waldron was elected to fill the vacancy.)
1775. Otis Baker, Caleb Hodgdon, (Elected to the regular Assembly at Portsmouth.)
1775. Shadrach Hodgdon, Stephen Evans; (Elected to attend a convention of the friends of Colonial liberty at Exeter May 17.) Otis Baker, Stephen Evans; (Elected to attend a similar convention at Exeter on the 21st Dec.
1776. Caleb Hodgdon, Stephen Evans.
1777, 1778, 1779. John Wentworth, Caleb Hodgdon.
1780. Joshua Winget, John Kielley.
1781, 1782. John Waldron, Caleb Hodgdon.
1783. John Waldron, James Calef.
1784. James Calef.
1785, 1786. John Waldron.
1787. Joshua Wingate.
1788. Dr. Ezra Green, to convention on Constitution of the United States.
1788. John Waldron (Mr. W. was afterward elected Senator and Andrew Torr was elected to fill the vacancy.)
1789. Andrew Torr.
1790, 1791. John Kielle.
1791. John Waldron to Constitutional Convention which met Sept. 7, 1791.
1792. John Kielle.
1793, 1794. Col. John Waldron.
1795. Andrew Torr, Richard Tripe.
1796. Capt. Moses Wingate, Richard Tripe.
1797. Moses Wingate, John Waldron.
1798. Col. John Waldron.
1799. Moses Wingate.
1800. Joseph Gage.
1801, 1802. Col. John Waldron.
1803, 1804, 1805, 1806. Daniel Henderson.
1807, 1808, 1809, 1810. Amos Cogswell.
1811. Tobias Tuttle.
1812. Amos Cogswell.
1813. Moses Hodgdon, Tobias Tuttle.
1814. Amos Cogswell, Tobias Tuttle.
1815. Amos Cogswell, Col. John Waldron.
1816. Daniel M. Durell, (M. C. 1807-9) John Williams, John Waldron.
1817. Andrew Pierce, John Williams.
1818. Andrew Pierce, Wm. Flagg.
1819. Andrew Pierce, Nathaniel W. Ela.
1820. Charles Woodman, Andrew Pierce.
1821,'1822. Charles Woodman, SPEAKER, Nathaniel W. Ela.
1823. Wm Hale, James Bartlett, Andrew Pierce, SPEAKER.
1824. James Bartlett, Andrew Pierce, Nathaniel W. Ela.
1825. James Bartlett, John Williams, Robert Rodgers.
1826. John Williams, James Bartlett, Daniel M. Christie, Sam'l Kimball.
1827, 1828. John Williams, D. M. Christie, Samuel Kimball, Eli Perkins.
1829. James Bartlett, John Wheeler, John Riley, Walter Sawyer.
1830. James Bartlett, D. M. Christie, Jacob Kittredge,
1831. D. M. Christie, Jacob K. Kittredge, Samuel W. Carr, Cyrus Goss.
1832. Samuel W. Carr, John P. Hale, Thos E. Sawyer, E. W. Fenner.
1833. Nathaniel Young, Wm. Hale, Jr., Thomas E. Sawyer, John H. White.
1834. John H. White, Thomas W. Kittredge, John B. H. Odion, Nathaniel Young.

1835. T. W. Kittredge, T. E. Sawyer, J. B. H. Odion.
1836. T. E. Sawyer, T. W. Kittredge, Andrew Pierce, Benjamin Wiggin.
1837. Noah Martin, Joseph H. Smith, Charles Ham, Daniel Hussey.
1838. T. E. Sawyer, George Wadleigh, Wm. P. Drew, Benjamin Wiggin.
1839. Daniel M. Christie, George Wadleigh, Wm. P. Drew, Oliver S. Horn.
1840. T. E. Sawyer, O. S. Horne, Jonas D. Townsend, Sam'l Drew.
1841. T. E. Sawyer, Andrew Peirce, Jonas D. Townsend, D. M. Christie.
1842. Andrew Peirce, Thos. T. Edgerly, Danl' Hussey, Nath'l Jenness.
1843. Andrew Peirce, Nath'l Jenness, Horace Clark.
1844. Charles Ham, James W. Cowan, Hanson Roberts, David Wilson, A. H. Otis.
1845. Andrew Peirce, Wells Waldron, Thomas E. Sawyer, Elijah Wadleigh.
1846. John P. Hale, SPEAKER, Thos. E. Sawyer, Nath'l Low, D. M. Christie, Elijah Wadleigh, Wells Waldron.
1847. Thos. E. Sawyer, Elijah Wadleigh, Wm. F. Estes, Darius T. Johnson, Nathaniel Low, Sam'l Hanson 2d
1848. George Wadleigh, S. Hanson 2d, Calvin Hale.
1849. D. M. Christie, Joseph T. Peaslee, Geo. Wadleigh, John H. Wiggins, James R. Moulton.
1850. T. E. Sawyer, Calvin Hale, James Austin, Thos. W. Kittredge, Benj. Wiggin, Wm. F. Estes.
1850. To the Constitutional Convention which met 6 Nov. 1850, Thomas E. Sawyer, Andrew Peirce, Shubael Varney, Asa Freeman, William Plaisted Drew, John H. Wiggins.
1851. Thomas W. Kittredge, Joseph Morrill, Benjamin Wiggin, William B. Wiggin, James Austin, William F. Estes.
1852. Geo. P. Folsom, Silas Moody, Joseph Morrill, John H. Wiggins, William B. Wiggin, Joseph Hanson 8d.
1853. None elected.
1854. James Bennett, George Mathewson, George P. Folsom, Silas Moody, Daniel H. Wendell, William Hale.
1855. Daniel M. Christie, Nathaniel Wiggin, James Bennett, William S. Stevens, Ivory Paul, Edmund J. Lane. These were the last before the City was organized.

MODERATORS OF TOWN MEETINGS

The earliest record of a town meeting is of 20 April 1644. There is no mention of any Moderator till 1659. In otherwise complete records frequently no such official is alluded to. We give a list of all on record. Many of the meetings were petty ones, for choosing a constable or drawing jurors, or the like, and often were called at convenient taverns. The number of Moderators indicates the number of town meetings in a year.

1659. Elder Hatevil Nutter.
1661. Elder William Wentworth.
1663. William Furber.
1664. Peter Coffin.
1675. Richard Walderne, Feb. 3, John Woodman, May 31.
1694, 1695, 1696. Job Clements.
1697. Capt. John Gerrish.
Record with date gone perhaps near this, — Woodman.
1702. Lt. James Davis.
1703. Richard Waldron.

1704-1712. Capt. John Gerrish.
1713. Capt. James Davis.
1714. Capt. John Gerrish.
1715-1717. Col. Richard Waldron, Capt. James Davis.
1717, 1718. No record.
1719. Col. Richard Waldron.
1720. Lt. Col. James Davis.
1721-1724. No record.
1725. Col. Richard Waldron.
1728. Lt. Col. James Davis, Capt. Francis Mathes, Nicholas Hartford, Capt. Thos. Millet.
1729. Lt. Col. James Davis.
1730. Capt. Thos. Millet, Col. James Davis, Paul Wentworth, Capt. Stephen Jones.
1731. Col. James Davis, Nicholas Harford.
1732. Capt. Thos. Millet, Paul Wentworth.
1733. Capt. Thomas Wallingford, Paul Wentworth, Capt. Thos. Millet.
1734. Capt. Paul Wentworth, Capt Thomas Millet.
1736. Capt. Thomas Millet, Capt. Paul Wentworth.
1737. Capt. Thomas Millet.
1738. Capt. Thomas Millet, John Winget.
1739. Lt. John Winget, Capt. Thomas Millet.
1740-1744. Capt. Thos. Millet, Capt. Thomas Wallingford, Lt. John Winget.
1745, 1746. Capt. Thos. Wallingford, Capt. Thomas Millet.
1747. John Wood, Capt John Winget.
1748. Col. Thos. Wallingford, Thomas Millet.
1749-1753. Capt. Thos. Millet, Capt. John Winget.
1754. Thos. Westbrook Waldron.
1755. Thomas Millet, James Young.
1756. Thomas Westbrook Waldron.
1757. John Gage, Thos. Westbrook Waldron.
1758. Capt. John Winget, T. W. Waldron, Col. John Gage.
1759, 1760. James Young, Capt. John Gage, Thomas Tuttle, Joseph Hanson, John Bickford.
1761. Ens. William Twombly, John Winget, Isaac Young, Otis Baker, Stephen Evans, Thomas Tuttle, William Hussey, James Young, John Bickford.
1762. Capt. John Winget, Moses Ham, Capt. T. W. Waldron, Daniel Young, Timothy Robinson, Col. John Gage, James Young, Ens. Stephen Roberts, Ebenezer Hanson, Jonathan Gage, Benjamin Hanson.
1763. Col. John Titcomb, Moses Varney, Col. Thomas W. Waldron, Thomas Tuttle, Solomon Hanson, Capt. John Gage, Natahniel Balch, James Kielle.
1764. Thomas Tuttle, Ebenezer Hanson, Capt. Thomas W. Waldron, Col. John Gage, Lieut. Joshua Wingate, Stephen Varney, Elijah Estes, Ephraim Ham, Peter Cushing.
1765. Solomon Emerson, John Horn, Jr., Capt. Thomas W. Waldron, Otis Baker, Ephraim Kimball, Sam'l Ham, David Watson.
1766. Capt. Shadrach Hodgdon, Dr. Moses Howe, Ichabod Hayes, Capt. Thomas W. Waldron, William Watson, Major John Titcomb, John Horn, 3d, Paul Brewster, Ens. Thomas Young, Thomas Davis, jr.
1767. James Calfe, Ambrose Bampton, Benjamin Evans, Capt. Thomas W. Waldron, John Horn, 3d, Capt. Caleb

Hodgdon, Daniel Peirce, Paul Willand, Joseph Varney.

1768. James Tuttle, Benjamin Peirce, Otis Baker, Capt. Stephen Evans, Capt. Thomas W. Waldron, Paul Hussey, Capt. Shadrach Hodgdon, Ezekiel Varney, Thomas Hanson, Capt. Samuell Gerrish, Aaron Wingate.

1769. Elijah Estes, Capt. Thomas W. Waldron, Deacon Daniel Ham, Thomas Tuttle, Nathaniel Cooper, Benjamin Church and Israel Hodgdon.

1770. Dr. Ezra Green, Lt. John Wingate, Joshua Perkins, Col. John Gage John Kielle, Capt. Shadrach Hodgdon, Isaac Hill, Benjamin Evans.

1771. Moses Sawyer, Capt. Thomas W. Waldron, Francis Drew, jr. Spencer Wentworth, Ichabod Horn.

1772. Lt. Joshua Wingate, Thomas W. Waldron, Thomas Tuttle.

1773. John Burnham Hanson, Thomas W. Waldron, Capt. John Waldron, Michael Reade, William Hussey.

1774. Jan. 10, Col. Otis Baker. First meeting on Revolutionary matters. March 28, Capt. Thomas W. Waldron, Paul Pinkham, Thomas Young. July 18, Capt. Stephen Evans. To appoint Delegates to the First Provincial Congress, Nov. 7, Richard Waldron. To act in reference to the Boston Port Bill. Dec. 26, Capt. Shadrach Hodgdon to choose Delegates to the 2d Provincial Congress.

1775. John Wentworth, jr., John Gage, Capt. Shadrach Hodgdon, John Burnham Hanson. June 5, Thomas W. Waldron. To act in regard to Committee of Safety, Joseph Bickford.

1776. March 26, John Gage. July 15, John Wentworth, Jr. On Expedition to Canada. Dec. 9, John Gage. For Provincial Congress.

1777. John Wentworth, jr., Col. John Wingate, Capt. John Gage.

1778. Otis Baker, Stephen Evans, Deacon Shadrach Hodgdon, John Wentworth, jr.

1779. Capt. John Gage, Deacon Shadrach Hodgdon, John Wentworth, jr.

1780. John Wentworth, Nov. 27, John Wentworth, jr. To choose Representaives and Delegates to settle place of goverment.

1781. John Wentworth, jr., Otis Baker, Capt. Shadrach Hodgdon, Col. Stephen Evans.

1782. Capt. John Gage, John Wentworth.

1783. John Wentworth, Otis Baker, Stephen Evans.

1784. John Wentworth.

1785. John Wentworth, John Gage Thomas Shannon.

1786. John Wentworth, Otis Baker.

1787. Stephen Evans, John Gage.

1788. Joshua Wingate, John Waldron, Otis Baker. Sept. 13, Peter Hodgdon, First Presidential Election, Joshua Wingate.

1789. Feb. 2, Samuel Evans, First election of Representatives to U. S. Congress. Col. John Waldron, Caleb Hodgdon, Daniel Hanson, John P. Gilman.

1790. Col. Joshua Wingate, Col. John Waldron, Benjamin Church, William Atkinson, Joseph Drew, Dr. Ezra Green, James Taylor, Edward Sise.

1791. Col. John Waldron, Eliphalet Ladd, Elijah Jenkins, William Tuttle, John Pinkham, Caleb Hodgdon, Thomas Jewett, Henry Mellen.

1792. Daniel Perkins, Col. John Waldron, Shadrach Hanson, Abraham Duncan, Nathaniel W. Ela, Caleb Hodgdon, Jr.

1793. James Taylor, Col. John Waldron, Abednego Robinson, Col. Amos Cogswell, Abimaaz Watson, David Tenny Foss Col. Caleb Hodgdon.

1794. John Kielle, John Waldron, Paul Kimball, Asa Tufts, Lt. Ephraim Ham, Col. Benjamin Titcomb, Ambrose Bampton, Col. Caleb Hodgdon.

1795. David Tuttle, John Waldron, James Varney, 3d, Joshua Pike, Ichabod Tebbetts, Dr. Ezra Greene, Dr. Carlton, Wm. Man, Wm. K. Atkinson.

1796. Paul Pinkham, Jr., John Waldron, Oliver Crosby, Daniel Libbey, Vaughan Jones, Capt. Samuel Wentworth, Wm. K. Atkinson, Stephen Willey, Dr. Ezra Greene, Col. Caleb Hodgdon.

1797. Daniel Henderson, Henry Mellen, Col. John Waldron, Wm. K. Atkinson, Thos. Calef, Nathaniel Horn, Col. Caleb Hodgdon.

1798. Richard Waldron, Col. John Waldron, Thos. Footman, Timothy Robinson, David Boardman, Deacon Benjamin Pierce, Samuel Evans, Col. Caleb Hodgdon.

1799. Joseph Watson, Col. John Waldron, Joseph Smith, Wm. Hale, Samuel Hanson, Jacob M. Currier, Dr. Ezra Greene, James Jewett.

1800. Nathaniel Ham, Jr., Timothy Hussey, Wm. Hale, Jonathan Hayes, Nicholas Peaslee, Tobias Tuttle, William Blake, Col. Caleb Hodgdon.

1801. Enoch Drew, Col. John Waldron, Philomon Chandler, Douglas Stackpole.

1802. Nathaniel Hanson, Benjamin Watson, John Waldron, Benjamin Hanson 3d.

1803. Israel Meserve, John Waldron, Dr. John Wheeler, Andrew Tuttle, Daniel Henderson.

1804. Dodavah Ham, William Perkins, John Waldron, Jonathan Gage, Amos Cogswell.

1805. James Varney, Jr. Wm. Runnels, Joseph Watson, John Waldron, Oliver Crosby, Daniel Titcomb, Clement Meserve, Thomas Young.

1806. Jacob Sawyer, Nathaniel Watson, John Waldron, Nathaniel W. Ela.

1807. Thomas Henderson, John Waldron, John Young, Andrew Torr, Col. Caleb Hodgdon, Stephen Coffin.

1808. John Waldron, Major Daniel Henderson, Daniel Roberts, Ebenezer Meserve.

1809. Nathaniel Hanson, William Runolds, John Waldron, Samuel Watson, William Blake, Jr., Dr. Ezra Greene, Dr. Jabez Dow.

1810. Hosea Sawyer, Horace Parmalee, John Waldron, Isaac Varney, George Pendexter, Benjamin Torr, Samuel Ladd.

1811. Benjamin Watson, John Waldron, Joseph Smith, Joseph Tuttle, Oliver Crosby, Ralph Twombly.

1812.--Joseph Tuttle, Moses L. Neal, Andrew Torr, Moses Hodgdon, Tobias Tuttle, William Hale, John Tebbets.

1813. Andrew Varney, William Hale, John Mann, James Tuttle, James Perkins, John Tebbetts, William Titcomb.

1814. Jonathan Rawson, Col. John Waldron, John Chadbourn, William Blake, Jr., Clement Meserve, James Coleman, William Hale, William K. Atkinson,

Daniel M. Durell, Jonathan Gage.
1815. James Whitehouse, Col. John Waldron, Asa Swasey, Andrew Pierce, Jonathan Hanson, Jr., David Tuttle.
1816. Isaac Twombly, Col. John Waldron, Daniel M. Durell, Benjamin Watson.
1817. William Perkins, Daniel M· Durell, Michael Reade, Amos Cogswell, James Richardson, James Coleman.
1818. James Farrington, Daniel Horne, Edward Sise, Reuben Varney, Daniel M. Durell.
1819. Jonathan Hanson, Jr., Isaac Watson, Daniel M. Durell, Moses L. Neal, James Bartlett.
1820. John W. Hayes, Jonathan Locke, William Hale, Alexander Scammell Chadbourne, John Kittredge, Andrew Pierce, James Whitehouse.
1821. James Bartlett, William Hale, Col. Amos Cogswell, Walter C. Green.
1822. Charles Woodman, William Perkins, Andrew Peirce.
1823. Capt. James Whitehouse, Andrew Peirce, Alphonzo Gerrish, Stephen Davis.
1824. Deacon Jonathan Locke, Andrew Peirce, John Samuel Durell, Jesse Varney, John P. Adams, James Bartlett, Daniel M. Christie.
1825. William Palmer, Andrew Peirce, Michael Reade, Dr. Jabez Dow, Andrew Varney, Capt. Moses Clements, George Piper.
1826. Job C. Waldron, Andrew Peirce, Dr. George Kittredge, David Peirce.
1827. Benjamin Boardman, David Pearsons, Andrew Peirce, Nathaniel Lamos, James Bartlett, Samuel Davis, Daniel M. Durell, Capt. Samuel Dunn.
1828. Jacob M. Currier, William Hale, Jr., Andrew Peirce, Charles Drew, Jonas C. March, James Bartlett, James B. Varney.
1829. Jacob M. Currier, Daniel Drew, James Bartlett, Capt. John Riley, William Hale, Jr.
1830. John Tapley, Samuel W. Carr.
1831. Thomas E. Sawyer, Samuel W. Carr, George Pendexter, Jeremiah Goodwin.
1832. Jacob M. Currier, John P. Hale, Thomas Bickford, George W. Kittredge, James S. Rowe, Benjamin Wiggin, John Riley, John Williams, Sam'l W. Carr.
1833. David Wilson, Ebenezer Faxon, George W. Kittredge, James B. Varney, John Williams, John Chadwick, George Pendexter, Thomas E. Sawyer.
1834. Andrew Peirce, Nathaniel Tibbetts, Samuel W. Carr, Oliver S. Horne, Andrew Peirce.
1835. Daniel Pinkham, Samuel W. Carr, John Riley, George W. Kittredge, Asa Perkins.
1836. John Currier, George W. Kittredge, David Peirce, William Frye, John P. Hale.
1837. George L. Whitehouse, John P. Hale, Thomas Wright, Nathaniel Wiggin.
1838. Samuel Ham, 3d, Moses Paul, Stephen Scruton, Thomas E. Sawyer, Daniel Johnson, Ezekiel Hurd.
1839. Samuel Wyatt, Rufus Flagg, Nathaniel Wiggin, Moses Paul, John S. H. Durell, Samuel Hanson, John S. Durell.
1840. Shubael Varney, Moses Paul, Samuel Ham, 3d.
1841. Joseph Hanson, 3d., William

Twombly, Shubael Varney, Thomas E. Sawyer, William N. Andrews, Nathaniel Tebbets, Simon L. Hartford, John P. Hale.

1842. Nathaniel Tibbetts, Thomas E. Sawyer, Asa Freeman, Joseph Hanson, Samuel Howard.

1843. Thomas E. Sawyer, Moses Paul, Ezekiel Hurd.

1844. Joseph H. Smith, Moses Paul.

1845. William Hale, jr., Ezekiel Hurd.

1846. William Hale, jr., Thomas E. Sawyer.

1847. Thomas E. Sawyer.

1848. Thomas E. Sawyer, William Hale, Jr.

1849. William Hale.

1850. George Quint, Thomas E. Sawyer, William Hale.

1851. Thomas E. Sawyer, Moses Paul.

1852. Thomas E. Sawyer.

1853. George T. Wentworth, Thomas E. Sawyer.

1854. Thomas E. Sawyer.

1855. Joseph D. Guppey, March 13; Charles A. Tufts, Aug. 15; the last town meeting, at which the city charter was accepted.

——

Mr. Editor:—The writer, in reading your list of Representatives from Dover, found that the list of dates and names in some cases did not agree with the record of services of the early Deacons of the Church at Oyster River, a subject the writer is looking up at the present time as supplementary to a historical sketch of the Congregational Church in Durham, N. H., and published by your paper, Feb. 17, 24, 1896.

For instance the Dover Town Records in regard to the service of Deacons Nathaniel Hill and Samuel Emerson do not show the actual services they rendered as shown by the records of the provincial assemblies. Your list from town records does not show Nathaniel Hill as Representative, while the provincial records give additional information and show that he was in attendance as a Deputy or Representative from Dover as follows:

At an adjourned session of provincial assembly 7 Aug. 1699, Nathaniel Hill.

1703, June 23 to 1703, Dec. 11. Nathaniel Hill.

1704, Feb. 8, to 1709, June 27 Lt. Nathaniel Hill.

June 30, 1709 to Nov. 5, 1714. Nathaniel Hill.

(Assemblies were summoned by writ, not at stated times, but summoned and dissolved at the pleasure of the President and Council, while New Hampshire was a Province. In early years, an Assembly continued in existence five years unless sooner dissolved; later three years.)

Capt. Tebbetts and Samuel Emerson are given in your Historical Memoranda as Representatives 1708, 1709, 1710, 1711, 1712, 1713, while provincial records give no mention of Samuel Emerson as ever being present at an assembly and (Capt) Samuel Tebbetts' name does not appear until 1715, and in place of Tebbetts and Emerson, we find (during same period) 1709 June 30 to 1714 Nov. 5, Nathaniel Hill, Stephen Jones, Ezekial Wentworth, etc.

Your list gives as representatives:

1689-1699. Lt. James Davis, also 1716, 1717, 1718, 1719 Capt. James Davis; while by assembly record James Davis appeared to have served as follows:

1698, April 5 to 1702, 9 Sept. Lt.

James Davis (with others) (not present at adjourned session Aug. 7, 1699, but there June 10, 1701.)
1715, Nov. 8, to 1716 May 18 James Davis and James Tebbetts.
1716, Aug 21 to Dec. 5. The same.
1717, Jan. 10 to Jan. 28, " "
1717, May 13 to 1722, June 28 " "
1722, July 2 to 1727, Nov. 21, James Davis (with others.)

There is another point to which I desire to call attention, you give as Representative Lt. James Davis, 1740, while the provincial records give Lt. Thos. Davis, 1740. It could not be Lieut. James Davis, for Durham was set off May, 1732, as a separate town and the first town meeting held in Durham June 26, 1732 "Col. James Davis, Esq.," was chosen moderator and served as moderator in Durham ten times including the year 1740 so he could not be the one, and Lt. Thomas Davis is correct.

You give Lieut. James Davis, Select man in 1733, doubtless Lt. Thomas Davis was intended for the same reason.

Lucien Thompson.

Durham, N. H. Dec. 20, 1897.

EARLY SETTLEMENTS IN DOVER.

The preceding matter concludes all that was in the first nine numbers as published in the Enquirer in 1850 with additional matter furnished by Dr. Quint in 1891.

No. 10 of the old series begins with the following concerning the first settlements of Dover, taken from Belknap's manuscript church record of the First Parish in Dover. J. S.

"Piscataqua River was first discovered by Capt. John Smith (in 1614,) who came from England on a fishing voyage and ranged the coast from Penobscot to Cape Cod.

"Capt. John Mason, Sir Ferdinando Gorges, and several other gentlemen, merchants and others, in the west of England belonging to Bristol, Exeter, Dorchester, Shrewsbury, Plymouth and other places, having obtained patents of the New England Council at Plymouth (England) or several parts of the country, and being encouraged by the plantation of New Plymouth, and the reports of fishermen who made voyages along the coast, projected and attempted a fishery about Piscataqua and in the spring of the year (1623) sent over Mr. David Thompson, a Scotsman, with Mr. Edward Hilton and his brother, Wm. Hilton, who had been fishmongers in London and some others, with all necessaries to begin a settlement. Mr. Thompson with some of the company settled on the west side of Piscataqua river, at a place called Little Harbor, where the first house was built, called Mason Hall."

The locality for more than a century has been called Odiorne's Point and is in the town of Rye. It is so called because a gentleman by that name purchased it about 125 years ago. J. S.

The two Hiltons set up their stages some distance above the mouth of the river at a place since called Northam and Dover. (At Dover Point).

"N. B. The Indian name of Hilton's (Dover) Point, the extremity of Dover Neck, was Wecohamet".

In 1890 Dr. Quint said the name was Wecanacohunt and that at Little Harbor was Pannaway. J. S.

"These settlements went on but slowly for seven years after, and in 1631 when Edward Colcott (who was afterwards chosen Governor by the Planters of Dover), first came over, there were but three houses in all that part of the country adjoining the Piscataqua River. There had been also some expense about Salt works."

"Two thirds of the patents belonged to some merchants of Bristol, the other third to some of Shrewsbury, and there was an agreement that the division should be made by indifferent men. Capt. (Thomas) Wiggin who was sent (in 1631) to superintend their affairs, after about one year's residence in the country, made a voyage to England, to procure more ample means for carrying on the plantation. In the meantime those of Bristol had sold their interest to the Lords Say and Brook, George Willys and William Whiting, who continued Wiggin in the agency, and procured a considerable number of families in the west of England, some of whom were of good estates and 'of some account for religion' to come over and increase the colony."

This was the first considerable accession the settlement received. Captain Wiggans (so his name is spelled upon the Records) upon his return arrived at Salem in the ship James, 10 Oct. 1633, after eight weeks' passage, and it was this year that the families arrived at Wecohamet (Wecanacohunt). Some of their names are ascertained and may be presented with other notices in some future article.

"They continued Capt. Wiggans in the agency for seven years, during which time the interest was not greatly advanced, the whole being sold to him at the expiration of that time for six hundred pounds."

Capt. Wiggans "had power of Governor hereabouts." The account of officers should therefore begin with him.

EARLY GOVERNMENT IN DOVER.

Dr. Quint says that under Edward Hilton, from 1623 to 1631 there could have been no civil organization. Nor did Thomas Wiggin, who came in 1631, returned in 1632, and led hither a re-enforcement in the autumn of 1633, bring with it any power of government. By some historians he has been absurdly styled "Governor." He was merely the agent of an English land and trading company. That company itself had no power of civil government. Capt. Wiggin had indeed the power to allot lands to settlers, and formal descriptions of some of these grants are extant, copied in the next decade. There is some reason to suppose that William Walderne may have made the original papers.

In the autumn of 1637, the people formed a "Combination" for government and Rev. George Burdett was placed at the head. It has been ridicuously stated that he "thrust out" Capt. Wiggin, a man who was never in. The statement is one of those perversions which a student into early New Hampshire history comes to expect as a matter of course. The simple fact was that in the absence of government, the growing colony found it necessary to organize. An independent government continued till a union with Massachusetts, 9 Oct., 1641. But an intermediate "Combination" had been made 22 Oct., 1640, whose records were in a volume extant in 1682, to which Gov. Cranfield and the historian Hubbard had access. Whether the volume was taken to England in tne Masonian trials, or never emerged from the hiding place where the people concealed it in those suits, is a matter of sad conjecture.

In connection with the above notice of errors, it may be well enough to allude to two or three others. One is that Thomas Roberts was never "Governor" in Dover; he was President of its Court—its Court, doubtless, being but little more than a board of selectmen. More stupid was the absurdity which imposed upon Hubbard a belief that Edward Colcord was once "Governor"; he was one of three men appointed to decide cases 20 shillings in value. Entirely inexcusable is the statement in some State publications, as in a Register now before us, that Dover was incorporated 22 Oct., 1641. Some blunderer took the month and day of the second Combination and affixed them to the year of union with Massachusetts and called the hybrid result the date of incorporation. Dover never was incorporated.

Dover was independent until annexed to Massachusetts, 9 October, 1641. At the next General Court, that of May, 1642, Savage says that William Walderne appeared from Dover and sat one day. The General Court held sessions in spring and autumn of each year. Deputies were chosen sometimes for one session, sometimes for the year.

THE END OF THE UNION WITH MASSACHUSETTS IN 1679.

The Commission establishing the Province of New Hampshire and appointing John Cutt President of the Council passed the Great Seal 18 Sept., 1679, and was publicly proclaimed at Portsmouth 22 Jan., 1679-80. The first General Assembly met 16 March 1679-80.

During the continuance of New Hampshire as a Province, Deputies were not chosen at stated times, but whenever an Assembly was summoned by writ, which, as well as the dissolution, was at the pleasure of the President and the Council. In early years an Assembly continued in existence for five years, unless sooner dissolved; later three years.

In 1651 Dover was fined £10, for not being represented at the General Court in Boston.

Capt. Richard Walderne was SPEAKER of the House during the sessions of the following years, 1666, 1667, 1668, 1673, 1674, 1675, and 1679.

(Rev. Dr. Quint had the following in his oration delivered July 4, 1890, at the laying of the corner stone of the new city building, which may be of interest in this connection in regard to the first settlement of Dover.)   J. S.

"Your invitations (to deliver the oration) mention a date far back of fifty years. They refer to the oldest extant official paper, and that is but a copy, found a few years since in the State paper office in London, of Dover municipality—if the word municipality I may use in this free sense.

It was the combination of forty-one citizens in 1640, two hundred and fifty years ago, to establish a government on this soil. I may barely refer to the fact, now established beyond question that our Wecanacohunt, or Dover Point, was coeval with Pannaway, or Little Harbor, in 1623; (that settlement at Little Harbor was afterwards deserted by every inhabitant, while that at Dover Point has been continuous): to the fact that the First Parish is the most ancient parish in the State, (dating from 1633) that the First Church was the first church organized on New Hampshire soil. And I now add that the claim of the Hampton church that it came thither as an organized church, or that the settlers of that town ever came there before 1639, is now so seriously questioned as to need new support. That in 1637 there was some kind of a combination on Piscataqua river, with its chief magistrate at Dover Point, is clear from the letters of Burdett to Laud, existing in their original in London, and Capt. John Underhill, famous in the Pequot war, as on the Zuyder Zee, ruled here in 1639. But in 1640 came the new Combination, and from that date, and by virtue of that agreement, there has been an uninterrupted government, town or city, to the day of this corner stone. This is therefore a day worthy of recognition. That Combination was purely Democratic. It originated with the people and by the people and for the people. It began with the first elements of native rights, that of establishing a government by the popular voice and without consent of king or lord."

THE FIRST RULERS IN DOVER.

Dr. Quint says:—An approximate list of the persons in charge of the early rule in Dover is as follows:

EDWARD HILTON from the spring of 1623 to 1631.

CAPT. THOMAS WIGGIN (Wiggans) superintended affairs for the English patentees from 1631 to 1637, except that he was in England 1632-3.

GEORGE BURDETT became head of the "Combination," and civil government was established in the autumn of 1637. He served a year or thereabouts.

CAPT. JOHN UNDERHILL became "Governor" and commander of the military in November or December 1638. He continued in office till March or April 1640, and in command of the militia still later.

THOMAS ROBERTS was made "President of the Court," that is, head of the magistrates, in March or April 1640. Apparently he served till the Union with Massachusetts in October, 1641; and the officials in power were continued in place by Massachusetts until further order, which order we do not find. The "magistrates" mentioned by Belknap were for the County of Dover and Portsmouth, not officials of Dover. Records are silent until 1647.

THE COMBINATION OF 1640.

At the Centennial celebration of the Declaration of Independence in Dover, July 4, 1876, Dr. Quint was the orator and in the course of his address spoke as follows concerning the Combination of 1640, which was the formal expression of what had been in existence, informally, from as early a date as 1637, as appears by Burdett's letters to Archbishop Laud, which still exist in the Public Record Office, London, England, and copies of two of which Dr. Quint then had in his possession. Dr. Quint spoke as follows:

J. S.

On the 22d day of October, 1640, the people of Dover established or renewed a formal government. The document, the earliest one of Dover history, should here be reproduced:

The body of this paper was preserved by Hubbard, but the names, except three, could not be found by Belknap. John S. Jenness, Esq., found a copy in the Public Record Office, London, and kindly gave me its use. The one herewith printed was made for me by Mr. Sainsbury. The names are given in three columns, as in the copy; as only a copy exists and not the original, doubtless some names are erroneously spelled.

DOVER'S MAGNA CHARTA.

Whereas, sundry mischeifes and inconveniences have befaln us, and more and greater may in regard of want of civill Government, his Gratious Ma'tie haveing hitherto setled no order for us to our knowledge:

Wee whose names are underwritten being Inhabitants upon the River Pascataquack have voluntarily agreed to combine ourselves into a body politique that we may the more comfortably enjoy the benefit of his Ma'ties Lawes together with all such Orders as shal bee concluded by a major part of the Freemen of our Society in case they bee not repugnant to the Lawes of England and administered in the behalfe of his Majesty.

And this wee have mutually promised and concluded to do and so to continue till his Excellent Ma'tie shall give other Order concerning us. In Witness whereof wee have hereto set our hands the two and twentieth day of October in the sixteenth yeare of the reign of our Sovereign Lord Charles by the grace of God King of Great Britain France and Ireland Defender of the Faith &c. Annoq Dom. 1640.

John Follet,	Thom. Larkham,
Robert Nanney,	Richard Waldern,
William Jones,	William Waldern
Philip Swaddon,	William Storer,
Richard Pinckhame,	William Furbur,
Bartholomew Hunt,	Thos. Layton,
William Bowden	Tho. Roberts,
John Wastill,	Bartholomew Smith,
John Heard,	Samuel Haines,
John Hall,	John Underhill,
Abel Camond,	Peter Garland,
Henry Beck,	John Dam,
Robert Huggins,	Steven Teddar,
Fran: Champernoon,	John Ugroufe,
Hansed Knowles,	Thomas Canning,
Edward Colcord,	John Phillips,
Henry Lahorn,	Tho: Dunstar,
Edward Starr,	James Nute,
Anthony Emery.	Richard Laham,
William Pomfret,	John Cross,
George Webb,	James Rawlins.

This is a true copy compared with ye Originall by mee

Edw. Cranfield.

[Indorsed.]

The Combination for Government by ye people at Pascataq 1640 Rec'd abt. 13th Febr. 82-3.

Dr. Quint in his centennial oration in this city in 1876 spoke as follows of the signers of the "Combination" of 1640 and its characteristics.

THE CHARACTERISTICS OF THE COMBINATION CONSIDERED.

Upon this earliest extant paper of our local history are the names of our forefathers. Some soon disappeared. Champernoon of ancient and eminent Devon house left our borders. The two ministers Larkham and Knollys returned to England. John Underhill was afterwards the scourge of the Indians beyond the Connecticut. But the names of Follett, Jones, Pinkham, Heard, Hall, Huggins, Waldron, Furber, Leighton, Roberts, Haines, Canney, Colcord, Nute, Emery and Rollins, are names familiar to the present generation. There is yet no sign of the Yankees degenerating, or dying out in Dover! The descendents of the signers of the "Combination" are as vigorous and independent as the forefathers.

In the absence of government, these settlers on a branch of the Piscataqua, fell back on the necessary human origin of government, the compact of the people. It antedated in practice by a hundred and thirty-six years, the principles announced in the Declaration of 1776. It was the proof that no act by any "gracious Majesty" was necessary to the existence of Government, and that the "body politique" could originate in a combination of individuals. Forty men on the shores of a river scarcely known across the ocean, were capable of establishing by their own act a Government. You will notice, also, its evident doctrine of perfect equality. There were no special privileges accorded to learned clergymen, on whose head the hands of a Bishop had been laid; nor to the scion of the knightly house whose pedigree was then five hundred years old, and in whose veins ran the blood of the Plantagenets. Their names are written in the same columns with those of obscure laborers, and with no marks of distinction. It was a pure democracy, "Such orders as shall be declared by a major part of the freemen of our Society." It was a perfect model of the simplest form of a democratic government, and of equal suffrage. Exeter had made a combination the year previous. The two papers are essentially alike, but you will see, if you compare them, that that of Dover omits all reference to the church, which that of Exeter makes foremost; and that ours is the simplest, most terse, a model of clearness and precision.

The political history of Dover, and in fact of New Hampshire, did not begin with a general government, and then a sub division into townships. The townships were first. They were independent of each other. A democracy on the falls of the Swamscot; a democracy on Strawberry Bank; a democracy on the upper Piscataqua. Experience showed the necessity of union but when they united and when they all came under the government whose seat was at Boston they retained almost all their independence. Dover transacted its own affairs in its own town meetings. It granted the land within its borders and its citizens held these lands in fee simple. It levied and collected its own taxes. It made its own municipal regulations. Our town records are full of legislation; legislation of a simple and homely kind; just such as we should expect of plain, sagacious, honest neighbors meeting together.

During the continuance of the union with Massachusetts Dover had its own Court and its own magistrates. No man could be taken out of his neighborhood for trial as to person or property. It was exempt from all taxes except for its own expenditures, and contributed nothing to the provincial Government. No person as a soldier could be drawn out of Dover without the consent of the town. Dover was essentially locally governed by itself during the forty years it was under the Massachusetts rule.

Still more remarkable was another concession. Massachusetts had a law that only church members could be voters; fundamental in its character. But it conceded that these towns should be exempted from this provision. All admitted inhabitants could vote "though they be not at present church-members." In fact the free spirit of Dover and Portsmouth would never have consented to the tyrannical statute, which, however necessary or justifiable in the origin of Massachusetts would have been absurd upon the Piscataqua. Few would have been the voters otherwise. With the original Episcopal element here and with the population which gravitated hither because of its freedom the churchly rule could not be endured. It was well. New Hampshire people never were tempted to, "Resolve first that the earth belongs to the saints; secondly that we are the saints." It never had to guard against the personal hypocrisy which such a rule tended to produce. In subsequent years it never sympathized with the persecution against the Quakers; the few stripes inflicted being by force of Massachusetts' laws; and Dover at one time being one-third made up of the Quakers. It had no tendencies toward the witchcraft persecutions and although it saw the phenomena it left them to die of themselves.

Although therefore our ancestors were for nearly forty years under the authority of Massachusetts that authority sat lightly. Dover was essentially locally governed by itself. It sent its deputies to the General Court. Major Richard Walderne, its deputy, was seven years Speaker of the Massachusetts House and yet Dover repeatedly passed such votes of instruction as this: "You shall stand to maintain our privileges by virtue of our articles of agreement and bring the proceedings of the Court that concern us in writing." And again: "Orders for the deputy for the General Court: he shall not with his consent pass any act impugning our privileges but shall enter his dissent against all such acts." And again: "You shall stand to maintain our privileges concerning military affairs that we may not be drawn out of our County of Dover and Portsmouth acc'g to our first agreement." The little Commonwealth here believed that "Eternal vigilance is the price of liberty," and it steadily and effectually maintained its power of local self-government against authority even so little distant and so lightly felt as that of Massachusetts Bay.

Thus we see citizens that our local government was founded by a race hardy in character and tenacious of liberty; that it was a voluntary democracy, and that in its union with Massachusetts which was a voluntary act, and utterly ignoring royal authority, it reserved local self-government and local liberties. It is not necessary to trace the same spirit through the period of New Hampshire's separate history as a royal province; it continued; and when the Revolution commenced, there was not a principle beneath it, which had not been the intelligent and practised belief of our fathers from the beginning. Their original character and their political habits alike made to them the great Declaration a natural and familiar expression of political truths.

When in 1640 these 41 persons met in town meeting for the transaction of their simple business, we may well wonder where they met and who was their moderator. That they met in their log meeting house near Dover Point is doubtless true, for our ancestors made the duty of a citizen as high as the duty of a church member, and put both into the common meeting house. The name meeting house was purposely used by our ancestors for it was the place where citizens met for worship or business. There they voted the taxes. There they elected their officers. There they ordered highways to be laid out. There they made grants of land. I do not think, however, that they laid any corner stone and the only lodge, my brethren, was "a lodge in some vast wilderness." That the first clerk was William Walderne is probably true, first of a line which has had no more able official than the one who has held this place for more than a tenth of this long history. Its first moderator could have been no other than the first signer of the combination Richard Walderne, who came here from Warwickshire, where he and Lord Brook, then simply Robert Greville had been boys together; who built the first mills upon the Cocheco, tradition says 250 years ago; who afterwards was for many years Speaker of the Massachusetts House and was the foremost man of New Hampshire and upon whose land this city hall is to stand. His fate in the destruction of Cochecho in 1689 is matter of history. But it is a noteworthy fact that while as magistrate for many years he sat in judgment in his own mansion which was destroyed in that massacre, the men who selected the site for the new court house just erected unconsciously placed it where a portion of that building covers a precise portion of the site of Richard Walderne's house.

The Dover Enquirer Oct. 22, 1850, contains No. 11 of the old series of Memoranda as follows:

EARLY SETTLERS OF DOVER.

Of Capt. Wiggans, the first "Governor" at Cochecho, Dr. Belknap says:

> "It appears from Ancient (Dover) Records that Wiggans had a power of granting lands to the settlers; but as trade was their principal object, they took up small lots, intending to build a compact town at Dover Neck. On the most inviting part of this eminence they built a meeting house which was afterward surrounded with an intrenchment and flankarts."

These lots were distributed in 1633 and a few years following. Other general divisions of land, of which there was plenty, were made in 1642 and 1648. Plenty of room then for good sized house lots.

The meeting house stood near the spot where now stands the lower school house on Dover Neck, and a low mound of earth around it still marks the locality of the old 'intrenchments,' though the wear of 217 years has lowered it a good deal and the plough of some vandal once cut off a portion. In the house there built, which probably remained until Major Waldron built a new one in 1653, first preached Mr. WILLIAM LEVERIDGE, of whom Belknap says:—

"Those that first enterprised that design, had some religious, as well as civil views, and therefore sent over with Capt. Wiggans in 1633, one Mr. (William) Leveridge, an able and worthy Puritan minister, with a promise of considerable allowance for his subsistence; but the encouragement proving too small for his maintenance, he removed to the southward toward Plymouth."

Mr. Leveridge had arrived at Salem 10 October, 1633, and immediately came to Dover. He remained here less than two years and left as stated above for 'want of support', his hearers falling into the habit of not paying according to agreement,—a habit which their successors in the church never entirely abandoned. He went to Boston, was admitted a member of the First church there 9 August 1635; was settled at Sandwich from 1640 to 1652; was employed as a missionary in 1657. He accompanied the first settlers to Huntingdon, L. I., and remained there until 1670, when he removed to Newtown, and died there. He is spoken of in Thompson's History of Long Island, at which place are found his posterity.

It was in 1635 that Richard Waldron settled here; the same who was so prominent an actor in New Hampshire until his death, 28 June, 1689. He came from Somersetshire, Eng., when 26 years old. About 1640 he built a saw mill at 'Cochecho lower falls' and another in 1649 and the same year sold a fourth part of the 'old mill on the South Side of the falls' to Joseph Austin, who came here about 1647 from Hampton, and is the ancestor of Elijah Austin, Esq., of Madbury, and others. The town granted, in 1648, to Mr. Waldron, the wood, whether oak or pine, of 1500 acres, for 'accommodation' to 'the sawmills he intended by God's permission to set up at Cochecho lower falls.' Joseph Austin had a like grant of 300 acres, for which he paid 20 shillings annual rent and Waldron £12. Grist mills were not built here very early but they were in time; and very likely there has been a succession of mills from that time until the 'old nail factory' took its position in 1821, on the north of the river, and "No. Two," usurped the 'mill privilege' on the South Side, and, with its associates, gave such an impetus to affairs that if the old Major himself were here, it would almost puzzle him to tell where, 'by God's permission he intended to set up his sawmills.'

But Dover Neck was the principal place of business for many years after 1635, and the town was tolerably large as to territory in those days. BLOODY POINT, now a part of Newington, then belonged to it. Its terrible name was given it, because in 1631 Capt. Neal and Capt. Wiggans came near shedding blood about the possession of this piece of land.

"But says" the worthy Mr. Hubbard, "both the litigants had so much wit in their anger as to waive the battle, each accounting himself to have done very manfully, in what was threatened; so as in respect, not of what did, but what might have fallen out, the place to this day retains the formidable name of BLOODY POINT." The OYSTER RIVER,(Shankhassick in the original Indian), now called Durham, was settled soon after, and perhaps then very thinly. Madbury had not then been sliced off to furnish a few more offices. A part or the whole of Lee was this side the line between Dover and Exeter when the line was accurately 'perambulated' in 1657, and this side of where the line would have been in 1635' if they had needed any. In the present towns of Somersworth and Rollinsford Elder William Wentworth, James Kid, Joseph Austin, and some few others, soon took possession of 'land lying near the great pond', 'land beyond the fresh marsh,' 'Indigo Hill,' 'between Cochecho and Quamphegan,' 'St. Alban's Cove,' 'Sligo,' and other equally definite localities. All these, besides 'Bellaman's Bank,' 'Dover Neck,' and 'Cochechae' were part and parcel of Dover, when it had that name in 1639. It lost the name in 1640, but soon recovered it.

The following is No. 12 of the Old series of Memoranda, Oct. 29, 1850.

EARLY MINISTERS IN DOVER.

The second minister of Dover was GEORGE BURDET, of whom Belknap's Manuscript Church History gives the following particulars:—

"In his room (that is, Mr. Leveridge), succeeded George Burdet, a person of better knowledge and learning than other abilities fit for that sacred function. This Burdet from a pretended quarrel with the Bishops and ceremonies of the Church of England, had about the year 1634, left Yarmouth in England, and coming over to Salem, was received as a member of the church there, (was admitted freeman there 2 September, 1635), and employed to preach among them for a year or more, being an able scholar and of plausible parts and carriage. But finding the discipline of the church too straight for his loose conscience, he removed hither (about 1637) where he continued for sometime in good esteem, at least in appearance, with Mr. Wiggans who had the power of a Governor hereabouts, until he declared himself of what sort he was; for the tree is not known but by its fruits."

"While he continued here he corresponded with Archbishop Laud, and a copy of a letter to the Archbishop, wrote by Burdet, was found in his study and to this effect, viz.:—'That he delayed going to England that he might fully inform himself of the state of the place as to allegiance, for it was not new discipline that was aimed at, but Sovereignty, etc.; that it was accounted perjury and treason in their General Court to speak of appeals to the King.' By the first ship that came in 1638, a letter was brought from the Archishop to Burdet, 'rendering him thanks for the care of his Majesty's service, and assuring him that they would take a time for a redress of the disorders which he informed them of. But by reason of much business which lay upon them, they could not at that time accomplish his desires.' This letter was by some means or other shown to the Governor of the Massachusetts."

"Not long after Mr. Burdet's coming

to Dover, by the assistance of some one who entertained a better opinion of him than ever he deserved, he invaded the civil government, and thrusting out Capt. Wiggans, who had been placed there by the Lords and others, he became Governor of the place as well as preacher. His true character was soon discovered. Being detected in some lewd actions, he made a precipitate removal (in 1638) to Agamenticus, now York, in the Province of Maine, where he assumed the rule and continued a course of injustice till the arrival of Thomas Gorges, their Governor, in 1640." He was brought to trial, fined and his cattle seized for payment. (There is a record of a law suit regarding these cattle, at Exeter.) "He appealed to the King, but his appeal not being admitted, he departed for England full of enmity against these plantations. When he arrived he found all in confusion." (It was in the commencement of the revolution of 1640, and the King had enough to do to take care of his own head, without troubling old Agamenticus. The people attended to Burdet, however, for as he fell in with the Royalsts he was taken prisoner by the Parliamentary party and put into prison, which is all we know of him save that he richly deserved it.)

"In the mean time (1633) several persons of good estate, and of some account for religion, were by the interests of the Lords and their gentlemen, induced to transplant themselves hither, so many as sufficient to make considerable of a township and following the example of the plantation about the Massachusetts, they soon after, namely, about the year 1638, attempted to gather themselves into a church state, and had officers ordained over them for that end. But for want of discretion, if not something else, in those that were called to that solemn work, they soon after fell into factions and strange confusions, one part taking it upon them to excommunicate and punish the other in church and state, an ordinary effect of loose and pragmatical spirits under any popular government, whether civil or ecclesiastical."

"While Mr. Burdet was here CAPT. JOHN UNDERHILL came," (in 1638) who had been convicted of various offences in the Bay Colony, "and the Governor of Massachusetts by desire of the General Court, wrote to Capt. Wiggans. Burdet and others of the plantation, to the effect that whereas there had been good correspondence between them formerly, they could not but be sensible of their entertaining and countenancing some whom they had cast out, etc., etc. To this Burdet returned a very scornful answer, which was very ill taken because he had sworn to their Government, and was a member of the church at Salem. But fearing lest he should take occasion to further misrepresent them to their enemies in England and judging that he would soon discover himself to the inhabitants of Piscataqua by his evil course, the Governor, by advice did not call him to account but wrote to Edward Hilton, a principal man in the plantation, declaring his ill dealing and advising them not to put themselves in his power, intimating also how ill it would relish with their Court and people if they should advance Capt. Underhill whom they had censured both in court and church; declaring also his former crimes together with some that had been brought out since his removal, and signifying that the church had sent for him to answer for his offences, but he refused unless his sentence of banishment were released, although the Court had granted him license."

But this letter was intercepted and opened by the persons mentioned therein, at which they were so enraged to send a false and malicious representation of the ill government to England. Capt. Underhill, who wrote a letter to Mr. Cotton, (Minister of Boston) full of threatenings and high words, and another to the Governor of a contrary strain, and in very fair terms asking forgiveness of what was past, and a bearing with human infirmaties, disavowing all purposes of revenge, etc."

OLD SERIES, N0. 13. NOV. 12, 1850.

We continue Dr. Belknap's Manuscript Church Record, a history of dissensions among the early settlers of Dover in relation to civil and ecclesiastical affairs:—

"The inhabitants of the Massachusetts were much offended with those at Piscataqua for encouraging those who were cast out, and they were themselves very soon sensible of their error in neglecting the Vine and the Fig Tree and putting their trust in the shadow of a Bramble: —for they soon found that Mr. Burdet, whom they had in a formal manner (in 1637) received for their Governor in room of Capt. Wiggans, who was sent by the Lords, being laid aside, and Capt. Underhill by them called to that place, (in 1638) they had not much advantage, save only that the latter was not so subtle and malicious, and therefore not so capable to do them mischief."

"Capt. Underhill, being possessed of his new dignity showed great disrespect to the Massachusetts Government, which they repaid by sending an account of his character and behavior to Mr. Hilton. But instead of showing any signs of remorse, he was much vexed that his faults should thus be made public among his own people. He was principally instrumental in calling a church of some of the looser sort at Dover, (there was already one) who had invited Knolles (his name was HANSERD KNOLLYS), to be their minister. This Knolles had come from England (where he was not much esteemed) in the year 1638, and was rejected by the Massachusetts for holding some of the Antinomian tenets, upon which he removed thither, and met with better acceptance. Underhill made use of him to write his commendation to the Governor of Massachusetts, styling him the Right Worshipful, their honored Governor, which moved the General Court to enquire of the principal inhabitants both here and at the river's mouth, whether it was with their privity, that he had sent such a defiance and whether they would encourage him in such practices against them. They all disclaimed his miscarriages, and showed their readiness to proceed against him whenever a regular information should be sent to them. After this his carriage was much abated for the chief of the people fell from him, and the rest little regarded him; but this did not abate his malice against the Bay Governor."

Mr. Knolles, who had formerly been forbid preaching here by Mr. Burdet, having by Underhill's interest been advanced to the ministerial office, (in 1639) to ingratiate himself further with his patron, wrote a letter to his friends in London, bitterly inveighing against the Government of Massachusetts, representing them as worse than the high commission court in England, and that there was no face of religion in the country;but a copy of this letter being sent over, of which he had notice from the Government, he was exceedingly perplexed, being convinced in his consience of the great wrong he had done them. Obtaining liberty and safe conduct from the Governor, he came to Boston, and upon a lecture day, most of the Magistrates and ministers being present, he made a very free and open confession of his offense and with great aggravation, so that all the assembly were as well satisfied as could be expected upon a verbal confession. He wrote also to his friends in London to the same effect, which he left with the Governor to be sent to them."

Dr. Quint remarks on the above as follows:

It is pretty well understood now that the chronicler suffered his prejudice to overrule his judgment with regard to Knollys. The plain truth seems to be that Mr. K. was a Baptist, a being regarded with as much aversion then by the venerable Puritans as now (1850) are Rationalists by Presbyterians, Parkerites by the original Unitarians, and Parkerites and Taylorites, by old school Orthodoxy. Mr. Knollys was charged with Antinomianism, a broad charge that could no more be argued against then, than the charge of Rationalism now (1850) and often applied with about the same propriety. Mr. Knollys was much esteemed in England; he did not write for Underhill as stated; nor did he ever confess anything more than indiscreet conduct. See Winthrop and Brook.

Dr. Belknap's Manuscript History of the Church proceeds as follows:

"About the same time (1640) Capt. Underhill being struck with sorrow and remorse, obtained license and came to Boston, where at the lecture, it being Court time, he made a public confession." (of any quantity of offenses. But the Boston people were not satisfied as to his repentance; and indeed coming back to Dover he proved that he was the same as ever.) "For to ingratiate himself with some gentlemen at the river's mouth, that had much dependance upon the Commissioners in England, he sent armed men to Exeter (of which Plantation he was also Governor), to fetch one Fish out of the officer's hands for speaking against the King, and when the Church and people of Dover desired him to forbear coming into Court until they had considered his case, and he had promised so to do, yet hearing that they were consulting to remove him from his station, he came in, took his place, grew passionate and would not stay to receive his dismission, nor receive it when it was sent after him. Yet they proceeded to choose one Mr. (Thomas) Roberts, President of the Court (and Governor) and sent back Fish to Exeter."

"Besides this in open Court the committed one of his fellow Magistrates for rising up and saying he would not sit there with an adulterer. Yet the chief matter for which they proceeded against him, was, that when he himself was the first man of them to break off their agreement with the Massachusetts, he had written to their Governor, to lay it upon the people, especially upon some of them."

"Soon after he wrote again to Boston to tender satisfaction; but not being satisfied about his repentance, they would not admit him to public speech and so he returned home the second time."

OLD SERIES NO. 14, NOV. 19, 1850.

BELKNAP'S MANUSCRIPT CHURCH RECORDS.

"Being cleared of Burdet, it (the plantation) was ridden by another Churchman, THOMAS LARKHAM. Coming to New England, and not favoring the discipline, he removed thither and the people of Dover were much taken with his public preaching, he being of good parts and well gifted. But not being able to maintain two ministers they resolved to cast off Mr. Knolles and embrace Mr. Larkham. Whereupon Mr. Knolles, making a virtue of necessity, gave place, and the other, soon after he was chosen, discovered himself by taking into the Church all that offered, though never so notoriously immoral and ignorant, if they would but promise amendment, and moreover fell into contensions with the people, taking upon him to rule all, even the Magistrates themselves. This occasioned a sharp dispute between him and Mr. Knolles, who either yet retained or on this occasion reassumed the pastoral office. Whereupon they were neither able quietly to divide into two churches nor to live peaceably together in one. The more religious sort adhering to Mr. Knolles, he in their name excommunicated Mr. Larkham, who in turn laid violent hands on Knolles, taking the hat from his head, pretending it was not paid for, but he was so civil as to send it back to him again. In this heat it began to grow to a tumult, and some of the Magistrates joined with Mr. Larkham and assembled in company to fetch Capt. Underhill before the Court; he also gathered some of their neighbors together to defend themselves and keep the peace, and so marched out to meet Mr. Larkham, one carrying a Bible on a halbud for an ensign, Mr Knolles being armed with a pistol. When Mr. Larkham saw them thus provided, he withdrew his party and went no farther, but sent down to Mr. Williams, Governor of Strawberrybank, for assistance, who came up with a company of armed men and beset Mr. Knolles's house, where Capt. Underhill was, kept a guard upon him night and day till they could call a court, and then, Mr. Williams sitting as Judge, they found Underhill and his company guilty of riot and set great fines upon them, and ordered him and some others to depart out of the Plantation."

"The cause of this eager persecution was because Capt. Underhill had procured a good part of the inhabitants to offer themselves to the Government of the Massachusetts, and being then prosecuted, they sent a petition to them for aid. The Governor and assistants commissioned Mr. Bradstreet, Hugh Peters of Salem and Mr. Dalton of Hampton, who came hither on foot to enquire into the matter and endeavor to make peace. They succeeded so well that Mr. Larkham was released from his excommunication, and Capt. Underhill and the rest from their sentence."

In 1640, September, "Capt. Underhill was brought to true and thorough remorse of conscience for his foul sins, and did openly, in a great assembly at Boston, on a lecture day, in the court time, and in ruthful habit, being accustomed to take great pride in his bravery and neatness, standing upon a form, lay open, with many deep sighs and abundance of tears, his wicked life," and the people of Dover were finally rid of him.

"Soon after (in 1640), Mr. Knolles left the scene of confusion, and in 1641, Mr. Larkham suddenly left to avoid the shame of a scandalous sin it was found he had committed."

So say the authorities, but Mr. Larkham had an action against John Richardson, 1642, 9 mo., 10, for falling timber on his land. The parties agreed.

"1640, March 4, Hanserd Knollys vs. Edward Starbuck, action of slander."

OLD SERIES NO. 15, NOV. 26, 1850.

BIOGRAPHICAL SKETCHES OF THE EARLY MINISTERS.

HANSERD KNOLLYS, the third minister of Dover, was born in Cawkwell, Lincolnshire, England, in 1598. He graduated at Cambridge, sustaining an excellent character. After graduation he was chosen master of the free school at Gainsborough, in the County of his birth. He was ordained deacon 29 June, 1629, and Presbyter the day following by the Bishop of Peterborough. Soon after he received from the Bishop of Lincoln, the vicarage of Humberston. He did not long hold it, but resigned in consequence of doubts as to the prevalent customs. About 1636, leaving the church entirely, he joined the Puritans, a step that ended in his leaving the country to find security, and coming to America.

After leaving Dover, he returned to England by invitation of his aged father, arriving there 24 Dec., 1641. After teaching sometime in his own house at Great Tower Hill, he was elected master of the free school in St. Mary Axe. He prospered, but left his school to preach to the soldiers in the Parliamentary army, which he continued to do until he saw the selfishness of the leaders. Returning to London he preached some little time, but being openly a Baptist, he suffered much persecution. He opened a meeting in Great St. Helens, but it was broken up, and his large congregation dispersed. He traveled on the continent for a short time, returned, and began to teach, also to preach to a congregation which met at Broken Wharf, Thames street, at the time of his death, which took place after a few days sickness, Sept. 2, 1691. He bore in England the character of a pious, devoted minister.

His wife died 13 April, 1671, and not far from that time his only son.

His published works were: (1) Christ Exalted,—A lost sinner sought and saved by Christ.—God's people a holy people. (These being the sum of three sermons preached in Soffolk, 1646). —(2)The Shining of a flaming fire in Zion; on baptism, being a reply to Mr. Saltonstall's Smoke of the Temple) –(3)A preface to Mr. Collier's book entitled, 'The Exaltation of Christ,' 1647.—(4) The Parable of the

Kingdom of Heaven explained, 1664.—(5) Grammatica Latine, Graecae et Hebraicae compendia, rhetoricae adumbratia:—item radicis Graecae et Hebraicae, omnes quae, in sacra scriptura veturis et novi testatemonti occurrent, 1665.—(6) An exposition of the whole book of Revelations, 1688.—(7) An Essay of Sacred Rhetoric used by the Holy Spirit in the Scripture of Truth, 1676.—(8) Last Legacy to the Church, 1692.—(9) Some account of his life to the year 1670, continued by Mr. Kiffin, 1692.—(10) The world that now is and that which is to come. (11) A defense of singing the praises of God. (12) Preface to Mr. Keach's Instructions for children.—(Condensed from books.)

An engraved likeness of Mr. Knolleys is in possession of Asa A. Tufts, Esq., of this town. [It is now (1898) in possession of Mrs. Caroline G. Hill, of Malden, Mass., daughter of Mr. Tufts.]

THOMAS LARKHAM, fourth minister of Dover, was born at Lynn, Dorsetshire, England, 4 May 1661. Graduated at Jesus College, Cambridge.—He was first settled at Northam, near Barnstaple, England, but being of the Puritan stamp, was followed by vexations and persecutions, so that at last he was forced to quit England. He came to Dover as previously related. He returned in 1641 to England, was settled in the ministry at Tavistock, where he bore an excellent character and had great success. He was ejected by the act of conformity in 1662, lived in great trouble from the persecution of the established church, and died in 1669, in the house of his son-in-law, where he was concealed by reason of fear of imprisonment. He left one son, Mr. G. Larkham, of Cockermouth. He wrote sermons on the attributes of God.—The Wedding Supper, a discourse on paying tithes. (Calamy condensed).

On the Town Records it is stated that Mr. Larkham owned lot Number 4, on the west side of Back River, in 1642, and that one hundred acres granted him by the town were sold to John Goddard.

OLD SERIES, NO. 16, Dec. 3, 1850.

TOWN RECORDS NO. 1.

We commence this week the publication of all the records in the early volumes of our Town Books excepting grants of lands and elections. The names of persons elected to office have been published in former numbers of these Memoranda, and the grants of land arranged under the names of the settlers to whom they were made, will appear in future numbers. We shall also insert a few extracts from other sources. If they are of little interest it may be said that had our records been better preserved, they would have been more interesting now and it is to prevent the loss of the remainder that we print them. The ancient orthography has been preserved in all cases where it was possible to obtain it.

1640.

(Under this date is the "Combination" article of 1640, which has already been published, but this "No. 16" has only three names, Thomas Larkham, Richard Walderne, and William Walderne, with a note that the other 38 names could not be found. The list was found in London, England, a few years ago, as given in a previous number of the new series. J. S.)

1641.
Act by which the Towns on the Piscataqua were admitted under the Jurisdiction of Massachusetts.

It is now ordered by the General Court holden at Boston the 9th of the 8th mo 1641, and with the Consent of the Inhabitants of the — — — —of Pascataway as followeth.

Imprimis that from henceforth the sayd Peopel Inhabitina thear ar and shall Be Accepted and Reputed under the government of the Massachusetts as the rest of the Inabetants within the sayd jureisdiction and also that they shall have the same order and way of Administration of Justice and way of kepping the Courte as is Established at Ipswich and Sallem. Also they shall Be Exemted from all publicke charges other than those that shall arise Among themself or from any occasion or course that may be taken To procure thear owne proper good or benefitt. Also theay shall inioy all Such lafull liberties of fishing, planting, falling timber as formerly they have Inioyed In the sayd River.

Mr Symion Bradstret Mr Israll Stoughton Mr Samewell Simones Mr william Tinge Mr Frances Willymes and Mr Edward hillton or anie fower of them whear of Mr Bradstret or Mr Stoughton to be one, these shall have the same power that the quarter Courts at Sallem and Ipswich have. Also the Inhabetants thear ar alowed to send too depeties from the hole River to the Court at Boston, also Mr. Braedstret Mr. Stoughton and they of the comishin apoynt too or three to Joyne with Mr. Willyams and Mr. hillton to govern the people as the magistrats heir tell the next Genarall Court take ferder order

OLD SERIES, NO. 17, DEC. 10, 1850.

TOWN RECORDS NO 2.
1642.

"At a Towne meeting 2d January 1642, It is this day ordered, that if any turbulent person shall molest any of the Townsmen appointed, or quarrel with them or contest against any of their law full accons, done according to Towne order, hee shall bee first admonished, and the second time fined 5s. and the third time 10s. for eurie such offence."

"1, 6 mo. '42. It is this day ordered that noe Inhabitant shall fall aboue Tenne trees for Clapboard or pipe staues untel he hath wrought ———— up, And hee that shall haue Aboue Tenn Trees fallen at any time not wrought up shall forfeit eurie Tree Tenne shillings."

Same date. "It is ordered that Mr. Danll Maud and Mary his wife shall enjoy the house they now dwell in during their liues, prouided hee continue amongst us as Teacher or pastor if please God to call him to it."

(Mr. Maud was the fifth minister of Dover. He came to this country as early as 1635, and was admitted a freeman by the Mass. Colony, Oct. 25, 1635. He settled in Boston and was a school master there several year. He came to Dover in 1642. After the departure of Mr. Larkham as mentioned in a previous number "the people (says Belknap) were thus left sometime without preaching but at last, in 1642, they obtained Mr. Daniel Maud, whom they enjoyed many years for their minister; he was a good man, of a serious spirit and a quiet, and peaceful disposition. He continued with them till his death."

He died in 1655. He had a wife, whose name, as appears by the above extract from the Records, was Mary, but left no children in this country.

1643.

Whereas it appears in this Courte that the Commissioners Appointed to lay outt the bounds between Douer and Strawberry Banke did not consider Strawberry Bancke as a Towne nor so exactly viewed the land one that side the Riuer as was needful, and thereupon lyd outt certaine to Douer which is Most Conuenient for Strawberry bank And certain lands to Strawberry banck which is Most Conuenient for Douer so Acknowledged to be by one of the said Commissioners in this Psent Courte, it is therefore finally Ordered that all the Marsh and Meddow grounds lyinge Against the Greatbay one Strawberry banck side shall belonge to the Towne of Douer together with fower hundred Ackers of Upland ground Adioyninge and lyinge as may bee most Conuenient for the Improueing & fencing In of said Meadow, the Remainder of the said to belonge to Strawberry Bancke, reseruing the due right to eu·ry one that hath propties in the same.

This A true Coppy of the Order of Courte taken out of the Courte Records
Edward Rawson, Secret.

Dated 10, 3 mo: 1643 & nomber 556.
8.1½ mo. 1643. It is this day ordered that noe man shall fall any timber for clapbrds or pipe staue planck or bords without approbation of the Townesmen.

(This was on public land. The manufacture of clapboards and pipe staves appears to have been a common business.)

OLD SERIES, NO. 18, DEC. 17, 1850.

TOWN RECORDS, NO. 3.

1644.

26th day of the 2nd Mo., 1644.—

It is this day ordered that Edward Starbuck, Richard Walderne and William Furber to bee Wearsmen for Cotcheco fall and River, during their lives or so long as they continue Inhabitants in the Towne and at any one of their deaths or departures out of Towne of the said falls wears and fishing to returne againe to the disposing of the Towne, to putt in another, paying yearly 6 thousand Alewives for the rent ot the Towne. The first they catch to bee imployed for the use of the Church and what fish is wanting for the Church's use, to bee delivered at common price, that is to say Three shillings a thousand at the utmost, and the first Salmon they catch to be given to our pastor or teacher; and none are to fish in the said fal's or wears but the above written. And further said wearsmen are bound to use all diligence in catching fish.

2ndly the said wearsmen are to have 6 thousand of fish each of them for their ground. 3dly Church officers are to bee served with fish. 4thly All that bear office in the commonwealth and 6thly the most ancient inhabitants to bee served with fish, and soe euie man a thousand of fish equally divided or so many as euie scull of fish afford and evie man to goe up for his fish and tend there for it in fishing season, and for the odd fish that comes before the scull to bee the wearsmen's if they exceed not above two or three hundred. After the Church shall have had six thousand of fish the next to bee served are the wearsmen. Those men that doe not use their fish themselves it shall bee at ye disposing of the wearsmen. And those that neglect to take their turne shall loose their fish for that time. And it is ordered that noe man shall molest the said wearsmen in their fishing upon paine of nineteen shillings for evie default.

1647.

primo. die, Nov. Mensis, (47.

At a publique Towne meeting it is this ordered yt William Pomfrett snell keep the Records of the Town and to record the Lands and Acts of the Town as hath bin given heretofore to p'ticular persons, or that shall bee hereafter.

27th 10th mo. '47. It is this day ordered yt Mr. Ambrose Gibbons, William Pomfrett, Anth. Emery, Rich. Walderne and Thomas Layton are to treat with Mr. Hate Evil Nutter and Company of Elders, concerning the erecting and setting up of a sawmill at Campron River and as the aforesaid parties shall agree it shall bee the Act of ye Towne.

(Here follows the order of the Town based upon the above order, specifying the terms upon which Elder Nutter and Company may erect their sawmill, and the privileges granted them of cutting trees, etc.)

19h of 11th mo, '47.

Wee the inhabitants and Townsmen in the order above specified have according to the order given us by the Towne agreed with Elder Nutter and Elder Starbuck And have given and granted unto them Acomodious and fitt place at the upper or lower fall for the erecting and setting up of a Saw Mill and what timber wood shall be necessary for the said use and purpose and to fall either Oak or Pine for sawying by the said mill and that there shall be allowed and payd for Evrie Tree for falling the same the sum of six pence unto the Towne for their use and this money to be payd either in bords or planck at— — — and shall have libetie to fall their trees in any place — — — Township as they in their discessions — — — and fitt: Prouided that if they shall — — — of Campron Riuer for Timber, they shall not fall above twenty Trees without the assent and consent of the Townsmen. Giuen under or hand the dae and yeare above written."

(It was customary to grant men the 'mill privelege and libety' to cut the wood on a certain number of acres of land of which they paid rent to the Town, either a fixed sum every year, or a small amount for each tree they cut. These rents were made a fund which was a part of the minister's salary, and so appropriated for many years. The wood so cut appears to have been made into pipe staves or clapboards. These were a 'marchantable commodity' and a legal tender to the minister.)

OLD SERIES, NO. 19 DEC. 24, 1850.

TOWN RECORDS, NO. 4.

1648.

22, 6 mo. 1648. It is ordered that Mr George Smith, William Pomfrett and John Hall being chosen shall have full power and authority to put an end to all controversies that shall at any time arise for the space of one whole year.

(This was the regular practice for many years. Their jurisdiction was quite limited.)

27 of the 9 mo. 1648. It is this (day) ordered at a publique Town meeting by the vote of said Town that all such person or persons that shall bee found absent without lawful cause from the Town meeting shall for such default pay the fine of six shillings.

Same Date. It is this day ordered at a publique Towne meeting that Richard Pinkham shall beat the drum on Lord's day to give notice for the time of meeting and to sweepe the meetinghouse for the which he shall be allowed six bushels of Indyan corn for his pay this yeare and to bee free from rates.

Same date. It is further ordered that the Towne Clerk shall have 12d. for recording evie home Lott and 19 d. for every out Lott. and giving a note under his hand for the same.

The 12th of the 10th mo. 48, is granted to Richard Walderne fifteen hundred of Trees either oke or pine for the accommodation of a Sawmill which he intendeth shortly by God's permission to erect and sett upp at or upon the Lower fall of the River Cochchechoe. The said Richard Walderne is to pay three pence per tree.

20th 10th mo, '48. It is this day ordered by us whose names are hereunto written who are the prudentiall men for the affaires of the Towne that George Walton shall pay twentie shillings for evie of wine that can appeare to bee drawn either by him or his appointment to any person or persons whatsoever since the time of his keeping an ordinary, and shall pay for the price of Two pipes and one hogshead of wine since the last Court the sum of fifty shillings upon demand made by us to any person chosen to receive the same.

Ambrose Gibbons, William Pomfrett, Tho. Layton Antho Emery.

1649.

28, 8 mo. 1649. The privilege at Belleme Bank was granted to William Pomfret, Thomas Layton and John Dam.

19, 9 mo. 1649. Oyster River falls were granted to Valentine Hill and Thomas Beard.

OLD SERIES, NO. 20., DEC. 31, 1850.

COURT RECORDS.

We give our readers this week some extracts from the Court Records which relate to Dover people and Dover matters.

164—, March 4. "Hanserd Knollys vs. Edward Starbuck, action of slaund—" What the verdict was we do not know.

1642, 9 mo, 10. "Tho: Larkham vsus John Richardson, an action for trespass for falling Timbers, agred."

1648, 6 mo 31. "George Webb presented for liuing Iule like a Swine."

This George Webb was here as early as 1642. He died here in 1649 or '50, and left no descendants. George Smith administered upon his estate in 1651. As there is no further mention of his swinish habits, we have the liberty to infer that he reformed.

1644, 8 mo. 2. "Elizabeth, wife of Mathew Gyles to be whipped or redeemed with a fine of 20 s. for revyling words against some of the members of the church" in Dover. So far as we understand the character of some of the folks in those days, she might have been justified.

"Ordered that William Joanes shall make a publique acknowledgment to Elder Starbuck and others he hath revyled, upon Lord's day come sennitt."—William left town.

1645—7—10. "John Baker fyned Ten shillings for drawing his sword and running after Indyans with it drawd, and to pay 2s. 6d. fees."

"John Baker admonished for trading with Indyans of the Sabbath day, and to pay 2s. 6d. fees."

John Baker psented for beating Richard Nason that he was black and blue and for throwing a fire shovel at his wife. 5s."

(John Baker lived at Cocheco as early as 1642, and had grants of lands then and at other times. His warlike propensities demanded a wider field and so the Town sent him to the "General Court" in 1650. He left town soon afterwards and the "Bakers" that were citizens years following were descendants of a more discreet warrior than John.)

1646, 6 mo, 26. "Itt is ordered that a prison be set up in Dover before the next Court at the cost and charge of the whole River before the next court upon the payne of ten pounds."

1648, 8 mo. 3. "The saide grand Jurye prsented Edward Starbuck for a fame or disturbing the peace of the church.

Edward Starbuck admonished for the same and discharged with — — — — — fee."

The saide grande Jury prsented Edward Starbuck for denyeinge to joyne with the churche in the ordinance of baptisme."

(We will give an account of the Elder and his troubles in some future number.)

1649, 2 mo. 24. (Old County of Norfolk Records.)—Edward Colcord vs. the town of Dover "for a debt of £20 wch was some time due to Mr. Burdett"—The town, it would seem, did not pay Mr. Burdett for his valuable services; and though "John Baker of Dover affirmed in court yt Rich. Waldin sayd he would take his oath that Mr. Colcord was really payd the debt of £20 to Mr. Burdett now in question," yet in spite of such satisfactory evidence, verdict was given for the plaintiff.

1651, 7 mo, 9. "George Walton prserted for abusing the Lord's day in carrieing boords and going to the Isle of Sholes, admonished."

"Phillip Cheslie, Thomas Ffootman, Thomas Johnson, and William Roberts prsented for goeing in the time of makeinge to the ordinarie on the afternoon the 25 may laste, admonishel."

"Thomas ffootman prsented for abusinge the constable Tho: Beard, fined for the same 13s 4d."

NOTE.—A correspondent inquires in reference to "Hate Evil Nutter and Company of Elders" who were mentioned in some of the preceding numbers of these "Memoranda," as having made a contract with the town for setting up a saw mill, etc., who the "& Company" was, and what was the origin and purpose of the association? The Town Records, we believe, give no other information as to the objects of the association, than that which has been mentioned, viz.— "the erecting and setting up a Saw Mill" —an enterprise which for those days, probably required, comparatively speaking, a combination of capital and skil[1] equal to that which is now necessary to establish a good sized Cotton Factory. The "& Company," we infer from the record of agreement published in No. 18, under date of "19th of 11th mo. 47," was "Elder Starbuck," his name being mentioned in connection with that of Elder Nutter as engaged in the enterprise.

The same correspondent states that he has "heard it said that Walderne is a distinct name from Waldron." The name is spelled both ways on the Towne Records and if it is a distinct name the difference was not recognized among the early settlers of the name in this town or their descendants. The name "Walden" is still common in some places in the State—whether a contraction of "Waldron" we know not.

OLD SERIES, NO 21, JAN. 7, 1851.

COURT RECORDS.

1652, 8 mo. 8. "James Newtt prsented for abusinge of authoritie. James Newtt bound for his good behauior for the same.

"Thomas ffursan prsented for ouer much drinkinge."

"James Newtt prsented for abusing Town Clarke in saying that he was a deceitfull man and had a deceitfull harte."

1656, June 27. "James Rollins being prsented for neglect of coming unto the publicke meeting is admonished, and to pay the fees of the Courte, two shillings & 6 pence."

1657, June 30. "Tho: Crawlie prsented for liuinge idle in his callinge, is admonished, with 2s. 6d. fees."

"Elizabeth Gils prsented for callinge John Alt constable, CONSTABLE ROGIE, is admonished, with 2s, 6d fees."

1659, 4 mo. 28. "The Jury prsented the Towne of Dover for the wayes between Hilton's Poynt and Quochecho. This Court Injoines the sd Towne to mend them between this and ye next court held at porchmouth, on penalty of £5 and fees of court."

They were notified also to "mend their wayes" between Oyster River Point and Mr. Hill's mill, and at ye head of Thomas Johnson's Creek.

The First Liquor Law in New Hampshire.

With a due regard to the public welfare and the pockets of the wine-sellers the court 'presented' all the ordinaries of Dover and Portsmouth for the crime of selling "wine at 8s. and Rumm at 16s. p. Gall."

There were also other scandalous irregularities, it being commonly reported that the men got drunk. But we who know what an excellent character Dover has always borne in respect to temperance may be allowed to believe that our ancestors must have been mistaken. Still, that they were confident in their own opinion, may be inferred from the following vote, passed the 30th of the same month.

The court hearing of this "suffering of psons to continue drinkinge to excess, as alsoe unto drunkenness, Quarrelling & fighting," & c.

"This court taking the same into their Serious consideration, accounting it there dutie by all due means to prevent the like abuses for ye future, doe order that henceforth noe wine Tavern shall either directly or indirectly suffer or permit any pson to have any Wine on the Sabbath day, neither shall they at any time sell any wine for more than 18d. a quart on penaltie of forfeiture of ye Licenses, and 5s. a pint for selling any on the Sabbath Day, or on evenings of ye Sabbath, excepting only to ffishermen of ye Lodg at there houses on ye Satterday night, half a pint a man, or to sick persons; and that no ordinary or house of common entertainment shall sell any strong Liquor on any pretence whatever.

This court doth ordr that henceforth only one Wine Tavern shall be Licensed at Dover," &c.

Persons at Oyster River (Durham) Fined and one woman put into stocks for Not attending church.

With due regard to the proprieties of life the authorities convicted and punished the following persons for not 'going to meetinge'—William Roberts of O. R. who had been absent 28 Sundays —William Williams, Sen., 8 days.—William Follett, 16 days.—James Smith, 14 days, "and one day confest to have been at a Quakr meeting," for which day he was fined 10s.—John Goddard 4 days, and twice at the Quakers.—Thomas Roberts 13 days —James Nute, Sen. wife and son 26 days, "and for entertaininge Quakers 4 hours in one day" he was fined 40s. an hour, "according to Law " Humphrey Varney "pleaded non conviction" for his absences, "unto whom the Law was this day read and he admonished."—Mary Hanson 13 days.— Richard Oates, wife and servant maid, 13 days.—Robert Burnham who had been to Strawberry Bank to meeting, and explained matters, which "showed him to the Courte not to be obstinate."—Jellian Pinkham, 13 days. Her husband refused to pay the fine, which was 5 shillings per day in each case, and she was adjudged to be set in the stocks one hour.

1661, June—"Tho: Canney of Douer desireing the court to ffree him from common training by reason he hath lost his eiesight, (it) is granted him."

1661, August 7.—"'The countie of Douer & Portsmouth prsented for want of sufficient Bridg for horse & ffoote ouer Chochecho Riuer. This court ord'rs that a Committee out of the Towne of Douer and Portsmouth be chosen to view Chochecho Riuer & if they find it needfull are Impowered to make a bridge for horse and ffoote and pay 2s 6d. fees court."

(If the last clause is to be literally understood, the committee was to pay costs! But our forefathers did not all understand grammar as well as they did more manly science.)

1667, Sept. 1.—"The grand jury prsented The Towne of Douer for want of Stocks, whipping post, standard weights and measures, a sealer of Leather, a pound, a watch house, powder match and bullets. The courte enjoyned ye sd Towne to provide them by ye next courte or pay flue pounds & fees 2s. 6d."

(Civilization would retrograde without its pleasant accompaniments of stocks and whipping posts. But the town did not learn by experience.)

1668, June 30.—"The Towne of Douer for want of a pr of stocks sentenced to get a pr by the next court of Associates or pay a fine of £5 and fees."

OLD SERIES, NO. 22, JAN. 14, 1851.

TOWN RECORDS.

1650.

1, 5 mo. 1650. Permission is given to "Mr. Thomas Wiggin and Edward Starbuck acomdation for ereickteing or setting downe a Sawemill at the secont fall of Cochechae Reuer with a Comedation of timber near ajasent." They are to pay 10 pounds rent after the mill is at work; and if they do not build it and set it at work within one year after the first of next July they are to pay 10 pounds. They also had land given them.

Same date. "Mr. Thomas Wiggin and Mr. Simon Bradstret" are granted "A comedation for a sawmill to be ereickerted by them and set up in the Riuer of niecknechewanicke aboue the first fall or at quampeheggun as also a Comedation of timber." £10 rent.

1651.

"At a towne meeting held the 14th of the 5th mo. '51, it is agreed upon by all the inhabetance of this towneship of Douer to Rayese and buey one hundred poundes by the year toward the maynte-nance of too menesters the one is to liue at Oyster Reuer, and the other at Douer, that is to say the minester that is to be called is to liue at Oyster Reuer. It is alsoe agreed apon yt the minester shall Changeabley exersies thear — — —some time at one plase and some time at the other a Cording As theay shall agree, and it is ferder agred apon yt Mr. Maud is to haue his fifty pounds ye yeare till thear is a noether minester Com to oyster reuer and after ye houndred pounds ye year is to be Equally deueided, yt is to say £50 to each menister."

It has not been hitherto known how early a minister was settled at Oyster River, in pursuance of this vote. Rev. John Buss, who began to preach there in 1678, has been supposed to be the first, though it was known that a meeting house was built there earlier, viz., in 1655, and the minister's house in 1656. But it seems a Mr. Fletcher was settled there in 1656, and left in 1657, after difficulty with the town, intending to return to England. A Mr. Fletcher is spoken of by Calamy as having been ejected in 1662, having lately returned from New England, and who returned thither after his ejection. It is probable this is the same person. His departure appears to have had something to do with the difficulties which were constantly existing between Oyster River and Dover Neck. For quite a number of years after his departure, the Oyster Riuer folks refused to pay 'rates' for the support of the ministry.

OLD SERIES, NO. 23, JAN. 21, 1850.

TOWN RECORDS.

1651.

8, 10 mo. 1651. "Mr. Ambrose Gibbons are to join with the selectmen" to bound the grants to the different sawmills.

There was evident need of this. In the generosity of the town it had granted wood or land twice or thrice over, and as a very natural consequence troubles arose. So this plan was adopted, which was a very sensible one, if it had been attended to in season. Next Spring, as appears below, under 1652, various grantees agreed to "rest contented with the decisions of these men," which they could not very well help.

1652.

"Whereas the I(n)habitants have granted to us liberty to erect certain sawmills with Accommodations of timber to belonge to each Pticular grant, now this testifieth that we whose names are under written doe Agree & promise to rest contented & satisfied with such decisions and Accommodatiuns of timber as shall be layd out and Agreed upon by such psons as the towne of Douer hath Deputed and sett out to bound the same.

Dated the 26th 4th mo.; (16)52.

  Simon Bradstreet
  Thomas Wiggin
  Edward Starbuck
  Valentine Hill
  Richard Walden

The mark of Joseph (X) Austin

7, 5 mo, 1652. Mr. Valentine Hill has "the whole accomodations of Lamprell River for the erectinge and settinge up a Sawmill or mills," with plenty of timber to saw up. £ 20 rent.

Same date. "Whereas there is some Scruples made by the Inhabitants of the towne of Dover conserning the fermness of such Grants as has been made by such as the towne hath formerly Deputed, we the presnt selekt men do hereby Rattefie and conferme all such grants as hath bin maed boeth of upland and marsh or medowe in the Greate bay to such as to whome the medoes were give and nowe doe possess them. Dated the 7th of the 5th Mo. 1652."

8, 7 mo. 1652. "Upon the petition of the inhabitants of Northam, Mr. Samuel Dudley, Mr. William Payne, Mr. Winslowe, mathew Boyes" are "to settle thier lemytes."

This Committee reported thus:—

That the utmost Bound on the west is a Creeke on the east sied of Lamprill River and from the end of that Creeke to Lamprill River forst fall and soe from the forst fall on a west and by north line six miles, and from newchawnick forst fall one—A north and by est line fower miles from a Creeke next Blowe Thomas Canne his house to a Certaine Cove near the mouth of the Great Bay called the hogstey Cove and all the marsh and meadowe ground lyning and butting on the Great Bay with Conveniente upland to sett thear hay."

"The 19 of October, 1652, it is ordered that the northern bounds of Dover shall extend from the falls of the newichewincke River upon a north and by west line fower miles."

At this same date, "in answer to a petition from the Inhabitants of Dover &

Exeter for a final determination of the Case between Dover & Exeter Concerninge ther bounds About Lamprill River," the line was thus settled.

"Agreed that the line formerly laid out shall stand, they takinge the pointe from the middle the bridge and the first fall one Lamprill River, and soe to Runne six miles west by North," with some specifications as to their equal right to the river.

OLD SERIES, NO. 24, JAN. 28, 1851.

TOWN RECORDS.

1652.

5, 10th mo. 1652. "Ordered that the inhabitants of the Necke of Lande of Dover shall have all the necke of Land below the Towne which is called the Swapme, and so to Hilton's point for to make an Ox Pasture."

The Town Orders the Erection of the First Meeting House by Major Walderne.

Same date. Mr. Richard Walderne has "accomedation" for his mills, "in consideration whereof the aforesaid Mr. Richard Walderne doth bind himself his heires administrators to erect a Meeting House upon the hill near Elder Nutters, the dementions of said House is to be forty feet longe, twenty six foot wide, sixteen foot stud, with six windows, two doores fitt for such a house with a tile covering, and to planck all the walls, with glass and nails for it and to be finished betwixt this and April next come twelve month, wch will be in the year 1654."

Same date. "Whereas Mr. Valentine Hil of Dover hath sett upp sawmill works at Oyster River," he has a grant of timber and land "half a mile to the East ward of Thomas Johnsons Creek," &c for which his rent is £10.

Same date. "Mr Valentine Hill has had permission at Lamprey River but has not yet done it."

Same date. "Whereas Captain Thomas Wiggins and Mr. Lyman Bradstreet haue sett upp Sawmill works at Quompehegon ffall," they are granted the trees on land a couple miles long and one mile broad. £10 rent.

Same date. Fresh Creek mill privelege is granted to "William Ffurber, William Wentworth, Henery Langster, Thomas Canney," £6 rent for the wood beside "tenn shillings for eury such mast as they make use of."

Same date. "Little Johns Creeke privelege is giuen Joseph Austin, and for the timbr he needs he is to pay £6 rent."

Same date. "Ordered that the Inhabitants of Douer Necke shall haue the land that lyeth west on the west side of the necke to make them a calves Pasture, from the Lott of John Hall & Phillip Lewis to the water side, to be fenced in by the inhabitants."

6, 10 mo., 1652. Mr. Richard Walderne has "Liberty to sett upp a saw mill upon the North side of the second ffall of the Riuer Cochecho," and has timber to correspond. £5 rent.

OLD SERIES, NO. 25, FEB. 4, 1851.

TOWN RECORDS.

1652.

"At A meting Selecktmen the 15th of

the 5 mo. Orderd maed and agreied upon by the Selecktmen as foelloweth. It is ordred yt Such as ar apoynted to lay out loetes shall Receue of these that haue loetes granted to them as followeth, that is to saye,

for Eury house loett 4d. p. Acker.

for Eury loett aboue a hondred Ackers 2d. p. aker.

for Eury loett under a hondred Ackers 3 d. p. aker.

At the same time it is ordred that the Clarke of the towne shall haue for the Recording eury house loett 12d.

and for eury Great loett too shillings and for Eurey Saewmill with Acomadations flue shillings."

2, 10 mo., 1652. The committee "laed out to Mr. Richard Walden of Douer who hath sett upp saw mill works at the lower ffall of Cochechae, two thirds of all the timbr lyinge & growinge betwixt Cochechae first ffall and ouer to the ffreshitt of Bellemyes Banck, and soe from the end of the swamp next Bellemyes banck and so westward betweene the Riuer of Cochechae & the ffreshitt that runneth to Bellomyes bancke & soe to the uttmost bounds of Douer. Exceptinge the trees granted to Joseph Austin as also upon Douer necke from a ledge of Rocke at a ffreshitt that runneth out of the woods. Against the lower side of the Mouth of ffresh Creek and from that ledge of Rocks at high water marke upon the necke of land three Quarters of A mile upon a South and by west line and from the end of that line upon A west and by north line tell he cometh to the next Grant—all the timbr within this tract of laud betwixt Cochechae Riuer & the line Afore mentioned Exceptinge what timbr is granted to Capt. Wiggan and Mr. Bra'street.

Prouided, The Inhabitants have liberty for the cuttinge of timbr Acordinge to the Order bearinge Date with these Psents." For this he is to pay £12 rent.

5, 10th mo, 1652. Mr. Walderne has a grant of "all the timbr beinge & growinge upon the land one the South side of Bellomyes Banck towards Oyster Riuer."

(The Major's grant must have been very extensive covering at least one half of the present limits of the town. His mill at the "lower ffall," of course, was somewhere near the Central Avenue Bridge.)

OLD SERIES, NO. 26, Feb. 11, 1851.

1655.

Daniel Maud was the fifth minister of Dover and succeeded Larkham, who left in 1641. Tired of unruly shepards the people had applied, after his departure, to the General Court at Boston, for their aid in procuring a minister of whom they should not be ashamed. The Court sent thm Mr. Daniel Maud in 1642, a "man of quiet and peaceable disposition" in which respect he differed greatly from his predecessors except the worthy Parson Leveridge. Mr. Maud had been a minister in England, is supposed to have arrived in Boston in 1635; was admitted freeman there 25 May, 1636 and ffiiated as "Schoolmaster" for some years. He was twice married, his last wife being Mary. He died early in the year 1655.

His will we publish so far as it can be made out; time has had some effect upon its appearance, and the writing itself is more unreadable than is usual even in papers of that date. Some few words we could not decipher and many others are worn off or effaced.

Rev. Daniel Maud's Will.

"I Daniel Maud in some weakness of body but in pfect memory, not knowing the time of removell out of this earthly tabernakle do here desier to make this my last wi— — & tes'ament comending my soule to the saruis of my Almighty Creator and most — — — and merciful redemer and my body to be layd in the place of ordenary buriall near to my last wife; desiring the Lord mercyfully provide for his people such as may hold on the work he hath among his people here with a further blessing than yet hath been among them, and for this end am willing to leave such few books as I haue for the use and benefit of such a one as may be fitt to have improvement, especially of those in the Hebrew tongue; but in case such a one be not had, to let them go to some of the next congregation as may have the use of them as York or Hampton, because learning is of relish with disuse; excepting one boke titled "Dei pass — — —orum" wch I would have left for Cambridge library, and my little Hebrew bible for Mr. Brock or any inferiour books, bokes for learning of — — be — — — to — — — — in learning.

And for my wife's children, seeing I recieved some of her debtes since my marriage of about £11 to have (if my estate will reach, to be coming to them, to the value of twenty ackers to be for their use when the — com to capableness to improve the same, beside what they have had allowed to them in every one a calfe now come up to a cowe-; my best outward receiving coat to mr Pembleton, and 14s. to mr. Cutts, wh there is 10s in my purse to be coming to him toward the answering of. 10s. to George Walton, wh Tho: Beard hath undertaken to satisfy for me. 4s. to goodwife Tucke of Hampton and 5s. to the French Doctor, wh there is — — — — — — — in my closet to satisfie for, wh I desire may come to them, and 20s. to one George feild then dwelling in boston, but he was removed fro— thence, as was sayd, to sudbury, wh I owed him for som conveighance of som comoditos hither fro Boston, some thing I am indebt to Mr. Newgate— about 7s. owed to mr. — — — — for some bokes wh I desire may be answered — — em — this is that I can, in psent call to mind Now I desire my well — — — — Mr. Brock, William Pomfret & John Hall to undertake — — — — — with them for their satisfaction of, if there be any remaining as — — — — —, to be in part taken to their own use or to such as are at want hereabout. One thing there is of som greater importance, wh is a little — — — — — wrapped in my deske wh I woul have comitted to Mr. Brock to put into the hands of mr. Dauenport, who, as I heard, is intended to go to England, that he would pruse, and for putting it forth I would leave it to his wise and godly ordering of —wh I think there is a trust of God in, and some benefit to redound to som by. There is a booke of mr Norton's which is entitled "Orthodox Euangelest," wh I would have my sister cotton to have, and another booke I borrowed of my bro Cotton is to come to his son Seaborn, of Mr. — — — — "agaynst Antichristin Idolatry," wh I shall leave upon the — — — — together with hers — — ye house. for som that is with me I should desire — — — that wh th— have full satisfaction when — — — time is out wh will be about the 7 of the next month, and a little — — — — wh was my wife's and a — — — in the closet wh Mrs — — — brought me the last weeke — — — — I have a — — — Susan Halsted & his brother and sister-in law who have no need of supplyes for me. I desire to be heartily remembered to those, they are ch — in years. And this is what I have in prsent to say. in witness whereof I have set to my hand and seele this 17th of this 11th month 1654. — — — Elizabeth Cotton, some other to Joseph and one to Sa —

By me Daniel Maud."
In presence of theese underwritten,
William Wantworth,
Job Clements,
Approved of in Court Jun the 26, 1655.
Renald Fernald,
Recorder.

OLD SERIES, NO. 27. FEB. 18, 1851.

DOVER TOWN RECORDS.

Our Town Records may be thus described.

I. The oldest book extant is marked on the cover, "Dover Old Book of Records," and is in very much the same state as our other old Records—that is out of binding and bearing marks of usage too hard for even its old fashioned parchment covers to endure. It contains 197 pages nearly entire. with a tolerable index. Its first record shows that it was commenced in 1647, but it has copies of matters earlier than that date, all of which have been published save the grants of land, tax lists for the years 1648, '9, 50, '7, '8, '9,—election of officers —votes relating to the ministry and education—preservation of trees,—settlement of town boundaries with Exeter, Portsmouth and Kittery,—and various other matters "too numerous to mention." The records extend regularly to about 1660, and here and there are interspersed records as late as 1753. It is mainly from this book that we have obtained the Town Records already published. We are glad to find that our plan meets the wishes of so many readers as is shown by the demand for the series and we intend to continue them as the copyist has leisure to arrange them.

II. A fragmen containing 17 loose leaves paged 13-29. It contains two lists of freemen, and various votes which are crossed as if copied into some other book, though into what book does not appear. They date 1653 and thereabouts.

III. A fragment of 16 leaves commencing page 5; it contains regular records of elections—instructions to delegates,—parish quarrels, grants, &c.— 1661—1670.

IV. Tax book, 1661, 1672, (1669 missing) It contains 32 pages in tolerable order, chiefly valuable for its names, all of which are published in the Genealogical Register, Boston, July, 1850.

V. Sixteen leaves, loose, torn, corner burned off, edges worn, beginning and end defective; mostly taken up with sales of land; has tax lists for 1675 and 1677 party destroyed, and a record or two earlier.

OLD SERIES, NO. 27. FEB. 18, 1851.

DOVER TOWN RECORDS.
(List of Books concluded).

VI. Records from 1686 to 1689 but containing scattered entries to 1726; elections, grants &c., for 60 pages; deficient at beginning and end, and twin brother to the preceding, if looks prove relationship.

VII. A gathering up of fragments; being 10 leaves or pieces of leaves saved from destruction and varying in size from a square inch up to nearly the size of a whole page.

VIII. A volume marked "Dover Town Book of Records, 8," containing 458 pages of usual record matter; commencing March 1693-4, and extending to 1757. This volume is in very good condition, except that the ink is faded in parts and the leaves torn, edges notched and out of binding.

IX. A "Highway" fragment of 6 pages, 1733-8.

X. A volume of "Births and Marriages" commencing about 1690 and containing a good deal of genealogical information for fifty years next following that date.

The records since 1757 are in good condition. A volume was lost some 30 years ago, one on highway matters; the Town Clerk said he lent it to one of the Selectmen, and the Selectman said he did not. Both agree the book was lost, and as both died soon after all chance of its recovery is also probably dead.

The date of records shows conclusively that somebody in old time was guilty of culpable neglect. Later clerks have done better, and we are glad to find that the books now are properly taken care of. Yet in their present condition the most careful usage injures them; and as it would be a preposterous idea to forbid access to them, the question very naturally occurs whether it would not be well for the town to follow the example of many towns and have the records dating earlier than 1757 copied and arranged.

OLD SERIES, NO. 28, FEB. 4, 1851.

DOVER TOWN RECORDS.

1654.

"Whereas we whose names are here underwritten are made choice of by the Towne of Douer and Kittery to lay outt the Deuideinge Bounds betweene the said Townes, we have Mutually concluded and Agreed that the great Riuer At newichawanacke shall be and remaine the Deuideinge bou -- d between the Aforesaid Townes, the one half of the said Riuer to Apptaine and belong unto the Towne of Douer on the South and the other half to the Towne of Kittery on the North. In confirmation hereof we haue Interchange — — — sett our hands this 4th of ye 2 mo (16)54.

   Nicholas Shapleigh
   Richard Walderne
   Edward Starbuck
The marke of Nicholas ⋈ Frost
The Marke of Richard ◯ Nason
   William ffurber."

1655.

16, 2mo. 1655, "It is agreed upon concerning 'setting comfortable maintenance of the ministry of Douer and Oyster Riuer, all the rent of the sawmills shall be set apartee into a Towne stocke, with two pence upon the pound to be rated upon the estates of all the inhabitants, and all such estates so appointed are to be put into the hands of any that shall be chosen Treasurer by the said Towne to receive the said, wch summ hath respect to the Rate is to be paid in money, Beauer, Beife, Poarke, wheat, Pease, Mault, Butter, cheeise, in one or any of these. This order to take place the 25th of June next and to continue one whole yeare"

1656.

10th, 1st mo. 1655-6. "It is agreed upon that Theare shall be noe more grantes maed either to any of the present Inhabitants or to any others until the grantes that are all Redey maed be laid out and Bounded and likewise that comaneidge be layed out to all our Inhabetants in our severall Respecktiue Places, as also noe ferder grants of land shall be maed to any but by the consent of every inhabetant, prouided that thear be power rsearved for the present selecktmen till the last of Febrearey next to Acommedate any Inhabetant ferder, as in thear wisdomes they see meat if any shall desire it, wich time being expired the present Ackts are hereby Rattified and confermed." (Annulled 9:9:'57.)

The same day the town confirms all previous grants and moreover.

"It is ferder agreed upon that whereas thear is squareell grants of land made by the towne to the Inhabetants, of wch some ar in contrevdrsey, wee doe hereby declare that we haue chosen Elder Wentfoerth, John Heard, John Bickford, William ffurber, left. Hall to bound any of our lands wch ar or shall be In contreuersey betwixt us and any of our inhabetants or nabers and likewise doe hereby ingage too Rest satisfied thear Deuelion whether it be more or lesse than our grants prouide, the persons actting herein be apon thear oethes to lay it out according to euery mans grant as neire as they Can to thear Best Judgments and understanding, wch being done by them or any three of Them afore menshened shall stand for a Currant Ackte and those persons to continew in this serues lett newe be chosen. taken upon oeth before Capt. Wiggins the day and year above mentioned."

30, 1 mo., 1656. "At a towne meeting holden the 30th of the first moenth, voted that thear shall be a house at Oyster Riu(er) Billed neier the meting house for the use of the menestrey, the demenshens as followeth, that is to say 36 feet long, 10 fooett broed, 12 fooet in the wall, with too chemueyes and to be seutabley feneshed."

Dec. 4, 1656. Mr. Valentine Hill and "one or too moer" are to be "a committee to run the line betweene Douer and exeter."

14, 11 mo. 1656. The pople in arrears as to "sawmill rents" are ordered to settle up.

Mr Valentine Hill has permission to turn part of the water of "Lampreele Riuer into Oyster Riuer for the supply of his mills."

OLD SERIES, NO. 29, APRIL 1, 1851.

TOWN RECORDS.

1657.

30, 1 mo, 1657. "It is ordered that the debety that shall be chosen for to goe to the Generall Court shall haue theitty shillings for his charges goeing and coming and his diet borne by the towne all the time of his atendance at the generall cort and 2s 6d. ye day all the time of his atendance the cort all this to stand tell the Towne see ferder base to allter it."

"At the same time will Pomfrett chosen to be clarke of the weites and likewise nomenatet to be Recorder of the Cortt."

"At the same towne metinge, Ordred that John Hall Decon, Tho ffootman, Peter Coffin haue power to call the townsmen belonging to the towne to acompt for all ccmpts belonging to the towne for the time past and to stand tell new be chosen and that theay shall Publickly declaer to the Inhabetants at a Publick towne metting."

"Mr. Val. Hill his Acoo: 16, (16)56-7 for Debteyes Charges.

	£	s	d
for himselfe 7 times 21 weeks to the General Cort	21	00	00
for his charges in goeing to and againe—time in the spring	6	00	00
for 6 time at the fall	4	10	00
for his horse 7 voyeges	7	00	00
for his horse charges at the springe	0	14	00
for his horse charges at the fall	1	06	00
for charges in goeing three times about mr flesher	3	00	00
for charges about him and his bringeing	2	00	00
for extreordenarey charges in expence in Boston ye time holee	4	00	00
for charges in Reaiesing ye meting hous at oyster Riuer	17	00	
for men's hier for underpeining the metting house	1	05	00
	51	5	6

"An Agreement Between Exiter & Dover. At a meeting in Exiter between certaine men of Dover & others of Exiter deputed by ye towne for setling of ye bounds be tween ye Townes. It was concluded by them whose names are hereunder wretten, that the west & by North Line from the lower falls of Lampreel Riuer running up into the country six miles shall stand, with these considerations followinge, to say, that ye lower fall of Puscassicke with ye mill thereon shall belonge to Exiter with Accomodation of Timber belonging thereto, beinge a Mile & a quarter from the Mill towards the upper fall with in ye Line & ye necke of Land possessed by John Godard, excepting the Marsh possessed at present by Exiter men to belonge to Douer. And for ye Land within ye Line with ye rest of ye Timber to belong to douer, prouided that Exiter shall haue free comonage far thear cattle upon the same Land. And also the owners of the mill shall haue the Necke of Land on the east side of Poscassicke Riuer, downe to Lampeel Riuer (only six pole by ye Riuer side excepted,) And also conuenient cartways from ye upper fall to ye Lower fall of ye said Riuer, As also ye owners of ye mills, to say, Mr Thomas Kemball, William Hilton & Robert Smart shall haue Sixty Acres of Land apeice for tillage to ly adjacent to their Mill on ye norwest side of the said Riuer, to hold & to haue the said Land to them and their Heires & Assignes foreuer without paying any Rates to Douer either for ye Mill or ye said Lands. Witness our hands the 14th of April 1657

    Edward Hilton
    Val: Hill
    John Bickford ○ Sen. his marks
    John Gilman,
    William ffurber"

OLD SERIES, NO. 30. APRIL 8, 1851.

TOWN RECORD.

1657.

"16th: 4:57. Capt. Walderne being Treasurer of the Towne of Douer:

	£	s	d
To a Rate 4th 10th month 54 for Cortes	8	13	04
To a Rate 15th 11th mo 55	86	04	06
To Soe much more of that Rate	59	15	10
To the Pronition Rate	73	00	02
To the Indian Corne Rate	86	10	01
To Rente Rec from toulend	50	00	00
To Rent at quampheagon	29	00	00
To a fine of Water Abit	16	00	00
To action money	3	10	00
To a fine of Phillip Chesley	5	00	00
To Rent of Richard Waldrerne — to April '57	51	00	00
To Bearer Reed	1	12	00
To deputies Charges	12	10	00
To 38 Masts at 10s per mast R per Richard Walderne	19	00	00
To Rent of Joseph Astin	24	00	00
To Rent of fresh creake	18	00	00
To Rent of quamphegon	10	00	00
To a fine of Goodman Giles	2	00	00
	515	15	11

Per Cont' credebtor (1657).

By Seuerall prentments is per Acco	541	07	03
By more to the Treasurer	20	00	00
	561	07	03
	515	15	11
	45	11	04
Richard Walderne Debtor now to the towne of Douer wch he hath not Brout in, Recd. from mr flecher	20	00	00
from Mr. Rayner	15	07	03
For a fine of James Kid's	10	00	00
	45	07	03
Rent to Balance	45	11	04
	00	04	01

"At a Publick Towne metting the 17th 4 mo. (16)57, ordered that homesoeuer ether Einglesh or Indian shall kill aney wolf or wolfes within this Township shall haue for soe doeing fower pounds for euery wolf soe kild, and the head brought to the metting house on Douer necke or deliuered to the constabell for that year to be Publicke declared"

'Ordred that the selecktmen that ar to be chosen to order the afaiers of the Towne theay shall be chosen the first second day of the second moenth yerly and that theay and All oether offecers shall Bring in thear accompts to the Towne or such as shall be chosen upon the same day to report them to the Towne, ye 17, 4 [57."

"At the same day mr fletcher and the towne haueing som discorse whe — he will leaue them he willingly manifested that he was not minded to stay aney longer but to Prepaer himself for old Eingland and could not Justly lay Aney Blame Apon the Towne"

"17, 4,16[57.] Ordred that if Aney of our Inhabetants shall fall aney trees for mastes Apon the comans of this towneship— — — shall paye for euery maste from 24 Iuches to 36 Inches, £3 10s., and from 14 to 18, 6s, and from 18 to 24, 8s."

"Aug. 1657. The Proposetions of Mr. Raner in his writing Bearing date the 18th of the 4th mo. 1657, conserning his yearly Alowance from the town is granted and excepted uppon the tarmes thearin he haith expressed him selfe. voeted at a Publicke Town meeting the last of August 1657"

The First Schoolmaster Elected in Dover.

"Charles Buckner chosen by vote A Scoellmaster for this towne"

"Voted this last of August 1657, that all tradesmen shall be free from paying Rates for thear trads for this Raet nowe past."

"9:9:57. layers out of land at Oyster Reuier chosen ar Ensin John Daues, Robert Bernam; for Douer necke, coechaohae and Bloody poynt, Ar chcsen Eld Wentwoerth, left. Hall, John Hall Deacon."

"21:10:57. At a Public meeting, ordred that from hencefoerth All our Inhabetants shall haue a Respeckte to the order mayd concerning falling of tember, wch is that noe man shall fall aboue fiue trees for claboard or Pipstaues befoer hee haeth (wrought?) up the said fiue trees, and hoesoe euer shal soe doe contreary to the former order shall be liable to the Peneallties befoer spesefied, and for moer streckter obseruation of this order the town haeth chosen Josephe Astien for this part of the towne shep and Thomas ffootman for Oyster Riuer hoe ar Alowed one halfe of the fines. likewise if aney other inhabetant shall informe and proue it hee shall haue the like part of the fines."

"(16)57, 10:31. Artickells of A Greement Betwins the Towneshep and our Inhabetants at Oyster Reiuer"

1 That is to say th Inhabetants of Oyster Reuer shall haue full liberty to Inioye one theerd part of the rentes of the townshep and other Reueneues that shall be dew to the same for Acomedatinge A ministrey Amongst them.

2. and till thay doe Inioy one thear they ar to contreybute to the ministrey of the necke of land of Douer, or at ani time when they ar with out Aboue fower moenths thay doeing the like to them in the like case

3 Thay of Oyster Reuer not exemptnge them selves from Anie other Publicke charges nor Rentes but shall be liabelle to all Sarvuice As formerly.

4. The Bounds of the Inhabetantce of Oyster Riuer for the Acomedatinge of the ministrey is the Inhabytants that are or shall Be seittuated from the next Rockey Poynt on the north side Belowe the moneth of sed Reiuer and from thence By Astrayt line too the head of Tho Johnsons Creeke to the Paeth thear, and from thence by a west line to the end of the towne Bounds. As also all Inhabetantes on the Soueth side of that line that ether are or shall be thear seittuated are likewise to pay to the ministrey thear exsipting all the Inhabetants on foxpoynt side that ar or shall bee in the letell Baye."

OLD SERIES, NO. 31.   APRIL 15, 1851.

DOVER TOWN RECORDS.

1658.

5, 2 mo. 1658. "At a publique Towne Meetinge held the 5:2mo:58.

The Salary of the First Schoolmaster in Dover.

It is agreed by ye selectmen together with ye Towne, that twenty pounds per annum shall be yearly raysed for the mayntenance of a skoolmaster in the Towne of Douer, that is to say for the teachinge of all the Children within the Township of Douer, the said schole master hauing the priuledge of all Strangers out of the Township aforesaid: The sd Master also to haue to reid, write, Cast acopmts, — — —— as the parents shall require.

At a meeting of the selectmen ye 26:2 mo. (16)58. It is agreed upon that the Rate that was last made for the cleeringe of the Towne debts shall goe forthwith to be leuied & gathered in by the Constables or whom the Seleckmen shall depute.

2dly, that in case it doth appeare that ye forty pound wch is to be paid for the agreement wch the owners be made appear to belonge to the propriators of the Marshes, although it now be paid by the whole Towne, that then the Propriators of the Marshes shal pay the said forty pounds back again to the towne."

3dly. They intend to apply to the Court regarding taxing sawmills &c.

Capt. Richard Walderne Instructed to Guard Dover Against the Puritans of Massachusetts.

19:2(16)58. Voeted at theis Publick metting that this order following shall Bee An Instrucktion for our Debetey that is to saye our Debety Capt. Richard Walderne shall not consent to the passing of anie Ackt conserning the infringing of our privileges conserning customes or the Beuer traid or anie preueleges wich formerly we haue Inioyed but shall Enter his dissent Against all such Acks as shall or may take away our former Riet and that or debetie doe Bring all such laws as are macked at this Cortt as other Debeties doe."

(1658):2:19.) At a Publicke Towne meetinge ye 19th of ye 2d mon :58.

Voted by the Inhabetants in general, a second time that the first iugagement & promise of the Towne unto Mr. Reiner of one hundred & twenty pounds yearely is ratifyed & confirmed to be made good unto him onely with annexinge thereto such prouisoes & limitations as will both stand with the true meaninge thereof & May secure the Towne from such burthens & pressures as are faered to come upon them thereby:

As first, that he except of Ministerey & office in the Chirroh, & continue therein accordinge to the Rule of Gods Word

2dly that mens estates generally in the Town be not obseruably decayed nor Rieuts belonginge to the Towne impared neither ye one, nor the other, from wha they are in the Townes present undertakeinge for one hundred & twenty pounds yeareley. But if so be the Towne be impared & decayed at any time in their estates & Rents then accordingly for such time & noe longer, the yearely stepende may be by the Towne be lowered, only if thereby the maintenance shall fall below one hundred pounds yearely without probability of its riseinge afterwards & that he cannott therewith Comfortably carry on family occasions, (he) may make use of some other help for his Comfortable Continuance hear, or remoueinge to some other place without offence:

3dly In case it be testified to him by the Towne or the major part thereof that their expenses for this or that present yeare ar aboue what they ar usually in respect to more than ordinary or urgent occasions, & that ye rise of their estates is not such as they can comfortably bear it & yet maek good the sum agreed upon, in such a case ye Towne may be at Liberty to take of from ye same summ with respect to such expenses for ye present time as may seem meet to them, prouided it be not aboue twenty pounds pr Annum."

"At a metinge of the Selecktmen the 10th 3 mo. (16)58, Ordered that all the comenage that is lieinge on Blo poynt side not yet granted out shall be for comenedg unto the inhabetants and that noe grant shall be maed without the consent of the inhabetants thearof."

28, 1, 1658-9. "Ordered that Douer neckt, oyster Ruier, cohechaew haue the same lebeter for thear comendge as was granted to Blode poynt."

10, 11mo 1658. "Voted that Lieftenant Hall, Deacon Hall, Robert Burnam shall lay out forthwith the Bounds of the Towne betweene Lampreell Riuer & Nichewaunicke Riuer, as Alsoe the head Line at our utmost Bounds."

also, the twenty acer lots W. of Back (Riuer) were to be rebounded

Dover Neck and Oyster River Meeting Houses Must be Cared for By Their Respective Neighborhoods.

10, 11mo. 1658. "It is this day voted hat the charges of the fitting the two meeting houses of Douer & Oyster Riuer Shall be carried on Distinct by the Neighbourhood or Inhabitants of each place, that is to say the charges of Douer Meetinge house by the neighbourhood of that, & the charges of Oyster Ruier meetinge house by the Neighbourhood of Oyster Riuer."

Vote to Place a Bell on the Meeting House.

21, 12 mo. 1658. "Voted by the said Inhabitants that the meetinge house on Douer Necke is to be underpindde, & catted & seeled with Boards, And a pulpett & seats conueinient are to be made & a Bell to be purchased And this to be paid by way of Rate upon each Mans estate according to the Law of the Country."

OLD SERIES, NO. 32, APRIL 22, 1851.

DOVER TOWN RECORDS.

1659.

6:4:1659. "Voted that All the Inhabetants of this townshep of Douer that haue taken thear oett of fidellity haue thear free voet in choies of thear Sellecktmen and all other offesers consarning the towne afaieres and that the former Ackt of the Choyse of Selleecktmen maed the 17th 4th mo. 57 in poynt of time is nullified and of no efeckt."

"At the same time ordred that the present Sellecktmen haue power to Re ceue the towne Bookes from the towne Clarke now in being and to take unto them soo maney of the inhabetants as theay shall see feett to vew the bockes and order such defeckts as theay shall see mett to be doen and to Give a discharge under thear hands to the sayd town clarke and likewise to delieuer the sayd bokes to the new towne clarke After he haeth taken his oeth."

"At the same time John Hall, Deacon, chosen towne clarke. (This could not be done by reson the Courtt wold not giue the then chosen Clarke his oeth.)

Same date. "And likewise the present seleckt men haue power to fernish the townes house that Mr. Reaner liveth in acording to Covenant, and to sell the sayd house to Mr. Reaner or aney other man as they see cause."

(1659:9:7. "At a Publick Towne meting holden the 7th of the 9th mo. '59 the Inhabetants of Oyster Riuer doe dene to Give in a lest of thear estates for the Preuention Raett as formerly theay haue doen."

(Also) "Giuen and granted unto Mr. John Rayner his now dwelling house wich was the townes house prouided for a menester we the Inhabetants of this towneshep of Douer we doe freely Giue unto the afoersayd Mr. Rayner the aforesayd house with all appertenances thear unto belonging to him and his heires for euer proueided that the afoersayd Mr. Rayner doe liue and die with us and ferder this doeth free the towne from Building aney other house for a menester for the time of his liuing Amonkest us and ferder it is agreied uppon that if in case that By anie prouidence that Mr. Rayner shall remoue from us that the Towne shall pay unto the afoersayd Mr. Rayner all such charges as nesesarey shall be maed apeir by him that the towne shall ether pay him his charges or or leue the sayd house to him to make his best advantege."

"At a publicke town meting holden the 7th of the 9th mo. 59, the Inhabetants of Oyster Riuer doe denie to Giue in a lest of thear Estates for the Prouition Rate as fomerly theay haue doen."

1660.

16:1:1660. "Voted that the Townsmen should make destres Apon the Inhabetants of Oyster Riuer for the Rents and Reuenewes and Rates Dew to the towne since mr flecher went a waye and the towne is to bear them out."

ORDERS FOR THE DEBETY, 25th 3 mo. 1660.

"1ly. That you should Indeure to procure as a comietione Couertt as hie as Porchmouth.

2ly. That you take cael to Reuers the order that Capt. Pemheuton haeth from the Generall court conserning the — — — — — — man.

3ly. That you wold stand to maintayne Preueidges consarning Melleterrie afayers, that we may not be drawne out of our county of Douer and Porchmouth accordinge to our first agreiment.

4ly. That you wold desire the solution of the Generall court conserning the choyse of Town offesers, whether or noe all that haue taken the oeth of fidiellity haue liberty to choese.

5ly. That you wold stand to maintayne our Preuelledges by vartue of our Artickells of a Grement and to bringe the Proseidings of the court that consarnes us, in writing."

"Mr. Reyner his Recet Douer the 12 4 1660."

"Rec of the treasure(r) and selecktmen for the towne of Douer for the three first yeires of my aboed thear and Being exsersied thear in way of ministrey the hole salaray for the sayd yeirses viz sixscoer Pounds per Anom: Allsoe Receued of the selleckmen for the Towne the foerth yeir twards the sallarey thear of the som of fourscore and nine Pounds Eaght shillings and six pence I say rec towards the fourth yeares salarey 89-8-6 the Rest of the salarey for the afoersay foure yeir Remainest due to me from the Towne at the date hear of nether is thear Any Acompt made between me and these lecktmen for the fifth year wich begings in July or thear abouts 1659 and Ends the same time of the yeir 1660 nether as consarning the Preuention Rate or anie part of the saleary for the saide yeare.

witness my hand John Reyner.

OLD SERIES, NO. 33. APRIL 29, 1851.

DOVER TOWN RECORDS.

1660.

13, 4 mo. 1660. "Voted that for time to Com in the choise of Prudentiall men thear shall be too chosen upon the neck of land and one in Euery Respectiue plase of the Towne."

"Roberd Burnum, John Daues, John Godder, John Martin, John Bickford, Richard Yorke, William Roberds, Tho Steuenson, Will Beard, Edward Patterson, will willyames, Phillp chesley, Thomas Johnson" did "protest against the Ackt."

After this vote, five "Prudentiall men" were chosen, viz.: "too" upon the Neck as above stated, and one each for Cochecho, Oyster River and Bloody Point. Before this no particular number appears to have been chosen — sometimes but two, both of which were probably from the Neck, as being the "seat of government."

Same date: "Voted that the present Selecktmen haue power from the towne with Elder Nutter, left. Hall, Richard Otes to treat with mr Broughton and make a final determenaton of the Defrence between the towne and him couserning the grant of the saymou fall"

1660 July 17. "We hose names are heir under written being chosen by the Towne of Douer are appoynted by thear order to heire and determine all such differences as apier Betwixt the inhabetants of the twothierds of the towne of Douer and the on third of the towne of Oyster Rieur, Doe conclude at Present as followeth that is to saye

1ly. first that from the first of April 1657 and so forward from yeir to yeir it is heirby mutually agreed upon that the naieghborhoed of Oyster Ruier shall inioy full Righte and interest of twenty pounds out of the Rents of the towne to be from lamprill Ruier grant Rent performed, as alsoe too peney Rate Rising from within themselves, boeth wich twenty pounds and too peney Rateis for the supply of the minestrey within themselves and to be ordred by themselfes for the end exprest.

2ly It is Agreed and determined that the sayd naigborhoed shall haue liberty from time to time to make choyse of a ministrey for thear acomedations prouided that they haue the approbation of the sayd towne or anie three adiasen Elders.

3ly. That in case the niegbberhoed of Oyster Ruier shall bee without a ministrey aboue fower moenths theay shall Return the twenty pounds aboue sayd unto the coman treseuery with Proporsenabell contrebution theay of Douer doeing the like to them in proportion in the like case and this mutually to be Donn so long as thear is defeckts of eather sied.

4ly It [is] ordred for the menistrey of Douer necke thear is sett aparte fitty five pounds of towne Rents with the too penie Rate uppon all the inhabetants except oyster Riuer is sett apart for the ministrey thear and in case this doe not make up the sallarey, then to be made up by a Rate upon the sayd Inhabetants, Blody poynt excepted only payinge the too penne Rate.

5ly It is ordred by the supply of cochechae thear is set apart fifteen pound of towne Rents for the minestrey thear in the winter seasone.

6ly It is agreed that the house of Mr Valentine Hill wich is his nowe dweling house at Rockey Poynt shall be within the line of Deuetion to Oyster Riuer.

Witness our hands this 17th of July 1660.

Valentine Hill   Richard Walderne
William Wentworth   Raphfe ball;
Richard Otes   william ffurber
John Daues   Roberd Burnam
William Willyames   William Roberds

1660:16—:13. "At ye same time Ordred by ye towne that there shall be forthwith a Rate made of an hundred pound for ye fittinge up ye meeting house on Douer Neck."

OLD SERIES, NO. 34, MAY 6, 1851.

Dover, Its Boundaries and Divisions.

The first mention we find of any particular boundaries of the town is recorded in Belknap, page 12, where it is said that in 1634, "Neal and Wiggin joined in surveying their respective patents and laying out the towns of Portsmouth and Northam," [Northham being the name once given to Dover.]—The authority for this assertion is found in a letter (printed as No. 6 in the Appendix,) the genuineness of which is a matter of dispute. Some great Antiquaries have held the letter to be "a forgery, and of the most palpable kind," while others equally great have lately brought to light papers which seem very strongly to restore the waning character of the document. We do not care to express an opinion on the subject at present, because in the first place, we do not know much about it, and in the next place it would do no good to the present article if we did. The letter describes the boundary of the town in a way that might do very well when nobody lived above the town, except Indians and wolves, but which, if a legal description at present, might bewilder the ideas of Rochester, Barrington and towns round about.

The boundaries of the town were certainly established by Commissioners appointed for the purpose by the Massachusetts Government just after the "Union," which took place 9, 8 mo. 1641.

The record of their doings we have been unable to find, either in the Massachusetts or New Hampshire Archives.

But it is probable that the limits were the same as those established in 1652 (an account of which will be found in its proper place,) with the exception that Bloody Point, (the Point opposite Dover Point,) was taken from Dover and given to Portsmouth. The Bloody Point people did not like this kind of decision and petitioned to be re-annexed as follows:

(1643) "To the Right Honble Gouernour and Honbl Assestants of the Massachusetts.

The humble peticon of the inhabetants of Blody poynt in the Riuer Pascataway.

Humbly showing unto your good Worpps that your peticoners the inhabitants of Bloody poynt being as they are informed orderd to be within the Towneship of Strawberry Banck, which was done altogeather against our consent, wee euer hauing beene within the Towneship of Douer & in combination with them at our entrance under your gouerment and had promise from you to inioy all our lawfull libertves for feling timber & the wch your peticoners are debarrd of which is upon record in your books and haue been formerly to thear great losse & damage. Alsoe your peticoners further shew unto your good Worpps that Strawberry Banck lieth 4 myles from them or therabouts whereby theay are all debarrd from hearng the Word by reason of the Tide falling out that we cannot goe but once a fortnight and then can stay but part of the day wch will rather be a day of toyle & labour, than rest unto the Lord & yet must be forced to pay for the mainetenance of their Minister. And sithence the Court they haue layd out to themselues 50, 100 or 200 Acres a (in) pts round about us penning us up & deniing us falling aney Timber without their leaue & makinge euery one that will haue of said Land to pay yearely 50s for C Acres & so after the rate for more or lesse, they being some 14 or 15 familyes liuing remote from one Another, scateringe upon the River 2 miles & 4, 5 or 6 mlye from us yet haue taken to themselues all our best- and adioyning to us.

Humbly Beseeching your gord Worpps to be pleased to take our case into your pious consideracons & to take some order for us that we may enioy our former liberty and may be in the same Towne ship we were of, And that the order of court may be confirmed wch was that our Neck should be in Douer Towne otherwise wee shall be forced to remoue with— — —to our undoing, being 12 poor familyes. And your poor peticoners shall be bound to pray your Worpps

The names of the Inhabetants that agree to this peticon.

*James Johnson   John Godard
*Thomas canning   *Henry Langstaffe
*Thomas ffursen   John Fayer(?)
william pray   Oliuer Trimings
William Jones   Philip Lewis
Thomas Trickey   *Raderic (unreadable)"
*These made their mark.

The result of the "Peticon" may be seen in No. 17 of these Memoranda, where it is found 10, 3 mo 1643, it was "Ordered that all the Marsh and Meddow ground lying Against the Great bay on Srawberry Banck side shall belonge to the Towne of Douer, together with fower hundred Akers of Upland ground Adioining and lyine as may be most Conueinent for Improuinge & fencing In of the said Meadow, the remainder of the sd ground to belonge to Strawberry Bancke, &c."

This territory with the terrible name remained a part of Douer till 1713.

Dover Neck, sometimes called Winnicohannet or Wecohamet, was settled in the spring or early part of the summer of 1623. Bloody Point must have been settled about 1634. A beginnng was made at Cochecho about 1635. Oyster River (Durham) settlement must have been commenced soon after the accession to the Colony in 1633. How soon those parts of Oyster River since called Lee, were entered, we have no means of determining but probably not to any considerable extent for some twenty years after. Somersworth was inhabited as early as 1650 and Madbury, then a part of Cochecho, apparently still earlier. All of these were part of Dover till 1713.

OLD SERIES, NO 35. MAY 13, 1851.

Upon the 8, 7 mo, 1652, upon petition of the inhabitants of Northam, certain men were appointed to "settle their lemytes" It was done thus:

"That the utmost Bound on the west is a Creeke on the east Sied of Lamprill River and from the end of that Creeke to Lamprill Riuer first fall on A North and by est line fower miles from a Creeke next Blowe Thomas Canne his house to a Certaine Coue near the mouth of the Great Bay called the hogstey Cove and all the marsh and meadowe ground lying and butting on the Great Bay with Conueniente uplande to selt thear hay"

"The 19th of October, 1652, it is ordered that the Northern bounds of Douer shall extend from the first fall of ne-wichawanick Reuer upon a north and by west line fower miles."

Between Dover and Exeter, "agreed that the line formerly laid out shall stand, theav takeinge the point from the middle of the bridge and the first fall on Lamprill Riuer and soe to Runne six miles west by north & c"

In 1654 the middle of the "Riuer newichawanacke" was determined to be the dividing line beween Dover and Kittery.

These were the general limits of the town. But the town was destined to make more towns than one. With the increase of prosperty men's desire for office increased. Particular was this evident at Oyster River.

"Our neighbors of Oyster Riuer," desirous of having a government of their own, discovered that it was very inconvenient for them, as it undoubtedly was, to go to meeting at Dover Neck; a good deal of difficulty rose about this matter, and it was at last decided in 1651, that Oyster River folks might have a minister of their own. They built a meeting house and a minister's house, and procured, in 1656, Rev. Mr Fletcher to preach in the one and live in the other. But Rev. Mr. Fletcher and the town could not agree, the town, and not the Oyster River people, retained the right of calling both ministers, out of which queer arrangement, trouble arose, as any man of sense might have foreseen. So Mr. Fletcher went away the next year. It appears that the town had no particular anxiety to procure another minister for that place; Mr. John Rayner preached at Dover Neck and was a very fine man, and everybody might go and hear him. This did not suit our neighbors, and in 1669 they applied to the General Court as follows:

Petition to the General Court of Massachusetts 1669, to have Oyster River made a Township.

"To the much honored General Court assembled at Boston, May 17. 1669, the humble petition of the inhabetants of Oyster Ruier is as followeth. The consideration of your prudent and pious care for the carriing on the main end of planting this colonie. In the settling religion and the promoting the welfare of souls in eurie part of it subject to your government, doth embolden us (who are also in some measure sensible of the great end we came into the world for the advancement of the glory of God in our own plantation) to present this humble address unto yourselues. It is not unknown to some of you that the inhabitants of Douer (of whom for the present we are part) manie years taking intocousideration the intolerable inconvenience of our traveil manie myles, part by land, part by water, manie times by both, to the publick worship of God and the necessarie stay of manie of us from publick worship, who cannot undergo the difficulties of travel to it, it was then publickly agreed and concluded that there should be two ministers at Douer, the one at oyster Riuer, the other at Douer neck, as appears by a town act bearing date the fourteenth of the fifth, fifty one, the means of calling and maintaining both which are one, yet while we continue with them there is noe power improued on our behalfe, to that end, nor have we anie of ourselves, whereby we haue a long time, and at present groan under intolerable inconveniences, our ministrie being greatly weakened, yea and hazarded thereby, hauing neither head nor hand, to move in order to calling when without, or setling and maintaining when obtained, and it being so difficult for us to attend civil meetings there that often most of us cannot be there, whence we are in danger to be neglected or not — — — taken care of, nor our affairs so well prouided for as if we were a township of ourselves, we being in all two hundred and twentie souls, near fiftie families, seventie and odd souldiers, a conuinient number of freemen, humbly request this honoured Court to grant us that so beneficiall a priuilege of becoming a township with such bounds as haue alreadie us, or shall be thought meet by this honoured Court, and for this end we have sent John Woodman, an inhabitant among us, and give him power to join anie with him, as he shall see meet for ye managicg of this our petition and prosecution of our further reasons, committed to him, should this honoured Court whose care we know extendeth to us among the rest of this colonie, vouchsafe us favourable answer to this request, where as now our hands and hearts are weakened, in the work, prouision for the ministree at a stay, the old and young in families too much neglected, others of good use who would join with us discouraged until we become a township, some readie to leaue us if things stand as they doe, we trust upon your grant you will soon find our number increasing, our hearts and hands strengthened in the work of God, our care more uigorous, for an able orthodox minister, our families instructed according to law, ourselues growing in truth and peace to God's glorie, our content and your good, and we shall not cease to pray God Almightie for a blessing upon you in all your weightie concerns and subscribe ourselues.

Yours in humble obseruance
John Bickford, Richard York, John Daues, William Beard, Robert Burnam, Phillip Chesley, Charles Adams, Steuen Jones, Walter Matthews, Nicholas Doe, uid, Elizabeth Drew, John Woodman, John Meader, Thomas Willie, John Hill, Thomas Edgerlie, William Perkinson, Benjamin Mathews, David Daniell, Thomas Drew, Joseph Field, Zachariahs Field, John Goddard, Matthew Williams, Edward Lethers, William Randall, William Pitman, Teag Royall, Salathiel Denbow, Barnard Pope, Joseph Stinson John Smith, James Smith, James Huckins, Robert Watson, Patricke Jemison, James Thomas, Walter Jackson, Francis Drew."

This was 1669.

The result of this petition is learned in part from the vote below: it would seem that some arrangement was made between the Neck and Oyster River in consequence of this advice. But the desires of the Oyster River people were not destroyed and in after years were accomplished:—

"Having heard the petitioners with what aleadged by Capt. Walderne in ye behalfe of Douer, That that town is not informed of this Motion, and by p(er)using many Pags presented in ye case together with what is granted & yielded on both hand. We have Grounds to hope there may be an agreement & Settlement of things betwixt you selues, wd we comend to you considering it best that they should jointly agree upon tarmes, ye wch may be most advantageous for each other & for Publick good: & for yt end Judge it mete to respit ye case till next session of this Court, when what they shall agree upon may be Confermed by this Court, or in case of Non agrement, These Petitioners to give notice in due season to theire Neighbours & brethren of thear Intendent further to prosecute this Motion of being a Township at the next session of this Court that soe they may haue opportunity to make answer thereto

May 25, 1669   John Pynchon
                 Edw: Johnson
                 William Parke

The Deputyes approue of the returne of the Comitte in answer to this prt. yor Honed mages to consenting hereto.

27 May, 1669   William Torrey Cleric
                Consented to by ye magists.
                Edw: Rawson Secreti.

OLD SERIES, NO. 36, MAY 20, 1851.

DOVER, ITS BOUNDARIES AND DIVISIONS.

Petition to the General Court of New Hampshire 1695, to have Oyster River made
A Township.

In 1695 the Oyster River people presented another petition to the Government (of New Hampshire now) praying for incorporation as a Parish. Here it is:—

'To the Honble John Usher Esqr., Leut. Governor, Comandr in cheif of his majists Province of New Hampshire, and to the Honrble the Councill, wee the Sub-

scribers, Inhabitants of Oyster Riuer
Humbly Petition and Pray That whereas his most Sacred Majesty King William has been pleased through his grace and favor to grant unto yor Honr by his Royall Comission (with ye Councill) full powers and authorities to Erect and Establish Townes within this his Majesties Province, and whereas wee yor petitioners have by devine providence Settled and inhabited that Part of his Majests Province Commonly called Oyster Riuer, and have found that by the Scituation of the placeas to distance from Douer or Exiter, but more Especially Douer, wee being forced to wander through the Woods, to yt place to meet to, and for ye Management of our affaires, are much Disadvantaged for ye Present in our Business and Estates, and hindered of adding a Town & People for the Honr of his Majesty in the Inlargement and Increase of his Province, Wee humbly supplicate that yor Honr would take it to yor Consideration and Grant that wee may have a Township Confirmed by your honours, wch wee humbly offer the bounds thereof may extend as followeth, to begin at the head of Rialls his Cove and so to run upon a North west line Seven Miles, and from thence with Dover line Paralell, untll wee meet with Exeter line, that yor Honr would be pleased to grant this Petition, which will not only be a great benefit Both to the Settlement of our minestrey—The population of the place, the Ease of the Subject, and the Strengthening and Advantaging this his Magists Province, but for an engagement for yor Petitioners ever to pray for the Safety and Increase of yor Honrs and prosperity.

John Woodman,
Stephen Jones
*Paul davis,
Samson Doe
*James Bunker Sen
Jeremiah Cromett
*James durgin
william willyoums
Elias Critchett
Nathaniell Meder
John Cromell
Jeremiah Burnum
John Smith
Thomas Bickford
John Pinder
francis mathes
Henry Nock
John Willey
Thomas Edgerly
*Ewdard Leathers
Henry marsh
Joseph Meder
Edward Wakeham
Philip Chastlie Sin
Thomas Chastlie Jun
George Chastlie"

William Jackson,
Joseph Bunker
John Smith
Joseph Jones
John Doe
John William
Thomas Williams
*William durgin
Henry Vines
*Phillup Cromel
John Meder Jr
*William tascet
*James (?) dere
*philip duly
*Ele meret
Joseph Jengens
*Jems Bonker
James Thomas
—— pitman
John Edgerly
*William durgin
Joseph Smith
Thomas wille
Thomas Chastlie
francis Pitman

*Those with a star made their mark.

We can find no action regarding this matter until 4 May 1716 when this petition or some other was thus answered:—

"In Answer to yt Petition of Capt. Nathl. Hill and the People of Oyster riuer.

That yt agreement of ye town of Douer wth yt Part of ye town called Oyster riuer abt maintaining a Minister among them at their own cost & charges be confirmied & yt ye new meeting house built ther be the place of ye publick worship of God in that District and Established a District parish wth all rights & privlieges belonging to a Parish with full power to call & Settle a Minister there and make Assesments for ye paymt of his Sallary & all other Parish charges equally on ye Several Inhabitants wthin yt distri3t & annually to choose fiue psons; freeholders wthin Said Parish to make ye tax and Manage all affairs of the Parish, & ye psors so chosen with a Justice of the Peace of this Province shall whenever they see cause call a Parish meeting to transact any Mattrs concerning ye Parish & yt ye first meeting be on Monday ye 14th Instant at ye aforesd New Meeting house & yt ye John Thompson, ye Psetn Constable of that District, notify ye Inhabitannts yre of and farther that Psons that have of late year paid to ye Ministre there, shall Continue to pay ye Proportion to him yt Shall Succeed in sdd office. 4 May 1716. By ordr of the house of representatives

     Theo: Atkinson, Cler.
eodm Die   In Councill
 Voted—a Concurrence His Honr: ye Lt. Govr: Assenting yre to
    R. Waldron, Cler: Con.

OLD SERIES, NO. 37., MAY 27, 1851.

DOVER, ITS BOUNDARIES AND DIVISIONS.

While the petition of Oyster River folks for incorporation as Parish was agitating, a general defining of boundaries was ordered by the Province, and those of Dover are thus recorded, 3 Auguts, 1701:—

"Dover bound Northerly to begin at ye Middle of Quamphegan Falls & soe up ye river ffour miles, or thereabt to a Marke tree by the river side wthin a mile of Whitehall and from ye Sd Quamphegan Falls down the River to Hilton's Point, and from thence to Kenneys creek and thence on a direct line to Hogsty cove toth ye Marishes on ye great bay & 400 acres upland Injning thereto as formerly laid out & from Hogsty Cove over to Lampril river mouth & Soe up ye river to ye upper ffalls wherever was formally a Saw mill commonly called Wadleigh's upper mill & thence west & by North into the woods two mile & thence to run a headline Nortberly to meet wth the head of the Northwd bound line on Nechowonnaoh river alwaies reserving unto ye town of Dover the whole privilege of ye sd Lampril river, Stream & Fall for ye erecting Mills, Dams, &c on either side the river wth out annoyance from the Town of Exeter & that noe Interruption be given by any to prevent the transportation of timber Down ye river to ye Lower Falls by making booms or otherwaise."

In 1713, the Parish of Newington was incorporated, and of course separated from Dover. This was composed of part of Portsmouth and that part of Dover which had been called Bloody Point. We can find no record of its incorporation and therefore no description of its boundaries, but as far as Dover is concerned, it took all the land south of the River which had been part of Dover. It left in Dover what are now the towns of Dover, Durham, Lee, Madbury, Somersworth, and Rollinsford. This was too much territory for one town and was diminished by the separation of Durham, (including Lee), which was incorporated 15 May, 1732, its boundaries being thus defined:—

"All those lands lying on the Southerly side of a West Northwest half a point north line from Johnson's creek at the Bridge in the county Rhoade, to the head line of Dover township and from the said Bridge South East & by East down to a Pine tree on a point or Neck of land called Cedar Point on the West side of the mouth of the Back River in Dover, be erected and made into a distinct & separate town by the name of Durham by the bounds aforesaid all the lands lying within the Township of Dover on the Southerly side of the lines aforsaid from Johnson's Bridge."

While the Durham folks were cutting off a piece at one end of the town, Somersworth people were at work at the other:—

"To his Excellency William Burnet, Esqr., Captain General and Governor in Chief in and over his Majesties Council and the Representatives of the sd Proivnce in General Assembly convened, the Petition of the Subscribers Inhabitants of the North East part of the Town of Dover, humbly sheweth,

That the Dwelling places of yor Petitioners are at a great distance from the house of the Publick Worship of God in the Town of Dover where yor Petitioners live, by which their attendance thereon is rendered very difficult more especially to the women and children of their families, and that in the Winter season and in Stormy Weather too they can not pay that Honor and Worship to God in Publick as in their hearts desire they could, therefore for the advancing the Interest of Religion and for the Accommodation of yor Petitioners, It is humbly prayed by them that yor Excellency and the Honourable Assembly will please to sett them of as a Parish for the maintaining the Publick worship of God amongst themselves, and that they be dismist from the Town of Dover as to the supporting of the settled minister there. And that the Bounds of that there Parish may begin at the Gulfe, a place so called at Cochecho river, and from thence to run to Varney's Hill, And from thence to the Town bounds on a North West point of the Compass, & yor Petitioners shall ever Pray as in duty bound.

Samuel Roberts, Paul Wentworth, Thomas Alden, Elezer ——, Lore Roberts, Jerimaiah Rawlings, Silvanus Nock, James hobs, Thomas Hobbs, William ——, George Ricker, Tho: Downs, Phillip yetton, Thomas nock, John Roberts, Samuel Randall, Samuel Casor, Marturin Ricker, Ephraim Ricker. Jos Ricker, Joshua Roberts, John Hall, Moses Tebbetts, William Downs, John Tebbetts, Benj. Peirce, Maturin ——, Zachariah Nock, Philip Stagpole, Thomas Miller, Nathl Perkins, Jun. Samuel Roberts, Benjamin waworth, John C——, William bushe, Joseph husey, Ichabod Tebbets, James Stagpole, Benjr Varney, Ebenezer Garland, Samuel Downs, Richard wintworth, Joseph Wintworth, John Connor, Thos waling ford, Moris hobs, Thomas Tebbets, Benjamin Stanton, Ebr Wentweorth, Samuel Jones, Joseph Pevey, Philip pappon (?), jems gupey, Josiah Clark, John Mason, Bejamin twomble, William Jones Daniel Plumer, Jazbeg Garland, Hugh Connor, Job Clements, John Roberts, Edward Ellis, Samuel Ally, William Thompson.

April 25, 1729. In the House of Representatives. The within Petition being

Read, voted the Petitioners serve that part of the town of Dover that they desire to be set off from with a copy of this Petition, to appear at the Generall Assembly Wednesday next to shew cause (if they can) why the prayer of the Petition should not be granted
In Coun: eod die
    Read and Concurred with
            R. Waldron, Cler. Con

It appears that the appointed day passed but Dover had not been notified. The matter therefore on May 1st was deferred until "the 8th inst. May, or if the Assembly be not sitting, then to appear the 2d day of the sitting of the next Generall Assembly."

No action appears to have been taken on the 8th day of May, but on the 14th, "Dover Petition was read and parties heard by Councill, and an order made for a Committee to go on the spot, and view the several Districts and Settle a Dividing line according to the best of their Judgments and that the Petitioners in the meantime be free from being Rated to the minister at the old Town &c., and the Majr part agreeing shall be accounted sufficient to make a return at the Next session—for Confirmation."

Somersworth Made a Parish.

The committee reported and on the 10th of Dec. 1729, in Council, "voted, That the Petitioners for a Parrish in the Northeast part of Dover have liberty to Bring in a Bill according to the Report of the Committee varying the Bounds from the head of fresh Creek to White Oak Tree as the Rhoad goes."

We can find no record of the passage of such a bill, in the Province Records, though such an one was undoubtedly passed.

The Parish of Somersworth Made a Town.

Another petition was presented 19 May, 1743, that the Parish be made a town. This was done on the 22 April 1754, the town taking the name of Somersworth, which the Parish had already borne, and possessing the same boundaries with the Parish. Thomas Wallingford, Esq., Capt. John Wentworth and Moses Stevens were appointed to call the first meeting of the voters.

Somersworth's Army in 1746,

23 July 1746, the Somersworth Army was composed of these persons.

"A True list of all the Train Souldiers In the Parish of Somersworth Undr Comd of Tho: Wallingford, Capt., are as followeth, viz:—Sergt. John Ricker, Sergt. Philip Stackpole, Sergt. Thomas Tebets, Sergt. William Wentworth, Corpo. Ebenezar Garland, Corpo. Samuel Joanes, Corpo. Samuel Randall.

Drummers—Thomas Stevens, Richard Goodin, and Samuel Downs.

Ebenezer Wentworth, John Wentworth, John Mason, Joseph Hussey, John Hall Daniel Goodin, Samuel Hall, James Hall Benja Wentworth, Ephraim Rickers, Meturin Rickers, Abram Mimmey, Samuel Nock, Elear Wyer, Henry Nock, Thomas Tebbett, junr, Benja Twombly, Ezekiel Wentworth, Ebnr Roberts, Thomas Wentworth, George Rickers, Senr., James Kenney, Robert Cole, Benja Stanton, James Clements, Moses Tebbets, Samuel Wentworth, John Vicker, John Lebrock, Samuel Austin, Benja Austin, Edward Eliot, George Ricker,

Jr., Samuel Wentworth, jun, Nathaniel Nock, Nock, Jonathan Ebenr Hearll, John Wentworth, Hatevil Roberts, William Hanson, Benja Roberts, Lemuel Perkins, Drisco Nock, William Stackpole, James Foye, Joseph Varney, jun., Elisha Crumel, Daniel Smith, Meturin Ricker, Benja Heard, James Stackpole, John Catland, Isaac Hanson, Daniel Hanson, Richard Philpot, John Sulevant, Samuel Allien, Edward Alliein, John Mazeet, Samuel Waymouth, James Nock, Love Roberts, jun. Ichabod Rawlins, Ebbenr Downs, jun, John Rickers, jun, Joshua Roberts, Tera Sprague, Daniel Libbee, Neal Vicker, Dodipher Garland, Richard Goodin, jun, Benja Warren, Samuel Roberts, Francis Roberts, Samll Downs, jun, Samell Jones, jun, Joseph Hussey, jun, Ebenr Roberts, jun, Job Clements jun, John Ferall, Zebun Ocason, Elizha Randall, Marke Wentworth, Joseph Richardson, Tristram Heard, William Chadwick, William Downs, Peter Clarke, John Downe, Noah Cross.

A True List as Alowed P me."

OLD SERIES, NO. 58, JUNE 3, 1851.

DOVER ITS BOUNDARIES AND DIVISIONS.

(Concluded.)

The dismembered town of Dover had a little rest after Durham was taken off until May 10, 1743, "sundry Persons Inhabitants of the Westerly part of the town of Dover & the Northerly part of Durham" petitioned to be set off as a Parish alleging particularly as a reason their distance from the meeting houses in Dover and Durham; they say that they were induced some years since at their own cost to build a meeting house Situated more conveniently, &c. They desired the boundaries of the proposed Parish might be thus:—

"Beginning at the Bridge over Johnson's Creek, so called, where the Dividing line between Dover & Durham crosses the County Road & from thence running as the said Road runs until it comes even with Joseph Jenkins his house & from thence to run on a North West & by North Course until it comes to the head of said Township, which boundaries would comprehend the Estates & habitations of yor Petitioners living in Dover, &c.

This was signed by Zachariah Pitman, Isaac Twombly, Hercules Mooney, Ely Demeritt, jun., Joseph Evans, Joseph Twombly, Thomas Bickford, John Evans Abram Clark, Daniel Mesarve, Henry Bickford, Joseph Jackson, James Huckins, Henry Bussell, James Clemens, Ralph Hall, Joseph hicks, William Dame, Junr. William Bussell, John Tasker, Morres fowler, Azariah Boody, Derry pitman, Robert Wille, Timothy Moses, Paul Gerrish Junr., Abel Leathers, John Demeret, John Bussell, Thomas Wille, Zachariah Edgerly, Job Demerett, John Roberts, Joseph Daniel, David Daniel, Samuel Davis, frances Drew, James Chesle, Samuel Chesle, Daniel Young, Ruben Chesle, John Huckins, William twombly, Henry tibbets, James Jackson, John foay, Jun, William Demeret, Robert Evens, Solomon Emerson, William Allen, Jonathan Daniel, Jacob Daniel, Nathaniel davis, William Hill, Joseph Rines, Samuel Davis, Junr, Stephen Pinkham, Benjamin Hall, Jonathan Hanson, Benjamin Wille, John Row."

Madbury Made a Parish.

The usual notice was ordered May 13, 1743, to be given to the towns concerned, and 24 August 1744, both parties being heard, the petitioners were granted leave to bring in a bill. No bill appears to have passed till 31 May, 1755, when the Parish of Madbury was constituted with the boundaries petitioned for. Solomon Emerson was authorized to call the first meeting of the voters.

A final and complete separation between Madbury and Dover was made by An act passed 26 May, 1768, which gave the Parish all the town powers and privileges which were not given by the Act of 31 May, 1755.

Lee Made a Parish.

The next separation was from Durham; 17 January, 1766, an Act was passed to erect a new Parish called Lee "in the upper or western end of the town of Durham," there being "a sufficient number of inhabitants," some of whom live more than eight miles from the place of Public Worship. The boundaries were thus described.

"Beginning at Paul Cheles house at Buck [or Beech] Hill (so called) then running North six Degrees East to the line between said Durham & Madbury, then running Westerly on said Line One Hundred & Twenty Four Rods, then beginning and running from to Newmarket Line to one mile and a half above the dwelling House of John Smart, and all the inhabitants dwelling on that shall dwell there and their Estates are hereby made a Parish by the Name of Lee."

The word Parish was used but the privileges were those of towns. "Joseph Sias, Gentn" was appointed to call the first meeting of the voters.

Rollinsford Made a Town.

The last division was made at a period so modern that it is hardly worth alluding to; but to make our article complete, and more particularly because this will be old five hundred years hence, we publish the fact that Rollinsford was taken from Somersworth 3 July, 1849, being described thus:

"All that part of the town of Somersworth in the County of Strafford, lying south of a line lying on the easterly line of said town at a point one hundred and fifteen rods southerly from Pray's brook, so called, on the line between lands of Moses Pray and Francis Plumer, and running thence in a straight line to the railroad crossing south of the dwelling house of Andrew Crockett, and thence in a straight line to a stone on the westerly line of said town at the point where the line between said town and Dover crosses the old road from Dover to Great Falls village," &c.

John B. Wentworth, William E. Griffin and Wm. W. Rollins were authorized to call the first meeting of the town.

We have thus recorded the various divisions and subdivisions of the old town of Dover. If all the territory it once embraced was now a single town it would form one with a population of 17,836. [Those figures were for 1850; the population now. 1898, is about 40,000].

This is evidently some improvement

since the spring day in 1623, when Edward and William Hilton and their party landed a Dover Neck.

Map of Old Dover.

OLD SERIES, NO. 39. JUNE 10, 1851.

DOVER TOWN RECORDS.

The Records which we publish today are the earliest in the fragment marked V referred to in our article No. 27; the thirty-two pages of which we shall publish entire.

The Records in this fragment like those in the preceding, display a very commendable independence in regard to orthography. We judge that the writer not only rejects the authority of any and every lexicographer, but even that of his own practice as it is difficult to find the same word spelt alike in two consecutive instances. "If A-s-h-a don't spell Asia, what does it spell?" said the old Sea Captain so if vu don't spell view, what does it spell?

As to the punctuation, if our readers find any punctuation marks (except in dates) they will please credit them to the generosity of the printer, for there is not a single mark in the whole thirty-two pages from which we copy.

A Booke of Orders for the Towne of Dover made the 4th 4th mo. 1661.

At a Publicke towne meitting holden the 5th 4th mo 1661,

Asoceates for the Court chosen wear Capt. Richard walldern and mr Edward hiilton.

At the same time Elder nutter William Pomfrett, John Dam sinyer chosen Coneskeners for small cases.

At the same time Elder Nutter, left Hall, William ffurber, John Goddard, Thomas Beard chosen Selectmens thear power was given a Cording to law.

William Pomfret chosen Comeshener with ye townsmen for a hole yeir or ontell a new Choyse. Elder Wentworth Chosen Moderatter.

The same day mr Peter Coffin Chosen Treashurer.

William Pomfret chosen Towne Clarke.

Ensin John Daues chosen Clarke of ye markett, layers out of land the same that was befoer left Hall, Elder Wentworth, John Hall Deacon, Roberd Burnum, John Daues, Henry lankster, William ffurber.

Saeruaiers the same that was befuer John Roberds, John heard, William Willyames sinyer.

The same Day Thomas harson and Thomas humphreyes tooke the oeth of fideillitie.

1661-64 14. A list of the names of the inhabetants of Dover Neck that have right of commenage to the ox pasture & calves pasture:—Mr. Thomas Kimball, Job Clements, Thomas Downes, Thomas Robırds, sen, The ministers house, Charles Buckner, William Pomfret, Thomas Beard, John Tuttle sen, Deacon John Hall, Thomas Leigh on, John Dam sen, Lieut. Ralph Hall, Elder Nutter, Joseph Austin, Phillip Cromwell, William ffurber, Jeremiah Tebets, Humphrey Varney, James Nute, Richard Pinkham.

—The above named were all land owners on Dover Neck but did not reside there. Regarding each of them some information will appear hereafter.

1662.

At A Towne meeting holden the 3th of 2d mo 1662.

The Constabells dr at this meting upon Complaynt Remeted from ther fines which Cort did fine them for want of — — — meseures.

Thomas Roberds Chosen Constabell for Douer Necke.

John heard senyer Chosen Constabell for Cochecha.

Charles Addames Chosen Constabell for oyster Reeuer.

Gran Jurymen Chosen, Tho laytton, Sar. John hall, John Bickford sinyer, Richard Catter, charles Buckner, Roberd Jones—[The last two names are crossed and the following entry made on the margin:] "20:2:1663 deckon hall chosen in this mans (Bucker) Room." (and lower down) "thomas hanson"

Jurey trials; left Hall, John Roberds, Phelep Cromwell, Roberd Burnum, Thomas ffotman, Thomas Beard.

Comesheners for small cases.

Capt Walderne, Elder Nutter, left hall. Asosiates for the Courtt.

Capt. Walderne, Capt. Pike.

At a Towne meting holden the 2th, 3th mo 1662.

Granted unto Capt Walter Barfoott fowerscoer foott in Breath of flates belowe hie water marke at sande poynt below the marke and 24 foott of upland, not intrenching apon anie former grant to be helt upon within on hole yer after the date heirof or Else to be voyd

Granted unto Cap Richard Walderne 24 foott of upland to jine to his former grant of flats at Saude poynt.

Cap Walldern at the same time Chosen Debety for the Generall Court for this yeir 1662.

At a Towne meting holden the 15th 4th mo (62: Voted that the Treshurer eowe capt Pembellton 10£ for the — —— —

At the same time Richar Rooe exspeled an inhabetant.

at the sam time Selectmen chosen, William Pomfrett, William Beard, John Woodman, Capt Walderne, Left Hall, and to stand till a new Choies

William Ffurber Comeshener.

Mr. Peter Coffin Chosen Treshurer.

The Selectmen Chosen the 15th, 4th mo 1662 have power to ackt in all prudentiall afayers Exsept gineing of land and Receuing inhabitants.

Mr. Peter Coffins grant at Sande poynt is Renewed tell the 29th of September.

John Scrieuen Exsepted an inhabetant the 15: mo (62.

At a Publicke Towne metting holden the 10th of the 9th mo. 1662.

Voted by the Inhabetants that thear shall a Rate forth with be maed for prouetion at a peney in the pound of all our inhabetants and all other Persons that are Ratabell in the Towneshep.

At a Publicke Towne meitting holden the 10th, 9th mo. (62.

Voted that all grants of land Granted unto the Inhabetants of Oyster Riuer that are not yet layd out ar to be layd out Acording to thear Grants, Each Inhabetants Bringing under the Two Townsmens hands wich ar thear, unto the towne Clarke and he shall record them and giue Copies of thear grants, prouided they intrench not apon anie former grant.

OLD SERIES, NO. 40, JUNE 24, 1851.

DOVER TOWN RECORDS.

1663.

At a Publick Towne meitting holden 20th, 2 mo 1663.

John Woodden Rec an Inhabetant to Improue his on land and as the Towne shall se Case to alowe him ferder Preuelege.

At the same time voted that the 22th of the 4th mo 1663 thear is a Publick Towne meitting to be holden for to Agitate Consarning the minestrey and Granteing of lands and Receuing inhabetants.

At a meitting of the freemen holden the 18th 4th 1663.

Capt Walderne chosen Deberty for the Generall Courtt at Boston for this Sationes.

His instructions was that he should not condescend to anething Concerning the Towne of Portsmouth but what was acted at our Publicke meitting holden the 20th 2th 1663 wich is as followeth:—

Voted the 20th 2th, 63 that our County Courtt should be altered to be holden the first Tuesday of the 8th monthe.

and likewise for a speacill Courtt,

voted alsoe to haue our Comesheners Courtt, formerly granted to our asotiates at our Coming in under the Gouerment for twenty Pound Cases.

At a Publicke Towne meitting holden the 20th, 2 mo, 63 Grand Jurymen chosen.

William ffurber, John beard, Tho Beard, John Dam sinyer, John Bickford sinyer.

Jury of trialls:—Antoney Nutter, John Martin, John woodman, Thomas umfreyes, Thomas nock, Jeddediae Andrues.

Constabell:—Jerremie Tebbetts, John heard, John meader.

At a Publick Towne Meitting holden the 20th, 2th, 1663.

Seleckmen Chosen for ye yeir or tell others Be Chosen.

Capt Walderne, left hall, Einsin John Daues, henery Langster, Robert Burnum, (not excepting of) John Bickford sinyer, (ye 22:4:)

Moderratter, —William ffurber.

Elder William Wentworth Comeshener.

Mr Peter Coffin, Tresserrer.

William Pomfrett Towne Clark.

John Daues Clark of the Market.

John hall Deacon, Clark of ye weites.

A Sotiates for this Courtt that is to be holden at Douer the last tuesday in June 1663, was chosen at Portsmouth by vote of the inhabetants of boeth townes the 12:3:1663.

ar Capt Pendellton 44 votes
Capt Walderne 38
Capt Picke 32
Mr Edward hillton 34
Mr. Richard Cutt 23

At a Towne meitting holden the 22th of the 4th mo 1662 men chosen to treat with mr Rainer.

Capt Richard Walderne, James newtt, William ffollett, Richard Otes.

At the same time James newtt Chosen to Be stuerd for the Towne at the ordenarey at the Courtt time

[Court Records 1663. "The Courtt allows Mr Rayners Daughters 20s for their paynes in attending ye Magestracy at yr fathers the time of the Court and order that ye Tresar of Douer pay it in to them."]

OLD SERIES, NO. 41, JULY 1, 1851.

DOVER TOWN RECORDS.

1664.

Att a meitting of the Seleckt—men the 17th of the first mo 1663-64.

Thomas Leighton, Sargt. John Roberds chosen to appraise goods taken by distress.

By the Seleckt men at the same time chose to goe in prambelation of the Townes bounds and to giue notes to Exsetoer to goe with them. The men chosen are Roberd Burnum, william ffollett to goe apon this seruise in Aprill next.

by the Selecktmen the 17th first month 1663-64. Ordred that Philep chesle shall goe forth in oyster Riuer to veu and inquire into seuerall Psons that doe transgres Towne orders abut Cuting tember for Pipe staues bceth in falling tember by such as haue noe right to fall ain tember, but transgress the towne ordr felling tember, wee the sellecktmen doe Impower Phelep Chesley to goe in to the woodes to veu to the sayd insarues, and to mak a Return to the Selecktmen.

At a meitting of the Townsmen the 17th of the first month 1663-64.

whereas hew doent hath Buell a house neir lamprill Riuer and hauin noe writ to anie land thear (we) due Grant him ten Ackers thear, Exchange of tenn Ackers from his thirty Ackers at Sandey Baucke, wich tenn ackers at Sandey Bauck is to Remaine the Townes.

At a Publicke Towne meittinge holden the 28th, 2 moenth, 64.

Capt wallden Chosen Deberty to the Generall Cort for this first setiones.

Capt Wallderne, left hall, Chosen to meitte with those of Porchmouth to open the votes for the asotiates.

At the same time Selecktmen chosen.

Capt Wallderne, henery Langster, Sargt John Roberts, Einsin John daues, Elder Wentworth, William Pomfrett, Comesheners, these to stand tell others be chosen.

Mr. Peter Coffin, chosen Moderator einsin John daues, Clarke of the markett.

At a Publicke Towne meittinge holden 28th 2 mo, 1663 William Pomfrett Chosen Towne Clark.

At the same time Phelep chesley and Pattricke Jemison chosen to lay out the hei ways from Oyster Riuer to Cochechae, and make the hiegways fitt for horse and foot and bring thear a Compt of thear charges to the Townsmen.

Constabells Chosen.

Juddediei Andres, William willyams Juner, Thomas hanson.

Grand Jurymen

Thomas Leighton, John hall Deacon, William Beard, Richard Catter, Sargt John hall, John louring John Allt.

Jury of trialls

leften hall, Eiensin John Daues, Thomas Roberds junier, henrey hobes, Phelep Cromwell.

left hall, John hall Deacon, apoyted to laye out the hie waye from lamp·ill falles to the watter sied betwixt John Godder and John Martin.

Associates for this Cort that is to be holden at Porchmouth the last Tuesday in June 1664 was Chosen by opining the votes of Boeth Townes at Porcl mouth the 8th of the 3th moneth 1664.

for Capt Pendleton 34
for Capt Pike 33
for Capt Walderne 36
for mr Richard Cutt 24
for mr Edward hillton 15

    Test Richard Walderne
    Richard Martin
    Nath ffrver
    R dish hall.

the 26th, 7th mo. 64.

At a Publick Towne meting Capt wallden chosen Denete for the Generale Corte by the freemen.

At a Publicke Towne meitting holden the 26th, 7th mo 64. Thomas Beard chosen to kepe Ordenarey.

At the sam tim John Screuen chosen Consta'ell

voted at the sam tim that thear shall forthwith a 2d Rat goe fuerth to pay Townes debts.

[The Rat here spoken of was a tax of 2 pence upon the pound, equivalent to five-sixth of one per cent, as anyone will readily perceive.]

Voted at the sam tim a peney Rat shall goe foerth for proneution for mr Raner.

At the sam tim Granted to John Martin the land wich now he possith where his dwelling house standeth to be maed up forty ackers, Beginning at the water sied, taking all the land Betwixt John Godder and Richard Yorke and see Running up in to the woods not intrenching apon anie former Grant.

at the sam tim Giuen and Granted unto left hall 20 ackers of land at the head of the 20 Acker lott ouer toe Back River, not intrenching apon anie former grant.

OLD SERIES, NO. 42., JULY 8, 1851.

DOVER TOWN RECORDS.

1665.

By the Seleckmen a meittinge holden the 15th 2th mo. (65.

Ordred that noe Parson that Cometh into this Towne as a Sarvant or By Pechasing of lands shall not be Excepted as An Iuhabetant in town of Douer untel he be Alowed or Exsepted by the Towne or the Sellecktmen.

Order for Building a Bell Tower for the Meeting House.

By the sellecktmen the 15th, 2th mo (65. Ordred that mr Peter Coffin shall be Impowered by this meittinge to A Gree with some work men to Build a Terrett apon the mettinge house for to hang the Bell wich we haue baught of Capt wallderne, and what it Cost to pay out of what credit the Neck of land hathe in your hand and if Cost moer wee doe in Gage to pay you apon the Towne a Compt.

    Richard Walderne
    Will Wentworth
    John Roberds

At a Publick Towne meittinge holden the 17th, 2th mo (65.

voted that Elder nutter and william Pomfrett ar to mett with Porchmouth men to open the votes for asotates

At ye same time.

John Daues chosen Constabell.
John Coaring Chosen Constabell.
Richard Catter Chosen Constabell.
Jurey of Trialls.

Peter Coffin, Rafe Twamley, Antoney nutter, John Marttin, John Robberds, Thomas Nock, Roberd Burnum.

Gran Jurey.

Job Clements, John Meder, John heard, John Bickford sinyer, John Woodman, Thomas Wiggin, John hill.

At the sam tim.

Capt Walderne Chosen Debetey for the Genarell Courte for this yeir.

voted at A Publick Towne metting holden the 14th 2th moenth 1661 (5?)

Order Concerning Valentine Hill's Sawmill at Lamprey River.

that whereas tnear was a grant made to mr vallintin hill of douer of a River called lamprill Riuer in the Towneshep of douer for to Ereckt Sawemill werke, and to Contunew his, or his assignes soe longe as he or theay kep possetion thearof; now know all to whom this may Conserne that in Case noe man doe appier to whold possertion and maek it known to the Sellecktmen of the said Towne within 6 moenths after the date heirof that then the Towne doeth Resolue to take into thear owne hands and dispose of it, or sell it for the use of the Towre to bear all Rareges.

and that a Copey of this be set up at some Publicke place at Boston and a nother at Douer.

Special Orders to Capt. Richard Walderne, Representative in the General Court in Boston.

At a meittinge of the Sellecktmen the 29th, 2th month 1665.

Orders for Capt Walderne, Debety for the General Courtt.

1. ordred that (he) wo(u)ld stand to mayntayne our preaeledges by virtu of Articklers of agreement, and to bring the proseding of the Court in writing.

2. That you move the Generall Courtt that our County Courtt may be Altred for time of it untill september.

3. that we desire thankfullness may be Returned unto the Court for ther Caer and Gouerment under his maijsty.

4. that whereas we ar Informed that seuerall persons haue made som writing in way of Complaynt against us, or som of our prosedings, we know noe Case theay haue so to doe and doe desier you to make all the Defence you can against them.

5. and that whear as our parts ar soe far destant from boston and the law dothe Inioyne all that will be maed freemen to apeir at boston that you wold petershon the Court that those that are Capabell to be maed free may be at our Countey Courte.

At a meittinge of the Sellecktmen the 28th July 1665.

All Acounts maed up with Thomas Beard for the Acounts Boeth for charges of the Asochaett Courtt and the Countey

Courtt last, with all thear Expenses that the sellecktmen haue Expended unto this day, wich some doeth Com to thirty three Pounds, and doe ordr the Treserrer to pay the same in Action money and fines of the Courte, and place it to the Towne a Count as witness our hands this day and yeir aboue written

     Richard Walderne
     Henry Lankster
     John Daues
     John Roberds.

Asotiates for this Countey Courtt that is toe Be holden the last Tewsday in June 1665, at Douer was Chosen by openning the votes the 5th, 3th mo. 1665.

Capt Pendellton	29
Capt Walderne	36
mr Richard Cutt	33
Capt Picke	35
Mr John Cutt	18

    Test
     John Cutt
     Hatevil Nutter
     Henrie Sherburne
     William Pomfrett.

[These last four names are autographs.]

OLD SERIES NO. 43, JULY 15, 1851.

DOVER TOWNE RECORDS.

1665.

At a Publick Towne mettinge holden the 10th of the 8th month 1665.

Thomas Whithouse Raeceued an inhabitant Apon these tarmes, as followeth, that is to say that the Towne not Being of a Capasety to giue a Comedation as heretofore doe Exsep him Apon noe other tarmes then what be by perchas he haeth B(ought) haueing Conviency for Cattel and noe other preueledg.

William Layton Receue at the same time apon the same tarmes.

At a meitting of the selecktmen the 25th, 10th mo. 1665 Georg Gooe forwarned to stay or haue anie habitation in the Towne of Douer.

Ordred By the sellecktmen the 28 of July 1665 that the Treasurer shall Pay for the keilling A wolfe in the yeir (63 as apeireth in a note under the Constabells hand in the hands of John Hall, Deacon, under the sellecktmen's hands that these 15 parsons shall Receue an Equall proportion of the money due for killing the wolf to Eurey man a like hose names ar heir under written.

John hall Deacon, John hall Juner, Jeremy Tebut, John lankster and 3 persons in Thomas Trickeys family, Mr. Thomas Wiggin, John Roberds Juner, Joseph Roberds, Thomas Leighton Juner, Thomas Whitehouse, Ralphf hall juner, Kinsley hall.

At a meitting of the sellecktmen holden the 25th, of 10th mo. 1665.

Ordered that whereas maney persons doe fall Timber and make staues without order and take in seuerall Inmates for that End, whearby the Towne and the Settled Inhabetants ar much Injured, these ar thearfoer to Impower John Roberds, Thomas Nock and Phelep Chesley, or aney too of them to make delegent sarch into all the Woods, and whear they find aney that hath transgres towne orders in making staues or falling timber what theay find theay shall sease for the use of the Towne, the informers shall haue the on halfe for thear Paaynes, and the other to be Returned into the Towne

Treasurey.

Order for Settling Disagreements Between Dover Neck and Oyster River.

By the selecktmen the 25:10:1665.

Ordered that whereas thear ar seuerall Deffrinces Apprehended to be betwixt the Inhabetants of Douer, and are principally with our naboers at Oyster Riuer these ar therfoer to desier all our naboers that have anie Greueances to meitt together and to propound what matter of deffrerance thear is and to state the Case Against the next Publick Towne meeting is apoynted the third monday in march, wich is the 19th day thearof, at the meitting house on Douer Neck thear to Discorce the sayd defiences for the settling of Peace amonghts us, or if it cannot be thear agreed, then to Chuse some others to heir and determine the same, and the Constabels of the Towne are heirby Ordred to giue notes to all Naboers in thear Respesktiue places to meitt for the End afoersayd.

1666.

At a Publick Towne Meitting holden the 19th day of the first month, (65 (66 [equivalent to O. S. 16 March, 1666.]

voted By the Generall Towne that All Deifrences and all Greuences that Are or shall Be Brought forthe then in the Towne in Generall unto Capt Roberd Pike, Mr Wencoell, Mr Elias Stillman to heir and determine the same, And what These Arbetraters suall determine and maek thear awaid, under thear hands by the last of this moenth of march the Towne doeth Ingage to stand to.

At the sam tim men Chosen to Declare all Grieuances to the Arbetrators ar Capt Richard Walderne, William ffurber Richard Otis, John Roberds, Thomas ffootman, Roberd Burrum, John Daues.

These Parsons ar apoynted to the End aforsayd on the 29th of the 1th month (66, and to declare the Case, and it is heirby ordred that Capt Richard Walldern doe mak the mind of the Towne knowne unto Capt Pike, Mr Wencoll, Mr Stillman, and to desier them to atend that sarues accordingly.

At a Publicke Towne mettinge holden the 19th of the first month (65 (66.

Tho Egerly, James Coffin, John Chirch, John fost, Roberd Evens, steuen Robinson.

These persons are Receued apon the same tarmes that Thomas whithouse and others wear Receued.

At the sam tim, Giuen unto walter Jackson 20 Ackers of land at the head of his own lot Betwixt the Cow path and the swan pe

---

OLD SERIES, NO. 44, JULY 22, 1851.

THE FIRST CHURCH IN DOVER.

It has been said by some that the First Church in Dover was organized in 1638; by others that Rev. Daniel Maud was the first regular minister of the Church. A bicenteunial sermon by Rev. David Root contains the former statement, which he derived from a statement in the margin of the Church Records, which was placed there some one hundred and twenty years after the time, and Hayward's New Hampshire Gazeteer has the second, which he derived doubtless from certain publications put forth by some antiquarians too dignified to investigate any sub-

culties of his troubled ministry we have already spoken. His character was bad, decidedly bad, and in 1638 the angry colonists drove him away. Rev. Hanserd Knollys had come to the settlement before Mr. Burdett's removal, but the latter, who had become Governor, had forbidden him to preach; on his departure Mr. Knollys began to preach.

A church was gathered in Jan., 1639, as has been stated, and Mr. Knollys became its pastor. It is a curious fact that this church, whose creed is untainted, at present, with any heresy, ancient or modern, should have been founded by a Baptist; and the fact that Mr. Knollys was a Baptist explains the vindictiveness with which his character was slandered by our devotedly pious, but not remarkably tolerant, neighbors of Massachusetts Bay.

The veritable Cotton Mather thought that Indians were descended from the Devil, and heretics were akin to both; and Baptists were the worst kind of heretics in his estimation. Hence the church was said to be composed of "the looser sort of people," referring to doctrines only; Knollys was called a slanderer, etc., etc., all of which the candid and unprejudiced reader will be satisfied was false. He did indeed make confession of indiscreet conduct, but throughout he gives indices of Christian virtue and ardent piety. The estimation in which he was held in England is sufficient answer to these slanders against him. There is even a religious publication society now existing in England which bears the name of the "Hanserd Knollys' Society."

Moreover in the difficulties between Knollys and Larkham "the more religious sort" adhered to Knollys; he left however, in 1640, and left the field to Thomas Larkham whose conduct in Dover was as disreputable as his after life in England was penitent. He returned to England in 1641.

The fifth minister, Daniel Maud, whose character is deservedly venerated, settled in Dover in 1642; of him also we have already spoken. He died here in 1655. His were the days when Richard Pinkham beat the drum to call the people to meeting. (The Salvation Army style of 1898.)

In 1653, the second meeting house was built. The first one was erected, according to tradition, by the Company which settled at Dover Point in 1633. They probably built in 1634, it being the latter part of the autumn of the previous year that they arrived.

The second house was built in 1653, by Major Richard Walderne, and stood on the spot nearly opposite where now (1898 stands the Dover Neck lower school house. The low mound of earth is still visible which marks the site of the "entrenchments and flankarts." In 1665 a "turrett" was built upon it and a bell placed therein to take the place of the original "drummer." This bell was purchased in England by Major Walderne.

The sixth minister of the First Church was Rev. John Rayner, a worthy successor to good old Parson Maud. He settled n 1655 and remained until his death in April 1669. The interests of the church did not suffer under his care no more than under his predecessor. The records of those days are unfortunately lost, and we are therefore unable to procure specific information as to the number of communicants, or other matters of interest. There were Deacons in those days. Deacon John Hall was "grave, not double tongued, not given to much wine, not greedy of filthy lucre," and he was also otherwise qualified as being the "husband of one wife, ruling his children and household well." The writer of this sketch loves to trace his descent from the old Deacon. There was Deacon John Dam, who dwelt on Bloody Point and lived to a good old age.

There were Elders, also:--Elder Wentworth, William Wentworth, was one. He used to preach at Cochecho sometimes, but oftener at Berwick, which was then a part of Kittery. Sometimes he dwelt in Exeter. When in Dover he seems to have made his habitation a little North East of Garrison Hill, the Elder had a large farm there.

(It is still owned by his descendants in 1898.) In times of danger he and his household used to go to Heard's Garrison which stood where Friend Bangs has his garden.(Now,1898,owned by Mr. Bangs's daughters.) Elder William had great reverence for the command to "increase and multiply and replenish the earth," as any one will see by the voluminous Wentworth Genealogy.

Edward Starbuck was another Elder of that period but he left for Nantucket before Parson Rayner died. Elder Starbuck was heretical; he refused to "join with the Church in the ordinance of Baptisme," and did divers other acts of a similar nature; he probably had not recovered from Parson Knollys's baptist preaching; the Court could not endure heresy and so Elder Starbuck and the Church parted company.

Elder Hatevil Nutter was another of the Elders. He lived on Dover Neck, pretty near the meeting house, just on the hill above it. He hated evil (as his name indicates) and disliked Quakers as zealously as Parson Rayner himself, and it may not be amiss to examine their gentle dealings with this sect before we consider who succeeded Parson Rayner in the ministerial office.

OLD SERIES, NO. 45, JULY 29, 1851.

DOVER TOWN RECORDS.

1666.

At a Publick Towne Meitting holden the 2th, 2th month, 1666,

william ffurber, Roberd Berune (Browne) chosen to meit with Porchmouth men to Carey the votes and Break up therfor asotiats.

Town Officers and Jurymen.

At a Publick Towne Meitting holden the 2th 2th month 1666,

Selectmen Chosen,

Capt Richard Walderne, Antoney Nutter, Roberd Burnum, John Marttin, Job Clements,

William ffurber Comesherner,

Comesherners for small cases,

Capt Walldern, Job Clemant, Elder Nutter,

Constabells Chosen,

Thomas Downes, Steuen Jones, Phelip Cromwell,

Jurey of Trials,

Peter Coffin, Eusin John Daues, Thomas Roberds John Scriuen, Thomas footman.

Grand Jurey,

Sargent John hall, Thomas Welley, John Allt, Richard Rowe, John hall, Deacon, Thomas Beard

At the same time voted that our selectmen shall take aney opertunety to Treat with the Selecktmen of Porchmoneth about the afaiers of the Countey and what theay shall see usefull for us to present at the next Towne Meitting.

At a Publick Towne Meitting holden the 9th of 2th month (66,

Town Votes Concerning the Common Land.

Voted that the Sellecktmen with others of our naboers now Chosen ar to Draw up something in writhing to present to the next Towne metinge Concerning the Right of Commanage and other things Consarning the Towne afaiers the men Chosen to jine with the Selecktmen ar Elder Nutter, Elder Wentworth, Thomas Leighton, henrey lankster, William ffurber, Richard Otis, Thomas ffoottman, William Roberds.

Town Auditors Appointed.

At the same time

Roberd Burnum, William ffurber, John Woodman, John hall Deacon, Richard Otes, these men ar Chosen to Adet (audit) all the Townes A Countes and to make thear Returne to the Towne.

Men Made Freemen of the Town.

The names of them that Desier to Be maed free ar John Martin, Antoney Nutter, John Daues, John Woodman, Thomas Roberds Juner.

[The freedom here spoken of is merely admission to certain privileges of citizenship. A. H. Q.]

By the Selleckmen,

Ordered that William Pomfrett shall Giue out Orders to mr Rayner for the Seuerall Rents deu from mills to be payed to him toward his sallery as also To giue mr Coffin order to Receue 15£ of Rent to pay Elder Wentworth for his paynes at Coechechae the last winter.

At A meitting of the Comesshenors At Porchmouth Chosen by the Towne of Douer to open the voetts for the Choies of Asocetiates for this present yeir (66.

Chosen

Capt Richard Walldern	57
Capt Roberd Pike	53
Mr. Richard Cutt	52
mr John Cutt	33
mr Elias Stileman	38

Test at.—Mr John Cutt
    mr Elias Stilman
    William ffurber
    Roberd Burnum

At A Publick meitting of the freemen holden the 14th, 3th monthe, 1666.

Capt Richard walldern Chosen Deberty for the Generall Courtt this present setions.

At a meitting of the Sellecktmen holden the 13th of July 1666.

Ordered that Richard Otes haeth liberty to Cutt all the Grass, wich is neir about the pond by Oyster Riuer, wich was knowne by the name of mr Whelrights marsh, and all other Grants belonging to mr hill thear abouts, and other spreings of marsh wich is not layd out to anie Pertickler persons, Apon Consideration the said Richard Otes is to pay to the towne, or to the Order of the Sellecktmen the some of three pounds and tenn shillings for this yeir; and we doe ferder order that the sayd Richard Otes shall Enioye all mr hills Right of marsh the next yeir, prouided he pay the sayd some of three pounds and tenn shillings to the selecktmen for the use of the Towne.

By the Selecktmen,

Ordered that the Constabells of the hole Towne that ar behind in making up thear accounts with the Treserrer, or the Selecktmen for the seuerall yeires as by the Pertickler Rates in the Towne book Doe appeir, and Cometed to them under the sellecktmens hands, with powr to take it by way of distress and finding by the Tresurrer his information that manev ar defecktive in not doeing A Cordinge to thear order, these ar thearfoer to giue notes to all the Constabells afoersayd that theay within 18 days after the date heirof make up thear accounts with the Tresurer and take his Reepts for the same and Returne the same to the sellecktmen, or Else theay may expeckt to be fined for Euery dayes necleckte after the sayd 18 days ar expired.

witness our hands this 14th day of July 1666.

  Richard Waldern John Martin
  Robert Burnum Antoney Nutter
    Job Clements.

OLD SERIES, NO. 46. AUG. 5, 1851.

By BALLARD SMITH of DURHAM.

Early Settlers at Oyster River.

[Note by John Scales.—At this point in the Memoranda Dr. Quint permitted Mr. Ballard Smith of Durham to furnish several articles. He began with the following:]

1633.

Among those who came to Dover Neck with Capt. Thomas Wiggans in 1633 were Francis Mathews. William Williams, John Goddard and Thomas Canney; these became early settlers at Oyster River. This river was called by the natives Shanknassic, but received its present name from the Colonists because of a large bed of oysters, which they found about half way between its falls and its mouth, at a spot nearly opposite what is now known as Bunker's bridge.

At the point of land formed by the confluence of Oyster River with Great Bay and the Pascataqua, now called Durham Point, Francis Mathews selected a site, made improvements and resided there for many years. His mother was the midwife of Henrietta Maria, at the birth of Charles II, and other children, and was a favorite of the Queen. Through his wife's influence he obtained a grant of the salt marsh at the Point, and afterwards at her solicitation other gifts of the adjoining marsh, until he became the owner of a large part of the North shore of Great Bay. At that time the marsh was highly valued for its grass, upon which the colonists depended for the sustenance of their cattle, as the uplands were not cultivated for grass; the attention of the first settlers being directed to the fisheries and trade with the Indians rather than agriculture.

The property of Francis Mathews at Durham Point descended to his grandson Francis Mathews, who held it until his death; it is now largely held by his descendants who, for some reason not explained, now spell the name Mathes. The site of the original settlement is very beautiful; it is just at the head of the main branch of the Pascataqua and com mands an extended view of Great Bay, Oyster and Bellamy rivers.

About the same time that that Frances Mathews settled at Durham Point, John Goddard obtained a grant upon the shore of Great Bay, and settled there prior to 1648. The Creek hard by, which divides for a short distance the counties of Strafford and Rockingham, still retains his name. He was a carpenter and acquired a very handsome estate. He was elected Selectman of Dover in 1661 and his name appears frequently on the town records.

Thomas Canney was a tailor and resided for many years at the "Neck" and was a man of some note as his name appears frequently on the town records. He came to be the owner of land on the North shore of Great Bay, near Crummit's mill creek and is supposed to have resided there for a short time.

William Williams obtained a grant of land from the town on the north side of Oyster river just below Bunker's creek and made improvements, which in a few years descended to his son Matthew and William Williams, Jr. The last named had a handsome estate, and resided upon the premises lately (1851) occupied by Ezekiel Twombly and now owned by Daniel and Joseph Smith. The property was retained by the family till after the Revolution and has been known as the Williams farm.

Ensign John Williams was elected a selectman of Durham soon after its incorporation, and was a man of influence in the town. John Williams, Jr., held the office frequently after the year 1741, and was active in procuring a settlement of a minister and in support of the church in the town. Jonathan Williams was the last one of the family of whom there is now (1851) any remembrance here, and his name is handed down as a signer of a document in 1779, which for its patriotic spirit is worthy of note here.

"Resolved that for the present we will sell no article for a higher price than the following, viz:—Indian corn 6£ per Bushel; old rye 6 do., New rye 6 do; Barley, 6 do; English Lay 39.0 per ton; Salt pork, best pieces, 15 per pound, veal 0:4 per lb.; Lamb 0:4 per lb.; Butter 0:15 per lb.; Sheeps wool (Sheared) £3:3 per lb."

Mr. Williams and the other merchants at Durham offered to sell for lower prices than the above when the merchants in Portsmouth and other towns would lower their prices; and would not sell for hard money but would take the Continental currency, and would "expose all persons whom we know to refuse paper money for such articles as they have to sell."

Charles Adams was another of the early settlers at Oyster River. Prior to 1648 he had a grant of land and adjoining that of Francis Mathews, on the south side of the river, near the mouth, of which he took possession, built a garrison, and made other improvements, and there resided till the destruction of his garrison by the Indians, and he and his family were murdered. He had several grants of land during his lifetime, one of which was near the Falls, where it is supposed his son Charles resided. It is supposed that his lineal descendants were Charles, Samuel, Dr. Samuel, Col. Winborn, a distinguished officer in the Revolution who fell at Stillwater, and Capt. Samuel who was also a Revolutionary soldier.

Col. Winborn Adams was engaged in the famous capture of powder from fort

William and Mary (now Fort Constitution) in December, 1774. The affair was described to the writer by Capt. Eleazer Bennett, who is now (1851) the only surviving member of the party of patriots, he being now 101 years old, but active in body and mind; he resides in Durham with his sons John and Eleazer Bennett, Jr. He at the time was in the employ of Gen. Sullivan at his mills at Packer's Falls. The General sent for him 'to come down and go to Portsmouth, and to go around among the neighbors and get any body else he could to come with him, as they were going to have some fun." He called upon several but all refused to go as they feared trouble.

The party as finally made up consisted of John Sullivan, Ebenezer Thompson, Winborn Adams, John Demeritt, John Griffin, Eleazer Bennett, Ebenezer Sullivan, Alpheus Chesley, Jonathan Chesley, Stephen Noble, Trueworthy Durgin, Peter French, John Spencer, Richard Davis, Isaac Small and Benjamin Small. It is supposed that Alexander Scammel was also a member of the party, but it is not known.

On the 13th of December, 1774, upon the reception of the news that the King had prohibited the exportation of gun powder or other military stores to the Colonies, it was determined by Gen. Sullivan and others to secure the powder and arms at the Fort, in anticipation of hostilities, which they saw must come. Accordingly on the evening of the same day, a party under the lead of John Sullivan, procured a "two cord gundalow" and dropped down the river, stopping at Portsmouth where they were re-enforced by a party headed by John Langdon, proceeded to the fort at the entrance to the harbor, scaled it, overpowered the garrison, bound the Captain, drove away the soldiers, and then removed to the boat 100 kegs of powder and 100 smaller arms with which they returned to "The Falls." A small part of the powder was taken by Captain Demeritt to his house at Madbury Corner, and the remainder was deposited under the pulpit of the old meeting-house at Durham (where now, 1898, is Sullivan's monument) from whence it was afterwards taken by the Patriots and used in the battle of Bunker Hill, and elsewhere about Boston.

The "gundalow" was furnished by Major Benjamin Mathes, who was too old to accompany the party; it was managed by three oars on each side, and started from the old wharf about half way between Gen. Sullivan's residence and the Falls.

It was bright moonlight, but a bitter cold night, and at the Fort the boat could not be brought nearer than a rod from the shore, so that in landing and bringing off the stores the men were obliged to wade through the water. The cold was so intense that their clothes froze on them, and their discomforts were increased, because that the strictest silence was enjoined, no fire was permitted, and no one was allowed to wear shoes, lest an accidental spark from the nails in the boot heels might ignite the powder.

This exploit was undoubtedly one of the boldest and bravest during the whole Revolution. It was four months before the battles of Lexington and Concord and was the first act that could be regarded as one of open and direct hostility conmitted by a military force against the Royal Government.

OLD SERIES, NO. 47, AUG. 19, 1851.

By BALLARD SMITH of DURHAM.

Of the Adams family at Oyster River, it is supposed that Charles, Jr., resided at the Falls in 1694, and escaped the fate of the rest. Samuel, another son of the original colonist, and his wife, were cruelly butchered; one or two of the family were carried into captivity, and fourteen were murdered, whose graves are now near the site of the old garrison.

Col. Winborn, supposed to be a grandson of Charles, Jr., was a Lieut. in the militia before the Revolution. He resided and kept a Tavern in the house now (1851) occupied by Fred Jenkins at the Falls, and was engaged in the purchase and sale of timber, of which Durham was then a very considerable depot. He was an active business man, and was for many years elected by the town surveyor of lumber. The town frequently held its meetings at his house, and after his death at the house of his widow, Mrs. Sarah Adams. He was a member of the Committee of Safety appointed by the town the 28th Nov. 1774; the committee consisted of James Gilmer, Valentine Mathes, George Ffrost, John Sullivan, Ebenezer Thompson, Capt. Thomas Chesley, John Smith 3d, Major Stephen Jones, Jonathan Chesley, Lieut. Winborn Adams, Moses Emerson, Alexander Scammel, Stephen Cogan, Joseph Stevens, John Griffin, Lt. Samuel Chesley, Jeremiah Burnham, Dr. Samuel Wigglesworth, Jonathan Woodman, 3d, Nathaniel Hill, Timothy Meder, Nathaniel Demeritt, and Francis Mathews.

At the same time the town appointed a committee of Correspondence of which the minister Rev. John Adams, was chairman, and directed the Selectmen "to add forthwith to the town stock of powder so as to make it up to 200 pounds and to lay in 400 pounds of bullets and 500 flints."

It is possible, and quite probable, that this vote of the town in November was what specially induced the party in December to go to Portsmouth and take the powder from the fort. This no doubt seemed the easiest and most expeditious way of putting in force the vote of the town.

The citizens of Durham were ardent Patriots; a large party left there immediately after hearing of the battle of Lexington. A town meeting was held 20 April, 1775, and voted that it would "pay any man that should set off equipped, as a soldier for Boston according as the Provincial Congress should determine, if it votes anything; otherwise the town will allow them a reasonable sum; and that those persons who are about to march, and are not able to furnish themselves, be furnished by the selectmen." Also elected Ebenezer Thompson, Moses Emerson, and John Smith, 3d, Deputies to attend the Provincial Congress forthwith

Soon after a company was organized of which Winborn Adams was Captain, John Griffin Lieut., and Trueworthy Durgin Ensign which rendezvoused at the residence of Capt. Benjamin Smith at the forks of the King's road and the road to Lubberland, near the bridge across

Lamprey river. Just before the company left for Boston Rev. John Adams the minister of the town preached a sermon to them, showing the soldiers their duty as patriots and Christians. He closed with a prayer which is said to have made the whole audience shed tears. This company was stationed for a while at Winter Hill and then accompanied the expedition to Canada.

[Note by Dr. Quint.—The first Charles Adams was born in or near 1623; he lived at O. R. till he was killed in 1694. His son Charles administered on the estate, the inventory of which was entered in April, 1695. His wife's name was Temperance. The first Charles is the one who "took the oath" of fidelity 21 June 1669, Charles, probably the second, was born in 1663, and his sister Sarah in 1671. There was a John Adams taxed at Cochecho from 1662 to 1668.]

Francis Mathews died prior to 1648. His widow, Thamarsin, had possession of his estate at Durham Point until her death in 1662. Their children were Benjamin, Walter and Martha; the last named married twice. 1, Snell, 2 Browne. Benjamin had issue, Francis, both of whom it is supposed resided at the homestead. Walter died in 1678; his will was proven 25 June of that year. He married Mary——; children, Samuel, Susanna, who married Young; Mary, who married Senter.

William Williams, Jr., the son of the first settler, married Margaret, daughter of Thomas Stevenson; their children were William, John and probably Henry. William was born in 1663; married Hannah Heard. John had a grant of land in 1717, and Henry in 1694.

John Goddard was freeman in 1668; his children were John, Benjamin and a daughter who married James Thomas; a daughter who married Arthur Bennett. He died about 1659; his inventory was entered 12 Nov. 1660. His widow, Welthen, married a Simons, and was living in 1681; his son John was born in 1642, and came to an untimely death about 1672 By his will dated July 2, 1672, he bequeathed his estate to his brother Benjamin and to the sons of his sisters, John Gilman, John Bennett and James Thomas, Jr.

Alexander Scammel, whose name has been mentioned as a citizen of Durham, was a student in Gen. Sullivan's office, and had charge of his business during his absence in the Continental Congress. He was appointed by the town a member of its first Committee of Safety, and it was supposed that he was engaged in the attack upon the Fort, and also was present at another affair which shows the spirit of the patriots of that day. Soon after the return of the party with the military stores from the fort, Governor Wentworth issued a proclamation declaring the perpetrators of the deed guilty of high treason, and called for their arrest. In open defiance of this proclamation Lieut. Adams, Major Sullivan, and other citizens of Durham, holding civil or military commissions from the King, assembled upon the common near the old meeting house, kindled a bonfire, and in the presence of a large number of persons, with becoming gravity and solemnity, burned their commissions, and the military clothing and other insignia which connected them in any way with the Royal Government.

Mr. Scammel was engaged to a young lady of the village, a sister of Mrs. Sullivan, and it is supposed that he intended to have returned to Durham at the close of the war. His death was a severe stroke to his betrothed, who consecrated herself to his memory, by a maidenhood continined to her death. His personal appearance was plain but preposessing he was considerably above six feet in height, and of a slight figure, of an amiable and engaging disposition, but nervous and excitable. It is said of him, that although of unquestioned courage, he never entered upon a battle, without tremor, and that it required some hard fighting to quiet his nerves. At the commencement of the war he was attached to the staff of Gen. Sullivan, afterwards had command of a regiment, and at his dath was acting Adjutant general.

OLD SERIES, NO. 28 AUG. 29, 1851.

By BALLARD SMITH of DURHAM.

The following is a copy of the manuscript (original in possession of Valentine Smith, Esq.,) from which Dr. Belknap obtained his account of the affair at Oyster River, as given in his history of New Hampshire. It contains more details and therefore seems worth preservation.

Destruction of Oyster River, July 18, 1694.

Deacon Burnum says the gate of his grandfather's yard was left open that night; there were ten Indians sent to surprise the Garrison--they were fatigued and fell asleep under the bank of the river near the house. It was a bright moonlight night; John Dean who lived at the falls on the north side, went out early to catch his horse, and returned to his house just after the dawn of day, when he was fired on by the enemy and slain. John Wille with his family was at Lt. Burnum's garrison; he had been kept up that night by the toothache. Upon hearing the gun he immediately alarmed the house and secured the gate; they called from the garrison to Ezekiel Pitman who lived at a gun-shot distance; their calling waked the Indians that were under the bank who immediately ran to Pitman's house; he burst a way thro' the end of his house that was next the garrison, when he with his family passed out the same instant the Indians got to his doors. The family took the advantage of the shade of some trees and got safe to the garrison—he understood there was 500 of the enemy; they did not fire on the garrison—they killed old Mr. Huckings that day.

Maj. Jones' acct—In the night the dogs barked much, his father tho't the wolves were about, got up and went some distance from the house to take care of sow and pigs, returned, went into a flanker, got on the top of it and sat there with his legs hanging down on the outside, when an Indian fired at him; he fell back, the bullet entered the flanker betwixt where his legs hung. A body of Indians were placed behind a rack a few rods from the garrison, from where they kept up a fire on the house.

There were several ungarrisoned houses in the neighborhood; some of the inhabetants made their way thro' the fire of the enemy and got to the garrison; a woman by the name of Chesley was shot thro' the breast as she ran and expired immediately. Several others of the same name were seized by the enemy and butchered; there were about five killed in that close neighborhood—the Watsons at a quarter of a mile distance were killed; Bunker's garrison stood. Edwin Small was in Jones' garrison Mrs. Burnum says Smith's garrison stood out: her grandmother Emerson was taken; the party that took her dismissed her aged mother who fled with her child and hid among the corn, another party came along and butchered them both.

Narrative of Mrs. Dean's Captivity and Escape.

After her husband was killed they took her and her daughter and carried them about a mile where they left them by the side of a spruce swamp, in the care of an old Indian who could speak English, while they went with a view to surprise a family that lived above. The Indian told her he had a violent headache and asked her what was good for it. She told him Occuba, the Indian name for rum; he had some with him of which he drank freely and soon fell asleep; then she took her daughter and escaped into the swamp: instead of coming down towards the inhabitants, her policy was to go up. She had just escaped from his sight when he missed her and she heard him call; she passed almost through the swamp and hid herself in a thicket, where she remained till in the night when she came down on the south side of the river till she got nearly opposite to where her house stood, which had been burned by the Indians; in looking across to the place where the house had stood she was greatly alarmed at seeing one of the posts which had not been burned down; at first she supposed it was an Indian, but watching a while she saw it did not move; then she ventured to the water where she found a canoe; she and her daughter got on board and paddled down the river about a quarter of a mile where she found the body of a man dead in the water; he had been shot that day by the Indians as he was attempting to swim across the river. She saw that Burnum's garrison was standing; so she landed near the house, but fearing it might be in possession of the enemy, she was in suspense for some time, doubting whether it was best to call, but at length she called, when, to her inexpressible joy, she was answered by friends who received her into the garrison.

OLD SERIES, NO. 49, SEPT. 2, 1851.

BY BALLARD SMITH of DURHAM.

[Continued.]

Destruction of Oyster River, July 18, 1694.

Mr. John Buss, who was preacher and physician, being absent, his family, which was somewhat large, together with a boy belonging to a neighbor, upon the first alarm left the house unseen by the Indians and secreted themselves among the trees where they lay till the enemy withdrew. The enemy came to the house, stripped of it some furniture which they carried with them and then set fire to the house, which was consumed together with a valuable library, and they killed a number of cows which were in the yard.

Ensn. John Davis was conversing, the evening before, about the Indians and gave his opinion there was no one within fifty miles; he, his wife and several children were butchered, his house burnt, two young daughters were captivated one of which after some years returned; the other entered a nunnery and continued there; his sister, a widow by the name of Smith, with her two sons, one of which was grown up, lived in the house with him; she was taken and carried into the woods and there killed; her eldest son escaping from the house to the river wa shot in the water; his body was found by Mrs. Dean as before stated; her youngest was killed at the house.

Jabez Davis says that his father, Moses Davis, with two of his sons, the day before, was at work on an out farm. The enemy passed by them; the dog discovered them; Davis then thought it was a bear, though afterwards suspected it was Indians and sat up all night. About an hour before day he heard the gun that killed Dean; he removed the things from his house into the bushes, and after finding by the firing that the whole town was attacked, set off and came down the river to a sawmill, where he discovered three Indians with Mrs. Dean and her daughter; they did not see him; two of them presently went in quest of him, while the other was left to take care of Mrs. Dean. He, with his sons hid in the woods till the next day, when they got to Burnum's garrison, he says it must be a mistake about Mrs. Dean's hiding in the spruce swamp for she was above it; no house below Jones' creek was consumed, except John Medar's which was abandoned; they set fire to Sergt. Davis's which he put out; there were three Indians waiting for him to come; he was fired on by them; he that moment stooped and the bullet split the body of a small tree just over his head; he shot an Indian that day at considerable distance; the Indian was carried off, his bones were found next year in a swamp hardby; another had a pack of valuable plunder; he was fired at; the bullet cut his belt when he quit his plunder.

Bunker's, Smith's and Davis's garrisons stood out; there was no great pains taken to reduce either. There were two Captains of the enemy; Capt. Nath'l had the command on the north side; he did not get to the lower settlement till after sunrise, so that the people who were inclined had time to get off by water, as were the Medars and others. A man by the name of Clark was killed by them in that part, and another by the name of Gellison as he was passing from one house to another after powder. A brother of the last mentioned was out likewise, when to avoid the enemy he jumped into a well, from which he was unable to get out, he remained there till the next day and died presently after he was taken out. Three Indians were sent off to attack the house of Mr. Tasker in what is now Madbury; Mr. Tasker had his family and one man with him in the house; an Indian looked into a small window and enquired whether it was not time for them to get up; Mr. Tasker immediately got up and discharged his gun through a hole in the house and mortally wounded one Indian, who, with bitter screeches was carried off by the others; the family immediately took to the woods and that night got to Woodman's garrison. He thinks old Mrs. Leathers and one or two others of the family were killed; the rest escaped into

OLD SERIES, NO. 50, SEPT. 9, 1851.

By BALLARD SMITH of DURHAM

Oyster River Massacre, July 18, 1694.

Kent upon hearing firing got up and looked out, when he saw a number of Indians by his house waiting for him; he was so surprised that he did not stop to awake his family, but secured himself in a drain that led from the house, where he lay all day; his family were presently after aroused by the firing, about which time the enemy that were around the house retired to assist their brethren that had besieged Drew's Garrison, which gave his wife an opportunity of escaping with her children. (What a coward that husband was in the cellar drain!)

Samuel Adams was killed, his wife, who was pregnant, was ripped up; the grave is still to be seen where fourteen persons lie buried. One or two of the Adams family were captivated.

The inhabitants of Great Bay were unmolested; it fell heaviest on the people by Little Bay, and on the South side of Oyster River. The two companies united at Durham Falls and together attacked Woodman's Garrison, without any other effect than their almost ruining the roof of the house. Those that were on the south side, after having finished their mischief below, collected on a green, a large shot gun distance from Burnum's Garrison, and showed their captives and affronted the garrison. One who had separated himself a little from the body and was making an indecent gesture, was fired at by a young man from the watch box and wounded badly just above his heel, whereupon they catched a horse belonging to Mr. Burnum whereon they mounted him and carried him to Winnipisseogee, where, on a beach of that pond, it is said some of the young men of the party had an inclination to practice horsemanship; the horse was mettlesome and several were thrown; at length they tied the legs of one under the belly of the horse; the horse started nimbly; the fellow soon lost his seat and came with head down and was presently dispatched; the Indians then shot the horse. There was an instance of this kind before at Casco.

Mr. Thomas Bickford kept his house alone; his family had been sent off on the tide; his house was not a garrison; he changed the appearance of his head; supposed he killed one Indian.

Edward Leathers's wife and a woman by the name of Jackson were killed William Leathers escaped by running.

Mr. John Edgerly says there were two families of Edgerlys, his grandfather Thomas and his uncle Thomas; his uncle lived at Amblers; upon hearing the Indians, he, his wife and her sister jumped out of bed, got down cellar, leaving their children in bed; the Indians came in killed the children and one or two persons living in the other end of the house were taken; they looked into the cellar but did not go down; they rifled the house and fired it; as soon as they were gone he put the fire out; his grandfather, son Joseph and a daughter were carried captive; the rest got into a canoe and as they were setting off the Indians fired upon them and mortally wounded his son Zachariah.

Mr. Joseph Drew says his father Thomas Drew had been married six months; he lived with his father and family; John Drew was put out of a window and escaped; there were fifteen; Benjamin was about nine years old; he was carried over Winnipiseogee where they set him to run through the Indians (run the gauntlet) that they might throw their hatchets and tomahawks at him, which they repeated till they dispatched him. His grandfather Francis, on a promise of quarter surrendered; they bound him; he got loose and it is supposed he killed one; his (the Indian's) bones were found in the house after it was burnt. Francis ran towards Adams's Garrison; there the Indians met him, took him, bound him and killed him with tomahawks; his wife was carried into the woods and was rendered so feeble with hunger they left her to die in the woods.

[The End.]

OLD SERIES, NO. 51, SEPT. 16, 1851.

By BALLARD SMITH of DURHAM.

The Early Settlers at Oyster River.

Philip Chesly (or Chasely at it is spelled on the records) "husband man," was at this plantation as early as 1644, and as was the case with most of the early settlers at Dover, had a grant of marsh and meadow upon Great Bay. His farm and residence was on the north shore at Lubberland, where a garrison was built which continued in possession of the family for four generations, but which has recently been torn down (1851) by William P. Channel, who owns a part of the farm, and resides near the site of the old house. He was freeman in 1665 and was twice married, having issue, Thomas, Phillip, Mary, who married Ralph Hall, son of Deacon John Hall, Esther, who married John Hall, grandson of Deacon John, and Hannah. His first wife Elizabeth was living in 1661, and his second, Joanna, is 1685. He conveyed the bulk of his property by deed of 28th of April, 1661, to his wife and children, some of whom were of nonage; gave land to his son Thomas on 12 August, 1663, and to his youngest son Philip, 29th Nov. 1664.

Thomas (2nd generation), who is thought to have lived at the homestead, married Elizabeth Thines about 1663; children Thomas, George, Joseph, Elizabeth who married Davis, Susannah who married Capt John Smith of Lubberland 17 June 1694, and Mary. He was selectman in 1688 and 1695; he had several grants of land from the town and was killed by the Indians near Johnson's reek 15 Nov. 1697. His will was entered 9 August, 1698.

Philip (2nd generation) was born about 1663; his wife was Sarah ——; children, Samuel, James, Philip, Ebenezer. He had a grant of 100 acres extending from Butler's Point, on the west side of the creek to "near ye Indian graves" (the old burying ground on Capt. Woodman's farm). His will was dated 18 Nov., 1695.

Thomas (3d generation) son of Thomas (2d) was constable in 1696; he was betrothed to be married to Miss Randall who lived not far from the present residence of Jeremiah Smith on the Mast Road. Just before the wedding was to have taken place, and while she was going home with a party of friends from the Falls, where she had probably been shopping, they were set upon by a party of Indians near where James Garland lived. She tried to escape, and ran towards a barn that stood near, with the hope of hiding herself, but was shot just as she was going into it, and fell across the stone at the door, where she soon bled to death. That stone has since been taken up to Ephraim Bunker's farm, and it is said that when there is a heavy dew the blood stains can still be seen (1851) upon it.

Mr. Chesley was greatly grieved at her death, and declared he would spend his life in fighting the savages: he took his gun and started out: he soon came upon a party of twelve Indians and the fight began; when it was ended he had killed eleven of them, single handed; the other escaped. It is thought Chesley was afterwards killed by the Indians near Oyster River. He was dead in 1708, leaving a son Samuel who was born in 1691; Samuel chose his uncle George for his guardian, 7 June 1708.

George (3) son of Thomas (2) had a wife Deliverence; he had a mill near the second falls of Oyster River, where he lived. He was dead in 1711.

Joseph (3) son of Thomas (2) lived on the homestead at Lubberland; his wife was Sarah ——; their children were Thomas, Joseph, James; his will was dated 13 April, 1730, and proved 7 June 1731. His executors were his brother-in law, Capt. John Smith, and Lieut. John Smith. He left the homestead to his eldest son Joseph.

Samuel (3) son of Philip (2) was Captain of a company at Oyster River, and is spoken of by Dr. Belknap, and others as a bold and worthy man; he earned a good name as an officer, and led his company in the first two expeditions against Port Royal; he frequently went out against the Indians and was killed by them at Oyster River 15 Sept., 1707; he had a grant 30 May, 1697: his widow Elizabeth, who was administratrix, married Amos Pinkham. Other facts about Philip (2) are given by A. H. Quint at page 205 in Genealogical Register of April 1851.

Joseph (4) son of Joseph (3), lived on the homestead at Lubberland without a wife till he became quite old; his neighbor, Dea. Ebenezer Smith, who lived near by at the Smith garrison, had a daughter, Comfort, very pretty and very wild; her father, who was proud and of strict behaviour, grieved at some of her hoidenish acts and, in a teasing way, said to her "You had better marry old Mr. Chesley." She took him at his word and started off at once to the field where Mr. Chesley was at work; she told him what her father had said and said she was willing to go and wed him. He was not unwilling and in spite of the wishes and the threats of her father they became husband and wife. At the time of her marriage she was sixteen and he was sixty. Their only child, Margaret, married Capt. Joseph Chase of Portsmouth. At the death of Joseph (4) the Chesley homestead was sold to Ebenezer Smith, Esq.

OLD SERIES NO. 52, SEPT. 23, 1851.

By BALLARD SMITH of DURHAM.

The Smith Family at Oyster River.

The Smiths at Oyster River were among the earliest settlers there, and the farms which they had at the first, have been kept by the kindred ever since. Ebenezer and Valentine Smith. Esqrs., and others, have been at much pains in getting the names of all who have sprung from the early stock, but there is still uncertainty as to some of the children of the first settler. The family traditions, heirlooms, old manuscripts, the town and other records, together, give the following.

George Smith, the first settler, is thought to have sprung from "the family" that dwelt for some two hundred years at old Haugh in County Chester, England, which was of kin to the Hatton that lived hard by (offspring of Sir Christopher, Lord Chancellor in the time of Elizabeth) and which afterward went to County Lincolnshire. He left England at Plymouth and came to "Boston when there were only a few huts built there, and not one cellar dug." Hence he came to Pascataqua. It has been "claimed" that he was son of a near kindred of Capt. John Smith, who came in early times to Virignia and was afterwards Admiral of New England; they say that he left England soon after the Captain's death and upon reaching the Pascataqua crossed to Smith's Isle (Star Island, Isles of Shoals) which had been given to Capt. John, but there is now no witness for the kindred, other than the claim and the likeness in the coat of arms.

If he went to the Shoals he must have come back soon, since he was at Dover "when it was but an infant plantation,"

and lived there till about 1652. While there (at Dover Neck) he was "Town Clarke, Recorder of the Court, Senior "Comeshener" for trials at law, Lieutenant of a company, and seemingly, a man of weight, worth and wealth. It is thought that together with other early settlers at Dover Neck he had a gift of marsh and meadows on Great Bay, and that his gift was laid out at Lubberland, where the Smith garrison stands. A coat of mail, cutlass, silver tankard, sets of silver buttons, etc., which are said to have been brought over by the first settler, have been handed down among the kindred as heirlooms. He left one son, Joseph, and, as is thought John Smith and James Smith were also his sons. Their mother after the death of her first husband became the wife of ——— Monday, who also died, and then of ——— Nason, by whom she had children who lived at Kittery (now Eliot.)

John (2) is thought to have lived at Lubberland until about 1674, and from him the homestead came to Capt. John, eldest son of his brother Joseph. An old manuscript that "John left his brother and went to Little Compton in Plymouth Colony on account of a young woman for whom he had great aversion and at the same time she had a passionate regard for him, insomuch that after he had absented himself she cut off a piece from one of her fingers and sent it to him enclosed in a letter." At Little Compton he married and had two daughters, who married at Boston.

James (2) bought about one hundred acres at Oyster River falls, where he kept an inn (ordinary) and carried on business. He was freeman in 1669; is wife

Sarah was daughter of John Davis; their children were John, James, Samuel, Mary, Sarah and two that died when children. "He died from a surfeit which he got by running to assist Capt. Floyd at Wheelwright's pond" His widow and Samuel were soon after killed by the Indians. Joseph died at sea.

John (3) married Elizabeth, daughter of Dr. Buss and had children, John, James, Joseph, Elizabeth, Mary, Hannah, Sarah and two that died when children. He died in his 41st year; his wife had a long life; his sister Mary married a Deane, Sarah married a Freeman, both dewlling at Cape Cod. Of his children James (4) is the only one now known to have stayed at Oyster River: he lived on the homestead of his grandfather; his wife's name was Mary; their son John (3), better known as Master Smith, from his having taught school, was born 24 Dec. 1736.

Master Smith was a busy and ardent Whig during the Revolution; he was one of the Committee of Safty; Town Clerk, Selectman, and Representative for many years, and was much beloved and highly respected by his townsmen. His first wife was Deborah, daughter of Thomas Chesley; they had two children, James who died at Dover and Thomas who was burned to death when a child. His second wife was Sarah, daughter of Rev. Wm. Parsons of South Hampton, by whom he had three children, Deborah, who died unwedded, William who died at Havana and Sarah (6) who married Major Seth S. Walker and resided at the homestead of James (2).

Joseph (2) the other son of George was born in 1640; he had a grant of land on the north side of Oyster River about half a mile above its mouth, adjoining a grant to William Williams; there he lived and died; his wife's name was Elizabeth. Their children were John, 16 June, 1687, Mary, married Samuel Page, Elizabeth, married James Pinkham and Samuel, born June 1687. Both sons soon became men of mark and worth in the town and provinces. He is said to have had a Quakerish leaning; he was the first clerk of the Dover Friends Monthly meeting (1702 and following) and was mindful of the Friends in his will. He died 15 Dec. 1727, well stricken with years. His wife 25 May, 1726. His gravestone says that "he was the first European who cultivated the soil in which his remains were deposited." His will is in the Probate office at Exeter.

Samuel (3) kept the homestead of his father, and John (3) had the garrison at Lubberland, Samuel (3) was town Clerk from 1739 to 1765; Selectman from 1744 to 1752; Representative, and about 1745 was one of the Royal Council. He died 2 May 1790, in his 75th year. By his wife Hannah he had twelve children, Samuel, Elizabeth, Mary, Hannah, Temperance, Patience, Sarah, Joseph, Benjamin, Jeremiah, John and Robert.

His son Joseph (4) (Major) was also town Clerk and Selectman for many years; he was born 12 March, 1724; died 16 July 1765; sons, Daniel, Joseph and Samuel. His widow Deborah married James Gilmore, Esq., of Portsmouth.

Daniel (5) (Major) was born 17 Oct. 1760; m. Mary Gilmore Dec. 1780; their daughter Joanna m., Ebenezer Meserve. Daniel's second wife was Mary Locke of Epsom; from him the homestead came to his son Winthrop (6), a man of great worth and highly respected by the community; he was b. 13 Jan. 1789; m. Eleanor Locke; he died 28 Aug. 1844. The old place of Joseph (3) is now (1851) owned by Daniel (7) and Joseph (7), sons of Major Winthrop.

John (3) eldest son of Joseph (2) kept the garrison at Lubberland, owned most of the north shore of Great Bay, and much land about the first fall of Lamprey river, so that it was a saying that "Capt. John Smith was sure to have all the land that 'Squire Mathes didn't own." He was Selectman of Dover, Captain of the Company on the south side of Oyster river in Indian times, and stoutly held his garrison against the French and Indians at the massacre in 1694. He married Susanna, daughter of Thomas Chesley; their children were:—John b. 18 May 1695; Elizabeth b. 1 Aug. 1697, who m. Robert Burnham; Joseph b. 7 Sept. 1701; Hannah b. 30 Sept. 1703; Samuel C. b. Feb. 1706; Benjamin. 22 March 1709; Ebenezer, b 6 June 1712; and Winthrop b 30 May 1714 died in 1728.

John (4) (Captain) m Mary Jones and is thought to have lived near Crummett's mill. Joseph (4) (Col) m Sarah Glidden; and her children John, Winthrop, Hannah, Israel, Gilman, Sarah, Winthrop, Hilton, Lydia, Susanna, Ichabod, Hilton, Andrew, Elizabeth, who m Col John Folsom, Mary who m Capt Herburtes Neal, and Joseph, (in all sixteen) He lived and died at Lamprey river.

Samuel (4) dwelt where Robert Channel now (1851) lives. m. Margaret Lendal' and had children:—Sarah, John, Susanna, and Margaret.

Benjamin (4) (Capt) like his father was a large landowner, had the old place at Lubberland where he built the house now owned by the kindred and also built and lived on the east side of Lamprey river, just opposite the bridge. He was Selectman, member of Committee of Safety in his 70th year; held many offices and was a man of mark in the town. He m Jemima daughter of Dea. Edward Hall of Newmarket; their children were Edward, John b 20 Sept 1732, and Mary. His second wife was Anna Veza, who had one son Samuel, C T March 1761. By a third wife, Sarah Clark, he had one son Benjamin, b 1769. Benjamin (4) d 13 Oct. 1791, in his 83d year. From him the old place at Lubberland came to his son John (5) (Lieut.) who m. Lydia, daughter of Hon. Thomas Millet of Dover; their children were: Benjamin, Thomas, Elizabeth, Jemima, John, Love, Lydia, Valentine and Ebenezer. John (5) like his father Benjamin was selectman, a warm Whig in the Revolution and a sturdy supporter of the church. He is said to have been frank, without selfishness, and so careful against himself in his dealings as to make it a saying that "the Lieut. was so straight that he leaned a little backwards." Like his father he was upwards of six feet in height, and lived out all his days. His wife died 4 March 1821 in her 87th year.

Ebenezer (4) (Deacon) fifth son of Capt. John (3) lived at the garrison: he was a man of great worth but like his brethren somewhat troubled with pride of kin. He m. Margaret Weeks of Greenland and had children, John (4) who m. Mary Jewett, Comfort who m. Joseph Chesley, Ebenezer, and Margaret who m. John Blydenburgh. His widow m. Hon.

George Frost of New Castle, both of whom lived and Judge Frost died at the Garrison.

Ebenezer (5) son of Dea. Ebenezer, was b. 13 March 1758, he was several years at the Dummer school (Newbury, Mass.); read law with Geo. Sullivan and opened an office in 1783 at the Falls. He m. Mehitable, daughter of Jacob Sheafe of Portsmouth, 5 May 1785; he was Representative six years and held other offices. He practiced at the bar more than forty years, and was President of the Strafford County Bar Association 28 years. He was Councillor for Strafford Co., an aid of Gov. Gilman and in 1798 was made Judge of the Superior Court, which office he declined. He was an able, upright, candid man, proud of his family and his town, a great friend of law and order and highly esteemed by all who knew him. He died 24 Sept. 1831. His wife died 4 Sept. 1843. Their children were Jacob, Ebenezer, Henry (Rev.) Alfred, Mehitable m. Ebenezer Coe, Mary m. Rev. J. K Young, Charles and four that died while children.

(This closes the Memoranda by Ballard Smith).

OLD SERIES, NO. 53. SEPT. 30, 1851.

EARLY SETTLERS IN DOVER.

So far as we can ascertain the only settlers in Dover in the spring of 1623 were Edward Hilton, William Hilton and Thomas Roberts and their families. There may have been and probably were others in the company but we do not know their names. There were probably some additions by immigration between 1623 and 1631 but there is no record of it till 1631 when Edward Colcord and Capt. Thomas Wiggans are known to have been here, the latter being sent over by the land proprietors as already stated. Wiggans went to England in 1632 and returned in 1633 bringing with him a large accession to the Colony. The names of families in Dover between 1623 and 1641 were Ault, Beard, Burdett, Canney, Colcott, Dam, Furber, Gibbons, Goddard, Hall, Heard, Hilton, Johnson, Knollys, Langstaff, Larkham, Leighton, Leveridge, Nute, Matthews, Nutter, Ordway, Pinkham, Pomfret, Roberts, Tibbetts, Tuttle, Walderne, Wiggans, York.

Regarding a few of these we are not absolutely certain and there are a dozen or more others who may have been here before 1641 but in all such cases we have followed the balance of probabilities. Of those dwelling in Dover between 1641 and 1700 we have found over 200 family names. Descendants of fifty or more families are now residing here and bearing the original family names. Nearly all the original settlers have descendants in Dover, of some other than the family name. The original stock is not dying out; it is still vigorous and promises to remain so for generations to come.

By diligently ransacking old records and by personal enquiry among the old members of many of these families we have procured some little information which is deemed worthy of preservation and which will appear in this paper. Regarding the families of Canney, Colcott, Furber, Hall, Heard, Leighton, Nutter Tebbetts and Walderne, all of Dover Neck, we still want information, particu larly, to render our articles more complete. We also want information of all families of Oyster River, Lee and Madbury, excepting those who have been noticed at some length already, and all the early Somersworth families.

For information regarding the families of Edward and William Hilton the interested are referred to the files of the Exeter-News Letter. To the full accounts published in that paper we can only add that it is stated in Dover Records that William sold his premises at Oyster River 7 July 1645, to Francis Matthews; that John was taxed at O. R. from 1648 to 1656 and was a "freeman" in 1655; and that Jonathan was taxed there in 1659.

Of Leveridge, Burdet, Larkham, Knollys and Underhill our readers have already enough. Mr. Ballard Smith has well written regarding the families of Chesley, Smith, Matthews, Goddard, Williams and Adams, all of Oyster River. We now earnestly request all persons having traditions or records relating to the early settlers of old Dover to communicate them to us. The records, either original or copied, and the traditions as traditions.

OLD SERIES, NO. 54, OCT. 7, 1851.

EARLY SETTLERS OF DOVER.

THOMAS ROBERTS was a dweller on Dover Neck at a very early period; how early we have no means of knowing certainly, but the uniform tradition of the family has stated that he settled at the Point with Edward and William Hilton in 1623.—The correct locality of his first residence is unknown, but it is probable it was very near that of the Hiltons, the site of which is still pointed out to the curious upon the extremity of Dover Point.

Not many years after Thomas Roberts moved further up the Neck and located himself upon the bank of the Fore River, on land now (1851) forming a part of the "Jerry Roberts estate" the spot on which he built and dwelt is still identified, though part of the soil on which his house stood has been washed away by the waters of the Pascataqua. It is nearly in a direct line east from the house now on that estate. The land which he then occupied has been preserved in the Roberts family in uninterrupted succession for two hundred and fifty years.

The first notice of him, apart from tradition, is found in Belknap's History (page 25) "that in 1638 the people of Dover chose Mr. Roberts President of the Court," in place of Capt. John Underhill, whom they had justly expelled for his conduct. His name appears also on the Town Records as being elected to fill various minor offices in the town, and also as receiving various grants of land at different times, though his possessions are said to have been comparatively small. He owned land on the east side of Dover Neck, and also on the west side of Back River, (Bellamy). Sewall in his history of the Quakers speaks of him as rebuking his sons Thomas and John who were Constables, for the excessive virulence with which they enforced the laws against the Quakers in 1662, and says that he had been a member of the church for more than twenty years, sustaining a good character.

Thomas Roberts died between 27 Sept., 1673 and 30 June, 1674, his will bearing the former date and the probate the latter. In it he gives the bulk of his property to Richard Rich, husband of his daughter Sarah and various legacies to the three children below mentioned. He was buried in the north east corner of the old burying ground on Dover Neck, where many of his descendants also lie.

His children were JOHN, b, 1629; THOMAS, b. 1633; HESTER, (wife of John Martin and being in Jersey in 1673) ANN, wife of James Philbrick of Hampton; ELIZABETH, wife of Benjamin Heard of Cochecho; and SARAH, wife of Richard Rich.

Thomas (2) son of Thomas (1) had a wife Mary, he lived on the homestead and appears to have died there. We have already spoken of his cruel treatment of the Quakers when he and his brother John were constables. He filled various other town offices as did his father and brother. We can find trace of but two children.—

Thomas (3) who died unmarried, and Nathaniel (3), but there were probably others and perhaps some of those whose connection we cannot identify on account of want of evidence.

John, (2) son of Thomas (1) as above, married Abigail, daughter of Elder Hatevil Nutter; she was living in 1674 and is mentioned in the will of her father. John is often called "Sargeant John"; he owned land near that upon which his father lived, and probably lived upon it; he was certainly a resident of the Neck and owned land west of Back (Bellamy) River, as well as marsh near the Great Bay. He was delegate to the New Hampshire convention which met in 1689.

Of his children were Joseph (3) and probably Hatevil (3).

NATHANIEL (3) son of Thomas as above lived in early life at a place called "House Point," but afterwards lived in a house that his son Paul had built on a spot a few feet distant from that now (1851) occupied by Andrew Varney, but which the early death of the builder had left vacant. He lived there until his death. Of his children by his wife Elizabeth Mason of Somersworth, were PAUL b, 18 Feb. 1706; who died a young man, unmarried MIRIAM, b. 4 Jan., 1708-9; THOMAS, b. 23 July, 1710, who built the house now (1851) standing on the eastern corner of Locust and Silver streets; he married a Jones of Durham and died without children; NATHANIEL, b. 22 April 1713, who was a sailor living at Somersworth, or Berwick; he married a Thompson and was lost at sea, leaving children, David, Isaac (lost at sea) George, Nathaniel and some daughters; AARON, b. 16 April 1716, who married Sarah, daughter of John Tibbetts; he inherited the land on which Andrew Varney now (1851) lives, and had children, Aaron (who left no children) John who lived at Rochester and had children, Silas of Alton, Daniel now (1851) living on Dover Neck and who is father of Alonzo Roberts, Esq ; Sarah who married Elijah Varney and had children; Hannah, who married Otis Tuttle; Tamsin who married Thomas Varney and had Andrew and others; Elizabeth who married Isaac Varney and is now (1851) living near "Little John's Creek"; and Abigail who married Jona-

MOSES who lived on the farm where the late Jerry Roberts lived, was born 22 June, 1718; the house in which he lived was burned about 1825. He married Elizabeth Whitehouse, daughter of Thomas and Rachel Whitehouse and born in 1725; he died, April 1808, having children, Anna who married Joshua Varney who lived and died on the farm where Nathaniel Jenness lives (1851); Thomas, who recieved the Jerry Roberts farm, he married Hannah Lamos, and died about 1825, having children: James, Jeremiah lately deceased, Elizabeth, wife of Nicholas Roberts, and Abigail, wife of Philip Tebbetts; James, who married Eunice Varney and lived and died in Farmington, leaving Jerry, now (1851) on Dover Neck and eight others Hannah, who died unmarried aged about twenty; Moses, who lived at Rochester, married Elsa Tebbets and had children Anna, Ezekiel Elizabeth, Moses, Lucy, Mary, Hannah and others; Elizabeth, who died unmarried at Dover Neck; Ephraim, b 27 March, 1772, lives at the Neck on the place where Thomas Canney settled in old times; he married Hannah Roberts, daughter of David and granddaughter of Nathaniel; his children were Amasa Roberts, Esq., who graduated from Dartmouth College in 1838; Emily, who is married to George Leighton and Andietta who married David L. Drew, and is now dead. Elizabeth born 3 Feb. 1722-3.

JOSEPH(3) son of John (2) married Elizabeth ————; he lived on the farm now owned by his great grandson Hanson Roberts; the house in which he lived was situated about 60 rods northeasterly from the present house. He had children, Joseph born 27 October 1695; John b. Dec. 1696; Elizabeth b. 13 March 1697; Abigail b. 16 July 1701; Stephen b. 20 Aug. 1704; who lived on the homestead and kept a public house there, near the western end of the then ferry to Kittery; he died in 1757, and had children of whom was Joseph, who died 26 June 1813, aged 66, who was father of Hanson Roberts; Ebenezer b. 24 Feb. 1705, Benjamin b. 20 Feb. 1709, Samuel and Lydia b. 11 April 1712; Mary b. 13 March 1716.

HATEVIL, (3), probably son of John (2) had wife Lydia. His will was dated 29 Aug. 1719; 3 March 1734-5; in it he mentioned his wife Lydia, and his children next mentioned:—SAMUEL b. 12 Dec. 1686, (who had wife Sarah and children Sarah b. 16 July 1717, Benjamin, 1 Sept. 1719, Lydia b. 16 May 1721, and Samuel b. 7 May 1723;) Abigail b. 29 July 1689; Joshua b. 10 Oct. 1698: Mary b. 20 July 1701.

There are records of other "Roberts" families which we can not connect with those already named, nor with each other, although it is almost certain they are thus connected. These are WILLIAM who was a resident of Oyster River apparently as early as 1645 when he witnessed a deed given by Darby Field of premises in that region. He was there in 1648; he had grants of land at various times, and was killed by the Indians in 1675 at the same time "with his son in-law." Whether or not he had sons we cannot ascertain.

There was a JOHN and Deborah who had children, Joanna b. 20 Oct. 1705; Sarah b. 18 Feb. 1708-9; Mary b. 20 July

1711; Phebe b. 20 July 1716; Ebenezer b. 5 Feb. 1721-2.

LOVE and Elizabeth had children, Hannah b. 10 May 1713; Love b. 21 April 1721.

JOHN and Frances Emery were m. 17 May 1720 and had children Deborah and Alexander, b. 15 Jan. 1725-6.

ENSIGN JOSEPH and wife Elizabeth had children Ephraim b. 23 March 1727; Joseph b. 7 Feb. 1729; Betty b. 21 April 1731; Mary b. 8 Oct. 1733; Abigail b. 18 Feb. 1736; Lydia b. 22 Oct. 1738.

OLD SERIES, NO. 55. OCT. 1, 1851.

DOVER TOWN RECORDS.

1666.

By ye sellecktmen the 3th of the 6m (66. Whereas the sellecktmen of the towne of Douer did make an order the 14th of July 1666 that all the Constabells of the Towne that haue not made up thear a Counts with the Tresurer or the sellecktmen acording to the orders and in the same order theay had 18 days time to doe the same, and not heiring of anything done by the Delinquents for the Cleiring themselves and knoweing no other way to bring the seuerall Constabells to account, and to bring in the Townes Estate Cometed to thear hands by the Seuerall Rates, Doe order that Euery man hoes name is heir under written for the neglect of order above said, doe fine each of them the sum of twenty shillings to be leved by the Marshall and for him to Return the said fines to the sellecktmen to be Improued for the Townes use.

John Bickford sinyer   Thomas Nock.
Wiliam Williams Juner, Jerremy Tebbut
John Woodman,   John heard,
John louring,   John Scriuen,
John Meader.

To the Marshall of Douer or his Debety.

You are required in his Magists name to leve by way of Execution uppon the Estate of these persons whose names are under written the som of twentey shillings apon each mans Estate, or for want there of the persons and is for satisfying of thear fines wich is imposed apon them for the Necklecckt of an order of the sellecktmen dated the 14th July (66 and Return the same to the sellecktmen to be Improued for the use of the Towne Dated the the 3th of August 1666.

At a metting of the freemen Called By the Constabells the 19th of the 7th month 1666.

Capt. Walldern Chosen Debetie for this present Generall Courte now to be holden the 11th of this present month.

At the sam tim voted By the freemen that Capt Walldern is to followe these Instrucktions following: First that he shall not ackt aneything to the Infrengment of our towne preueledges.

2dly That he shall not acct aneything for the hendrance, or stopping of aney person or persons that his maghsty hath sent for.

At a metting of the sellecktmen at Cochechae th. 26 9 mo (66

Ordered that Thomas Terner Be warned out of the Towne by Ensin John Daues and John Bickford and that he depart a Cording to lawe.

Ordered that the wife of William Risley

95

be warned out of the Towne By Antoney Nutter.

At the same meting henrey kerk Apoynted to keep Ordenarey at Douer and to stand till next County Courts Appon his Good behauer.

Phellep Cromewell Sworn to be Constabell the 3th of the 10th month 1666.

At a meitting of the sellecktmen the 27th 12th mo. 1666.

Ordered that whereas maney InConuiences and damages Coming apon the Towne By seuerall of our Inhabetants Taking in seuerall Parsons, boeth men and women, do heir by order that none of our Inhabetants shall from hence forth Admitt or Entertaine anie Inmate, or sudgener, or saruent to be hired, or taken into thear houses, uppon the Penalty of nintine shillings fine to the Towne, Besides all other Damedges the Towne sufireth By Such Persons taken in

     Richard Walldern
Townsmen Job Clement
     Antoney Nutter

At a Publick Towne meitting holden the 11th of March 1666.

Voted that whereas seuerall of our grants Maed to our Inhabatants Run to them and thear heires and Assignes, the other Grants Run to such particler parson; Nowe that all our Inhabatants may haue and Inioye Proprietes Aliek in an Euery pertickler Grant made unto them; Wee Order that all Grants that Run to aney Pertickler Persou, his wrighte shall be as good as those that Runs to them thear heires and Asoynes. This is entered into the great booke.

At the same day voted that the Selecktmen shall fortwith make a Rate to Defray the Publick Charge of the Towne for killing Woolfes to this day, and debetes charges and what charge Mrs. hill and her charges, prouided (it) exceed not 3 half pence apon the pound.

At A Publick Town meitting holden the 11th March, 1666,

Voted That finding seuerall great Grants maed to seuerall persons, and alsoe seuerall persons taken in to be Inhabetants, and not accomedated with land according to the Townes Engagement, and not knowing whether thear will be anie moer to grant when all former grants be fullfilled, doe order from hencefowerd that noe Person shall be taken in as an Inhabetant to have anie land granted to them untill all other grants be layd out according to grant, and alsoe the Towne booke be Examined and Euery mans grant be drawne out By some person with left William Pomfrett, and likewise a lest of all our Inhabetants whoe then are and howe maney, that the Towne may see how maney we are to take Care of.

At the aforsayd Publick meitting

Ordered and voted by the hole towne

That whereas the Towne is given to understand that Roberd Wadley and some others doe Intrude and build or make waste of our timber within our Towne Bounds; for stoping any such intruders or trespassers have Ordered and apoynted Will ffurber and Richard Otes to forewarne them and apoynt them (to) Come before the Prudentiall Men; otherwise to arrest them in an action to trespass to the next County Court; and doe by these presents apoynt them lawfull attorneys to procicquet any such parsons in the Townes behalfe.

OLD SERIES, NO. 56, OCT. 28, 1851.

DOVER TOWN RECORDS.

1667.

At a Publick Towne meitting holden the 8th of the 2th monthe, 1667.
Sellecktmen chosen.
Capt. Richard Walldern, Mr. Job Clements, Sargeant William Furber, Ensin John Daues, Corporall Antony Nutter.

William Pomfret Comeshener

At a Publick Towne meitting holden 8th of the 2th monthe, 1667.
Comesheners for small Causes to stand that wear formerly chosen wich was
Capt Walldern, Elder Nutter, mr Job Clemants.

At the same time voted that mr Job Clemants, and William Pomfrett are chosen to open the votes for the Choise of Asotiaets

At the same time William ffurber and henrey kerk voted to be sealers of letter.

Grand Jurey, John Bickford sinyur, Thomas Edgerly, John Couring, Richard Catter, John Chirch

Jurei of Trial, Mr Job Clemants, Philip Cromwell, Thomas Roberds Juner, henery hobes, Antony Nutter, John Woodman, John Dam, Juner.

Constabells at the same time Chosen ar James Coffin, Thomas Chesley.

At a meitting of the Sellecktmen of Dover and Porchmouth at the towne of Porchmouth the 7th of may, 1667, Remeding seueral Inconuences.

It is mutually agreed and ordred Betweine them that whereas By Custome the Public charge boeth of Court and County haue bin carried on by each Towne destinoktly for the Time past. Now, for the futer all Charges Referring to the Publick shall be Borne Joyntly By the County and that a County Treasurer to bee Chosen aCording to lawe.

Henrey Sherburne
James Pendleton
John Hunkinge
Richard Sloper
Phillip lewes
Sellecktmen of Porchmouth.

Richard Wallderne
Job Clemants
William ffurber
John Daues
Antoney Nutter
Sellecktmen of Douer.

At a meitting of the freemen the 9th of the 3th month 1667 Capt. Richard Wallderne Chosen Debety for the Generall Court for this hoell yeir.

Instruction to Capt. Richard Wallderne Debety for the General Court.

Imprimis, that he standeth to mayntaine our liberties and preueledges.

2dly That he make known to the Generall Court the Papers receued from Maijor Shapleigh Conserning Pattin write to Pertickler Parsons and the Towne In Generall, as alsoe to Desier the General Court to end sum Declaration Coasarning the same, or to take other laws as they See feitt in thear wisdom

3dly Not to Ingage the Towne By Compolsion To Bueld fortifications.

4th To Consuelt with the Debeties of Porchmouth Conserning the Enlargement of the County

At A meitting of the Sellecktmen,

Wee the Sellecktmen doe order the three half penny Rate made ouer the hoele town to be delivered to Capt. Richard Walderne By the scuerall Constabels of the town and for him to Despose the same a Cording to the sellecktmens order from time to time.

Asctiats for thes Countey Courtt that is to be holden the last Tuesday in 1667, In June at Douer was Chosen by opening the voets the 13th of the 3 mo.

Capt. Walderne 33
Capt. Pike 32
Mr. John Cutt 26
Mr. Richard Cutt 27
Mr. Eellias Stillman 24

Teste Job Clemants
phellep lewes
Richard Sloper
William Pomfrett

At A meiting of the Sellecktmen the 4th, 5th mo (67.

Rickned with Stiuen Jones the 4th July 1667 about keeping Mrs. hill and her child the yeir past and ar debtors to him on the Townes a Compte the sum of twenty flue pounds, wich is to be allowed him and taken in part pay for Thomas Johnsons Estate at Oyster Riuer when the deds are made of land from the Towne a Cording to the Court order, whereby it is ordred a Cording to the lawe of Estates. This is ordred by the Sellecktmen the day aboue writen, with the Consent of the sayd steuen Jones.

NOTE BY DR. QUINT. Mrs. Hill was widow of Valentine Hill who was of Boston about 1643 and came to Dover. He was a man of considerable property, being at one time the highest tax payer in Dover. He lived at Oyster River, where he had extensive grants of mill privileges, land and timber. He was Representative 1653-5, and 7. He died about 1660. The child spoken of was Nathaniel Hill, his only son and was born the last of March 1659-60, and was recognized as his legal heir in 1697.

Nathaniel lived at Oyster River and was Representative and a man of much influence in the town. His descendants still live in Durham.

TOWN RECORDS.

By the Sellectmen 4th 5th (67.—It is Agreid with left Coffin to Build the forte about the metting house on douer neck one hundred foot square with two Sconces of sixteen foot square, and all the timber to be twelfe inches thicke, and the wall to be Eaght foot hige, with sells and Braces, and the sellecktmen with the melletory ofecers haue agreed to pay him an hundred pounds in days workes, at 2s 6d p day, and alsoe to all persons Concerned in the worke on day to help to Rayse the worke at so many on day as he shall apoynt.

NOTE BY DR. QUINT.—The mound where this fort was constructed around the meeting house still exists (and can be seen in passing along the road at the present time, 1851). The building of this fort is the first intimation we have of the construction of any defense against the Indians. The colonist of Dover had been unmolested, as yet, although there had been troubles in the south at an early period; nor did any open act of hostility occur here until the breaking out of King

Philip's War in 1675. But the construction of the defences imply that at this period, 1667, suspicions were entertained as to the dispositions of the savages. Nor is it wonderful that the friendly relations, which had continued for forty-three years between the English and the Indians should be at last sundered by acts of insult and aggression which were daily committed by the English.

There were laws, indeed, forbidding all ill treatment of the Indians, but these laws were a nullity, and the once generous and frank Indians brooded over their wrongs in sullen and revengeful silence until their opportunity for revenge came. How these wrongs were avenged the stories of Philip's war, the history of the bloody morning of the 28th of Jure, 1689, the desolation of Salmon Falls and Oyster River and the years that followed, can tell the reader who wishes to learn the history of those times.

TOWN RECORDS.

The votes opened for the Countey Tresuerer the 13th of the 7th monthe Mr Nathanell frier Chosen Treserrer for this Countey of Douer and Porchmouth,

T. stat Phellep lewes,
William Pumfrett

At a Putlick Towne meitting 3:8:(67. Ordred that Euery Indian that shall kill aney wolfe within the township of Douer and Bring the head into some publicke ofecer the sayd Indian is to have thirty shillings for euery wolfe as he shall kill, and noe more, and that the former order conserning Indians killing wolfes is nulled.

At the sam tim ordred that the sellecktmen are to treate with John Chirch Conserning Naomies Child, and to put the child to him, agreinge with him for the takinge of the child and satisfyinge him in land, prouided theay do not Exseid Sixtie ackers to giue to him for taking the child.

At the sam time voted that the Sellecktmen shall make a rate 2d ½ per £ ouer the hole Towneshep

Voted at the sam tim that the Sellecktmen shall treat with the Sellecktmen of Porchmouth about the settelling the Countey and Countey Charges and how to be leued.

OLD SERIES, NO. 57, NOV. 4, 1851.

DOVER VILLAGE (COCHECHO) IN 1780.

DOVER VILLAGE now is not what it was in 1780. This is a commonplace sort of a commencement, but when one really thinks of it, he will find a good deal of meaning in it. In 1780 our grandfathers were alive and flourishing brisk young men; small clothes and shoe buckles adorned their nether extremities, and sound sense filled their powdered heads. Times have changed in other things besides small clothes since our grandfathers' day. Instead of riding double on venerable horses of good constitutions and steady habits over the hills and down the valleys of Cochecho we follow spluttering locomotives of more speed and less discretion straight through the whole on a dead level. Then the mail went to Boston one week and came back the next. People then knew nothing of the Washingtonians or the Sons of Temperance, but drank their home made cider and Holland gin whenever it suited their appetites. There were some tough guzzlers in those days. Their port wine was unacquainted with logwood and their brandy was not villianous, as now.

In 1730 cotton factories were unheard of at Cochecho lower falls, and people built ships at Dover Neck. Boys were boys then and youth were not above reverencing age. Girls could spin and weave and help their mothers do house work; pianos were unknown; no gaudy pins or flaming ribbons bedecked the girls of that day.

In walking about town to consider the state of things in 1780, or thereabouts, we will commence with the angle formed by the junction of the Dover Neck and Portsmouth roads, the former the old highway to "Strawberry Bank," over which have travelled Royal Governors and their Counsellors "in good old Provincial times when we lived under the King"and Republican Presidents and obsequious demagogues, while we live under the people. Famous men have travelled up this road and some equally in-famous;—the latter is a road of comparatively modern date.

Looking down the road towards "Libby's Bridge," you will notice a large house on the Durham road, not far beyond the Bellamy, familiarly known as "Dunn's Tavern." This was a tavern in 1780. COL. BENJAMIN TITCOMBE was then its host, a man of commendable character and doing a fair business; he died of consumption, 4 June 1799, aged 56 years. From the bridge no house, as now, was to be found until the turn in the road was reached where the "Pottery" now is. Here there was in ancient time a small house whose owner's name is forgotten; and near it was one inhabited by Jonathan Hanson a blacksmith who lived and died there.— There was then no house upon that side of the street before reaching one standing where the "William Perkins house" now is.

In the angle formed by the union of the Dover Neck and the Portsmouth roads, or rather a few rods south of it, stood a house belonging to Capt. John Riley. Opposite this and on the east side of the Dover Neck road was the "Old Cushing House," then an old house in fact, as well as in name. Parson Cushing, the minister of Dover from 1717 to 1769, lived there and probably died there in that very house; it almost tumbled down of itself, at last, and was finally taken down about 1820. Near the Cushing house was another large house whose owner's name we do not know, and just below that a small house occupied by Josiah Folsom, who was long known as "Barber Folsom." Where the late Samuel Watson lived, formerly stood a house inhabited by Elijah Estes, grandfather to Israel Estes; he died 28th, 11 mo, 1788, aged 67; the house was torn down when Samuel Watson built the one now standing.

We have said there were no houses on the west side of Pleasant st. to the angle in the road to the Wm. Perkins lot. The houses now standing there were built at a later period. The "Chandler" house was built by Philemon Chandler who came here in 1792. The next house now inhabited by Alfred W. Pike, Esq., was the

Parsonage House in olden times. It was not n existence at the period of which we are writing (1780), but was erected at the settlement of Robert Gray, minister of the First Church. It was deemed worthy of remembrance that no rum was used at the raising of the frame, an event of startling importance in 1787. In those days the men engaged in raising could never fix the ridgepole until their cry "the ridge pole wont suit! the ridgepole wont suit!" was answered by passing up a junk bottle of rum. A drink from that bottle passed from mouth to mouth always made the ridgepole fit into place marvellously quick, after the last man had had his sip of rum. At the raising of the parsonage no rum was used; instead they sang the following:—"Jerry is gone and Robert is come, So we'll put on the ridgepole without any rum,"— alluding to Jeremy Belknap and Robert Gray.

The Pine Hill burying ground was in existence in 1780, and indeed forty years and more before that, it having been appropriated for its present use about 1735. We will not stop to examine its old grave stones now.

A school house stands next in 1851; a school house stood there before this, built in 1790; and one there once had a bell upon it. What a curious place for a school house; a grave yard on one side and a Quaker meeting house upon the other Next to the Quaker meeting house was and is the "Osborn house;" it was built by Marble Osborn and is now occupied by his son, Daniel Osborn. Where the Tredick house stands, David Hanson lived. On the other side of the way, just north of the Parsonage was the house occupied by Gershom Lord, the potter, who died a very old man. Jonathan Hanson's house and his brother Benjamin's were the next north on that side. Enoch Hoag lived next; he was a Quaker and afterwards moved to Sandwich. Moses Hanson's house came next. These two houses were taken down and the large three story house now standing there was erected by Stephen Hanson in 1807 or 8.

[Now, 1898, occupied by the Cressey family.— Ed.]

The next house was the Palmer house on the corner of Spring street; the Davis house was built later by James Remick. Richard Canney lived in the Palmer house, a fisherman, who afterwards moved to Great Island and died there.

Opposite Richard Canney's house was the Old Jail, where now is the Niles house. In 1780 or thereabouts, Thomas Footman was Jailer. He had under his care the well remembered Elisha Thomas, who was executed for murder 3 June, 1788.

OLD SERIES, NO. 53, NOV. 11, 1851.

DOVER VILLAGE IN 1780.

Next north of Richard Canney's on the same side of Pleasant st (Central avenue) dwelt Col. Theophilus Dame. He was "a fine old gentleman." He was High Sheriff for many years when that office gave its possessor a great deal of importance. It is said that when he cut the rope at the execution of Thomas, he shed tears. He died 20 Jan. 1780. His house stood where Dr. Low's now does; it was taken down by Capt. James Whitehouse. The next house was John Remick's. He was in the freighting business on the river, but afterwards went to Rochester and turned farmer; he died in Rochester. The house was hauled off to Portland street; Esquire John Williams built the house now owned and occupied by Hon. John P. Hale; another near adjoining was torn down at the same time, that in which Betty Young used to live: a third stood on the same lot in which the noted Betty Marshall lived and died. She was a physican and somewhat famous in her profession; she was probably the first woman physician in New Hampshire; she died 19 Sept, 1792. Her brother John Marshall was the one known as "Old Master Marshall," from his occupation as school teabcer.

At little southwest of Jeremy Perkins's store at the Corner, and perhaps in its rear, was a house in which lived Samuel Bragg, who came here from Ipswich, and carried the mail through a large part of the "up country". He was the father of Samuel Bragg, Jr., the Printer, who lived with him and after him, and had a printing office snug by. The first office was burnt and a second was erected, which afterwards shared the same fate. A son of Mr. Bragg senior married daughter of Eliphalet Ladd, said to have been first printer in Dover. He published the "Political Repository and Stratford Recorder," from 15 July 1790, to 19 Jan. 1792; and the "Phoenix" from January 1792, to 29 Aug. 1795: the "Phoenix" was so called to commemorate the fire.

After the last date Samuel Bragg, Jr., conducted the paper, and gave it the name, "The Dover Sun." It was continued by him till about 1812, when it passed into the hands of John Mann, by whom it was published to a late period, under various names.

There was no house on the east side of Pleasant street from the old jail to the end of Court street. The "Wheeler house" in which Deacon E. J. Lane lives, was built about 1790, by James Remick. The store occupied by John H. Wheeler was built in 1800. Before that date a blacksmith shop stood near it, occupied by Mr. Isarel Estes, this was burnt in 1792. When the store was built in 1800 the street in front was so low that a man could walk under the front sill.

On the corner of Silver and Pleasant streets, where the Perkins block stands, Christine Baker once kept tavern. This was about 1735. At a later period Dr. Cheney Smith live there in a little one story house in which a Toppan kept store in 1790. This building was moved off; one account says to Field's Plains; another says it was placed on Col. Baker's premises and was promoted to the dignity of a variety store, under the charge of Amos Cogswell, Col. Baker's son-in-law.

DR. CHENEY SMITH was a physician in Dover in 1750. He died about 1756.

Going up the south side of Silver street the first house met with in 1780 is still standing, under the name of the "Dr. Dow house." Many years before that Capt. Gage lived there. He married a Twombly of Rochester. In that house "Marm Becky" Twombly, sister to the Captain's wife, kept school a good many years. Thomas Footman lived there after Capt. Gage, and sometimes kept tavern. He was the former jailor.

Long years ago a Quaker meeting house stood on the corner of Locust and Silver streets where Friend Jacob K. Purinton now lives. This meeting house was built before 1720 and had vanished before 1780, as well as the burying ground attached. In 1780 George Watson, the tailor, lived there; his house was previously a sort of business house for Friends' meetings; it was taken away but a few years ago. The tailor did considerable business in that little house; it answered for his home and his workshop. He died 8 Oct. 1800, aged 52.

Near the house in which J. S. H Durell now lives stood the house then occupied by Nathaniel Ham. His wife was Hannah, daughter of Capt. Dudley Watson and his wife Christine Baker, daughter of Christine before mentioned. They were married 1 Aug. 1771.

Above that there was no house before reaching the Alden place. Where the jail now is in 1790 stood a small house inhabited by John Lindsey, a tailor, who died of consumption 6 Oct 1794.

Where Wm. H. Alden now lives and in the same house, Nathaniel Watson once lived; this house occupies the place of one which Watson took down when he built the present one. He kept tavern in both; Sometime since 1780 Daniel Randall lived in the house opposite the Tole-End road: he afterwards moved to Tuftonborough.

Some little distance north on the Tole-End road would be seen the "Coffin House," in which Eliphalet Coffin formerly lived. He was born 11 Sept., 1742 and died 4 Aug. 1808. There was a Coffin house formerly, near the sight of the present one, built by Eliphalet's father Tristram, who died in 1758. This Tristram was son of Tristram and grandson of Hon. Peter Coffin, who came to Dover from Newbury, Mass.

Turning about and coming down Silver street on the north side, we find a goodly row of houses of unquestionable antiquity. No one can doubt this who stops to look at the Jeremy Belknap house with its antique door knocker adding to its venerable appearance. There lived REV. DR. JEREMY BEKNAP, the Historian of New Hampshire, the minister of the First Parish for nineteen years, a part of which was during the Revolutionary war. In 1780 he was in the midst of his hardest troubles.

In that old house Dr. Belknap wrote his History of New Hampshire, a work which will be remembered when the political hacks, who are now anxious to surpass him, will have been deservedly forgotten. Though deficient in some qualities of a great historian, yet for accuracy, industry and honesty, Dr. Belknap has never been surpassed.

DR. BELKNAP was born in Boston 4 June, 1744; graduated from Harvard College in 1762; was ordained at Dover, Colleague with Rev. Jonathan Cushing, 18 Feb. 1767; was dismissed 11 Sept. 1786, after a series of difficulties which his people should have been ashamed to cause; he was installed pastor of the Federal street church in Boston, 4 April 1787, and died 20 June 1798.

Next east of the Belknap house stood that of COL. OTIS BAKER, a distinguished man in his day. His whole name was Otis Archelaus Sharonton Baker. He was born in 1727, was twice married and died 27 Oct. 1801, having been a member of the Provincial Congress, State Senator and Judge of the Court of Common Pleas. He left a large number of descendants, among whom are Sharonton Baker and John B. Wheeler. The old house was burned down about 1830 and the late Michael Whidden built another a few feet south west of the former site

The next house standing in 1780 is still in existence, and is now inhabited by John H. White, Esq. This was built by Capt. Wm. Twombly who lived there (when he was not at sea) and died there.

OLD SERIES NO. 59., NOV. 18, 1851

DOVER VILLAGE IN 1780.

The house now owned and occupied by HON. ANDREW PIERCE was built in 1786 by Henry Mellen, Esq., a lawyer who came to Dover from Massachusetts. He died in 1807. The next house to that (on Silver street) was built and inhabited long before 1780; Capt John Tebbetts lived there when not at sea. He was lost at sea. This house was a famous place for suppers and parties in Widow Tebbets' day. The FISH AND POTATOE CLUB held its regular sessions there, in the back room. The widow kept a very respectable tavern.

Dr. Greene lived in the house next east in 1780, or would have lived there had he not been at sea about that time, —long before he moved into the house where he died, which was built about 1800. DR. EZRA GREEN was born in Malden, 17 June, 1746, O. S.; graduated from Dartmouth College in 1765, studied medicine with Dr. Sprague of his native town, and came to Dover to practice in 1768 or 69. He remained here until the Revolution began when he joined the army as surgeon. He was with the army a year and a half. In October 1777, he enlisted as surgeon under the noted John Paul Jones, in the Ranger, and remained in this station until October 1778, when he returned to Dover. In the spring of 1779 he again went on a cruise in the Ranger and returned in the latter part of the year. He was off again in 1780 and 1781 after which he returned to Dover and quietly settled down to practice his profession, and remained here until his death. He was the first Postmaster of Dover, when the delivery of the office extended to the White Mountains. For many years he was the chief merchant in town, his store standing near his residence He married Susanna Hayes of Dover in 1779; he died in Dover July 27, 1847, aged 101 years, 1 month and 10 days.

The house in which Dr. Green lived in 1780 was afterwards inhabited by 'SQUIRE MOSES HODGDON; John J. Hodgdon now lives in it.

The Austin house now standing on the corner of Locust and Silver streets is a comparatively modern house. The land which it occupies formed the larger part of two house lots in 1780, one of which Moses Sawyer occupied and the other William Watson. The latter person died 25 January, 1800, aged 67. His house was removed when Elijah Austin built the one now occupying the site.

In 1780 a narrow lane run a few rods north where Locust street is now located; at the north end of the Lane and facing Silver street stood the house occupied by

LIEUT. SAMUEL STACKPOLE, a Revolutionary soldier. He was born in that part of Rollinsford known as Sligo, October, 1740; he lived at the end of the lane many years; removed to Rochester and died there, having had eleven children, one of whom, Samuel, now living in Dover, is the father of DR. PAUL A. STACKPOLE and others.

On the east side of the lane was the house which Thomas Roberts built a great many years ago. He was born 23 July, 1710, and died without children,—about 1790. Nathaniel Cooper lived there after Roberts; he was Town Clerk from 1788 to 1795, when he died, aged 53 years. His wife was a Hayes, mother to Dr. Green's wife. He was succeeded in the office of Clerk by his son Walter, who continued in office till 1799. Walter was Cashier of the Strafford Bank many years.

Patty Cooper, his sister, kept school in the old house; her scholars are grandfathers now. There were two other sisters also; this composed the whole family.

The next house was the Peirce house, which was old in 1780, but still bidding fair to outlive many younger ones. DEACON BENJAMIN PEIRCE, of honored memory, lived and died here. He was Deacon of the First Church, Selectman of the town for many years, and held other offices.

The Old Freeman house, still standing, was once the Tebbetts house, and earlier still the Calef house. Col. James Calef is said to have built this house, and it has been standing for a time "whereof the memory of man runneth not to the contrary." Major Ebenezer Tebbets lived in it after Calef; he came here from Rochester; he had a son Samuel and a daughter who married a Shannon, and others. A Joseph Allen once lived there and had a store on the "Landing."

On the east side of Tuttle square stands the house of the late Mr. George Andrews. This was built about 1800 by Thomas Folsom, a tinman, or goldsmith; he married Ednah Ela, sister of the late Nathaiel Ela, the tavern keeper. Folsom had his workshop in the house.

Next north, at the corner to Central and Court streets, was a little one story house owned by Isaac Watson, though he did not live there. This was an old thing; has long been gone.

The First Parish church now standing was built in 1829; its predecessor on the same spot was dedicated 13 December, 1758. The predecessor to that of 1758 stood on Pine Hill, a few rods northwest of the Cushing tomb. It was erected in 1714 and taken down in 1760. This had no steeple and the bell hung on the school house near by. The meeting house used before this one stood on the old lot on Dover Neck. It was built in 1653 and was standing in 1720. It succeeded the one built in 1634, or there about, a short distance south of the second house.

The "old Court House" was not in existence in 1780. Richard Tripe built it about 1791. Previously the courts were held in the meeting house over the way. The Legislature held its sessions in the "Old Court House" in 1792.

The Dover Hotel which has been a public house for a hundred years or more is probably the oldest in the State; it was kept in 1780 by Jonathan Gage. It is supposed it was built by Joseph Hanson, whose daughter Rebecca, Gage married, and from whom he received it. This Joseph Hanson was son of Tobias Hanson and Ann Lord, his wife, and was born 10 Jan. 1704. Tobias was son of the Tobias who was killed by the Indians 10 May 1693, and grandson of Thomas Hanson, the first settler of the name, who died in 1666. Joseph married (1) Rebecca Shepard born in 1708, died 19 April 1736, leaving one child Ephraim, born 15 June, 1728. Joseph married (2) Sarah Scammon, who died 2 Sept. 1738, leaving Humphrey, born 27 August, 1738, who married Joanna Watson. Joseph married (3) Susanna Burnum, born 1 March 1715-16. She had Rebecca, born 28 Dec., 1739, (who married Jonathan Gage, the Dover Hotel man, and had Susanna, born 30 Oct. 1759, Hannah b. 25 Jan. 1763, Elizabeth born 4 June, 1768, Peggy born 25 Jan. 1771, and Joseph H. born 4 March, 1779;) John Burnum born 29 Nov. 1741, w o married Elizabeth Rogers. Joseph Hanson died 5 Sept. 1758; his last wife died 4th March 1758.

"The Pendexter house" was a house of respectable age in 1780. and was then inhabited by John Burnum Hanson spoken of above who was found drowned in the Cochecho river 17 Dec. 1788.

The house now inhabited by David L. Drew was occupied by Dominicus Hanson, a great many years ago. He probably received it from his father Humphrey, (brother of John B.) who married Joanna, daughter of Isaac Watson, great grandfather to Seth. They had children: —Dominicus b. 19 Dec. 1760, Sarah b. 22 Sept. 1762, Joseph b. 18 Dec. 1764, Elizabeth b. 12 May 1767; all were born in Dover and probably in the house in which David L. Drew now lives, and near which many of them with their ancestors now lie buried. The Hansons would seem to have owned a large share of land thereabouts and there were plenty of the race to inherit it; their entire genealogy we omit, for several good reasons, but particularly because it would fill the whole pages of the Enquirer and an extra besides.

Looking from the old house towards the east would be seen the house now inhabited by Seth Watson; in 1780 it was occupied by Seth's grandfather Benjamin, who was born in Dover 3 April 1734 and died in the old house 31 Jan. 1785.

CORRECTION.—The date of the death of Col. Theophilus Dame was 10 January, 1800 instead of 20 Jan. 1780, as given in No. 58.

OLD SERIES, NO. 60, NOV. 25, 1751.

DOVER VILLAGE IN 1780.

When Col. Amos Cogswell first came to Dover he moved into a little house that stood where Church street joins Central avenue. In that house in 1780 William Brewster lived. Col. Cogswell lived in it a short time and then moved into what was and is known as the Cogswell house; this house formerly stood on the site of the New Hampshire Hotel, but was afterwards moved a few rods north. Col. Cogswell was born in Haverhill, Mass., 2 October, 1753, and died at Dover 28 Jan., 1826. He was a Revolutionary soldier and helped form the Society of Cincinnati. In the course of his life here he was

Representative, State Senator, Presidential Elector, besides holding many other places of trust. He had five children.

Going north from the Cogswell house the next one was the Dr. Kittredge house; it was standing in 1780 and is standing on the corner of Kirkland street and Central avenue. Abraham Hanson lived there then. We suppose Abraham was the son of Ephraim, the brother of John Burnum, and born 15 July, 1759. This Ephriam married Margaret Lord, and had children, Joseph, b, 1 Oct. 1756 and Abraham just mentioned. He died 24 March, 1772; his wife died 21 Aug. 1769, aged 31 years.

There was a house in 1780 where the late Hon. William Hale built the one now standing, which is said to have been built in 1750. A Hodge built it and lived in it; it was removed when Mr. Hale built there. HON. WILLIAM HALE was born in Portsmouth 6 Aug. 1765; he spent some years at Barrington in trade with his oldest brother Judge Samuel Hale;he settled in Dover in 1795,. His long life illustrates what may be accomplished by prudence, honesty and untiring industry united with sound judgment and common sense. He was often in public office, having been State Representative, State Senator from 1797 to 1801, Counsellor from 1803 to 1805, and Representative in Congress from 1809 to 1811, and from 1813 to 1817 but his continuance in office is not a test of the estimation in which he was held. He died universally lamented 8 Nov. 1848.

The house where HON. ASA FREEMAN now lives was occupied for many years by Hon. Wm. King Atkinson who died about 1820. It was built by Dr. Wigglesworth and Col. James Calef. Dr. Wigglesworth was for many years a physician in Dover; he afterward removed to Lee and lived on"the Hill"and died there about 1795, without children. His wife was Polly, daughter of George Waldron brother of Thomas Westbrook Waldron. COL. JAMES CALEF was a noted man here in old times. His wife was a Calef, a cousin of his. Some of his singular transactions are well remembered. His family discipline was peculiarly firm and strict, it being his custom to correct any fancied misdemeanors in his wife by carefully imprisoning her in the cellar where she usually had sufficent time for meditation upon her offence.

The Durell house is thought to be a hundred years old. This was built by Dr. Wigglesworth. In 1780 it was inhabited by JOHN WENTWORTH, Jr. who was born 17 July, 1745, graduated from Harvard College in 1768 commenced to practice law here in Dover in 1773. He was member of the New Hampshire House, Councellor, Committee of Safety, Senator and four times was elected Delegate to Congress. He died in Dover 10 Jan. 1787 of consumption having had seven children one of whom, Paul, now lives in Concord.

In 1780 there were no other houses in the village on the south side of the river. The first one erected in the vicinity of Central Square, after 1780, was the house in which Joseph Evans lived, and which stood a few feet back of the west end of Cocheco block the land where that Block now stands was formerly more elevated than now. The level extended back some rods towards the "Flats," where there was a sudden descent on three sides. On the brow of this elevation Joseph Evans built a house in 1790; it was afterwards removed and the surface lowered. Joseph Evans was son of COL. STEPHEN EVANS who lived on Main street; of him we shall speak by and by. Joseph was a graduate of Harvard College; he married Elizabeth, daughter of Thomas Westbrook Waldron, and died 30 Aug., 1797. His wife was born 3 Jan. 1761, and died 8 Dec., 1820. Some of his children are living.

The "Bickford house" was built in 1794. Our readers will remember the house which stood on the hill which was cut away when the Varney Block was built: it looked for a long time as if ready to pitch down into the street some day. This house was built by Mrs. Bickford and Deborah Coffin, daughter of Tristram Coffin, before spoken of. In digging the garden once belonging to this house the workman hit upon a sleeper of the "old Coffin Garrison," memorable for its capture by the Indians in 1689, and in digging away the hill there was found a weight of undoubted antiquity; which is now in possession of Asa Tufts, Esq., who says that the position of the Garrison house was about sixty feet from Central avenue, on the north line of Orchard street. The well known accuracy of Mr. Tufts is sufficient authority. But there were none of these houses standing here in 1780. And while Central square has changed marvellously as to buildings it has changed little less as to surface. In 1780 there was a deep gully occupying the southern half of that part of Washington street which fronts Cochecho Block and a corresponding ridge in the other half. There was a brook in it, which is still running though covered up; this brook which was a large one in 1820 came down back of the Town Hall, forming at that spot a quagmire of unimpeachable respectability. The hill which we have spoken of as situated where Varney's Block now is ran across Central avenue into the Factory yard. No 4. mill stands in what was a very deep hollow in 1780.

There was a sort of bridge where the Central avenue bridge now is, in 1780, but it did not last long. The freshet of November, 1785, carried this away as well as all the bridges on all the branches of the Pascataqua river, save one small one somewhere in Durham. This freshet is still remembered by the "oldest inhabitant" as the "greatest freshet that ever was."

The water covered all the lands in every direction. The neck which connects the point back of the High School was entirely overflowed and the land now occupied by the houses on First street was completely stripped of everything movable. The mills were partly carried away, and all the lumber near them, which was not hastily removed.

The lower (Washington street) bridge was speedily rebuilt, but the place of the upper one was not supplied (except by ferry) until the occupation of the water power by the Cocheco Manufacturing Company in 1822.

There was another freshet here in June, 1798, remembered particularly from the drowning of a boy. At that time ferry boats were kept on the river and usually someone could be found to "set over" any person desiring to cross. At the time of the freshet in 1798 a young woman wished to go across and called a boy who was sitting on the opposite shore, "Academy hill," to come over for her. After some hesitancy he attempted to comply; but hardly had he left the north shore when the rushing torrent, which would have defied the strength of a man, only mocked the efforts' of a boy of 12, and hurried him with the quickness of thought over the falls, in the sight of persons who could give him no aid. His body was found some days after at the "Gulf." His name was Burrows and he was the son of a widow.

There were no mills on the north side of the Cochecho in 1780; there had been some in 1660, but how long they lasted nobody knows; the Coffins afterwards had mills there, but they had been destroyed long before 1780.

In this connection the name of our river deserves notice. It has been ill treated in a most serious manner. Every person seems to have felt himself authorized to manage its orthography in any way he chose; hence all sorts of ways of spelling it have prevailed.

The first record in which we meet the name is in 1642, and in that the name is spelt CUTTCHECHOE, the pronunciation of which is evident. In 1648 it is spelt COCBCHECHOE and so pronounced for many years. In 1650 COCHECHAE is met with for once, and the pronunciation of this manner of spelling was that usually followed about 1670. In later times the pronunciation of the last syllable had reverted to the original form, that of the first and second remaining as it was so that Cochecho became the name; this is seen to be almost the exact original pronunciation and has been well settled for years. The spelling KECHEACHY was used occasionally a few years after 1700, but it never came into general use. The form QUOCHECHO is an unmitigated barbarism so is COCHECO, although its unfortunate adoption by the Manufacturing Company of this place has given some credit to that form. The form COCHECHO is best supported by old examples and is at present generally adopted by all who know anything of its origin. Regarding its derivation and meaning we shall have better opportunity to speak in a future article of the rivers, hills, etc., of Dover.

OLD SERIES NO. 59., NOV. 18, 1851

DOVER VILLAGE IN 1780.

On the north side of the river there were in the village proper three dwelling houses and their out buildings, a tavern, a cooper's shop, a store, three barns, a grist mill, sawmill, and a burying ground.

The cooper shop was on the Landing; it stood where the Ela's Tavern so long kept its doors open to travellers. A few trees were scattered here and there, the remants of the thick pine forest which once covered that part of our village. The road crossed the lower bridge, and wound up the hill very nearly as it does now, save that modern improvement has lowered the hill and filled up the valley. In going up that hill in 1780 the first house met was that of Col. Evans, which stood nearly where the Deacon Jenness house now stands. The Ham house was next: it stood upon the exact site of the building which Nathaniel Tebbetts erected a few years ago, and which Dr. Jefferson Smith now occupies. The Waldron house was in its old position, across Second street and facing Franklin square, and its two barns were across the road on the site where now stands the American House. Capt. Shannon kept a tavern just north of Central avenue bridge, and Friend Ham's father lived where Friend Ham now lives. These were all the houses standing in the village on the north side in 1780.

Starting at the Washington street bridge, on the east side and south of the road the observer now finds two buildings occupied by William Hale. The lower one of these is the older, and was built soon after 1780 by Capt. William Horne, the "Capt of the Troop." There was a building that occupied very nearly the position of the present store of Mr. Hale, erected about the same time as the lower one, but the great freshet of 1785, before mentioned, almost entirely demolished the upper one, and twisting the lower one off its foundations; these buildings were much less elevated than at present. After the freshet the present store was erected.

On the other side of the street is the "Alden store," or what was known for many years as the "Jewett store." This was built about 1790. On the corner of Main and Washington streets, was a small black building which many of our readers will remember, as it was only taken away a few years since when the Peirce and Nutter block was erected; this was built by Col. Calef about 1790; Moses Emery built one just above the Tavern lot. The Tavern was built by Nathaniel Ela, in 1794, but it was not used as such till 1800. He lived previously in the Horne House, which stands on Main street, next above the vacant lot. On this vacant lot was a house of Capt. Samuel Gerrish's; it was built about 1788 by Maj. Tebbetts for Capt. Gerrish who was then away at sea in Tibbett's employ. This house was moved some years ago and now stands on the orner of Third and Chestnut streets.

About 1786 Col. Jonathan Moulton built a house on the corner of Portland and Belknap streets; he himself resided in Hampton, but a son occupied the house at Dover and took care of the wharf which the Colonel built about the same time. The house owned and occupied by Michael Reade was built in 1785 by his father who bore the same name; its interior presents fine specimens of the substantial and handsome work of that time.

COL. STEPHEN EVANS lived next above. His house was a few feet northwest of the present "Jenness house"; his store is still standing on the corner of School and Main streets. Col. Evans was a man of wealth, and, in 1770 was busily engaged in trade and ship building. He was a soldier, too; had served at the capture of Louisburg in the French war, and at the taking of Burgoyne in later times. He was the youngest child of Benjamin and Marcy Evans, and was born 13 Nov. 1724. Benjamin was son of Robert Evans (born 1665, died 1753,) and grandson of Robert, the first immigrant of that name, who was killed 28 June, 1689, by the Indians Benjamin, Col. Stephen's father, was killed by the Indians 15 Sept. 1725. Col. Evans died about 1808; he had three times married, and left eight children. His house was taken down after it became very old.

Next above Col. Evans' in olden times was the Moses Horn house; Moses lived in it after the first Michael Reade. This we have already spoken of.

Looking then toward Garrison Hill would be seen in 1780 the two Waldron barns where the American House now is. Between these and Friend Ham's house was a continuous line of stone wall. On the other side of the road was a board fence enclosing a pasture.

In 1780 on the north side of the Fall were mills—a grist mill and a sawmill. Similar erections have occupied this place for 210 years, except the time when it was necessary to rebuild them; they were burned twice; first on 3d Jan. 1682, as recorded in Rev. Mr. Pike's Journal; —"Col. Walderne's mill burct down in a very rainy night." It was burned a second time in 1689, when the Indians burned the whole town and killed Major Walderne. These mills remained in possession of his descendants until the property was sold to the Cocheco Manufaturing Co. by Daniel Waldron. In 1780 a "mill house," a structure of logs, stood within the present limits of the "yard", a little north of the present machine shop.

Very nearly on the corner Central and First street was Capt. Shannon's Tavern; it faced to the East. Capt. Thomas Shannon, the host, came from Portsmouth, where he was born; he "served his time" with Thomas Westbrook Waldron, and settled here as a tavern keeper. He married 28 Feb. 1771, Lilian Watson, a sister to George, the Tailor, who lived on Silver street. Afterwards Capt. Shannon moved to Farmington where he died, but he was buried in Rochester. He had several children among whom was Dr. Richard Shannon, who married Polly Tibhets, daughter of Major Ebenezer, and went to Saco—a daughter who married a Barker, and son William who died of fever in the war of 1812.

THE WALDRON MANSION.

The Waldron mansion was in its prime in 1780. Few persons now looking on the old "Boarding House," would imagine that that house was once a stately mansion of olden times. In 1780, when Thomas Westbrook Waldron was living there, the house was in good repair and filled with all the appliances that the wealth of its owner could so easily procure. Remains of the curiously carved work of its old dining hall are still visible, but the paintings which adorned its walls and the solid old fashioned mahogany furniture which ministered to the ease of its occupants, are now but matters of tradition. It formerly stood fronting upon Franklin square, being situated upon an elevated spot with its garden running towards the river, which was, of course, in full view. The orchard was in the rear of the house, and beyond that a field skirted with woods. In that field was the "red oak spring," where "Tamsin Mesarve" chatted too long with her lover. This spring was situated a few feet west of the house of William B. Wiggin, and the same distance from the street. The spring and the oak were in existence in 1825, but both have vanished.

The frame of the Waldron mansion was

raised in 1763. Men came from far and near to help raise the, "Great House," and stories are still told of the marvellous quantities of grog furnished on that occasion. The Waldrons were very wealthy and the tradition is that the grog was dipped from buckets with silver drinking cups; the crowd became very indignant at some undiscovered thief who stole the silver cup from which he drank his grog. One grog bearer on that occasion was Richard Hanson who was then a youth of thirteen years; he died in 1840, having been born in 1750.

This house is said to have stood on the exact site of the old Garrison House which was burned by the Indians in 1689, and to sustain this tradition it is said that the workmen in digging the cellar found the remnant of a silver spoon partly destroyed by the fire of 1689.

On the other hand it is said that the garrison house stood where Central avenue now is, and that a person now living remembers how that the mowers always left untouched the remains of the old cellar which was visible in their childhood.

There must have been rare and royal good times in that old mansion. If the old timers could speak they would doubtless tell us of very interesting stories of the generous hospitality of its wealthy owner, who was one of the great and influential men of his day. Young and old have been carried from that old house and its stately owners felt in the midst of their wealth and honors that the hollow pageantry of grief only mocked the sorrow of the stricken in heart.

This house now is a dwelling house cut up into tenements. Modern improvement demanded the erection of Morrill's Block; so the old spring was covered up; the old oak was cut down, the old house was wheeled back into line with its neighbors. An old house removed from it foundations loses the power of conjuring up fantasies; so let the deeds of the olden time and the fashion of their highborn dames be forgotten.

THOMAS WESTBROOK WALDRON, a distinguished man in his day, died 3 April, 1785, and was buried in the old family burying ground east of St. John's Methodist Episcopal church. The mansion was then placed in the care of a tenant and the young heirs were carried to Portsmouth where they remained for many years.

The old burying ground probably contains the dust of Major Richard Walderne. Tradition says that his remains were collected from the ashes of the fire of 1689 and buried, probably in this old burying ground as it is known to have been a burying ground before 1700, and that land was a part of the Walderne estate This grave yard was once considerably larger than at present. When the whole of the surrounding land was sold, by some mistake the whole of the grave yard was not reserved, and a strip along Durell street was cut off and the graves were obliterated.

This closes our sketch of Dover village in 1780; our grandfathers were as full of life then as we are now; how will it be seventy years hence?

NOTE by John Scales.—As it may be of interest to many readers of Dr. Quint's Memoranda, in the next issue will be given a list of old houses that are now (1898) standing which he records as standing in 1780; they are now the ancient houses of Dover and Dr. Quint's record has made them historic. Many names that were familiar in 1850 are now only a hearsay, or are entirely unknown to the large majority of the people of Dover now.

Old Houses in Dover in 1898 that Were Standing in 1780.

By JOHN SCALES.

Dover, "Old Dover," is 275 years old this month, or in the May preceeding, hence any house is not considered "old" unless it is considerably more than one hundred years old. Of the houses which are near the century mark, and a little past it, there are many; but of the real "old" stock there are about 25, of which 21 are mentioned in Dr. Quint's Memoranda as in existence in 1780, and were "old" to that generation, so that when we add 118 years to the age they then had, it gives them an average of 175 years

Mr. Joseph A. Peirce, son of the late Hon. Andrew Peirce, the first Mayor of Dover, has lived in Dover all his life, and is perfectly familiar with what Dr. Quint describes in the Historical Memoranda, in the numbers preceding this article; hence as a matter of record of the changes since 1850 Mr. Peirce very kindly accompanied the writer, one day recently, and pointed out the "old" houses which were standing in 1780 and are now in existence in this year, 1898. They are as follows:

1. The Palmer house on the corner of Spring street and Central avenue; supposed to be 180 years old.

2. The Dr. Dow house on the corner of Silver and Locust streets; it is supposed to be 175 years old. Mrs. M. E. H. G. Dow owns and resides in it.

3. The Alden house on the corner of Silver and Rutland streets, now owned and occupied by Mrs. John J. Hanson; this is about 145 years old.

4. The Coffin house on the corner of Washington and Arch street, now occupied by Mr. I. Smith Brewster. It is at least 180 years old.

5. The Hon. John H. White house on the north side of Silver street and opposite the beginning of Elm street, now occupied by John H. Blanchard and George W. Parker. It is supposed to be about 160 years old.

6. The Hon. Andrew Peirce house, No. 51 and 53 Silver street, now occupied by G. Fisher Piper and his sister, Miss Mary S. Piper. It is 112 years old.

7. The Capt. John Tebbetts house, Nos. 43 and 45 Silver street, now occupied by Capt. B. O. Reynolds and Mrs. Wallingford; it is undoubtedly 180 years old.

8. The Dr. Greene house, Nos. 37 and 39 Silver street, now owned and occupied by Job Burleigh and Miss Mary P. Thompson. It is, no doubt, 180 years old and perhaps older.

9 The house that stood where the Austin house stands on the corner of Silver and Locust streets was moved to Atkinson street by Hon Andrew Peirce and is standing there, and bears the numbers 70 and 72; it is 175 years old.

10. The Deacon Benjamin Peirce house, No. 25 Silver street, adjoining J. Y. Wingate's, is owned and occupied by Mrs. Sarah E. Nason. It is 175 years old.

11. The Freeman house is Nos. 17 and 19 Silver street, now owned and occupied by Miss Fanny A. Drew, and is probably 190 years old.

12. The old Dover Hotel, on Tuttle square, owned by the Misses Woodman.

13. The Pendexter house east of the Hotel building, on the corner of Hanson

street, owned and occupied by Mrs. John R. Varney; supposed to be 175 years old.

14 The Drew house on the south side of Hanson street.

15. The Cogswell house on the corner of Angle street and Central avenue; 150 years old.

16. The Dr. Kittredge house on the corner of Kirkland street and Central avenue, 150 years old.

17. The Atkinson house now on top of Law's block, 150 years old.

18. The Durell house, next adjoining the Belknap church; probably 160 years old. This is the last of the number on the south side of the river.

19. The first mentioned by Dr. Quint on the North side of the river that is now standing and was standing in 1780, is the Micahel Reade house, which is the second house south of the corner of School and Main street. It is about 180 years old.

20. The Col. Evans house is the third house north of the corner of School street, on Main street and the end stands at an angle to the street and is reduced in size in the rear, but shows its age by its style in contrast with those around it; it is probably 175 years old.

21. Last but not least of all the old houses is the "Waldron Mansion" on Second street in the rear of Morrill's Block, and opposite the Court House where the Major Waldron garrison stood and was burned by the Indians in 1689; 135 years old.

Of the houses outside of the Dover Village of 1780 there are at least four which are more than 150 years old. The Guppey house, on Portland street near the Rollinsford line was built in 1690 and is in remarkably good state of preservation. It has been in the possession of the Guppey family since 1767, when Capt James Guppey bought it and came here from Portsmouth to live, that is his family lived here, and he did when not at sea, as he was a sea captain of high repute.

The Ham house at the foot of Garrison (Varney's) hill is known to have been in existence in 1696, and some have a tradition that it was built in 1680, and was not attacked by the Indians on 28 June 1689, because Mr. Eben Varney who built the house was a Quaker, and maintained such friendly terms with the Indians that they did not molest his house or his family. The chimney in it is undoubtedly the oldest in Dover, and is a marvel in size and stability.

The house on Gov. Sawyer's farm on the Dover Point road is known to be more than 150 years old, but just what year it was built is not known by any record yet found.

The Drew garrison on Spruce Lane, Back River district, is the only garrison house now standing in the whole territory of "old Dover," since the Woodman garrison was burned at Durham (Oyster River) in November, 1896. Just how old it is not known, but it was undoubtedly built more than 200 years ago, and is remarkably well preserved, and should be henceforth kept with the greatest care as the last of the many garrisons that once existed in the oldest town in New Hampshire.

OLD SERIES, NO. 62, DEC. 16, 1851.

DOVER TOWN RECORDS.

1668.

At a Publick Towne Meitting holden 20th 2d 1668.

Gran Jurey—Sargt John hall, Thomas Leighton, Richard York, John beard, will Beard, Deacon hall, Sargt William ffurber,

Jurey of Trialles,—left. Coffen, Roberd Burnum, John Parnall, Walter Mathews, Roberd Evenes, Flexsander wallderne, Thomas Edgerly,—John Dam, Juner, Constabell.

Sarvaers of highways.—left Coffin Roberd Burnum, Antoney Nutter, Sargant John Roberds, these fower men are chosen Seruaiers for the highwayes to be dereckted By the Sellecktmen Conserning the laying out and mending the highways belongin to the Towne.

Ordrd that Capt Walderne and Ro. burnum Chosen to overse the work of the ministers house at Oyster Riuer, and that left Coffen and william ffollett shall not ackt anie thing without the aforsayd Capt. Waldern and Roberd Burnum; and what they shall consent unto shall be the ackt of the Towne for fenishing the house.

John Dam. Juner at a Publick Towne Meitting holden the 20th 2 month (68, chosen Constabells of Dover.

At a Publick meitting holden the 20th 2 mo,. '68.

Sellecktmen Chosen.—Capt. Walderne, Elder Wentworth, Roberd Burnum, left Coffin, Sargt John Roberds.—Mr. John Clements Chosen Comeshener. These ar to stand for an hole veir.

Ordrd that the new Townsmen ar to Receue a Compt from old Townsmen, and what theay shall find the Towne in debte theay shall have power to make a Rate over the hole Towne for the paing the Towne debtes a Cording to thear Deseresion, and alsoe the fineshing the ministers house at Oyster Riuer.

Voted and ordrd that the Sellecktmen, now in Being, have power to make a Rate ouer the Neck cf Douer, Cochecha, Blodey Poynt, for the som cf forty five pounds.

At the same time Capt. Walderne Chosen Debety for the Generall Courte for this hole yeir.

At a Publick Towne meitting holden the 14th, 7mo. 1668.

William Perkinson chosen Constabell for the Towne of Douer.

At A meitting of the Sellecktmen the 21th, 7th mo. 1668. Nickloes Doe Receued an Inhabetant apon the same tarmes Thomas Whithouse was Receued in the yeir 1665.

At A Publick Town meitting holden the 14th 7th (68. Ordrd by the Sellecktmen that forthwith the Constabell shall take of William Williams, sinyer, by way of distress, the som of nintine shillings for a fine for a Breach of a Towne order for entertaining Naomie hull.

At a Publick Towne meitting holden the 17th 7th (68, ordered by the Sellecktmen that John hance shall haue fower pounds for killing a wolfe payd him by the Towne.

OLD SERIES NO. 33, DEC. 23, 1851.

DOVER TOWN RECORDS.

1669.

By the Sellecktmen the 15th first mo. (68-69. Ordered that all that haue been Constabells in the Towne of Douer, that haue not a discharge from the Towne for what Rates weare Cometed to them that theay appeir Befoer the selecktmen to make up thear a Counts the 22 day of this Instant mor the on Douer Neck at left Pomfretts house at 9 of the clocke in the morning. Apon Penelty of such fines as the Sellecktmen shall Impose. Dated this 15 March 1668-69.

At a meittinge of the Sellecktmen the 29th 1 mo. 1669.—It is Ordered and we haue appoynted left Peter Coffin, Antoney Nutter, William ffollett, Roberd Burnum, william Roberds, Richard Otes, william ffurber, to goa to Lamprill Riuer the 6 day of April next to meitt with Exeter to Goe A prambulation a Cording to the law and set Bound marks Betwixt the too Townes, the day is apoynted by the Sellecktmen of Boeth towns.

Richard Wallderne,
William Wentworth,
John Roberds,
Sellecktmen of Douer.

At A Towne metting holden the 3th of 3th mo. 1669 – Roberd Wadleigh Receiued an Inhabetant A Cording to the Tenewer of the last Inhabetant Receued.

At the same time that the Request of Elder wentworth and som of the Bretheren, left Coffin, Einsin daues, Thomas Beard, Antoney Nutter, these are Chosen to Joyn with the Chirch in thear agetation,

At A Publick Towne Meitting holden the 3th of 13th mo.--Constabells Chosen, Antoney Nutter for this present yeir.

Jurey of Trialles,—Job Clemants Einsin John Daues, James Coffen, Samewell wentford, Josefe Smith, Tho Roberds Juner.

Townesmen Chosen,—Capt. walldern, henrey lankster, left Coffin, Job Clemants, Roberd Burnum;—Einsin John Daues, Comeshener.— At the sam tim Capt Walldern Chosen Debety for the General Courte.

Ordered at a Publick Towne meitting holden the 3th of the 8th mo 1669, that the lote Granted unto william kakett and sold unto Thomas hanson seinyer, and by him giuen to Thomas hanson, his son, is Remoued adjoining to Tobias hanson Sixty ackers.

At the same time Job Clemants and William Pomfrett chosen to open the votes with them that are deputed by our nabers of Porchmoueth for the choice of Asotiates for the Countey Couert.

At a Publick Towne meitting 3th of the 8th mo, 1669.—Giuen and granted unto Thomas Perkins by the consent of the Inhabetants of the Neck of land of Douer, formerly Granted to him and now at this meitting Confermed to him, one house lot, 3 ackers and a halfe on the Esterne side of Douer Neck to be layd out by them that are apoynted.

Votes for Sotiats
Mr Stillman	35
mr. Richard Cutt	31
Capt Walldern	46
Capt. Pike	43
John Cutt	23

At A Training the 21 June 1669 thos persones following haue taken the oeth of fledelity.

Samewell Wentwort,
Tho Canney,
Tho Edgerley,
Beniamen heard,
John foste,
Tho Hanson,
John Gerrish,
James Smeth,
John Wentworth,
Roberd Euens,
Charles Adames,
Beiniam Mathews,
Richard Row,
John York,
Will Perkins,
Tho welley,
Tho Perkins,
will Shuckforth.

At a Towne meitting holden the 29th June 1669, Joh Clemants, John Daues, Peter Coffin chosen Comesheners for small Cases, Thomas Edgerly, Chosen Constabell.

At A Publicke Towne meitting holden the 22th 5th mo 1669,—Voted that for the Accomedation of the Minestrey on Douer Neck is set apart forty pounds of mill Rents and a peney Ratt in prouition apon the Estates of all the Inhaberants of the Towne of Douer, Exsepting Oyster Riuer, and this order to stand for one yeir, the peney Rate to be payd in October or Nouember, or a free contribution what Euerey man will free giue.

Voted that the £40 of mill Rents be appropriated for the minestre of Douer Neck this day.

At the sam tim ordred that henrey lankster, will ffarber, Antoney Nutter are apoynted to giue notes (notice) unto the Towne of hampton to apoynt thear men to lay out the highway from Blodey Poynt to Hampton, and to Joyn with them in laying out the sayd highway. betwixt this (date) and the last of October.

At ye sam tim voted that thear shall be a ministers house built apon Douer Neck; the dementions is as followeth yt is to say, 44 feet in lenketh, 20 foot wide, 14 foot betwine Joist and Joist, with a stack of Brick chimneyes and a sellar 16 foot squaer; this house to be Buellded at the charge of the hole town in General.

Whearas at A Publicke Towne meitting holden the 22th July 1669, the Towne granted to Mr. John Ranyer A Call to ofetial in the ministrey untill the 22th of July next insuing, wich will be in the yeir 1670.—At a Towne meitting holden the 27th of September (69, Mr John Rayner gaue in his Exseptance to that sarues.

NOTE by Dr. Quint —This was John Reyner the younger,. In our next number we will give some account of the first John Rayner.

OLD SERIES, NO 65, JAN. 6, 1852

JOHN REYNER, SIXTH MINISTER OF DOVER.

John Reyner, sixth minister of the Church in Dover, was born in England. He came to America in 1635 and settled at Plymouth, Mass., in 1636, where he remained eighteen years. Owing to causes mentioned below his connection at Plymouth was dissolved in 1654, and in 1655 he settled in Dover.

His character and the causes of his removing from Plymouth is explained by the following extract from the Church Records in that town.

"He was a man of meek and humble spirit, sound in the truth, and in every way irreproachable in his life and conversation. He was richly accomplished with such gifts and graces as were befittng his place and calling, being wise, faithful, grave and sober, a louer of good men, not greedy with the matters of the world and armed with much faith, patience and meekness, moued with much courage in the cause of God, was an able, faithful and laborious preacher of the Gospel, and a wise orderer of the affairs of the Church, and had an excellent habit of training up children in a catachetical way in the grounds of Christian Religion."

"So that by loss of him ignorance ensued among the vulgar, and also much licentiousness and profaneness among the younger sort. His remoual was partly occasioned by the unhappy differences then subsisting in the church at Barnstable which much afflicted the church at Plymouth, and partly by the going away of divers of the Church, yea some of the most eminent among them, to other places, and partly by the unsettled state of the church, too many of the members being leauened with prejudice against a learned ministry by means of sectaries then spreading in the land."

"After leauing Plymouth he resided that winter at Boston, where the General Court recommended him to the North Church, and in the spring went back to resettle, if the people had complied with a proposition made by him. But they not doing it, to their sorrow, and being inuited to Douer he settled there, and continued in the ministry till his death, which was April, 1669."

At Dover M. Rayner proved a very worthy successor to Mr. Maud and was universally esteemed by his people. He excited, however, the dislike of the Quakers by his opposition to their doctrines and his support of the law against them. Probably both parties were to blame.

The town gave Mr. Reyner a house and a few acres of land, 7th, 9th mo. 1659, which was confirmed to his heirs by vote of the town 29th May, 1671. His house stood near the school house on Dover Neck, and its site is still discernable. It can be found by any one who will follow the following directions: Walk down the road from the south east corner of the old meeting house lot fourteen rods, cross directly towards the east and continue in a straight line a little more than four rods beyond the fence on the east side of the road; one will then have reached two apple trees standing on the edge of an old cellar; the cellar marks the site of Parson Reynor's house.

Mr. Reyner was assisted in his ministry during the last few years of his life by his son John Reyner, Jr. He died in April 1669, his will being dated 19 April. Frances, his wife, administered on his estate, as she did also on that of her son John, afterwards. In 1679 she petitioned the General Court to appoint Mr. Richard Martyn, Capt. Thomas, Daniel and Antony Nutter, to assist her in her duties regarding these estates, and that also the court would order the selectmen of Dover to collect what taxes were due the ministry and the arrarges of mill rents. On the 10th of June 1679 the court passed orders agreeable to her petition.

Mr. Reyner's children were as follows: JACHIN of Rowley who married 12 Nov. 1662, Elizabeth Denison; she died 8 July 1708, having had children: Edward, born 6 July, 1671, Jachin, born 31 Jan.

1673-4, Annate born 16 July, 1678, Jachin born 16 Jan. 1681.-2.

JOSEPH born 1640, died 1652.

JOHN born 1643, who succeeded his father in the ministry in 1669, and died without issue 21 Dec. 1676.

HANNAH who married Job Lane of Bellerica,. Also Elizabeth, Dorothy, Abigail and Judith.

Mr. Reyner had a brother Humphrey who was Representative of Rowley in 1649, and died in 1660 In it the devises property to "son Wigglesworth" for the use of "grand child Mercy;" to Rowley church; to Samuel Philips, to grand children, Umphrey Hobson, John Hobson, William Hobson; his wife executrix: —"I request my dear brother John Reyner, pastor of Douer, and Deacon Jewett of Rowley to oversee this my last will and testament."

Here is Rev. John Reyner's will:—

"In the name and fear of God amen Know all men to whom these presents shall come that I, John Reyner of Douer in New England, being in my good and sound understanding and memorie, willing to set my house in order, do therefore make and declare this my last will and testament; hereby revoking and annulling all former wills of this nature whatsoever.

Imprimis, I giue and bequeath my soul into the hands of Him who gaue it, my blessed God and Father; and my bodie I commit to the earth, to be decently buried; in hope of a glorious resurrection among the just; the manner of which I leave to the discretion of my executrix, and worthy friends hereafter named, resting assured of their care and readiness to yield assistance, as to the things herein concerned, at all convenient times, especially when and wherein desired, to the utmost of their power. After my debts which I shall ow to anie person be truly payd, and necessary funeral expences satisfied — — — — of my dear loue and tender affection to my wife and desire of her comfortable subsisting and being confident of her care of and motherly affection to her children, I will and bequeath to her my whole estate in New England; in or out of this jurisdiction, houses, lands, chattels, moveables, rents, debts, and whatsoeuer else is, or may be, anie part of, or belonging to the same: (excepting such legacies as hereafter in this my will shall by me be disposed other wayes) to be by her injoyed and improued, to her own use and benefit, together with the rents of my land in Old-England, lying and being in the Countie of Yorke, in the town of Gilderso e, in the Parish of Batly, either already due, or that hereafter shall be, during the terme of her naturall life, (she remaining my widow;) but in case she shall see good to change her condition and enter into marriage; then my will is that my whole estate immediately before such change of condition be equally diuided into parts, and that she injoy one halfe of this estate in New Eng land, aforesaid, together with one third of the rents of that in Old England, as aboue; the other halfe of my estate here in New England, with the other two thirds of the rents of the aforesaid lands in Old England, upon her entering into married state, as also that halfe left in her hands, with the one third of the rents of that in Old England as afforesaid at her decease the whole (in case she marrie not) be so disposed and equally diuided that my fiue children, John, Elizabeth, Dorotha, Abigail and Judith, my natural son and daughters, by this my last will may haue each equal benefit by, and portions out of the said estate both in New England and Old, yet that the particular parts, or parcells of the said estate, here or there, or elsewhere (if anie be) be settled upon the persons, to whom hereafter bequeathed to my son Jachin Reyner of Rowley, and daughter Hannah Lane, wife to Joh Lane of Bilerica; to each of which I haue giuen their full portions as my estate will reach, I will and bequeath the old silver beer bowle and so much monie as shall be ten shillings more than the worth of the cup— one of them to haue the cup, the other the monie, Jachin to haue his choise; the cup is that which I had with their mother.

To my son John Reyner I will and bequeath by these presents my Librarie books and manuscripts (except such English books as his mother shall make choise of for her use; this besides an equal proportion with anie of his sisters as aforesaid.

Item, I do by these presents will and bequeath my lard in Old England in the countie of York, as above said, to my son John, his heirs and assignes, to haue and hold foreuer in fee simple, and doe hereby engage him to dispose of the rents as is aboue specefied, during my wife, his mother's life, and so long after as my aforementioned four daughters, Elizabeth, Dorotha, Abigail and Judith, or anie of them shall leaue their part of the principal in his hands, not exceeding the term of twentie years, they standing to the loss or gain of the said estate according to interest therein and being at equall charges for recouerie of the same, if attended with anie difficulties. My will also is that my son John enjoy my housing and land on Douer Neck, and my four caughters, Elizabeth, Dorothie, Abigail, Judith, my land lying in the woods near Cochecha, being equally diuided among them, a due respect being had by the deuiders to the qualtie as well as quantitie of the said land, or anie part or share thereof, yet not contradicting the promises, viz.:—that everie and each everie of my aboue named fiue children, my son John and daughters Elizabeth, Dorotha, Abigail and Judith have equal shares in, benefit by and portions of my whole estate, in New England and Old, elsewhere if anie (excepting the aboue named legacies bequeathed to my sons Jachin and John and daughter Hanna, viz—cup, monie and Librarie, as also 10 pounds which I give my wife & to dispose of at her decease as she shall see good) all which estate of myn in what place soeuer, as aforesaid I doe by this last will and testament bequeath to my aboue named fiue children, John, Elizabeth, Dorotha, Abigail and Judith, according to the promises what anie haue receiued (not herein excepted) to be considered as part of their share; my will is also that if anie of my four children yet unmarried shall by God's prouidence be so disposed as to enter upon marriage, during the time the estate remayneth in their mother's hands or possession, there be some suitable encouragement as the will affords (her own need duly first considered) giue to each one as the case shall require.

I constitute and appoint my beloued wife Frances Reyner sole executrix of this my last will and testament, and intreat my worthy friends, mr. Richard Walderne and mr. Joshua Moody to be helpful to my wife and children by their faithful counsel and aduice, or other wayes as God shall enable:—

In signe of eurie and all the promises, I hereto set my hand and seal this nineteenth day of Aprill in the year of our Lord one thousand six hundred and sixtie and nine. If anie of the aboue said flue children decease before actual possession they haue libertie to dispose of their rights, being of age.

John Reyner,.

Signed, sealed and deliuered in presence of us

Testes. Hateuil Nutter
Jonh Hall

The last will and testament of mr John Reyner, sen'r, deceased, Broughte into ye Countie Courte held at Douer ye 30: June 1679 & proued by El'er Hateuil Nutter & John Hall, who tooke oath therunto & yt mr Reyner declared it to be soe.

Elias Stileman, Cleric.

NOTE BY DR. QUINT.—The compiler of these articles is happy to acknowledge his indebtedness to Asa A. Tufts, Esq., for many of the facts brought to light. Indeed but for his previous labors the field of investigation would have been little else than a wilderness. The writer owes his thanks also to the Towne Clerk, Charles Emery Soule, and to Deacon E. J. Lane, chairman of the Board of Selectmen, for the facilities they have afforded for examining the Town Records; and to Hon. John H. White, the accommodating Register of Probate; may he be Register, or something better, a thousand years.

OLD SERIES, NO 66, JAN. 13, 1852

DOVER TOWN RECORDS.

1669.

At a Publick Towne meitting holden the 27th of September 1669.

Left Coffin is chosen in the Behalfe of the Towne of Douer to goe to the Generall Courte next Insuing to Answer the Complaynt about the Devision line betwixt Oyster Riuer and the other parts of Doner, a Cording to a warrant under the secketares hand, Bearing date 21st July 1669, and that the selecktmen are apoynted to giue him his orders and power to constetute anie Aturney under him.

At A publick Towne meitting holden the 27th September 1669.

Whereas seuerall of our nabers of Oyster Riuer haue preferd a petishon to the Generail Courte in May last for to Rend from Douer and to be Towne of themselves, though some of us did then declare against anie such acktings and wayes, heiring that there is a ferder proseding at this next Generall Courte, nowe lest wee hoes names ar heir under written shold be inualued and Brought under some pertickler mens ackting, doe, in the Publick Towne meitting, protest against anie suche ackting as Braking of from Douer, or anie peteishing to the Generall Courte for that end, but doe desier to hold to the former agrement with the Town.

At a Publicke Towne meitting holden the 27th September 1669.

Whereas thear is some pretended defrence betwixt our nabers at Oyster Riuer, and some Complaynt made to the Generall Courte our deuisinall line betwixt them ard the other parts of the towne, and being desired by the Courte at Boston, in May last, that they wold meit and Chuse some persons to heir and detirmine the same, it is thearfoer for preuention of ferder trobell to the Generall Courte, and the finall endinge all dfrences mutually chosen at this publicke meitting, the day and the yeir aboue sayd, Capt Roberd Pike, Capt. John Wincole and Mr Samewell Dalton and what three or anie too of them shall oetermine, wee doe agree to rest satisfied thearwith. This was voted and past as an order of the Towne at this publick Towne meitting

At A Publick Towne meitting holden the 22th July 1669, uoted.

That whearas thear is some Complaynt made to the Generall Courte last, by the Inhabetants of Oyster riuer, against the other parts of the Towne of Douer, and the Courte apon heiring the defrince did aduise and Desier the parties wold meite together at a Towne meitting and thear — — -- — — — themselues, this day there is this tender made to the inhabetants of Oyster Riuer that if theay please to make knowne their Greuances and to discos them together, and in case wee doe Agree, to chuse mr Moody, or some other persons, they may hear and determine the defrence, and not to spend money to goe to Genarall Courte anie moer; all these tenders was refused.

At a Publicke Towne meittıng holden the 6th October 1669.

1ly. Ordered that Oyster Riuer shall Build a meiting house at thear one order and apon thear a Count, and what Charg was out About the hands befoer Steuen Jones began, is to bee apon the Publicke acount, and what Stephen Jones his worke that he haeth done shall be payd by the Inhabetants of Oyster Riuer and all the Inhabetants within deuidng line a Cording to former Order and that for tin e to come Douer is to bullde thear ministers house apon thear owne a Count, and not to call for anie helpe of Oyster Riuer, and Oyster Riuer is not to Call to the Rent of the Towne for anie helpe for the futter.

2ly Ordered At the same time whear as our nabers of Oyster Riuer haue by seuerall orders of the Towne bin impowered to order thear Afares about the Rasinge maintenance for the meinstrey thear and minstares house and meiting house and other Charges thear about, it is ended as followeth: -.

That the sellecktmen or men that shall be Chosen from yeir to yeir with too other men Chosen at the Towne meitting, shall haue power amonkest themselues to make Rates for the use aforesayd, and for the present the Towne have Chosen Einsin John Daues and John Bickford to Jine with Roberd Burnum sellecktman (of O. R.) for the use aboue sayd.

3ly Ordered, whearas lamprill Riuer Grant Being formerly granted to Oyster Riuer by ackte of the Courte for the a Comedation of Minestrey thear, and finding for this seuerall yeirs the Towne Can find noe persone to pay the Rents for the present supply of mayntenance of the minstrey at Oyster Riuer, doe grant that theay shall haue the £10 per annum from Roberd Wadley grant, and £10 from Oyster Riuer grant, and when there shall be anie thing Re Couered from lamprill grant it shall be ordred and disposed by the hole towne.

4ly. At the same time ordered that all the ackts in Publicke town meitting shall not be of force unles it be ackted one hour befoer sone sett.

5ly. At the same time ordred that all the a Counts that are as yet not perfected are now foerthwith to be leuied by the Selecktmen, and all old Rates to be brought in, and in case the towne is in debt the Selecktmen shall houe power with Einsin John Daues to make a Rate to Cleir the Towne Deotes.

At a Publick Towne meiting holden the -- month, 1669.

Uoted that hoe soeuer of our inhabetants, or anie other men, shall fall anie tember for to Carey away downe the Riuer, or aney whear to sell, shall forfeit 10s for Euery such tree, Exsepting the old timber — — — all Ready fallen, to Cut or sell of the Commons.

This order is more full by law by order of the Selecktmen.

At the same time ordered that A Comete shall be Chosen, which is at this present meitting Chosen, Capt. Wallden left Coffin, Roberd Burnum, Job Clemmants, John Woodman, Philip Cromwell, Autoney Nutter, these are to draw up sumthing Consarnin the Comenedy and other Publick busineses to present at the next Publick meitting wich will be the first Monday in March next insuing.

Ordered that homsoeuer of our inhabetants, or Anev other person not being an Inhabetant, shall fall any Trees for flerwooi to sell to aney person out of this Townshipe, Apon the Comons thearcf shall forfeit ten shillings for Eurey such tree so fallen, Exsepting old Trees formerly fallen.

1670.

At A Publicke Towne Meitting holden the 7th 1th mo, '69-70.

Selecktmen Chosen for this yeir

Will ffurber, Will Wentworth, Phelep Cromwell, Tho Roberds, Juner, John Woodman.

At ye same time Comesheners for small Cases,—Sarg Will ffurber sinyer, henrey Lankster, John Woodman.

Left Coffin Comeshener with the Selecktmen.

At ye same time Gran Jurey men Chosen,—Job Clemants sinver, John Screuen, John Allt, Richard Cutter, John Meader, Beniamin Mathews.

Juey of Trials,—Peter Coffin, John Woodman, Phillep Cromwell, Stephen Jones, Roberd Burnum.

At ye same time Constabells Chosen,—Joseph Smeth and Thomas Canney.

NOTE BY DR. QUINT.—Here ends the fragments of thirty two pages, marked III which we have now published entire, verbatim et literatim

---

OLD SERIES, NO. 67, JAN. 20, 1852.

THE NUTTERS.

HATEVIL NUTTER, Elder and occasional preacher, was born in England, 1603, or thereabouts, as appears from a deposition of the Elder when he once testified regarding some disputed land titles. He was probably one of the "Company of persons of good estate and of some account for religion," who were induced to leave England with Capt. Wiggans in 1633 and to help found on Dover Neck a compact town." He testified in the aforesaid deposition that he was here in 1637; he took a lot of Capt. Wiggans that year which was rebounded in 1640, as follows:—"Butting on ye Fore River East, and on ye west upon ye High street on ye north upon ye lot of Samewell Haynes, and on ye south upon ye Lott of William Story."

He also owned lot No. 20 on the west side of Back River, and at various times received grants of land in localites that cannot now be defined. It is sufficient to say that his house stood about fifteen rods N. E. from the nearest corner of the second meeting house lot at Dover Neck. In the remnant of an old cellar two pear trees are now standing.

In 1643 the Elder had a grant of land between Lamprill and Oyster Rivers which was laid out in 1662 to Antony, his son. He had a grant of 200 acres "next Wm. Sheppalds" "for a farm," 2, 12 mo. 1658. In April 1669 he gave the Welchman's Cove property to his son Antony, and after his (Antony's) death, to Antony's son John. He gave to John Wingate "husband of daughter Mary," land, etc., on Dover Neck, 13 Feb. 1670.

The Elder was a very respectable man indeed. He filled various offices in Church and State, and possessed a reasonable share of this world's goods; these considerations procured for him that respect which the moral worth of a rich man always excites. He was conspicuous and active in the prosecution of the Quakers, as is manifest by what the Quaker historian Sewel says in giving an account of the whipping of the Quakers by order of the court; Sewell says:—"and all this (whipping) in the presence of one Hate Evil Nutwell, (Nutter) a Ruling Elder who stirred up the Constabelles to this wicked action and so proved that he bore a wrong name."—He was an able and influential man and stood up boldly and conscientiously for the Church and the teachings of sound doctrine as he understood it. He believed the Quakers were wrong and that their teachings were pernicious as set forth by those who were whipped. The Quakers had liberty to go elsewhere; as they did not exercise that liberty Elder Nutter believed it was right to force them to go. No doubt both parties were wrong but the worthy Elder should be judged by the standard of that day not of the present day, to get a correct estimate of his character.

Elder Nutter died in a good old age. His will was dated 28 Dec. 1674 (he being "about 71 years of age") and proved 29 June 1675. To his "present wife Annie" he gave the use of his dwelling house, orchard, marsh in Great Bay, etc., all of it to go to his son Antony after her decease. To his son Antony he gave the mill grant at Lamprey River, one third of the moveables, etc., and one fourth of his 200 acres of land in "Cochecho woods," marsh east of Back River, and the other third of the personal property. John Reyner and

John Roberts were witnesses. The Elder's children therefore were:—

ANTONY, born in 1630; Mary who married John Winget before 1670; a daughter who married Thomas Leighton, and was dead in 1674; Abigail who married Thomas Roberts and probably others.

ANTONY (2) son of the Elder as above, lived for a time at Dover Neck, but afterwards moved to Welchman's Cove on Bloody Point side. He was a man of note, as well as his father, though his genius was developed in a different sphere: his father was a strong and ardent Church man; Antony was a soldier, and in 1667 was "Corporal;" in 1668 he was "Leftenant;" his house at Bloody Point was a Garrison of which he was commander in-chief. He was also a man much engaged in public affairs: he was Selectman for several years, and Representative in the General Court six years, certain, and perhaps more.

He took a conspicuous part in the controversy that the early settlers of New Hampshire had with Mason who claimed to own all the land and attempted to collect rents from those who had settled here, resulting in a lawsuit that lasted nearly a century. In Vol. I., pages 578, 579, 580 and 581 of the Provincial Papers of New Hampshire can be read an account of an affair in which Antony Nutter showed his independence of and contempt for the Masonian claim. The story in brief is this:

In December 1684, Capt. Thomas Wiggin of Exeter, son of the Capt. Thomas who came here in 1633, and Antony Nutter went to Newcastle (Great Island,) and at the house of Deputy Governor Barefoot had an interview with Mason who was stopping there, in regard to the land claims. Nutter was Constable, then one of the most important offices in the Province. The interview took place in Barefoot's kitchen, where there was a large, old fashioned fire place. After discussing the question some time, Capt. Wiggin at length refused in very emphatic language to pay a cent for rents. Thereupon Mason ordered him to leave the house. Capt. Wiggin refused to go, claiming that Mason had no right to order him out of Barefoot's house. Mason appealed to Barefoot; Barefoot said the house and servants were Mason's as long as he remained in the Province. Mason then took Wiggin by the collar and attempted to push him out at the open door. Wiggin resisted and snatched off Mason's cravat and then clinched him and threw him into the fireplace, where there was a good fire for December weather; he then commenced to choke Mason, who was bellowing for help to get him out of the fire and Wiggin's clutches; the servants heard the row and came in and with their assistance Barefoot succeeded in pulling Wiggin off from Mason.

Capt. Wiggin then turned his attention to the Deputy Governor and threw him into the fire and choked him severely, Mason was furious and ordered a servant to bring in his sword that he might defend himself against the valliant and stalwart Provincial Captain. The sword was brought in, but when Mason attempted to use it, he was prevented by Antony Nutter, the equally stalwart Constable, who very deliberately took the sword from Mason's hands, and restored order all around; after which the Captain and the Constable left the house, having completely subdued their foes.

The account describes Wiggin as a tall and large man, with great strength; Mason says that by being thrown into the fire place he had his left foot scorched which badly swelled afterwards, and his coat, periwig and stockings burned, in addition to being almost choked to death.

Barefoot testified that the result of his being thrown into the fire was that he had two ribs broken, by falling on the andirons, one tooth knocked out, and his velvet cap was badly scorched in the live coals, which was only saved from complete destruction by a servant's grabbing it there from.

The servants testified that "a tall, big man, called Antony Nutter, was walking about the room in a laughing manner" during the fracas, and that when they appealed to him to pull Wiggin from Mason and stop the fight, as an officer of the King was bound to do under ordinary circumstances, he would do not do anything except "walk around in a laughing manner;" as long as Captain Wiggin had the upper hand in the fracas the Constable was content to look on and laugh, but when the servants brought in Mason's sword Nutter very quietly and promptly interfered and took the sword from Mason and restored order. The Captain and the Constable then departed.

Of course warrants were issued for the arrest of Wiggin and Nutter but they were not disturbed, as no officer could be found who would dare to attack those "tall, big men."

Antony married Sarah, daughter of Henry Langstaff; she outlived him. He died 19 February, 1686. Their children were:—

JOHN; Hatevil; Henry and Sarah who married Capt. Nathaniel Hill.

JOHN (3) son of Lieutenant Antony as above, resided on Bloody Point side. He had children, probably,

JOHN (4) whose will was dated 16 August 1746; proved 29 April 1747; he married, but died without issue; MATHIAS, JAMES and HATEVIL.

HATEVIL (3) son of Antony (2) lived also in Newington. He was twice married and died in 1745 His will was dated 12 Nov. 1745; proved 25 Dec. 1745. In that he gave to his wife Sarah all of his moveables, including his "negro Caesar." To his two sons Hatevil and Antony he gave all his lands in Rochester; to his sons John and Joshua all his lands in Newington; to his five daughters Eleanor, Sarah (Walker,) Abigail (Dam,) Elizabeth (Rawlings,) and Olive he gave £10 each.

He therefore had children by his first wife; Hatevil Antony, Eleanor and Sarah; and by his second wife—John born 24 Feb. 1721, Joshua, Abigail, Elizabeth and Olive.

HENRY (3) son of Antony (2) lived in Newington and died about 1739-40, his will was dated 24 Dec. 1739; proved 19 Jan. 1739-40. He gave to Mary, his wife the use of all his estate in Newington: to his son Samuel, who was also his Executor, all the estate after his mother's decease excepting that son Valentine was to have £50, son Joseph the lands in Rochester, daughter Elizabeth (Crockett) £10, and daughter Mary £10. We know of no other children but those named in his will.

JOHN (4) son of Hatevil (3) and grandson of Antony (2) was born 24 Feb. 1721; he married 17 Nov. 1747, Anna Sims, who was born 20 Oct, 1727, and died 11 Aug. 1793. He lived in Newington. He died 19 Sept. 1776. Their children were:—

HATEVIL, born 1 Dec., 1748; Mary, born 25 Aug. 1750; Hannah born 12 June, 1752, and died 12 June 1764; Dorothy. born 5 Aug, 1754; John born 5 March 1757; —— born 17 Feb. 1764; Hannah b. 4 July, 1767, and Abigail b. 21 April 1769, died 28 Aug. 1850.

We believe that descendants of these are living in Newington. Others of the family are scattered over Strafford County and vicinity.

OLD SERIES, NO. 68. JANUARY 27, 1852

DOVER, ITS BOUNDARIES AND DIVISONS: ADDITIONAL.

In No. 27 (old series) of these Memoanda we referred to NEWINGTON as being incorporated in 1713, but said that we had not been able to find any official record of this transaction. There was none in the office of Secretary of State at Concord, but we have since procured the followig from another source.

A meeting of the inhabetants of the place now known as Newington, was held 21 Jan., 1712 at the meeting house which they had already erected, to "confer about heiring a minister among them". The inhabitants were probably nearly equally divided between Dover and Portsmouth. Of these families dwelling on Bloody Point (the Dover section) where Dam, Rollins, Bickford, Lankstar, Trickey, Shackford, Pomeroy, Furber, Knight, Nutter, Leighton and Downs, most or all of whom were descendants of early Bloody Point settlers.

At the meeting above mentioned measures were taken to procure a minister; and as it was not proper for those paying for the support of the ministry at Newington should be taxed elsewhere, a petition was presented to the General Court to erect a certain part of the towns of Dover and Portsmouth into a new Parish, by which act only could they be freed from the form the taxes demanded by the law for the maintenance of the Ministry in their respective towns.

The petition and the action held thereon were as follows:—

PROVINCIAL COUNCIL RECORDS

The Petition of the Inhabitants of Bloody Point was read at the board in the words following:—

To his Excellency Joseph Dudley, Esq. Cap(tain) General & Governor in chief in and over her Maj(estys) Province of the Massachusets Bay, New Hampshire, and the house of Representatives now in General Assembly convened:—

The Petition of the Inhabitants of Bloody Point, within the limits of the Township of Dover with some from the outskirts of Portsmouth, most Humbly sheweth:—

That your Petitioners living so remote from the Public worship of God, and under great inconvenience to Attend the same, have of late erected a meeting house and obtained a Tract of Sixty

Acres of Land for the Accommodation of a minister among them, with a firm resolution, (by the Divine Assistance) of giving him an honorable — — — — — to the utmost of their ability. But the taxes demanded of us from whence we Come off do place us under so insuperable difficulties of doing as otherwise we wish.

Wherefore (we) most humbly pray that your Excelency (who hitherto hath distinguished yourself from others in the Publick worship of God) would please so aid that we your Petitioners by Maintaining the minister, (and) School among ourselves, may be Exempted from all the other charges, save only the Province Tax of the Assembly.

All which we humbly conceive to be most reasonable, and whereas nothing now is wanting to effect the same but your Concurrence, we most humbly — — — that — — — — — — — our request herein. And your Petitioners shall pray as in duty bound &c., &c, &c.

George Huntress, Edward Row, John Dam, Wm Hoyt, Joseph Richards, Sam'll Rawlings, Joseph Rawlings Sam'll Thompson, Richard Downing, Wm Furber, Jethro Bickford, Clement Meserve, Thomas Bickford, John Fabyan, Sam'll Huntress, Nathan Knight, John Hodsdon, John Pickerin, 3d., Henry Langstar Benjamin Richards, John Downing, John Knight, Thomas Trickey, Andrew Peters, John Knight (2), John ————, John Bickford, John Rawlings, Hatevil Nutter, William Witham, James Rawlings, Clement Meserve Moses Dam, Alexander Hodsdon, Henry Nutter, William Shackford, Thomas Leighton, Richard Pomeroy, Joshua Crocket, John Hudson, John Nutter, Abel Peavey, Tho Row, Edward Pevey, John Quint, John Trickey, James Gray, John Carter, Henry Bennet, Benjamin Bickford, Richard Nason, Thomas Downes.

15th July 1713.

In Council read and the good intention of the Petitioners approved, and ordered that the Selectmen of the Town of Dover be notified to appear by Nine O'clock tomorrow in the forenoon at the Council Board.

Charles Story, Secr'y.

Copy ex'd; P. Theodore Atkinson Jun'r., Secr'y

16th July 1713.

Upon hearing the Selectmen of Dover and Parties to the Petition.

Ordered that the Petition be granted and the Place made a Parish by themselves. they forthwith establishing An Able Orthodox and Learned Minister among them And be henceforth acquitted from the support of the ministry of Dover and Portsmouth.

And upon representation of the great alteration this makes in the town of Dover, Ord. that there be a meeting house built at Cocheco, much nearer the Centre of the Inhabitants of the said Town.

Ordered that the selectmen of the Town of Dover give early notice to the Town to choose proper persons to attend the next Sessions of the General Assembly To shew cause why that at Cocheco may not be the Place of Public Worship for the future, or any other considerations there pon.

Voted in Council, sent down to the House of Representatives for Concurrence

Charles Story, Sec'y

16th July 1713. Concurred with the Council, by order of the House of Representatives.

Sam'l Keais, Clerk.

Copy exam'd. P. Theodore Atkinson Junor, Sec.

Col. Waldron and Mark Hunking of the Council and Mr. Speaker Gerrish, George Jaffrey, John Downing and Samuel Weeks of the House, were appointed to run the line between Greenland and Newington.

Upon the 6 August 1713 the inhabitants assembled under their act of incorporation to pass such vots regarding town officers as were necessary. The main thing was "to consult together what offer to make Mr. Fisk in order to be settled in sd Parish"

Capt John Knight was chosen Moderator of the meeting, John Dam, Town Clerk, and it was voted that "Ensign Jon. Fabyan and Mr. John Downing, Jurer, should have power as selectmen for the year ensuing";

It was voted to offer a sallary of £80 per annum to Rev. Mr. Fisk, but Mr. Fisk declined and was paid for the fifteen Sabbaths he had officiated as minister. Rev. John Emerson preached three Sabbaths and a Thanksgiving, but he also concluded not to settle at Newington; so he received £4 for his service and went his way.

REV. JOSEPH ADAMS accepted the invitation that was then given him by the committee, which we almost forgot to mention consisted of Capt. John Knight, Lieut. John Downing, Ensign John Fabyans (plenty of the church militant at any rate) Mr. John Dam, Mr. George Bunter, Thomas Leighton, and the aforesaid Joseph Adams was thereupon settled, and remained a great many years.

OLD SERIES, NO. 69, MARCH 23, 1859

THE STARBUCK FAMILY.

EDWARD STARBUCK, born in 1604 is said to have come to Dover from Derbyshire, England. He is first mentioned as receiving 3 , 6 mo. 1643, a grant of forty acres of land on each side of "Fresh River," "at Cutchechoe, next above the lot of John Baker, at the little water brooke and alsoe one platt of Marsh above Cutcheshoe great Marsh that the brooke that runs out of the great river runs through, first discovered by Richard Walderne, Edward Colcord, Edward Starbuck and William Furber." He had other grants at different times; one was a marsh in the Great Bay in 1643; another was a small privilege at Cochecho, second falls (with Thomas Wiggin) with timber to accommodate in 1650, and various others, so that he was evidently a man of large possessions of land and tradition says he was large in body.

He was Represntative in the General Court of Massachusetts in 1643 and 1646; he was an Elder in the Church and enjoyed various other tokens of respect given him by his fellow citizens. In fact he might have lived very comfortably at Dover and died in the midst of his family, respected and contented, but for one unfortunate difficulty—he became a heretic. It is not easy to ascertain at this late day the peculiarities of his tenets; oblivion has swept off all traces save a few paragraphs in the records of the County Court.

On the 8d of the 8th mo. 1648, the grand Jury "presented Edward Starbuck for a fi e for disturbing the peace of the Church. Edward Starbuck was admonished for the same and was discharged with — — — — fee."

"I he saide grande Jurye presented Edwarde Starbuck for denyinge to Joyne with the Churche in the ordinance of baptism."

In view of these deeds of his, he was recognized to appear at the next Court of Assistants at Boston "to answer to such offences as have by him been committed against the law con erning Anabaptists; and furthermore that he shall be of peaceable and good behaviour towards all men, and especially towards the Reverend Teacher of Dover."

We cannot, of course, ascertain with certainty in what particulars the Elder was an Anabaptist.—But that he agreed in any considerable decree with the raving fanatics who bore that name in Germany, we do not believe. It is probable that he differed from the established Cnurch only in regard to "the ordinance of baptism," he supposing and believing that immersion was the Scripture method of performing that rite, and that infants were not fit subjects for its performance, while the good old Parson Maud held to precisely the opposite view The Elder's arguments on this subject might easily make him liable to the charge of "disturbing the peace of the Church," for theological disputes on points that admit of no demonstration generally end in a quarrel.

Now about this time the Baptists were making considerable disturbance in New England, so much so that the Government of Massachusetts Bay found it necessary to enact quite stringent laws to suppress such dangerous heresy. Old Parson Knollys, the founder of the Church here, was himself considerably tinctured with it, though it is doubtful whether he avowed his belief very strenuously until after his return to England. They whipped one man in Massachusetts for refusing to have his child baptised, though even this did not seem to change his opinion. The people at Dover were of course alarmed and when the Elder began to broach his heretical notions, they employed the means above quoted to convince him of his error. Their arguments were more strong than convincing, owing to his unfortunate obstinacy, and though the Elder managed to get along tolerably quietly for quite a number of years, at last he concluded to leave the Reverend Teacher of Dover to himself and emigrate to some more congenial clime.

So in 1659 Elder Starbuck went off on an exploring expedition. In the course of his travels he met Thomas Macy and his family (then troubled with a somewhat similar inability to convince the people of Newbury), James Coffin, (a youth of about nineteen) and Isaac Coleman, a boy of twelve. These adventurers set sail in an open boat in the autumn of 1659 and in due time arrived at the Island of Nantucket, an eligible situation for men who liked plenty of water. They settled first at Matical but afterwards moved to a more central place now called Cambridge.

The next spring the Elder came back to Dover to get his family. His daughters Sarah and Abigail were married and remained in Dover, but his wife Katherine went with him and Nathaniel, Dorcas and Jethro, his remaining children. So they settled down peacefully at Nantucket and Dover lost a good citizen. He became a leading man in his new place of abode being at one time the Magistrate of the Island and always enjoying the esteem of his fellow citizens. He died 4, 19 mo, 1690.

The children of the Elder were —NATHANIEL, born 1636, Dorcas, Sarah, Abigail, Jethro; the last named was killed 27 May 1663, by a cart running over him. The others had families as follows:

NATHANIEL (2) married Mary daughter of Tristram Coffin, Senior, and b. 20 Feb. 1645.

Nathaniel was a wealthy man; he is also said to have been a man of no mean abilities but was outshone by the superior capacity of his wife, a woman of uncommon powers of mind. She had been baptized by Peter Folger in Waputequat Pond but years afterwards became convinced of Friends' principles, and became a preacher among them, as did his son Nathaniel and his daughter Priscilla. A "Public Friend" who was acquainted with her calls her "The Great Woman." On account of her superior judgment she was often consulted in public affairs of the Towne, as well as in religious matters. She died 13, 9 mo. 1717. Nathaniel died 6, 6 mo. 1719.

They had children:—MARY born 1663, the first white child born in Nantucket; she married James Gardner son of Richard. ELIZABETH, b. 9 Sept. 1665, she married first her cousin, Peter Coffin, Jr., second marriage Nathaniel Barkard, Jr.—NATHANIEL b. 9 Aug, 1668; he married his cousin Dinah Coffin, daughter of James, and died in 1752.—JETHRO, b. 14 Dec. 1671; he married his cousin Dorcas Gayer, and died 12, 8 mo, 1770.—BARNABAS, b. 1673, died 1733. —EUNICE b. 11 April 1674, who married George Gardner, son of John.— HEPSIBAH, who married Thomas Hathaway of Dartmouth, Mass.—ANN died single, as also PAUL.

DORCAS (2) married William Gayer; she died about 1696; he died after a second and childless marriage 23, 7 mo. 1710. Their children were:— Damaris b. 24 Oct. 1673, married 17 Aug. 1692. Nathaniel Coffin, son of James; from them was descended Admiral Sir Isaac Coffin, famous in the annals of the Island. Dorcas b. 29 Aug. 1675; married 6 Dec. 1694, her cousin Jethro Starbuck as above:—William b. 3 June 1677; he married in England his cousin Elizabeth Gayer, daughter of John and died in England, a wealthy man, in 1712 or 13.

SARAH (2) is the subject of considerable difference of accounts. Tradition represents her to have married Benjamin Austin and the same authority makes another and nameless daughter to have been the wife of Humphrey Varney. But from an examination of the Town Records we are convinced that she married (1) William Story about 1658; (2) Joseph Austin about 1659 or '60, who was dead in 1663; (3) Humphrey Varney. For "widow Sarah Storie" is represented to have married Joseph Austin when William Story's inventory was entered, and Joseph Austin in his will speaks of "my brother Peter Coffin" and after Joseph Austin's death Elder Starbuck; confirms to his "son-in-law Humphrey Varney" husband of "Sarah," land formerly given by him to his "son-in-law Joseph Austin." If this is correct we are inclined to think that Sarah had children in her third marriage, by which she became ancestress to a race of infinite numbers.

Abigail (2) married (Hon.) Peter Coffin of Dover, son of Tristram, Senior, and lived in Dover. Peter was a noted man in his day, "a gentleman very serviceable in Church and State," as the writer of his obituary said after the death of Peter 21 March, 1715. He was Councillor, Judge and active in other official positions, he had a garrison house at Dover (Cochecho) which was captured by the Indians in 1689, when Peter lost considerable hard money which grieved him sorely.

They had children:—Abigail, born in 1657 who married Daniel Davidson; Eliphalet, who died single; Peter, born 20 Aug. 1660, married his cousin Elizabeth Starbuck; Jethro, born 16 Sep. 1663, married Mary Gardiner, daughter of John; Tristram, born 1665, married Deborah Colcord; Elizabeth m. John Gilman; Edward b. 20 Feb. 1669, m. Ann Gardner, daughter of John, and died childless; Robert, married Joanna Gilman; Judith b. 1672.

The Starbuck family has ever been respectable. The Elder was a man of great worth and appears to have been so looked upon in Dover notwithstanding the persecution he there experienced. His descendants have been, so far as we learn of them, men of worth; many of them are now worthy and respected, not for their wealth merely but for those qualities which always command esteem.

Our Dover ancestors were not perfect. The enforcing of a law against theoretical opinions regarding baptism proves that, at least, they were sometimes wrong in their views; and the treatment of the Quakers, of which we shall in some future number give an account, increases our regret that human passions should have suffered so far to obscure their sense of justice and weaken their feelings of humanity. They were, many of them at least, good men but they were men after all.

The writer of this article returns his thanks to Mr. Peter C. Folger of Nantucket for valuable aid in giving him the substance of the facts contained in this article.

OLD SERIES, NO. 70, MARCH 30, 1852

DOVER TOWN RECORDS.

1673.

The following Records are from the fragments marked V mentioned in Memoranda No. 27.

These leaves are very imperfect and many omissions are thus made necessary in publishing them. In consequence of these imperfections the records of 1671 and 1672 are lost.

At A Meitting of the freemen on the forth of the — — — — — — 1673

Capt. Richard Wallderne chosen Debety to goe to the Cortt apon a warrant from the Gouerner and Counsell to Consult for the Safety of the Collenie.

At A Meitting of the Selleckmen the twenty fifth of January libertey is Granted by the sayd selleckmen to John Roberds and Jeremy Tebbets of Douer for to improue Six Ackers of land in the Comon lyinge of the Ester sied of the paeth that doeth Goe unto the watering place on Douer Necke, Neir unto Thomas Perkins his house wich land is for to be Improued by them Seven yeir for thear use and then for to be Returned unto the Townes use and to be left playnse for feding Ground.

     Antony Nutter
     Roberd Burnum
     John Gerrish
      Selleektmen.

At a Towne Meitting holden the 2th of the first — — — '73—'74. Joseph Cany Chosen Constabell

Jurey of Trialls.—Mr Jno. Euins, Sergt Burnum, Jno Tuttle, Tho. Canney, Junr, Jno Woodman, James Niewte, Junr.

Grand Jurey,— Mr Job Clements, Senr, Jno Dam, Junr., Jno Hill, Jno Winget, Jno Frost, James Huckins, Jno Symons.

Ye Surveyors ffor ye high wayes ye same, yt were chosen ye last year to Stand ffor this yeir — —.

73—'74 —Nickloes hareson noted by the Towne to ofesbeat Noe long-r as A Celler of pipe staues.

Selectmen:—Capt Walderne, Jno Roberts, Antho. Nutter, Jno Wingett, Jno Gerrish, Roberd Burnum, Jno Woodman.

[The following in a later handwriting]

At a meiting held the 19th 3th m. — — .— — — Capt Rich — - .— — — — — — — — — .— — — — —

At A Meitting of the sellecktmen of Douer this 18th of the 6th month '74

Ordered and apoynted the parsons their under Named to Rune over headline, as formerly from Nechewanick Riuer unto our utmost Bounds on the South Side of Lamprill Riuer; the parsons that are apoynted Are Einsin John Daues, Sargant Robert Burnu n, Deacon John Hall, John Gerrish and John Wingett, and theay, or the major part of them to apoynt the most Conuenent time for the doing it befor winter.

At the same apon Complaynt of James Newett, Sinyer that Phillep Cromwell taketh in his highway and trespaseth the Comon, we, the Selecktmen have apoynted Sargint John Roberds and Deacon John Hall to goe to the place and take Notes of what is donen and giue an a Count at our next Meitting that we may Regulate the same a Cording to Equitie.

At A Publick Towne Meitting holden the — — — — — th mo (74.
— — — — — — —whear ther was
— — — — — —order that Euery
— — - — — keld in the Township
— — — — — — said partie snold
— — — — — — — —whearas now
— — — — — — it shall be but
— — — — — — wolfe.

At A Meitting of the Selleckmen the 20th 9th mo (74. Whea — — — — — a fower acker loct Giue — — — — — Grented nnto henrey hob — — — — — Acker lott was granted — — — — — side of huckellberrey hill a — — — — in the possession of Joseph — .— — — — said lott being found to be — — — — land that Aprope — — — — — — —

To Publick was the sele — — — —

from the Gouerner and Counsell to Consult for the Safety of the Collenie.

At A Meitting of the Selleckmen the twenty fifth of January libertey is Granted by the sayd selleckmen to John Roberds and Jeremy Tebbets of Douer for to improue six Ackers of land in the Comon lyinge of the Ester sied of the paeth that doeth Goe unto the watering place on Douer Neoke, Neir unto Thomas Perkins his house wich land is for to be Improued by them Seven yeir for thear use and then for to be Returned unto the Townes use and to be left plavnse for feding Ground.

     Antony Nutter
     Roberd Burnum
     John Gerrish
      Selleoktmen.

At a Towne Meitting holden the 2th of the first — — '73 – '74. Joseph Cany Chosen Constabell

Jurey of Trialls.—Mr Jno. Euins, Sergt Burnum, Jno Tuttle, Tho. Canney, Junr, Jno Woodman, James Niewte, Junr.

Grand Jurey,— Mr Job Clements, Senr, Jno Dam, Junr., Jno Hill, Jno Winget, Jno Frost, James Huckins, Jno Symons.

Ye Surveyors ffor ye high wayes ye same, yt were chosen ye last year to Stand ffor this yeir — —.

73—'74—Nihckloes areson noted by the Towne to ofesheat Noe longer as A Celler of pipe staues.

Selectmen:—Capt Walderne, Jno Roberts, Antho. Nutter, Jno Wingett, Jno Gerrish, Roberd Burnum, Jno Woodman.

[The following in a later handwriting.]

At a meiting held the 19th 3th m. — — — — — Capt Rich — - — — —
— — — — — — — — — — — —

At A Meitting of the sellecktmen of Douer this 18th of the 6th month '74

Ordered and apoynted the parsons their under Named to Rune over headline, as formerly from Nechewanick Riuer unto our utmost Bounds on the South Side of Lamprill Riuer; the parsons that are apoynted Are Einsin John Daues, Sargant Robert Burnum, Deacon John Hall, John Gerrish and John Wingett, and theay, or the major part of them to apoynt the most Conuenent time for the doing it befor winter.

At the same apon Complaynt of James Newett, Sinyer that Phillep Cromwell taketh in his highway and trespaseth the Comon, we, the Selecktmen have apoynted Sargint John Roberds and Deacon John Hall to goe to the place and take Notes of what is douen and giue an a Count at our next Meiting that we may Regulate the same a Cording to Equitie.

At A Publick Towne Meitting holden the — — — — — th mo (4.
— — — — — — —wheⱥr ther was
— — — — — — —order that Euery
— — - — — keld in the Township
— — — — — — said partie shold
— — — — — — — —whearas now
- — — — — — it shall be but
— — — - — — wolfe.

At A Meitting of the Selleckmen the 20th 9th mo (74. Whea — — — — a fower acker lott Giue— — — — — Granted unto henrey hob — — — — Acker lott was granted — — — — side of huckellberrey hill a — — — — in the possession of Joseph— — — — — said lott being found to be — — — — land that Aprope — — — — — — To Publick was the sele — — — —

doe thearfoer order and apoynt Dehall, Sargant John Roberts to lay oute his said fower ackers of land on either side of the paeth that goeth to lettell John's Cricke on the North side of ye swamp at the foott of huckellberry hill.

At A meitting of the Sellecktmen the 20, 9th month (74.—Whearas John Roberds and John Hill wear apoynted to vew the fence of Phellip Comwell whearin he had trespassed on the Townes Common in setting his fence as we goe to James Newtes, for the preseruing our writes of highwayes and Commons doe order that Phillip Cromwell doe forthwith Remoue his fence and sett it a Cording to his owne Bounds that we may haue our old wayes to Pass in, Apon the penaltie of haueing his fence pulled downe and alsoe fined.

OLD SERIES NO. 71, APRIL 13, 1852.

THE PINKHAM FAMILY.

The observing Antiquarian cannot fail to be struck with the wonderful coincidences in family ancestries with which he will be sure to meet in the traditions of all families which ever had any ancestors. Occasionally there were "two brothers" who settled in America, more rarely "four," but in the great majority of cases there were just "three brothers who came over," and settled here and there about the country. This universal belief is easiest accounted for on the supposition that all mankind have an indistinct tradition of Shem, Ham and Japhet, whose history of "three brothers" and their navigating propensities they mix up with their own immediate family history by the same confusion of ideas which makes every man who is at a loss for the name of his great grand father stoutly affirm that his grandfather came straight from England. If this tradition should chance to be found among the Malay and Indians, it would go far towards relieving many honest old ladies of both sexes from the terrible fear which Professor Agassiz has produced by his theory regarding the "unity of the race."

Regarding the PINKHAM family, tradition tells, of course, of the "three brothers who came over." One, it says, settled on Dover Neck, one at Oyster River and one at Bloody Point,—a tradition which is entirely without foundation. Perhaps the family story that the Isle of Wight was its former residence may be entitled to more credit. But without referring to the Apocrypha more than is necessary, it is certain that RICHARD PINKHAM, the first ancestor of the name who came over was the gentleman who was ordered by the vote of the Town in 1648 to "beat the drumme" on Lord's day to call the people to meeting. He was here too in 1642, and perhaps earlier. The spot where he early dwelt is said to be the same on which stood the Pinkham garrison, which Richard afterwards made his habitation. The precise situation of this is easily pointed out, inasmuch as it continued to be a dwelling house until one side of it fell down seven and twenty years ago; that event rendered it necessary for the family to move which they did as soon as possible into a new house standing about five rods from the old one.

After passing the house of Hanson Roberts on Dover Neck a traveller will notice a lane on the west side of the road leading towards the river. On the north side of the lane is a house now occupied by Elijah Pinkham, a man of more than 80 years who owns land once owned by his ancestor Richard. About four rods directly west of his house was the garrison house, half of which was taken down about two years after the wind had demolished the other half. The spot on which the fortress stood in ancient days presented a few months ago the aspect of a flourishing cabbage yard.

RICHARD lived on Dover Neck and died there. He appears to have been a man of good character and had his share of public offices. In 1671 he conveyed the bulk of his property to his son John who engaged to support him.

Of the children of Richard we know the names of but three: RICHARD, JOHN and THOMAS, who was taxed on Dover Neck 1667-68, and then vanishes.

RICHARD (2) son of Richard (1) as above, married Elizabeth, daughter of the second Thomas Leighton. He was a carpenter and lived on Dover Neck owning a lot fronting on High street. He conveyed to Thomas Tibbets the High street premises 2 May 1699, to his nephew Amos 12 May 1709 land which formerly belonged to the first Thomas Leighton; to his son Tristram land 22 Feb. 1736-7; to his son Richard lot No. 70 in the first division at Rochester, 2 Dec. 1730-1; he received land 18 April 1699 from Thomas Leighton, eldest son and heir to Thomas, deceased, grandson to Thomas the first and brother to Elizabeth, Richard Pinkham's wife. Richard (2) had children:

RICHARD, TRISTRAM, JOHN b. 19 Aug. 1696.

John (2) son of Richard (1) and the one who was to support his father was first taxed on Dover Neck in 1665; he first assumed the care of his father, legally, and took possession of the homestead in 1671, just before the time when it became necessary to build garrisons and carry guns to meeting. He married a daughter of the first Richard Otis, of Cochecho, apparently named Rose, regarding whose ancestry many curious particulars may be found in the genealogy of the Otis family which was published in the 2d No. for the year 1851 of the Genealogical Register, a work published in Boston, and very necessary to all who care to remember that they ever had any grandfather.

JOHN PINKHAM (2) had at least nine children viz.:—Richard who had a wife Elizabeth, and perhaps was the Richard who at the age of 85 married 27 Nov. 1757, widow Mary Welch, aged 76, (at Kittery). Thomas (who had a wife Marcy and children Richard, to whom he gave property 22 Oct. 1736, Benjamin to whom he gave property 23 Aug. 1736, Ebenezer to whom he gave property 15 March 1736-7); Amos (who married Elizabeth widow of Samuel Chesley killed 15 Sept. 1707, and had children, Hannah b. 10 Jan 1713-14 Joanna b. 11 Aug. 1718;) Otis (whose family will be given below;) Solomon who had a grant of land 23 June 1701;) James (who m. Elizabeth daughter of Joseph Smith (2) as recorded in No. 42 of these Memoranda, and had children,

James b. 21 July 1714, Wesla b. 4 Oct. 1716, Mary b. 14 Sept. 1719, baptized 22 May 1720, Lois b. 2 March 1721-2, baptized 8 July 1722, Hannah b. 16 Sept. 1722, baptized 25 Oct. 1724, Sarah baptized 4 June 1727, and Jonathan baptized 3 May 1730;) Rose (who m. (1) James Tuttle, (2) Thomas Canney and whose children are recorded in the "Otis" Genealogy; Elizabeth (probably the one who m. Samuel Nute 18 March 1718-19) and Sarah.

This John (2) gave to his eldest son Richard land at Cochecho 19 June 1714; to his son Otis land 16 March 1721-22; to his son Amos 4 July 1715, certain lands on condition that he pay to each sister above named £5; this land and conditions he transferred to his brother Otis 8 August 1720.

OTIS (3) son of John (2) m. 22, 9 mo. 1721, Abigail, daughter of Ephraim and Rose Austin Tibbetts, b. 12, 6 mo. 1701. Otis inherited the old homestead. He died about 1763, and his inventory was entered 30 Nov. 1764 by his widow Abigail. He had children.

SAMUEL, b. 26 Sept. 1722, m. Susanna Canney; Ann b. 30 April 1724 and died unmarried; Rose b. 18 March 1725-6 and m. James Tuttle of whom we will speak under "Tuttle;" Paul b. 3, 4 mo. 1730, (m. Rose daughter of Joseph Austin.) He died 16 3 mo. 1819, having children, Nicholas b. 3, 11 mo. 1755, died 1, 10 mo. 1770, Joseph b. 8 mo. 1757, m. Elizabeth Green, 1788 and died 1845, having had Nicholas b 1789 and died unmarried, Jeremiah G. b. 1791, m. widow Louisa Heard and is living, Sarah b. 94, m. Joseph Tuttle, known as "Friend Joseph" (who lives on the Neck) Elizabeth b. 1797, who is in Ohio, Joseph b. 1800, who died unmarried, Hannah b 1804, m. Levi Sawyer and is living at Garrison Hill, Rose b. 1807, m. Samuel Dunn and is dead, Rebecca b. 1809, m. Jacob K. Purinton and died in 1834, leaving Mary E. and Sarah A.; —Otis b. 25, 8 mo. 1759 who was lost at sea; Silas b. 9, 11 mo. 1764 who died 10 9 mo. 1796; Rose b. 1, 12 mo. 1766 who married Jonathan Hanson; Paul b. 1, 12 mo. 1768; John b. 29, 8 mo. 1739.

JOHN (4) the last named received the homestead, garrison and all, from his father; he married Phebe Tibbets, b. 5 April, 1744, d. 24 Jan. 1828. John d. 14, 8 mo. 1815. They had children:—

ELIZABETH, b. 13, 1 mo. 1762, m. David Roberts, of whom see "ROBERTS"; Otis b. 23, 3 mo. 1765 m. Hannah Young and died in Milton 5, 1 mo. 1814 leaving descendants; Edmund b. 3, 10 mo. 1767, m. Miriam Gould and went to Maine and was living when last heard from; Elijah b. 15 Dec. 1769, m. Eunice Tuttle and has had Rose who m. John Young and Phebe (now dead) who m. Charles Thompson. Elijah is still living on the homestead as we have before mentioned. Joseph and Benjamin b 18, Jan. 1772; Joseph m. Sarah Young, lived and died in Tuftonborough; he had children among whom is Enoch, now living at Dover Point. Benjamin m. Nancy Davis, who is still living; his son Daniel is also living on the Neck; Enoch b. 14 Feb. 1774; his wife was Elizabeth, dau. of Richard Tripe, she is living childless, he was a sailor and though successful in business "never owned a foot of land"; he determined at last to marry, go one more voyage and settle down on his return; he married, sailed immediately, but never returned; he died at sea.—Sarah b. 4 Sept. 1776, she is dead.—Nicholas b. 10 Jan. 1779; he m. Abigail Lamos and lived at Dover, J. Burley Pinkham and others are his children.—Abigail b. 12 March 1781, died unmarried at the homestead 17 Aug. 1809.—Phebe b. 20 June 1783, m. John Jackson a sea Captain who lives at Belfast, she died 28 Oct. 1810, having two children, Frank and Elizabeth. John b. 8 Jan. 1787, d. 29 May following. Samuel b. 22 July 1788 m. Lydia Ham; he lived in Brookfield, d. 1 April 1825, havin two children, Nathaniel and E. J. Pinkham.

Our readers will perceive that the homestead has never been out of possession of the family since it was first occupied. The house upon it is situated in a pleasant field, sloping gently toward Bellamy river and commanding a view of the stream and the dark woods covering its opposite shore, whose quiet beauty might well content the generations that have made the spot their resting places in the journey of life.

OLD SERIES, NO. 72, APRIL 20, 1852.

DOVER TOWN RECORDS.

1674.

At A Publick Towne meting holden the 4th of 11th mo (74.

For the selling of land to pay Towne debtes we the Inhabitants whose names ar heir under writen Doe Desent from that ackett.

John Dam Sinyer, Thomas Leighton,
Thomas Beard, John Tuttell,
Thomas Roberds, William Pomfrett

In a Publick Towne Meeting holden ye 3 february 1674:—

Major Walderne chosen Moderator for this present meeting. (This is a later hand).

Three fourths of the next page of the record is gone. From the remainder we find that certain persons had become possessors of small tracts of land for which each one "engageth to pay" on or before a certain specified time. The only names remaining are Peter Coffin, John Wingett, Thomas Cany, Joseph Cany, Jeremiah Tibbitt, John Hall, Mr. Rayner and James Newt.

The next page on the same leaf informs us that the "Committee chosen and appoynted for ye selling land" have concluded to sell ten acres to Zacherias Field, and that said ten acres were laid out by John Hall and John Evens. In some undefinable locality. The said committee also sold to Jerimie Tibitt, who was, by the way, ancestor of most of the Tibbereses who flourish in this vicinity. Some dealings to the amount of five pounds were had with John Michill and John Woodman, but what those dealings refer to, the rats have deprived us of the pleasure of communicating. The next piece of record informs us that two grants of land to John Hill and ——— were laid out 18 Nov. 1678, by John Davis and Robert Burnum: "these two grants are laid out and bounded as follows: 65 rods along ye shore from

Thomas Humphreyes — — next John Alts long Creeke near ye mill and from thence (?) went nor west 90 rods to marked tree, marked T. C., and from yt it runs east south east till it come to ye same brook it began at."

The next page continues the list of those who owe the towne for land, among whom were Thomas Pirkins, Isaac Stoakes; "John Wingett Refuseth to hold ye Neck of Land at Lamperel Riuer but serendereth it up to ye Towne again; so John was released from payment. Leiftenant Petter Coffin but all this right which Wingett had given up, for £150, part of which he paid by crediting the town for money which it owed him, and the remainder he gave his note for.

We are also informed that "Whereas Henery Tibitt, Phillip Cromwell and Thomas Whitehouse Could not haue thiere land where they proposed the Towne had granted them Liberty to have it laid out elsewhere."

The sudden fit of economy that possessed the town continued, as also the desire to pay off the debts of the town by selling land. So.

"Att a Meiting of the Committee for selling land held at Oyster Riuer ye 3tn of — — — 1675, Sold to John Alt the tenn acres." Sold also to Thomas Edgerly considerable, and some to William Beard, Edward Leathers, William Williams, Senor, Nicholas Follett, William Pitman and Phillip Follet. These were all Oyster River and Madbury folks. There were four acres laid out to Edward Leathers, who was some years earlier, however. His early residence put to flight the story that the Leatherses were descended from straggling gypsies who settled hereabouts in 1750. There ancestor was here as early as 1660, and we belieue had no more connection with the gypsies than he had with the man in the moon.

The traditions are great things. We met an old man the other day who gave his father's and grandfather's names correctly and finished by tracing his descent from Benning Wentworth the last Royal Governor of New Hampshire who wouldn't leave Portsmouth until the rebels pointed a cannon at his door. Moreover he said this Benning Wentworth "came over" with Elder Wentworth and these two were the first settlers of Somersworth and lived there!

It was a pity to spoil so good a story by reminding the informant that the last Royal Governor was named John; that he was born about thirty years after the death of his grandfather's grandfather Elder William (with whom he never 'came over') that the informants own grandfather was old enough to be Gov. John's father rather than his descendant and besides that his own pedigree was exactly known.

OLD SERIES, NO. 73, APRIL 27. 1852.

DOVER TOWN RECORDS.

1675.

Att a Publick Towne Meeting held at Douer ye 31 of May 1675.

Mr. Clements chosen moderator for this day; (he declined) John Woodman chosen in his stead.

Votted yt whereas there was an order

made of giuing liberty to ye Inhabitants for ye buying of land and a Committee chosen to sell, these are therefore to Conferme ye said lands to whom yee lands is sold to have and to hold to them their heirs and assigns, forever, with all ye priveleges and apertinances thereunto belonging excepting timber formerly granted in mill grants.

Same date.—Voted that John Pierce shall have liberty to buy 10 acres of land near Thomas Chesleys where ye Committee shall appoynt. Others had similar liberty, viz--Richard Rich (then three names lost) Phillip Cromwell, Phillip Benmore, Joseph lieftenant Petter Coffin, James Newt Junior, David Larkin.

Same date.—Votted yt all ye land ungranted above Little Johns Creek on ye west of ye way yt goes to Celamyes Bank shall lye Common forever.

The next record contains entries of Peter Coffin's having had a grant of a hundred acres of land 7th 10 mo. 1656 which is now (31 May 1675) laid out to him "a little above ye third falls in Cochecho."

May 24, 1675 "Michaell Braun Senior" had a grant of ten acres out of land, "next Henery Langsters land on ye east side of the conterie high way."

The same date ten acres were laid out to James Huckins "Joyning to ye north end of his home lott" which was on the south side of the brook which runs into ye freshet at ye head of ye Creek (Thomas Johnson's).

John Wingate had ten acres joining his land; John Gerrish 10 acres: Deacon John Hall 10 acres "from a white oake marked I. H. being at ye north west corner of six acres of land laid out to Joseph Caney beyond Hucklbury Hill on ye east side of ye Road which doth lead to litle Johns Creek."—John Hall Junior 10 acres joining that "laid out to his fathers as above. Sargent (Antony) Nutter bought some and so did Peter Coffin Joseph Caney and John Woodman.

Sargent John Roberts bought ten acres which was laid out to join his fathers land at Little Johns Creek.—Thomas Beard ten acres was to join those of John Hall, Junior spoken of above.—Thomas Downes, Thomas Roberts, John Migell, Mr. Clements, Phillip Cromwell, Thomas Whitehouse, William Roberts, and John Tuttle each bought ten acres the price varying from five to twenty shillings per acre.

Land between Lamprell River and Goddards Creek which Peter Coffin bought of the town for 150 pounds as previously related, he sold 25 June 1675 to Richard Waldern.

Then follow more ten acre lot sales. James Newt Senior, John Tuttle, Henery Langster, John Evans, Richard Rich, Thomas Perkins, Ichabod Rollins and Isaac Stoakes, had shares.

July 15, 1675 the bills were footed up. Those who had paid were "Zacherhias feild, James Smith, Mr. Trickey, William ffurber, Sargent John Hall, Jeremiah Tibetts, humphrey varney, Mr. Rich, Thomas dowes, Joseph Cany, Thomas Roberds, Philip Cromwell, Henery Tibutts, Thomas Whitehouse, Thomas Cany, John Tuttle, Mr. Clement James Newt, Junior" and various other persons whose names are torn off.

"Voted that Sargant william ffurber, Sargant Antony Nutter and John Wood man are chosen & apoyted a Co nete to treat & discuse with the selectmen of Portsmouth & of the Isle of Shoals, or other meet prsons of thes towns for to state or propose some way for the Reasing of Morys for the defreing & sattifing of such prson, or prsons as have suffered (?) either by ther estattes or services (?) in the present warr with the Indians & what they do hearin to make Report to the Towne."

Another specimen of troublons times; "wheras ye Sellecktmen neglected ye making a prouition Rate this present yeare according to ye former order, by reason of ye troubles of ye times, it is votted yt ye Sellectmen shall make prouision Rate for this present yeare according to ye last yeares Rate, making abatement of such mens estates as they see Just cause for at their descretion."

OLD SERIES, NO. 74, MAY 4, 1852.

DOVER TOWN RECORDS.

1675.

The next record is that of the "Provision Rate" for the year 1675. The persons taxed were of—

DOVER NECK AND COCHECHO.

Mr. Nutter	James Newt Senior
Deacon Hall	Mr. Clements
Deacon Dam	Abraham Newt
Joseph Canie	John Hall Junior
Thomas Canie, Jr.	Richard Rich
Henery Tibit	John dereie
Philip Benmore	Tho: Teare
John Pinkham	Ralph Welch
Jeremi Tibits	Zacharie fleeld
Tho: Beard	Nathaniell Stevens
Tho: Perkins	ginkin Jones
Isaac Stockes	John Ham
Tho· Roberts	William Horne
Jo: Tuttle	Tho: Hamett
Philip Crumell	John Elis
Rich :Pinckham	Humphire Varnie
Tho: Whitehouse	(nine names missing)
John Roberts	david Larking
Leftenant Pomfrit	Tho: Austin
James Newt, Junior	Tho: Haines
Mr. Clements	Capt. Walderne
Jonathan Watson	Tno: Leighton
Thomas Paine	Richard Otis
John Daues	John Gearish
John Heard	Tho: Hanson
Mr. George Waldern	Robert Evans
Ralf Twamlie	gershom Wentworth
Ezekiel Wentworth	James Coffen
George Ricker & brother	
William Taskett	Tho Downes
widdow Hanson	Mark Giles
John Church	Benjamin Head

OF BLOODY POINT were:—

Sargant Hall	Henerie Langster
william ffurber Jr.	william ffurber,
Antony Nutter	Edward Allin

and eight names are missing.

OF OYSTER RIVER were:—

Ensign Daues	
James Huckins	Tho: Edgerlie
John Alt	John Hill.
John Bickford	John Meader
Tho: willie	Wm. Williams, Jr.
Joseph Smith	Phillip Cheslie, sr.
Stephen Jones	wakler Jackson
Robert Watson	Edward Leathers
John Daues Junior	James Smith
Tho & Phill'p cheslie	William Hill
John York	John Godard
Nicholas dow	Benjamin York

Charles Adams
Joseph Stimson
Steephin Willie
Joseph ffield
Tho: Moris
Nicholas Follett
Robert Burnum

dauid daniel

Nathaniel Lummack
ffrancis drew
william Pittmans
William Follett

Samuel Willie
Nicholas Haris
——Stimson
John Dow
william durgin
John Woodman
William Williams, [Senior
Mr. John Cutt [Non-Resident.(
Salathiel Denbow
Benjamin Mathews
william Perkins
george goe

"This prouision is to be paid at ye price followeth:—wheat 5s 6d p bushel; Indian corne 4s p bushel; pease 4s p bushel; beef 2d ½ p pound; pork 4d p pound; barlie 4s p bushel; butter 5 i p pound."

There were other names in the list to which the word "nothing" had been added; viz:—

Isaac Stockes
Rich Pinckham
Jos. Bickford (O R)
Philip Comell (O R)
ffrances hynck (of Bl. Pt)

Capt. Barfoott
Elder Wentworth
John Migel (O. R.)
Teage Reall (O. R)

The highest tax payer on the above list was Capt Walderne who paid £2-7-4, the second was John Roberds who paid £1-16 8⅓; the third was Job Clements paying £1-15-6½; the fourth was Richard Otis, paying £1-5 7½; the lowest on the list were John Elis and six or seven others, each of whom paid 2s 6d.

OLD SERIES, NO. 75. MAY 11, 1852.

DOVER TOWN RECORDS.

1676.

We learn from the next complete record that "Mr Clements, senior, John Bekford, senior, Ensign Daues, Thomas Beard were fined 6p each for smoking Tobacco in ye Towne meetting.

At a publick m— — — — — — — the second Anno— — — — — — — — whereas wee are inform— — — — — — sent to ye Cuntrie dated at — — — — one Thousand six hundred— — — — — certain petition presented— — — — — petiioners prayeth to his Maj— — — — gouerner of us knowing also— — — — Inherit or Lands did bona ffide— — — That wee neuer that ye said— — — — Shewed us or our Gouernors any Law in that wee haue lived long & happily— — gouernment to our great content.

It being also certainly known in all — within ye latitude ye Northernmost pt Mas— — —then bounds of ye Bay Collinie.

ffurther Considering also that ye seat of our present Indian war is principally here in these parts of ye Countrie we haue by their assitance of ye Massachusets render ye ptection of the Almightie god defended our Land & Estates, hitherto with ye expense of our monie and blood.

Therefore it is unanimously agreed Upon, Voted and Ordered that our trusty and well beloved Richard Walderne, Sarjant Majr doe in the name and behalf of our Towne petision his Majist that he would Interpose his Roayall athoritie & afford us his wonted fauor that wee be not disturbed by said Mr. Mason or any other, but continue peaceably in our present Just rights under his Majests Massachusetts bay gouernment."

BY DR. QUINT. The petition is one spoken of by Belknap (page 86) who has quoted from it in such a manner as partly to supply the vacancies existing in our records. It shows the deep repugnance which the people of Dover had to the claims of Mason which they would have, of course, as the success of his claim would have deprived them of their homes, and their strong desire to continue under the Massachusetts Bay Colony.

It was evident that the separation from that province was to be but the preparatory step for enforcing the claim of Mason who demanded that he be acknowledged as owner of large tracts of land granted in 1621, including the territory of Dover, and that the inhabitants should pay him annual rents. This reduction to vassalage could not be submittted to; the claim was the cause of long and bitter controversies, which only ended long after the death of the original settlers.

It is not my place to describe the difficulties, even if sufficiently acquainted with the facts; it is sufficient to say that although New Hampshire was constitued a separate Province in accordance with the wishes of Mason and his friends, and much to the dissatisfaction of the inhabitants, yet the final results of the controversy was not injurious to the interests of the people.

"At a publicke Towne Meeting holden 5th of March 1676.

Chosen Selectmen,—Major Walderne, Mr. Clements, Leiftenant Nutter, Ensigne Daues, Sargant Roberts.

Chosen Jurey of Tryalls,—Mr. Richard Walderne, Junior, Mr. Gerrish, Leiftenant Nutter, Thomas Roberts, John Wingett, John Woodman, Thomas Edgerly.

Chosen Grand Jurey,—Mr. Job Clements, senior, John Dam Junior, Thomas Whitehouse, John Bickford, senior, John Hill, Gershom Wentworth.

Chosen Constabels,—John Ham, James Smith.

The last record in this fragment is that of a tax list, dated 3 July 1677. The names are principally the same as those in the preceding tax list. There are some additional ones. William Perkinson, William Borden, John Michamore, Abraham Clark (these of O. R;) widow Canie (instead of Thomas) widow Benmore (instead of Philip) Silvanus Nock, widow Tibbitt (instead of Henry) Henery Hobs, John Windiet, John ffoss, Peter Coffin, John Nasson, Richard Nasson, Benjamin Nasson, Joseph Sanders, Tho: Young, Tho: Homes, (these of D. N. and Cochecho); Isaac Trickie, Mr. William Henderson, Elihue Gulison "and three men," Richard Scammon, James Green, Stephen Howel, Steiphin Seavie (these of Bloody Point. The highest tax this year was paid by Captain Walderne £1—4—10, the next by John Gerrish, £1—3—5; the next by John Roberts 18s—1¾ the next by Richard Otis, 13s—1½; the next by Antony Nutter 13 s.

OLD SERIES, NO. 77. JUNE 1, 1852.

JOHN REYNER, JR.

JOHN REYNER, JR., seventh minister of Dover was son of John Reyner, his immediate predecessor; it is probable he was born in Plymouth, Mass., in 1643. He graduated from Harvard College in

1663, taking the third rank in a class of seven. After his graduation he engaged in suitable preparatory studies, and became, about 1667, assistant to his father at Dover. Immediately upon his father's death 22 July 1669, he was invited to officiate as minister for one year; he accepted the invitation and doubtless remained in that position from that date till he died, although he was not regularly settled until 21 July 1671. He took the freeman's oath 12th June 1670. It is worthy of notice that he was the first minister of Dover who was born and educated in America.

He is spoken of by those acquainted with him as giving great promise of future usefulness. Fitch says "he possessed a double portion of his father's spirit,"—no slight praise to the mind of those who appreciate the excellencies of one of the best ministers of which the early history of New Hampshire speaks. If he resembled his father, then he was man possessed of a strong mind, well cultivated and enriched by learning, of ardent piety and warm heart, and filled with deep longings to fulfil the duties of his calling. But his comparatively early death cut short all anticipations.

He died 21 Dec. 1676, at Braintree, Mass., while he was apparently on a visit there. He was doubtless childless, and probably unmarried, as his mother administered upon his estate.

In his day the meetings were held in the meeting house on Dover Neck; it was the one which was fortified not far from his time. There was then no other in the vicinity, save one at Oyster River, and that was unoccupied by a regular minister. Even when that at Oyster River was used, the shortest journey which some of the congregation were compelled to make, was six or seven miles; while the distance of some who attended the preaching of John Reyner, Jr., was that from Salmon Falls to the lower school house on Dover Neck. In those days men and women deemed this sacrifice of personal comfort of little account, when it enabled them to listen to the word of the truth; but the aged and infirm were debarred from this privilege by the length of the required journey, and that doubtless was the principal cause of the first subdivisions of the old town; indeed this is stated at various times as the principal reason why the petitions for such sub divisions should be favorably answered.

The salary of the minister at that period was paid partly in money and partly in provision: the former amounting to £40 was derived from the mill rents which were received from the occupants of the various mill seats upon the streams of Dover, partly as compensation for the timber which they had liberty to cut from the town lands, and partly, it would seem, as rent for use of the water power, which appears to have been retained in the ownership of the town for sometime after this period.

The "provision rate" as its name implies, was paid in provisions according to the scale of prices yearly established. This tax was annually assessed, about this period, at a penny in the pound, equivalent to five twelfths of one per cent. In the time of John Reyner, Jr., this amounted to not far form £30 more. But the payers of mill rents were often very dilatory in meeting their engagements and probably the provision was not always on hand when wanted.

The town showed its liberality, however, in appropriating £70 towards building him a house, although the former one was still standing and was in his possession.

OLD SERIES, NO. 78. JUNE 8, 1852.

DOVER TOWN RECORDS.

1658.

The fragment of a volume of Town Records which we numbered II. in article 27 is composed of nine leaves, (commencing with page 13) partly filled with records which are crossed as if copied into other books. Some of the entries we find so copied, but the larger part do not appear elsewhere. We shall print the whole distinguishing with a star those which are crossed.

* At a publick Towne metting held the 5:2 mo (58, orders for the Debety for the Genarall Cort:—

That he shall not, with his Consent pas anie ackt Conserning the infrenginge our prueleges Cons.rning Costomes or Reuer Trade or anie priveledges that formerly we haue enioyed, but shall enter his dissent Against all such ackts as shall, or may infringe our preuleges, and that he shall bring (home) all such laws are made at this Cort.

Same date. * It is agreed by ye Selectmen together with ye Towne that twenty pounds per. annum shall be yearly raysed for the Mayntenance of a Schoolmaster in the Towne of Douer:—

That is to say for the teachinge of all the children within the Towneship of Douer. the said Schole Master hauinge the preveleges of all Strangers out of the Towneship. The sd Master also teach to read, write, cast a Compt, and Latine, as the parents shall require.

* At a metting of the Selectmen the 21:2 mo (58. Granted unto Tho: Terner and will Hilton lebertie to Gather three score and ten loed of pine knotes to Be gathered upen the comenes, upon the Neck, betwine Oyster Riuer and Back Riuer, prouided theay Come not into anie menes grantes and in Consederation heirof, the afoersayed Tho: and William haue Ingaeged To pay unto Tho: Caney three pounds tenn shillings betwine tue date heireof and the 29th of September.

* John Bickford Credetor £2-7-10 and his Rate payd.

* Granted unto William Williams, Juner, a small tract of land lieing Botweine Mathew Willyames his loett, and the loett of will willyames not intrenceinge upon anie former grants, and likiwise to leue a suefetient Cartway.

* At a meitting of the Selectmen and Comeshener 26th :2 mo (58.

It is agrede apon that the Rate yt was last maed for the Cleareing the Towne debts shall foertwith to be leued and gathered in by the Constabells, or whom Selectmen shall deput.

2 ly That if in Case it doeth apeir that the 40th wich is to be payd for the agreiment with the owners be maed apeier to belong to the proprieters of the marshes, although it now be paid by the hole Towne, that then the proprieters of the marshes shall pay the sayd £40 back agayne to the Towne.

3ly That we do make Choice of left Hall and Robert Burnum to put up a petetion to the next Cort at Porchmouth for thear soelcution Conserninge the Mills not being Raeted and other veseble estates Conserning the mills.

4ly If anie of the Inhabitants do justly find themselues to be ouer rated they may Repaier to the present Sellecktmen, or anie three of them apon Juste Case theay shall haue Relese, and likiwise if it be found that anie of our Inhabetantes Be not Rated a Cording to thear Reall and usebelle states as theay waer at the makinge of the Rate theay are to be Brought into the Rate nowe; and that the persons home this order Conserneth shall apeir at Douer at left Hall his house apon the 10 day of May at 9 of the Clocke in the Morning.

Then follows this entry by a later hand:—

"October the 22:1722, Then Perrused this Book."

After the above—

*At a metinge of the Sellecktmen the 26th mo (58.—We the Sellecktmen doe approiate and ay out for the use of the Towne parsell or groue of Pines, trees lieinge and beinge on the north west sied of the let ll Bay half a mile or thearabout from a Crecke Comauly Called the Long Creck Bounded apon the Soeth by Tho Willey his grant.

*John Bickford, Tho ffootman, John Daues apoynted to lay out the hie wayes for Oyster Riuer, and the hundred ackers of land granted to the Inhabetants of the Poynt for the cutting of wood.

*Left Ralphf Hall, Tho. Leighton, John Dam, Apoynted to lay out the hiewayes for Douer Neck.

*Granted Richard Bray 20 acres of upland at the head of his lot, not intrenching apon anie former grants.

* At A Publicke Towne miettinge holden the 10th of 11th mo (58.

—Certain matters were transacted the records of which are printed under the year 1658, in No. 31. There are only verbal differences in the two records, except that the following was included in the leaves from which we are now copying—

*At ye sam tim uoted yt the former order Conserning Running ye line at ye head of our Towneship, giuen by order of ye Towne to Corprall ffurber, Peter Coffen, is uoted nulled, and new (men) chosen.

Richard Huberd, Henrey Browne, Patrick Jameson, Edward Earwin, Walter Jackson, James Merry, Tho Doutey, James Eare, James Medellton, these all Reciued as inhabetants.

* At the sam tim appointed:—

Elder Nutter, Tho: Leighton, John Dam, will Storey, left Hall to lay out and Bound the 20 acre lots ouer Back Riuer according to the former grants.

James (illegitle) lot is excepted.

OLD SERIES. NO. 79, JUNE 13, 1852.

DOVER TOWN RECORDS.

1658.

By The Selecktmen 11:11:58.

Thomas Welley chosen to krep the ordenary untell the Court at Oyster Riuer. In Regard to John Bickford his laying the ordenary downe, that the place should not be destituted of Entertainment for Strangers and the supply of the place, we the afoersayd Selecktmen doe order that Tho Welley shall kepe the ordenerary, and that John Bickford shall not kepe selling ether wine or beir or ainy other thing as an ordenary.

Tho: Caney Tho Leighton Ralph Hall
Roberd Burnum Tho: ffootman

* At a meetinge of the neighbourhood of Douer Neck, Cocheche & Bioody Pointe the 21th day of 12 Mo: (58.

NOTE BY DR. QUINT.—The vote was passed regarding furnishing the meeting house on Dover Neck, buying a bell, etc., which is printed in No. 31. It is succeeded by the following

* At the same time voted that Elder Nutter is to Joyne Assistance with the three prudentiall Men now in beinge upon the said Notice of Douer or the makinge of a Rate to discharge the foersaid work about the Meeting House.

* At the same time uoted that Elder Nutter, Leiftenant Pomfrett & Lieftenant Hall haue power to hier men and see to the manageinge of the foersaid worke.

—Then follows a list of the freemen which was printed in the Genealogical Register, Vol. 4, after which it is recorded that:—

* Henry Tebetes was chosen Constabell the 5th 2 mo. 1653.

Mr. Valtine Hill chosen Debety for the Generall Corte the 27th first mo (58. Mr. Hill chosen to set with the Magestrates in Corte.

Capt. Walldern, Mr. Hill, Wm, Pomfrett chosen to end small cases.

—The next page upon which is any record contains a list of those who have taken "ye oath," which was also printed in the Gen. Reg. Vol. 4.

* Voted that the Townsmen, now in being, haue power to call Capt. wallden to a Compt for all the writings that Conserne the Towne preueleges and else. These Townsmen haue the same power the former had. (No date).

* At a Towne mettinge holden the 19th 2 mo (58:—Granted to will ffollet 3 Acceres of upland at Belleameyes Bank, more one hundred acres of upland at the south west sied of Belleameyes Banke freshett, not intrenching apon aney former sayells, or grants.

* At the same time granted to Joseph Asten liberty to fall tember apon the Coman, as other inhabetants, for his saw mill at Little John's Creake; twenty shillings abated f his Rent per yeir.

* At a publicke Towne mettinge holden the 5:2 mo: (58

Orders for the Debety for the Generall Cort That he shall not with his Consent pass anie ackt conserninge the infringinge our preueleges Conserning Customes, or Riuer Traed, or anie preueleges that formerly we haue enioyed, but shall enter his dissent Against all such ackts as shall, or may, infringe our preucleges, and that he shall bring all such leaues (home) as are made at this Cort.

—At the same time was passed a vote relating to a school master, which was printed in No. 31.

This is the last of the fragment; in copying from it we have taken the records in the order of pages, whether they entered upside down, or right side up, or crossways, of each of which style of records specimens may be found in this fragment.

147

OLD SERIES, NO. 80. JUNE 22, 1852.

DOVER TOWN RECORDS.

1661 to 1689.

A book of twenty-two leaves, containing tax lists beginning in 1661, with records of other kinds interspersed. The names of the persons taxed have already been published in the Gen. Reg. and their repetition is needless; we therefore shall publish only the regular records with an occasional glance at the tax lists.

The first tax list is that of Oyster River, and embraces the names of 5 persons, besides the estate of "mr hill" and "the Johnson," This rate is dated "4:9 mo. in the year (61.''

The second rate was made in 1662 and was "over the whole town," and was made to pay Mr. Rayner the amount due him as salary and was to be paid in provisions at the following rate:—

"Beffe at 3d ½ per lb; Pork at 4½; Wheat at 6s per bushell; Malt at 6s; Barley at 6s; Pease at 5s."

At this time twenty eight tax payers resided on Dover Neck, who were blessed with the labors of "Thomas Umphries stiller;" twenty nine lived at Cochecho and were taxed there, as was also "William ffollet Bellemes banke" and "Quamhegon mill;" on Bloody Point were twelve taxpayers and at Oyster River forty-two.

In the tax list for 1663 the only matter worthy of notice is the proof of the antiquity of the local name "Toll End."

From the tax list of 1664 it appears that "white oak pipe staues" were worth £4 per thousand; "pine bords" 45s per thousand; "hoggshead staues" 5s per thousand; "red oke pipe staues," £3 per thousand; "barrell staues," 40s per thousand.

After the tax lists of 1665, 1666, 1667, 1668, appears the following records.

At A Publicke Towne Metting this 5 March 1667, uoted and Granted A Confermance of ye former Grant of 60 Ackers of land Granted about Neamey's child, as also tenn Ackers more of marsh and Swampe, all ye 70 Ackers Granted to mr Petter Coffin Considerance of what he hath paid to John Church to take ye child and to kepe her from all Charge to ye Towne of Douer from this Daye and forward until she be 20 yeare old, and yᵉ Selectmen Are herby Impowered to make a full End About this Agrement with mr. Petter Coffin and Indent rs for ye child to John Church. Voted,

At ye same time ordered or Voted:—

Whereas Severall Inconueniences Doe Arise by Reson of some Defeculty, or Errors in our Towne Grants and lying out more land ye Retarne thereof, and Recording ye Same, for ye Preuenting all Diferance Amongst our Naighbors and settling Peace Amongst us, haue Apoynted these persons A Comitty, Capt. Richard Walderae, Left Peter Coffin, William Furber, William ffollet, Roberd Burnum, to take all our Records and Examine them and to Agree with some man to write and Draw out of our Towne Booke what they see Necessary to be Done About ye Premises and to make Returne of what they shall find may tend to aney Difering About ye Same; and also to Draw up sumthing which they consuue may conduce to Peace; and what Charge is Expended to place to ye Towne account and make Returne to ye Towne what they Doe. 5. March 1667-8, noted Generall.

Same Date. noted that Capt. Waldern' Ensign John Daues, Mr Job Clemants, Are hereby Impowered to treat with the present Sellecktmen of Porchmouth about the Running the line from Caneyes Creek and hogstie Cone and what they shall, and Doe agree apon, shall be for a finall Determination, or end of that Diffrence, and stand as a Towne Ackt as if the town were all Present to Ackt the Same.

—The tax list for 1669 is missing. From that for 1670 we learn that prices of beef, pork, &c. remained firm, and also that butter was 4d per pound; cheese 6d; Indian corn 4s per bushel. After the list of 1671, '72 are the following records.

A Publick Towne Meeting Appoynted to be held at ye meeting house Apon Douer Neck, 28 October 1689, the Inhabetants of sd Towne being met noted the sd meeting to be Legall.

At A Publicke Towne meeting held at Douer this 28th October 1689.

Voted yt Lieut Jno Tuttle is choosen to open ye uotes at Portsmouth for ye choyce of A Comisioner by ye majority of votes for ye joyning with ye Commissioners of ye United Collories and to joyne with ye Rest of ye Representatiues of this Prouince. In giuing such Instructions to ye set Commissioners as shall be thought meet for ye Vigrous Maingment of ye present war.

—This was a few months after the destruction of Cochecho, an account of which will be printed hereafter, embracing several interesting original letters relative to the affair, which have never yet been published.

New Hampshire, Douer Neck
ln New England.

At a publick Towne Metting held Jan. 1, 1689:—Whereas, this Prouince since ye last Renolution in ye Massachusetts Collony haue been destitute of Gouernment, and has hetherto waighted theyr Majties order, for a settlement thereof, wi h not yett Ariuing and seeing A present necessity of falling into sume Method of Gouernment In order to our defence Against ye Common enemy.

Voted, Nemine Contradicent.

That six persons be chosen in this town as Commissioners to meet with ye Commissioners of ye other towns of ye Prouince to Confer about and Resolue upon A method of Gouernment within this Prouince, and what ye sd Commissioners of ye whole Prouince, or ye Mayn Part ot them shall conclude upon and Agree as to ye settlement of Gouernment among us, Wee, ye Inhabitants of Douer, shall hold as Good & Vallued to all Intents and purposes, hereby obliging ourselues to yeald all Redey obeudiants thereunto untill theyre Majties order sball arriue for ye settlement of Gouernment ouer us.

The persons chosen by ye Majority of votes of ye Towne are Capt. Jon Woodman: Capt Jno Gerrish: Liften Jno. Tuttle: Mr Tho Edgerly: Liften Jno Roberts· Mr. Nicolas Follet.

This Passed A clear vote In ye Towne metting In Douer Meetting house this first Day of January, 1689.

OLD SERIES, NO. 81, JULY 6, 1852.

DOVER TOWN RECORDS.

1689.

Jan. 30, 1689, A Publick Towne Metting held in Douer.

A vote past in sd Towne metting that it was legally called and the (Moderator) to preside.

January ye 30th 1689. At a Publicke Towne metting. Then Chosen for the Counsall for the Prouince Capt John Gerrish and Capt. John Wood man to be of the Councell, and also the votes given in destintly for the President, Secretary and Treshurer of the Prouince and separately seled up in papers to be opened by the Comishoners of the Prouince.

—The records then return to 1671.

At A meitting of the sellecktmen the 19th first month (71. Ordred That all the Constabells of the Towne of Douer are by the 15th day of April next to make up thear a Counts with the Treserrer of the Towne by that day for all the old areares of what is wanting. Behind of old Rates in thear hands; but in Case theay should Neckleckt heir In theay may Expeckt to hier from the sellecktmen forthwith whoe will deal with them a Cording to lawe.

At the Same time ordred by the sellecktmen that the Tresurrer of the Towne doe take care forwith to repaer the Cluse about the metting house and place it to the Townes a Count.

Whereas there was an order maed that left Coffin should prouide Ameneshen for the Towne a Cording to Lawe deliuered by him unto Capt. Wallderne the 22th of the first month Too barralles of Powder and mach.

At a metting of the freemen holden ye 16th of ye secont month 1672 Capt Richard Wallderne and left Peter Coffin Chosen Debeties for the Towne of Douer to goe to the Generarll Court for this yeir.

At A metting of the Sellecktmen the 28th 2th mo 1671 baue ordred to sease all the timber that is found Cutt ard Cared to the water sied wich is ether at Oyster Riuer or at the Foer Riuer, or Carrid to Bellamies Bank mill, wich timber did belonge to the Grant of letell Johns Cricke grant, and likewise to giue notice to all persons that haue Cutt the timber, or lay Clame to it that theay appier befoer us to giue thear answer theartoo on the 15th day of the 3th month, next, at the house of William Pomfret on Douer Necke, and then yt the Constabell and Phellip Cromwell are heirby impowered to giue notice to all the persons aboue Expressed and likewise the selling the timber, and this shall be your warrant.

Dated this 28th day of April 1671.

At the same time ordred that whereas thear are seueral Rates in the hands of seuerall Constabells of maney yeires standing and seueral Rents and other Reuenewes behind whereby the Towne is much Ingerd and lieth in debt to seuerall persons, and for the gathering of all the old Areares Boeth of Rates and Rents and for paying the sd soms to seuerall persons According to the Sellecktmens orders, Doe Apoynt Phellep Cromwell, and Impower him to demand and Receiue the same and to dispose the pay acording to order, and this shall be his warrant. Dated this 28th April, 1671.

Witness our hands as Sellecktmen of Doner.

   Capt Richard Wallderne
   William ffurber
   John Danes
     his
   Thomas (T. R.) Roberts
     mark.

At A meitting of the freemen 15th of 3th mo (71, legally assembled, Capt. Richard Waldrne and left Richard Croocke of boston Chosen Debeties for the Generall Courte for this howell yeir.

At the same time Capt Richard Walderne chosen Comeshener for Associates and for Treseurer.

Deacon John Hall the 13th of Janewary, 71, Agried with all By the Sellockmen to Sweep the meetting house and Rirg the Bell for ore holl yeir from the date aboue writen, and to haue for that sarnes the Some of £3.

At A Publike Towne meitting held the 13th of ye first mo (70 (71.

Ordred that the first Monday in March shall be A Publick Towne meitting yeirly for the Choise Sellecktmen and other towne afaires and other publick ofecers.

At A meitting of the Sellecktmen ye 16th April 1617, 71, It is ordred that Phellep Cromet shall haue lebertie to kep a ferey at lamprill riuer for passing all peopell and horse ouer the sd Riuer and shall be Alowed for Euery person 2d, and for horse and man 6d, and this ordr to stand untell the County Court take order about it.

At A Publick Towne meitting holden ye first month (71.

Sellecktmen chosen—Capt. Richard Walldern, left Petter Coffin, henrey lankster, Roberd Burnum, Antoney Nutter

Job Clemants, Comeshoner.

Constabells—William Shuckforth John Rane.

Gran Jurey.—Job Clemants, sinyer, John Bickford, sinyer, James Coffin, Richard Rowe, John Michiel.

Jurey Trialls—William ffurber Thomas Casey, Juner, Joseph ball, John Chirch. Kinsin John Daues.

Left Coffin chosen Tressuerrer for this yeir 71 (72, or untell another be chosen

At A Publick Towne meitting holden ye 13th of fitst mo 70 (71.

Seleckmen Chosen.—Capt. Walldern, Phillep Cromwell, Thomas Roherds, Juner, William ffurber, Einsin John Dau s.

Job Clemants—Comeshener.

John Winget Chosen Constabell.

Beniamen Mathewes, Constabell.

Jurey Trialls—John Gerrish, Antoney Nutter, Roberd Euenes, Tho. Roherds, Phellep Cromwell, John Woodman, Stephen Jones

Gran Jurey—Roberd Burnum, John hill, John foste, John hamm, Henery lanskter, Deacon Hall, Deacon Dam.

left Coffin, Antoney Nutter, Roberd Burnum, John Roherds, these fower Chosen seruaires for the high wayes and to take their orders from the Sellecktmen now in being.

At ye same time

For the better Incoredgement of Mr. John Rayner in the minestry the Town doth order the forty pounds of mill Rents with the peney Rate to be payd to him yeirly soe longe as he Conteneweth merister of the Towne of Douer. This peney Rate to be leuied on the Inhabetants of Douer Neck Cochecho, Bloody Poynt and Oyster Riuer a Cording to thear Artekels.

Voted ye 13th, 1 mo.

And ferder It is ordred that the Sellecktmen have power to treat with Mr. John Rayner and to agree with him for his bi'lding for himself Conuenient houesing, not Exsieding seventy pounds. Voted ye 13th, 1 mo.

Voted, it is this day ordred that twenty Ackers of swamp land to be layd out for the use of the minestrey, nor to be allenated without the Consent of Euerie Inhabetant; the place is the Great Swamp apon the Neck of land to be bounded and laid out by the Sellecktmen.

—This is the last record in the book from which we have been last copying.

OLD SERIES, NO 82. JULY 13, 1852.

DOVER TOWN RECORDS.

1686.

We commence today the publication of the fragment marked VI. in our description of the Dover Records. This fragment of 30 leaves contains records of various votes commencing Sept. 13, 1686 and ending in 1689; others commencing in 1702 and ending in 1716, (these being records mainly of annual elections,) and others of various dates scattered through the book, placed apparently wherever the Clerk found a vacancy.

Upon the top of the first page is an entry in a different hand writing from that which follows: viz:—

John Tutle chosen pound keeper.

The first regular record is the following which is hardly legible in the original and moreover is partly destroyed as are many other records in the book.

September 13 1686. At a generall Towne meitting then held of the freemen of the towne of Douer at the meeting houæe.

It was then acted that Sellecktmen which are Chosen for this yeir be Impowered to laye out the high wayes for his Majesties & Cuntries use in the Conuenient — — the sard selectmen shall see fitt, or any three of them in all parts of the township of Douer and make their return to the Clarke within 28 daies.

It is alsoe voted and agreed on at the same meeting to — — —& pay the Minister of Douer Sixtie pounds, to the Minister of Oyster Riuer fortie pounds for the yeir ensuing from the tenth day of June last, to be paid them in such Species and prices — — — —

  Pine bords at 20 s p
  Beife at 2d
  Wheate at 5s p bushel
  Pease at 4s p bushel
  Barlie at 3s p bush
  Indian (corn) at 3s p bush

Oyster Riuer to pay thear parte according to what was formerlie agreed on to thear minister.

This ackt was past by a Jenerall vote in a Towne meitting

  Approved by us
    Peter — — —
    Jno. — — —

Rich Otis s n'r doth decent from this vote.

James Nute Jun'r doth Decent from this vote.

Sept. 13 1686.

In Jenerall Towne meeting brought from the other side — — — — —

It is alsoe ackted at the sayd meeting that Jon Euens the Towne Clarke shall haue 20s per yeir allowed him as — — — — besides his fees as long as he shall supplie the office of Towne Clarke.

Nov. 2d 1686. Then Laid out the high wayes according to order bearing date Sept. 23, 1686.

That is to say from Willies Creeke unto Oyster Riuer falls and — — — — to Bellimans bainke falls, neare along as the path goes fouer Rods in breadth as it was formerly laid out by John Bickford and John Woodman by a Towne order.

Wee haue bin Uppon the high wayes betwixt Oyster Riuer and Lamper Riuer & have laid out the high wayes as the path goes to be fouer Rod wide from Oyster Riuer to Lamper Riuer falls, or about fortie Rods aboue it as may be most conuenient.

We haue laid out a high way from Oyster Riuer falls — — — ffreshet, or ouer the riuer into the Commons by — — — nalls of fouer Rod wide neare as the path now goes.

      John Woodman
      Thomas Edgerlie
      Nicholas Harris
      John Winget
      John Tuttle
        Sellectmen.

A a Jenerall Towne meeting of the free holders of Douer held at Douer on the 18th day of Oct. 1686.

Then voted William Partredge to be Constabell for Douer. And then voted Samuel Burnum to be Constabell for Oyster Riuer. And then voted Thomas Tibbits to be Constabell for Douer.

It is alsoe voted at the aforesaid towne meeting that all the books of former Records & all Papers of transactions which doe Concerne the affaers of the towneship of Douer, that the said books and papers be deliuered into the hands of the Selectmen; & the said Selectmen to take good notice of the said books and papers; and soe to deliuer them to John Euens, the Towne Clarke to be by him kept for the use of the Towne of Douer; this is past by vote.

—The next entry in the book is dated 31 May 173— and its printing is therefore deferred until that year is reached in order.

At a Generall Towne meeting of the freeholders of Douer held at the Meeting house at Douer Neck 27 April 1687.

It is voted that Zacharias ffield & John Knight be surveyors of the highwayes between Jonsons Creek & Bellemans bank Riuer for the year ensuing.

At the same meeting it is voted that the Selectmen have power to make a Rate to the valew of ffifteen pounds upon the Inhabitants of the Township of Douer for the releef of the Widd Dorothy Roberts & to be Implyed for her use, to be paid in such species as followeth,(and for the use of the poor) as:

Wheat 5s; Indian Corne 3s, pease 4s; porke at 3d per pound; beiff at 2d the pound.

It is alsoe ordered and voted at the meeting afoer said that Lieut. John Roberts is Chosen a Culler of Staues, and Nicholas Harriss & John Daues of Oyster Riuer to be Cullers alsoe, or either of them for the Township of Douer.

OLD SERIES, NO. 83. JULY 20, 1852.

DOVER TOWN RECORDS.

1687.

At a jeneral towne Meeting held at the Meeting house on Douer Neck of all the freeholders & Inhabitants of the towne of Douer the Tenth day of August, 1687.

It was then voted that Mr. Job Clemens was to be Commissioner According to the order directed to the Constables from Mr. John Usshier, Esq., Treasurer. At the said town Meeting

John Winget, John Tuttell, William ffurber, Junr, Thomas Cheslie, Senr, John Woodman Chosen Selectmen.

At the same towne meeting

Thomas Peaine, Joseph Kent Chosen Constables.

May 19, 1688. Majr Richard Waldern did this day take a revew of the bounds of the four hundred acres of Land which he purchased of the Towneship of Douer, at Six score acres to the hundred upon consideration of building the Meeting House. (And there was in Compaynie) Mr. John Gerrish & Mr. Joseph Gerrish, Robert Euans, Senr, Zacharie ffieild, John Euens. The bounds are as followeth according to the Returne) from a oake on the brow of the hill on the South side of the mill dam of bellemans banke (south, south west) 260 rods to a pitch pinne on the plains marked R. W., near the house which Thomas Drew, Junr, hath erected, (the which pine is cutt dowre) but there are stones laid on the stump of the said pine and from that (North north east) to bellimans bank Riuer to a hemlock marked R. W. and soe the said Riuer bounding the said land on the north to the mill dam.

May 21, 1688. At a Jenerall Towne meeting of the free holders of the Towne of Douer, held at the meeting house of Douer for the chewsing of town officers.

John Tuttle, Thomas Cheslie, William ffurber, Tristram Coffin, Thomas Edgerlie, James Huckins, Chosen to be Selectmen.

At the same meeting.

Mr. Job Clements Chosen Comisioner.

And John Church, Thomas Drew, Senr, Thomas Roberts, Junr, Chosen Constables.

1689 March 18. Then laid out at the head of William Beards Creek A Certaine parcell of Land there on the west side of the Creeke for the Conuenience of a landing place and high wayes; the bounds of the said land and high wayes are as followeth:—

At the Creeke 8 rods wide & from thence following North & by West unto the North side of John Woodmans land North Nor west unto the King his high waye & from the head of the said Woodman his land ffourcty rods North east unto A Certaine p cell of Rocks there, Where wee haue appointed & Laid out two high wayes of 4 rods wide; an Runs ouer the Brooke neare North west, & then north north east & by east unto the high waye unto Newtowne: and from the foresaid Rocks Another high waye runs North west & by north on the North side of the aforesaid John Woodman his land into the Commons.

These landing places and high wayes were laid out by vertue of a order from the townsmen bearing date Sept. 24, 1688,

By us—John Woodman
James Huckins.

Jno Tuttle
Will ffurber
Tristram Coffin
Thomas Edgerlie
Tho Cheslie
James Huckins
Selectmen.

1689.—At a Jenerall towne meeting of the ffreeholders of — —

—The records of that time close with the preceding sentence. During that disastrous year probably no more meetings were held, nor for several years succeeding. The estates of those who perished on the 28th of June were not settled untill four or five years at least had passed; and such a check was given to the prosperity of the settlers that meetings were neither necessary nor expedient. The next records to be found after that period are those relating to land titles, commencing in the spring of 1693-4. These will be examined at the proper time. At present we shall continue printing the remaining records in the leaves before us.

The first of these is a record dated 13 May, 1673, and reads as follows:

Whereas there was a contrauersie betweene Ensigne John Daues of Oyster Riuer & Joseph Smith of the Same place About som Land, wee whose names are under written, who are appointed by the Towne, haue vewed the Land and bounded Ensigne Daues his Land as followeth:—beginning at a white oake tree at stonny brooke Coue near Joseph Smith his fence which mark was owned by William Roberts, who was one that first laid out booth the Lotts, and Runn upon a north north east line at the head of ye Lott, which Line took off Eighteen Rods of his Lott, haue left sufficient of Land to make good Joseph Smith his Lott; & all the East side of Ensigne Daues his Land is to stand as it was first Laid out and the West Corner att the head is bounded by a Red oake tree.

William Wentworth
John ☒ (mark) Bickford
John ☒ (mark) Heard

OLD SERIES, NO. 84, JULY 27, 1852.

DOVER TOWNE RECORDS.

1701.

May 20th, 1701.

By the Comette Chosen by freeholders of the town of Douer for suruaing and laying out Conuenant High wayes in the Seuerall Parts of this town.

First ordred that the high way to the spring neare the backe Coue bee Left open from the way that Leads to the back coue to the afouer sd Spring and soe clear thro in to the Swamp by the head of ye Creek as in Antient times.

June the 6th 1701.

By the Comittee Chosen by the freeholders of the Towne of Douer for ordering and stateing high wayes for the Conuenience of the Inhabitants within this Township of Douer.

Voted that a Conuenient high way of fouer Rods wide be laid out from the Mast Path to the Cheslie mill, on Oyster Riuer and ouer the Freshett and to Runn by Edward Smalls and Clear threw to the old waye formerly Laid out into the Comons by Edward Smalls and soe to Lamperels second falls, maintaining the same breadth

Test. Wm. ffurber, Clark of sd Comitte.

The aboue grant voated and Confearmed in Publick meeting ye 27th of October, 1701

Test, Jno Tuttle, Towe Clark.

Whereas as Complaint hauing been made to us the subscribers hereof concerning A highway at bellemies bank which sd waye Edward Euens had stopped up and fenced in, and wee being upon the place and veved the ground haue ordered and stated the sd high waye for the Conueniance of his Majts subjects as followeth viz.—

From a stake in the ground by the Kings Road that leads to Cochecho and soe Eastward as the Stakes are sett in sd Euens his field till it comes to sd Euens his fence and from thence as the way now goes a Cross the Neck till it Comes to the Landing place, opposite to fresh Creek its mouth with ten Rods Square of Land for a Landing place, and also a high waye of fower Rods wide as the way goes from huctlebary Hill to the watering gutt and so A Long as the path now goes ouer the hill to the westward of Joseph Robbarts his house, till it Comes to the Cross way that Leads to billemies banck; and doo order these wayes to lie open for the Publick use of his Majestie his subjects, for Euer; and that the Towne Clark doo Record the Same.

Witness our hands this 25th day of April Ano dom 1699.

    John Woodman
    Job Clements
     Justises of Peace.

   James Daues
   Ezekiel Wentworth
   Nathaniel Hill
     Selectmen.

June ye 6th 1701. By the Comitte Chosen by the ffreeholders of the Towne of Douer for ordering and stateing highwayes for the Conueniency of the Inhabitants within this Towneship of Douer:—

Voted that all that land at ye head of Oyster Riuer that was formerlie made use for a Landing place be left open as formerly for the Conueniency of the people for Transportation of goods, and that the Mast Path from Oyster Riuer falls to Utmost bounds of the Towneship as it now goes be Stated a highway fower Rods wide.

Test William ffurber, Clark.

The aboue grant voted and Confirmed in publick Towne meeting ye 27th October 1701.

Test. Jno Tuttle, Towne Clark.

June ye 6th 1701, by the Comitte Chosen by the freeholders of the Towne of Douer for ordering and Stateing highwayes for the Conueniency of the Inhabitants within this Towneship of Douer.

That a highway be stated from mr Harrison, his house, to broad Coue freshett and so to the highway from Bloody Poynt Road to Stephens, his poynt, on broad Coue, where it shall be thought most fitt

Test by ye Comitte
   Will ffurber, Clark.

The aboue mentioned highwayes voted and Confirmed in publick Towne meeting 27 of October 1701.

Test, Jno Tuttle, Towne Clark.

June ye 11th 1701, by ye Comitte Chosen by ye freeholders of the Towne of douer for ordeiing and stateing highwaies for the Conueniency of the Inhabitants within this Towneship of douer Voated that a highway be Laid out from Fox poynt to the way that leads from Bloody poynt Road to broad Coue where it may be most conuenient.

Test Wm. ffurber, Clark of sd Comitte.

The aboue gract voted in a Publick Towne meeting ye 27th of October 1701.

Test Jno Tuttle, Town Clark.

Whereas wee the subscribers hereof being chosen with others to be a Comitte to suruaie and Lay out highwaies in the seueral parts of the Towne of douer for the Conueniency of the Inhabitants, and being desired by Lt. James Daues and Joseph Meader to lay out a highway from the heads of their Lottes to the King his road, thoro fair Road according to a vote in generall Towne meeting, ye 27th October 1701, and being Apon the place or ground with John Gerrish, Esqr., one of his Majts Justes of Peace, haue laid out as followeth Viz—from two stumps at or near the aforesaid Dauis and Meader, their Land, at about fower Rods distance, and to Rune about 12 Rods north westerly, then turning moer westerly keeping the hey land till it comes to a hemlock tree in the norwest Corner of Mathew Williams, his forty acre grant, in the Tenure of Joseph Smith, and so to the old path that leads to Abraham Clarks and so Clear Thoro to the king his thorofair Road as the way now goes, to be fower Rods wide.

Giuen under our hands this 29th of October 1701.

    Jno Tuttle
    Will ffurber
    Tristram Heard

Of the Comitte
Jno Gerrish, Just, Pc.

OLD SERIES, NO. 85, Aug. 10, 1852.

DOVER TOWN RECORDS.

Douer Aprill ye 6th, 1702.

Being Leagally Called is held A Publick Towne meeting at the meeting house on Douer Neck.

ffirst, Ltt James Dauis chosen modderator.

2ly Samnell Tebbets, Jno Meade, Jonr., Joseph Jones, Zekiell Wentworth, Jno Downing chosen selectmen.

3ly Thomas Tebbetts, Ltt will ffurber, asssessors.

4ly Sargt Thomas Robbarts, Sargt Jeremiah burnum, Ralph Hall, a Comitte to call the Sellectmen to account.

5ly Silvanus Nock, Samll Emerson Jonathan Woodman, Thomas Leighton, Constables.

6ly Will Lam, Ephraim Wentworth, Philip Cheslie, Abraham Benick Benjamin Bickford, suruaiers of heywaies

7ly Jno Church, A Lott Laier in the Room of Samll Heard.

8ly Tho Pots, Jos Dauis, Jethro Furber, Cullers of staues, these officers still continnoo.

9ly mr Job Clements, Timothy Robbison, Sarchers and Sealers of Leather. These officers still continnoo.

At ye aboue sd meeting voated that Mr. Richard Waldron shall haue a grant of — — — —fall of Cochecha Riuer, commonly called Haies fall, with due regard to the falls below, ye sd Waldron puying thirty shillings p year therefor the Rent to begin ye 24 day of June 1704.

At ye aboue sd meeting voated that mr Waldron haue six pounds Abatement for Timbr to com ———of ye Lower fall.

Wee the subscribers hereof being chosen by the ffreeholders of the Town of Douer for stateing and laying out Conuenient hey waies in the seuerall parts of the Towne haue according to a Voat of the Towne laid out a way of 2 Rods wide from the Road that Leads from Little Johns Creek threw to ye watering gutt way and bounded as followeth beginning at white pine tree marked H.X by Little Johns Creek Road from thence Easterly on the south side of the gully at the South west Corner of Thomas White-Louse his land and Runs bearing ye same bredth to a maple Tree in the northwest Corner of Board his lot leauing the sd Tree on the north and a pine on the south at 2 Rods distance markt H. Each of them and so on the south side of A Pine marked H. on the watering gut way, then threw the South East Corner of Samuell Tebbets his fence to the said watering gut way.

februrary ye 20, 1702-3.
   Jno Tuttle
   Thos Tebbets
   Ezekiel Wentworth
   Tristram Heard
    of the Committee.
   Jno Meader
   Samll Tebbets
      Selectmen.

——nday ye fifth day of Aprill 1703 being Lawfully called is held a Public Towne meeting at the meeting house on Douer Neck for chosing Towne officers and other affairs proper to be acted on such day.

Mr Richard Waldron chosen Moderator

Thomas Robberts, Senr, Tobias Hanson, Joseph Jones, ffrancis Mathes, Jno Dam Junr Chosen selectmen (The names of Joseph Jones and ffrancis Mathes are crossed and the "renounce serves" are added.)

Ltt will ffurber, John harrison, senr, assessers.

Job Clements—Jones, Ezekiell wentworth A Comitte to examine ye selectmes accompts.

Abraham Nute, Thomas Hanson, senr, John willey, Jno downing Constables.

Thomas whitbous for douer neck, will dam for ye bellemans bank, Benjamin Wentworth for Cochecha; will Jackson from Oyster Riuer to bellemans bank; samson dou from Lamprell Riuer to Oyster Riuer.——Jno Nutter Survaiers of heywaies.

At the aboue sd meeting Voated that ye Comitte formerly chosen for stating and Laying out Conueanient heywaies in seuerall pts of the Towne be still continued for Laying out those that are all Reddy Stated and upon Reasonable Requests are Impoiored to Lay them out in Euery pt of ye Towne, and shall be paid for theyr seruis out of ye Towne Treasuery.

Att a Publick Towne meeting held at ye meeting house on Douer Neck the 5th day of April 1703.

Whereas the Reauerant Mr. John Pike has seuerall Times signified To this Towne that he was minded to moue to Salisbary and by the Remoual of his family has giuen us just Cause to Expect the same, in answer thereto Voated that Captt Jno Gerrish, Mr Rich Waldron, and Capt Jno Tuttle are hereby chosen and invested with full power from the Towne to Joyne with the present selectmen to make up accounts with ye sd Mr Pike and orders for the payment of such arrears as is yet behinde and allsoe to treat with him in order to his further Continuance amongst us and take his answer and make Report to the towne thereof. Passed in the meeting aboue sd.

Jno Tuttle, Towne Clark.

Att a Publick Towne meeting held at ye meeting house on Douer Neck ye 5th of April 1702.

Voated that whereas the mill Rent was formerly Sequestered and sett apart for the use of ye ministry of ye Towne of Douer to be applied two thirds of sd Rents to the use and support of the minister at Douer Neck, and one third part of sd Rents too be applyed to the Use and Support of the minister at Oyster Riuer. Voated that the sd Rents be still Continued and applyed to the Uses aforesaid and not otherwaies disposed of. Past.

We the subscribers hereof have Laid out the highway from oyster bed to oyster Riuer, through the Country road to the durty gutt by Abraham Clark his house, beginning at ye Usuall wadeing place att oyster bed at a Pine tree on the East and white oak on the West at 4 Rods distance markt H each of them, from thence North Easterly to the west side of ffollet his Rocky hill, aboue ffollet his barn, and then it Runes on the East side of the next Rocky hill by James Bunker his barn and from thence to the Cartway at the head of Bunker Creek and so a Long threw as the old way formerly Lay till it comes to a Rock at the Southwest Corner of Nath Lamos his Land, from thence as it is markt till it comes to the bridge at durty gutt, to Lye 4 Rods wide Clear threw, and allso a highway from that leads from Ltt Dauis his house, beginning att a white oak marked H I B and 4 Rods in bredth a Long by the head of Joseph Bunker his land from thence to the King's thorro fair Road.

Laid out this 9th of Aprill 1703 by us
Jno Tuttle
Jere Burnum
James Dauis
of the Comitte.

OLD SERIES, No. 86, AUG. 24, 1852.

DOVER TOWN RECORDS.

1703.

Att a Publick Towne meeting held at ye meeting house on Douer Neck ye 17 day of May 1703.

Then Chosen Richard Waldron moderator.

Samuel Cheslie, Robert Huckins selectmen in the Roome of James Jones and ffrancis Mathes who refused to serue on that seruis.

Jno Haise Constable.

We the subscribers hereof being chosen by the ffreeholders of the Towne of Douer to suruaie and Lay out Conuenient heywaies in ye seuerall pts of ye Towneship of Douer and being ordered by the selectmen of the town to Lay out the Landing place at ye head of Oyster Riuer and heywaie into the woods according to a vote of the Towne of ye 27th of October

1701, which accordingly wee haue done as followeth:—Begioning att high water mark by George Chesley his fence, so from high water mark by ye fence eight rods northwesterly or as the sd fence now layes, which is near thereabouts, from thence west on be south twenty nine Rods to the Top of the hill by Bartholomew Stephenson his house, from thence nor-norwest to a pitch pine markt H standing on the East side of ye mast path which Leads from Oyster Riuer falls, from thence west to the fence on the west side of the aforesaid path, then southward as ye sd fence now goes tell it comes to the fresh Riuer aboue the saw-mill, all which Land thus Laid out to Lay open for a Public Landing Place and alsoe the mast path is Laid out fower Rods in bredth as ye sd path now lyeth or Leadeth from ye sd Landing place to the outmost of our Towne bounds for a publick heywaie. Wee haue alsoe Laid out a highway from ye Chesley mill at Oyster Riuer to the mast path to be fower Rods in bredth a Long as ye path now Ledeth from sd mill to ye mast path as may appear by fower trees markt H and standing at ye fower Corners of ye sd way.

This Lauding place and high waies aboue mentioned Laid out according to order this 14 of June 1703.

By us, John Tuttle
Jetem Burnum
Tristram Heard
James Dauis
of ye Comitte

Present Jno Woodman Esq., justs Pc.
We ye subscribers here of being upon ye ground, or spott att ye Second fall of ye Riuer Cochecho haue Laid a Conuenient Logg hill accomadable to the mill Erected on sd fall as followeth, beginning att ye Taill of sd mill from thence flue Rods by ye Riuer side, from thence west line Ten Rods, from thence on a nor-west and be west line to sd Riuer, all which sd Land between ye aboue sd Line and sd Riuer we haue Laid out for acomadation to ye fall at Tole End, and alsoe haue Renewed ye bounds of ye Antiant Cartway that leads from sd fall into ye swamp on A West an south poynt to an oak and a pine about flue Rods disstante markt H Each of them, from thence to Run as ye way Now goes at the same bredth till it meet with the other way that Leads from broad Turne into sd swamp.

March ye 4th 1703-4

Jno Tuttle, Senr
James Dauis
Thomas Tebbets
Ezekiel Wentworth

Tuesday ye 25 April 1704 being Legally Called is held A Publick Towne meeting at ye meeting house on Douer Neck.

ffirst, Captt Jno Gerrish Chosen moderator

2ly Sargent Thomas Robbarts, Mr. Will ffrost, ffrancis Mathes, Captt Samll Chesley, mr Jno Damm, Chosen Selectmen.

3ly Ltt Wm. ffurber, Mr. Robert Huckins, Chosen assessors:

4ly Mr. Job Clements, Ens Stephen Jones, Mr. Ezekiel Wentworth, a Comitte to examine ye Selectmens account.

5ly Jno Tuttle, Junr, Henry Nock, John Pinder, Josep Rollings Constables

6ly The suruaiers Last year Chosen for ye Repairing highwaies be Continued to pursue ye same office ye year ensueing

7lly For as much as it is found by Experience that it is very greuious to ye Selectmen to be Exposed to the great Trouble of going from house to house to take an Inventory in order to make an assossment for Redressing greuience for ye time to Come. Voated that ye Selectmens orders posted in Ye publick meeting places in ye Respective pts of this Towne shall be accounted sufficient notis to bring their accts to the Selectmen in their Repective places. These that shall neglect so to do, it shall be accounted Lawfull for ye Selectmen to Rate by -- -- -- and doome.--

Past.

April 30, 1705.

Prsuant to An order Recd from Jno Pickering Speaker of Ye House of Representatiues Importing and giuing Notis to ye ffreeholders of ye Towne of douer to meet together at their usual place for Choyse of 2 princable men to Jcyn with ye Representatiues to debate and determine matters Relating to mr Allen his claims; the ffreeholders being met prsuant thereto on the day aboue sd haue Chosen Capt Gerrish moderator, Mr. Richard Waldron, Esqr., Captt John Tuttle to Joyn with ye Representatiues of sd Province and then Invested with full power to hear, debate and determine matters relating to mr Allen his claim.

Monday ye 27th day of May Ano dom 1705.

Being Legally called is held a Publick Towne Meeting at ye meeting house, Douer Neck, for ye Choyce of Towne officers

ffirst Chosen Capt Jno Gerrish, Esqr. modderator

2ly Samll Emerson, Rich Waldron, Esqr, Capt Jno Knight, Joseph Meader Jonathan Woodman Selectmen.

3ly Ezekiell Wentworth, Joseph Jones, Assessors.

4ly Lt Thomas Tebbets, Tristram Heard and Joseph Smith, A Comitte --

5ly Ralph Hall, Jno Hoyt, George Chesley Jno Waldron, Constables.

6ly Thomas Robbarts, senr, Joseph Tibbets george Ricords (Ricker) Philip Chesley, Jno doo, Jno Dam, Junr, Suruaiers of highwaies.

7ly Captt. Jno Tuttle, Chosen Towne Treasurer

OLD SERIES, NO. 87, SEPT. 7, 1852.

DOVER TOWN RECORDS.

Monday ye 22th of Aprill 1706, being Legally Called is held a Publick Towne meeting at ye meeting house on Douer Neck.

ffirst Captt Gerrish moderator.

2ly Thomas Robbarts, sen, Mr Richard Waldron, Joseph Jones, Capt Samll Cheslee, Capt Knight Chosen selectmen.

3ly Capt James Dauis, Sargt Thomas Robarts, Junr, Chosen assessors.

4ly Ltt Thomas Tebbets, Mr Jos Smith, Mr Tristram Heard, A Comitte--

5ly Jno Meader, Junr, Jno Wheeler, Sargt Thos downes, Hatevell Nutter Constables.

6ly Capt Knight, Jos Robarts, Tobias Hanson, Jno Leighton, nath Pittman Abraham Bennet, Suruaires of high waies.

7ly The Comitte furmerly Chosen and Apoynted by ye Town to Lay out ye high waies be still Continued and Impowered to Lay out ye waies in ye seuerall Parts of ye Towne, according to grants.

8ly Voated that the distance is as followeth for the suruaiers to keep in Repair; ye Inhabitants of Douer Neck from Hiltons Poynt to Abraham Clark his house; ye Inhabitants of ye northside of Oyster Riuer, from Oyster Riuer falls to Lamprill Riuer falls: Cochecha, from Cochecha to Salmon Falls.

9ly Suruaiers of fences for Douer Neck, Sargt Thomas Robarts, senr, Mr. Samll Emerson; Bloody Poynt, Capt Knight, Captt Hill; Cochecha Richard Waldron, Esq., Ezekiell Wentworth; oyster Riuer Captt Cheslee, mr Jos Jones.

10ly Joseph Dauis, Edward Euens Cooper, Cullers of staues.

Monday ye 5th May 1707 being Legally called is held a Publick Towne meeting att ye meeting house on Douer Neck for ye Choyse of Towne officers and wtt other occasions may occur for ye benefitt of ye Towne.

ffirst Captt Jno Gerrish, Chosen moderator

2ly Thomas Robarts, senr, Richard Waldron, Esq., Captt Jno Knight, Mr Joseph Jones, Sargt ffrancis Mathes, Selectmen.

3ly Captt James Dauis, Sargt Thomas Robarts, Junr, assessors.

4ly Mr Joseph Smith, mr Tristram Heard, Sargt Samll Tibbets, Comitte

5ly Pomfret Dam, Jno Ham, Junr, mr will Jackson, Junr, Jno downing, Constables.

6ly Captt Knight, Jos Robarts, Tobias Hanson, Jno Leighton, Nath Pittman Suruaiers of high waies.

7ly Ens Stephen Jones Lott Layer.

Att a Publick Towne meeting held at ye meeting house on Douer Neck ye 17 of November 1707.

ffirst Captt Jno Gerrish Chosen moderater.

2ly Captt Jno Tuttle chosen assembly man

3ly Voated that mr Pike haue fifteen Pounds P Annum added to his sallery of £65 and one third thereof be pd in money, other ⅔ ds in Prouition, as formerly, and that ye mill Rents as they shall be Reced shall be a Part of his said sallery.

Pasd in ye meeting aboue sd.
Pasd in ye meeting aboue sd.

Att a Publick Towne meeting held in ye meeting house on Douer Neck ye 10th day of May 1708.

ffirst Captt Gerrish Esq., Chosen moderater.

Thomas Robarts senr, Richard Waldron Esq , Captt John Knight. Mr. ffrancis Mathes, Mr Joseph Jones chosen Selectmen.

2 ly Captt James Dauis, Mr. Joseph Robbarts, assessors.

3ly Mr Joseph Smith, Mr. Samll Tebbets, Mr Tristram Heard a Comittee.

4ly Richard Pinkham, Henery Nutter, william ffrost, John Amoler, Constables.

5ly mr Philip Chesley, Mr Ezekiell Wentworth, Lt John Downing, Captt John Tuttle chosen to Joyne with ye Selectmen as a Comitte to take care for the repairing or builuing such bridge or bridges this year as may be thought necessary for ye Passing over such Riuer or Riuers as belong to ye Towne Pticularly and — — — over Cochecha Riuer and derect orders and Regulate ye same, accorôing as sd Comitte or ye Major part of them — — — -- — shall think fitt, defraying ye charge thereof out of ye Towne stock to be Raised by Ye selecmen or as the other Towne Charge.

6ly Captt Knight, Tobias Hanson, John Leighton, Thomas wille, Rich Randall, John Cromitt, Survaiers of high waies.

7ly Ye present Selectmen survaiers of fences.

Att a Publick Towne meeting held at ye meeting house on Douer Neck ye 10th day of May 1708.

Voated that whereas Seuerall Persons make Scruples about Paying their mill Rents according to their Conditions made with ye Towne, that John Tuttle ye present Treasurer of ye Towne for the time being is hereby impowered to use all Lawfull meanes by actions or other waies about Recouering ye same.

Past in ye meeting aboue sd.

Monday 9th of May 1709 being Leagally called is held a Publick Towne meeting in ye meeting house on Douer Neck; then chosen.

ffirst Captt Gerrish Esq. moŋerator

2ly Sargt Tho Robards, senr, Richard Waldron Esqr, mr Joseph Jones, mr ffrancis Mathes, Capt John Knight, Selectmen.

3ly Capt James Dauis, Ltt Thomas Tebbets, Assessors.

4ly mr Joseph Smith, Capt Tristram Heard Sargt Samll Tebbets Comitte

5ly Petter Varney, Tho Hanson, Junr, Ens. Jno Knight, mr Philip Chesley, Constables.

6ly Capt Jno Knight, Jno Leighton, Tho Willey, Rich Randle, Jno Crumet, Jno Wentworth Survaiers of highwaies.

7ly Sargtt Meader, Sargtt Woodman Joseph Robards, Jno Bickford, Ephraim Wentworth, Henry Tebets, benja bickford, Jno Ham Junr, viewers of fences.

Where as Complaint has been made to the Towne that the pound on Douer Neck is not sufficient to answer the seueral pts of ye Towne it is ordered that the Inhabitants, or any part of them Liveing at Cochecha, oyster Riuer and Bloody Poynt shall haue Liberty of building a Pound in all or Each the sd places at their owne Cost and Charge & that ye same be holden and accounted the Towne pound or pounds & ye keepers thereof and his fees from time to time be appoynted, ordered and directed by ye Selectmen of ye Towne for ye time being, Voated

Whereas there was fower pole wide Reserued by ye Lott Laiers that Laid out the Range of Lotts betweeen St Albands and Quamphegan abutting on Nechewanicke Riuer to be Laid at ye same bredth a Cross ye sd Lotts where yo Towne should see most meet and Conuenient for a highway for her Majts good subjects that should haue occasion to pass and Repass, that we the subscribers being chosen and appoynted by ye Towne of douer to be a Comitte to survaie and Lay out Publick highwaies in ye seuerall parts of ye Towne for yᵉ Conueniency of ye Inhabitants; pursuant thereto we haue Laid out ye aforesd way a Cross the aforesd Rang of Lotts in manner following:

Beginning at ye East End of ye old way that Leads from the head of fresh Creek to St. Albans Cove, and from that end of that way it Runs north ward downe ye hill and over ye fresbet that vents into St. Albans Coue at ye old wadeing place here and from thence Runes a Long between Lt Hatevell Robarts his house and barn and so on ye west side of Sligo garrison and Runes a Long between Silvanus Nock his house and barn keeping ye same Course as ye way now lies till it Comes to that way that Riurs downe on ye north side of Thomas Cannie his Lott to ye old wade ing place opposite to Chadburn his mill hen Trending Eastward downe ye sd way till it Comes to ye mouth of a little Creek on ye South side of James Stackpole his house,then it Trends north- ward ouer ye sd Creek and Runes a Long between ye Riuer and Stackpole his fence till it Comes to a stake about 16 Rods to the Southward of ye north East Corner thereof, then Trending Westward between two hills and to the Westward of Joseph Abbott his fence till it Comes to that way that Comes downe out of ye woods to Quamphegan falls on ye north- ern side of ye aforesd Joseph Abbott his fence and then Trending Eastward downe ye sd aforesd way till it Comes to ye usual watering place at ye taill of Quamphegan mill on ye west side of ye Riuer; ye aboue sd high way thus Laid out and bounded ye 12th day of Octob r 1709 by ye susbcriters

    Thomas Tibbets
    Tristram Heard
    Ezekiell Wentworth
     Of ye Comitte

OLD SERIES, NO. 88. SEPT. 14, 1852.

BIOGRAPHICAL SKETCHES.

CAPTAIN THOMAS WIGGANS, modernized in Wiggins, has already been alluded to as the first gentleman who en- joyed the honors and emoluments per- taining to the office of Governor of the Colony at Dover Neck. Those days, when Capt. Wiggans ruled, were the Golden Age of Dover's history, when Colonists and Indians lived together in peace. The Governor and his subjects improved the condition of the country by hiring Indians to kill the bears and wolves, leaving their descendants to kill the In- dians.

Captain Thomas was here in 1631, be- ing sent over by the proprietors of the territory; he soon returned to England to secure colonists to enlarge and improve the plantation;he came here again in the fall of 1633, having prevailed upon "some men of good estates and of some account for religion" to come with him. He granted lots to the new comers on Dover Neck, where they built "a com- pact town." They laid out "High street" immediately, which remains to the present time as it was first located. Parallel with this, on the west side, about a third of the way to the river was "Low" street; these were connected by cross streets, called "Lanes", one of which was "Dirty Lane" and led to the landing on Bellamy River at Back Cove. There were other side streets that led to the Fore River on the East.

They immediately built a meeting house of logs, of course, being Chris- tians; soon they built a tannery being barefooted; a brewery being Englishmen; a whipping post and stocks being Puritans, and later a jail being the sons of Adam. A part of this record and considerable more was found recorded on William Walderne's papers, which were handed down in the family. Whether Capt. Wiggans, or his predecessors the Hiltons, paid the right owners for the land has never been accurately ascertained. On the whole we think they did.

The supplanting of Governor Wiggans in office by Mr. George Burdet has been already noticed in these papers and affords a melancholy instance of the instatility of human affairs. He bore his reverse of fortune manfully, however, and kept at work steadily.

Capt. Wiggans is said to have resided at Hampton in 1645. If so he returned to Dover. He was here in 1650 when he received a grant of the mill privilege at Cochecho second falls and timber to correspond; and in company with Elder Starbuck he built mills about 1651. He had also grants of land near his mill.

The records as published in the Exeter News-Letter say that he was elected Assistant from 1650 to 1654, and as Assistant had a seat on the bench of Common Pleas. He died about 1667 He had sons Thomas and Andrew; the latter was taxed in Dover in 1659, and married a daughter of Simon Bradstreet, and granddaughter of Governor Thomas Dudley.

WILLIAM POMFRET (Pumfret, Pomfrett) was of Dover in 1639 when he bought premises on Dover Neck, of Thomas Johnson who moved to Oyster River about that time. He had lot number 12 west of Back River in 1642, and in 1643 had a grant of land at the extreme point between Cochecho and Newichawaunock Rivers. He was elected Town Clerk 9, 7 mo. 1647 and continued to hold that office till about 1680; he was Selectman at different periods; rejoiced in the title of Lieutenant and held various town offices and stations of honor, trusts, importance and profit. He owned a saw-mill at Bellamy, two-thirds of which he sold to William Follet and Philip Lewis 16, 5 mo 1651, for four pounds. On 26 March 1679, he gave land to his grandson Pomfret Whitehouse.

The Lieutenant was an educated man, and was well to do in the world. He posessed a large porperty for those days and paid a very respectable tax. Like many other substantial citizens he was occasionally the object of calumny. For example, James Nute once said Lieutenant Pomfret was a "deceiptful man and had a deceptful heart," but James Nute was promptly admonished for thus abusing a man in authority, and apparently reformed. The Lieutenant was Town Clerk for more than thirty years. One year the Town elected another Clerk, but the Court promptly refused to administer the oath of office, hence the Lieutenant held on. He was a good Clerk and wrote a good hand till his hand grew tremulous with age and another took his pen.

He died 7 August 1680. No sons can be heard of, but he had two daughters; Elizabeth who married Thomas Whitehouse, and Martha who married William Dam.

THOMAS MILLET, according to tradition, came from England to Cape Ann with his father when fourteen years of age, that he had a brother John, but no sisters; but the fact that their were

Millets there at a much earlier period renders the tradition of doubtful authority. Thomas came from Cape Ann to Dover while a young man, and unmarried. For the greater part of his life he was engaged in ship building. A grandson says that he settled first at Oyster River and built there one ship; but perceiving that he could find better convenience at Dover Neck he removed to that place; he purchased considerable land, most of it from the Hilton family, 9 June 1721, part of which was on Dover Neck and part at Tole End. He resided at Dover Neck during the remainder of his life dwelling on the premises where Calvin Coleman now (1852) lives. The Henderson farm was a part of his property, being purchased by him of Captain Beard.

Captain Millet was a man of property and character. As to his public life he was a Selectman of Dover in 1732-4-8, '40-50, 52-5. He was Moderator of Towne Meetings 1730 32-4-8, '40, 44-49, 53, 55. He was Representative of Dover in 1731, 33, 39, 44, 49, 52, 55, and probably in other years of which no record was made. He was also Judge S. C. 1740, 42. He died 1763.

Capt. Millet married —— Bunker of Durham and had thirteen children, of whom seven died young, six of diphtheria those who lived to maturity were; a son who went to England and died there of small pox, Abigail b 1723, married 16 Oct. 1750, Col. John Wentworth; they had eight children and she died 15 July 1767; Hannah who married a Hambleton of Berwick; Lydia, b. 1734, married Lieut. John Smith of Luberland; they had 9 children and she died 4 March 1821; Susan married Capt. Stephen Jones; and Elizabeth who married Howard Henderson and had seven children, and died Nov. 1813.

HOWARD HENDERSON, father to the one just mentioned came to Dover not far from 1720; settled near the lower falls of Bellamy River. Tradition says that in early life he was a sailor, and that he was present at the memorable capture of Gibralter by the English 24 July 1704. He died in 1772 at the age of 100 years.

He married a Roberts of Dover and they had children;—Howard b. 1718; Richmond who moved to Rochester.

HOWARD, son of the first Howard married as has been stated, Elizabeth daughter of Thomas Millet. He was a shipmaster and ship builder, living near Bloody Point Ferry, which he run. He died Nov. 1791. His children were:—

BENJAMIN, who married and left no children; he was lost at sea during the Revolution.

STEPHEN, who died in Dover unmarried.

DANIEL who married and left children Howard of New York, Henry of Baltimore, William of New Orleans, and others.

LOVE who married Silvanus Tripe.

BETSEY who married a Hatch.

Thomas, b. 25 October 1771, and now (1852) a hearty and vigorous man.

OLD SERIES, NO. 89. 21 SEPT. 1852.

THE QUAKERS OR FRIENDS IN DOVER.

In 1662 some travelling Quakers came to Dover and were treated with a severity which has been greatly blamed. To enable us to judge of this matter impartially, it is necessary to notice the circumstances under which the laws were enacted, and the character of the punished.

The sect originated in the north of England about the year 1644, at a time when men's minds were in a feverish state of excitement inflamed with a zeal to reform Church and State, morbidly religious, and suddenly freed from the bonds which had long repressed free thought and free speech. George Fox, the founder of the system of faith, was a contemplative and profoundly pious man, but, we think, visionary and constitutionally hypochondriacal. Meditations on divine things produced in him a diseased state of mind, though he firmly grasped glorious truths, which the belief of neither churchmen nor dissenters could comprehend. His thoughts found no response in their hearts and he met with no sympathy.

He was led to question the christianity of those who ridiculed his most cherished belief, and who only stared at his peculiar views The theory of the "Inner Light," one of the most divine, if true, that man ever advanced, they thought was caused by and led to licentiousness: while in fact that complete upheaving of the foundations of belief which attended the English Revolution of 1640, necessitated a return to simpler and more correct systems. Amid what we consider erroneous in the writings of Fox, there gleams forth many a beautiful ray of religious truth; and, with many faults of conduct, we behold many more instances of apostolic devotion. Had George Fox been a philosopher in name, as he was in reality, he would have been a follower of Descartes; but being a theologian, he became the leader of the "People called Quakers."

The theory of the "Inner Light" was bitterly opposed by Catholic, Protestant and Puritan. Yet it arose from that now acknowledged truth, that the standard of upright conduct lies in the man's own heart. It is a wonderful fact, yet not unparalleled in the history of doctrines, that one form of this, the essential theory of Quakerism, so bitterly opposed at that time, should now be so universally adopted even in the systems of Theological Professors. It was opposed by the Romanist, for it strikes at the very root of his system, in its form of the right of private judgment. Equally did it demolish the claims of a church which differed from the last named mainly in the fact that Rome and London were so far apart. The Puritan hated it, because his doctrine snatched infalibility from the Pope only to give it to the Synod.

We can easily see that such a doctrine would be violently opposed, and not without some pretense of fairness, when we consider how liable it is to abuse. To transfer the standard of action entirely to one's own consciousness would suffice were all men honest; but to allow the performance of every deed which a man asserted the "Inner Light" dictated, were totally subversive of order and government. We see its results most plainly in the conduct of the frenzied fanatic whose impiety could not long shelter itself under the guise of Quakerism. Our Quaker Friends themselves have been forced to give suitable officers the power of "judging whether the Ministry be sound," that is, of submitting the Inner Light of one man to the scrutiny of three or four other inner lights, and hereby preventing extravagancies, which roused the moral sense of the community against their actors.

The character of George Fox was not the character of many of his immediate followers. The enticing nature of this favorite doctrine drew crowds of visionary enthusiasts, who delighted to advance their crude thoughts and fantastic notions under the assumed authority of divine guidance. They claimed the name of "Friends," but they were not entitled to wear it. It were difficult to trace any resemblance between the Ranter of that time and the man of peace, who is now only remarkable for the quietness of his guarded demeanor, and whose precision of language is often time so elaborate as to be painful. Nor do we now see the proselyting spirit which sent one fair missionary to Rome to convert the Pope, and another to Constantinople to make a Quaker of the Grand Turk.

It is needless to relate the silly actions of men disowned by their nominal associates, or the wicked deeds which brought the name of Quaker into contempt. They were not really chargeable upon Quakerism; their authors were not acknowleged as Quakers by the reflecting and sober part of the sect. But they claimed full communion hence brought on the whole society an odium which it was hard to remove, an odium the more deserved inasmuch as some Quaker writers justify and applaud the most disgusting indecencies.

The reputation of these Ranters reached New England and filled its inhabitants with consternation. What if they should come to disturb them in their chosen refuge. As if gifted with knowledge that they were not wanted, the Ranters came to Massachusetts, and in the course of their stay fully justified the character which had preceded them. They were at first sent out of the Colony, but this was of no use for they came back immediately. A law was passed banishing them from the jurisdiction, with the penalty of losing their ears if they returned.

This only brought them in greater numbers, for it held out to them the glory of persecution, a glory which men earnestly love. Another law made the penalty of a second return death.

Why was this severity used? The Puritan regarded himself as chosen of God for a great work, that of founding a Christian Commonwealth. He had for that purpose gone to a remote part of the world, purchased land far from civilized man, and fondly trusted that he might educate his children away from the contaminations of the old world. Had he not a right to exclude all who differed from him? There was wilderness enough for others; the boundless continent was before them; why should they envy the Puritan's dearly bought share? So be excluded, peaceably but firmly, all who troubled him. Vain hope! The world's history might have taught him the impossibility of its ever being realized.

But were the Ranters dangerous to community? The records of these times tell us that men and women marched through the streets denouncing "woe upon all the inhabitants of the land;" they proclaimed that Governors and Judges were trees that cumbered the ground and must be cut down; in the house of worship they blasphemed with words against a "carnal Christ;" one man considered himself directed of God to imitate the faith of Abraham, and was in the act of sacrificing his son when the cries of the lad brought him aid. Nor were they content with such exhibitions; they went farther, and two women re-enacted the famed legend of Godiva of Coventry, though without her excuse Such conduct should have sent them to the mad house rather than to jail. "Bismillah!" said the Sultan, reverently taking his pipe from his mouth, "the woman is crazy!" and she was treated with that espect which is always paid to the insane or inspired, which is all the same thing in Turkey. Would not our ancestors have done better to imitate this example? It seems evident that some were partially insane; doubtless the cruel treatment to which they were subjected increased their frenzy. But had they not been so, an undiscriminating law was unjust; violations of public order were properly punished; but Quakerism as a system of doctrines was out of their jurisdiction. Moreover some, indeed many, who suffered were sane God-fearing men whose blood still cries out against the persecutions of these the Quakers of later years are the successors. An besides the impolicy and injustice of maltreating these persons, though there might be ome show of propriety in excluding them from Puritan Massachusetts this reason would not apply to New Hampshire; our "fishing and trading" ancestors were by no means Puritans.

With this necessary explanation of the character of these persecuted persons, and recalling the fact that Dover was then subject to the laws of Massachusetts, we turn to the consideration of the treatment which they encountered here.

OLD SERIES, NO. 90.   SEPT. 28, 1852.

THE PEOPLE CALLED QUAKERS.

The following accounts of the coming of Quakers to Dover are taken from George Bishop's "New England judged by the Spirit of the Lord" the first part of which was published in 1661 and the second in 1667, the whole being republished in 1702-3. The reader must keep in mind the fact that the narrative is written by a man who was too deeply interested in the events to be an impartial historian. He says:

"In the year 1662 Mary Tomkins and Alice Ambrose, who came from Old England, and George Preston and Edward Wharton of Salem aforesaid, came to Pascataqua River, and, passing up, landed at the town aforesaid (Dover;) whither to go it was with them from the Lord; where they had a good opportunity in the Inn with the people that resorted to them; who reasoned with them concerning their Faith and Hope which to the people being made manifest, some to the Thuth thereof confessed; others not being able to gainsay the Truth, ran to Rayner their Priest and told him that such a people were come to town; and that they had discoursed with them about their Religion and were not able to contradict what they said, and therefore desired him to come forth and help them. "Or else" said they "we are like to be run on ground."

At this the Priest chafed and fretted and asked the people "why they came amongst them?" To which they answered, "Sir, it is so that we have been amongst them and if you come not forth to help up we are on ground," and said the Priest's wife, "which do you like best, my husband or the Quakers?" Said one of them "we shall tell you that after your husband hath been with them."

Whereupon in came Rayner in a fretting and forward manner, saying "what came ye here for, seeing the Laws of the Country are against such as you?"

"What hast thou against us?" replied Mary Tomkins. "You deny Magistrates," said the Priest, "and Ministers and the Churches of Christ." "Thou sayest so," replied Mary. "And you deny the Three Persons in the Trinity," said the Priest. To which Mary answered, "take notice, People, the Man falsely accuseth us; for Godly Magistrates and the Ministers of Christ we own, and the Church of Christ we own, and that there are Three that bear Record in Heaven, which three are the Father, Word and Spirit, that we own; but for the three Persons in the Trinity, that is for thee to prove."

"I will prove three Persons in the Trinity" said the Priest. "Thou sayest so" said George Preston, "but prove it by the Scriptures". "Yes" replied Rayner, "by that I will prove it where it is said 'and he is the express image of his Father's Person," "But" said one, that is falsely translated." "Yea, it is" replied a learned man for in the Greek it is not person but susbtance." "But" said the Priest, it is Person, and so there is one Person." "Thou sayest so" said George, "but prove thy other Two if thou canst." Said the Priest, "there are three Somethings," and so in a rage flung away, calling to his people at the window to go away from amongst them; bu Mary soon after got after him and spake to him to come back and not leave his people amongst them he called wolves; but away packt the Priest; whereupon she said unto the People, "Is not this the hireling that flies and leaves the flock?"

So Truth came over them all and there was great sorrow for the Lord and many were Convinced of the Truth that day. And notwithstanding the terror of your wicked Laws many waxed bold and invited them to their homes and they had at that time a great and good meeting amongst them, and the Power of the Lord reached them that day

Having had this good Service at that time at Dover, for the Lord, they passed away into the Province of Mayne, being invited to Major Shapleigh's."

If Parson Raynor had "written a book" he would have presented a different view of this theological discussion. The account of his "fretting" was very evidently drawn from Bishop's imagination; it is totally opposed to all other accounts of Mr Raynor's character.

But the Quakers did not remain long in Maine for —"towards winter it came into the hearts of Alice Ambrose, Mary

Tomkins and Ann Coleman to go and visit the seed of God amongst them that had reached the Truth in Pascataqua River, where they were not long, but a flood of persecution arose, by the instigation of the Priest who caused them to be apprehended by virtue of your Cart-Law; and order was made to whip and pass them away as followeth:—

'To the Constabels of Dover, Hampton, Salisbury, Newbury, Rowley, Ipswich, Winham, Linn, Boston, Roxbury, Dedham, and until these vagabond Quakers are out of this jurisdiction:—

You, and every one of you, are required, in the King's Majesty's name, to take these vagabond Quakers Anna Coleman, Mary Tomkins and Alice Ambrose, and make them fast to the carts tail, and drawing the cart through your several towns, to whip them upon their naked backs not exceeding ten stripes a piece on each of them in each town; and so to convey them from Constable to Constable till they are out of this jurisdiction, as you will answer it at your peril; and this shall be your warrant

Per me Richard Walderne.
At Dover, dated Dec. 22, 1662."

"A cruel warrant through eleven townships by name and whatsoever else were in that Jurisdiction to whip three tender women, and one of them little and crooked, with ten stripes a piece at each Place, in the bitter cold weather, in such a length of ground, near 80 miles, enough to have beaten their flesh raw and their Bones. Oh the Mercies of the Wicked, how are they cruelties! The Devil certainly bore through that warrant (and as men used to say) Top and Top gallant, no interruption."

"Your warrant was through these Towns, ten stripes a piece, enough to sink down any Man whom God did not uphold; but this out runs the Law in the Constables, as the Proverb is; there is eleven named, which according to the rate of ten in a place, is one hundred and ten a piece, laid on so as, if it were possible, the knots might kiss the Bones every stroke. And yet this was not enough; if any more towns through them they must go. From whom sprung this unreasonable Warrant and who influenced all this? And through whose instigation were they apprehended? And who drew the Warrant? Omne malum saith the proverb, incipit a Sacerdote; that is, All evil begins from the Priest; or from the Priest all evil hath its beginning.—

Priest Rayner aforesaid (who could not evince his own Position, but, as hath been said instead of proving three Persons in the Trinity by the Scripture said "They were three Somethings;" and so fled away, being not able to stand before the Power and Force of Truth in these Servants of the Lord, and sets on his Deputy Magistrate Waldren,* and makes him to serve his purpose; and turns his Clerk too rather than fail and draws the Warrant as indeed it carries with it the face of the Priest.

By reason of whom they were brought before Walden who began to tell them of your Law against Quakers. Mary Tomkins replied "so there was a Law

---

*"This Walden keeps a Sawmill and is a log sawyer, but that day that he sentenced these women, his wife caused to have handcuffs put on."

that Daniel should not pray to his God" "Yes" said Walden, "and Daniel suffered and so shall you." (See how he appears influenced by his Priest's Spirit Mad and Blind;) and so demands Alice Ambrose her name, though he had it in the Warrant.

"My name" said she "is written in the Lamb's Book of Life." He answered "nobody here knows the Book and for this you shall suffer."

So in a very cold day your Deputy Walden caused these women to be stripped naked from the middle upward and tyed to a Cart and after a while cruelly whipped them † whilst the Priest stood and looked on and laughed at it, which some of the Friends seeing testified against for which Walden put two of them (Eliakim Wardel of Hampton and William Fourbush of Dover in the Stocks.—

Having dispatched them in this Town, and made way to carry them over the waters and through woods to another; the women denyed to go unless they had a Copy of their Warrant so your Executioner sought to set them on Horseback, but they slid off; then they endeavored to tie each to a man on Horseback; that would not do neither, nor any course they took till the Copy was given, in-somuch that the Constable ‡ professed that he was almost wearied with them. But the Copy being given them, they went with the Executioner to Hampton; and through dirt and snow at Salisbury, halfway the Leg Deep, the Constable forced them after the Cart's tayl at which he whipped them, under which cruelty and sore usage, the tender women traversing their way through all, was a hard spectacle to those who had in them anything of tenderness; but the Presence of the Lord was so with them (in the extremity of their sufferings) that they sung in the midst of them to the astonishment of their enemies."

This disgraceful sentence was executed no farther than Salisbury.

OLD SERIES, NO. 91. OCT. 12, 1852.

THE PEOPLE CALLED QUAKERS.

But these gentle dealings did not reclaim the wanderers After their release they passed a short time at Major Shapleigh's, in Kittery; but when,

—"After a little space, from Major Shapleigh's they returned again to Dover the place of their late barberous Execution and there visited their Friends who had both received and suffered with them; where being met together on the next first day of the week, after their coming together, whilst they were in Prayer, the Constabels Thomas Roberts aforesaid and his brother John, like sons

†The tender women they tyed with Ropes to the cart at Dover to be whipped, which being very cruel, James Heard asked whether those were the Cords of the Covenant."

‡"The Constable of Dover's name was Thomas Roberts, who looking pittifully the same night through his extream Toyl to bring the Servants of the Lord thither to be whipped as they had been at Dover, they were so far above his cruelty that they made some good thing for his refreshment which he took.

of Belial, having put on their old Cloaths with their aprons, on purpose to carry on their Drudgery, [taking Alice Ambrose] the one by the one Arm and the other by the other Arm, they unmercifully dragged her out of Doors, with her Face towards the snow which was knee deep, over stumps and old Trees near a Mile: in the way of which when they had wearied themselves, they commanded two others to help them and so laid her up Prisoner in a very wicked man's house, (Thomas Canny's,) which when they had done they made haste with the rest that were with them to fetch Mary Tomkins; whom as they were dragging along with her face towards the Snow, the poor Father of these two wicked Constabels, following after Lamenting and Crying "Wo that ever he was the Father of such wicked children" (From this man, Thomas Roberts, whose Labour was at an end, and who had lived in Dover thirty years and a Member of their Church above twenty years, they took his cow away which gave him and his wife a little Milk, for not coming to their worship. So thither they haled Mary Tomkins also and kept them both all night in the same house; and in the morning, it being exceedingly cold, they got into a certain Boat or Canoo or kind of Trow, hewed out of the Body of a tree which the Indians use in the water, and in it they determined to have the three women down to the harbor's mouth; and there put them in threatening that they would now so do with them that they would be troubled with them no more. Whither to go the three women were not willing they forced them down a very steep place, in deep snow and furiously they took Mary Tomkins by the arms and dragged her* on her Back over the stumps of Trees, down a very steep hill to the water side, so that she was much bruised and after was dying away; and Alice Ambrose they plucked violently into the water and kept swimming by the Canoo, being in danger of of drowning or to be frozen to death; (what acts of violence and cruelty are here! And Ann Colman they put in great danger of her life also in view of their enemies, in great hazzard; and in all probability they had destroyed them quite according as they had said viz, That they would do so now as that they would be troubled with them no more; but on a sudden a great Tempest arose and so their cruel and wicked purpose was hindered and back they had them to the House again and kept Prisoners there till Midnight and then they cruelly turned them all out of doors in the frost and snow, Alice Ambrose's cloaths being before frozen like Boards, and it was much and to no other thing could it be attributed but to the arm of the Lord that Alice especially and the rest had not been killed; such unmercifulness to their fellow creatures lodgest in the Breasts of these wicked Men who doubtless thought by these Things to have dispatched them; but the Hand of the Lord who keeps all those who wait upon him, preserved and upheld them; to whom be the glory, Amen."

Neither imprisonment, fines nor starvation could daunt these fearless disciples of the Inner Light.—Shew them a whipping post, they clung to it; a prison, they entered it; a halter, and they put their necks in it.

*"Edward Waymouth was the wicked one that dragged her. Hate Evil Nutter, a ruling Elder, was present, stirring up the Constables to do this thing for which no warrant had they as ever could be known or did appear; for, procuring none, they turned them out at Midnight as is related."

Others, fascinated by the glory of persecution, came to the place of its affliction:

"George Preston, Edward Wharton, Mary Tompkins, Alice Ambrose, alias Gray, having been at Dover (Neck) * * * * passed from hence over the water to a place called Oyster River, where on the first day of the week, the women went to Priest Hull's place of worship; who standing before the Old Man, he began to be troubled; and having spoken something against women's preaching he was confounded and knew not well what to say; whereupon Mary standing up and declaring the truth to the people, John Hill in his wrath thrust her down from the place where she stood, with his own hands and the Priest pinched her arms, whereupon they were had out of the place of worship; but in the afternoon they had their meeting, unto which came most of the Priest's Hearers, when truth gave the Priest such a blow that day, that a little while after the Priest left his Market place and went to the Isles of Shoals, three leagues in the sea."

Another aspirant for martyrdom soon came, Elizabeth Hooton. Bishop says:

"Then at Dover for asking Priest Rayner aforesaid, a Question, she was put in the Stocks and kept in prison four days, in the cold weather, being an ancient woman, which might have cost her her life, but the Lord preserved her; Richard Walden aforesaid (whose wife, it is said, begged the office of Deputy Magistrate for him that he might mischief Friends,) being he who executed this cruelty through the instigation of the Priest, as before he had done to others of whom I have made mention; more cold storms she endured and Persecution in the service of the Truth in these Parts than she was able to express, being made a strength to Friends, and leaving the others without excuse."

She says of herself:

"I was imprisoned also at Hampton and Dover, where a wicked Constable came with a warrant and fetched away a poor old man's heifer (Thomas Roberts' probably) who had little else to maintain him, for £3 6s. fine imposed on him by a Fine of 5s. a day for not hearing their teacher, which was a horrible oppression five times worse than the Bishop's law, which is but one shilling a day for not coming to hear their Common prayer. I being present asked him "who made that warrant?" He said "the Treasurer, Peter Coffin." But he read it "in His Majesty's name;" I asked him "who was that Majesty?" He said "the King." Then said I, "in the King's name restore the poor man's heifer, for he hath made no such law." But he would not. So I went to Peter Coffin the Treasurer and cleared my conscience unto him and told him "that he had done contrary to God's law and the King's law in taking away the poor man's cow, for that the King had sent to them That their Church members should not make laws by themselves excluding others." He told me that he would take away more yet. But the Lord stopped him in that purpose.— From him I went to Richard Walden the Magistrate, to whom I said, "yesterday thou and thy wife were at a fast and to-day a poor man's cow is taken away in his Majesty's name by a warrant." I asked him if he made that warrant. He said "no." I said, "then make a warrant to fetch him again."—But he answered, "if I had a cow he would fetch her." I said it was contrary to God's law and to the King's. "Then," said he," "it is the Devil's law." I answered "then thou mayest take it home; as thou sayest it is the Devil's law so say I, for thou hast said it." Then I bid him him repeat and turn from these wicked laws and wicked actions or else God would cut them off. From him I went again to the Constable and bid him return the poor man his Cow again, for he did not as he would be done by. But he answered, "if the Magistrate commanded him to take away the man's Life, he must do it." So you may see by what law these men act in persecuting the just, as Walden said himself "it is the Devil's law." So a Company of blood thirsty men are, &c. &c."

OLD SERIES, NO. 92, OCT. 19, 1852.

THE PEOPLE CALLED QUAKERS.

The Magistrates did not visit the burden of punishment upon strangers alone; they also dealt with their own delinquents. For absence from public worship on the Sabbath the law required a fine of five shillings each day; for attending a Quaker meeting the penalty was the payment of ten shillings; for permitting a Quaker to rest in his house the hospitable criminal must pay forty shillings per hour. These penalties were now inflicted; the records of the Court tell us that William Roberts of Oyster River had been absent from public worship on twenty-eight Sabbaths; William Williams, sen., eight days; William Follet, sixteen days; James Smith fourteen days, "and one day contest to have been at a Quaker meeting;" John Goddard had been absent four days and had heard the Quakers twice; Thomas Roberts, sen., thirteen days, for which his cow was taken as has been already related; James Nute, sen., and wife and son, twenty-six days, "and for entertaining Quakers four hours in one day" he was fined £8; Humphrey Varney pleaded "non-convicted" for his absences, "unto whom the law was this day read and he admonished;" Mary Hanson had been absent thirteen days; Robert Burnum "had been to Strawberry Bank" to meeting, and explained the matter, "which showed him to the Court not to be obstinate;" Jelian Pinkham, thirteen days.

These fines were rigorously exacted, and such treatment had precisely the effect which might have been expected. The very sufferings of the Quakers had aroused the sympathy of those who probably would never have been interested in their teachings save by interest in themselves. The steadfastness with which these oppressed persons bore their afflictions did more to spread their tenets than a score of preachers. And it is worthy of notice, that the Quakers have flourished best in the very places of their sufferings, while many of the descendants of their persecutors embraced their faith. Of such were the posterity of Edward Weymouth and Thomas and John Roberts, who have earnestly upheld the faith which their fathers persecuted.

"In the year 1663 on the 4th day of the 5th month Edward Wharton aforesaid, being at Pascataqua River, and hearing of the cruelties done by your Court of Dover, was pressed in Spirit forthwith to repair to the Court where your Magistrates being assembled he cry'd aloud and said, "Wo to all oppressors and Persecutors, for the indignation of the Lord is against them. Therefore, Friends, whilst you have time prize the day of his Patience and cease to do evil and learn to do well; ye who spoil the Poor and devour the Needy, ye who lay Traps and Snares for the innocent."

"These words of advice and counsel and denunciation of Judgement against that which oppresses and persecutes the innocent, were very hard to your Court, and Thomas Wiggans aforesaid (an old bloody Professor) being in a great rage, cryed out, "Where is the Constable? Where is the Constable?" The Marshal coming they had him to the stocks and put in his legs and so held him till having consulted what to do, they had him in again, and then William Hathorne of Salem, who sat at that time Judge of the Court, demanded of him "wherefore he came thither?" who answered, "to bear my testimony for the Truth against Persecution and Violence." Whereupon the said Wiggans fell to ging ra gain, to whom Edward said, "Thomas Wiggans, Thomas Wiggans, thou shouldst not rage so; thou art old and very gray, and thou art an old Persecutor; it's time for thee to give over, for thou mayst be drawing near to thy grave." Which gave an issue to an order to whip him through three towns, ten stripes at each town."

Jeremy Tibbets Constable having received the warrant he was bid to have Edward away and tye him to the carts tail and whip him through the town. To which Edward manfully answered as he was passing from them, "Friends, I fear not the worst ye may be suffered to do unto me, neither do I seek for any favor at your hands." And to William Hathorne he said, "O William, O William, the Lord will surely visit thee."

"So to a pair of cart wheels he was tyed with a great rope about his middle and a number of people to draw them about, then the Executioner cruelly whipped him (as in the warrant) and having loosed him, told him "That he must prepare to receive the like at the next town which was about fourteen miles from thence through the woods; which being a long way for a man to travel on foot whose back was so torn already, to serve their pleasure in his own Execution, he told them he should not go unless they provided a horse for him or that they dragged him thither, whereupon your Executioner Complaining to your Court, this order according to this Copy was issued forth as followeth:"

"To the Constables of Dover or either of them:

These are to require you That whereas Edward Wharton a Vagabond Quaker hath been sentenced according to Law and at present a Horse, according to that sentence, cannot be obtained, These are in his Majesty's name to and require you to commit the said Edward to the Prison at Dover, there to remain in close Custody till the next second day of the week; and there you are to execute the said sentence according to Warrant formerly delivered unto you; hereof you are not to fail.

Dover the 4th of the 5th month 1663.
Thomas Wiggans,
William Hathorne,
Eliazer Husher."

This sentence was executed.

"At another time Thomas Newhouse, John Liddal, Edward Wharton, Jane Millard, Ann Coleman, in a first day of the week, coming to your worship house in Dover, were by Walden's Command (of whom I have formerly spoken) haled to prison, where after he had caused them to be detained almost two weeks though he confessed That for aught he Knew they might be such as were spoken of in the 11th of Hebrews, yet he must execute the Law against them, and so set them at Liberty. The people promised That the Priest Rayner should give them a fair reasoning when his worship was done; but he broke their word and packed away; and though the women followed him to his house yet he would not turn but clapt to his door, having taken out the Key and turned Anna Coleman out of the house."

NOTE BY JOHN SCALES.—At the close of the above No. 92 was the statement, "To be continued," but I have looked through the whole series of Memoranda and fail to find any further mention of "The People Called Quakers." Dr. Quint evidently intended to continue the subject but never found the time or the material to do so.

OLD SERIES, NO. 93, NOV. 9, 1852.

THE HILTONS.

EDWARD and WILLIAM HILTON were brothers and came together from London to Pascataqua in the spring of the year 1623. They had been fishmongers, and were therefore selected for the enterprise which should be supported mainly by fishing. The Company of Laconia sent them over, the magnitudes of whose designs was only equalled by the magnitude of their failure. The colonists were directed to discover mines, cultivate the vine, trade with the Indians and commence fisheries—these operations being expected to fill the pockets of the enterprising projectors without any particular trouble on their part. How many were in the first party of colonists nobody knows the only names which have come down to us being those of David Thompson, the Hiltons and Thomas Roberts; and even that the last is rightly quoted is not certain. The Hiltons settled at Dover Point.

The settlement did not advance very rapidly. Instead of pouring money into the pockets of the merchants before mentioned, it was very efficacious in drawing it out. Nor did the colonists fare much better. Nearly ten years after the commencement of the settlement the people of Dover received their principle supplies of grain from Massachusetts and Virginia and had them ground at the Boston Windmill.

In 1633 a large accession was made to the colony of which the Hiltons were the Pioneers, composed of men of very various characters. Some of them were of "good repute for religion," but the Massachusetts government regarded Edward Hilton as "the principle man in the settlement," and depended on his assistance in maintaining order. The troubles at Dover Neck were ended by the annexation of the young republic to Massachusetts, which was brought about largely by Mr. Hilton.

EDWARD HILTON was of English birth, but we can find no mention of its date, nor is it known whether he brought a wife with him; if he did he was more fortunate than most of the first settlers; if he did not he soon after obtained one. His first wife was the mother of his children, but what her maiden name was is not known; his second wife was Catherine, widow of James Treworthy of Kittery.

Mr. Hilton was the first named in the list of magistrates of Dover in 1641, but removed from Dover shortly afterward to Exeter. A large grant of land had been made to him by the authorities of the latter town on the "4th day of the 1st week of 10th month 1639", and he removed to that town previous to 1652, for in that year it was "Voted that Mr. Hilton be requested to go along with Mr. Dudley to the General Court to assist him." In 1653, another grant of about two miles square, comprising the whole village of Newfields, was made to him in regard to his charges in setting up a saw mill." Here he is supposed to have settled, and considerable part of this grant has remained to this day the property of his descendants. He died in the beginning of the year 1671; the letters of administration were granted by Capt. Richard Walderne 6 March 1671; his property was appraised at £2,304.

The children of Edward Hilton were, EDWARD; WILLIAM (a Captain who died about 1690, leaving a son Richard who administered on his estate and who married a daughter of his uncle Edward;) SAMUEL, of whom we know nothing; CHARLES of whom there is no record; a Daughter who married Christopher Palmer of Hampton; and a daughter who married Henry Moulton.

EDWARD (2) remained at Exeter. On the 7th of January, 1660, he made a large purchase of Wadononamin, the Indian Chief who was otherwise known as John Johnson; he was Sagamore of Washuck, where he dwelled; he sold this land to Hilton, as he says, as well for the love he bore to the Englishmen generally, and also especially to Edward Hilton of Pascataqua, eldest son of Edward Hilton of the same Pascataqua, Gentleman, "as for divers other reasonable causes and considerations him there to moving, voluntarily gave and granted to the said Edward all his lands of whatever nature, quality or kind soever, lying bounded between the two branches of Lampreel River, called Washucke, being about six miles, and a neck of land * * * * reserving however one half (if need be) of convenient planting land for and during his (the grantor's) natural life." This land is thought to lie in Newmarket, Epping and Lee.

His wife was Ann Dudley, who was born 16 October 1641; she was daughter of Rev. Samuel Dudley of Exeter and granddaughter of Thomas Dudley the second Governor of Massachusetts Bay; her mother was originally Mary Winthrop, daughter of John Winthrop, the first Governor. Mr. Hilton died 28 April 1699, his wife surviving him.

The children of EDWARD (2) and Ann (Dudley) Hilton were: WINTHROP b. about 1671; DUDLEY; JOSEPH b. ab. 1681; JANE who married Richard Mattoon of Newmarket; ANN who married Richard Hilton; MARY who married Joseph Hall of Exeter; SOBRIETY who married Jonathan Hilton.

COL. WINTHROP HILTON (3) son of EDWARD (2) was born about 1671. He became the leading man of the Province, and had the chief command in one or more expeditions to the Eastward. In 1706 he was appointed Judge of the Court of Common Pleas; he took his seat on the bench on the first Tuesday in December of that year and continued in office until his death. A short time before his death he was appointed a Councillor for the Province, but does not appear to have taken his seat at the Council Board.

While engaged with his men in peeling bark in that part of Exeter which is now Epping, on the 23 of June 1710, he was killed by the Indians, and was buried with the honors due to his rank and character, in his own field on the western bank of the river; the field is still owned by his descendants, and the brief inscription on his moss covered monument is still legible (1853). A Silver headed cane once owned by Col. Hilton is now (1852) in possession of Hon. John Kelley of Exeter.

His wife was Ann Wilson, who afterwards married Captain Jonathan Wadleigh of Exeter; she died 8 March 1744.

The children of COL. WINTHROP (3) and Ann (Wilson)Hilton were—JUDITH who married William Pike; ANN who married Ebenezer Pierpont of Roxbury, Mass., and had children Ebenezer, John, William, Benjamin and Ann; DEBORAH who married Samuel Thing, ELIZABETH who married John Dudley; BRIDGET who married Arthur Gilman; WINTHROP born 21 Dec. 1710.

OLD SERIES, NO. 94. NOV. 16, 1852.

THE HILTONS.

DUDLEY HILTON (3) son of Edward (2) lived in that part of Exeter which is now South Newmarket. He married Mercy, daughter of Hon. Kingsley Hall and grand daughter of Ralph Hall of Dover and Exeter. Dudley was with his brother, Col. Winthrop, when attacked by the Indians, 23 June, 1710, and was never afterwards heard of by his friend. He was probably carried into captivity, and died among the enemy. His children were, ELIZABETH wife of Christopher Robinson:) ANN (wife of Nathaniel Ladd, Jr.,) MARY b Oct. 1709, (who married Kingsley James.).

JOSEPH (3) son of Edward (2) was born about 1681, and died at the age of 84. His first wife was Hannah, daughter of Richard Jose of Portsmouth;—their only child was HANNAH. His second wife was Rebecca Adams; their children were, ISRAEL b. 10 Oct. 1717, (who went to the Southern States;) JOSEPH (was a blacksmith and went to the Carolinas;) THEODORE (of New Market, who married Mary Sinclair); DUDLEY (who married Sarah Taylor.).

RICHARD (3) son of Capt. William (2) married Ann, daughter of Edward (2), of their children were, RICHARD (whose wife was Elizabeth, and who died before his father;) BENJAMIN; SAMUEL; WILLIAM; EDWARD (who died in 1776, leaving a wife and five children,) viz: Josiah, of whose children was Col. Richard (6) of Newmarket; Edward, whose daughter Betsey, married Winthrop Hilton; Betsey (Smart;) Mary (Brackett;) Love (Pickering).

WINTHROP (4) son of Col. Winthrop (3), born 21 Dec. 1710, lived on the paternal farm, was a Colonel in the militia, and died 26 Dec. 1781. He married Martha, daughter of Joshua Weeks and widow of Chase Wiggin; she died 31 March 1769. Their children were, WINTHROP b. 7 Oct. 1737; ICHABOD b. 22 June 1740; ANN b. 19 July 1745, (who married John Burleigh of Newmarket,) and died 26 Oct. 1769, leaving an only child, Martha, b. 29 Aug. 1769, who married Col. Eben Thompson of Portsmouth.

THEODORE (4) son of Joseph (3) and grandson of Edward (2) lived in New market; he married Mary Sinclair of Stratham; they had children, COL. JOSEPH (of Deerfield, who died in 1826;) RICHARD (of Shapleigh;) WILLIAM (of Cornville;) NATHANIEL (of Portsmouth:) MARY (who married John Marston of Newmarket;) ANNA (wife of Philip Davis of Fayette, Me).

DUDLEY (4) son of Joseph (3) and grandson of Edward (2) lived also in New Market. He married Sarah Taylor; their children were, DUDLEY (of Parsonsfield, Me.;) DANIEL (of New Market;) GEORGE (of New Market;) WARD (of New Market;) NATHAN (of Deerfield;) (ANNA who married Maj. Wm. Norris of New Market.)

WINTHROP (5) son of Winthrop (4), and grandson of Col. Winthrop (3), born 2 Oct. 1737, married, 5 Sept. 1762, Sarah, daughter of Col. Joseph Smith of New Market; he was wounded by the fall of a tree in Northwood, 11 Jan. 1775, and died the next day, having children, ANDREW b. 8 Aug. 1763; WINTHROP b. 26 Sept. 1766; SARAH b. 27 Sept. 1772; —ICHABOD b 23 Nov. 1774.

ICHABOD (5) brother of Winthrop (5) last spoken of, b. 22 June 1740, married Susanna Smith, a sister of his brother Winthrop's wife; he died 25 March 1822, she died 9 Oct. 1794; their children were, SUSANNA b. 18 March 1767 (married Levi Mead of Northwood:) WINTHROP.

GEORGE (5) son of Dudley (4) and descendant of Joseph (3) and Edward) (2,) married Mary Wiggin of Stratham. Their only child, GEORGE OLIVER, resides in New Market; has been a member of the N. H. House of Representatives, and was whig candidate for Senator from District No. 2, the present year.

ANDREW (6) son of Winthrop (5) and descendant of Winthrop (4), Col. Winthrop (3) and Edward (2) born at New Market 8 Aug. 1763; he married, 25 March 1784, Deborah, daughter of Col. Samuel Gilman of New Market; she was born 5 March 1767 and died 8 Feb. 1835; he died 18 Jan. 1838. Children were, CLARISSA b. 11 Dec. 1785 (married Samuel Ham;) DEBORAH b. 17 May 1788; SARAH b. 5 June 1790 (married Samuel Langley;) SUSAN b. 4 July

1792 (married Hon. John Kelly;) ANN b. 15 Nov. 1794 (married Daniel Langley;) ELIZA b. 10 June 1787 (married John Farnham;) ANDREW b. 14 Aug. 1799, died 1 Oct. 1815; JOHN of Lynn, b. 11 Feb.1802) married Sally Clark of Lynn;) THOMAS J. b 7 May 1804 (married Elizabeth Coombs;) JOSEPH S. b. 5 Jan. 1808, died 30 March 1810; MARY J. b. 19 Dec. 1809.

WINTHROP (6) son of Winthrop (5) and descended as Andrew (6) last mentioned, born 26 Sept. 1788.—He married, in 1795, Abigail Hilton; their children were, ELIZABETH b. 22 April 1796 (married Eliphalet Dearborn of Epping;) WINTHROP S. b. 12 Sept. 1800; ABIGAIL b. Aug. 1803; MARTHA ANN b. 5 Nov. 1809; MARY JANE, b. 21 June 1812.

WINTHROP (6) son of Ichabod (5) and a descendant of Winthrop (4), Col. Winthrop (3) and Edward (2), married (1) Betsey Folsom, who died 8 March 1800; they had only JOHN F. of LYNN, who married Lydia Moore. WINTHROP (6) married (2) Theodate Jenness; he died 5 Oct. 1817; children were, ELIZABETH F.; MARY ANN; WINTHROP; FRANCIS J; SUSAN S. (married Bruce;) MARTHA W.; ANDREW J.

OLD SERIES, NO. 95, NOV. 23, 1852.

JOHN UNDERHILL.

CAPT. JOHN UNDERHILL, "Governor" of Dover in 1638, was a strange character, and deserves our notice as much for his peculiar mixture of soldier and theologian, as for his various adventures. He had been an officer in the British forces and had served with reputation in the Netherlands, in Ireland and at Cadiz, when John Winthrop, the father of the colony of Massachusetts Bay prevailed upon him to accompany the colonists of 1630. In a well founded anticipation of difficulties with the natives, it was thought that the military abilities of an experienced soldier might be serviceable in training the rough valor of the colonists into shape.

He became early a member of the First Church in Boston, being numbered 57 on their list, and was elected one of the Boston delegates to the first General Assembly, held in 1634. Winthrop speaks of him occasionally as he was performing various petty services in the ordinary routine of affairs, which was interrupted however by a visit to his friends in the Low Countries (where he had married his wife,) for which he left Boston in Nov. 1634 "in Mr. Babb's ship," and from which he had returned before January 1635-6. The difficulties with the Pequods in 1636 and 1637 gave him employment congenial to his taste; in the latter year he was sent to defend Saybrook against the Dutch and Indians, which we suppose he did, and in the same year he was a member of the Ancient and Honorable Artillery Company.

Had the Captain confined himself to the legitimate duties of his business he might have remained in good esteem, and Dover would have had one Governor the less. But he seems to have had a great deal of activity in his composition which must be exercised some way or other. The ordinary duties of instructing the citizens in the mysteries of military science, varied by an occasional chase after vagabond Indians were not sufficient.—So the subtle wit and nimble tongue of Mistress Anne Hutchinson ultimately involved him in disgrace. The disputants of the day being unable to cope with the fair theologian in argument, the only method remaining by which the truth might be sustained, was that of silencing by force the adherents of these errors to which they affixed the odious name of Antinomianism. Capt. Underhill was very much of her opinion in matters of religion, as was the great majority of the Boston Church; so when Rev. Mr. Wheelwright, a teacher of the new heresy, was adjudged guilty of sedition, &c, because of the sentiments of a certain sermon, the restless Captain, justly indignant at the outrageous decision, meddled with what he would have let alone if he had been wise. He prominently assisted in the preparation of a paper which was immediately numerously signed and presented to the Court in 1638, 1, 9, in which it was affirmed that Mr. Wheelwright was innocent, and that the Court had condemned the truth of Christ, with divers other scandalous and seditious speeches. For this offence against the dignity of the authorities, Capt. Underhill "with several others of the principal" were immediately disfranchised and deprived of all offices.. The Captain endeavored to argue the case; "he insisted much upon the liberty which all states do allow to military officers for plainness of speech, &c., and that he himself had spoken sometimes as freely to Count Nassau." but it was of no use; the Captain was obliged to submit. And to prevent all mischiefs which might be perpetrated by this race of heretics, a large number of persons of which the Captain was first on the list, were ordered by name "to deliver in at Mr. Cane's house at Boston all such guns, pistols, swords, powder, shot, and match as they shall bee owners of, or have in their custody;" and they were strictly forbidden to buy any more.

Underhill's occupation being gone he made a short visit to England, but he soon returned, intending to remove to the plantation of Mr. Wheelwright who was our neighbor at Exeter But before he went he concluded to ask the General Court for the three hundred acres of land they once promised him, and at the same time acknowledge his former errors. This the Court thought an excellent opportunity to question him about certain rash speeches he had made in the ship in which he had just come over. He had compared the Massachusetts men to the Scribes and Pharises, and likened them to Paul in the days of his persecuting principles; he had talked nonsense also about his "religious assurance" coming to this mind while he was taking a pipe, and he had labored with some success to advance his peculiarities of doctrine on ship-board. The first charge he denied but it was proved by unimpeachable testimony; as to the second, he thought that as Paul was converted while persecuting, so peculiar favor might be manifested to him while making "a moderate use of the creature called tobacco."— This plea was very unsatisfactory; and the added charges of licentiousness that followed, which, though true, were not proved, induced the Court to banish him out of their jurisdiction. So in the autumn of 1638 he came to Dover.

Soon after he had left Boston, full proof of his licentiousness came to light; the church sent to him to come and be tried, offering to procure a safe-conduct. When he refused, in which he probably acted very wisely, the Governor, by direction of the Court, wrote to Burdet, Wiggans and others of this plantation, to the effect that they should take it very ill if the Pascataqua people should favor the Massachusetts refugees. To this Burdet, the then Governor, returned an answer which for various reasons was peculiarly offensive. So the Governor wrote next to Edward Hilton, giving a full expose of the delinquencies of the Captain, and warning him against suffering Underhill's advancement. But it was too late; the letter stopped first in Underhill's hands, and besides he had already in Nov. 1638 been elected Governor in place of Burdet, who was thus served in the same manner as he treated Wiggans.

Underhill was exceedingly indignant at the contents of the letter, and he did not hesitate to express his resentment freely in private, but to the Governor of the Massachusetts he sent a very mild and penitent missive. But such was the effect of the news upon the people here, that the best men turned against him. Even Parson Knolly repented of favoring him, though he had sympathized with Underhill at first, probably because his own religious tenets had been distasteful to the theology of the stricter Puritans. Influenced partly, perhaps, by the conviction of his growing unpopularity, Underhill obtained a safe conduct and went to Boston, where, upon a lecture day (1639-40, 1, 5,) he publicly confessed the various crimes with which he had been charged, but his confession was so mixed with excuses and extenuations that it was exceedingly unsatisfactory. Nor did his after conduct show a change. Returning to Dover he attempted to conciliate certain men at Strawberry Bank, who were peculiarly zealous for the Royal authority and opposed to that of Massachusetts. But the people had become thoroughly disgusted with him, and removed him from his office. They were the more angry with him because, when by his influence the plan of union with Massachusetts in 1639 had been broken off, he had laid the blame of it, in his letters to Boston, upon the people.

But in Sept. 1640, he appears to have become really penitent, and "did openly, in a great assembly, at Boston, on a lecture day, in the Court time, and in a ruthful habit, being accustomed to take great pride in his bravery and neatness, standing upon a form, lay open with many deep sighs and abundant tears, his wicked life." Winthrop devotes a page and a half to a narration of the circumstances, but it is sufficient to say that he was freed from a punishment which he richly deserved.

For nearly two years he was without employment either in a military capacity or any other. He was not popular, notwithstanding his repentance; in Sept. 1641, happening to be in Boston, he was arrested for trial on the old charges from which he had once been released. But this manifest injustice was not suffered to proceed far; he was acquitted by acclamation."

Shortly after this, the New York government invited him to enter its service, and he visited their territory to examine the prospect. He was well inclined to accept the offer; his long service in the Netherland had given him command of the language, and his wife, who had clung to him, woman like, through good and ill, was desirous to be with the people of her own race. So returning to Boston he asked permission of the church to remove. But hearing that he had offers also from Stamford, Ct., where there was a church of the true faith, they recommended him to settle there. He submissively consented, and the church fitted him out and furnished a pinnace to convey his family and substance.

In his new position he appears to have had a new character. He was a delegate from Stamford to the General Court in 1643, and was appointed Assistant Justice. A war breaking out in that year between the Dutch and Indians, he was offered and accepted the post of commander of the former, and for nearly three years was engaged in the contests which were ended in the summer of 1646 by the severe but decisive victory at Strickland's Plain. He afterwards settled at Flushing, L. I.; he was efficient in exposing the intrigues of the Dutch Treasurer with the Indians in 1652, and offered his services to the Commissioners of the United Colonies. It may have been under their orders that he attacked Fat Neck. In 1665 he was delegate from Oyster Bay to the Assembly held at Hampstead by Governor Nicolls, and was appointed Under-Sheriff of the North Riding of Yorkshire (Queens' Co.) In 1667 the Matinecoe Indians gave him 150 acres of land, which was in his family in 1828, and very likely is there now. He is supposed to have died at Oyster Bay in 1672. His descendants have principally exchanged his warlike habiliments for the garb of the Quaker, and have been influential and respected.

We might have entered into a description of the Antinomian tenets, which caused his first difficulties, but it would not be interesting to our readers; and besides that, the fact is, we don't exactly understand them ourselves. We might draw a moral from his life also, but that the reader can do as well as we.

OLD SERIES, NO. 96. NOV. 30, 1852.

JOHN PIKE.

JOHN PIKE, ninth minister of Dover, born in Salisbury, Mass., 15 May 1645 was son of Hon. Robert Pike of Salisbury, who was for many years one of the Assistants of the Massachusetts Government, and who died 11 Dec. 1706 aged 90. Graduated at H. C. in 1675, his name stands first in the list of his class. How long or under what auspices he pursued the study of Theology does not appear; his settlement at Dover took place 31 Aug. 1681, but he says in his Journal that he "came to Dover for the work of the ministry 1 Nov. 1678."

The salary of Mr. Pike in 1686 was £60, to be paid principally in provisions. The prices current of that time ranged thus: Pine boards 20s. per M.s; pork 3d per pound; beef 2d; wheat 5s per bushel; pease 4s per bushel; barley 3s per bushel, and Indian corn the same.

The desolation of Cochecho on the 28th June 1689 caused the removal of Mr. Pike and his family to Portsmouth, though without dissolving the connection between pastor and people; that was a more tenacious bond then than now. He remained at Portsmouth until the 24 Oct. 1690, when he went to Hampton where he preached for several months.— The death of Rev. Seaborn Cotton (19 April 1686), had made a vacancy at that place which his son John Cotton (born 8 May 1658) had been invited to fill; he had declined the call, though but temporarily, for when it was afterward renewed, he accepted it and became in 1696 fourth minister of Hampton; but at this time he was preaching at Portsmouth, while Mr. Pike was at Hampton. The stay of the latter was but short; for although the church gave him an invitation to become their pastor, he declined it, hoping that his services might be again required at Dover. On the 4 Feb. 1691, he removed to Newbury, and again to Portsmouth 6 Oct. 1692, having been offered the station of chaplain at Pemaquid, which place he reached on the 26 Oct., after a passage of ten days. It is somewhat remarkable, by the way, that the author of the article on SEBASTIAN RALE, in Sparks' American Biography, should have known of Mr. Pike only as "probably an officer in his Majesty's service." He returned to Portsmouth 13 July 1695, and remained there until 11 Nov. 1698, when he came again to Dover with his family.

He removed again to his native place 21 Oct. 1702, and remained there a year or two, when he returned to Dover; here he remained until his death.

Of these removals he speaks in the valuable Journal which he kept for many years, which is printed in the third volume of the N. H. Historical Collections. The reasons of these frequent changes of residence are found in the constant difficulties with the Indians, and not in any changeableness in the man. Testimony as to his personal character is very explicit. Rev. Jabez Fitch characterizes him as "a person of great humility, meekness and patience, much mortification to the world, and without gall or guile." Cotton Mather says that he was "much beholden to him" for some of the information contained in that chaotic work The Magnalia. Mr. Wise of South Berwick used to say that Mr. Pike never preached a sermon which was not worthy of the press. Dr. Belknap learned that "he was esteemed as an extraordinary preacher and a man of true godliness. He was a grave and venerable person, and generally preached without notes. Those well acquainted with him have given him the character of a very considerable Divine." Some of his sermons were in existence when Dr. Belknap wrote. Doubtless Mr. Pike was worthy to rank with his predecessors Daniel Maud and the Reyners, father and son; these men with their immediate successors gave to Dover for a century and a quarter a ministry surpassed by very few towns in the early history of our country, and they did much to remove the evils which the dissolute conduct of earlier ministers had produced; yet not entirely could they retrieve the past; that can never be done.

Mr. Pike married Sarah, second daughter of Mr. Joshua Moody, 5 May 1681.

she died about 1705; Farmer says that he died upon the 10th March 1710, but his will seems to render this impossible. Some particulars regarding his family may be gathered from his Will, which follows below. The exact connection between Rev. John Pike of Dover, and Rev. James Pike of Somersworth, whose son was the well known Nicholas Pike, may be worthy of mention:—John Pike of Newbury in 1635, removed to Salisbury, and died 29 May, 1654, leaving two sons, John of Newbury, and Robert of Salisbury.—Of the children of John (2) was Joseph born 26 Dec. 1638, killed by the Indians 4 Sept. 1694. Rev. James Pike was grandson to this Joseph. Rev. John Pike was son to Robert and grandson to the first John, and was therefore first cousin to the grandfather of James.

Here is a copy of the Will of Rev. John Pike.

Dover the 6th of March 1709.

I John Pike of Dover minister of the Gospel, being sick & weak of body but of sound & perfect mind & memory do make this my last will & testament in manner & form following—

Imprimis—I bequeath my soul to God who gave it & my body to ye grave to be decently interd according to ye discretion of my Execuirs hereafter named.

Item—I give to my son Nathaniel the one halfe of that Farm or estate of house land & marsh that was formerly in Goldway with all privileges & appurtenances thereunto belonging, I having already given him by deed of Gift the other halfe of sd estate, soe that now he shall have ye whole to him his heirs & assigns forever, also that wch was Mr. Wosters orchard & hoeing — — — standing just before it, accounted about two acres & all th — I give to my sd son Nathl with this proviso that he j — — — with his brother Robert in paying an equal proportion — — — charge of bringing up their brother Soloman to school — — — he arrive to the age of fifteen year—

Item—I give to my son Robert that part of my land lying upon the Little River between the comon High way & a place call'd Foxhill, containing about acres sixteen wth all the housing theron & all priviledges & appurtenances thereon belonging wth this proviso that he joyn with his brother Nathl in paying an equal proportion of ye charge of bringing up their brother Solomon to school till he to ye age of fifteen years, & then take care to dispose of him as he & his brother Nathl shall think mos for his advantage, also I give Robert one third part of my meadow in joynt with his two younger brothers—

Item—I give to my sons Joshua & Solomon in equal proportion that whole parcell of land lying on the Northwest side of Little River containing three score Acres more or less with two thirds of my meadow in joynt with their brother Robert, wch meadow is comonly called Great Meadows & it is to be understood all the land & meadow before mentioned lies in the town of Salisbury in ye province of the Massachusetts—

It—I give to my daughter Hannah two twenty acre lotts lying a little way over the river, to the Eastds of Capt Trews Jr Salisbury & one halfe of the Lott comonly called the Leach lott in Salisbury—

It—I give to my daughter Mercy one halfe of a Six score lott lying betwixt

Amesbury & Haverhill formerly bought by my Father of Wm. Huntingdon & one halfe of ye lot comonly call'd ye Leach Lott in Salisbury—

It—I give to Joseph Stockman Junr twenty acres out of the sixscore acre lott lying between Amesbury & Haverhill & to my neices Dorothy Light & Sarah Pike daughter of Robert Pike each of them twenty acres out of the sixscore acre lott aforesd—

It—I give all my moveable estate into the hands of my Executrs to defray the charge of my Funeral & pay my just debts & ye remainder to be equally divided between my daughters Hannah & Mercy.

And ffinally I make my two elder sons Executrs of this my last will & testament to whome also I give a lott of abt thirty acres in a place call'd Mill Division in Amesbury & a ten acre lott at Salisbury at a place call'd ye run—the better to enable them to pay my debts.

Signed, sealed & declared to be his last will & testament in presence of Samuel Tebets, John Ambler, Sarah Cutt.

JOHN PIKE { SEAL }

Province of New Hampshire 10th March 1709.

Samuel Tebets John Ambler and Sarah Cutt personally appearing before me Richard Waldron Esqr Judge of Probate of Wills, and granting letters of Administration: made oath that they were present and see John Pike signe, seal and declare this instrument in writing to be his last will and Testament, and that he was of sound deposing minde and memory at the doeing thereof to the best of their knowledge.

RICHD WALDRON.

OLD SERIES, NO. 97, DEC 21, 1852.

EDWARD COLCOTT.

In No. 10 of these Memoranda are the words:—"in 1631 when Edward Colcott, who was afterwards chosen Governor by the planters of Dover, first came over, &c." To the word "first," PASSA-CONAWAY next week made objections, believing as he did in the authenticity of the deed purporting to be given by his namesake in 1629 to Rev. Mr. Wheelwright, with which the said Mr. Edward Colcott is somehow mixed up We do not pretend to decide when learned Antiquarians disagree, but we object to the statement that he was ever Governor of Dover. We do it because we can find no place for him between 1633 and 1641, which was the only period when Dover had Governors of its own.—He was here, however, or rather round about here, now at Dover, tomorrow at Exeter, next day after at Hampton. The fact is he was a very active man, and not very well liked, as will appear from the following petition:—

"To the Right Worshipful and much honored General Court now assembled at Boston the complaint of severall psons whose names are underwritten to which many others might be added if desired.

Humbly sheweth,

That whereas it hath been much observed & a long time taken notice of, that Edward Colcord a man notoriously — — — hath many years vitiously liued, to himself, and disorderly towards others, what by vexatious suits, and fradulent dealings, in seuerall respects, by cheating and cozening, by wresting mens estates out of their hands, by colour of law, by reuiling their psons, by fomenting of strifes, by raising discord among neighbors, by false swearing—before a Court, by takeing all advantages to insure — men whereby hee might get some thinge to himselfe, it may seeme strange, that this man hath runn this Course, without any restraint, unlesse beeing debarred from pleading & being made incapable of giuing testimony, but what by his fair speeches deluding many by subtle contriuances, and underhand practices he hath hitherto euaded the hand of justice, the time was, that proceeding so farr as to lash out against the Worshipfull Captaine Wiggin in casting four slanders upon him, there was an intent by some to haue wrought out theise Villaines to a — before authority which the same Edward Colcord fearing, and foreseeing his condign puuishment, made an escape and rann away from the towne wherein he liued, & the places adjacent quickly perceined by their peace and quietness what a blessing it was to be freed from such an incendary, hee trauelling from place to place till euery place was weary of him, supposing that by length of time injuries might be forgotten and the heat of our spirits somewhat allayed, he returned againe & for a short season applied himselfe to some orderly liuing, but a man habittuated in all manner of wickednesse is not so easily reclaimed, he taking up his former wont persisting in the same and that nothing might be warting, to fill up his measure, he hath anew vilified the cheifest of our magistrats and abused them by opprobrious terms.

The subscribers to this complaint hauing a deep sense of theise mischiefs and expecting no end therof from him, that their — — might be secured and the names goods of other preserued, haue drawne forth a portrature or charge of this Colcord & present to the wise — — of that much honored Court, not knowing any other way -- — -- remedy of the aforesaid euils.

The subscribers hereunto will be ready to make good what charges are giuen in this complaint

Thomas Coleman, Timothy dalton, John Brown, John ———, William Godfry, Robert Tuck, Thomas ffilbrook, william ffeffeiled, Humphrey Wilson, wilfful——, Robert Nam——(?)"

It was doubtless not all pleasing to Mr Colcott or Colcord that the Court took the same view of the subject with Parson Dalton and his friends, but they did as may be seen by the following.

"Att ye Court held at Hampton ye 8th 8th mo 1661 upon the Complaint preferred against Edward Colcord at the Generall Court & referd to this Court to hear and determine; This Court haveing found him guilty of many notaole misdemeanors & crimes, some agt Authority & some agt prsons in authority, Some cheiting of men in their estates, some in causing needlesse & vexatious suites in law, & other disturbances among the people, Hee is sentenced as followeth. viz: to pay a fine of flue pound to ye Treasurer of this County; 2ly to bee committed to the house of Correction at Boston, not theare to bee discharged, unless there bee bond taken to the value of —— with sufficient sureties for his good behauior & in particular that hee sue no man at any time hereafter without putting in good security to satisfye ye partie sued what shall be recouered of him by Auchoritie from time to time & Costs.

This is a true copie taken out of the Records for Norfolk as attest,

Tho Bradbury, rec.

The constable is to see these orders of Court forthwith put in execution.

Tho; Bradbury, rec."

That he had friends nowever is proved by the fact that Robert Page, Ffrancis Page, Thomas Page, Christopher Palmer, Will: moulton, Henry Dow, Moaries hobes, william hilton, ——Tucke, and James Philbrick became his sureties, "till next Salisbury Court."

—But we must reserve some other documents in relation to him until our next.

OLD SERIES, NO 98, DEC. 28, 1898.

EDWARD COLCOTT.

It were not at all strange if the dislike to this gentleman (as exhibited in the documents published last week) originated principally from his espousal of the claims of the proprietors in preference to that of the inhabitants, a course which might easily account for his summary conviction, considering that our Massachusetts Rulers of old times were usually convinced that every man who opposed them must be a villain. The vexatious suits probably referred to this fact. This difficulty is pretty strongly hinted at in a paper dated seven years previous, which we herewith publish:

"To the Right Worshipfull the Governour and Magistrates and Debuties of the generall Courte now assembled in Boston,

The Humble Petition of the Inhabitants of the Towne of Dover,

Sheweth,

That whereas your poor petitioners were taken under the government of the mattachusetts by the extent of the line of the patent of the mattachusets; and likewise the people there are accepted and reputed under the government as the rest of the Inhabitants within the said Jurisdiction; as also a Committee chosen to bounde out ye Towne wch accordingly was done, and afterwards conformid at the generall Courte as the Acts do more fully declare, Therefore Wee, your poore petitioners do humbly crave protection in our habitations & rights according to the Lawes and liberties of this Jurisdiction, and likewise that some order might be taken to restraine such as doe disturbe and molest us in our habitations by challenginge us by Patent, and threateninge of us, and sayinge that Wee plant upon their Ground, and that wee must give them such rents (as they please) for cuttinge grasse and Timber, or else they will take all from us, so by this meanes the people are many of them disquietted not only by the Patent but also by the threats of EDWRD COLCORDE, who wth others of his Pretended owners do report that they have fourteen shares and that they are the greatest Owners in the Country, wch Patent wee conceiue (under fauour) will be made void, if it be well looked into. So hopeinge euer to enjoy protection within

your Jurisdiction,
(1654)   Wee shall ever pray,
                    Richard Walderne.

Mr. Colcord was not depressed by the result of the accusation against him. In 1679 he is still living and keeps his eyes open to his own advantage; having become "an Antient Inhabitant" he has learned what party is best and now speaks a good word for the Massachusetts people, though not without expecting a consideration:

"To the Honoured Gouernor & Councill now assembled in boston.

when Maior waldrine went from the Genneral Court of Boston about May last was two years, when he returned through Hampton he requested me, Edward Colcord to Come to his house wheare he showed me the Complaint yt was put in to his Maiesty against the Massachusetts Maiestrates wr in he said the said Mason had charged the Maiestrates sume things to this purpose wch I heare relate yt they had taken away the Gouerment of the people; & burnt the houses & banished seueral persons; upon wch Maior waldrine desireinge me being an Antient Inhabitant in these parts, to speak wh seuerall Inhabitants theire yt weare antient inhabitants to speake to the truth theireof, who gaue in or testimoneys to the truth for yor Honours vindecation; & to accomplish this it Cost me Eighteen dayes tyme; & one weeke Cominge heither wch was in the prime of Sumer; for wch I desire Satisfaction.
                    Edward Colcord.
Boston 6th March 1678-89."

A marginal note adds—
"I hope yor honours will giue me at least tenne pounds for I really desarue it & more; for I was noe sunner absent but post was sent after me."

Edward got into difficulty again; the Court Records present the following:

The Case of Edward Colcord for abuse offered to his wife att Diuers times as Doth appear by Euidenc, the President and Councill Doth order thatt the sayd Edward Colcord shall Continnow in prison till hampton Court next, unless he can Gitt baile to the Vallue of fortie pounds too keep the peace towards all persons and speciall towards his wife and Children till the Court take further order Conserning him.   29 June 1681.

Edward Colcord moveing the Council (who hath sentenced him to prison there to be kept until he can Giue seaurity of 40£ for his Good Apearing to his wife and family thatt stands in fear of their liues if he be att liberty) which by Reason of his Restraint Cannott find wt to Answer as if he had some time allowed him to attaine the same, the Council doth further order thatt he haue three weeks or a month's liberty to poure sufficient suerties to the sd some of 40£; and if in the meane time he shall Committ any outt Rage or any wise abuse his wife or Children upon any of their Complaints to Authority made by them, that then he shall forfitt to the Treasurer of this puence, all that Right he hath or ought to haue into all or any part of thatt maintinance the Councill hath allotted him for his support Duering his life outt of whatt Euer Estate he hath or pretendeth to haue, and be forthwith Committed to prison without baile or monie prise ther to be kept Duering the Councils pleasure; to be Committed by such of the Councill as the Complaint

be made unto.
   by order of ye Council,
 30 June 1681.
    Samll Dalton Recdr.
 What became of Edward afterward we don't just now remember. We believe, however, that his children were excellent citizens and much respected, and that the descendants of that name have stood fair in the community.

OLD SERIES, NO. 99, JAN. 11, 1853.

MISCELLANEOUS.

 In 1652 John Ault deposes that he was at Dover in 1635. Richard York does the same. Elder Hatevil Nutter was here in 1636; William Furber in 1637.

 To the Honoed Generall Court now assembled at Boston.

 The petition of Richard Walden In the behalfe of the Towne of Dover,

 Humbly Showeth,

  That wr as this Honoed Court granted & confirmed unto Mr Edw Rawson, 200 Acers of Land layd out at chutt checno River; which Land the Inhabitant of Dover do declare & find to bee Included in there bounds & haue disposed yre of to severall of ym selues whom to tne Ministry haue beene Constantly rated; And haue olsoe procured Mr Rawson aforsd to accept of Two hundred Acers of Land elsewhere, Cleare of the Towne of Douer's Lyne.

 The prmises Considered, your petitioner humbly desireth this Honord court would bee pleased to grant the sd Edw Rawson in Lew of that grant of Land aboue expressed Two hundred Acers of Land else wr, fur wch yor petitioner shall bee further Ingaged to pray for yor continewed prosperity, & eur remajne yor humble servant,

    Richard Waldene."

(This was agreed to 29 May 1661.)

 In the Massachusetts Archives is the record of the following receipt:

 "Received by me, Obadiah Bruen, of Thomas Larkham for my share in the plantation of Pascataquack Impr in money & bevur three pound, in Corne flue bushells twenty shillings, six yards of woolen cloth forty snillings and a heifer Cow foer pound, in all the sume of ten pounds. witness my hand this 24 June 1642.   Obadiah Bruen.

This is A True Copie Compared with the originall that was on file & test in its steed is Attest by

   Edw: Rawson Secrty
   Nich: scamon "

 This Bruen was of Cape Ann. He had bought this share of RICHARD PERCIVALL of Shrewsbury, England, 22 October 1635. LARKHAM sold all his interest in the plantation to William Walderne and Ferdinando Gorges, 13 Sept. 1642.

 Another record relates to Mr. Larkham also:

 "The Accompt of goods in the Custody of mr Larkham wch doe belong unto the whole adventurers.

Impr one great Iron Pott.

Itt one fouling piece the barrell flue foote.

Itt 3 pr of musket moulds, one pr sheep sheres

Itt 2 beast tobacco pipes,oneGreat knife.

2ps,—5 dozen Awle blades, 1 dozen Cod hookes

4 lb 1-2 lead, one sickle, one bearing bill-itt one—sawe and two moosecoates. Itt a key of the barn dore.

I acknouledge it
Vera Copia.   Thom. Larkham.
The key nicolas (Scamon had?) of Mr. Larkham and is in his custody,

This is A true Copie Compard to the Originall yt was on file & test in its steed as Attests
Edward Rawson, Secrety.
Nich: Scamon."

1652-8-21. James Wall testifies that he and William Chadbourne and John Goddard "came over" about 1634 "for themselves and as agents" and were placed at Newichwannock; that they there "built a sawmill" and a "stamping mi'l for corne," and bought upland of the Indians; that they held this land for three or four years, and they deeded it then to Thomas Spencer (son-in-law to said James Wall) who now lives on it.

1661 April 15. Valentine Hill's inventory was entered by Nich. Shapleigh, Richard Walderne and Peter Coffin, at £2532-6-8.

[1642 (?)] To the Honord Court.
The inhabitants of Douer desire Mr Ambrose Gibbons to be a Comisionr to sit wth our honord Magistrate.
William Walderne
in behalf of the towne.
The petition was granted.

"This Court being informed of great misdemeanors committed by Edward Starbuck of Dover, professor of Anabaptism for wch he is to be proceeded agt at ye next Court of Assistants if euideuce an be prepared by that time & it beinge very far for witesses to travayle to Boston at that season of ye year It it therefore ordred by this Court that the Secretary shall giue —— to Capt Tho: wiggin & mr Geo. Smith to send for such pson as they shall haue notice to be able to testifie in the sd Cause, & to take their testimonies upon Oath & Certifie the same to the Secretary so soone as may be that further proceedings may be —— as the Court shall require.

The mags haue passed this with Reference to the Concurrence of or — — —
Jo: winthrop: Gour.
(1648?) Wm Torrey by orders.

1651 Sept 6. There beinge no deputy appearinge from the Towne of douer neither this nor the last session of this Court, The Deputs thinke meete that the sd Towne of douer shall be fined ten pounds for their neglect with reference to the Consent of or honord ma— hereunto.
William Torrey, Cleric.
15 (8) 51.   Consend to by ye magists.
Edw: Rawson Secrety.

OLD SERIES, NO. 100, JAN. 25, 1853-

MISCELLANEOUS.

Some of the following papers have been printed, but are now republished from new copies to ensure correctness

"The Generall Court ordering that their petitionrs Jno Allen Nicholas Shapleigh Thomas Lake might make a breife declaration of ther Right in the 2 patents Swascott & Douer. (1654.)

Wee humbly prsent to this honnord Court as follo 1. That Mr. Edward Hilton was posses of this land about ye year 1638 wch is aboute 26 years agoe.

2. Mr. Hilton sold the sd Land to

some merchants of Bristoll who had it in possession for about 2 yeares.

3. The Lord Say the Lord Brooke, Sir Richard Saltonstall Sir Arthur Heselrig mr Bovsill Mr Wyllys mr Whyting mr Hewett & others bought ye sd land of ye Bristoll merchants and they haue pd 2150 pounds. they being writt unto by the Gour & Majestrts of ye Massachusetts who Incuraged them to perchas the sd land of the Bristoll men In Respect they feared some ill neighbourhoode ffrom them, as some in this honnored Court may please to Remember.

4. The Lords & Gentlemen posse(sse)d and Injoyed the sd Land (so purchased) about 9 yeares & placed more Inhabitants at Douer some of which came ouer at ther Cost & Charges & had ther Seuerall Lottes sett fforth Unto them.

5. The 14th of ye 4 mo; 1641, Mr. Wyllys Mr Whyting mr Saltonstall mr Holicke mr Makepeace themselues & ptners putt ye sd pattents under the Gouernment of ye sd Massachusetts Reserueing 1-3 of Douer pattent & the whole of ye South pt of the Riuer to ye Lords & Gentlemen & the sd Court Confirmed the sd Lands on them their heires & assignes ffor euer as by the sd Contract ffully appeares the 14th 4 mo: 1641, & the 2-3 of Doue Pattent should Remayne to the Inhabitants of Douer.

6 The 7 mo 1642 Mr Samuel Dudley & others weare appoynted by the Court to lay out ye limetts of Douer According to ye agree(m)ent with Mr Whyting & Company & that nothing be don to ye prejudice of mr Whyting & Company appeare P ye Court Record 7 mo 1642.

7. The 7 mo 1653 the Marsh & mid-dows in ye Great Bay & 400 aces of Upland was Granted to douer Reseruing the Right to ye proprietors.

Now wee humbly pray this honnored Court to take Into Consideration that this Conditionall Grant to Douer was 2 yeares 3 monthse after yor Contract wth mr Whyting & Compa. And 15 yeares after the owners had porchassed & possessd it, Dureing wch time the whole patcents was twice sold & seuerall pts alsoe; And alsoe it was Injoyed by the owners 13 years before this honored Court Challenged any Intrest in ye sd land by the extent of yor pattent. And thatt this honored Court will be pleased to Graunt a diuission of ye sd land According as yo haue fformerly ordered.

To the Honed Gener: Court of the Massachusets in Botson these prsents show this tenth of October 1665.

Mav it please the Honored Court

Whereas we the Inhabitants of Douer haue receiued Creditable information that the Inhabitants of some of the townes borderinge upon ye River of Pascataqua haue petitioned his Majesty or Dread Sovoraigne with respect to wrongs and usurpations they sustaine in the Prsent Gouernment under which they reside, for an alteration to be made amongst them in the Gouernment as his Majesty to please to order the same: We thought it necessary beinge orderly assembled in a Townes meeting to Cleare orselves for or owne part by these prsens from hauing any hand in any such Petition or Remonstrance and in case any such act hath passed we looke at it as unworthy misrepresentation of us the Inhabitants of Dover to his Majesty as beinge done without any either Consent or Meetinge for Congnian ce of the Towne or the Major part thereof. Furthermore as its or bounden Duty so upon this occasion we profess the same that God assistinge we shall continue in or faith and Allegiance to his Majtie: by adheringe to the prsent Government Established by his Roial Charter in the Colony of the Masshchusets accordinge to the Articles of Agrement. We beseech the Lord for his presence in the midst of you and his blessinge upon all your publick and weighty occasions and humbly take Leaue.

    Richard Walderne
    William Wentworth   } select
    John Roberts   } men
    John Davis

It was voted at a publick townes meetinge Octobr 10, 1665 that the Contents hereof be pisented to ye Gen: Court as the Townes act and that it be prsented to all the rest of or neibors to subscribe their hand as any willinge

John Reyner   Hate-evil Nutter
Peter Coffin   John Woodman
*Henry Tibbuts   *John Heard
William ffurber   *Thomas Canny
Thomas Nock   John Dam
Jeremiah Tibbuts   John Hall
Thomas Downs   John Bickford
*Richard Cater   *Richard Roe
*Charles Addams   John ffrost
*William Laiton   John Chirch
Steuen Jones   Thomas Leighton
John Loveringe   *William Beard
*Roberd Euenes

This is A Trew Cope Taken from the Oridgenall
            P me William Pomfrett,
                  Towne Clarke.

The Gennerall Court of the Massachusets Jurisdiction in New England.
To Joseph Dudley, Esqr.

Whereas you are chosen & Appointed by the Authority of the Generall Court sitting in Boston the twenty third day of may 1677 to keep the County Court of Douer & yorke for the yeare ensuing with the Associates of thosa Counties chosen bv the sayd Counties and allowed of by the Generall Court, which sayd Courts were to haue been kept in Douer the last tuesday in June last and in york on the 1st tuesday In July, which sayd Court by Reason of the troubles in those parts occasioned by the Indian warr, was by the Council Adjourned till the last wendesday in October and that of work on the first tuesday in November next, These are therefore to Impower & Authorize you to Repaire thither and accordingly with the sayd Associates to kepe the sayd Courts according to Law & the sayd Adjournment.

In testimony whereof the Seal of the Colony is here unto Affixed. Dated in Boston the 26th of October 1677.

—— *Those thus marked, made their marks.

OLD SERIES, NO. 101, FEB. 8, 1853.

DOVER TOWN RECORDS.

At A publick Towne meeting held at ye meeting house on douer neck the 22d day of May 1710,

first. Capt Gerrish Esqr Chosen moderator.

2ly. Thomas Robards Senr, Richd

waldr(on) Esqr., mr Joseph Jones, Ens ffrances Mathes, Captt knight, Chosen Selectmen.

3ly. Captt James Dauis, Ltt Tebbets, assesters.

4ly. mr Joseph Smith, Sargtt Small Tebbets, Captt Tristram Heard, a Comitte.

5ly. Thomas whitehouse, Jabez garland, Abraham benet, william hoyt, Constables.

6ly. The Suruaiers of highwaies that was Last year Continued this year.

vewers of fences that w(ere) Last year Continued.

7ly. Captt hill, Ltt downing, Chosen to Joyn with the Rest of the Comitte formerly Chosen to Lay highwaies.

at the Aboue sd meeting voated that the Towne Aduance Tenn Pounds towards defraying the Charge of mr Pikes furerall.

At A Publick Towne Meeting held at the Meeting house on douer Neck the 22th day of may 1710.

Whereas by the death of the Reauer and Mr Pike the Town is at present destitute of a settled minister & the Inhabitants there of haueing Considered the necessity of a supply as soon as may be,

Captt Jno Gerrish Esqr, Richard waldron Esqr, Captt Jno knight, Captt Jno Tuttle, Captt Nathl Hill, mr Ezekill wentworth and Ltt Thomas Tebbetts are desiered to take Care as often as they Can to procure a Person to preach with us on the Lord's daies and as soon as possible to write or send to mr Seuer (Sever) to Endeuer to obtain his Companie a month or more in order to a Constant settlement among us as we shal agree; and for his Incuriagement to Lett him know that if by gods prouidence he doo settle amongst us his sallery shall not be Less than eighty pounds pr Anum money, and one hundred pounds paiable in too years toward the purches of house and Land as he sees meet and that who Euer preaches among us untill a settlement shall haue Tweney shillings Every day and subsistan(ce) for him self and hors paid out of the Towne Treasuery.

(MR. NICHOLAS SEVER, here referred to, was ordained here 11 April 1711, and remained until the spring of 1715, when he was dismissed "on account of an impediment of his speech." An account of him will appear hereafter.)

Att a Publick Towne meeting held at the meeting house on douer neck the 9th of october 1710,

Mark Giles Chosen Constable.

monday ye 18th of december 1710 being Legually Called is held a publick Towne meeting at the meting house on douer neck;

first. Captt Jno Gerrish Esqr Chosen moderator.

2ly. Voated that the minister that it shall pleas god by his prouirce to settle amongst us shall haue Ten Acres of Land for his Incourigement to build a house on, ouer and aboue the hundred pounds — — in order to his settlement.

3ly. Voated that there shall be six pounds added to the ministers sallery of Eighty pounds, to procure him wood.

at the aboue sd meeting,

4ly. Voated and ordered that there be fifty or sixty Acres of the most conueniant Comon Land on bloody poynt side be sequestered and sett apart to be secured for the use of the minienstry wh it shall please god to direct a settlement of that kinde amongst them there and Captt Jno knight and Ltt Jno downing are Chosen to Call upon the Lott Laiers on that side to Lay the Land out and make Return of Record of their dooings therein and the sd knight and downing are hereby Impowered to take Care that the Land so Laid out be secuered and and preseuered to the use affore sd and not other waies disposed of.

Test Jno Tuttle Towne Clark.

mond(ay) the 7th of may 1711 be(i)ng Legually Called is held a publick Towne meeting at the meeting house on douer neck,

first, Captt gerrish Esqr Chosen moderator.

2ly. Sargtt Joseph Robbards, Richard waldron, Esqr, John Smith senr, Sargtt Joseph Meder, Captt Jno knight, Chosen Selectmen.

3ly. Captt James dauis, Ltt Thomas Tebbets, assessers.

4ly. mr Joseph Smith, Ltt Tristram Heard, Sargtt Samll Tebets, Commissioners.

5ly. Corpll Thomas Robbards, Jno wingit, Robbard Huckins, Richard downing, Coustables.

6ly. The Suruaiers of highwaies that was Last year Contmued this Insueing year

7ly. drovers Chosen for douer neck Samll Tebbets & Joseph beard; for Cochecha, Thomas Hanson, John waldron for oyster Riuer, James bunker & Jno willy senr; bloody poynt, benjamin bickford sen, will hoyt

viewers of fences the same that was Last year.

8ly. Voated and ordered that from and after the first day of april next Inueing, no person presume to turn any gees upon the Comons in douer on penalty of forfitting the same, and that it shall and may be Lawful for Any person to kill any such gees as he shall finde on the Comons as well as in his owne Land, for they shall be accounted as wilde gees from and after the first day of aprill which will be in the year 1712.

Past in Publick Towne meeting 7 may 17(11)

monday ye 12th: of may 1712 being Leaugually Called is held a Publick Towne meeting att the meeting house on douer neck.

first. Captt Jno Gerrish Esqr Chosen moderator.

2dly. Joseph Robbards 47, Richard waldron Esqr 53, Jno Smith 27, Joseph Meder senr, 29, Ltt Jno downing 36, Chosen Selectmen. (We suppose the figures express the number of votes given to each.)

3dly. Captt Tebbets, Ens. Mathes, Chosen assessers.

4ly. mr Joseph Smith, Ltt Heard, Sargt Samll Tebbets, Chosen a Comitte.

5ly Joseph Tebbets, benjamin wentworth (Refuseth to serue,) benjamin waymouth, Amos Pinkham, moses dam, Chosen Constables.

6ly. Ens knight. Jno Leighton, Thomas willy, Jno Cromelt, Jno wintworth, Rich Randle, Petter Varney, Chosen Suruaiers of highwaies.

7ly. drouers the same that ye Last year.

3ly. Vewers of fences the same yt was Last year.

att he aboue sd meeting,

Captt Tebbets, Ltt Heard. Ltt burnum, Captt Tuttle, Chosen a Comite to Vew the Land between Joseph Jenkins, John bunker and Storys Maud and Report to the next Publick Towne meeting to se if Captt dauis Can haue his Land and a highway Complyd with here.

OLD SERIES, NO. 102, MAR. 29, 1853.

DOVER TOWN RECORDS.

Monday ye 15 of december 1712 being Loagually Called is held a publick Town meeting at the meeting house on dover neck.

first, Captt Jno Gerrish Chosen moderator.

2ly, Voated that a sufficient boom be erected and built fort — — over Cochecho River and that the whole Charg be defrayed out of the Towne Treasurey as other publick Tow(n) charges are.

3ly, at the above sd meeting voated that the bridges over belemies Bank River and oyster River be built and that the Char there of be defrayed out of the publick Treasurey as other Town Charges are.

4ly, at the above sd meeting voated that twent five pounds be paid out of the Towne Treasury towards the building a boome over Lampreel River for passage for man and hors till further order.

5ly, A Comitte be Chosen to Joyn with the selectmen to order that affair are as followeth, Jno Tuttle, Captt Timo Gerrish, Lt heard, Tho hanson, Jno Bickford, Ens knight, mr Abrm benick, mr Jcs Chesly, mr Joseph Jones.

Monday ye 25th of may 1713, being Legually Called is held a publick Towne meeting att the meeting house on dover neck

ffirst, Captt Gerrish Esqr Chosen moderator.

2ly. Lt Joseph Robbarts, Coll Richd Waldron, Sargtt Jos Meder senr, John Smith senr, Ltt Jno downing, Chosen selectmen.

3ly, Captt Tebbets, Ens Mathes, chosen assessers.

4ly, mr Joseph Smith, Lt Tristra'n heard, Sargt Samll Tebbets chosen Comitte.

5ly, nath Robbards, James heard, Thos draw sen, Eleazar Coleman, chosen Constables.

6ly, Captt Tebbets, Captt Timo Gerrish Ltt Robbarts, Ltt heard chosen Lott Layers to fill up the Comitee formerly chosen to that service.

nath Robard Refuseth to sarve in the Constables offis being chosen therennto and has pd his fine, (£)05-0 0.

James Mussey chosen to supply his place.

James heard Refuses to serve Constable pd his fine 05-0 0

John hanson chosen Constable in his stead Refused and paid part of his fine, 04-10 0

monday ye 17th of Augst 1713 being Legually Called is held a publick Towne meeting at the meeting house on dover neck.

first, Captt James Davis chosen moderator.

2ly. Captt Tebbets, Ens. heard, mr Samll Emerson, chosen to Represent the Towne att the next sessions of the general assembly to shew Reasons why the meeting house at Cochecho should not be Stated the place of publick worship for the futuer.

3ly. benjamin wentworth senr chosen Constable.

4ly, Captt Tebbets, Ltt downing, John Tuttle, chosen to Joyn with Portsmouth men to Run the line from Cany's Creak to hogsti Cove.

5ly, for preuention of cutting wood in ye Comons on dover neok and between Cochecha and fresh Creek or Cochecha poynt to Transport out of the Towne it is ordered that from hence forward no person Cutt any wood within these Preuints but for their own use or for sume Inhabitant nor after a month time after ye date hereof transport or Cause to be transported any such wood on penaltie of paying ten shillings a tree for Cutting or three shillings a Cord for Transporting, to be paid one half to the Informer, the other half to the poor of ye Towne.

Voated in the above sd meeting.

---

monday ye 17th of may 1714, being Leagually Called, is held a Publick Towne meeting at the meeting house on dover neck for the Choyce of Towne officers and other publick affaiers proper to be acted in public Towne meeting.

first, Captt Gerrish Esqr chosen moderator.

2dly, Ltt Joseph Robbarts, Collonell waldron, mr Joseph Jones, Ens ffrances Mathes, Ltt Jno downing, Selectmen.

3d ly. Captt Tebbets, John Smith, assessors.

4ly, Captt James dauis, mr william ffrost, Sargtt Thos Robbarts Senr, Comitte.

5ly, Joseph Jenkins, Joseph hanson, Joseph davis, Samll huntres, Constables.

6 ly. Abraham Clark, Jno Rawlings, Jno williams, Petter Varney, Jno knight Jno wentworth, Survaiors of high waies.

7ly. Survaiers of fences the same that was Last year.

8ly, Voated that mr Sever preach ye next Lord's day at Cochecha and so Every other Lord's day this sumer and till A finall settlement be directed.

---

monday the 14th day of June 1714 being Leagually Called is held a publick Towne meeting att the meeting house on dover nexk.

first, Captt Jno Gerrish chosen moderator. (No further).

Monday ye 27th of Septter 1714, being Leagually Called is held a publick Towne meeting att the meeting house on dover neck for the choyse of a Constable to supply Cochecha part of this Town by Reason of Joseph Hanson's Refusall.

first, Captt Gerrish chosen moddorator.

2ly. John Richards chosen Constable in ye Roome of Jos. Hanson. benedictus Tarr In Joseph Jenkins Roome.

---

monday the 29th of October 1714, being Leagually Called is held a publick Towne meeting at the meeting house on dover neck.

first, Captt John gerrish Esqr chosen modderator.

2ly, John Haise Chosen Constable to supply the vacancy mad by John Ricor's Refusall.

3ly. mr Samll Emerson chosen Constable in the Room of benedictus tarr and qualified accordingly.

4ly. Elleazar bickford chosen Culler of staves.

Att A publick Towne meeting held at the meeting house on dover neck the 11th of Aprill 1715 for the Choyce of Assembly men

first, Captt James davis chosen moderator.

2d ly. Captt Timothy Gerrish, (19) Ens Stephen Jones (19) Captt John downing, (29) chosen assembly men.

Monday ye 30th of may 1715, being Leagually Calle(d) is held A Publick Towne meeting at the meeting house on dover Neck for the choyce of Towne officers.

first, Collonell Richd Waldron chosen moderator

2ly, Capt Tebbets 75, Tobias Hanson 53, Joseph Meder 86, John Ambler 78, Sargt Thomas Robarts 89, selectmen.

3 ly, Lft Jos Robards, mr Jos Jones, assessors.

4 ly, Captt James davis, Captt Timo Gerrish, Sargtt Samll Tebbets, Commissioners.

5ly, John Cany, Love Robbarts, John Tomson senr, Constables.

6 ly, Survaiers of high wales; Thomas young, Thomas downes, John bickford, Joseph Chesley, Samll Smith, Abram benck.

7 ly, Viewer of fences the same that was Last year.

whereas There have been and are from Time to Time sundry Trespassers upon the Towne's Commans by fenceing in the same without any grant from the Towne, to the prejudice of the severall Inhabitants, Voated that Captt Jno Tuttle and mr Samll Emerson for and in behalf of the Towne doo prosecutte at Law all such Trespers and offenders and they the sd Capt John Tuttle and mr Samll Emerson or Either of them are hereby Constituted and appoynted Authorized and Impowered by themselves or substitutes to act and doo the uttmost the Law will allow that the Towne Rights and priveledges may be preserved for the benefett of the Inhabitants there of and the selectmen for the Time being Take Care to pay any extraordinary Charg they may be at in this affair.

Voated in the meeting Above sd Test— John Tuttle Towne Cloark.

OLD SERIES, NO. 103, APRIL 5, 1853

DOVER TOWN RECORDS.

Monday ye 25th day of July 1715 being Legually Called is held a publick Towne meeting at the meeting house on dover neck.

first, Captt James davis chosen moderator.

2ly. Israell hoigsdun Chosen Constable to supply the vacancy made by the Refusall of John Canny.

3ly, John Wentworth Chosen Constable to supply the Vacancy made by Loue Robbarts Refusall.

(Pity it is that some of our modern patriots had not lived in those days, in order to teach our simple ancestors that it was not the mark of a good citizen to decline office!)

To the selectmen of douer in public

Towne meeting: My humble petition to you is that you will be so kinde to me as to grant me a highway out to the Country Road, that is to say, to the highway that goeth from willeyes Creek to oyster Riuer falls, for I am pened up by bartholomew Stephenson to Eight foot or near there about which you are senceble of when you were at neighbour Wakeham's about the highwaiys and saw your selves the way to be too or three Rods in bredth. So Rest your to serue July; 25; 1715. James Langley.

Voated in answer to the within petition that the two Rods Left by the suruaiers from the head of the petioners Land be Left open to the highway that Leads from willeyes Creek to oysterRiuer falls for the use of the petitioner & other of his Majts good subjects.

Test. Jno Tuttle Towne Clark.

———

Wee whose names are under Written being chosen by the Towne of douer with others to suruaie and Lay out high waies in The seuerall pts of the Towne and being desiered of James Langley to Lay out a way of too Rod wide beginning at will Drews old possession joyning to the bond high way so Runing sow west and by west to a pine tree on the south East side of this highway and so keeping the two Rods in breadth to a little hill Leaueing the Spring Seuen Rods on the nor west side of the highway, keeping the same breadth southsouth west to the highway that goeth from willeyes Creek to osyter Riuer falls to a white oke markt H I S and william drews wood lott on the sonth east of this highway.

James Davis

Jeremiah burnum
Thomas Tebbets.
Recorded may ye 28; 1716.

———

Att A publick Towne Meeting held at the meeting house of dover neck for the Choyce of Assembly men (1715;

first, Collonel waldron moderator.

2ly, Voated, that no Voats be Received in publick Towne meeting for the futuer but such as are delivered by the hand of the Voater and not sent by the hand of another man.

(From this it would seem that voting by proxy, at town meetings was not uncommon in those days—a practice, which, if continued to this time, would probably be more convenient to office seekers than conducive to the purity of elections).

3ly, Sargtt Samll Tebbetts, Captt James davis, chosen assemblemen.

———

OLD SERIES, NO. 104, APRIL 19, 1853

———

RICHARD WALDRON.
I. Settlement.

———

No name is more prominent in early New Hampshire history, than that of Waldron. Identified as its various members have been with the prosperity of the State, our readers will pardon us, if we devote more space than usual in our biographical notices, to the head of this family.

RICHARD WALDRON, or WALDERNE rather, as he spelt his name, was born, according to tradition, in Somersetshire, England, in 1609. He came to America, (says the fragment of a letter from James Jeffrey to Councillor Richard Waldron, grandson of the subject of this article,) with "Mr. Hilton or Mr. Wiggin, (in 1635) to See the Country; he stayed about two Years & returned to England and there Marryed a Gentlewoman of a very good family (whose parents were very unwilling She should come away) her names are not remembered, nor of wt place. Your Great Grandfather did not come with your Grandfather."

Upon his first visit Richard Walderne seems to have purchased land of Capt. Wiggans upon Dover Neck, and to have made arrangements for settlement; on his final return he purchased a large tract of land at Cochecho lower falls, where, in 1640, or a little earlier perhaps, it is said that he made his residence. Probably he also built a sawmill in 1640, as in 1649 in a deed to Joseph Austin he conveys part of the "old mill." This was the origin of the settlement long known as COCHECHO, and now the central part of the flourishing city of DOVER.

Soon after his settlement he purchased a large amount of standing timber from the town, to engage in the preparation of lumber, pipe-staves, &c, which speedily became the main business of the town. He erected a sawmill, apparently the second, in 1649, (James Wall of Exeter, a carpenter, being the builder,) which was finished previous to 2, 8 mo.; a constant succession of mills have since occupied the spot. Here, too, on the north side of Cochecho lower falls he rescued land from the wilderness for a farm; here he made his home and here found his grave.

Some of these town grants are the following:

1, 6, 1642. Given and granted by the Towne unto Richard Walderne fifty Acres of upland at Cuttchechoe. The said land joyning to the fall at ye fresh River, and the River on the South side of the same. More, 30, 6, 1643, three score acres of upland next adjoyning to his old planting ground at Cuttchecohe aforesaid, on the lower side of the River, opposite to his house, the River lying on the north side of the said Land. More, 1, 6, 1642, att the Marsh at the upper end of Cuttchechoe Marsh lying west from John Baker his ten Acres, bounded with a Rock on the Northside of the said Marsh which lyeth between ye Marsh of ye said Richard Walderne. More Sixe Acres of Marsh being the thirteenth Lott in the said Marsh. More 18, 4, 1648, Three lotts of Marsh conteyning by estimation Sixe Acres apece more or lesse, which were William Waldernes, one whereof being knowne by the name of the Ninth Acre Lott was Henry Beoks, one more known by the (name of the) Tenth Acre Lott which was the said William Waldernes, and the other known by the (name of the) Eleventh acre Lott which was Hateuill Nutters; and all lying in the before mentioned Marsh of the said Richard Walderne.

"The 12th of the 10th Mo 48" there was granted unto Richard Walderne "fifteen hundred of Trees either of oke or pine" for the "accummodation" of a Saw-mill which he intendeth shortly by God's permission to erect and sett upp at or uppon the Lower fall of Cochebchoe." He was to pay 3d for every tree he should cut.

5, 10, 1652, He has further "accommodation" for his saw-mill "in consideration whereof the aforesaid Mr. Richard Wald erne doth bind himself, his heires and administators to erect a Meeting House upon the hill near Elder Nutters, the dementions of said House is to be forty foot long twenty six foot wide, sixteen foot studd, with six windows, two doors, fitt for such a house, with a tile covering, and to planck all the walls, with glass and nail for it, and to be finished betwixt this and April next, come twelve month, wch will be in the year 1654."

6, 10, 1652. He has "Liberty to set up a saw-mill upon the North side of the second ffall of the River of Cochecho" with timber corresponding, for which £5 will be the annual rent.

2, 10, 1652. The Committee for granting land &c. laid out to "Mr. Richard Walden of Douer who hath set upp sawmill works at the lower ffall of Cochechoe, two thirds of all the timber lying & growinge betwixt Cochechae first ffall and ouer to the ffreshitt of Bellemeys Bank, and so from the end of the swamp next Bellamyes Banck and soe westward between the Riuer of Cochechae & the freshitt that runneth to Bellamys banck & so to the uttmost bounds of Douer, Excepting the trees granted to Joseph Austin, as also upon Dover necke from a ledg of Rocke at a ffreshitt that runneth out of the woods Agaist the lower side of the Marsh of ffresh creek and from that ledge of Rocks at high water marke upon the neck of land three Quarters of A mile upon a South and by west line, and from the end of that line upon A west & by North line tell he cometh to the next Grant—all the timber within this tract of land betwixt Cochecha Riuer & the line afore mentioned, Exceptinge what Timber is graunted to Capt. Wiggin & Mr. Bradstreet. Provided, The Inhabitants have liberty for the Cuttinge of timbr Accordinge to the order bareinge Date with these Psents." For this he was to pay £12 yearly rent.

5, 10 1652. Mr. Walderne has granted to him "all the timbr being & growing upon the land one the South side of Bellemyes banck lyeinge one the North side of the path from Bellemeys Banck towards Oyster Riuer."

2, 3, 1662. Granted urto Capt. Richard Waldern, 24 fett of upland to join to his former grants of flats at Sandy Point.

The records of other grants have been doubtless lost in the rough usage to which the Dover Towne Records have been subjected. Enough remains however to show that Waldron was a comparatively wealthy man at the time of his enigration.

Of his affairs for the few years following his settlement, no other certain means of knowledge are open; it is said, however, that his house speedily became a post for the Indian Trade in furs; it was the frontier house then, the forests above stretching away to Canada.

OLD SERIES, NO. 104. ARPIL 19 1853.

MAJOR RICHARD WALDERNE.

II TOWN EMPLOYMENTS.

The first notice of his participation in public affairs is found in his signature to the "Combination" to establish a form of government at Dover, a measure rendered necessary by the disorders into which the people had fallen. The paper bears date 22 October, 1640, and was signed by 41 men, Walderne's name being second upon the list and following that of Thomas Larkham, the minister. As this is found in Hubbard's New England, in Farmer's Belknap and in these Memoranda, it is needless to reprint it. It is enough to say that it established a form of government by freeholders, for the time in which it was in operation. It ceased to exist when Dover became a part of Massachusetts, 9, 9, 1641.

Walderne was early and frequently engaged in the business of the town. He was Town Treasurer for many years, and Commissioner for Small Cases; was Selectman in 1647 (when the town records commence,) in 1651, 1662-9, 1671-2, 1674-7, and was undoubtedly similarly employed in years where records are destroyed. In addition to these comparative unimportant offices, he was invariably chosen to act in behalf of the Towne when difficulties arose, as they frequently did, between Dover and its neighbors. The Dover Records make frequent mention of them, thus: 20, 2, 1644 "It is this day ordered that Mr. Edward Starbuck, RICHARD WALDERNE and William Furber to bee Wearsmen for Cotchico fall and Riuer, during their lives, &c"—27, 10, 1647, "ordered yt Mr Ambrose Gibbons, William Pomfret, Nath. Emerey, RICH WALDERNE and Thomas Leighton are to treat with" certain parties regarding saw-mills priveleges. 22, 4, 1663, "men chosen to treat with Mr. Rayner, CAPT. RICHARD WALDERNE, William Follet, James Nute, Richard Otis". 28, 2, 1664, "CAPT. WALDERNE, Left. Hall chosen to meet with those of Portsmouth to open the votes for Associates." 15, 2, 1665, "ordered That Mr Peter Coffin shall be impowered by this writing to agree with some workman to build a turret upon the meeting house for to hang the bell which we have bought of CAPT. WALLDERNE, &c."—19, 1, 1665-6, all "grievances" are referred by the town vote to Capt. Robert Pike, Mr. Wincoll, Mr. Elias Stillman, CAPT. RICHARD WALLDERNE," was selected "to make the mind of the town known" to these gentlemen. 20, 2, 1668, CAPT. WALLDERN and four others were made a Committee to "treat with the town of Portsmouth about the public affairs of the county, &c." At the same time "CAPT. WALDERNE and Robert Burnum chosen to oversee the work of the ministers' house at Oyster river, &c." In 1669, CAPT. WALLDERNE and six others were chosen to "draw up something concerning commonage and other public busines-, &c."

OLD SERIES NO. 105, APRIL 26, 1853.

III. PUBLIC OFFICES.

In 1652, Walderne was chosen to represent the town in the Genneral Court which met at Boston; he was again elected in 1656 and thence annually until 1675 when the Indian war required his presence at home: in 1677 he was rechosen and also in 1679. In 1666 he was elected Speaker of the House, which at that time consisted of forty-three members representing thirty-nine towns; he was continued in this office the two next years next succeeding and was re-elected in 1673, 4, 5 and 9, when his membership ceased.

The "County of Norfolk" was established in 1643; it was composed of Salisbury, Haverhill, Hampton, Exeter, Portsmouth and Dover. Salisbury was the shire town, but Dover, and Portsmouth were situated so far from that place that they were allowed to hold a separate Court of their own; this privilege was secured, indeed, by the articles of Union. The Court of the "County of Dover and Portsmouth," was generally held twice a year, being at each place alternately. Its five Magistrates, at first appointed by the General Court, were afterwards elected by joint ballot of the two towns and formed the "Court of Associates." Of this Court, Walderne was a member of 1661 and probably earlier. The town Records furnish proof of his election from 1661 to 1667 and in 1669; they indicate, perhaps, the estimation in which he was held, in the fact that at every election save one he received a higher number of votes than were given to any other candidates.

IV. THE QUAKERS.

During this term of office as a Magistrate, the conduct of the Quakers came under his supervision—The laws of the Province against this people were then severe and rigidly executed. The Quakers were literally outcasts from the pale of society. Three women of the persecuted sect visited Dover in 1662; their object was doubtless to teach their doctrines, their manner not needlessly gentle, irritated as they were by the severities of a Puritan code. On their first visit they were suffered to depart unharmed; on their second, the aid of the law was invoked; our ancestry may have been sincere, but that the religious zeal of three weak women could justify a sentence of ten lashes on the bare back in each of eleven towns, in the depths of winter, is repugnant to every sentiment of humanity or justice. The deeds of our ancestry may be palliated, they cannot be justified. It is not strange that such dealings failed to reclaim the wanderers, nor that the Quakers increased faster in Dover, the only place of persecution, than in any other town in New Hampshire; nor is it wonderful that some of this people regarded Walderne's death, years afterwards as the righteous retribution of heaven upon a persecutor. But it is charitable to suppose that Walderne's heart, and his duty as a Magistrate, were at variance.

V. BUSINESS.

During this period, as through his whole life, Walderne was actively engaged in business. In addition to his mills at the lower falls of Cochecho, he had others at the second falls and at Bellamy.—That he was engaged in commerce is inferred from the following:

"Upon a motion made to this Court by Capt. Walderne who hath extraordinary occasions referring to the leading away of a shippe, The deputes are willing for the prsent to dismiss him the Court if or honod magistrates please to consent thereto.

William Torrey, Cleric.
Consented unto by the Magistrates
Jo Endecott, Govr."

His trading operations were extended in 1668, to Penacook, now Concord; in 1658, his name heads the list of grantees of a tract eight miles square, which were given under certain conditions regarding the number of families which should settle in a given period. These conditions were not complied with, and the fort and trading house were abandoned in 1668, when a circumstance occurred which gives the matter its main interest. In May of that year a murder was committed; Thomas Dickinson, a white man, was killed by an Indian under the influence of strong drink. The selling of liquors to Indians, was at that time, strictly prohibited; so gross a violation of law, as seemed to have been committed in furnishing strong drink to the Indian, was taken up by the General Court. Capt. Walderne and Peter Coffin were accused of the deed.—The sending of liquors from Cochecho, the intoxication of the Indian thereby, the circumstances of the murder, the summary punishment inflicted by the Indians, the stoic resignation of the criminal, were easily proved Of sending the liquors to Penacook Capt. Walderne was acquitted, from his own oath, the testimony of his son Paul and that of Peter Coffin. Coffin was convicted and fined £50.

VI. MALCONTENTS DEFEATED.

Somewhere near 1662 complaints went to the King, about territorial Limits, which were a constant source of contention. To decide upon these, and to examine and determine disputed matters generally, Col. Richard Nichols, Sir Robert Carr, Kt. George Cartright, and Samuel Maverick were appointed Commissioners with almost royal powers. In the course of their labors they came to New Hampshire. Finding a few persons discontented, they offered to release the people from the control of the Massachusetts government, and make New Hampshire a royal province, supposing that the opportunity would be gladly received. On the contrary, the mass of the inhabitants utterly refused to assent to such an arrangement; and as Abraham Corbet, a malcontent of Portsmouth, had framed a petition, complaining of the Massachusetts government, which a few men signed, the people of Dover, as well as of other towns, embraced the occasion to declare their satisfaction with their political connexion. Walderne was the leader of the people in this matter. The following paper apparently drawn up by him is of value:

20 July 1665
May it please the Honored Councell &c,

Having soo sure a hand it is a parte of our fidelity by these Presents to give you a brief Acount of some late transactions here as having Relation to the Publick. the 10th of this Prsent; Warrants Being sent to our Constables from the King's Commissioners in these partes to Call the Town together the day following at the place of meeting to hear a Letter from his Majesty lately come to their hands, the Constables forthwith gave notice thereof to the Mayin part of The Town Before it came to the Krowledge of Capt. Walderne though therepuon it was stopped from the notice of others, yett the following day the meeting Being Assembled and the Letter Read, they were required to Choose two men to meet at the Harbours mouth on the 6th day following, there to Feceve with others their Instructions as Concerning ffortification. Inquiry being made who must have liberty of voting herein answer was returned all and every one, which liberty we fear will bee Improved by our Inhabitants in future meetings to our disturbances, the 6th day ffollowing notwithstanding Letters and Warrants Sent, such as were chosen by the Towne proceeded to meet according to appointment, where poverty Being pleaded as rendering them uncapable to manage such a work, they were showed the place ffor ffortification & Left to their Liberty till they were better able. forthwith upon the place was prsented By the hands of Abraham Corbet a petition to His Majesty ffor the Inhabitants of New Hampshire as they called it to Be taken from under the Massichusetts government under his own to which sundry at the same time sett to their hands, since which time carryed about to procure more. this Week A Court is kept at Wells & rumors are given out of their keeping a Court Shortly at their return here — — — if intended by them. wee exp(ect) it will bee a suddaine busynesse before any Intelligence Can bee given thereeof to youselvs. having credible information of these premises wee Comit them to your wisdom & consideration Besceching the Lord to direct you to do as Concerning them & all your soe weighty occasions wch may issue in the Good & wealle of all Concerned therein.

Remaining your Humble Servants,

Richard Waldern
henery (his mark) langstafe
John Dauis
John Robearts
} selectmen of douer.

The machinations of Corbet and the other enemies of Massachusetts, were defeated. The people well understood that their own interests were best guarded by their union, and that separation was only intended to further the aims of the discontented men. The Commissioners soon returned to Europe; and though the King was much irritated at their reception, the people experienced no immediate danger from the royal displeasure.

OLD SERIES NO. 106, MAY 8, 1853.

RICHARD WALDERNE.

VII. INDIAN TROUBLES.

Forty years had passed away since Walderne settled at Coch-cho; in these the Indians and the colonists had lived in peace. This was now to be changed. Men should go to their fields armed, suspecting a foe behind every tree. Families should crowd into close garrison houses for the long summers and roam in the forests only when the snows of winter protected them from savage attacks. They should worship in the same humble edifice where he had weekly met, but the house of God should be within a fortress, and sentinels should pace in its enclosure.

In 1675 the colonists at Dover Neck were able to defend themselves with comparative ease. The beautiful swell of land on which they dwelt was made a peninsula by the Bellamy, the Newichwannick and the Cochecho, which seeming at first glance to offer easy access by canoes was yet defended by the freedom with which the eye could sweep the waters in every direction; the inhabitants were numerous also; this territory was seldom called upon to defend itself therefore; and it may be that it was guarded in later years by a separate treaty which tradition, (for the honor of our ancestors we hope untruly,) says was made by the inhabitants of Dover Neck.

But at Cochecho, the forty families which had gathered, some near, some remote, around the lower falls constituted a frontier settlement. The forests above them stretched away to Canada, alive with Indians who knew every path in the forests, who were skilled in the use of fire arms through the indiscreet bounties which Dover itself had offered, and who had many a cause for hatred to the whites. No inhabitant however deserted his home. They were indeed partially prepared; suspicions of Indian friendship had been raised some years previous; in 1667 the bulwark was raised around their plain house of worship, and doubtless the garrison houses which were so common on the actual breaking out of warfare, were then erected.

The first general war with the Indians commenced in 1675. For several years previous, only the fear which the power of the whites excited, and the influence of a few old men had kept them quiet; love had little to do with it. The cordiality which had welcomed the settlers, ended long previous; increasing encroachments on Indian hunting grounds to supply an increasing population, excited their alarm; the contempt openly expressed for the Indians grated harshly upon their sensitive feelings; the overreaching habits of traders who acted upon the principle that it was a praiseworthy deed to cheat an Indian, exasperated their sense of justice. While laws pretending to guard their rights were as inoperative as laws not sustained by public opinion must ever be, and cases of individual hardship and cruelty were not unknown, it is only wonderful how they were kept inactive so long. But they were brooding over real and fancied wrongs; and when the impetuous young men of Philip of Pokanoket forced him into a war in which he saw foreshadowed only the destruction of his people, it needs not the theory of a general conspiracy to account for the fires which blazed all along the frontier. Each town had its own ground for enmity; and the torch which the Wampanoags applied to Swanzey was the signal for a hoped for, but scarcely planned war, which in twenty days, was felt at the northeastern extremities of the colonies.

As soon as the first blow was struck the Massachusetts government prepared for general defence. The towns on the Pascataqua were especially exposed; their defence was confided to Walderne, who, in 1675, was appointed commander of the militia of those towns with the rank of Major, which was conferred upon him either then or just previous.

All that could be done in this vicinity, was to act entirely upon the defensive. The account therefore, of the strife around the Pascataqua is but the history of a series of petty and irritating attacks which were made and ended in a night.

The first bloodshed, was at Oyster River, in September, 1675, when the Indians "burned two houses belonging to two persons named Chesley, killed two men in a canoe, and carried away two captives," (both of whom made their escape soon after.) One person (Goodman Robinson of Exeter) was killed on the road from that place to Hampton and one (Charles Raulet,) captured, but he soon escaped.—A few days after, the house of Richard Tozer at Newickwannock was attacked, where thirteen out of fifteen women and children, were saved by the devotion of a young girl eighteen years old; she saw the enemy coming, shut the door and held it until they cut it to pieces with their hatchets; as they entered they struck her to the floor, left her for dead, and went in pursuit of the fugitives, whom the heroic girl had given an opportunity for escape; she herself entirely recovered; yet the heroine's name at least ought to have been preserved. Some pursuit was attempted when some houses had been burned and some grain destroyed, but it met with no success: immediately afterwards, five or six houses were burnt at Oyster River, and two persons (William Roberts and his son-in-law) were killed. In such a tantalizing kind of warfare, the force under the command of Walderne could not be brought to bear effectively in any one point; chafed as he was, he was obliged to content himself with being always on the alert, and ready to give aid where it was needed. Some twenty young men, however, mainly of Dover, obtained permission of him, to follow the trail of a party, but their attempt met with no success, except that they killed two out of a party of five Indians whom they accidentally discovered near a deserted house.

A letter dated 25 Sept. 1675, from Walderne, is of great historical value; but as it was recently published (January) in the N. E. Hist. Gen. Register, we omit it

The whole country was now aroused, the labors of the farm and the forest were suspended, and the inhabitants were crowded into garrison houses, the heavy timber walls of which, gave them the aspect and security of fortresses. In this condition they did not forget their ancestry, and 7th of October was a day of fasting and prayer.

On the 16th of October, Salmon Falls was again attacked. Lieut. Roger Plaisted sent out seven men from his garrison, to make discovery of the position of the enemy, all of whom were cut off. Venturing out next day, with twenty men to bury the dead, he himself was killed. Major Charles Frost, of Sturgeon Creek, (who was under Walderne's command,) came to Newichwannock the day following, but the enemy had retreated. His own house was soon attacked and was bravely defended; frustrated in this attempt, the Indians committed all possible devastation along the river, until opposite Portsmouth, when they were dispersed by the firing of cannon, and were pursued with so much energy that they were forced to abandon their plunder to secure their own safety. These continued assaults kept the inhabitants in alarm; but the severity of the following winter aided the colonists more than their defences; for the Indians pinched by famine, were forced to sue for peace, and applied to Major Walderne for his mediation. A peace was concluded at Cochecho with the whole body of Eastern Indians, 3 July, 1676, Walderne, Shapleigh and Daniel signing the treaty in behalf of the whites. A copy of this paper is printed in Drake's Book of the Indians, p. 699. But this peace was short lived. The death of Philip, in August 1676, instead of ending the difficulties, as it was hoped it would, only increased them; for some of his allies, fearing their total extermination, now that the Massachusetts government, freed of its greatest enemy, could turn its attention entirely to them, fled to their brethren of Penacook, Ossipee and Pequawket. The Penacooks had not been engaged in the late disturbances; those of Ossipee and Pequawket had made peace. Some of the southern Indians also fled to the Kennebec. It was for the interest of these refugees to excite the tribes to renewed war, both for their own safety and to gratify their earnest desire for revenge for their own defeat. Troubles were excited by these means, and the government forced to engage again in hostilities, ordered two companies thither under the command of Capt. Joseph Syll and Capt. William Hathorne. Dover was in their line of march, and on the 6th of September they arrived at Cochecho. It was most unfortunate.

OLD SERIES, NO. 107, MAY 10, 1853

RICHARD WALDERNE.

VIII. THE SHAM FIGHT.

There were gathered at Cochecho, some four hundred Indians; for though the war had again broken out on the Kennebec, there was peace on the Pascataqua. Of these, two hundred were refugees, who had fled thither for protection. All of them were on terms of peace with Major Walderne, and considered themselves as perfectly safe. But the Massachusetts government had ordered their troops to seize all southern Indians wherever they might be found. In obedience to these orders Capts. Syll and Hathorne told Major Walderne that they must seize these Indians by force. The Major dissuaded them from this purpose, well knowing the bloodshed that would follow such an attempt, and contrived a strategem to accomplish the purpose.— He proposed to the Indians to have a sham fight, the next day; they agreed to it; the Indians formed one party, and the troops of Walderne (including those under Capt. Ffrost of Kittery,) with the two companies, formed the other. In the midst of their fight, the whites suddenly surrounded the whole body of Indians and made them prisoners, almost without exception, before the Indians were aware of the intended deception. The captives were disarmed immediately; the southern Indians present were sent to Boston; the others were set at liberty. Of those sent to Boston some five or six were hung for past offences, and the remainder sold into slavery.

This action of Major Walderne has excited different opinions in different persons. By those who recognize the necessity of unqualified military obedience, it is commended. This was the view of Major Walderne. It is said, and probably with truth, that he was opposed to the affair, both on the ground of policy and of honor; but the orders of his government were imperative, and he would not set the example of insubordination; he well knew that he was exposing himslef to the hatred of a people who never forgave an injury, but he never feared an enemy. Those who prefer honor to discipline will condemn his conduct: we cannot, of course, settle the question, though our own opinion is easily formed. The Indians never forgave him; they did not understand why they should be punished for acts of open warfare committed in the South, when peace had been made at the North. They could not comprehend the policy which treated them as rebels, who were born free; and when some who were sold into slavery escaped, and returned to the woods of the Cochecho, they hoarded up their vengeance until the bloody morning of the 28th of June, 1689.

The companies of Captains Syll and Hathorne passed on to the East, taking with them a reinforcement from Walderne's men. But the Eastern settlements had been generally destroyed or deserted, and they turned from their fruitless expedition, to Pascataqua. Some information led them to march to the Ossipee ponds on the 1st of November, but finding no sign of an enemy, they returned to Newichwannock, within nine days after their departure.

The following letter, copied from the Massachusetts Archives, will explain the state of affairs at the time of its date:—

"Portsmo, 19, 8r, 1676.

Much Honrd

Being upon occasion of ye Alarms lately recd fro ye Enemy mett togethr at Portsmo thought meet to give yor Honers our sense of Mattrs in ys pt of ye Country in ye best Manur yt upon ye place in ys prsent Hurry wee are able to get. How things are now at Wells and York wee know not but prsume yorselves will be informed ere yt comes to yor hand P ye Post sent fro ye Commandr in Chiefe wch (as was undrstood) went thro ye Towne ys Morning. Only thus much we have learnt yt ye Enenmy is Numorous & about those pts having carried all clear before him so far as Wells. That hee is pceeding towards us & so on toward yorselves ye Enemy intimates & ye thing itself speaks. What is meet to be now don is wth yorselves to say rather than for us to suggest, however beeing so deeply & nextly cons rned humbly craue leaue to offer to Consider (ati)n whether ye securing of what is left bee not or next Work rather than ye Attempting to regan wt is lost, unless there were strength enough to doe both. It seemes little available to endeaur ought in ye More Eastern places yt are already conquered, unless there bee several Garrisons made & kept wth pro-uision & Amminition & what may be suitable for a Recruit upon all Occasiors, wch to do (at least ys Winter) cannot say yt ye profit will amend for ye charge. Sure wee are yt orselves (yt is ye County of Northfolk wch Douer & Portsmo.) are so far from being capeable of Spareing any fforces for yt Expedition yt wee find orselues so thinned & weakened by thoes yt are out already yt there is nothing but ye singular Providence of God hath preuented our being utterly run down. The Enemy observes or Motions & knows or strngth (weakness rather) bettr yn wee are willing hea should & Pbably had been with us ere this had not ye Highest Power ruled him. And that Hauer-hill,

Exettr, &c are in like prdicament wth Douer &c seems apparent, & hence as incapeable of spareing Men. In true(?) there is an Army out in Yorkshire wch will doubtless doe what may bee done yet there is room enough for ye Enemy to slipp by them unobserved, & if so, what so, what a Condition we are in is evident. Our own men are not enough to maintain or own places if any Assault bee made & yet many of ors are now on the other side of the Pasnataq. River. Wee expect an Onsett in one place or other Qeuery day & can expect no Reliefe fro those yt are so far fro home. If it should be thought meet yt all ye Men yt are come to us & other parts — — fr m ye deserted & unguarded Eastern Country should bee ordered to ye Places yt are left on theyr own side of ye Riuer, yt so ors may bee recalled to theyr seuerall towns, it might possible bee not unavailable to ye End. Especially if with all some Indians might bee ordered to those parts too bee upon a perpetuall Scout from place to place. Wee design not a lessening or discouragt of ye Army who rather need strengtheng & Incourag mt, for we verily think yt if by ye good Hand of Providence ye Army had not been there, all ye Parts on ye other side of ye Riuer had been possest by the Enemy & perhaps orselves too ere ys Time. But what we aim at is that orselves also may bee put into a Capacity to defend orselues. Wee are apt to fear we have been too bold with your Honors, but woe are sure our Intentions are good, & or Condition very bad except ye Lord of Hosts appear for us speedily, & wee would be found in ye Use of Meanes, commending or Case to him yt is able to protect in ye Use of Meanes, commending in order thereunto, & Remain

Mch Honrd yor Humble Seruts
  Richard Walderne
  John Cutt
  Tho: Daniel
  Robert Pike
  Richard Martyn
  Wm. Vaughan."

It has been said already, that two hundred of the Indians captured on the 7th of September, were sent to Boston for trial. The following letter which relates to this matter, may be of interest:—

"Dover, 10th September 1676.

Much Hond

The Indns being now on board & Comeing towards you, Wee yt haue been Soe far Impr— — about yme Thought it conuenient to Inform how ffar they haue kept the Pease Made wth us & who of those are concerned therein vizt Penicooks, Wonolonsets, Waymesists & Piscataq Indns there being not any belonging further Eastwd come in — — — nor any other of those belonging to ye South Side of Mirimack euer Included in our Pease —those of ym yt had made ye Pease comeing in to Comply wth yt, the others to get Shelter under ym but yt they should be all treated alike as here they were wee humbly Conceive no Reason wee not being able to charge those yt had made ye Pease wth any breach of Articles saue only yt of entertaining our Southern Enemies but by yt meanes we came to surprise Soe many of ym. There ar Seueral of Piscataq Indns here who before ye Pease had been very Active Against us but since haue all liu'd quietly & Attended Order but yor

Pleasures being to haue all sent down to determine their Case at Boston, hath been Attended keeping here about 10 young men of ym to Serue in ye Army wth their familie & Some old men & theirs wth Wonolansets Relations. Yesterday came in 2 Squawes informing yt one eyd Jno & Jethro were designing ye Surprizing of Canonicus & bringing in desireing Some of our old Menn to come to Aduise wth him about it, I forthwith sent out there to ffurther ye design. Wee haue Information from Jewel's Island yt the former newes is not Soe bad being not aboue 10 in all kill'd and wounded being unexpectedly Surprized. if yr be Any obs(t)ructions in ye ffurther Prosecution of ye enemy now by ye — — our people will quickly desert their Country Shall Add no more at Prsent, but Remain in much Honr.

   Yor Humble Servnts,
    Richard Waldern
    Nic Snapleigh
    Tho Daniel "

OLD SERIES, NO. 108, MAY 17, 1853.

RICHARD WALDERNE.
VIII. THE SHAM FIGHT.

Another letter, copied from the Massachusetts Archives, throws light upon the fate of the captured Indians.

    "Cochecha, 2 9 ber 1676.
Majr Gookin

Hond Sir, I recd yors of 25th 9ber concerning Some Indns wch you say it is Alledg'd I promis(d) life & liberty to. time Prmits mee not at prsent to inlarge but for Answer in Short you may Please to know I promised neither Peter Jethro nor any other of yt Compa life or liberty, it was not in my Power to doe it. all yt I promise(d) was to Peter Jethro vizt: That if he would use his Endeauor & be Instrumental In ye bringing in one eyed Jno &c I would acquain ye Gouenr wth wh Seruice he had done & Improue my Interest in his behalfe that I Acquainted ye Honrd Council wit if it had been their Pleasure to haue Saued more of ym it would not haue trouble mee. as to ye Squaw you Mention belonging to one of Capt. Hunking's souldiers there was S(uch) a one left of ye first great Compa of Indns (sent?)down wch Capt Hunking desir'd might stay here til himselfe & her husband Came back from Eastward wch I consented to, and how She came among yt Compa I know not. I requiring none to geo yr to Boston but those that came in after ye Armies departure neither Knew I a word of it at Boston wn I disposed ym Soe yt twas her own fault in not Acquainting mee wth it but if Said Squaw be n t Sent off I shall be freely Willing to re-imburse those Gent wt they Gave mee for her yt She may be Sett at liberty. being wholy Inocent as to wt I'me Charg'd wth I intend ere long to be at Boston wn I doubt not but Shall giue you full Satisfaction there about.
 I am Sr Yor humble Serut
    Richard Waldern."

IX. A SHORT PEACE.

The war was ended for a long time, by a treaty between the whites and Penobscots, concluded on the 6th of September, MOGG having been deputed to act for the Indians and agreeing to articles of peace at Boston, whither he had been sent from Pascataqua. These articles were afterwards ratified by Madokawando. Vessels were therefore sent to the Penobscot, to procure the release of captives, Mogg being still retained as hostage. Some few captives were obtained, but Mogg escaped, and his treacherous purposes were soon displayed. It was soon after discovered, also that Narragansett Indians were still scattered amongst those of the East; three of them were decoyed into the wigwams of Cocnecho and were slain, the cut of their hair betraying them. Such circumstances convinced the colonists that the peace would be of very short continuance, and it was judged proper for the whites to strike the first blow. The Bay Government determined upon a winter expedition.

X. EXPEDITION TO THE EAST.

Four hundred men were equipped (including sixty Natick Indians,) and were dispatched for the eastward, under the command of Major Walderne, the expedition sailing in the first week of February 1677, after a day of fasting and prayer, Here follow his instructions:

"Instructions for Major Rich. Walderne.

You shal repaire to Blacke point, wth the 60 soldiers under capt ffrost that you are authorized by ye council to raise in Dover, Portsmouth & Yorkshire, by the 8 of febr, where you are to take under your comand the other forces from Boston & Salem under the comand of Capt Hunking & Leiftenant Fiske & other — — officers, from whence wth all expedition wth the aduice of your Comanders — — you shall aduance towards the enemy at Kinnebeck or elsewhere, & according to the proposed designe, endeauor wth all silence & secresy to surprize them in their quarters, wherein if it please God to succeed you, you shall do your utmost endeauor to save & rescue the English prisoners.

If you fail in this designe you shall assay by alle means in your power to disturb & destroy the enemy, unless you have such overtures from them as may give some competent assurance that an honorable & safe peace may be concluded with them — wherein you must avoyd all trifling and delayes & wth all possible speed make a dispatch of the affaire not trusting them without first deliuery of all the Captiunes & vessels in their hands.

If you should, in conclusion, find it necessary to leaue a garrison in Kinnebeck wee must leaue it to your discretion.

You shall use utmost expedition as winds & other advantages will permit, lest ye season be lost and charges seem without profit.

Praying God to be with you
past   E. —— R. —— S.
24 Janury 1676 (7).

"F, L. G. wth the consent of the Council.

To Major Richard Walderne

whereas you are apoynted Cor in Chief of the forces Now to be raised agt the enemy the — — in the East for the — — — all haue ordered the rendevous of the sd forces at Black point the 8 of febr next — — hereby ordered & authorized you to take under your Comand

& conduct the sd forces woh you are to require to obey & attend your orders & Comands as their Comander in Cnief, & you to leade, conduct & order the sd forces for the best seruice of the country against the Comon enemy whom you are to endeavor to surprize, kill & destroy by all means in your power & all soulders, officers & — — under you are required to yield obedience — endeavor to recover the English prisoners from out of their possession, you are also to govern the forces under your Comand according to the laws enacted by the Genrall Ct, to attend all such orders comands as you shall receive from time to time from the generall Court Councills or other Supe rior authority.

Given in 29 jan. 1676-7.

past. E. R. S."

This expedition proved fruitless. But few events in it are worthy of remembrance. A parley at Casco was attended with no important result. Another parley was held at the mouth of the Kennebeck. It was mutually agreed to lay aside arms, and negotiate for the ransom of prisoners. The Indians demanded twelve beaver skins for each, with some good liquor, but only three captives could be obtained. Another parley was proposed when Walderne, Ffrost and three others landed under a mutual promise that no weapons should be worn on either side. But Walderne espied the point of a lance under a board, and searching further, found other weapons, and taking and brandishing one towards them, exclaimed, "Perfidious wretches you intended to get our goods and then kill us, did you?" They were thunderstruck yet one, more daring than the rest, seized the weapon, and strove to wrest it from Walderne's hand. Capt Ffrost laid hold of Megunnaway, one of the barbarous murderers of Thomas Brackett and neighbors and dragged him into his vessel. Meanwhile an athletic squaw caught up a bundle of guns and ran for the woods. At that instant a reinforcement arrived from the vessel, when the Indians scattered in all directions, pursued by the soldiers. In this affray Sagamore Maltahouse and an old Powow were capsized in a canoe and drowned, and five others were captured. One thousand pounds of beef were taken, and some other booty. Megunnaway, grown in crime, was shot. Two more Indians were killed at Arrowsick Island. The expedition returned to Boston on the 11th of March, without the loss of a man.

XI. AT HOME.

After this expedition was ended, the Major returned home, and busied himself with the duties of his charge here. Though the war continued a year longer, but little took place about Dover. But one instance of alarm is recorded as having occurred in its immediate vicinity during the year. Sometime in March, the presence of hostile Indians in the woods near Cochecho, was discovered, and Walderne sent out eight of his Indians of whom Blind Will was one, to obtain information. These were all surprized by a company of Mohawks, who, nominally in alliance with the English, spared neither friend nor foe. Two or three of the scouting party escaped the others were killed or taken; Blind Will was dragged away by his hair, and being wounded perished on a neck of land formed at the junction of the Isinglass and Cochecho rivers, which was long called "Blind Will's Neck." It was first thought that the death of Blind Will was fortunate but the result proved otherwise; for the friendly Indians became suspicious that the Mohawks were engaged to destroy rather than assist them.

OLD SERIES, NO. 109, MAY 24, 1853.

RICHARD WALDERNE.

The following letter gives us some information not hitherto published—

"Cochecha, 18th April, 1677.
May it Please yor honor:

I have lately Recd Some lines from Majr Gookin intimating an order of ye honrd Council for ye Sending mee 10 Indns to releive & Strengthen ys pts, wch ffauour I gratefully Acknowledge but of the Said 10 are but 2 come from Cambridge & 3 from Ipswch, 2 ye latter being old & unfitt for Seruise wch must dismisse again to Saue Charges.

Majr Gookin hints yt ye Indns Auersion to coming hither is not wthout Some Reasons of weight wtbout telling mee what they are but am since better Informed of their Complaints from ye Secretary, vizt, of my Improueing them to labour about my own ocations wthout any Allowance & their dissatisfaction wth my Pronisions. ffor ye fformer I did Employ Some of ym. 5 or 6 days but pd ym for it to their full satisfaction. Indeed wn I Sent out men to Cut wood ffor ye ffire they Went out wth ym as our English Souldiers use to doe to prouide wood to make ymselves a fire. I think some of ym in my Absence were ordred 2 or three dayes to Cutt bushes on ye Side of ye Comon Road without wch no Post or other could Passe without danger of being cutt off by an unseen enemy.

As to their Prouision know not why they should (complain) unlesse because I did not keep a Maid to dress their Vituals for ym but ordered ym to do it ymselves. I did not discouer any Kind of dissatisfaction till Peter Ephraim came & after yt nothing wd content ym but they must goe home. Wn I had ye 1st intimation of three Indns Seen up Mirrimack I had ordred 20 forthwith to haue gone out but through the Sd Peter's means they were grown Soe high & ungouernable was fforc't to dismisse them.

Since my last we haue been & are almost daily Alarmed by ye Enemy. An Acct of ye Mischeif done Presume yor honrs haue already had.

11th inst. 2 men more kill'd at Wells. 12th. 2 men, one woman, & 4 children kill'd at York & 2 houses burnt. 13th, a house burnt at Kittery & old people taken Captiue by Simon & 3 more but they gaue ym ther liberty again without any damage to their psons. 14th, a house surpriz'd on South SidePascatway & 2 young women carried away thence. 16th, a man kill'd at Greenland and his house burnt, another Sett on fire but ye Enemy was beaten off & ye ffire put out by Some of our men who then recouer'd alsoe one of ye young women taken 2 days before who sts there was but 4 Indns; they run Sculking about in Small pties like Wolves. we have had pties of men after ym in all qrters wch haue

Sometimes Recouer'd Something they
haue Stolen. but Can't certainly Say
they have kill'd any of ym; Capt ffrost is
after ym in Yorkshire. from Black
point you will haue ye Intelligence of ye
Enemies March, ffrom Capt Scottow, to
whome haue Sent Some letters froth
— — — —I add noe more at prsent but
Comend you to God's Protection who
hath hitherto & is able still to be our or
Guard.

    resting Sr Yor Very humble Serut
           Richard Walderne."

XII. PEACE

In the spring of the year 1678, a peace
was concluded at Casco, Major Shapliegh of Kittery, Captain Francis Champernoon and Mr. Fryer of Portsmouth
acting for the whites. The following
paper has reference to this matter:

"For Major Walderne & Major Pendleton.

from your selves by seueral letters we
have receiued Information of Squando &
the other Indians case their Desire
further to hear the English of — —
parts for a firm peace & that Major
Shapleigh & Champernoon are Desired to
Aduance in that matter as most acceptable to the Indians. if themselves or
any other persons be Judged Suitable by
your selves for such an occasion te obtayned to hear them they may In the
name of the Gouernor & Council promise them a Safe Conduct comeing and returning hither in way of treaty whether
anything Concluded or not as they formerly Haue if otherwise they may take
the Indians Demands of which ours-lves
hear may Consider & give Answer In
the Mean time aduising as ye Spring
cometh on to be upon your watch and
guard your own Security.

    not else but Remajne S — —
      your freind & Seruant
      Edwd Rawson Secret & — —
       — — of the Councill."
9th of March 77.

By the terms of this treaty the captives were restored and the deserted settlements permitted to be re-occupied, the
whites paying one peck of corn annually
for each family as an acknowledgement
to the Indians of the possession of the
lands. Thus a tedious and distressing
war was ended by a disgraceful peace,
though perhaps its terms were as favorable as the colonists had a right to expect.

XIII. THE LAND TITLES DISPUTED.

During the troubles that ended with
the peace of 1678, another enemy, of a
different character, arose to vex the inhabitants of Dover; or rather an old one
renewed his attacks. Robert Mason,
grandson of John Mason, the original
Proprietor of the Province, petitioned the
King in 1677, for a 'restoration' of the
property which he claimed under the
original Patents. The matter was referred by the English Government, 17
May 1675, to the Attorney General, Sir
William Jones and the Solicitor General,
Sir Francis Winnington for their opinion
as to the legality of the claim. Their report was in favor of the validity of Mason's title. These lands were now under
the control of the Massachusetts Government which was regularly informed of
the decision, and directed to send agents

to England, who should make answer to Mason's complaints. At the same time, Edward Randolph, a man of great energy and bitterly hostile to the Bay Government, who was sent over as the messenger of the Lords of Trade, was disaulrected to inform himself as to the 'state of the country,' this charge being understood to mean that he should manufacture as much public sentiment against the Massachusetts Government as was necessary to justify the separation of New Hampshire from Massachusetts, a deed already secretly decided upon. Randolph met no friendly reception in the latter province and came into New Hampshire, trusting to meet with better success.—He found a few persons discontented, but the people generally highly offended; for their separation from Massachusetts was to be only the prelude to their own reduction to a state of tenantry on the soil which they had defended at so much expense of blood and treasure. Prominent in opposition to Randolph and to the whole series of measures in which he was interested, was Major Walderne. His prominent position in Dover, and indeed in the whole province, caused the people to turn their eyes upon him as a leader. Apart from his own important interest in the title to the soil, he was ready to assist his fellow citizens, and he immediately took that position of leader in opposition to Mason's claim which he retained throughout the whole struggle. In this town the inhabitants 'protested against the claim of Mason, declared they had bone-fide purchased their lands of the Indians, recognized their subjection to the overnment of the Massachusetts, &c., &c.,' and appointed Major Walderne to petition the King in their behalf.

XIV. A NEW GOVERNMENT.

After various proceedings it was finally concluded in England that Mason's claim to the land could only be tried upon the place, and it was therefore necessary to create a new government there. Before this was done, however, Mason was forced to promise that he would ask no back rents for any time preceding the 24th of June 1679, and that he would make out titles to all of the lands in their possession to them and theirs forever, provided they would pay a sixpense in the pound according to the yearly value of all houses which they had built and lands which they had improved. On the 8th of Sept. 1679, the territory lying between Massachusetts and Maine was constituted a separate Province; John Cutt was appointed President, Richard Martyn, William Vaughan, and Thomas Daniel of Portsmouth, John Gilman of Exeter, Christopher Hussey of Hampton, and Richard Walderne of Dover, were appointed Counsellors.

The commissions were received, by the gentlemen named, with much reluctance, but for fear of worse usage, they accepted them. Under this charter Walderne was appointed Vice President of the Province, and commander of the military establishment, which was composed of one foot company in each town, one troop of horse, and one company of artillery at the fort.

OLD SERIES, NO. 110, MAY 31, 1853.

RICHARD WALDERNE.

On the 30th of December, 1680, Mason arrived from England to enforce his claims, bringing with him a mandamus to admit him to a seat in the Council. But instead of having the disputed claims brought to trial, he commenced issuing arbitrary orders to the people, requiring them to take leases of him, forbidding them to cut firewood, and the like. Such proceedings became so intolerable, that the Council forbade them, and, at last, Mason departed for England, exceedingly irritated at his reception. The manner in which his orders had been treated, may be inferred from the following:

"Robert Mason Esqr Proprietor of the Province of New Hampshire maketh oath, That the Writing hereto annexed is a true Copy of the Declaration which he caused to be set up at the usual places in the several towns of the sd Province, And that Major Richard Waldern did say to this deponent, That no such Papers should be set up to amuse the People and did show unto this Depount one of the afore sd Declaracons or some part thereof that he had pulled down. Robert Mason.

Taken upon Oath the 17th of October 1684, before me
R. Chamberlain Just. P"

XV. PRESIDENT PRO-TEM, CHIEF, JUSTICE.

John Cutt died on the 27th of March, 1681, and Walderne, who was his deputy, succeeded to his office, as President of the Province; this post he occupied until the arrival of Edward Cranfield, 4 October. Of course, while Walderne was at the head of the government, nothing was done regarding the claims of Mason, who was then in England—The appointment of Cranfield was made in pursuance of an arrangement in which Mason's interest in the whole province was mortgaged to him for twenty-one years. Cranfield was therefore, a party directly interested in Mason's claims and this was the cause of the rancor with which he pursued those who opposed his purposes. Only six days after his arrival, he suspended Walderne and Martyn from the Council, on frivolous pretexts, but this use of his power, only served to render him odious in the very commencement of his administration. Ashamed, perhaps, of this action, on the 14th of November, he restored them to their places.

The Assembly met on the same day, but after a short period of harmony, their opposition to his measures became so irritating, that the Governor adjourned the Assembly. Its next session was no more to his mind, and he then dissolved it, an act which aroused the anger of the whole body of the people, unused as they were to such proceedings—One person, Edward Gove, a member of the Assembly, from Hampton, endeavored in a half-crazy manner, to excite the people to arms, but however, much they were dissatisfied with the government, they had no sympathy with Gove's wild proceeding. His attempt failed entirely. He himself was brought to trial on an accusation of high treason.

—A special court was created, 15 Feb.'y 1683, of which Walderne was Judge. Gove was convicted, being the first and last man convicted of High Treason in the State of New Hampshire, and the horrible sentence of the law was passed upon him, by Major Walderne; it is said that the Judge shed tears as he pronounced the sentence.*

In pursuance of the previous arrangements the Governor called upon the inhabitants, 14 Feb'y 1683, to take leases of Mason within one month.—But this, of course, was out of the question. Within the month, however, Walderne, accompanied by John Winget, and Thomas Roberts, all large land owners, waited upon the Governor. He directed them to see Mason; the proposition of Walderne, that the whole affair should be referred to the King, was refused, and there was therefore no way of avoiding a series of legal quarrels.

Walderne was again suspended from the Council, as also Martyn and Gilman. "The judicial courts were also filled with officers proper for the intended business. Some who had always been disaffected to the country, and others who had been awed by threats and promises, took leases from Mason; and these served for under sheriffs, jurors, evidences, and other necessary persons."

"Things being thus prepared, Mason began his law-suits, by a writ against Major Walderne (who had always distinguished himself in opposition to his claim,) for holding lands and felling timber, to the amount of four thousand pounds. The Major appeared in Court, and challenged every one of the jury as interested persons, some of them having taken leases of Mason, and all of them having lands which he claimed. The Judge then caused the oath of voire dire to be administered to each juror, purporting "that he was not concerned in the lands in question, and that he should neither gain nor lose by the cause." Upon which the Major said aloud to the people present, "that his was a leading case, and that if he were cast they must all become tenants of Mason, and that all persons in the province being interested, none of them could legally be of the jury." The cause, however, went on but he made no defence, asserted no title, and gave no evidence. Judgement was given against him, and at the next court of sessions he was fined for "mutinous and seditious words."

Suits were instituted against many other land owners, and decided in the same summary manner. In Dover, besides Walderne, there were John Heard, sen., William Horne, Jenkin Jones, William Furbur jun., John Hall jun., Joseph Field, Nathaniel Hill, James Huckins, William Tasker, Zachary Field,

---

*Gove was not executed, but carried to England and confined in the Tower of London, several years, when he was finally pardoned and permitted to return home, and his estate was restored to him. The house in which he lived, or some portion of it, is still standing, in Seabrook, formerly a part of Hampton, and a Pear tree, which, tradition says, he brought with him from England, is yet flourishing in "a green old age" on the premises. He did not live many years after his return, and always contended that a slow poison had been administered to him while in prison. His descendants are numerous in Seabrook, Hampton, and other parts of the State.

Philip Chesley jun., Thomas Chesley, Robert Burnham, Antony Nutter, William Furtur, sen., Thomas Paine, Charles Adams, Thomas Edgerly, Henry Langstaffe, Thomas Stevenson, John Meader, John Woodman, John Windiet John Davis sen., Joseph Beard, John Roberts, Joseph Stevenson, Samuel Hill, Philip Lewis, John Gerrish, John Hill, Joseph Hall, Thomas Roberts, sen. and perhaps others, who were thus declared dispossessed. From seven to twelve cases were dispatched each day—Some executions were levied; but the officer could neither retain possession, nor find purchasers, so that the property soon reverted to its owners.—These matters went on, until the representations of Nathaniel Weare so influenced the Board of Trade that they ordered Cranfield to suspend the suit—Executions however, were issued after this; the success which they met with may be learned from an incident which occurred in Dover; certain officers attempting to levy an execution, were driven off; they returned on the Sabbath, with warrants to apprehend the rioters; a tumult ensued, which was ended by a young girl's knocking down one of the officers with her Bible; such a spirit it was useless to resist.

The suits were suspended, however, and were not resumed until long after Walderne's death. It is unnecessary for us, therefore, to say more than that in the final decision, the rights of the colonists were fully reserved.

OLD SERIES NO. 111, JUNE 7, 1853.

RICHARD WALDERNE.

XVII. DEATH.

For eleven years there had been profound peace upon the Pascataqua and its branches. At Cochecho the former habits of trade were revived and whites and Indians mingled freely.

Means of safety were not neglected however,—Seven garrison houses were still preserved, into which the neighboring families gathered at night. Walderne's, Heard's, Otis's and Paine's stood upon the north side of the river; those of the Coffins, father and son, and Gerrish's, were upon the south. The timber walls around them were impregnable by open attacks and their gates were well secured by bolts and bars.

The Indians who were captured at the sham fight in 1677, had never forgiven Walderne for his share in that event. Some of them who had been destined to slavery, after finding no purchasers among the nations to whom they were offered and after having been left at Tangier, had succeeded in returning home; these had cherished a relentless thirst for revenge. The Pennacooks, it is true, had no such reasons for hostility, for though their sachem and a hundred others were captured on that occasion, they were immediately released; but they regarded his conduct as a breach of faith worthy of punishment, the memory of old wrongs also was revived; and when Kankamagus, who imagined himself illtreated, had fled in 1686 to the Androscoggin for safety from the Mohawks, who nominally allies to the whites, yet spared neither friend nor foe, his dissatisfaction was doubtless strengthened by the emissaries of Baron de St Castiens, the Frenchman who lived in half feudal state on the banks of the Penobscot. Wonalanset, son of the venerable Passaconaway, had always remembered his father's dying charge to live at peace with the whites; but Kankamagus, Sachem of the Pennacooks, formed a league with the Pequawkets and the remnant of the fugitives to gratify their desire for revenge, and aided by Mesandowit, a sachem second in authority to himself prepared for an attack upon Cochecho.

Without the knowledge of any preconcerted plan, the people of Dover, in June, became suspicious of Indian friendship. Larger numbers of Indians seemed gathering than was usual for purposes of trade. Many strange faces were among them, whose scrutiny of the defences of the place excited notice. — Walderne, however, could not be convinced of danger. Some of the people came to him with their fears, "go plant your pumpkins," said he merrily; "I will tell you when the Indians will break out." A day or two previous to the time decided upon, some squaws endeavored to alarm the whites by vague intimations of danger. Thus one of them repeatedly recited the words:

"O Major Walderne, you great sagamore What will you do, Indians at your door;" but she was not understood until the transactions themselves had given only too vivid a meaning to her words. On the evening of the 27th, a young man told him that the town was full of Indians, and that the people were much alarmed. "I know the Indians very well, and there is no danger," was the reply. Long experience had made him presumptuous. But though Major Walderne was so fatally confident, information of the expected attack had already been sent to the Massachusetts government by Major Henchman of Chelmsford in a letter of which the following is a copy.

"Hond' Sir—This day, two Indians came from Pennacook, viz Job Maramsquad and Peter Muckamug, who report that damage will undoubtedly be done within a few days at Pascataqua, and that Major Walderne, in particular is threatened; and that Tulimutt fears that mischief will quickly be done at Dunstable. The Indians can give a more particular account to your honor. They say, if damage be done, the blame shall not be on them, having given a faithful account of what they hear; and are upon that report moved to leave their habitation and corn at Pennacook. Sir, I was very loth to trouble you and to expose myself to the censure and derision of some of the confident people, that would pretend to make sport with what I send down by Capt. Tom (alias Thomas Ukqucakussennum).

I am constrained from a sense of my duty, and from love to my countrymen, to give the information as above So with my humble service to your honor, and prayers for the safety of an endangered people—

I am sir your humble servant
    Tho: Hinchman."
June 22 (1689).

Mr. Danforth communicated the information to Gov Bradstreet, who, with the Council ordered a messenger to the Cocheco with the following

  Boston 27 of June: 1689.
"Honord Sir.

The Governor and Council haveing this day received a Letter from Major Henchman of Chelmsford that some Indians are come into them; who report that there is a gathering of some Indians in or about Penecooke with designe of mischief to English, amongst the said Indians one Hawkies (Kankamagus), is said to be a principle designer and that they have a particular designe against yourselfe and Mr. Peter Coffin which the Councill thought it necessary presently to dispatch Advice Thereof to give you notice that you take care of yor own Safeguard, they intending to endeavour to betray you on a pretention of Trade. Please forthwith to Signify the import hereof to Mr Coffin and others as you shall thinke necessary and Advise of what Information you may receive at any time of the Indians motions.

By Order in Councill
Isa: Addington Secry.

For Major Rich'd Walderne
and Mr. Peter Coffin or Either
of them.
At Cochecha.
These with all possible (speed)."

The messenger hastened towards Cochecho; he would have been in season, but he was unavoidably detained at Newbury ferry, and he reached the place only on the morning of the 28th.

On the evening of the 27th June 1689, two squaws, according to the previously arranged plan, applied at each garrison house for liberty to sleep in them; this was often done in time of peace and they were readily admitted into Walderne's, Heard's, the elder Coffin's and Otis's. At their own request they were shown how to open the doors and   tes in case they wished to leave the house in the night. They told the Major that a number of Indians were coming to trade with him the next day, and Mesandowit who was at supper, said "Brother Walderne, what would you do if the strange Indians should come?" "I could assemble a hundred men by lifting up my finger," carelessly answered the Major. No watch was kept, and the family retired to rest.

In the hours of deepest quiet, the gates were opened the Indians who were waiting without, immediately entered, placed a guard at the gate and rushed into the Major's apartment. Awakened by the noise he sprang from his bed, seized a sword, and though nearly eighty years old, drove them through the two or three rooms; but returning for other arms, they came behind him, stunned him with a hatchet, and overpowered him; drawing him into the hall they then placed him in an elbow chair on a long table with a derisive cry "who shall judge Indians now?'" They then obliged the members of the family to get them some supper; when they had finished eating they cut the Major across the breast with knives, each one with a stroke saying "I cross out my account." Cutting off his nose and ears they thrust them into his mouth, and when he was falling down, spent with the loss of blood, one of them held his own sword beneath him, he fell upon it and his sufferings were ended.

OLD SERIES, NO. 175, AUG. 6, 1857.

NOTE BY JOHN SCALES.—In order to bring the Walderne family matter in consecutive order for the convenience of the readers, the numbers of the Memoranda from 111 to 175 are skipped for the present and will be taken up later, after all of the Walderre memoranda is completed.

THE WALDERNE-WALDRON FAMILY.

Some time since we gave a voluminous account of the life of Major Waldron of Cochecho in its early days. For want of certain information we omitted a genealogy of the family—a defect we are now able to supply. Recent researches in England, conducted mainly by the eminent antiquary and genealogist, H. G. Somerby, Esq., enable us to print even a pedigree of the Major's ancestors,—which would have still longer eluded search but for the fact brought out in our columns that the true name of this family was not Waldron, but Walderne: this important distinction changed the direction of a search previously carried on for "Waldron" and speedily brought to view the family history.

Richard Walderne was not a native of Somersetshire as has been asserted, nor was he born as Belknap has it in 1609; the date is disproved by a deposition of his own which compares with the table now published; and the family was of Alcester in Warwickshire.

Commencing with the earliest ancestor on record, we find Edward Walderne (1) of Alcester; he was buried there 13 Jan 1590, having had a wife Joan, and children (Fam. 1) George; Edward; William baptized 15 April 1561.

George (2) (Fam. 1) was also of Alcester; he was there married 8 July 1576 to Joan Shallard or Shaylorde, who was buried 27 July 1577, he was 12 April 1588. Of his children (perhaps the only child) (Fam 2) was William, bapt 25 July 1577.

Edward (2) of Fam. 1. was of Alcester, He mar. 3 Oct. 1574, Mary, daughter of Robert Hunt; he was buried 11 Febr. 1619. Children (Fam. 3.)

—Edward bapt. 13 Feb. 1576: Rose bapt. 25 June 1577, buried, 17 June 1585: John (2) bapt. 13 March 1579: William bapt 21 Jan. 1582, buried 4 May 1588.

William (2) of Fam. 1 also of Alcester, mar. 22 June 1584, Agnes Dislin; she was buried 24 June 1621. Children. (Fam. 4.)—Elizabeth bapt. 14 Nov. 1586, buried 7 Feb. 1601: Margery bapt. 8 Nov. 1588: Elinor bapt. 4 April 1591, buried 6 Jan. 1592; Edward bapt. 15 Oct. 1592; Alice bapt. 29 June 1595; Susan bapt. 12 Feb. 1598; John bapt. 28 May 1601, buried 26 Dec. 1626.

WILLIAM (3) of Fam. 2, of Alcester, (the Major's father,) mar. 26 of Nov. 1600, Catharine Raven; he was buried 25 Dec. 1636. Children were (Fam. 5).

—William, bp. 18 Oct. 1601, of whom by and by; George bapt. 26 April 1603: John bapt. 25 of Oct. 1606. Thomas bapt. 27 of Oct. 1608, bur. 7 Dec. 1633; Foulke bapt. 3 March 1610; Robert bapt 9 April 1612, "of London, citizen and leather dresser of St. Bride's parish;" Elizabeth bapt. 10 Oct. 1613; Richard bapt. 6 Jan. 1615 (the Major;) Katherine bapt. 7 Feb. 1618; Alexander bapt. 6 April 1620; Humphrey, bapt. 4 Aug. 1622, buried 25 of June 1624, Edward "of Alcester 1650," and of Kidminister

Worcester. 20 April 1658, but of what age is unknown.

Of the English branches,

EDWARD (3) of Fam. 3, mar. 18 Oct. 1607, Mary Clough; had children, (Fam 6.)

— Eleanor, bapt. 20 Sept., 1608 mar. 5 Feb. 1627, John Hemming; Mary bapt. 7 April 1610; Margaret bapt. 8 Oct. 1612 mar 16 April 1632, Robert Eaden; John bapt. 14 Aug. 1614; William bapt. 24 May 1616, buried 30 Oct. 1617.

EDWARD (3) of Fam. 4, mar. 7 July 1633, Alice Maunde, and had children, Fam. 7.

—Alice bapt. 20 July 1634, bur. 12 Aug. 1635; Edward bapt. 10 April 1636; William bapt. 8 March 1640.

Returning to the Major's immediate family—WILLIAM 4 came to Dover perhaps with his brother. Various papers to and from him are in existence, but none of particular interest. He owned some property among which were some shares of the Dover plantation. He was in office somewhat; was Recorder in 1641 to 1646, by virtue of which office he recorded deeds of land "on a pese of paper" which, copied, from the basis of our early Towne Record; was Amciale (that is, a sort of side judge) in 1642 was Deputy to General Court at Boston in 1646, in which his most memorable deed was to back up the town's credit which had suffered some by neglect to foot up previous "deputy's charges,". He was a member of the church here, but unfortunately, being a little overcome by liquor, as we are told, was drowned at Kennebunk in 1646. His affairs were found to be in considerable confusion having had a great many irons in the fire, some had got scorched.

Geo. Smith. was appointed to succeed him as recorder, at the court of Nov. 1646, and he and Elder Starbuck were appointed (on petition of the Major) to sort out William's papers, give private individuals such as belonged to them, and hand over the public documents to the court. Quite a variety of creditors importuned the General Court (which then did all sorts of business) for the court to devise a way by which "wee may be putt into some course how to come by the estate of ye sd William Walderne, to be divided amongst vs proportionally, according to our debts;" this was in Oct. 1647, and Capt. Wiggin and Edw. Rawson were appointed to administer; in May 1649 the administrators were paid for their services, the former 30s, the latter 40, and the estate was passed over to Elder Nutter and John Hall "to dispose of as they judge may best tend to the improvement of the estate and to be ready to be accomptable when the Courte shall thinke meete to call for it, ffor ye sattisfaccon of the creditors." How much satisfaction the creditors got out of it we are unable to say, but we don't think it was a great deal, as in 1666, when Richard Scammon of Portsmouth (who had married William's only daughter, Prudence) petitioned to have William's share of the Shrewsbury part of Swamscot patent placed in his hands, it was done only on his giving security to the "creditors"; we hope they lived long enough to see the end of it. As to his family we know nothing except these items:—Fam. 8. His only daughter Prudence married Richard Scammon of Portsmouth. In a pedigree compiled from a bill in chancery at the Tower of London he is still supposed to be "living in New England, beyond the seas," in 1654, "having issue Christopher and many other children" of this Christopher we have no trace:—William b. 1642, taxed in Dover 1664 is called "nephew of Major Walderne," and in all probability was son of William 4. "George Wallden," taxed at Cochecho 1659-1672, may have been another.—Alexander, at one time of New Castle, "a relative of Maj. Walderne" d. 7 June 1676, and William, taxed together as "Elexander & William Walden" in 1664, (the first taxed alone in 1665 and again in 1667) at Cochecho, may have been others. So may John Wallden, who was taxed at Cochecho 1672, It ought to be noticed that Alexander made his will 7 June 1670, in which he leaves his property to his "brother Edward in Old England," brother Samuel and to the wife of Robert Taprell. How many of these were Wm.'s children, it is hard to tell; Prudence certainly was, and was the only daughter, Christopher must have been; William probably was; of the rest, perhaps they were, and then, again, perhaps they were not.

George (4) of Fam. 5, brother to the Major was, "of Alcester, Chandler, 1650;" he married 3—May 1635, Bridget Rice, and had children, Elizabeth bapt. 22 March 1636; Mary bapt. 1 Aug. 1637, William bapt. 4 Aug. 1639.

Either one of the Major's brothers married a Stone of Bristol, or else a Stone married one of the Major's sisters; which we don't know but evidently a neice of the Major's by one of these arrangements came over and resided with her uncle at Dover until she got married, which probably was not very long; she married Joseph Hall, son of Sergeant John Hall of Dover, which John made his will 29 Aug. 1677 and who left wife Elizabeth and son Joseph, and Sarah and another daughter who married a Dame: Joseph Hall who married the Major's neice died of small pox (he lived in Greenland up to that time) 19 Dec. 1685, the disconsolate widow mar. 7 Aug. 1687, Col. Thos. Packer of Portsmouth, and of course removed there, with her daughter Elizabeth, she died 14 Aug. 1717 æ 62; her tombstone is still standing in Greenland, with this inscription: "Here lieth ye body of Mrs. Elizabeth Packer, wife of Col. Thomas Packer, aged 62 years: deceased Aug. 14, 1717."

In our next number we will speak of the Major's own family.

OLD SERIES, NO. 176, SEPT. 3, 1857.

WALDERNE-WALDRON FAMILY.

RICHARD WALDERNE, 4 (of Fam. 5,) familiarly known as "the old Major," was born in Alcester, England in 1615, or the very last of 1614. He came over here to look about in 1635, (probably) went home and married "a Gentlewoman of a very good family, (whose parents were very unwilling she should come away,") which is not to be wondered at, considering the state of society here at that time, returned with his bride in 1637, located first on Dover Neck, as we learn by a list of inhabitants there in early times, but came up to Cochecho, where he lived and died.

Of his public services we need make no mention, as they are fully described in Nos. 104—111 of these memoranda. His house stood either on Second street, on the site of the late Waldron house, about 20 feet west of the southwest corner of Morrill's Block, or else a little lower down on Central avenue; our own opinion is that the latter is the true tradition inasmuch as one aged member of the family, now living distinctly remembers how the traditionary spot of her childhood was left uncultivated and it is most probable that when a new house was built, it was placed on a little different site. In either case, the garden sloped down to the river and in later days the orchard stretched westward on Second street, where a few trees of the latter orchard of Daniel Waldron are still standing in the garden of George Quint, in good order yet. The Major's spring was a little south of the south line of 2nd street, and a few feet west of the house of W. B. Wiggin, but is closed up; it was called 'Red Oak Spring.' The Major's mills were on the north side of the river, where the Machine shops now are, as well as on the south side. His home property stretched from below the falls a long distance up the river on its north side, and from the south line of the Academy lot north, to above Friend Ham's house. Besides, he owned either the soil or the timber of thousands of acres in various places.

The Major's first wife died and he married (2) Annie, (probably a sister of Richard Scammon,) who died 7 Feb. 1635. The Major was killed, as everybody knows 28 June 1689, his house was burned over his head, but tradition says that his bones were collected and buried in the very old burying ground east of the Methodist church, which was doubtless a family burying place. His children were, (Fam. 10), —Paul, who died about 1669 in Algiers, probably, being employed in a ship of his father's (the preceding year he was at Penacook;) Timothy, who died a student in Harvard College; Richard, b. 1650; Anna mar Rev. Joseph Gerrish; Elnathan b. 6 July 1659, died 10 Dec. 1659; Esther b. 1 Dec. 1660, mar. Henry Elkins, Abraham Lee, Richard Jose and somebody else, (one at a time, of course) and last of all the woman died also, in the Isle of Jersey; Mary, b. 14 Sept. 1663, died young; Eleazer, b. 1 May 1665; Elizabeth, b. 8 Oct. 1666, mar. John Gerrish of Dover; Maria b. 17 July, 1668, died aged about 14. Of these children, Elnathan, Esther and Mary, were born in Boston; all after perhaps all before were born in Dover.

Of the Major's children, Paul is disposed of.—For TIMOTHY, we have hunted at Cambridge, but the absence of early records forbids success: RICHARD we will speak of below. Anna, who mar. Rev. Joseph Gerrish of Windham, had children, but how many we do not know; her husband was a son of Capt. Wm. Gerrish of Newbury; and was b. 23 March, 1650; one of their children was Elizabeth, who mar. Rev. Joseph Green of Salem Village. ELNATHAN died young. How many children, if any, Esther had in the course of her four marriages we are totally ignorant; her first husband, Henry Elkins, was a son of Henry Elkins of Hampton; her second, a "chymist," she married 21 June 1686; he was killed 28 June 1689, and she was carried into captivity by the Indians; after her return she married Richard Jose, son of Sheriff Richard of Portsmouth, but had a further opportunity to marry, and married somebody whose name is lost to history. Mary died young, and so probably did ELEAZER. ELIZABETH mar. John Gerrish, son of Capt. Wm. Gerrish of Newbury, b. 15 May 1645; he "took the oath" of fidelity in Dover, 21 June 1669; the old Major gave him 1 June 1669, part of the Mill at Bellamy, where Gerrish lived, and also a hundred acres of land; also 6 May 1670, a house partly finished; John was an enterprising man, being Representative in 1684, member of Convention in 1689, and Judge; they had children; Richard, John, Paul, Nathaniel, Timothy, b. 1684, and probably others, all of whom we need say nothing now, except that Richard became a Judge also, and that descendants still live here. MARIA, ("Marah") died young. So that Richard, Anna, Gerrish and Elizabeth Gerrish are the only children who seem to have left descendants, Richard's children being the only ones to perpetuate the name.

RICHARD 5, son of the Major, b. in 1650, early moved to Portsmouth, where he was living when news of his father's murder arrived, 28 June 1689. He was educated as a Merchant under Governor Willoughby, at Charlestown. He was a leading man, not only in Portsmouth, but in the Province. He was a member of the Convention of 1690, a Representative in 1691-2, was a Counsellor in 1681, Chief Justice of C. C. P., Judge of Probate; and Colonel. He was twice married, (1) to Hannah, daughter of President Cutt who died 14 Feb. 1602; (2) 6 Feb. 1692-3, to Eleanor, daughter of Major William Vaughan, who was born 5 March 1669-70, died Sept. 1727. He died 3 Nov. 1730. His will was as follows:

In the name of God ame, The 6th day of April, 1730.

I Richard Waldon of Portsmouth in New Hampshire Esq. laboring under bodily indispositions and the infirmity of an advanced age, but of sound and perfect mind and memory, Do constitute and ordain and appoint this to be my last will and Testament. My soul I commit into the hands of Almighty God, relying on the merits of a crucified Saviour for pardon and acceptance, and my body to the earth which I will shall have a decent Interment according to the discretion of my Executors hereafter named. And touching the temporal and worldly Estate wherewith it hath pleased God to bless me I do order give and dispose of the same in manner and form following —That is to say—

Imprim'—I will that all my just Debts and funeral charges be paid and discharged with all convenient speed.

Item. I give and bequeath to my beloved daughter Margaret Russell and her heirs forever Three hundred and fifty pounds in Province bills of credit to be paid by my Executor within two years after my decease which with what I gave her at her marriage makes up the sum of five hundred pounds.

Item. I give and bequeath to my beloved daughter Anna Rust and her heirs forever three hundred & fifty pounds in Province bills of credit to be paid by my Executor within two years after my decease which with what I gave her at her marriage makes up the sum of five hundred pounds.

Item. I give and bequeath to my beloved daughter Abigail Saltonstal and her heirs forever Three hundred and fifty pounds in Province Bills of credit to te paid by my Executor within two years after my decease which with what I gave her at her marriage makes up the sum of five hundred pounds

Item. I give and bequeath to the children of my beloved son William Waldron deceased and their heirs forever four hundred and fifty pounds in Province Bills of credit to be paid by my Executor as follows (vizt) one hundred pounds to my daughter-in-law their mother within one year after my decease to be improved at her discretion towards subsistence and education of the said children, the remaining part to be paid within two years after my decease to their said mother and my son-in law Mr. Eleazer Russell whom I appoint feofees in trust of the said sum the same to be disposed of at loan upon interest and the interest to be paid annually and applied towards the subsistance and education of the said children, and when they arrive to lawful age that is the males to twenty one and the females to eighteen years, or marry then to be paid respectively one third part of the said sum by the said feofees which with what I have before given my said Daughter in law makes up the sum of five hundred pounds.

Item. I will that my plate, bedding and clock with all my household stuff be divided into five equal parts, one fifth of which I give to my son Richard, one fifth to My daughter Margaret, one fifth to my daughter Anna, one fifth to my daughter Abigail, and the remaining fifth to the children of my son William to be disposed of to the best advantage by their mother and the produce to be improved towards their subsistance and education.

Item. I give my beloved sister Anna Gerrish as a token of my love the sum of Ten pounds in province bills to be paid by my Executor within twelve months after my decease.

I give to my beloved sister-in-law Eliza Vaughn as an acknowledgement of her kindness and tender regard towards me in my sickness the sum of Ten pounds in Province bills to be paid by my Executor within twelve months after my decease.

Lastly I give and bequeath unto my beloved and only son Richard Waldron and his heirs and assigns forever all the residue and remaining part of my Estate not before disposed of (viz) all my houses lands tenements hereditaments mills mill streams slaves cattle money goods chattels bills bonds books and papers and every other thing whatsoever belonging or appertaining unto me wheresoever the same is or may be found whether it be real or personal and of what kind or nature soever. And furthermore I do hereby constitute, ordain and appoint my said son Richard Waldron sole Executor as well as residuary Legatee of this my last will and Testament. In witness whereof I have hereunto set my hand and affixed my seal the day and year before written.

    Richd Waldron. (Seal.)

Signed, sealed, published and declared by Richd. Waldron Esq. to be my last will and testament in presence of us witnesses.

W. Fellows, Sam'l Hart, Micha. Whidden, Josh. Peirce.

RICHARD had children as follows. (Fam 11) Samuel b. 1681, died aged about eleven months; (and by second wife), Richard b. 21 Feb. 1693–4; Margaret b. 16 Nov. 1695, mar. 18 May 1721, Eleazer Russell and died 20 May 1753; William b. 1697; Annie b. 1699, mar. Rev. Henry Rust of Stratham, (minister from 1718 to his death in 1749) and died in 1734; Abigail b. 1702, mar. Judge Richard Saltonstall of Haverhill in 1726, and died in 1735; Eleanor b. 1704, died unmarried in 1724.

OLD SERIES, NO. 177, OCT. 8, 1857

WALDERNE-WALDRON FAMILY.

RICHARD WALDRON (6) of Fam. 11, born 21 Feb. 1693-4, graduated at Harvard College in 1712. He lived first at Dover but soon removed to Portsmouth where he resided for the remainder of his life. He was a public man and "did the State some service;" in 1728 he was appointed Councillor, and soon after Secretary of the Province, and and in 1737 Judge of Probate; as to this latter office it is unfortunate that when his house burned down 21 May 1736, a large part of the early probate records were destroyed. Secretary Waldron was a firm friend to Gov. Belcher, and so long as the latter was Governor, Waldron retained his office; but when Belcher was succeeded by Gov. Wentworth, the new executive suspended Waldron from the councillor-ship, and removed him from his Secretaryship and Judgeship. Party feeling then ran high, and Waldron became the head of the opposition; in 1749 he was elected representative from Hampton and was immediately chosen Speaker; the Governor negatived the choice, but the assembly denied his legal power to do any such thing; neither party would yield, and this controversy continued for three years, Secretary Waldron was a professor of religion and zealously attached to the church of which he was a member He died 23 Aug. 1753.

His wife was Elizabeth, daughter of Thomas Westbrook, Esq., born 26 Nov. 1701, whom he married 31 Dec. 1718; their children were (Fam. 12.)—Richard b. 20 Dec. 1719, lost at sea 1745; Thomas Westbrook b. 26 July 1721; William b. 8 Mar. 1723-4, died 22 Sept. 1741; Elizabeth b. 3 Feb. 1729-30, d. 13 Apr. 1732; George b. 1 May 1732, d. 1 Sept. 1805; Elizabeth b. 17 May 1734. d. 1745; Eleanor b. 13 Nov. 1736, d. 5 Sept. 1741; William b. 12 Dec. 1741, died aged 17 months.

MARGARET (6) of Fam. 11, married, 18 May 1721, Eleazer Russell of Barnstable, who was educated at Harvard, and was son of a clergyman.—They had children;

Eleazer b. 21 May 1722, d. 18 Sept. 1798; Eleanor b. 7 Feb. 17.3-4; Margaret b. 12 Nov. 1726; Benjamin b, 13 April 1729, died master of a ship on the Coast of Africa; Martha b 15 Nov. 1732, d. 21 Sept. 1798; Anna b. 6 Oct. 1734, d, 28 Feb. 1816.

WILLIAM (6) of Fam. 11, born 1697, was a minister; his name appears as that of the first person admitted to our First

Church during the ministry of Parson Cushing, 30 March 1718. He grad. at H. C. 1717, and was ordained 22 May 1722, first pastor of the Brick Church, Boston, (which was afterwards merged into the Second Church, of which Chandler Robbins is now pastor). Rev. Dr. Robbins, in his admirable history of the Second Church thus speaks of Mr. Waldron: "His ministry of only five years was too short to make full proof of his plans and capacities of usefulness; but few clergymen have been more affectionately commemorated by their professional associates.—The Library of our church contains a volume of sermons which were preached on the occasion of his death by the most celebrated of his compeers. In reading these, it is doubtless necessary to make considerable allowance for the naturally exaggerated encomiums of warm personal friendship and freshly excited sympathy. But when this is done to the fullest extent, there remains indubitable evidence that the character of the first minister of the New Brick church was of more than ordinary worth. To a finished education was superadded the still more excellent qualification for the ministry, the grace of early piety. His most intimate friend, Dr. Cooper, dwells particularly upon this characteristic, and illustrates it by a brief anecdote which has so much of the savor of that old time that I am tempted to repeat it. "In his early childhood," says Dr Cooper, "a particular Providence set the wheel of prayer agoing, and I believe it never fully stopped afterwards. This he once gave me an account of in a retired conversation, and I suppose I was the only person to whom he mentioned it. His dear parents were going somewhere by water, when a storm arose with sudden gusts of wind, when it was supposed they were returning home. The little boy heard his family speak of the danger they might be in. This so alarmed his fear, that he went away alone to seek God in their behalf, and pray that they might be preserved and returned in safety. And, having begun thus successfully to pray for his parents, he afterwards began to pray for himself. I also know, said he, that, while at college, he was one of those young students who used to meet on the evening of the Lord's day, for prayer and other exercises of social religion."

"As a preacher, he was remarkable for soundness of argument, plainness and directness of speech, and gravity of manner. His temper was naturally obliging and his affections warm, while at the same time, he was too independent to stoop to any little acts to conciliate favor, too stern in his integrity ever to prostitute his conscience. He was like most of the clergy of New England, a hearty patriot, and a steady friend and advocate of all civil privileges which the people then enjoyed. He was, also, a strict and very zealous Congregationalist. If he had lived longer, there is no doubt that he would have exerted a powerful influence in the community, and have left more conspicuous memorials upon the records of this church. But Providence had another destiny in store for him.—His death took place on the 11th of September, 1727. "He died," says Cotton Mather, "nobly. So to die is indeed no dying. 'Tis but flying away, with the wings of the morning, into the paradise of God." Hist. See. Ch. pp. 181-3.

William Waldron married Eliza Allen of Martha's Vineyard who survived him. That they had children is clear from the will of William's father, at least two sons besides one daughter (Fam. 13); this daughter, Elizabeth, married in 1756 Josiah Quincy, (father of Josiah Quincy, Jr. the patriot by a former marriage;) she was his second wife, and had one daughter, Elizabeth, (born 1757, married in 1785 Benjamin Guild Esq., and died 1825;) Elizabeth (the mother) died in 1759, and Mr. Quincy married again.

Regarding the descendants of the other children of Col. Richard Waldron we have no means of information. Richard and William were the only sons; whether the name was perpetuated through William we have acknowledged our ignorance.—It was through Secretary Richard however as the table of Fam. 12 shows; he had only two sons who lived to adult age and left issue, viz Thomas Westbrook and George.

OLD SERIES. NO 184, MAR, 25, 1858.

WALDERNE-WALDRON FAMILY.

We have said all we care to say about the descendants of old Major Richard Waldron. But there were in Dover other Waldrons, a distinct family, of some note, and connected with the Major's branch, tradition says, in England. Of this family we propose to record various particulars.

JOHN WALDRON is mentioned in John Heard's will (dated 21 April 1687,) as "my prentice."—Tradition (communicated to us by J. Waldron's great granddaughter) says that "Master Heard," a sailor, picked him up in the streets of a seaport town in England and carried him off unceremoniously after the fashion prevalent on the coast of Africa. Master Heard brought him to Dover and kept him as "chore boy." Poorly clad and having a hard time of it generally, he excited the kind sympathies of a Mrs. Horne, past whose doors he used to drive the cows to pasture, and who did him many a kindness—the last of which was to marry him when she became a widow. She lived where the late Stephen P. Palmer (who married a Horne) resided, and we suppose was widow of William Horne who was killed 28 June 1689, whose property mainly went to sons John, William and Thomas.

John Waldron acquired considerable property; probably Mrs. Horne brought him a little, and his own industry brought him more. He lived, we are informed, where Taylor Page now lives.

He died in 1740. By his will, which was dated 12 May 1740 and proved 30 July following, he gave to his wife Mary (perhaps a second wife) one half of the homestead, the whole of which was to go, after her decease, to son Richard; to son John jr. (besides the hundred acres where "he lives,") lands in Rochester "which I bought of the Twomblys," and "all my wearing apparel;" to daughter Elizabeth, wife of Ezra Kimball, £30 and 30 acres which were bought "of Rayner,"—a part of old Parson Rayner's grant near the present poor farm or else thefarm itself*; to daughter Anne, wife of Timothy Ro'erts, 70 acres in Rochester, 40 of which joined land which Dea. Gershom Wentworth bought of 'Squire Atkinson: to daughter Mehitable, wife ot James Chesley £30 and 30 acres in Dover, purchased "of Rayner;" to daughter Sarah, wife of Isaac Linby, the same as to Mehitable; to grandsons John Waldron, Richard Kimball, John Roberts, and Samuel Libbey, lands in Rochester; son Richard (executor) was residuary legatee.

John had children (Fam. 1.)—Sarah, Bridget, Richard, John, b. 1698; Elizabeth, Anne, Mehitable, Sarah.

These children we dispose of as follows:

SARAH and BRIDGET died in this wise; the first being seven years old and the second five, they were one day turning the calves into a pasture rear the house, when nine Indians suddenly appeared, seized them and with an axe cut off their heads on a log before the door and in full view of their agonized mother. The Indians carried their heads away, but after taking off the scalps threw them into some bushes where their father found them some weeks afterward.

RICHARD (?) lived on the homestead; a part of his cellar was said to be under Taylor Page's house a few years since, and we presume nobody has carried it away. He inherited as we have seen above. His wife was a Smith of Durham, and he had children, (Fam. 2).

—John (Col) b. 1740, Hannah, Betsy, Mary, Joseph b. 16 May 1744; Samuel, James. For their families see below.

JOHN (2) lived in Dover; he died 4 July 1778, aged 80, having had children (Fam. 3.)

—John, William, Ephraim, Bridget, Ebenezer. Of these we know nothing further.

ELIZABETH (?) married Ezra Kimball; they had children. Tradition says they lived in Farmington.

ANNE (2) mar. Timothy Roberts, and had at least one son, viz. John, (Fam. 4).

MEHITABLE (2) married James Chesley (born 18 May 1706, d 16 Oct. 1777, son of James, grandson of Philip, and great grandson of Philip of Dover 1644) They had children, (Fam. 5).

—Tamsin (who married, 1st John Twombly, son of John, and married 2d, Col. Otis Baker,—having by her first marriage, three children, viz. Sarah and Hannah, who died young, and Tamsin b. 18 Sept. 1756 who married John Waldron,—and by her second marriage seven children, viz. Lydia b. 12 May 1759 and mar. 1st. Capt. Samuel Wallingford, and 2d Col. Amos Cogswell, Ebenezer b. 22 Dec. 1760, (father of Sharanton Baker of Dover,) John b. 12 Dec. 1762, Mehitable b, 21 April, and married Capt. William Twombly and recently deceased in Dover, Otis b. 8 Aug. 1766, James Chesley b. 15 April, 1768, (father to Mrs. John H. Wheeler of Dover,) and Thomas b. 21 Jan. 1770; Hannah, who married Rev. Avery Hall, a native of Connecticut, ordained minister at Rochester 15 Oct. 1766, resigned 1C April 1775, and who had two children; Ebenezer, who died suddenly unmarried; James and Otis both of whom died of consumption unmarried. MEHITABLE, wife of James Chesley, died 21 Aug. 1776, and the disconsolate widower then seventy years old, married 4 April 1777, Lydia, daughter of Isaac Horne, who had attained the venerable age of twenty two.

SARAH (2) married Isaac Libbey, and had at least one son, viz., Samuel (Fam. 6.)

*"Reyner's brook," sometimes incorrectly called "Reynard's brook," got its name through this grant. This brook is the one which crosses the road east of the Almshouse, and runs into the Cochecho a little above "Watso's and Waldron's mills," lately called "Tricker's mills," and now no mills at all.

OLD SERIES, NO. 185, APRIL 8, 1858.

WALDERNE-WALDRON FAMILY.

Those of the next generation were as follows;—

COL. JOHN WALDRON (3) of Fam. 2, will be remembered by not a few of our readers. He lived on the homestead, but owned considerable other property,— among which was (in part) the place where his grandson Hon. Ezekiel Hurd resides, that where Jacob Clark lives, and the land where William Wendell has a farm. He was a man of note, often in public office and possessing a wide influence, especially in the days of the old Republican party, of which he was a devoted adherent and in which he was a leader. Records of his public offices show that he was a member of the Provincial Legislature which met at Portsmouth in 1774, of the Revolutionary Convention held at Exeter in 1775, and a Representative of Dover in at least the years 1782, '3, '5, '6, '8, '97, '8. 1801, '3, and 1815; he was also a Delegate to the Constitutional Convention in 1791, and Senator in 1788, '90 '2, and 1803, '6. It is said that he was Moderator of our town meeting in twenty-nine out of thirty successive years, an office for which his clear, strong voice, his energy and decision, particularly qualified him. It is narrated as an evidence of his strong views, that once in high party times, in declaring his vote, he added (giving the real numbers) "so many for America and so many for England." It is worthy of notice perhaps that at one election he was chosen moderator, lot layer, highway surveyor, overseer of the poor, Representative, and Senator.

Col. Waldron was Colonel in the Revolutionary army. He had held commission in the militia before, and when war broke out he was appointed Colonel; his regiment of 700 men he enlisted nigh self, and marched them to Cambridge. His service was not long, the death of his wife recalled him to take care of a family, the youngest of which was but three weeks old.

He was married four times; 1st to Joanna Shepherd of Salisbury, Mass., who died 1 Sept. 1775, 2d to Polly Winn, who died 19 July 1799; 3d to the widow of John Wentworth, jr., (originally Margaret Ffrost of Newcastle, born 3 Dec. 1747, died 30 Sept. 1805,) and 4th to Mary, widow of Rev. Caleb Prentiss of Reading, Mass., who had deceased 7 Feb. 1803. Col. John died 31 Aug. 1827. By his first wife he had five children; by the second, four; by the others, none. Children were (Fam. 7,) — Abigail, who married John Hurd of Dover, uncle to Ezekiel, and who survives her, he still living in New Durham, they having had nine or ten children; Jeremiah who

Married Mary Scott of Machias, Me., lived in Farmington and had children among whom was Elder William H. Waldron and George P. now of Dubuque; Richard who married Mary Hanson (aunt to Israel) lived at Long Hill on the farm adjoining that of the almshouse, and had four children, one of whom was first Lorenzo Rollins; a daughter who married a Wentworth and died childless a good many years ago; Joana b. 1775, married Ezekiel Hurd (who died in 1814; fever 27 Feb. 1800, aged 27) and died 10 Aug. 1840, having had three children, viz., Mary B. (Hon.) Ezekiel is of Hurd, and Eliza B. who died unmarried March, 1853; by second wife,— Timothy Winn who moved to Bath, and died having had two children of Rochester; now dead; Susan married Steven Hale of Royalston, Me. and died leaving children; Mary B. married Zachariah Wyman of Woburn, and died leaving children; Eliza married Capt. Benjamin Stanton of Bath, Me., and died leaving two children.

HANNAH (3) of Family 2, married Capt. Elisha Shapleigh of Kittery and had ten children (Fam. 9.)

MARY (3) of Family 2, married 23 March 1768, Capt Elijah Clements of Somersworth who lived near the present farm of Wm. H. Rollins; they had two children (Fam. 10.)

JOSEPH (3) of Family 2 lived near Oliver S. Horn's present farm. He married Tamson Twombly (b. 18 Sept 1759 daughter of Capt. John Twombly, who lived near Isreal Ricker's at Littleworth, and married Tamson whose second husband was Col. Otis Baker as narrated above) Joseph died 8 April 1821; his wife died 11 March 1823. Children were (Fam. 11), Mary b. 13 Jan. 1773, died young; Moses b. 14 July, 1774, late of Rochester, and left children; Joseph b. 10 April 1775, left Betsey, dau of Winthrop Watson (son to Col. Dudley Watson and Christine (Otis) Baker, famous in Indian captivities) and had nine children; James b. 23, August 1778, died single in Sarah b. 13 March 1781, married George W. Quimby and died in 1855, leaving children (among whom the wife of Joseph Morrill Esq., of this town;) Olive and Samuel died young; Olive b. 4 April 1787, married James Ham and is now or was lately of Rochester; Mehitable b. 25 July 1789, married Henry Quimby and is of Dover; Mary b. 14 March 1796, married John Plummer and had seven children, and died in 1836.

RICHARD (3) of Fam. 2, married Elizabeth Clements, b. 1754, daughter of Job Clements of Dover, and Aunt to Charles Clements of this city. He owned the almshouse farm. They had children (Fam. 12.)

JOB C; RICHARD (father to Richard Waldron now of Dover;) Mrs. Canney (mother of T. J. Canney;) Mrs. Fowler (mother to the Fowlers, late of the firm Fowler & Plummer,) who lives in Durham; Mrs. McDuffee.

SAMUEL (3) of Family 2 married a Gage and died childless.

JAMES (3) of Fam. 2, mar. Betsey Pickering, lived in Rochester, and had two children now living.

WALDERNE—WALDRON FAMILY

(NOTE BY JOHN SCALES. As it is claimed by many prominent members of the Family in the line of Col John Waldron that Dr. Quint was in error in regard to the ancestory of the distinguished Col. John Waldron, I requested John Waldron, Esq., of Farmington to furnish me with what information he has in regard to the question. In response I have received the following from him and his wife, Mrs. Adelaide Cilley Waldron, the gifted authoress. It will be found very valuable in correction of Rev Dr. Quint's errors.)

After the publication of Dr Quint's Historical Memoranda No. 352, the great grandson and namesake of Col. John Walderne or Waldron, talked with Dr. Quint about the "too many Johns" who had perplexed the historian, and informed him that nothing was ever heard or known in this branch of the family of the kidnapping story, although it may have been true of some John Waldron, not the Col's ancestor.

COL. JOHN WALDERNE, who had used this spelling until common usage made all of the name to be known and spelled, as now, "Waldron," "was a son of Richard Walderne, gentleman," as mentioned in the latter's will. This Richard was son of John, who was son of William, brother of Major Richard; the two brothers came from England to Dover together about 1635. This is the undisputed tradition of this line of Waldrons. Old books at the Waldron homestead in Farmington, given by Col. John to his son Jeremiah, whose son William H. inherited and gave to his son John (the present owner,) have written in them "Richard Walderne." Old letters in possession of the same family show that this Captain Richard and Col Thomas Westbrook Waldron, called each other "cousin." Letters from the Rust connection addressed the Col as "Dear Cousin John."

The several generations have been marked by those ineffaceable personal tricks of feature and manner which tell the tale of a common heritage, and from one "old resident" to another the tradition of certain resemblances has been passed along, outside the traditions of the family itself. The John Waldron who paid taxes at Cochecho (in Dover) in 1672 is held by the men of this line to be their John, who was nephew of Major Richard, and grand father of Col. John of the Revolution. John and Mary were and are such common names that it is quite natural there should have been confusion in connection with them, and Dr Quint admitted that he had to use a good deal of guess work in the midst of the probabilities and possibilities of so remote a past. Although of course he did the best that he could do in reconciling dates and personalities.

The oldest members of this line, who could remember a great grand father, always spoke of the old Major Richard as one of the famliy, and there is no trace of anything to the contrary having been thought of. So far as choice goes, it makes no difference to me whether I am on the one or the other family, but it is natural to hold the traditions of one's own people, and no one in this line ever has had any reason to set our especial tradition aside in favor of one which has never been alluded to by any of our forbears, nor has any substantiary records

It may interest some readers to know there are many clergymen named in the records of the Walderne-Waldron family; among this number are two widely known Roman Catholic Priests; John Waldron who died at Detroit, and Edmund Quincy Sheaf Waldron, who died in Maryland, President of Boromeo College in Baltimore. A John Waldron is engaged in the paper business in Boston, which firm was established in 1857. He lives in Somerville.

The English "Notes and Queries" inquired some time ago if the name of Waldron occurs in the list of Baronets of Nova Scotia. There are Knights whose titles date farther back than 1707. The inquirer said that once his father's house was rented by Sir John Waldron, a Nova Scotia baronet, and adds, —"We children were not accustomed to the ordinary baronet of the period, but I well remember the interest with which we discussed the question of what a Nova Scotia baronet might be; and our interest was deepened when Sir John himself appeared —a gentleman of tragic aspect, dark, melancholy, Byronic, and enveloped in a cloak of sable hue."

There are Waldrons in Digby, N. S and in New Brunswick, and there are a few western towns named Waldron. The name itself is that referred to by Dr. John Fiske when he said that an amazing number of good, old English families were Dutch or German. A clergyman of the name from New York told me that his father spoke pure Dutch. To the Heraldry office it makes little difference whether one writes his name Walderne, Waldron, Walderon or Walrond The arms of all these bear three bull's heads. The name comes from the Teutoic root, and signifies a ruler of lands or woods; or one who governs.

It is odd that so many of the family name have owned and worked logging swamps and saw mills; first for personal convenience, and afterwards for purposes of gain, but in all cases with a strong predilection for the lumber business, after the fashion of the distinguished Major Walderne of old Dover.

The lad stolen by Heard in England may have been known to belong to the family of which Major Richard was one. The spellings of the sir name do not count for much, as even in autograph papers one finds Walden, Wallden, Walderne, and Waldern, applied indiscriminately. One of my family is addressed invariably by a Dover gentleman as "Mr. Waldring."

It is reckoned an advantage to have a good name by inheritance, provided one does credit to it himself. It is interesting also to observe the "cropping out" of family peculiarities, and the Waldron ways have that definite character which cannot fail to be recognized in one generation after another.

The men seem to have been temperate in habit, patriotic, deliberate, but tenacious of a once adopted opinion; kindly when undisturbed, but relentless when once aroused to anger; easy and plausible of speech inclined to the gown rather than the sword, but hard fighters when the sword is taken in hand; and with all possessed with a more than common keen sense of humor. The most widely known men of the name have been of a noticeable personal appearance, so far as portraits, tradition and observation inform us.

OLD SERIES NO. 112.   JULY 8, 1853.

DOVER TOWN RECORDS—1716.

Whereas there has been of late an unhappy difference between the inhabitance of Dover Neck and Cochecho with reference to the ministry and a meeting house there; in order for an amicable union and for the maintaining of Peace and Christian Love amongst us, the subscribers hereto, viz., Richard Walderne Esqr., Capt. Timo Gerrish, Ltt. Tristram Heard, Ens. Paul Wentworth, Sargt. John Ham and Mr. William Ffrost on behalf of the inhabitants of Cochecho, and Capt. Thomas Tebbets, Ltt. Joseph Roberts, Mr. Sam'l Tibbets, Mr. Thomas Roberts, Sr., and Ens. Joseph Beard, in behalf of the inhabitants of Dover Neck have unanimously agreed to join together in calling a Minister to preach at the new meeting house at Cochecho every Sabbath day in the months of November, December, January, February, March and April; and every other Sabbath in the months of May, June, July, August, September, October, and the remainder of the year, viz. - that he preach every other Sabbath in the last six months mentioned, for the people at the old meeing house in Dover (Neck) and that in the same Rate made for the finishing the new meeting house, money shall be raised not exceeding ten pounds for the better Repairing of the old meeting house, but in case at the public Town meeting the Town by major vote of the Inhabetants consent not to this agreement, then we the subscribers in behalf of the Inhabetants of Dover Neck, viz. Capt. Thomas Tebbets, Ltt. Joseph Roberts, Mr Sam'l. Tibbets, Mr. Thomas Roberts, Sr. and Mr. Joseph Beard, do hereby oblige ourselves to Joyne with the Inhabitants of Co hecha to Call a minister and pay our proportion of his yearly salary, and further upon due compliance with this agreement by the town in general, the new meeting house at Cochecha to become the Towns meiting house, they paying in equal proportion towards the decent finishing the same, with a proviso, that whosoever is granted the privilege of building a pew therein for the accommodation of himself and family, shall pay ten pounds towards the building and finishing the said meeting house

In witness whereof we the parties before named oblige ourselves each to the other to perform on our parts every Article in the foregoing argument, to which we have hereunto set our hands this 11th day of May 1716.

Tho. Tebbets   Richard Waldron
Tho. Roberts   Timo Gerrish
Jos. Robbarts   Tristram Heard
Samll Tebbetts   William Ffrost
Jos. Beard   John Ham
                      Paul Wentworth.

At a publick Town Meeting held at the meeting house on Dover Neck the 28th day of May 1716.

Voted a concurrence with the foregoing articles, and that the same be Recorded in the Towne book

John Tuttle descents from the vote.

At the above sd meeting Voated that Ltt. Joseph Robbarts and Mr. Sam'l Tebbetts of Dover Neck, and Capt. Timo. Gerrish, Lt. Tristram Heard Cochecha do Joyn with the present selectmen Viz. Richard Waldron Esqr., Capt Thos Tebbets and Ens Paul Wentwouth as a Comitte to Call a minister in order to a settlement according to Agreement between sundry the Inhabitants of dover neck and Cochecha to which the Towne have consented as appears on Record in the dover Towne book.

———

Monday may the 28 day 1716 being Legually Called is held a publick Towne meeting at the meeting house on dover neck for Choyce of Towne officers and what other business of a public nature be offered.

first Collonell waldron Chosen moderator.

2ly. Captt Thos Tebbets 56, Collonell Waldron 58, Ens. Paul wentworth 48, Sargtt Jos Meder 65. Mr Jno Ambler 67.

3ly. Captt Timo Gerrish, Mr Philip Chesley, assessors.

4ly. Ltt Heard, Ens. mathes, Ens. beard, Comition(er)s.

5ly. Joseph Chesle Chosen Constable daniel meserve chosen constable, Thomas horne chosen Constable in the place of ben. wentworth, mr benjamin wentworth Junr chosen (Con)stable Refuseth to serve and (paid) his fine of five pounds.

6ly. Timothy Robinson, Jno Smith, Stephen Jenkins, Thos downes, will hill, Jos Jeukins, sarvairs of highwaies.

———

OLD SERIES NO. 113, JULY 12, 1853.

———

DOVER TOWN RECORDS.

———

Monday the 20th of Augt 1716 being Leagally Called pursuant to precept directed by the Sheriff for the choyce of assembly is held a public Towne meeting at ye meeting house on dover Neok fcr that servis.

1st, Collonall Waldron Chosen modderator.

2ly, Samll Tebbetts, Captt Davis chosen assembly men.

———

monday the seventh of Janry 1716-7, being Leagually Called is held a public Towne meeting (at the meeting) house on dover neck for the choyce of assembly men.

first. Collonall Waldron Chosen moderator.

2ly. Sargtt Samll Tebbetts 81. Captt James Davis 82, Chosen assembly men.

at the above sd meeting voated that the Comitte formerly chosen for calling a minister in order to a settlement do offer him ninety pounds a year sallary for his Incuridgment.

Thomas Ash decents. Samll Emerson decents. Thomas (who?) decents.—Nicholas Harfor and Joseph hall decents.

at ye said meeting, Ens. Joseph heard Sarg benja wentworth, Sargt Jno waldron, Chosen to Joyn with the Comitte formerly Chosen to Call a minister.

———

Monday ye 25 of March 1717 being Legually Called is held a publick Towne meeting att the meeting house on dover neck for the Choyce of Two assembly men pursuant to a precept directed for the purpas.

1st. Collonall Waldron chosen moderator.

2ly. Sargtt Samll Tebbets chosen assembly man.

3ly. Captt James — —. chosen assembly man.

4ly. Voated that the assembly men for the futuer shall have fower shillings a day for their servis in generall assembly for the Towne of dover.

---

monday ye 20th may 1717 is held a publick Towne meeting at the meeting house on dover neck.

first. Collonall Waldron chosen moderator.

2ly. Capt. Thos. Tebetts 107, Colonell Waldron 094. Ens paul Wentworth 079, Ltt Joseph Jones, 090, mr philip Chesle 091, chosen selecttmen.

3ly. Captt gerrish, Cappt Mathes, chosen Assessors.

4ly. Ltt heard, Ltt John Smith, Ensin Joseph heard, Comitions.

5ly. Henry Tebbets, morris hobs James durgin, chosen Constables. david watson Excepted in the Room of moses hobbs.

6ly. Timy Robison, Joseph Jenkins, for dover neck back river, mr benjamin wentworth, Cochecha; James nock, James burnam and philep duly, oyster River: Survaiers of high waies.

7ly. Vers of fences; Semll Conell (?) Thomas Robbards Junr for dover (neck and) back River; paul gerrish, benjamin wentworth Junr for Cochecha; sill nock for sligo; James nute, Joseph Tebbetts for back River; Jno Smith, John Edgerly on the south of oyster River; Jno williams, william Jackson on the north.

8ly. Capt Tebets pound keeper; Sargt Tebets, Ensj Joseph beard, drouers; Tobias hanson, pound keeper; Thomas hanson Jno waldron, drouers; for Cochecho James burnam pound kee(pe)r; John davis, william durgin, drouers on the south side; will hill on the north side of oyster River.

Continued and Carried over to the other side.

(On the next page the date, &c is repeated.)

9ly. for as much as this meeting is Informed that the money granted by a voat of the Towne for the glazing and seating of the new meeting house at Cochecho is found Insufficient to doo it for Conveniancy, Voated that if Any gentleman will be so kind as to advance tweaty or thirty pounds for that servis that it may be decently fitted for the present occations and trust the towne for the same till next year that money shall then be Raised to Reimburs them and they first paid.

10ly. Voated and granted to the Inhabitants of this Towne Commonly Called Quakers ten acres of land for a pasture for the better Inatling them to accommodate their Travelling friends this Land to be laid out in some Convenient place between the watering place or gutt and Cochecho not intrenching upon Any of our former grants. Test John Tuttle Towne Clarke.

at the above sd meeting Voated and granted unto Mr Nicholas Harfor the Libberty of keeping a ferry from beck's slip to Kittery he keeping sufficient boat or gundelo for the sole transportation of man and horse over sd ferry for which servis his fee shall be for a single person 2, for man and hors six pence.

at the above sd meeting that that the Comitte formerly chosen for Laying out highwaies be still Continued in their places and that Capt. Tim'y Gerrish be added to them to fill up the vacancy made by the death of mr Ezekiel wentworth

At a Publick Towne meeting held at the meeting house at Coobecha ffebruary the 2d day 1718-19.
first. Coll Waldron chosen modderator.
2ly. Voated a substantiall standing brijg be built over Lamprill River.
3ly. Voated Captt Samll Emerson, Captt Samll Tebets, Captt Paul gerrish, Ltt Joseph Jones, chosen with the selectmen to be a Comitte to view the Place and agree workmen to build sd bridg according to sd Voat and the selectmen shall Raise money in the next Towne Rate to defray the charg thereof.

ODD SERIES, NO 114, AUG. 2, 1853

TEBBETS.

HENRY TEBBETS was the ancestor of probably all persons bearing the name in New England, although there was a Walter Tebbets who died in Salem Ms. in 1651. The orthography of the name varies remarkably; t, e, b, i, p, u, are interchanged, doubled and omitted in our early records in every variety of spelling which would bear torturing into a distant resemblance to the sir-name of Henry above mentioned. This Henry lived on Dover Neck; in 1643 he owned a house lot bounded E. by Wm. Furber's, N, by John Heard's, S. by Geo. Walton's W. by the common, and therefore it was near the site of the lower school house. A grant of land in 1656 was laid out between St. Albans and Quamphegan, which was in the family in succeeding generations. Henry was taxed in 1648 and to 1675 each year as a resident of the Neck. He seems to have died in 1676, as in 1677 "widow Tibitt and her son Jeremi" were taxed in his place. Henry's wife seems to have been an Austin, inasmuch as on the 12 Nov. 1677 it is agreed by "Mary Tippit and Jere Tippit her son" that her youngest son shall "serve his uncle Matthew Austin." Of the children of Henry 1 were Jeremy b. before 1636; Thomas; daughter who

NOTE BY JOHN SCALES—After the preceding was published and came to the attention of Chas. W. Tebbetts, Esq., he informed me that the Teubetts Memoranda by Dr. Quint contains many errors, and that he will furnish a corrected Memoranda to publish in the place of it, sometime in the course of a few weeks. Therefore the next Memoranda in order is taken up and will be continued until the Tebbetts corrected Memoranda is ready.

OLD SERIES, NO. 115, AUG. 9, 1853.

WALTON.

GEORGE WALTON was born in England in 1615 or 1616, as appears by deposition. The name of Walton is not uncommon there; thus, in the visitation of Durham, Eng., in 1615, a George Walton of Shaicklackhall had arms confirmed to him. Also, in the Visitation of Essex in 1634 is a pedigree of Waltons of four descents, in which George Walton is mentioned as being eighteen years of age, i. e. born in 1616.

GEORGE WALTON was of Exeter, N. H. in 1639 when he signed the "Combination;" in 1648 he was of Dover; 20, 10, 1648, he was licensed to keep an "ordinary," for which privilege he was to pay twenty shillings for every pipe of wine which he might sell. He went to Great Island about 1650; 8, 1 mo., 1651 he sued Humphrey Chatbourne because the house which said Humphrey had built for Walton was not built according to contract, and won the case. He was not so fortunate 7, 9 mo,, 1651, when he was "admonished" for abusing the Lord's day in carrying board's and going to the Isles of Shoals." Various purchases, suits, &c., are recorded of him but none of any special importance. He died in 1686.

Alice, his wife, is said by Sewell (Vol. 1, p 417;) in 1664 to be "reputed one of the most godly women thereabouts." Of this her descendent, who writes this article, is properly proud.

Of the children of George and Alice Walton were George b. 1649 (alive in 1671;) Martha (who mar. Edward West, of Portsmouth and had son John before 12 July 1665:) Dorcas (living in 1666;) child (drowned 5 May 1657;) Shadrack b. 1648; Mary (probably who married Samuel Rand 14, 1 1679;) and doubtless others connected with the Taprells, Robys, and Truworthys mentioned in his will.

His will we here insert:

The Last Will and Testament of George Walton, sen. being of sound judgment and perfect memory, in manner and form following.

Imprimis. I do appoint and constitute Alice, my now wife, my Executr of all my estate after my debts are satisfied, funeral charges paid, and legacies herein given and bequeathed, discharged, to be by her disposed, ordered and given as she sees good and meet.

Item. I give and bequeath unto my son Shadrach Walton, the nine acres of meadow, be it more or less, which I have formerly possessed, to him and his heirs forever.

Item. I give and bequeath unto Alice Taprell and Priscilla Taprell, each eight acres of land, on the Great Island, to be laid and appointed unto them of my out land between the Highway going to the ferry and the Little Harbor and Matthew Estes and his brother Richard

Item. I give and bequeath to Grace Taprell, the house her mother died in, to her and heirs forever.

I give and bequeath to Samuel Walton the remainder of said out land next Little Harbor, not laid out to Priscilla and Alice Taprell, and seven acres of marsh, part of the twenty acres granted me by Mr. Mason; the remaining four acres not disposed of, I give also to my son Shadrack and his heirs forever.

Item. I give and bequeath unto Thomas Roby, ten acres of the land I have a deed for from Mr. Mason, of forty acres in the long — —, and twenty acres of said forty I give and bequeath unto Walton Roby: the remainder being ten acres I give and bequeath unto Elizabeth Treworthy. Each legacy being to remain to the heirs and successors of each legatee forever, not to be possessed by either or any of them, until either or any of them come to age or my executor shall see convenient and fit.

Lastly for a final and full conclusion of this, my last Will and Testament, I do declare that my mind and full intent is, that my said Executor shall enjoy and possess the whole during her life, or till she see cause otherwise to deliver it up to any or either said legatees now under age shall be and come to full age, not before.

The fourteenth day of February, sixteen hundred and eighty-five; George Walton did declare the above written to be his last will, in the presence of
    Robert Mason,
    William Bockham.

That the above written instrument was the last will and Testament of the above named George Walton, Robert Mason, Esq., and William Bockham made oath the ninth of March, sixteen hundred and eighty-five-six.
    R. Chamberlain, Secretary.

SHADRACK 2 was born in 1658, was a resident of Great Island and a man of wealth. He was Ensign in 1657, was engaged in the Indian wars of 1707, was Major of the N. H. troops in the unfortunate attack on Port Royal in 1707, and their Colonel in the reduction of the place in 1710; he was Colonel of the Rangers in the winter of the same year. He was appointed a Councillor by Mandamus in 1716, and was senior member and President in 1733. He was Judge C. C. P. 1695 to 1698, Judge S. C. 1698-9, and again Judge C. C. P. 1716 to 1737. He died 3 Oct. 1741. Of his children were,—George; Benjamin (H. C. 1739;) Elizabeth (m. Keese;) Abigail (m. Long;) Sarah (m. Sheafe:) Mary (m. Randall,) and was grandmother to Benjamin Randall, the well known founder of the Freewill Baptist Denomination.)

Here follows his will:

In the name of God, Amen; I Shadrack Walton, of the Town of New Castle in the Province of New Hampshire, Esquire, being of a sound mind and memory and knowing that it is appointed unto all men once to die, do make and ordain this my last Will and Testament, touching that Estate which God in his good providence has given me, which I give, devise and bequeath in manner and form following.

Imprimis, my will is that my just debts and funeral charges and expenses be first paid out of my present estate by my executors herein hereafter named, within a reasonable time after my decease.

Item, all the remainder of my personal estate I give and bequeath unto my well beloved wife, to be at her own disposal as she shall see fit for her comfortable support, and for that end I also devise and bequeath unto her, the sole use and improvement of all my real estate, be the same in the Province of New Hampshire or elsewhere, for and during the term of her Natural Life.

Item. I give and bequeath unto my son George Walton (over and above what I have already given him out of the estate by deed and other ways) five Pounds, to be paid him by the surviving Executor of this my last Will and Testament according to the direction of my Executor aforesaid, the said sum of five pounds to be paid to my son George, after the decease of his mother, my said wife.

Item. I will, devise and bequeath all the residue of my Estate after the payment of all my debts, funeral charges, and the said Legacy to my said son George, and after the decease of my said wife all my lands and other real estate of what nature or kind soever and wheresoever, to and among my children, viz., Benjamin Walton, Elizabeth Keese, Abigail Long, Sarah Sheafe, Mary Randall, to have and hold, to them their heirs and assigns forever, in equal shares to be divided.

Lastly. I do hereby revoke, disannul and make void all other Wills and Tesments by me in any manner heretofore made, ratifying and confirming this and no other to be my last Will and Testament, and by these presents constitute and appoint my said wife and my said son Benjamin to be Executors of this my last Will and Testament. In witness whereof I have hereunto set my hand and seal the fifth day of December Anno Domini seventeen hundred and thirty seven, and in the eleventh year of the reign of our Sovereign Lord, George the Second, by the grace of God, of Great Britain, France and Ireland, King. Defender of the Faith, &c.

Mem. There are two words viz · land and what interlined on the other side, before signing, &c.

    Shadrack Walton (L. S)

Signed, sealed, published and pronounced by the said Shadrack Walton as his last Will and Testament in presence of us.

  John Wentworth Junr
  Peter Greley
  William Parker

There was a George Walton of Newington, who with his wife Frances, deeded to their son George land, 17 Nov. 1732, granted to them in common with the other heirs of the late Hon. Samuel Allen. They were also witnesses to a deed from James Randall in 1713, who, we think, was the husband of Mary Walton. George may have been the son of George 1 but we know nothing about it. Walton has been a not uncommon name in Portsmouth.

OLD SERIES, NO. 116, AUG. 23, 1853.

COCHECHO IN JUNE 1689.

In former articles we recounted the fate of Major Walderne, 27 June 1689. From that point we will continue our relation of the trouble with the Indians.

There were, as has been previously stated, seven garrison houses at Cochecho. Belknap speaks of but five, but he is clearly in error (a rare thing with him;) two others are spoken of in contemporary papers, viz. Paine's and Gerrish's.

After the death of Major Walderne and the removal of the family by the Indians, his house was burnt. Otis's garrison was captured in a similar manner to Walderne's; the owner, Richard Otis, was killed either in rising up in bed or on looking out the window; his son Stephen and daughter Hannah were killed, the latter, a child of two years, having her head dashed against the stairs, the wife and infant child of Richard Otis, and two children of Stephen Otis, (Stephen and Nathaniel) were carried captives to Canada. Three other daughters of Richard were carried away but were recaptured in Conway. Heard's garrison was saved; the door had been opened and the Indians were entering, when William Wentworth, who had been awakened by the barking of a dog, pushed them out, shut the door and falling on his back, held it until the people came to his assistance; two bullets came through the door but both missed him.

The elder Coffin's house was similarly captured, but as the Indians had no particular enmity to him, they contented themselves with pillaging his house; finding a bag of money, they forced him to scatter it by the handfuls while they amused themselves by scrambling for it. His son had refused to receive the squaws on the previous evening, but the Indians coming to his house, threatened to kill his father before his eyes unless he surrendered; to save his father's life he did so; these captives were placed in an empty dwelling, but in the confusion they escaped. Of Paine's garrison in its connection with this attack we know nothing; Gerrish's escaped.

Five or six houses were burnt, as were the mills upon the lower falls. Twenty-three persons were killed, and twenty-nine carried away captive. Their names were preserved only in part; of the killed were Maj. Waldron, Abraham Lee, his son-in-law, Robert Evans, Richard Otis, Stephen Otis, Hannah Otis, Joseph Dug Joseph Duncan, Daniel Lunt, Joseph Saunders, Joseph Buss, William Buss, Will'am Arm, William Horn, the widow of Thomas Hanson; of the other eight we know nothing. Of the captured were Joseph Chase, Mrs. Lee, (daughter of Maj. Waldron,) the wife of Tobias Hanson, the wife of Richard Otis, Sarah Gerrish, Christine and three other daughters of Richard Otis, Nathaniel Otis, Stephen Otis, John Church. We cannot find the names of the remaining seventeen.

An incident which relieves the sickening character of the details should be recorded. We give in the peculiar language of Cotton Mather,

"Mrs. Elizabeth Heard, a Widow of good Estate, a Mother of many Children, and a Daughter of Mr. Hull, a Reverend Minister formerly Living at Piscataqua, now lived at Quochecho; happening to be at Portsmouth on the day before Quochecho was cut off, she returned thither in the Night with one Daughter and Three Sons, all Masters of Families. When they came near Quochecho they were astonished with a Prodigious Noise of Indians, Howling, Shooting, Shouting and Roaring, according to their manners in making an Assault. Their Distress for their Families carried them still further up the River, till they secretly and silently passed by some Numbers of the Raging Savages. They landed about an Hundred Rods from Major Waldern's Garrison; and running up the Hill they saw many Lights in the Windows of the Garrison, which they concluded the English within had set up for the Direction of those who might seek a Refuge there. Coming to the Gate they desired Entrance; which not being readily granted, they called earnestly, and bounced and knocked and cried out of their unkindness within, that they would not open to them in this Extremity. No answer being yet made, they began to doubt whether all was well; and one of th young Men then climbing up the Wall, saw a horrible Tawny in the Entry, with a Gun in his hand. A grevious Consternation seiz'd now upon them; and Mrs. Heard, sitting down without the Gate through Despair and Faintness, unable to stir any further, charged her Children to shift for themselves, for she must unavoidably there end her days They finding it impossible to carry her with them, with heavy Hearts forsook her, but then coming better to herself, she fled and hid among the Barberry Bushes in the Garden: And then hastening from thence because the Daylight advanced, she sheltered herself (though seen by Two of the Indians) in a Thicket of other Bushes, about Thirty Rods from the House. Here she had not been long before an Indian came towards her, with a Pistol in his Hand: The Indian came up to her, and stared her in the Face, but said nothing to her, nor she to him. He went a little way back, and came again, and stared upon her as before, but said nothing; whereupon she asked, what he would have. He still said nothing, but went away to the House Co-hooping, and returned to her no more. Being thus unaccountably preserved, she made several Essays to pass the River, but found herself unable to do it; and finding all Places on that side the River fill'd with Blood, and Fire, and Hideous Outcries, thereupon she returned to her old Bush and there poured out her ardent Prayers to God for help in this Distress. She continued in the Bush nutil the Garrison was Burnt, and the Enemy was gone; and then stole a long by the River side, until she came to a Boom, where she passed over.

Many sad Effects of Cruelty she saw left by the Indians in her way; until arriving at Captain Gerrish's Garrison, she there found a Refuge from the Storm; and here she soon had the Satisfaction to understand, that her own Garrison, though one of the first that was assaulted, had been bravely Defended and Maintained against the Adversary. This gentle woman's Garrison was the most extream Frontier of the Province, and more Obnoxious than any other, and more uncapable of Relie; nevertheless, by her Presence and Corage it held out all the War, ever for Ten Years together; and the Persons in it have enjoyed very Eminent Preservations. The garrison had been deserted, she had accepted Offers that were made her by her Friend of Living in more safety at Portsmouth; which would have been a Damage to the Town and Land: But by her Encouragement this Post was thus kept; and she is yet Living (1698) in much Esteem among her Neighbors."

The act most to our purpose in this connection, the chronicler, perhaps from ignorance, omitted.—It is this: when the four hundred Indians were captured at Cochecho in 1676, one, a young man, escaped and took refuge with Mrs. Heard. She concealed him, and he afterwards escaped. This Indian, she supposed, was the one who gazed at her so earnestly in her dangerous hiding place on the morning of the attack; the memory of a kindness, an Indian seldom forgets.

OLD SERIES NO. 117, AUG. 30, 1853.

COCHECHO IN JUNE 1689.

On the morning after the massacre the

people poured in from all parts of the town, but the enemy had vanished. Pursuit was made which resulted in the recapture of three daughters of Richard Otis, who were overtaken near the present town of Conway; no other good was accomplished, for the suddenness of the attack and the celerity of the departure alike baffled all efforts. Further attacks were however expected, and information was immediately sent to Portsmouth to the son of Major Waldron, a resident of that town, who despatched a messenger to Salisbury with the following letter:

Portsmouth, 28th June 1689, about 8 o'clock, morning.

Just now came ashore here from Cocheca, John Ham and his wife, who went hence last night homeward, (with Mrs. Heard,) (they living within a mile of Major Waldron,) and about break of day going up the river in a canoe they heard guns fired, but notwithstanding proceeded to land at Major Waldron's landing place, by which time it began to be light, and they saw about twenty indians near Mr. Coffin's garrison, shooting and shouting, as many more about Richard Otis's and Thomas Pain's, but saw their way to Major Waldron's where they intended immediately to secure themselves; but coming to the gate and calling and knocking, could receive no answer, yet saw a light in one of the chambers and one of them say (looking through a crack of the gate) that he saw sundry Indians within the garrison, which supposed had murthered Major Waldron and his family; and thereupon they betook themselves to make an escape, which they did, and met one of Otis's sons, who also escaped from his father's garrison, informing that his father and the rest of the family were killed. Quickly after they set sundry houses on fire. This is all the account we have at present, which, being given in a surprise may admit of some alterations; but doubtless the most of those at or about Cochecha are destroyed.

The above account was related to me.
Richard Waldron, Jr.

Accompanying the preceding was the following:

Portsmouth, 28th June, 1689.
Major Robert Pike,
Honoured Sir,

Herewith send you an account of the Indians surprising Cochecha this morning, which we pray you immediately to post away to the honourable the governor and council in Boston, and forward our present assistance, wherein the whole country is immediately concerned. We are, sir, your most humble servants,

Richard Martyn
Wm. Vaughan
Richard Waldron, Jr.
Tho. Grafton
Samuel Wentworth
Ben. Hull

To the Honourable Major Robert Pike, at Salisbury—Haste, post haste.

It was received by Major Pike, who forwarded the papers immediately to the Governor at Boston, with the following addition:

"Salisbury, June 28, 1689, about noon
Much Honoured,

After due respect, these are only to give your honours the sad account of the last night's providence at Cocheca, as by the enclosed, the particulars whereof are awful. The only wise God, who is the keeper that neither slumbereth nor sleepeth, is pleased to permit what is done. Possibly it may be either better or worse than this account renders it. As soon as I get more intelligence, shall, God willing, speed it to your honours, praying your speedy order or advice in so solemn a case I have despatched the intelligence to other towns, with advice to look to yourselves. Shall not be wanting to serve in what I may. Should have waited on your honours now, had I been well. Shall not now come except by you commanded, till this bustle be abated. That the only wise God may direct all your weighty affairs, is the prayer of your honour's most humble servant, Robert Pike."

To the much Honoured Symon Bradstreet, Esq., Governour, and the Honoured Council now sitting at Boston, these present with all speed. Haste, post haste.

This paper is endorsed—
"Received about 12 at night upon Friday the 28th June."

The following answer was returned to Portsmouth:

Boston 29th June 1689.

Gentlemen—The sad account given by yourselves of the awful hand of God in permitting the heathen to make such desolations upon Cocheca and destruction of the inhabitants thereof, being forwarded by the hand of Major Robert Pike arrived the last night about twelve o'clock; notice thereof was immediately despatched to our out towns that so they may provide for their security and defence; and the narative you give of the matter was laid before the whole Convention this morning who are concerned for you as friends and neighbors and look at the whole to be involved in this unhappy conjuncture and trouble given by the heathen, and are very ready to yield you all assistance as they may be capable, and do think it necessary that (if it be not done already) you would fall into some form or constitution for the exercise of government, so far as may be necessary for your safety and convenience of your peace, and to intend such further acts as the present emergencies require—this Convention not thinking it meet, under their present circumstances, to exert any authority within your Province. Praying God to direct in all the arduous affairs the poor people of this country have at present to engage in, and to rebuke all our enemies desiring you would give us advice from time to time of the occurrences with you.

Gentlemen, your humble servant,

Isaac Addington, Sec'ry.

Per or er of the Convention.

Dated as above said.

Voted by the Representatives in the affirmative.

Attest, Ebenezer Prout, Clerk.

Consented to by the Governor and Council, 29th June 1689.

Isaac Addington, Sec'ry.

For Messrs. Richard Martyn,
Wm. Vaughan, Richard Waldron, &c.
at Portsmouth these with all speed.

This paper is endorsed.

"Despatched upon Saturday the 29th of June '89 at 12 o'clock at noon.

Accompanying the above is the draft of a letter which we suppose was written by the Governor:

Gentlemen,—We have read yours, informing of God's severe humbling hand, suffering the enemy with so much violence and rage, to destroy and lay waste before them so sudden a surprisal. We must all say the Lord is righteous; we have sinned. It is not as you well know, in our power to direct in your matters authoritatively, but as friends, and under our (one) prince, are ready, to our utmost to yield our assistance in helping you with ammunition or anything in our power, men or moneys. It remains with yourselves to meet and consider your own circumstances, and put yourselves in such a way (if not so at present) as may accommodate the present emergency in the best manner ye may, and let us know what you desire, and we shall serve you to our power. Our present circumstances do not advantage us to impress men, or levy money, but must do as we can. God help us all to humble ourselves under God's mighty hands.

Aid was immediately despatched to Cochecho, though no further attack was then made.

OLD SERIES NO. 118, SEPT. 6, 1853.

COCHECHO IN JUNE 1689.

The condition of Cochecho a week after the attack will appear from the following letter from Wm. Vaughan and Richard Waldron:

"From Capt. Gerrish's garrison at Cochechae 5th July 1698.
May it please yor Honrs,

On Wensday evening Majr. Appleton h Between 40 and 50 men (most of Ipswich) arrived here Accompaned wth Majr. Pike and yesterday morning wth wt additional force we could make, marcht into the woods upon the track of the enemy abt. 12 miles to make what Discovery they could, but returned in ye Evening wthout any further Discovery Save ye deade body of one of the captive men they carried hence, nor since or last has any of the enemy been seen hereabout we fear we shall not long be quiet but doubtless the main body are wth drawn to a considerable distance.

We cannot but gratefully acknowledge yor honrs Favour in taking such care for or releif and Assistance, & are bold heartily to pray the continuance of the Same wth out wch we cannot possibly Subsist, in or last wee humbly offerd or opinion of the necessity of a small pty of men whereby or people may be enabled to prserve their selves and cattle & the sd. Souldiers ready upon any assault here or elsewhere to march to their assistance, wch wee are Comonly too late for Wee have obtained of majr. Appleton with his compa. (who wd not stay wth out him) to continue wth us at prsent (the rest being Volunteers wd be under no comand & Soe are all wth drawn) & must beg upon his removal another Supply else sd people will be utterly discourg'd & necessitated to quitt their Stations at last, for or neighbrs hereabt can yeild us noe assistance expecting daily ye Enemies assault on ym, soe are standing on their own Guard. We beg Pdon for this trouble & remain, Much Honrd, yor most humble Servts
Wm. Vaughan
Richd. Waldron."

The preceding letter is in Waldron's

handwriting. The following was from Major Appleton, commander of the soldiers sent to the relief of the Cochecho:

"Cochecho 14th July 1689.
Much Honrd

I have yors of 11th Inst. wherein you are pleased to Aduise (Upon my remouall) to leaue the imprest men here under ye conduct of Lift Greenleaf(,) now you may please to know yt of Imprest men here are only 10 from Salem & 6 from Rowley wch witn the 20 that came last make but 56 and Mr. Greenleaf not being here know not his inclination to this affair & should I leave those 36 they are so ung(ov)ernable would Doe but little Seruice, for Newbery men here are none those that came were Vulenters and forthwth more Willingly returned home. So that I humbly propose in order to seruing the people that are here left to prseruing the place that an addition of (34?) men to these 36 wth a Discreet Conduct may suffice at present for this place, wch I beg yor Honrs to Considr and fauer me with an answer forth with for besides the Afflicting Providence of God Upon my family befor I came from hence in bereauing me of two children, I have Just now aduice of the death of a third together with the indisposition of my wife & the Exterordinary illness of another of my children all of which necessitates my hasting home, however I am so Disposed to the Defence of the Countery and the Preceruation of this place in order to it yt am very unwilling to giue ye people of this place any Discoragment by my renoual, till I have yor Honrs Answer, herto wch I humbly pray you to hasten wth all expedition and if you se cause to send yor possetiue order for the stay of these men of Salem & Rowley that were Imprest men, who are full of expectation of returning home wth me. As to the enemy we have had no appearance to any Considerable number, but sundery Skulking rogues are Daily Seen both here(.) at Kittery & Oyster river or employment here hath been to range the Wods an to guard & assist the people in setting in their corn which we are still daily Psuing

this wth my Humble seruce is all at Psent

from your Humble serut,
Samll Appleton."

Several years passed away before Cochecho recovered its former vigor; the inhabitants indeed principally returned to their houses or rebuilt them, but the loss of so many persons was a severe blow to its prosperity. Before 1700 however, it had assumed its former importance, and though occasionally harrassed by the enemy it was never again the subject of so destructive an attack.

OLD SERIES, NO. 119, SEPT. 13, 1853.

COCHECHO IN JUNE 1689.

Another extract from Mather, relating some of the personal incidents connected with the devastation of Cochecho, may be interesting and form a fitting conclusion to our "Memoranda" under this head:

"Mrs. Sarah Gerrish, Daughter to Captain John Gerrish, of Quochecho, a very Beautiful and Ingenious Damsel about Seven years of Age, lodg'd at the Garrison of her affectionate Grandfather, Major Waldrerne, when the Indians brought an horrible Destruction upon it. She was always very fearful of the Indians, but what fear may we think now Surprised her, when they fiercely bid her go into such a chamber and call the People out? Finding only a little child in the Chamber, she got into the Bed with the child, and hid herself in the Cloaths as well as she could. The Fell Salvages quickly pull'd her out, and made her Dress for a March, but led her away with no more than one Stockin upon her, a terrible March through the thick Woods and a Thousand other Miseries, till they came to the Norway Plains. From thence they made her go to the end of Winnopisseug Lake, and from thence to the Eastward, through horrid Swamps, where sometimes they must Scramble over huge Trees fallen by the Storm or age for a vast way together, and sometimes they must Climb up Long, Steep, Tiresome, and almost Inaccessible Mountains. Her First Mastor was one Sebundowit, a dull sort of Fellow, and not such a Devil as many of 'em were; but he sold her to a Fellow that was a more harsh and mad sort of a Dragon, and he carried her away to Canada.

A long and a sad Journey she had of it, through the midst of an hideous Desart, in the midst of a dreadful Winter. And who can enumerate the Frights that she endured before the end of her Journey? Once her Master commanded her to loosen some of her uppergarments, and stand against a Tree while he charged his Gun; whereat the poor child shrieked out, He's going to kill me? God knows what he was going to do; but the Villain having charged his Gun, he call'd her from the Tree, and forebore doing her any Damage. Another time her Master ordered her to run along the Shore with some Indian Girls, while he paddled up the River in his Canoe. As they were upon a Precipice, a Tawny Wench violently pushed her Headlong into the River: But it so fell out, that in that very Place the Bushes hung over the Water; so that getting hold of them she recovered herself. The Indians asked her how she became so wet? But she durst not say how, through dread of the young Indians, who were always very Abusive to her when they had her alone. Moreover, once being spent with Travelling all Day, and Lying Spent and Wet at Night, she fell into so profound a Sleep that in the Morning she waked not. The Barbarous Indians left her Asleep and covered with Snow, but at length waking, what Agonies may you imagine she was in, to find herself a Prey for Bears and Wolves, and without any Sustenance, in an howling Wilderness many Scores of Leagues from any Plantation? She ran crying after them; and Providence having ordered a snow to fall, by means whereof she Tracked them until she overtook them. Now the young Indianes began to Terrifie her with daily Intimations, That she was quickly to be Roasted unto Death, and one Evening much Fuel was prepared between Two Logs, which they told her was for her. A mighty Fire being made, her Master call'd her to him, and told her that she should presently be Burnt Alive. — At first she stood Amazed; afterwards she burst into Tears; and then hung about the Tygre, and begged of him with an irrepressible anguish, that he would save her from the Fire. Hereupon the Master so relented as to tell her, That if she would be a good Girl she should not be Burnt.

At last they arrived at Canada, and she was carried unto the Lord Intendant's House, where many Persons of Quality took much notice of her. It was a Week after this that she remained in the Indian Hands before the Price of her Ransom could be agreed on. But then the Lady Intendant sent her to the Nunnery, where she was comfortably provided for, and it was the Design as was said, for to have her brought up in the Romish Religion, an then have Married her unto the Son of the Lord Intendant. She was kindly used there, until Sir William Phips lying before Quebeck, did, upon exchange of prisoners, obtain her Liberty. After sixteen Months Captivity she was restored unto her friends; who had the Consolation of having this their Desireable Daughter again with them, returned from the Dead; but coming to be Sixteen Years Old, in the Month of July 1697, Death, by a malignant Feavur, more Irrecoverably took her from them.

OLD SERIES, NO. 120, OCT. 4, 1853.

WATSON.

JONATHAN WATSON was a resident upon the "Upper Neck" as early as 1675. Whether he was a relative of Robert Watson of Oyster River does not appear. (Robert was born in 1641, purchased land at O. R. of Walter and Jane Jackson 14 Dec. 1663, married Hannah Beard, and was killed in 1694; his inventory was entered in 1703 by said Hannah, who had previously to that date married John Amblar.) JONATHAN owned land upon the Neck and also near Tole-End. He appears to have been twice married. 1, Abigail, daughter of Rev. Samuel and Elizabeth Dudley; and 2, to Elizabeth ———. He gave all his property to his wife 9, 8, 1714, and died soon after. She conveyed the property, 13 Sept. 1721, to her sons David, William and Isaac, the latter receiving the homestead.

Of the children of Jonathan 1 whose names we can ascertain were (Fam. 1—Daniel; Samuel; David; William "of New York, Mariner;" Isaac; Daughter, m. Eliezer Young of Dover.

Of DANIEL 2 we find no trace except that his name occurs in a deed.

SAMUEL 2 had wife Mary, and (Fam. 2,) child Winthrop b. 11 Jan'y 1723 in Dover; there may be others.

DAVID 2, born before 1684, had wife Mary: he was dead in 1747. He owned land on Silver and Pleasant Streets, in the corner of which Jeremy Perkins' store now stands; this tract was sold by his children Dudley; Mercy, Sarah and Mary, to their brothers Jonathan and Winthrop, 20 Oct. 1747. Children therefore were (Fam. 3,)—Dudley Mercy, baptized 2 June 1742, mar. Benj. Hanson; Sarah, m. Nathaniel Doe; Mary, m. William Cushing (probably the fourth child of Rev. Jonathan Cushing and born 26 Dec. 1723;) Jonathan of Exeter in 1747; Winthrop, of Exeter in 1747.

One of the sons of Jonathan Watson, but which we cannot ascertain, had William, b. 1738. (Fam. 4).

ISAAC 2 lived on the farm now owned and occupied by his great grandson Seth Watson. He mar. 1, Elizabeth —— —— who died before 1745; he mar. 2, Joanna————. He was dead in 1754, and his widow Joanna and son Joseph administered upon his estate which was finally divided in 1795. Widow Joanna became a member of the First Church 13 July 1755. She died 28 Oct. 1784. Children were (Fam. 5)—Benjamin, b. 3 April 1734; Keziah; Isaac, who was dead in 1795; Joseph; William; Jonathan; John; Elizabeth, bapt. 5 Oct. 1755, mar. Francis Drew; Joanna bapt. 16 June 1742, (married Humphrey Hanson, son of Joseph and Sarah Hanson and born 27 Aug. 1738, died 13 Nov. 1766,) and had Dominicus b. 19 Mar. 1760; Joseph b. 18 Dec. 1764, Sarah b. 22 Dec. 1762; Elizabeth b. 12 May 1767; David, dead in 1795; Servia bapt. 5 Oct. 1765, mar. Lieut. Samuel Stackpole, grandfather of Dr. Paul A. &c. of this town; George bapt. 5 Oct. 1755, dead in 1795.

DUDLEY 3 son of David and Mary Watson as in Fam. 3, mar. Christine Baker, daughter of Capt. Thomas Baker and his wife Christine (Otis) whose captivity among the Indians after the attack on Dover in 1689 is recorded by Belknap and more fully by the author of the "Otis Genealogy" in N. E. Hist. Gen. Register. Dudley was "Captain" and lived in Dover, doubtless at Tole-End. He was baptized and admitted to the First Church 17 Oct. 1736. Children were (Fam. 6,--Dudley bapt. 17 Oct. 1736; Lucy bapt. 18 Feb. 1739, mar. Aaron Ham, lived in Rochester, and had five daughters; David bapt. 14 June 1741, died young; Thomas bap. 10 Aug. 1743; Samuel bapt. 7 April 1745, died young; Winthrop; Mary bapt. 15 April 1750 m 14 of Mar. 1775 Heard Roberts of Dover and Rochester and had four sons and one daughter; Hannah bapt. 17 May 1752, m. 1 Aug. 1771, Nathaniel Ham of Dover and had three sons and one daughter; Otis Baker bapt. 30 Sept. 1753; Sarah bapt. 18 July 1756, mar. Richard Garland of Bartlett, N. H. (who was born at Rochester 28 May 1763, and was living two years since,) and died 17 Feb. 1814, having had five sons and three dau.; Lydia bapt. 24 Feb. 1760 mar. Richard Hayes of Madbury, bapt. had six sons and five dau; and died 22 April, 1850.

WILLIAM 3 of Fam. 4, lived on the spot where O. L. Reynolds now lives; he married Lucy, dau. of Joshua and Lucy (Baker) Stackpole. Children were, (Fam. 7,)—Benjamin, whose son Jeremiah recently deceased in Barrington; Himeous, of Barrington; William, died at sea married; Nathaniel, lived and died in Danvers, Mass.; John died at sea unmarried; Frederick, removed to the state of New York; Fenton, died unmarried in Salem, Mass.; Joseph, died in Dover, unmarried; Elizabeth, mar. Ezekiel Varney of Rutland; Abigail mar. —— Tracy of Dover and died without children.

BENJAMIN 3 son of Isaac Watson as in Fam. 5 lived on land received in part from his father, it being the farm of Seth Watson. He mar. Lydia, dau. of Isaac and Susanna Hanson, b. 5 Nov. —; he died in Dover 29 Jan. 1785 and his wife Lydia was appointed adm'x 8 June, 1785. Children were (Fam. 8,)—Susan b. 2 May 1768, drowned in youth; Susan b. 15 April 1770, mar. 1, Lowis Wentworth, 2 Thomas Burleigh, and had by her first marriage Susan (now living) and one other who died in infancy; Benjamin b. 26 June 1772; Samuel b. 7 July 1774; Isaac b. 21 April 1777; Sarah b. 6 July 1780, mar. Samuel Hanson and died childless; John b. 8 May 1782, died at sea 17 Oct. 1799.

JOSEPH 3 of Fam 5, had wife Elizabeth; was dead in 1795; and had children, (Fam. 9)—Isaac b. 11 Jan.'y 1760; James b. 8 Mar. 1763; Sarah b. Jan'y 1766.

JONATHAN 3 of Fam. 5, removed to Scarboro, Me.; he married Olive Seavey, who died there before 1800. Children born in Scarboro' were (Fam. 10,)— Jonathan b. 1 April 1771, who married Hannah Millikin (born in Buxton 23 April 1782,) had Ann and others and died in Saco in 1850; Lillias; Ann.

THOMAS 4 son of Dudley 3 as in Fam. 6, mar. at Dover, 31 Dec. 1770, Abigail Horne, and had children (Fam. 11,)—Aaron (on the old homestead at Tole-End;) Dudley, died in Rochester; Daughter, mar. Benj. Horne; Abigail and Lydia, died unmarried.

OTIS BAKER 4 son of Dudley 3 as in Fam. 6, mar. Charity Horne of Dover, settled in Sandwich, and died there 11 Mar. 1815; his wife died in S. 22 July 1848, aged about 85. Children, (Fam. 12,)—Christine, died about four years old; Polly, b. ab. 1789, m. David Eldridge of Sandwich and is now living there: Christine, b. 23 June 1791, mar.

her cousin Paul Horn, and lives in Sandwich; James H. b. 1793, m. Sarah Keazer of Groton. Ms. and both live at Sandwich; David b. 1795; Jonathan b. 1796. m. 1, Adeline Tebbets of Dover, 2, Elizabeth Burnham of Dover; Esther b. 1803, lives at Sandwich; Sophia, b. 1806, lives at Sandwich; Eleazer H b 1813, lives at Sandwich.

BENJAMIN 4 son of Benjamin 3 as in Fam. 8, mar Elizabeth Whitehouse, dau. of Richard and Hannah (Goodwin) Whitehouse of Rollinsford, born 27 July 1772. He lived in Dover on the homestead a part of which probably descended directly from his grandfather Jonathan. He died 16 Nov. 1847; his widow resides with her son Seth. Children, (Fam. 13,)— b. 13 Dec. 1799; Benjamin m. Whitehouse, and had Elizabeth and John Adams b. 10 Dec. 1830; Lydia, (mar. Jeremy Perkins of Dover and has had children Charles Edwin, now dead,) Sarah Elizabeth, Jerry William (dead,) Lydia Augusta. Isabella (is dead,) Daniel Libbey, John Henry (died 16 Nov. 1849, Isabella, Ann Louisa, Harriet Ella;) Andrew; Andrew 2d; Susan; Samuel d. Oct. 1810; Sarah Hanson, (mar. Oliver L. Reynolds, and has had children Cecilia Amanda b. 13 Mar. 1832 died 1 Mar. 1850;Juliete b. 29 Nov. 1833; Benjamin Oliver, b. 3 Dec. 1836;) Elizabeth b. 4 Feb. 1813, (mar. Hon. Thomas E. Sawyer, and died 1 Dec. 1847, having had Charles Walter, Mary Elizabeth, Ruth Ann b. 8 July 1835, d. 13 Aug. 1835, Edward, Sarah Ellen b. 2 June 1838, d. 8 Jan'y 1842, Thomas b. 28 Oct. 1840, d. 8 Aug. 1842, Ruth Ellen b. 9 May 1843, d. 27 Aug. 1848, Son b. 25 Nov. 1847, d. same day;) Isaac and Seth (twins) 1815, of whom Seth m. 1 widow Ann Berry, dau. of Jonathan and Hannah (Milliken) Watson of Fam. 10, b. 5 April 1815; she died in Dover, having had Benjamin b. 28 Jan. 1847, died 24 Aug. 1848, and Benjamin Seth b. 11 June 1849; Seth mar. 2 Lydia A. Horne of Dover.

SAMUEL 4 son of Benjamin as in Fam 8 mar. 19 Sept. 1803, Priscilla, daughter of Caleb Hodgdon, b. 31 Jan. 1779: his residence is well known:he died 14 April 1847; his wife had died 31 Oct. 1822. (Children Fam 14) —Nancy b. 1 Feb. 1804, mar. 20 Mar. 1824, Stephen Davis, and died 24 Jan. 1842, having had two children, one of whom is Ann Elizabeth; Elizabeth; Horace P. mar. Betsey C. Ham of Rochester; Susan b. 2 Oct. 1810, d. 10 Mar. 1811; Lydia; Lucy b. 21 Dec. 1815, d. 2 Sept. 1817.

We are unable to locate the following: Lillias Watson m. Thomas Shannon 28 Feb. 1771.

Alice Watson m. Thomas Thompson 27 Sept. 1772.

Isaac Watson m. Mary Hogg 31 Mar. 1774.

—— —— Watson (probably of Exeter in 1741) was baptized 3 Jan. 1742.

Those wishing to trace the genealogy to the Stackpole family after intermarriages with the Watsons will find it at length in the Genealogical Register for July 1851, commencing page 217.

OLD SERIES NO. 121. OCT. 11, 1853

DOVER TOWN RECORDS.

At a Public Towne meeting held at the meeting house at Cochecho ffebruary the 2d day 1718-19.

first. Coll waldron Chosen modderator.

2ly Voated a substantiall Standing bridg be built over Lampril Riuer.

3ly. Voated Captt Samll Emerson, Captt Samll Tebbetts, Capt. Paul Gerrish, Ltt Joseph Jones Chosen with the Selectmen to be a Comitte to View the Place and agree (with) workmen to build sd bridg according to sd Voat and the Selectmen shall Raise money in the next Towne Rate to defray the charg there of.

---

whereas Seueral of our Inhabetance Belonging to the Towne ship of Douer haue giuen in A Petistion by way of Complaint for the want of a highway to be Laid out for the Conuenuance of the Inhabetance to goe Downe Riuer from the Road yt goeth to madberey, across to the other Road and wee whose names are underwritten who are Impowered by Law to Lay out Public and Priuit high wayes in aney Part of our Township for the Convenancy of the Inhabetance Pursuant thear unto wee being on the place have Laid out a high way of two Rods in Bredth beginning on the south side of Edward Euines house and soe to go southerly between John bussels Land and Joseph Daniels Twenty acre Lot and Runing Down to Ltt Joseph Jones Land and soe Turning west and be South by sd Jones Line keeping the same bredth of Two Rods and so Runing to sd Jones nor west Corner bound mark then Turning South and by East by sd Jonesis Line. Taking of a Corner of thomas willies Land keeping the same bredth till it Comes to ye highway that Leads to the Kings Thorow fare Road between the too whit pines stan(d)ing by the sd Road

Laid out and Stated by us: the 26 Day of may 1720.

    Thomas tebbets
    Thomas Robarts
    Tobias Hanson
    John Smith,
      Selectmen.

----

whearas Seauerall of the Inhabetance belongin to the Down of Douer haue made Application to us the subscribers for a highway to goe from the Road way that Leads from Knights farme to madbery and from that way Threw John Tebbets is Land Down to Bellomaus banck freshet we have Laid out a high way of three Rods wide from John tebhets is Sow west Corner bound mark in sd tebbets is Land and from thence upon a north poynt of the Compas 80 Rods Down within three Rods of a whit Pine standing near sd Riuer which is John Tebbets is bound mark and from thence turning Easterly by sd Riuer Leauing the way on the high ground whils it Comes to a hemlock marked with H oppersite against John Hansors Land being three Rods from the Riuer all which Land is about two Acors or thear abouts and for Sattisfaction thear of we haue measured and Laid out to sd Tebbets fower acos of Common land on the South Side of his Land being Eight Rods from his old bound mark to a stake and Soe keeping the same bredth upon an Est piut of the Compas Eighty Rods to the Extent of his Bounds and this highway to be Left open to pas and Repas for the Inhabetance of the town of Douer by the Last Day of Aprel next ensuing from the Date hearof September the 5: 1720 as witnes our hands.

    Thomas Tebbets
    Tobias Hanson
      Selectmen.

Trustrum Heard chosen by the selectmen.

It is the Rquest of thirty Eight of the Inhabetance of the Parrish of oyster Riuer to haue a high way of Three Rods to bee Laid out from a highway that Leads to willeys Creek to ye Kings Thorowfare Road that Leads to Lampereel Riuer and it is Laid out as folneth beginning att the hed of the Lane att a Place Called Teem hill and so along be(t)ween fransis Matheus Trelue Acre Lot and the Lott hee bought of John wille and ouer the South Corner of Matheus is Seauenteen acor Lott and over the north Corner of the Poynt wood Lottand see along whear the Path now goes and on the north East side of a grate Rock and soe on the north side of John Willeys indwelling hous and so Down to tne Long marsh and over the Marsh to the highway that Leads from oyster Riuer foils to Lamperell Riuer Bridg This highway Laid out and bounded the 22 Day of Feoruary 1720 21 by us,

    Thomas tebbets
    John Smith
    fransis Mathues,

----

march ye 16th 1721-2.

Then Laid out a highway upon Dover neck from the high street Down to the fower Riuer which way is Laid out as folleth: begining att a Rock by the sd

Street fower Rod wide up on an Esterlye Line Down to the fore Riuer to a Landing Place which is Comandly known and Called by the name of becks Slip which high way shall be Six Rod wide at the Said Landing Place and keep that bredth Ten Rods up from the River on said way by us

     Joseph Roberts
     Tobias Hanson
     Timothy Robertson
       Selectmen.

Aduertisement.

These may Certify whome it may Concarne that John Smith of Louberland has got in his Coustity A Stray mare of a black Roone Coller In defferent Large and if aney Person Cann Lay A Just Clame to the same Paying the Charg of Keepping and Crying may obtaine the same mare.

December the 13th 1722.

Att a meetting of the selectmen att Douer the 13th Day of march 1722-3.

they then gaue Liberty that John Parell of Douer shall keep a ferrey ouer the back Riuer from his hous or Landing Place ouer to Sargt Drews usall Landing Place and for his seruis the sd Parll is to Receue one Penney for Every Inbaletance soe Carrid ouer sd Riuer aud 2 Pence for Strangers.

Test Thomas Tebbets Town Clark.
march ye 13th 1722-3.

Douer ye 24: (1) 1724 Att a meetting of the selectmen the Day and Year aboue sd ordred that a highway of fower Rod wide be Laid out from quamphegon to Indigo Hill and so into the woods to the Comones, and Capt. Thomas Tebbets, Capt Pauel Gerish, Ltt Hateuill Roberts, is Appointed a Comitte to Lay out the same.

the aboue written order is as may appere

Test Thomas Tebbets Towne Clark.
march ye 25th 1724.

Douer ye 28th march 1724.

At a meetting of the Selectmen this Day they finding nothing upon Record of a high way Euer Laid out from Cochecha to Douer which way Think necessary to be Don & accordingly order that the said high way shall begin att the Contrary rode that Comes ouer Bellomas Banck River on the western side of the meetting hous at Cochecha & from thence Douer Neck Downe to the Spring near Capt. millitis house and from thence betwene the Land of Capt millite & the Land of apt John Tuttle Late Desesed Downe to Hilltons Point as it has heatherto been in use kaeping the Biedth of fower Rod throughout the same and suothing more whear the Badues of the way Requires it.

     Stephen Jones
     John Smith
     Benjamin wentworth.
     Nicklas Harfott
       Selectmen.

OLD SERIES, NO. 122, OCT. 25, 1953

THE HALL FAMILY.

In 1650, the assessors found in Dover three John Halls, viz. John, John Jr., and Sargeant John.

These three Johns came from England; from what part we do not know; indeed finding it rather difficult to locate rightly all the John Halls in this country, we let the old country alone very willingly. Thus it is sometimes hard to distinguish the first John above mentioned from John Jr. and these two from Sargeant John, and these from John Jr's son John and nephew John and two John grandsons; we congratulate ourselves however in hoping that we have been literally accurate in this as we shall show by and by; yet we own to some perplexity in always distinguishing, in our note book, these Dover Johns from John of Middletown, Ct. and his son John the Deacon, and the John who came from Coventry to Charlestown, in 1630, or thereabouts and afterwards went to Yarmouth with his son John and the other thirteen children most of whom doubtless had each a John; besides the John of Cambridge who certainly had a son John born in 1660, which last John had two Johns himself, one of whom had another at the earliest convenient opportunity; then there was John of Roxbury in 1634, and John of Hadley, and John of Newbury, and John of Barnstable, and John who went from Boston to New Haven about 1650 and afterwards to Wallingford where he and his son John were Selectmen, to say nothing of John of Bradford, and John of Taunton, and John of Scituate, and John of Groton, and John of Lynn, and John of Salisbury,—all of whom, flourishing before 1700, impress upon us the conviction that, either John Hall moved quite frequently or else he had several namesakes.

But this article concerns itself with only the three Dover Johns and their descendants.

We said that three John Halls lived in Dover in 1650. Of these the first is said and supposed to be father to the second, but nobody knows. Before attending to them however, we will dispose of Sargeant John.

SARGEANT JOHN HALL was of Dover in 1642, as appears by a record on Mr. William Walderne's "pese of paper" which we think can apply only to him; according to that record he owned lot No. 19, on the west side of Back River; at that time he lived on Dover Neck; but in 1649 he exchanged these Dover Neck premises with Elder Nutter for others on Bloody Point side, from which time he is designated as "of Bloody Point" or "of Greenland" indifferently; he lived so near the dividing line between Dover and Portsmouth that he was occasionally taxed in both places; of this he complained 27 June 1656, and afterwards his tax was regularly divided. He is probably the John whose name occasionally appears on the Portsmouth Records.

His will was dated 29 Aug. 1677; in it he gave property to his wife Elizabeth, to son Joseph, to daughter Sarah, and to his grand daughter Abigail Dame who was then under age. Of his children were—Joseph, who married Elizabeth Smith, a niece of Major Waldron's and died of Small Pox 1 Dec. 1695, leaving Elizabeth, (and perhaps others) who went to Portsmouth with her mother who mar. 7 Aug. 1687, Thomas Packer of that place; (whether John of New Castle in 1713 was of this branch I cannot ascertain;) Daughter, who mar. John (?) Dame; Sarah, who was living in 1718-19, when she sold land to Richard Rooks.

If the John first mentioned in the tax list of 1650 was father to John Jr., he had other children also; for John (the Jr.) b. 1617, Ralph b. 1619, and Stephen, who lived in Massachusetts probably in Stow, were brothers. (Fam. 1.)

JOHN 2 b. 1617, first appears in 1650; he may have come over earlier, but we can find nothing definite as to that. In 1652 he owned on Dover Neck a lot next to the church whose site is still pointed out; there he lived. In that year he had a lot joining the "calves pasture"; 19,8 1656, he had a grant laid out of thirty acres of upland joining his marsh; the same year he had a grant of land "butting on John Roberts' on the north and east, adjoining James Rawlins' on the south and east, and so by his own marsh bounds;" this was on Bloody Point side. In 1657 he is first called Deacon; 11, 11 1658, he had a grant of 100 acres of upland next Jeremie Tebbets in the tract from Cochecho to Salmon Falls, a part of which he deeded to Job Clements 11, 4, 1662; some of this property descended to his great grand children; from the fact of his owning this land, he is erroneously named in one of the volumes of the N. H. Historical Society, as among the first settlers of Somersworth. 8 June 1675, "Deacon Hall bought land of ye Committee." 10, 12, 1677 "whereas 20 acre lots were granted to the inhabitants on the west side of Back River, as appears recorded" in 1642, George Webb's lot is laid out to Deacon Hall. 1 Feb. 1685, on account of his "age and weakness he deeded half of his property to his son Ralph." He was Town Clerk. Lot Layer, Commissioner, Selectman, &c., at various times. He married (1?) Elizabeth, daughter of Thomas Laighton; and died about 1693-4. Of his children were, (Fam. 2)—John b. ab. 1649; Ralph; Hatevil; Nathaniel; Grace b. 16 May 1663-4; and probably others.

The similarity between the circumstances of this son and father, with those of two individuals in Connecticut, is remarkable. John of Middletown, Ct., died there 26 May 1673, "in the 86th year of his life and 40th of his living in America," having mar. Anna, dau. of John Wilcox of M., who died 20 July, 1673, aged 56 he had settled at M. about 1650 when the first John of Dover disappears; both had sons named John who were both Deacons; the Connecticut Deacon John went to Middletown about 1672, married there, Oct. 1874, Mary, daughter of Thomas Hubbard of M. and died 22 Jan. 1693-4, aged 75, having been Town Clerk several years; his wife, died 29 June 1709, having had one child which died young. The Dover and Middletown Deacons died the same season, at about the same age.

RALPH 2 b. 1619, was of Exeter in 1639; tradition says that he was thereabouts prior to Mr. Wheelwright's settling there; perhaps he was; he was there at any rate when he signed the "Combination" where his autograph still appears. Whether he remained there until his removal to Dover in 1650, we do not know but we are inclined to think he is the Ralph who turns up at "misticke side" and who mortgaged, 17, 10, 1647, to Thomas Gardiner of Roxbury land which he "bought of Edward Burton" at said locality; as also the "Ralph hall of Charlestowne" who conveyed, 15, 7, 1648, 20 acres on Mystick side, to William Brackenbury of Charles towne; and whose last sale there appears when "Ralph hall and mary his wife" convey 60 acres of land in Charlestown, 2, 2, 1649, to Richard Cooke of that place. However Ralph moved to Dover in 1650, and remained there fourteen years, during which time he was honored with the rank of Lieutenant, became "Commissioner of small Cases," Selectman," &c. His premises on Dover Neck he sold 19 Oct. 1664, to John Reyner, "sometime teacher at Dover." He was a delegate from Exeter to the first New Hampshire Assembly which met in 1680, and consisted of eleven men. Ralph was living in 1690. His wife was Mary, and they had children, (Fam. 3)— Mary b. 15 Jan. 1647, died July 1648; Huldah b. 16 April 1649, of whom we find no further trace; Mary (prob.) b. —— — - mar. 13 Jan. 1668--9, Edward Smith at Exeter, Ralph, died 6 June 1671; Samuel, died 1690; Joseph; Kinsley b. 1652; Sarah, died 16 July 1662.

JOHN 3 of Fam. 2 b. ab. 1649, is first mentioned in 1670; he lived on Dover Neck; June 1693-4, he received a grant of 40 acres joining his twenty acre lot west of Back River, and also 100 acres east of Cochecho River. He appears to have been a tavern keeper, as he gave bonds 6 Dec. 1693 for that business. He was Representative to the N. H. Assembly in 1698, but died before the expiration of the year. He mar. 8 Nov. 1671, Abigail, dau. of John Roberts; after his death she mar. Thomas Downes of Cochecho, who was killed by "ye Indian salvages" in 1711. 3 Aug. 1698 John eldest son and heir of JOHN late deceased, sold to John Tuttle land formerly belonging to grandfather (Deacon) John. Thomas and Joseph being witnesses. 19 April 1700, the estate of JOHN was appraised by Ralph Hall and John Tuttle. 10 Dec. 1700, Thomas and Joseph were appointed administrators, their mother Abigail Downes having declined the office. The children of John and Abigail were, (Fam. 4—John b. 27 June 1673; Thomas b. 19 June 1675; Abigail b. 24 Feb. 1679; Joseph ?; Sarah who mar. Gershom Downes son of her mother's husband.

OLD SERIES NO. 123, NOV. 1, 1853.

THE HALL FAMILY.

RALPH 3 of Fam. 2, is first mentioned on receiving land of his father 1 Feb. 1685. 11 July 1694, he had a grant of 20 acres on Fresh Creek; in 1702 was "auditor;" 25 Jan. 1704 he received of Richard and Elizabeth Pinkham land formerly belonging to "our grand father Thomas Layton." In 1706 he was dead; 4 Mar. 1706, John and James his sons, were appointed administrator In the division of the estate £15 were reserved for Jonathan "a sick and weak child" and the remainder divided among the seven sons below mentioned, the oldest according to custom receiving double portion. In 1735 Ralph and Benjamin sons of RALPH 3 deceased, together with Joseph, attorney of the heirs of James, deceased, sell lands which were laid out to said RALPH by the town in place of land- lost in a lawsuit with Richard Waldron who claimed upon a prior grant. RALPH married Mary, dau. of Philip Chesley, and had children, (Fam. 5)—John, of whom nothing further; James, dead in 1735; Jonathan who doubtless left no issue; Isaac, who removed according to tradition, to Medford, Ms.; Benjamin b. June 1702; Ralph; Joseph b. 26 Mar. 1706.

HATEVIL 3 of Fam. 2, married Mercy ——; he lived at Back River. Of his family (Fam. 6,) we find but one, viz.—Hatevil b. 15 Feb. 1706-7.

JOSEPH 3 of Fam. 3, was born in Dover during his fathers residence there; he returned to Exeter with his father in 1664 and there he died. His wife was Mary daughter of the second Edward Hilton by his wife Ann. dau. of Rev. Samuel Dudley and grand daughter of Governors Winthrop and Dudley. Of his children were (Fam. 7)—Joseph; Edward.

KINSLEY 3 of Fam. 3, born in 1652 in Dover, resided for the greater part of his life in Exeter, but in 1718 we find him at Beverly, Mass. He was appointed Counseller in 1698 and not far from that time became Judge S. C.; how long he held the latter office we do not know. He died about 1736, having been twice married, viz. (1) 25 Sept. 1674 to Elizabeth, dau. of Rev. Samuel Dudley of Exeter, and (2) to a Woodbury of Beverly, who died 24 Jan. 1728-9 aged 64. Of Kinsley's children were (Fam. 8)— Josiah; Paul b. 1689, Elizabeth; Mary, who died before her father, having married John Harris, and leaving one child; Mary, born 23 July 1707, and married 13 Nov. 1733, to Herbert Waters and having Herbert b. 8 Aug. 1735, and apparently married (2) Jonathan Jones; Mercy, who m. Dudley Hilton.

JOHN 4 of Fam. 4, lived either on Dover Neck or in Somersworth or both; he had 100 acres laid out for him 23 July 1720 which had been an unlocated grant to his grandfather Deacon John; 23 Dec. 1718 John and Esther and their cousin Philip Chesley settle matters relating to inherited property; various other deeds to and from this John Hall are on record at Exeter. He mar. Esther, daughter of Thomas Chesley and had (Fam. 9) —John; James; Samuel; and two daughters, one of whom mar. an Evans; of the last four we know nothing.

THOMAS 4 of Fam. 4, appears as a witness to a deed in 1698; was joint administrator of his father's estate in 1700; owned with Joseph part of the mill at Cochecho second Falls in 1702; had a 100 acre grant to his father located 4 July 1721. He was dead in 1732 when his eldest son, James, declined administering and desired that his bro. Thomas be appointed; their mother Mary had previously refused. He lived in Oyster River boundaries; of his children were, (Fam. 10)—James; Thomas; Joseph, b. 13 April 1707; of none of these have we further records.

JOSEPH 4 of Fam. 4, was alive in 1730, had wife Esther and child, (Fam. 11,)—Abigail b. 3, July 1708.

BENJAMIN 4 of Fam. 5, was apprenticed 16 July 1709 to "William Damm, weaver;" he lived, when free and settled, in "ye west part of ye Town," now Madbury, until in 1735 when he removed to Barrington, where he died in 1779 or 1780. 30 Dec. 1741, our church record tell us that Rev. Jonathan Cushing bptized "Benjamin Hall and Frances his wife and their children viz: Benjamin, Isaac, Joseph, John and Abigail:" another record reads "1772, Benjamin Hall's house burned in the spring." Benjamin married Frances Willey of Lee, and had (Fam. 12,—Benjamin b. 12 Dec 1730, Isaac; Joseph, who died young probably of throat distemper by which disease "several died;" John; Abigail b. 1741, died young; Samuel b. 1743, died at home unmarried Feb. 1776; Mary, who married Ebenezer Kelley and lived at Strafford Ridge.

RALPH 4 of Fam. 5, lived in Dover until about 1755, when he moved to Barrington, forsaking the old home whose foundation lines are still perceptible near to "Hall's spring" on Dover Neck, where his father and grandfather had lived. In the latter part of his life he lived with his son Joseph upon lands now occupied by his great grandson Joseph of Strafford; on that land he and his wife were buried. He married Elizabeth Willey of Lee, and had children, (Fam. 13,)—Elizabeth m. Joseph Daniels of Barrington, and had Joseph and others; Frances, mar. Sam. Foss of Barrington, and had Ralph, John, Joseph, Lois (Ham,) Abigail (Tebbets;) Solomon,; Ralph, m. a Davis and died in or near Jackson, N. H.; Lois d. young; Joseph b. 11 Dec. 1741; Deborah, m. John Hall; Abigail; Sobriety, m. 19 June 1777, Nicholas Brock of B., and had Ralph, Isaac, Nicholas, John, Ezra, Betsey.

JOSEPH 4 of Fam. 5, was a resident of Dover, and died here 14 Nov. 1782. He married Peniel Bean, and had children, (Fam. 14,)—Anna, bapt. 29 July 1733, mar. a Kelley and had Reuben, Obadiah; Mary, bapt. 23 May 1756, m. ——and had Elijah, Daniel, Micajah, Huldah; Joseph bapt. 5 Nov. 1738; Daniel bapt. 22 Aug. 1742, had one child, Hannah; Abigail, bapt. 7 Oct. 1744, and mar. Hawkins; Samuel, born 19 Mar. 1747, bapt. 3 May; Hannah bapt 2 April 1749, mar. Reuben Long and had John, Reuben; John; Peniel, m. Scribner and had Bradstreet, John, Joseph, &c.

HATEVIL 4 of Fam. 6, born in Dover 15 Feb. 1708-9; he m. 1 April 1733, Sarah Furbush of Kittery; removed from the homestead at Back River to Falmouth about 1753, and died there 28 Nov. 1797. His children, (Fam. 15,)—Dorothy b. 23 Aug 1733, mar. 20 Jan. 1753, in Dover, Geo. Leighton, they became Quakers; children were Peletiah, Jedediah, Sarah, Hatevil, Abigail, David, Paul, Silas, Daniel b. 24 Mar. 1735-6; Hatevil b. 24 Mar. 1736-7; Mercy b. 6 Oct. 1738, m. Joseph Leighton in Dover, and had Susanna, Hannah, Andrew, Stephen, Mary, Ezekiel, Lydia, Daniel, Betsey, Robert, Sara; Abigail b. 12 Feb. 1739-40, m. Isaac Allen, and died 12 Feb. 1825, having Catharine, Sarah, Robert, David, Mary, Dorcas, Isaac; Ebenezer, b 20 July 1741; William b. 6 Dec 1742; John b. 19 June 1744; Jedediah b. 21 June 1748; Andrew b. 15 Sept. 1750; Nicholas b. 8 Mar. 1753; Paul; Silas.

JOSEPH 4 of Fam. 7 resided in Exeter where he was much respected and often in public office. He was twice married; (1) to Mary —— b. 168?, d. 1 April 1755; (2) to Eunice b. 1696 d. 27 Mar. 1790. He died 1767. Ch. (Fam. 16)

—Love b. 10 June 1716; Mary m. Sargeant; Sarah m. John Burleigh of New Market and had John, Sarah (Hill), Deborah, Rebecca.

EDWARD 4 of Fam. 7 resided in New Market. He was taken captive by the Indians (Belknap p. 102) in July 1706 but escaped after several years captivity. He mar. (1) Mary Wilson who d. 2 Dec. 1737 aged 57 years and 22 days; m. (2) Hannah widow of Josiah Hall originally Hannah Lord of Ipswich. Children, (Fam. 17)—Anna, m. 5 April 1730, Rev. John Moody of Newmarket and had Mary b. Mar. 1731; —— mar. Rev. —— Page; —— m. John Burgin of Newmarket, grandfather of the late Judge Hall Burgin; Jemima m. Capt. Benjamin Smith; —— m. Joseph Merrill of Stratham.

OLD SERIES NO. 124, NOV. 8, 1853.

THE HALL FAMILY.

JOSIAH 4 of Fam. 8, mar. Mary Woodbury of Beverly. being published in Beverly 30 Mar. 1712; he mar. (2) 10 May 1719, Hannah, widow of John Light and dau. of Robert Lord of Ipswich. I am inclined to think that he returned to Exeter or that he never left that place. He died 16 Oct. 1729. His children were, (Fam. 17)—Elizabeth who mar. Tobias Lear and was grandmother of the Tobias Lear who was Gen. Washington's Private Secretary; Mary; and by his second wife, Kingsley, b. 11 Nov. 1720; Josiah b. 31 Oct. 1721; Dudley b. 20 Jan. 1722-3; Samuel b. 20 April 1724; Abigail b. 20 June 1726; Paul b. 18 April 1728; of these six all but Samuel and Abigail died young.

PAUL of Fam. 8, had wife Mercy, who outlived him, and died 29 Dec. 1726, leaving (Fam. 18)—Elizabeth, who mar. Daniel Grant, and had Paul B., Daniel of Gilmanton, James father of Francis, Daniel, Samuel.

ELIZABETH 4 of Fam. 8, m. Francis James, and had (Fam. 19)— Kinsley b. 19 Feb. 1708-9, mar. 5 Nov. 1735, Mary dau. of Dudley Hilton, b. 22 Oct. 1709, and had Elizabeth b. 15 Sept. 1736, d. 27 Feb. 1737, Mary b. 10 Dec. 1737, Lois b. 30 Sept. 1739 and m. Theophilus Lyford, Kingsley H., b. 1741 d. unm. 1810: Ann who m. (1) Thomas Lyford, and (2) Col. Giddings and d. 12 Aug. 1813; Dudley b. 5 Nov. 1713, m. (1) 5 March 1740-1, Mary, dau. of John and Hannah Light, and (2) 12 July 1753; Tirzah Emery, and had by first wife, Abigail b. 8 June 1742 m. Josiah Weeks (whose son Nathaniel of Gilmanton was father to Joshua and Nathaniel of Exeter,) Dudley b. 8 Sept. 1744, d. 8 May 1763, Robert b. 9 Sept. 1746, d. 8 Feb. 1748-9 and by second wife, Tizzah b. 15 May 1755 who became second wife of Dea. Samuel Brooks, Caleb of Gilmanton, Joshua, Mary who m. Caleb Emery of Sanford, Me.; Francis b. 16 Feb. 17 4-15, m. 27 Jan. 1736-7, Abigail Leighton b. 7 Nov. 1713; Benjamin, whose dau. Elizabeth died in Tuftonborough some twenty years ago in the family of Francis Piper her son.

MERCY 4 of Fam. 8, m. (1) Dudley Hilton, son of the second Edward Hilton and brother of Mary, wife of Joseph Hall. Dudley was with his brother

Winthrop 23 June 1710, when they were attacked by the Indians and Winthrop killed; Dudley was never afterward heard of. She mar. (2) Nathaniel Ladd. Her children were, (Fam. 20)—Elizabeth, who m Christopher Robinson, who died at Cape Breton leaving two daughters, one of whom m. Barnabas Palmer of Wakefield and the other a Davis of Rocheter; Ann, m. Nath. Ladd, Jr.; Mary m. Kinsley James; by second husband, she had Dudley; Paul.

JOHN 5 of Fam. 9, lived in Somersworth, now Rollinsford, on the farm where John Wentworth now lives; he m. (1) Anna Morrill of Kittery, (intention of marriage being entered at K 17 Aug. 1728;) he mar. (2) 17 Oct. 1743, Sarah Stackpole of Somersworth; he died in S. 19 Oct. 1789, and was buried in the "Carr burial place;" his second wife died Jan. 1804 aged 86. Children were, (Fam. 21) Samuel b. 1 Mar. 1736; Anna b. 19 Sept. 1737, m. John Tucker of Portsmouth; John b. 24 Mar. 1740, and died aged 5 or 6; by second wife, William, b. 10 July 1745; Mary b. 25 May 1748, probably died young; Ruth b. 1 Mar. 1750; Lucy b. 26 Nov. 1751, m. Peter Ball of Portsmouth; Silas b. 9 May 1753, N. S.; Philip b.15 May 1755, died at sea unm; Marcy b. 9 Dec. 1758; John b. 1 Nov. 1763, died 19 Aug. 1786. unm.

BENJAMIN 5 of Fam. 12, resid d in Barrington, a farmer; he was some time in the Rev. Army, going to Cambridge immediately on the breaking out of the war; the gun which he used there, and a ball cartridge which he brought home, are still preserved by his descendants He mar. in 1756 Sarah Huckins, b 6 May 1733, a dau. of James Huckins of Madbury who died in the army in the old French war. Benjamin died 30 Oct. 1810 and his wife 7 April 1821. Children (Fam. 22)—Ebenezer b. 8 Aug. 1756; Abigail b. Sept. 1758, m. George Berry of Strafford and d. 14 July 1791, having children Susan, Benjamin, John, George, Isaac, Abigail; Hannah b. 7 Jan 1761, d. 23 March 1783, having mar. Nathan Foss and had Nathan who d. aged 20 days; Frances b. 28 Aug. 1763, d. unm. 29 Jan. 1848; Jonathan b. 29 April 1766; Sarah b. 22 July 1768, m. Jonathan Clarke, and had Mary, Sally, Hannah, Rhoda, Jonathan, Lois; Mary b. 9 Mar. 1772; Benjamin b. 3 May 1772; Benjamin b. 3 May 1775; d. June 1776, John and Lois b. 27 Sept. 1777, John dying Jan. 1778.

ISAAC 4 of Fam. 12, m. his cousin Elizabeth Willey of Lee, lived where his father lived and there died. Children (Fam. 23)—Elijah, m. Tasker and has seven children; Elisha m. Marjory Meal and had five children of which Elijah b. Mar. 1783 now lives at Bow Pond. Stephen m. Louges and lives in Montpelier; Esther m. Samuel Clay d. 1885 Isaac b. 16 m. Betsey Caverly had eleven chil. and is living in Barrington; Joanna b. April 1769 m. Libbey had two children all dead; Benjamin m. Glover had four children; Mary; Betsey m. Smallcorn had 3 children; Samuel never returned from sea; Hannah m. Samuel Demeritt, no children; Phebe, four times married; Keziah, m. Solomon Demeritt, three children; Patience b. 16 Nov. 1782 m. Andrew Meserve, has had 10 children, of whom was Mary Ann m. Dr. John S. Fernald of

Barrington, Isaac H. the successful Superintendent of Roxbury City Farm, and Curtis Coe b. 28 Mar. 1816. grad. Dart. Coll. 18 —; Jacob, m. three times and had 16 children.

JOHN 5 of Fam. 12, m. his cousin Deborah Hall, lived at Bow Pond and had, (Fam. 24) — Winthrop; Israel (now of Bow Pond:) Mary; Abigail; Sobriety, m. Israel Caswell; Hannah; Samuel (of Bow Pond;) John died young; Daniel (of Rochester;) Deborah m. Isaac Hall.

SOLOMAN 5 of Fam. 13, m. (1) Abigail Davis (2) Widow Tamson Ayers, (3) Charity Johnson, lived in Barrington and died Sept. 1818 having had (Fam. 25) — Solomon, who m. Joanna Morrill of Northwood, died in Nashua, having Prudence b. 1799, Rhoda b. 1801, Asa; Love; Daniel b. 8 July 1769: John, had wife Nancy; Hatevil b. 21 June 1779; Moses, moved to Vermont; Charity, m. her cousin Samuel Hall; Sally, d. unm.; Mary, m. John Davis of Nottingham; Tamson, m. a Ward and rem. to Vt., Abigail m. Israel Fierce of Barrington (b. Aug. 1772,) and have John D. b. 28 Feb. 1811, m. Tamson Hall. Hall, who m. Mar. 18?9 Sally Hall, Moses. Alfred.

JOSEPH of Fam. 13. was a resident of Strafford, was Ruling Elder in the church and is well remembered for estimable qualities; he m. 4 Aug. 1764, Mary, daughter of Samuel and Mary (Dowse) Foss of Barrington, b. 25 Mar 1745; she died May 1822; he died in Dec. 1826. Ch. -(Fam. 26) — Mary b. 17 Feb. 1765, m. 6 Feb. 1783 in Rochester Ephraim Holmes, and lives in Strafford S. P.; Joseph, b. 8 July 1767, settled in Barnstead, m. (1) Mary Garland who d. 20 Feb. 1794, (2) Mary S. dau. of Eld. Benj. Randall, b. in New Castle 24 Feb. 1774, d. in Barnstead 23 Feb 1843, and himself died 27 April 1844, having had nine childhren, of whom Joseph possesses the homestead; Soloman b. 25 June 1769, m. Lydia Scruton who d. Aug. 1845, and d. in Barnstead 24 Oct. 1852 having had twelve children, of whom George had his farm; Betsey b. 25 Mar. 1772, m. Samuel York, and d. in Barnstead 4 Sept. 1845, having three children; Samuel b. 8 Aug. 1774, m. Charity, daughter of Soloman Hall, who d. Nov. 1845, owned his father's home farm and d. there 26 June 1845, having had eight children, of whom Joseph is upon the homestead and Ralph (Representative, &c.) resides in Greenland; Abigail b. 31 Jan. 1777, d. unm.; Lois b. 18 Mar. 1779, m. Wm. Sanders, lives in Ossipee, and has five children; Sally b. 13 Dec. 1782, m. Wm. Berry b. 1 Feb. 1779, and d. in Strafford 8 Sept. 845, having five children; Israel b. 17 Mar. 1785, resides in Strafford, has been Selectman, Representative, &c. m. (1) Hannah Sanders, b. 3 April 1787; (2) Mary Sanders, b. 6 Jan. 1792, and has had eleven children.

ABIGAIL 5 of Fam. 13. m. Samuel Berry of Barrington; children, (Fam. 27) — John b. 10 Jan. 1778, m. June 1796 Hannah Garland, b. 8 Oct. 1778; he died in Barnstead, formerly Representative, Councillor, and Warden of the N. H. State Prison; William, Joseph, Polly G., Abigail, John Freeman; Samuel m. Rachel Otis of Strafford and had Hezekiah, Rachel, Jane (Hayes;) Jonathan, m. Betsey Towle, and had nine children; Abigail m. John Stiles and had twelve children; Eleanor, m. John Clark and had seven children.

THE HALL FAMILY.

JOSEPH 5 of Fam. 14, m. —— and had (Fam. 28)—Joseph; Dorcas; Nathan; Betsey; Elias; Josiah; Polly; Benjamin.

SAMUEL 5 of Fam. 14, m. (1) 26 Aug. 1773, Bridget Gilman of East Town (Wakefield;) he m. (2) Hannah Leighton of Barrington. He died 19 April, 1831. Children (Fam. 29) - John b. 5 April 1774; Anna b. 29 April 1777; Joshua G. b. 19 July 1779; (and by second wife,) Andrew b. 10 Dec. 1786; Bridget b. 1 Sept. 1778; Jeremiah b. 12 Sept. 1794; James b. 2 Nov. 1796; Ira b. 13 Dec. 1800.

DANIEL 5 of Fam. 15, m. in Falmouth, where he removed, Lorana Winslow, b. in F. 1 July 1737; he was the first of the family who removed to Maine, which was about 1754; he returned to Dover and induced his parents, brothers and sisters to remove; he died in Falmouth 18 Dec. 1788; his wife d. 14 Aug. 1793. Ch. (Fam. 30)—Winslow b. 7 Sept. 1758; Mercy b. 19 Aug. 1761; William b. 11 Nov. 1763, d. 6 Oct. 1813; Stephen b. 23 Jan. 1767, d. 12 July 1843; Rachel b. 18 July 1769, d. 11 Dec. 1849; Simeon b. 12 July 1771, d. in infancy; Anna b. 1 Sept. 1774, d. 28 Aug. 1844; Betsey b. 28 June 1778, (m. 26 Jan. 1796, Robert Purinton b. 26 Sept. 1771, lived in Poland, Me., where he d. 3 Mar. 1836 and she 8 Dec. 1852, having ch. Lavina b. 5 Dec. 1796, Amos b. 17 Jan. 1799, Winslow H. b. 11 Nov. 1800, James M. b. 23 Feb. 1803, d. at Ponce Porto Rico 28 Dec. 1831, William b. 12 Feb. 1804, Mary Ann b. 1 Dec. 1806, George b. 30 Nov. 1808, Harriet b. 31 Jan. 1811, m. Moses G. Dow of Norway, Me. and d. there 23 April 1843, Emily Jane b. 12 Mar. 1816, m. James N. Hall of Norway and d. there 1 Nov. 1844) Simeon b. 3 May 1781.

HATEVIL 5 of Fam. 15, m. (1) Ruth Winslow, (2) Ann Jenkins; he d. in Buckfield, Me. 10 May 1804; Children (Fam. 31)—Job; Ruth; Sarah; Hezekiah; Enoch Submit; John, Hatevil; Abigail; Nathan; Dorcas; Margaret; Shadrach.

EBENEZER 5 of Fam. 15, m. Hannah Anderson, and died in Gorham, Me., 26 Aug. 1807. Children (Fam. 32)—Abraham; Isaac; Dorothy; Israel Bethshua; Ebenezer; Daniel.

WILLIAM 5 of Fam. 15, m. (1) Betsey Cox, (2) Elizabeth Wilson, and d. 18 Aug. 1811. Children (Fam. 33)— Elijah; Timothy; Trial; Robert; Israel; Jeremiah; Betsey; Sarah; Mary.

JOHN 5 of Fam. 15, m. Grace Sprague, removed to near Jonesboro' and d. there 18 June 1804. Ch. (Fam. 34)— Sarah; Love; Abigail; Syloma Hatevil; Lucy; Charity; John; Dorothy; Anne; William; Daniel; Grace; Simeon; Joel.

JEDEDIAH 5 of Fam. 15, m. (1) Hannah dau. of Joseph and Elizabeth (Hussey) Tebbets b. 1 Mar. 1753;(2) Elizabeth Clough and removed "Down East." Children (Fam 35)—Peter; Joel; Elizabeth;Aaron; Moses; Abigail; Daniel Jonathan Ann Dorcas.

ANDREW 5 of Fam. 15, m. Jane Merrill and d. 23 Aug. 1831. Children (Fam. 36)—Jane; Edmund; Polly; Amos George; Josiah; Henry.

NICHOLAS 5 of Fam. 15 m. (1) Experience Stone, (2) Emma Sawyer, and d. 13 Sept. 1835. Children (Fam. 37.— Esther, Meriam; Noah; Lot; Greenfield; Experience; Comfort; Solomon, Ephraim; Osney.

PAUL 5 of Fam. 15 m. (1) Sarah Neal, (2) Keziah Hanson; he resided in Brunswick and d. there 12 April 1841. Children (Fam. 38)—Johnson; Olive; Daniel; Neal; William; Sarah, Hanson; Patience; Betsey; James.

SILAS 5 of Fam. 15 m. (1) Mary Gould, (2) Hannah Neal. He lived first at Falmouth but removed to Raymond, Me. there he d. 26 Jan. 1843. Children (Fam. 39)—Samuel; Mary; Dorothy; James; Frances; Peace; Sarah; Andrew; John; Paul; Olive; Silas; Miltimore; Augusta; Hannah.

LOVE 5 of Fam. 16 m. Israel Bartlett of Newbury, and had (Fam. 40)—Joseph H.; Sarah m. (1) Col. Winborn Adams (2) Col. Hubbard; Israel (Hon.;) Mary b 17 Aug. 1751, m. 22 Sept. 1771 Gen. Henry Dearborn of the Rev. Army and d. 22 Oct. 1778; Josiah; Thomas (a Judge.)

REBECCA 5 of Fam. 16 m. Samuel Adams a physician of Durham, N. H., and had (Fam. 41)—Winborn who was a distinguished officer of the Revolution and fell at Stillwater in Sept. 1777; his wife was Sarah Bartlett; he had a son Samuel, ho was a Captain at Stillwater as aid-de-camp to Gov. Sullivan at the time of the Exeter mob and who m. a daughter of Hon. Wm. Parker of Exeter, dying at Portsmouth and having seven children.

MARY 5 of Fam. 17, m. John Langdon of Portsmouth, and had children (Fam. 42)—Woolbury (Hon.;) John b. 1740; Mary, m. Storer; Elizabeth, m. Barrel; Martha m. (1) Barrel, (2) Simpson, (3) Gov. James Sullivan; Abigail. Of these children, JOHN was the most noted. He entered early upon a sea faring life but was driven from it by the Revolutionary troubles, when he immediately took decidedly American ground; 13 Dec. 1774 he was engaged in the removal of the stores from the fort at Newcastle; in 1775 and 1776 was delegate to the general Congress; took command of an independent company of Cadets and was present at Burgoyne's surrender, served in R. I. with a detachment of his company, and was present when Gen. Sullivan brought off the American troops. He was member and Speaker of the N. H. House of Representatives in 1776 and '77; was Judge C C. P. in 1776 but resigned the next year; in 1778 was agent under Congress for building ships of war, and was continental agent for N. H ; in 1779 was President of the N. H. Convention for regulating the currency, and from 1777 to 1782, was Speaker of the N. H. House of R.; in 1780 he was a Commissioner to raise men and procure provisions for the army; and 13 June 1783 was again elected delegate to Congress. In 1784 and '85 he was member of the N. H. Senate and in the latter year President of the State; in 1788 he was delegate to the convention which framed the Constitution of the United States. In March 1788 he was elected Rep. in N. H. Legislature and Speaker of the House, but took the office of Governor to which he was simultaneously chosen. In Nov. 1788 he was elected a member of the senate of the U. S. and became the first presiding officer of that body, was re-elected Senator in 1794. Later in life he was nominated for Vice President but declined on account of age. From 1801 to 1805 he was Rep. in N. H. Legislature, in 1804 and '5 was Speaker, and from 1805 to 1808 and 1810 and '11 was Governor. The degree of L. L. D. was given by D. C. in 1805. He died in Portsmouth 18 Sept. 1819.

Of his patriotism, the following speaks emphatically: "In one of the darkest periods of the revolution, when our means were small, the Provincial Legislature was in session in Exeter, the resources of the country were at the lowest ebb, despair was on every mind, when John Langdon arose in that assembly and made this remarkable speech: 'I have two thousand dollars in specie. I will pledge my plate for as much more. I have eighty hogshead of Tobago Rum, which will be sold for the service of the State. The country shall have it all. If we succeed in establishing our Liberty I shall be repaid; if not, property is of no value'. Such a proposition reanimated every one; called hope back to all, and, and the Governor said, 'We can now raise a New Hampshire regiment and my friend John Stark can command it.' The regiment was raised and fought the battle of Bennington."

SAMUEL 5 of Fam. 17, lived in Exeter. He had (Fam. 43)—Kinsley b 11 Oct. 1760, m. Honor Rundlett; Sarah m. Dea. Samuel Gilman; Abigail, m. Joseph Elbridge; Merribah, m. Benjamin Hodge; Elizabeth, m. Henry Ranlet.

KINSLEY 5 (JAMES) of Fam. 19, m. 5 Nov. 1735, Mary dau. of Dudley Hilton b. 22 Oct. 1709. Ch. (Fam. 44)—Elizabeth b. 15 Sept. 1736, d. 27 Feb. 1737; Mary b. 10 Dec. 1737; Lois b. 30 Sept. 1739, m. Theophilus Lyford, Kinsley H. b. 1742, d. unm. in 1810; Ann m. (1) Thomas Lyford, (2) Col. Gidings, and died 12 Aug. 1813.

DUDLEY 5 of Fam. 19, m. (1) 5 Mar. 1740-1, Mary, dau. of John and Hannah Light; he m. (2) 12 July 1753, Tizzah Emery. Children (Fam 45)—Abigail b. 8 June 1742, m, Josiah Weeks (whose son Nathaniel of Gilmanton was father to Joshua and Nathaniel of Exeter;) Dudley b. 8 Sept. 1744, d. 8 May 1765; Robert b. 9 Sept. 1746, d. 8 Feb. 1748-9; by second wife, Tizzah b. 15 May 1755, who was second wife of Dea. Samuel Brooks; Caleb, of Gilmanton; Joshua; Mary, m. Caleb Emery of Sanford, Me.

———

Thus far we have given six generations, including some five hundred descendants of the JOHN HALL first mentioned. Other records, containing later generations are in the hands of the compiler and are open to all who are therein interested. In them are found Joseph Hall of Barnstead, Ralph of Greenland, Josiah and Winslow of Dover, Charles E. of Boston, Joshua G. of Wakefield, Joshua E. of Windham. Me., Joseph of Strafford, Thomas B. of Lee, Winslow of Portland, Me; and of other names Hon. Josiah Bartlett of Lee, John Neal of Portland, Neal Dow of Portland, Valentine Smith of Durham, Hall Roberts of Concord, &c., &c. Their records it is needless to give.

DOVER TOWN RECORDS.

Att a public Towne meetting held at Dover ye 18th day of September 1724, Voted that Capt. Paul Garish & Capt. Benjamin wentworth are appointed Agents or Atturneys for the Towne aforesd Joyntly or Seauerally to Prosecute all actions of Trespas upon the Townes Comans allredy begun or hear after to begin and to subsicute atturneys under them as they se ease.

we the subscribers being Desired by Saueral of the Inhabetance of the Town of Douer to Lay out a Livh way out from the thorow fare Rode that leads from bellomars Banck to oyster River falls, we have Laide it out three Rods wide as folloeth: it begins at a stake on the norwest side of the thorow fare Road and from that stake it Runs norwest about two Degres westerle Thirty o e Rods and (a) half to a Pich Pine tree markt with H. W. and from Pich Pine it Runs north a half a poynt Esterly about afower Rods to a whit oak tree Standing near the freshet marked H. W. and from that whit oak it Runs north north East about three degrees northerly over the freshet near the mill forty nine Rods and from thence it Runs north three Degrees westerly seauen Rods and from thence it Runs norwest twenty one Rods to John Bunckers bound mark and soe his Line the bounds to the End of sd Line so keping the same tredth As the path no v Goes tell it comes to the way that Leads from Bellomans Banck to madbery.

Layd out the 9th of August 1725.
franses mathes
James nute
John Smith
                    Selectmen.

At a meeting of the freeholders of Douer Parish at Cochecha meeting house the 16th Day of august 1725.

first. Cornall waldron chosen moderat r.

2d. voted that our minister mr. Jorathan Cushing's Sallery that the Towne gaue him of one hundred Pound in the yeare 1717, shall be made as Good to him as it was at his first settlement amongst us.

3dly. voted that there shall be 50 pounds anuelly added to his first hundred Pounds to make his Sallery good.

march the 26:1726.

At a meeting of the Selectmen at Cochecha the Humble Request of nicolas Harford Humbly Sheweth,

that whereas sd Harford has A grant of Liberty to keep a ferrey ouer the foer Riuer viz. from Dover Neck to Kittery, which Liberty was granted in the year 1717, and sd harford hath been at a grate Charg in building Conuenancies for said ferrey and But Little Proffet at Present nor Likely to be for maney yeares, and Considering the frailty of Life and the grate Charg he hath been at and no assurance of sd ferrey any Longer then his one Life by vertu of the former grant, humbly Prayeth that the sd ferrey may be confirmed unto him and his heires.

at the above sd metting ye selectmen gaue their Co sent that the sd ferey should be Confirmed unto ye sd nicolas Harford's heires.

Test Thomas Tebbets Towne Clark.

at a publick Towne meeting at Cochecho ye 28th Day of march 1726,
Capt. Samuell Emerson Chosen in the Rume of Capt. Benjamin wentworth Desesed to Joyn with Capt. Paul Gerrish to Prosecute at Law any Person or persons that Trespass on our Towne Comons.
Test Thomas Tebbetts Town Clark.

At a meeting of the select men ye 23 of September 1726, then ordeied the Charg of Laying out and Recording of the aboue sd highway shall be on the Towne's account
Test Thomas Tebbets Towne Clark.

Dover ye 22 August 1726
At a meeting of the selectmen this Day
whereas more than 40 of ye Inhabetance have Petistied for a highway to be Laid out from madbery Road to New Towne Road for accommodation of the Inhabetance their abouts, ordered that Capt. fransis Mathus mr John Smith & mr James Nute be Desird to vew the Land and Lay out A high Way whear it may be most Conuenant without aney Charge to the Towne.
as attest Thomas Tebbets Town Clarke

whereas forty of the Inhabetance of the Towne of Douer Petisened that there might be a highway Laid out from the thorow fare Rode that leads from Sallmon falls to Cochecha for the Conuenancey of the Inhabetance to get into the Comaus, at a meeting of the Selectmen at Dover the 6th of march 1726-7, then ordeied that franses Mathes, nicholas Harford and James Nute Lay out the aboue said highway and make Returne thereof & we ye subscribers hauing ben on the Spot haue Layd it out two Rods wide as followeth: we began on the norwest Side of the aboue Said Road between the Land of Thomas wallinford and the Land of John Tebbets 44 Rods near nor west, then it Runs near northeast 32 Rods between the Land of Samuel Corsons and the Land of wallinfords, then it Runs north 40 Rods upon wallinfords Land, then it Runs 60 Rods between the Land of Richard Rooks and the Land of the aboue sd wallingford, then it Runs near norwest and be west 48 Rods upon the Land of Judeth Tebbets, Then it Runs westerle 80 Rods upon the Land of James Canney, then it Runs west sow west 20 Rods between the Land of Geoarge Ricor and the Land of the afforesaid Cenrey, then it Runs 46 Rod upon the Land of william Jones, then it Runs 320 Rods upon Samuel Jones Land, then it Runs 40 Rods upon Ebenezer Downes Land, then it Runs 60 Rods upon wentworth Land, then it Runs 60 Rods upon Samuell Downes Land, then it Runs 60 Rod upon william Daues Land and then by Church is Land to the Coman.
Layd out the 9th of march 1726 7.
    Nicholas Harford
    James nute
    franses mathes
        Selectmen.

march ye 23d 1726 7.
The Selectmen then layd out at high way from the Back River up to the Contrary Road Betwen Thomas Roterds Land and the Land that is now in the Pesestion of Thomas Cenue, bounded as folloeth; beginning at sail River upon

the Bank 4 Rods upon the upland and then it Runs 32 Rods upon a north east Line Between Thomas Roberds Land and said Riuer neare the mouth of Little Johns Creek and then it Runs 38 Rods north East and East half a Poynt Easterly Between the Land that is now in Posestion of Thomas Canne and the afore said Thomas Roberds Land where the sd Roberds fence now Standeth up to the Contray Road that Leads from Hiltons pint up to Cochecha 2 Rods wide haueing Reserued the Springs and watering place on the north side of Thomas Roberds his house to Lay Comon as it is now for Ever.

fransis mathes
James nute
Nicolas Harford,
Selectmen.

OLD SERIES, NO. 127, DEC. 20, 1853.

THE INDIANS.

The first Indian war in New Hampshire did not end with the destruction of Cochecho in the summer of 1689; it continued five years longer. Yet though that first severe blow upon the frontier made the inhabitants tremulously sensitive to rumors and indications of trouble from that time Cochecho was comparatively unharmed. Other parts of this and the neighboring towns were not so fortunate.

Thus after the massacre at Cochecho not all of the Indians immediately left for Canada, whither a part went with the captives. Two days after, as the following letter shows, they were at Oyster River:

Hampton, July 30, 1689.

Major Pike Sir: Thes are to informe you that this last night There came news to me ffrom Exeter that one of Philllip Cromwells Sons came yesterday from oyster River where were 20 Indiens Seen and seueral Houses Burning. About 20 English ishued out to beat them off a many guns were herd g o off but he coming away while it was a doing we haue not as yett any account of what harme is ther done and we thank you for your care about our — — — Althoug no help could be procured there is but a few could be procured with us the notice was so suddaine but thos that are gon went yesterday when it was almost night they were willing to stay no longer. When I have account father from Oyster River I will sennd it to you Lot Els at present

ffrom your ffriend
Samuell Sherburne.

The result of this attack we are unable to learn. Belknap does not allude to it at all, and the Massachusetts State Papers, in which the letter is filed, present no additional information.

Belknap tells us however of an affair of the succeeding August. Indians, watching in the woods about Oyster River, noticed how many men belonged to the garrison of James Huckians: they counted eighteen. Seeing them all go out to work one morning, they got between them and the garrison and killed all of them but one. In the house were two boys, some women and children; it was attacked, but the boys defended it manfully until it was set on fire, when on promises of safety to all, they surrendered. Three or four of the children, however, were killed and the others of the party carried off. One of the boys escaped the next day and told the story. He, or some other of the children, became himself an Indian fighter and was father to a son who, a soldier, died in the army of the old French war.

Upon the other side of Cochecho also, there was trouble. A united campaign for the first time was entered upon. Three parties of French and Indians were detached from Canada by Count de Frontenac: the one burned Schenectady; the second surprised Salmon Falls; the third destroyed Casco.

At Salmon Falls the attack was as unexpected as at Cochecho. Sieur Hertel, a French officer of energy, led through the forests and amidst snows, a company of fifty two men from Trios Rivieres,— there being among them Wahwa, better known as Hoophood, a noted warrior, commanding twenty-five Indians. They reached Salmon Falls 18 March 1690, and at daybreak attacked the garrison from three directions. The surprised people made a vigorous resistance, but when thirty of their travest were killed, including nearly every man, the fifty four remaining, nearly all women and children, surrendered. The enemy burned twenty structures, including houses, barns and mills, (Charlevoix says twenty seven,) destroying many cattle in the barns, committed depredations as far as Quamphegan, and retreated. A hundred men were hastily collected from the neighboring towns and pursued them. Hertel, encumbered with captives, expected to be overtaken; he posted himself therefore beyond a narrow bridge on Wooster's river in Berwick. The pursuers arrived and attacked him, but after two hours of warm fighting, extending into the darkness of the night, they found themselves unable to force his position and retired, taking with them one prisoner, a Frenchman. Hertel sent the captives, with part of his force, to Canada; himself was next, resulting in similar success, at the burning of Casco.

From their date the following letters possess a peculiar interest. They have never, we believe, been before printed, and they correct one or two slight errors in published history:

Portsmo March 18: 1689-90.
10 a clock.

Much Honrd

Wee are Just now infor red that ye Indian Enemy this morning Attacqued Salmon falls and have surprised all the families above the fort wch are about 10 or 12, & have also taken possession of the fort & of Loves house where several families lived.

Wm. Plaisted who gives this information made his Escape from Capt. Wincols house wch was twice assaulted by ye Enemy but they were beaten of by six or seven English men whome he left in possession of sd house when he came a way from thence to give this advice & pray for relife he saw not above twenty Indians; we have already sent away from the banks between twenty and thirty men, & have sent to our other Towns for further releife; we now here see the smoaks rise so yt they are burning all before them: We humbly pray a thorough & serious Consideration of the condition of this pt of ye Country, and yt such measures may be forthwith taken as in yr Honrs wisdome shall be thought most Conducive to the preservation thereof: this is the hole of wt information we can at present give, as soon as we have A further accot you may expect to hear further from

Much Honrd yor Humble servts
Wm. Vaughan
Richd Martyn.

OLD SERIES, NO. 128, DEC. 27, 1853.

THE INDIANS—CONTINUED.

Portsmo 19 March 1689-90.
Much Honrd

Yesterdy we gave accot of ye dreadful destruction of Salmon ffalls the perticulars whereof pleas to take as followeth.

The enemy made their onset between break of the day & sun rise when most were a bed & no watch kept neither in fort nor house they presently took possession of ye fort to prevent any of us doing it & so carried all before them by surprise, none of our men being able to get together into a body to oppose them, so that in the place were kild & taken between ffourscore and 100 persons, of wch between twenty and Thirty able men, the fort and upwards of twenty houses burnt, most of the Cattle burnt in the houses or otherwise kil'd which were very considerable, from thence the enemy proceeded to Quampregan where lived onely Thomas Holmes who upon the Alarm retired from his house to a small Garrison built near his Saw mill wheither also some of Salmon falls yt made their escape fled, about 30 of the Enemies surrounded Holmes house but met with noe opposition then till fourteen men of uus came up from ye lower part of ye Town & undisaryed by ye Enemy, made a shot npon yt party of Indians at Holmes house, sundry of ym standing before the door at who shot t ey say three Enemy fell, ye rest run into the house & broke through ye backside thereof, & being more numerous than ours forced our men to retire, some of them got safe home & five Escaped to Holmes Garrison, only one of ours wounded in the Encounter, then the Enemy burnt Holmes house & proceeded about a mile lower down & turnt the ministrs house wth two more & assaulted Spencers Garrison but were repel'd & so retired. James Plaisted who was taken at Salmon falls was set

by Hopehood (Commander in chief of the Indians) wth a Flag of Truce in Tno: Holmes for ye surrender of his Garrison promising liberty to depart upon his soe doing, but Plaisted returned nor was ye Garrison surrendered.

The sd Plaisted who was in ye Enemies. baud many hours Informs yt he saw of ye Enemy one hundred and fifty men well accoutred & Guesses them to be about one half ffrench, upon their taking possession of ye ffort he said that ten of them ffrench & Indians made A dance wcn Hopehood told him were all office rs. he also told him of his Brother Gooden who lived in Loves house was going to be try'd for his life by A Councill of Warr, for yt in their taking Loves house ye sd Gooden had kil'd one ffrench & mortally wounded another, & further that there was Eight french ships designed for Pascataqua River to destroy ye same:

The Alarm being given to all Adjacent Towns in ordr to their releife we sent about thirty men from this Town, as many went from Duer, & A party from York together wtn wt could be got from their own Town, but before they could unite their force it was neare eight & then they marcht wth about 10 men under Comand of Capt Jo Hamont Comandr of ye uper part of Kittery. the scouts yt went before just as they came wth in sight of salmon falls Disovered one of ye Enemy whc was binding up his pack & staying behind his Company fell into our hand which proved to be a ffre chman whose Examination in short we here wth send you & tomorrow mornin intend to send the person toward you by land none by Water being just ready to gne: our ffores proceeded in pursuit of ye Enemy & about 2 miles above ye ffort of Salmon falls at the farther huose up in the woods there discovered them about ye settling of ye sunn. our men presently fell upon them & they as resolutely opposed them, in short the fight lasted as long as they could see friends from Enemies, in which we left three men, one of York, another of Cochecho kill upon ye place 6 or seven

wounded some is feared mortally wt damage we did the Enemy we cant at present say: This is all ye accot we can at present give, tomorrow intend you shall hear again from us. we intrem subscribe ourselves Honrd Srs
   Yor humble Servts:
    Wm. Vaughan
    Richd Martyn.

Portsmo: 19th March 1689-99.
Upon examination of the french man taken at Salmon ffalls he said
Their Company that Attaq'd Salmon ffalls consisted of sixty men 30 French & 30 Indians who came from Canady the beginning of ffeubr from a Town called three Rivers lying above Cabeck, t at they have not been near any English Plantation since they came out till now but waited about twenty or thirty miles off, severall days for a party of 20 or 30 Indians who promised to meet & Joyn wth them but came not, that they have lived wholly upon hunting, yt they came by ordr of the ffrench Govr at Canada & t at by both ffrench and Indians are in pay at ten Livers p month. The said Govr is Comt Fontenack yt arrived from ffrance last yeare in A man of war with severall merchant Ships wch went away again in 8ber. only two ships remain in Canada of Twenty-five Guns a piece. That two parties of ffrench & Indians of three hundred men in a Company came out about the same time. they came, but whether they were design'd he saith he knows not. That he knows nothing of the Mischiefe done near Albany, that they intended to carry their captives to Canada & there sell them. yt their design was not against this place when they first came forth but principally against Monsieur Tyng & the place where he lived but he saaith the Indians who were their principle pilots did often Vary in their Opinions about wt place to fall upon, cant understand whether it were Mr. Tyng of Merrimack River or Casco Bay. That they saw no Considerable Company of Indians in their March only a few in some places hunting, that they brought out wth them two pounds of powder & sixty bullets a piece, that their are sundry English Captives at Canada but he saw only three, two girls and a boy, that the ffrench are able to raise four or five thousand men in Canada able to bear arms, & yt they have Thirty two Companies of fifty men in a company in constant pay. trac the ffrench Capt name of this Company is Monsieur Aretall; his son being his Lieut.

These communications were forwarded to Boston.

Attacks, but less appalling, followed the disastrous blow upon Salmon Falls and Casco. By the destruction of the latter the inhabitants of Maine were driven back to Wells. The Indians followed them and in the same month (My) a party under Hoophood attacked the inhabitants of Fox Point in Newington, then of Dover; they burned several houses, killed about fourteen people and carried away six captive. Pursuers recovered some of the captives, and wounded Hoophood, who was soon after, to the great joy of the whites, mistaken by his allies for an Iroquois and killed.

On the fourth of July, eight persons, swimming at Lamprey river, were killed, and a boy captured. In the fight the enemy attacked Captain Hilton's garrison at Exeter, but with no success, save to kill a few whites. The day following is more memorable.

The provincial authority at Portsmouth had determined to send an expedition into the forests against the Indians. Capt. Wiswall was designated for this service; it being deemed advisable to join another Captain with him, members volunteered, of whom Capt. Floyd was selected by lot. A hundred men rendezvoused at Dover, and started westward. On Sunday morning, 6 July, the advanced scouts reported an Indian trail. They followed it and overtook the enemy on the borders of Wheelwright's pond: an engagement followed—in which each man fought for himself, in the Indian custom. After hours of fighting Wiswall, Flagg, his lieutenant, Walker, his sergeant, and twelve others, having fallen, and the bulk of the remainder being rather exhausted by the heat of the summer day, Floyd retreated, the Indians however doing the same. Floyd was blamed afterwards, but clearly without cause.

Few attacks were made in this vicinity for two years following: for the Indians in a conference at Sagahock made a truce which continued until June 1691, a month longer, strange to say, than the time agreed upon: then Wells was attacked, but unsuccessfully; two men were killed at Exeter, and in September, twenty-one persons were killed or captured at Rye. But a new and more energetic plan of guarding the frontiers by the constant ranging of sufficiently strong scouting parties from one post to another, being adopted, the only incidents which took place during the succeeding winter were that a party which fired upon a young man in the woods of Cochecho was followed and all excepting one man slain; that Tobias Hanson was killed at Dover 10 May, 1693; and that mischief was perpetrated upon "one poor family which they took at Oyster River."

Further quiet was obtained also by a treaty of peace concluded at Pemnaquid 11 Aug. 1693, signed by thirteen Indian chiefs, four other Indians, and three English interpreters. The Indians then acknowledged their subjection to the English Crown, promised to abandon the French alliance, to return their captives, to forbear the gratification of private revenge, and, with sad mockery, to keep a perpetual peace. To Dover, with the rest of the province, this treaty gave a happy breathing time, their continued alertness, the wasting of their property, the inability of cultivating their lands and the destruction of their men, had well nigh exhausted and dispirited the people.

The peace was short; French cunning found a new element by which to excite Indian hate. Religious fanaticism was added by the labors of tireless French missionaries, and through this Sieur de Villieu, commander upon the Penobscot, in 1694, broke the treaty. The first blow fell upon Oyster River.

OLD SERIES NO. 129, JAN. 3, 1854.

THE INDIANS—CONTINUED.

As profound a peace existed in July, 1694, as in June 1689. In the latter time the first notice of war was read in the destruction of Cochecho; in the former a still more stunning blow awoke the inhabitants, in another part of the stricken town to the horrors of Indian butchery.

Though by virtue of solemn and unrevoked treaties there was peace upon the Pascataqua, a deliberate attack was talked of in the streets of Quebec two months before its occurrence. Madok wando was persuaded not to comply with his engagements for returning captives principally, it is said, by the agency of M. Thury, a French missionary to the Indians. Wrongs, real or fancied, were appealed to; religious fanaticism was aroused; a bounty was offered for scalps; and in July, 1694, Sieur de Villieu led two hundred and fifty Indians, of the St. John, Penobscot and Norridgewocks tribes, attended by two priests, against Oyster River.

There were eleven garrison houses about the falls, but no danger being thought of, some families were in their ordinary defenseless dwellings; some of the fortified houses themselves were without powder, and one of them was not even closed at night so secure did the inhabitants feel. John Davis, conversing the evening previous to the attack on the fact that not long bef re Indians were seen in the woods, gave it as his opinion that there was not then an Indian within fifty miles; yet Moses, his nephew, not satisfied but that an alarm which his dog had given him in the day time and which he then thought a bear occasioned, arose from the presence of the enemy.

On Tuesday evening 17 July, the enemy approached the falls. Concealing themselves in the woods, at night they divided into two sections, one for each side of the river. Small parties were to place themselves near every house, awaiting through the moonlight to sight the signal of the first guns for a simultaneous attack.

The signal was given too soon. John Dean, who lived near the falls, on their north side, intending to leave home in the morning, arose before day to catch his horse; as he returned an Indian could not restrain his impetuosity, and fired. He killed Dean; but the firing disconcerted the whole plan; some parties who had far to go had not reached their stations; and though the attack immediately commenced, the inhabitants were alarmed and some had time to prepare for defence. But for this accident principally, the whole settlement would have perished.

The details of the attack are the following:

The inhabitants of the unfortified houses ran for the garrisons; a few succeeded; more were killed. Five Chesleys, near Jones' garrison, were shot; Robert Watson and his family, save his wife, a quarter of a mile away, were all cut off. Kent, awoke by the firings, looked from his window and saw Indians waiting for him to go out; in his fear he did not awake his family but hid in a drain, and lay there all day; his wife and children, awoke by the continued tumult, escaped while the Indians had left their house to assist in reducing Drew's Garrison. Ezekiel Pitman and his family, a gun-shot distance from Burnum's Garrison, were awoke by shouts to them from that place; they escaped through one end of the house as the Indians entered the other, and in the shade of trees, escaped to the Garrison. James Huckins, whose family had nearly all been killed in 1689, was himself shot at this time. Mrs. Emerson was taken, with her mother and child; the latter two the party dismiss d; they hid among corn, but other Indians came along and butchered them both. Mrs. Dean, wife of John, with her daughter, was captured when her husband was shot, taken to a spruce swamp and tha the others might pursue Moses Davis, left in the care of an old Indian; the latter, able to speak English, told her he had a violent headache, and asked her the remedy; "cccapee", she answered, that is "rum"; he drank freely and went to sleep; taking her daughter she immediately ran; she heard him calling after her, but she hid in a thicket, lay there until light, then went down the river in a canoe to Burnum's Garrison, and there found safety. Ensign John Davis, remaining in his own house, surrendered on the promise of safety; but he, his wife and several children, were killed, his house burnt, and two daughters made captives; one of them became a nun in Canada, the other finally returned—His sister, a widow named Smith, who lived with him, with two sons was carried into the woods and killed; her oldest son escaped to the river, but was there shot.

Moses Davis, who had watched uneasily all night, heard the first gun; speedily finding the whole town attacked he started down the river; he was pursued, but baffled search in the woods and the next day with his family entered Burnum's Garrison. Sargeant Davis's house was set on fire, but he extinguished the flames; as he left it one of three Indians waiting, fired upon him; he stooped and the bullet split a sapling just over his head; he escaped to Col. Davis's. Edward Leathers' wife was killed, and a woman named Jackson. William Leathers escaped by running. A man named Clark, and a Gellison, the latter going from one house to another for powder, were shot near Davis's garrison. Thomas Edgerly lived at Amblars; hearing the firing, he, his wife, and her sister hid in the cellar; their children were killed, and one or two persons in another part of the house were taken; the Indians fired the house but when they had gone, Edgerly extinguished the flames.

John Buss, the preacher and physician was absent; his family on the first alarm, left the house and secreted themselves among some trees near by. The enemy entered the house, stripped it of furniture and set fire to it; the valuable library was consumed. The house of Mr. Tasker, in the bounds of Madbury, was entrusted to three Indians; one of them, looking into a window, asked "isn't it time to get up?" Tasker, who had another man with him in the house, answered the savage by loading his gun and shooting him; the family then took to the woods and safely reached Woodman's Garrison.

Thomas Bickford lived near the river; his house was not properly fortified but it had around it a palisade. Alarmed before the enemy had reached his house, he sent off his family (mainly one of young children,) in a boat, and prepared to defend his home alone; by often changing his dress, giving orders as if he had others with him, and firing as often and from as many different positions as possible, he succeeded; despairing of success the enemy withdrew.

Five of the Garrison houses were destroyed.—That of Charles Adams was entered without resistance. The owner, a man of seventy years, Samuel and his wife, and others to the number of fourteen, were killed; they were afterward buried in one grave. Joseph Beard with his family abandoned his garrison, escaping down the river. So did John Meder, then sixty four years old, and who lived until 1712 or perhaps longer. Thomas Edgerly, father of the Thomas already mentioned, left his garrison and attempted to escape, but himself, his son Joseph, and a daughter were captured others of his family entered a canoe, and were saved, with the exception of Zachariah, a son of Thomas, who was shot as he stepped on board. Thomas Drew surrendered his garrison on promise of safety; there were fifteen persons in it. He was bound, but releasing himself, in the struggle killed one Indian; he ran towards Adams' garrison, but the Indians there took him, bound him, and killed him with tomahawks; his wife was made captive, but becoming feeble on the march towards Canada, was left in the woods to die; his son Benjamin, a boy of nine, was taken as far as Winnepissiogee, was there made to run the gauntlet as a mark for hatchets, and so killed; another son John, by being early let out of a window, escaped; Thomas, who had been married a few months previous, was carried to Canada, his wife to Norridgewock; both afterwards returned, he after two years captivity, she after four; and they became parents of a large family.

Seven garrisons were successfully defended. The first alarmed was Burnum's. The gate of this garrison was open and there were ten Indians lying under the bank of the river, who sent to surprise it had through fatigue fallen asleep. In the garrison was John Willey and his family; he was kept awake that night by a toothache, and he heard the gun which shot John Dean an hour before day. He shut the gate and alarmed the garrison, who shouting to Ezekiel Pitman, their neighbor, awoke the Indians. The house was thus saved. The fate of Bickford's house, erroneously enumerated with the Garrisons by Belknap, has already been described. Bunker's Garrison was successfully defended by the owner, James Bunker. his son James, and others—The Davis garrison, unfortunately containing but part of the Davis families, was stoutly defended by its owner, James Davis, afterwards Colonel and a brave officer, and "Sergeant" Davis, the families being sent off by water. No very severe attack was made upon this house, nor upon that of Bunker, nor upon Capt. John Smith's at Lubberland; indeed, on the shore of Great Bay little injury was done. Less was accomplished by the enemy at the Falls also than would have resulted had it not been that the leader of the enemy assigned to the north side of the river did not reach the lower settlements until after sunrise, when the inhabitants had escaped.

Capt. Stephen Jones in the early morning heard a furious barking of the dogs; he supposed it was caused by wolves; he went out therefore, to secure some swine; returning, he sat upon a flankart, with his feet hanging outwards; seeing the flash of a gun he fell back, when a bullet entered the log on which he had been sitting; from that moment a constant but effectual fire was kept up upon the garrison, from behind a rock near by.

The party upon the south side of th

river, having finished their work, assembled on a green in sight of Burnum's garrison, showing their captives and insulting the whites. Here a young man in a sentry box shot one of them who, imagining he was out of reach, was mocking the garrison; him they took away upon a horse of Mr. Burnum's.

Both parties at last met at the falls, and proceeded together to attack Woodman's garrison; this fortification, then owned by Jonathan Woodman, still standing near Durham village and owned by his descendant, Nathan Woodman, now bears in its logs the bullet shot into them that morning. But they were unable to capture it, and supposing that the men of the neighboring towns would soon be in pursuit, they left the bodies and smoking houses of the desolated settlement and started for Canada. Not however until the French priests, who in these hours of bloodshed, had amused themselves with writing with chalk on the pulpit of the meeting house, had twice said mass.

NOTE.—In No. 127 of these Memoranda the letter of Samuel Sherburne to Major Pike, which is spoken of as being written two days after the massacre at Cocheco, is dated "July 30, 1689." A correspondent inquires if this is right? There is evidently an error somewhere, as the affair at Cocheco, it is well known, took place on the 28th, June. But on recurring to the manuscript of the copyist we find that the printer has "followed copy."

OLD SERIES, NO. 130, JAN. 17, 1854.

THE INDIANS—CONTINUED.

In the attack on Oyster River the enemy seems to have lost but four men; one shot by Ensign Davis; one killed by Francis Drew; one mortally wounded by William (?) Tasker; and one killed by Thomas Bickford. They destroyed five garrisons, eight dwellings, much cattle, desolated a tract six miles in width, and killed or carried away ninety four persons.

The names of the killed so far as preserved are these: John Dean; James Huckins; five Chesleys; Robert Watson (and others of his family;) Mrs. Emerson's mother and sister; Ensign John Davis and wife and several children, and his sister Smith and two sons a Clark; a Gellison; a brother of the last named who jumped into a well and there died; Samuel Adams, his wife and twelve others of his family; Edward Leathers's wife; a woman named Jackson; some children of Thomas Edgerly, Jr's, Zachariah, son of Thomas Edgerly; Francis Drew, his wife and his son Benjamin. For the Scalps of these Frontenac paid the stipulated price. Of the captured were two daughters of Ensign John Davis, one of whom never returned; one or two of Samuel Adams's family; one or two persons in the house of Thomas Edgerly, Jr.; Thomas Edgerly, a daughter and his son Joseph; Thomas Drew and his wife. The names of the others, killed or captured, are lost.

Letters written on the morning of the attack are here given:

Portsmo July 18th (1694).

Just now arrived a post from Oyster River. The Indians have destroyed the place killed & burned all they could N-re —— have Escaped and are too badly wounded doe not Know but they be all over our ffrontiers

wait yr Honors Motion
Tho Packer.

May please yor Exy:
9 in ye Morning New Castle July 18th: 1694.

Just now have Received the Enclosed acco. our prouince all in arms desire your Exy forthwith to (send) one or Two hundred men with Arms & Aminution for the defence of the place and to parsue the enimie: we fear Se u hrall other or Towns in the province are be sett.

—— —— burnt from ye head of oyster River to ye mouth of it on both sides tho: Edgerly & his son wounded making their Escape and judge the wholl place is Cutt off.

Nott doubting of Yor Ready Assistance I subscribe Yor Esq's Humble Seruat John Usher.

(To Geo. Phipps.)

May it Pleas yor Excell. (rec. 21 July 1694).

Since the Lft Governrs of 18th Inst; anoth is Come to our hand. the Indians verie Numerous. Not less than three hundred. Douie who signed the Peace was there, a Woman who was Douie's Servant ma e her Escape, by reason of his being drunck. Faith Douie did tell her that thay deid Expect 600 Indeians more that the Mangwaits were joyned wth them, and judge So Le Southern Indians were there. There is two Fryars among the Indiaus who af er Victory Said Mass twice, the Indeians did Spred 6 or 7 miles, and engaged all at once. Oyster River in a manner Ruinede, only abt 20 houses left, the rest layd waste. unless we have a supply of men from yourself Oyster Riuer n ust be deserted. If Ovster Riuer be des rted, the Enimie will have an inlett in to the whole Countrey, for the Majess Service & Security of the Countrey desire you would forthwith Supply us wth one hundred men wth amunition & Provision to be Posted for preservation of these Out places. we are dispatching Some Soldiers into our Outward Garrisons according to the ability of this Province upon the Alarn s wth all expedition. We dispatched from the Severall Townes one third of the Militia in this Province for Releafe of Oyster River, but before they came there the Eni:.ie was drawn of and could not be met with; its Judged Eighty psons Killd & taken. abundeance of Cattle Killd. last Night three Indiars Seen several Guns fired. Judg the Enlmie is still bordering upon us, but we vant assistance to pers ie them, the Euimie being so numerous; Desire that Orders may be given to Justices and all Constables for the dispatch of Expresses; Not doubting of yor Rediness to assist us, we being ready to afford our assitance according to our ability, to your parts case the Enimie snould Invade yours. We Cranue your answer by this ——ess.

By ordr of the Lt Govern & Couniel.
Wm. Redford: Dept Secrs.

The apprehensi ns of further violence were unhappily realized. Not all of the body who attacked Oyster River returned immediatetly; while one portion under Toxus, a Norridgewock, went westward, a smaller party crossed the Piscataqua, and killed Irsula Cutt, (widow of the President Cutt) and three others. baymakers. That day Col. Richard Waldron had promised to dine with her but the arrival of friends prevented it; while at dinner in his own house he heard of her death.

In July 1695, two men were killed at Exeter. On the 7 May 1696, John Church was killed and scalped at Cochecho. Various person were killed at Portsmouth on the 26 June, and the recapture at Breakfast Hill in Rye took place the next day, of which an account is here unnecessary. On the 26 July the people of Dover were waylaid and fired upon as they were returning home from meeting. Nicholas Otis, Mary Downs, and Mary Jones were killed; Richard Otis, Anthony Lowden, and Experience Heard were wounded; John Tucker, Nicholas Otis, Jr., and Judith Ricker were captured. As all these persons appear to have lived between Waldron's Garrison and Garrison Hill, it is probable that the attack was between the upper falls and the brow of the hill before reaching Otis' Garrison.

Of affairs at Exeter, of the killing of Major Frost at Kittery, of the threatened invasion by sea, our purpose forbids minute accounts. Dover soil was no more molested during that war, and the war itself soon ended.

The peace of Ryswick, concluded in Europe 20 September 1697, forced the French Governor Frontenac to withdraw his protection and assistance from the Indians, as France and England were no longer at war.

He advised the Indians therefore to bury the hatchet. Themselves wearied with fighting, pinched by want, and divided in their own councils, at last they concluded a peace at Casco, 9 January, 1699. Among other promises it was agreed that captives should be returned; some indeed had in 1695 been ransomed; among these were John Key sen and John Key, Jr. of Cochecho, Elizabeth Smart and Cisca Brackett of Oyster River. Others in the hands of the French at that time, memorials of the fate of Cochecho in 1689 and Oyster River in 1694, were Abigail Willev, Judy Willey, Elizabeth Willey, John Skyly, Sarah White, and Samuel Rand, (a boy,) of Oyster River; Grizel Otis, Christian Otis, John Otis, (a boy), Rose Otis, a girl, Stephen Otis, (inhabitants of the ill-fated Otis Garrison,) John Anthony, (a boy,) and Obadiah Preble, of Cochecho; and Joseph Perkins, (a boy,) Abigail Curlin, Lydia Langley, (a girl,) Mary Swarten, Abigail Brackett, Elizabeth Squire, John Persons, (a boy,) Ro- and Young, (a boy,) Ruth Persons, Mary Sayward, Esther Saywarde, and H. S. Short, (a boy,) of Dover, but of unknown locality. How many of these ever returned it is impossible to tell. Christina Otis, returned; Rose, her sister, did also and married John Pinkham; John Otis probably remained in Canada; Stephen certainly did; so did their mother-in-law Grizel, who married there. Others doubtless did also and so were finally lost to their friends; for the treaty stipulations were not fairly carried out in this particular, and to the settlers the horrors of border warfare were succeeded by the deep grief of knowing that children, educated in another faith than that of their ancestry, were alienated in heart, calling strangers to their blood fathers and mothers.

―――

*** The above particulars, differing in some slight points from published history, we have drawn from original documents of which the most important is the manuscript in the hands of Valentine Smith, Esq., of Durham, already presented to our readers.

OLD SERIES, NO. 173, MAY 28, 1857.

THE COFFIN FAMILY.

In the Boston News Letter of 25th March 1715, we found the following obituary.

On Monday, the 21st Courant, Died at Exeter the Honourable Peter Coffin, Esq., in the 85th year of his Age, who was late Judge of His Majesty's Superiour Court of Judicature, and First Member of His Majesty's Council of this Province; a Gentleman very Servicable both in church and State. We have now a Severe Storm of Snow.

The latter sentence is out of our line: the preceding suggests the following.

The Honourable Peter Coffin, Esq., was long a resident of Dover. His father was TRISTRAM COFFIN, a native of the parish of Brixton, near Plymouth, Devonshire, England, a son of Peter (1) and Joanna Coffin, and born in 1609. TRISTRAM sen. (2) married Dionis Stevens, and after the death of his father, came to New England in 1642, bringing with him his mother, (who died in May 1661, aged 77;) his two sisters, Eunice and Mary, and his wife and five children, viz., Peter, Tristram, Elizabeth, James and John. He at first came to Salisbury, went thence to Haverhill the same year, thence to Newbury, about 1648, thence in 1654 or 5, to Salisbury, where he signs his name, "Tristram Coffyn, Commissioner of Salisbury;" in 1659 a company was formed in Salisbury who purchased nine tenths of Nantucket, and Tristram removed thither in 1660 with his wife, his mother and four of his children, viz., James, John, Stephen and Mary. There he died 2 Oct. 1681, aged 72.— His children therefore were, Peter (our Peter) born in 1630; Tristram b. 1632; Elizabeth, mar. Stephen Greenleaf; James b. 12 Aug. 1640; John b. in England, died in Haverhill 1642; Mary b. in Haverhill, 20 Feb. 1645, John b. in Newbury 11th May 1652.

As to Tristram's sisters, while we think of it, we will say that Eunice married William Butler; and his sister Mary married Alexander Adams of Boston.

As to his children: PETER (3) of Dover, we will attend to by and by. TRISTRAM (3) was a merchant tailor, and lived in Newbury. He married Judith Somerby, widow of Henry Somerby and daughter of Captain Edmund Greenleaf, he died 4th of Feb. 1704, and his widow 15 Dec. 1705, aged 80, leaving 177 descendants. Their children were Judith, b. 4 Dec. 1653, Deborah b. 10th Nov. 1655; Mary, b. 12th Nov. 1657; James, b. 22 April, 1659; John b. 8 Spt. 1660. d. 13th of May 1677; Lydia, b. 22 April 1662; Enoch, b. 21 Jan. 1663, d. 12 Nov. 1675; Stephen, b. 18 Aug. 1664; Peter, b. 27 July 1667; Nathaniel b. 22 March 1669. JAMES (3) mar. 3 Dec. 1663, Mary Severance of Salisbury, in 1659 running across Thomas Macy and his family, who on account of Baptist notions had found Newbury rather unpleasant, Isaac Coleman a boy of twelve, and Elder Starbuck, whom the people of Dover had tried to reason out of his Baptist ideas, but failed on account of his uncommon obstinacy,—James and all these took an open boat in 1659 and set sail or the oars, we don't know which. In due time they arrived at Nantucket, a place possessing unsurpassable water privileges, and there they settled. James and his wife replenished Nanatucket with fourteen children, and he died 28 July 1720. What his children's names were we don't know, except that DINAH married her cousin Nathaniel Starbuck, son of Nathaniel and grandson of Elder Edward above mentioned, and that Nathaniel mar. 17 Aug. 1793, Damaris Gayer, dau. of William Gayer, who married Dorcas Starbuck, daughter of the Elder, and was the progenitor of Admiral Sir Isaac Coffin, famous in the annals of the isle and the British Navy. Whether Capt. Coffin, in "Moby Dick" is any relation, we have not ascertained. — MARY (3) mar. Nathaniel, son of Elder Edward Starbuck, of whom we have spoken at length in our "Starbuck" article. He was a wealthy man of no mean abilities, but was decidedly outshone by his wife. She was a Baptist at first; was baptised, indeed, by Peter Folger in Waitpeetequat Pond, but she became "convinced of Friend's principles," and became a preacher among that people, as did also her children Nathaniel and Priscetta.— She was often consulted in town affairs as well as Spiritual in that amphibious territory; she died 13, 9, 1717, having nine children, whose names we need not again publish. JOHN (3) mar. Deborah Austin, and had seven children; he lived in Nantucket; died in 1711. STEPHEN (3) mar. Mary Bunker, and had eight or nine children; he died in 1725.

We may as well insert Tristram's (3) grand children. JAMES (4) mar. 16 Nov. 1685, Florence Hook, and had children. Judith b. 7 Oct. 1686; Elizabeth; Sarah b. 7 20 Aug. 1689; Mary b. 18 Jan. 1691; Lydia b. 1692; Tristram b. 19 Oct. 1694; Daniel b. 10 May, 1696; Eleanor b. 16 May, 1698; Joanna b. 2 May 1701; James and Florence b. 1 Jan. 1705. PETER (4) mar. Apphia Dole, and moved to Gloucester had children: Hannah b. 3 March, 1688; Judith b. 9 Oct. 1693; Tristram b. 10 Aug. 1636; Richard, Sarah b. 24 Aug. 1701; Apphia STEPHEN (4) mar. 1685, Sarah Atkinson, and had children. Sarah b. 16 May 1686; Tristram b. 14 Jan. 1688; Tristram b. 6 March 1689; Lydia b. 12 July 1691; Judith b. 23 Feb. 1693; John b. 20 Jan. 1695 — Stephen (4) died 31 Aug. 1725. Hon. NATHANIEL (4) mar. 23 Mar. 1693, Sarah Dole, and had children. John b. 21 Jan. 1694; Eno h b. 7 Feb. 1696, Apphia b. 9 June 1698; Brocklebank; Samuel b. 24 Aug. 1700; Joseph b. 30 Dec. 1702; Jane b. 5 Aug. 1705; Edmund b. 19 March 1708; Moses b. 11 June 1711. He died 20 Feb. 1748.

Before turning to Peter we notice also that the descendants of Tristram (2) Coffin in 1722 amounted to 1138, and in 1728 to 1582, reckoning only blood descendants. Of these, our Peter's number at the latter date was 168.

Any body interested in further details of the Nantucket Coffins will find a long story of names and dates in the Gen. Reg. for 1853.

The Honourable Peter Coffin Esq., (3) who settled in Dover, was born in England in 1630, and came first to Newbury.

Tradition says his father was a Royalist, and was perhaps the only man who came to New England on account of Oliver Cromwell's success. The exact date of his coming to Dover, we cannot obtain; he was not taxed in 1648, but was in 1657. His name thenceforward is frequently met with in our town books. He became a large land owner, although not many grants appear; the main record we find, is the following; 30, 11, 1670. 70 acres; these were located 17, 12, 1672, "according to that order Sixty acars of ye sayed land lyeth on yo north side of ye great Mast path goeing into ye Swamp the south est Corner bounded by a marked tree at the west end of Plum pudding hill & see by the head of Capt. Waldern's land to ye hihgway that goeth to Tole End & from thence along by ye land yt sd Coffin bought of Thomas Nock to ye bridge over ye brooke goeing to tole end only Reserveing liberty on ye sd land for a Cartway for ye use of ye towne if required & from ye sd bridge fourty fower Rodd westerly if it is laid out & bounded on ye south side by the great mast way into ye swamp about seven score Rods from Plum pudding hill to a rock on ye top of a hill on ye si e of ye path & from hence Uppon a straight line to ye North west corner of it." The other ten acres were laid out on "the south side of the above mast path," bounded N. by the mast path, E. by the land formerly laid out to said Coffin, "to ye path yt goeth to Muchadoe."

Peter doubtless had other grants from the town; one of 870 acres in 1667 to reimburse some expenses is not located. He bought land also, and some he probably received with his wife, who was a daughter of Elder Starbuck. Elder conveyed, 20, 5, 1652, to Peter, "Cocheche upper ffalls granted to him by Dover, 6 Dec. 1650, with all the "accomodations of water & timber. About the time he went to Nantucket, the Elder conveyed, 9 Mar. 1659--60, to "my Son in Law, peter Coffion all my houses & Lands marsh & Meadows Situate and lying within the Jurisdicktion of Dover, with all appurtinances thereunto belonging & also all my household goods or imple ucats with in dores or without to him the sd peter &c. Also "all my cattle and beasts of all sorts. We shouldn't be surprised to find that the old Coffin estate can e in this batch. Some of it he sold,--uplaud "formerly the land of Edward Starbuck granted by Dover on the S. E. side of Great Bay, to John Hall, and gave possession "with twigg and Turfe 25, 10, 1662.

OLD S RIES, NO. 174, JUNE 4, 1887.

THE COFFIN FAMILY.

Whereabouts in Dover Peter Coffin lived at first, we have no means of ascertaini g, except that it was at Cocheoho, and possibly near the spot where in 1689 his Garrison stood.

Peter was a man of note. He was a Selectman in 1660, '8 and '9, 1672 and '5 While Dover sent representatives to Boston, he was one in 1672, '3 and '9, and in 1680 was one of the Representatives to the first N. H. Assenbly from Dover. In 1657 he was one of two appointed by Massachusetts General Court to lay out 200 acres to Edward Rawson above Dover Bounds, which they did 4 May 1657, said land being on both sides of "Kachecha River," a little below the Indian path," which said "path lyeth about 8 miles above Peter Coffin's howse." The General Courts elected him in 1663 as one of the three to settle up Valentine Hill's troublesome estate, which they did in the course of twenty or thirty years. In 1666 he was one of the committee to see about fortifying Portsmouth so as to "receive great gunns." In 1668, however, Peter experienced "great gunns" himself. In June of that year a man was slain up at Penacook, (Concord) by a drunken Indian; the matter was investigated and the Indians testified that they had "several runlets of strong licquors" from Thomas Payne and Thomas Dickinson (who was killed) who sold it at Capt. Walten's "trucking house" up there in behalf of the Captain, his son Paul and Peter Coffin. This being contrary to law these three were examined, and al three denied any interest in the liquor business. The General Court thereupon directed them to clear themselves by oath. The Captain and his son Paul did so, but Peter didn't exactly like to swear about it, and owned up, so the Court fined him £50.

In 1666 the General Court made a bargain with Lieut. Peter for some masts which were to be a present to his Majesty; in 1668 they were delivered. 15 May 1672 he was paid, receiving £100 for the masts, and for "his own care and paynes in procuring the said masts," a couple hundred acres of upland, and "thirty or forty acres of meadow, "where he can fined it not yet layed out, which wee suppose he may well deserve, & will be no less satisfying to him." The latter statement we will guarantee for considerable less than the market rates, and beg nobody to feel any trouble as to his having found it. Peter liked property.

Peter was occasionally Moderator of the town meeting, an office, alas, never more to be filled in Dover. He was also a commissioner to settle small cases, was juryman, and now and then "perambulated town lines." He was moreover Town Treasurer, (for which office he had a peculiar fitness) being elected in 1661 and onward; (a rather ingenious vote was passed in 1662, that the "Treshurer is to eowe capt. Pembellton, &c. &c.;) as Treasurer, we suppose, he was directed by the town in 1665 to "AGree with some workman to Build a Terrett upon the meeting house for to hang the Bell which we have Bought of Capt. wallcern;" and also in 1667 to build around the church the fortification whose remnants still exist.

In 1689 Peter's house at Cochecho was destroyed in the Indian attack of 27 June, as was also his son's. One of these garrisons stood about 60 feet from Central street on the north line of Orchard street. In digging away the bank which formerly occupied the west side of Central street, the workmen found part of a sill and a metal weight, both of which were remnants either of Peter's residence and business, or of his sons. When, the right of the attack, the squaws asked to sleep by the fire, Pe er gave them permission, and the squaws let in the savages. The other Coffin garrison stood on the high ground south of the residence of Thomas H. Cushing, Esq., perhaps near that of Mr. A. Folsom. We have always held the idea that the son referred to was Peter until examination convinced us of the contrary. Belknap gives no name, and Peter, jr., was an inhabitant of Nantucket at that time; the garrison, we think, was Tristram's. The story is that the son would not let the Indians in, but that after the capture of the old gentleman's house they brought the family in front of the other, threatening to kill them unless the son surrendered; filial affection prevailed, and he opened his doors; but the two families being left in a deserted house, escaped while the captors were busy. The Indians were wags in their way, and made Peter bring out his bags of hard money and throw up the specie by handfuls, while they laughingly scrambled for it; it hurt Peter's feelings.

In 1692 he was appointed Councillor, a position which he held till he was Senior at the Board.—He was also a Justice; when appointed we do not know, but he was in office at the time of Rev. Mr. Moody's trial in 1684, for refusing to administer the Lord's supper to Gov. Cranfield and others in the "Prayer Book" form, and voted to condemn him, the bench being four to two. This decision was a blow at liberty of conscience, but Coffin thought it of little consequence, saying "It is a nine days wonder, and will soon be forgotten." He was also appointed Judge Sup. Court for New Hampshire, which position he occupied until he died at Exeter 21 March 1715.

PETER married Abigail, daughter of Elder Edward Starbuck of Dover. Their children were Abigail, b. 20 Oct. 1657, mar. Maj. Davison of Ipswich, Mass., who moved to Newbury; Peter b. 20 Aug. 1660, of whom more by and by; Joshua b. 16 Sept. 1663. Tristram b. 18 Jan. 1665, married Deborah Colcord; Edward b. 20 Feb. 1669, mar. Anna Gardner, daughter of John Gardner, and died childless; Judith b. 4 Feb. 1672; Elizabeth b. 27 Jan. 1680, mar. Col. John Gilman of Exeter; Elizabeth b. ——, died single; Jethro b. ——, mar. Mary Gardner; Perne or Parnel b. ——, burnt in childhood.

We come now to the families of the children of Lieut. Peter Coffin (3) of Dover

Abigail (4) who mar. Maj. Daniel Davison of Ipswich, we will say nothing further about.

Peter (4) b. 20 Aug. 1660 mar. 15 Aug. 1682, his cousin, Elizabeth Starbuck of Nantucket, daughter of Nathaniel, and granddaughter of Elder Edward. The tradition is that Peter said he wasn't going to stay in Dover to be killed by the Indians and so moved off to Nantucket: the latter part of which tradition is verified by the records of his childrens' birth at Nantucket, as follows:

Abigail b. 9 July 1683; Tristram b. 23 April 1685; Nathaniel b. 26 March 1687; Samuel b. 26 Feb. 1689; Barnabas b. 12 Feb. 1690-1.

Joshua (4) we know nothing about.

Tristram (4) b. 18 Jan. 1665, lived in Dover: he is we have no doubt that son of Peter which had a garrison here in 1689, that stood somewhere near Thomas H. Cushing's. He inherited the Dover estate. His wife was Deborah Colcord b. 21, 3, 1664, a daughter of Edward

OLD SERIES NO. 182, DEC. 31, 1857

THE COFFINS.

(Continued from No. 174).

Of the next generation of Coffins we have but little to say. We did intend to go into the matter pre ty fully, but were frightened out of it by the following paragraph in a letter from the Hon. Joshua Coffin, the learned historian of Newbury. "If you will examine the history of Newbury, you will find that the descendants of Tristram Coffin, sen., who were born between 1652 and 1728 were 1582, of whom 1128 were living in 1728. In about the same ratio they have been increasing ever since, so that if you want a list as full as possible you will have enough to do for the rest of your days." We concluded therefore to let alone all except Dover.

Eliphalet (5) born 13 Jan. 1689, son of Tristram, son of Old Peter of Dover, mar. 11 Feb. 1710, Judith Noyes. He lived in Exeter. His will was dated 15 Jan. 1734-5; proved 13 Sept. 1736, in it he gave to wife Judith "all my moveable estate within doors and without, and my mulatto girl named Tiona and my negro girl named Peg," &c. &c., together with use of all his real estate; to son Peter, his dwelling house, his negro Jack, some pasture, marsh, &c. a hundred acres at Lamperele river, two acres in Dover with orchard upon it, his right in the sawmill at Dover, and all other Dover property except Starbuck's meadow; to daughters Abigail, Eleanor and Judith Coffin, his "great meadow" in Dover, called Starbuck's meadow,

Colcord of Hampton, and he had four children, viz:

Abigail b. 30 May 1686, mar. Bartholomew Thing; Eliphalet b. 13 Jan. 1689, m. 11 Feb. 1710, Judith Noyes; Parnell b. ——, mar. Benjamin Thing; Tristram b. about 1691, mar. (.) 15 Nov. 1710. Jane Heard of Kittery, (2) Hannah Smith.

Edward (4) died childless.

Judith (4) we know nothing of.

Elizabeth (4) who mar. Col. John Gilman of Exeter, who was b. 19 Jan. 1677, and had seven children; she died 10th July 1720, and her husband m ar. (2) Elizabeth, widow of Hon. Robert Hale, and daughter of Nathaniel Clark of Newbury. Of Elizabeth's (4) desecendants was her son, Hon. Peter Gilman, a Counsellor and Brigadier General; and ancestor to Jacob B. Moore, Esq., Mary, wife of Charles W. Brewster Joanna, wife of Rev. Dr. William Cogswell, and others.

Eliphalet (4) died single.

Jothro (4) mar. Mary Gardner. and lived in Nantucket. He had children. Margaret b. 19 June 1689, mar. (1) Rev. John Wilson, (2) Rev. Samuel Tennes; Priscilla b. 26 Dec. 1691, mar. John Gardner; John b. 12 April 1694, m ar. Lydia Gardner; Josiah b. 28 July 1698, mar. (1) Susanna Coffin, (2) Parnell Coffin; Abagail b. 12, 13, 1700-1 mar. (1) Nathaniel Woodbury of Bristol, (2) Elakim Swain; Peter (?) Edward (?) Robert b. 21, 2, 1704; Perne or Parnel (4) was b. rnt in childhood.

containing by estimation a hundred acres, together with some other property in Exeter, Judith having a hundred pounds before division; to Eliphalet Gilman, his right in the sawmill and grist mill upon Exeter falls. Peter was executor.

Eliphalet and Judith had children (Fam.—).

—Abigail b. 13 Nov. 1711, m. 2 Dec. 1731, Dr. Josiah Gilman, and d. 22 Oct. 1775; (Rev.) Peter b. 9 Dec. 1713, was minister at Kingston, mar. (1) 29 Jan. 1739, Dorothy Gookin, dau. of Rev. Nathaniel Gookin of Hampton, (and had five children,) (2) 19 July 1749, Elizabeth Green of Boston; Eliphalet b. Nov. 1715, drowned 3 May 1722; Judith b. 1717, mar. 1 Jan 1740, Rev. Nathaniel Gookin, son of the old Parson Gookin, and d. 24 July 1741; Deborah b. 11 Feb. 1721, d. 25 Sept. 1721.

Tristram (5) born about 1691 inherited the Dover property. He was twice married; (1) 15 Nov. 1719, to Jane Heard of Kittery, (2) to Hannah Smith. He lived near the Coffin house recently sold, in a house which he built and which many of our readers remember. We don't know much about him, in fact he died a hundred years ago; but he was a Captain,— "Captain of a Troop of Horse, enlisted out of the towns of Dover and Durham," being commissioned 6 November 1732. In later years he was lame and walked with a cane.

Tristram Coffin made his will 27 April 1761 in which he calls himself a "gentleman;" after piously disposing of his soul he distributes his other property in the following manner his wife Hannah is to have the use of the west room and chamber in his house as much cellar as she needs, the use of one third of his barn and homestead with firewood enough to keep one good fire going—all this while she is a widow and a third of all household goods and live stock and a bed whether or no; son Eliphalet is to have the homestead the right in the lower falls, two thirds of live stock and his cart and wheels; two daughters Abigail Gennis or Jennis and Jane Colcot all his lands in Rochester; two daughters Susanna (afterwards Bickford) Deborah and Parnel, (afterwards Evans,) the land near Cochecho Bridge where he used to live, (that is, where Varney's Block stands and so on to the site of City Hall;') son-in-law Joseph Ham had £5; Abigail Jennis £50; Jane Colcot, Susanna, Deborah, Parnel, each £200 all old Tenor. Eliphalet was executor; the will was proved 26 Aug. 1761.

His children were, by first wife,

—Abigail b. 16 July 1728, baptised 30 July 1721, mar. (1) Benj. Sleeper of Kingston, (2) Richard Jennings of Rye; Jane b. 11 Mar. 1721-2, bapt. 18 Mar. 1722, mar. Edward Colcord of Newmarket; Tristram b. 2 Feb. 1723-4 bart. 22 Jan. d. 10 Feb; (by second wife,) Deborah b. —, d. a child; John b. —, bapt. 21 June 1730, d. about 1736; Susanna b.—, bapt. 24 Nov. 1732, mar. Lemuel Bickford; Hannah b.—, bapt. March 1735, mar. Joseph Ham of Dover; Deborah b. 31 Aug. 1738, bapt. 17 Sept. 1738; Eliphalet b. 11 Sept. 1742, bapt. 24 Oct. 1742; Parnel b. 21 June 1741, bapt. 23 June 1745, mar. 25 Dec. 1783, Nathaniel Evans, and lived on the Littleworth Road.

Of their children Mrs. Bickford, Deborah and Eliphalet remained on the old property. The first two abandoned the old house but built, at a slight distance, the house which stood on the bank that was dug away a few years ago to make place for Varney's Block on Central St. Our readers will remember it; as they will also the fact that only within a few years have the buildings on the corner of Washington and Central streets been erected; a few years only will carry us back to the old orchard (it had villainous apples), which occupied the south side of Washington St. adjoining the Academy land. The Coffin property was in two lots. Originally the Waldron property took a small strip of the south side of the river, bounded by a line which started where Central Block and Varney's Block unite, and ran in a tolerably direct line westward, (the southern line coinciding with the southern line of the Academy lot which Daniel Waldron gave and which covered the land where Central Block now stands which was leased for 999 years) united near Fayette street or more exactly to the west line of Thomas Goldsmith's land, then turning south ran in a narrow strip a little across the present southern line of Washington Street, where it branched east to Central street, (reaching it on the south line of the City Hall lot,) and south to Silver Street; this Coffin lot therefore was nearly square, enclosed on three sides by the Waldron property and bordered by Central street from the north end of Varney's block to the building next south of the City Hall. The other and main part of the Coffin estate commenced near "Long Hill Spring" on the south side of the river and followed it up nearly to the second (or Whittier's falls. The Waldron strip which ran southward from the river and thus divided the Coffin property, was sold (with the Atkinson field) to Messrs. Atkinson and Hale. They built, the former the house now Asa Freeman's, the latter the Hale house; and they sold the Belknap and other lots on Silver street.

Washington street was run up through the first Coffin lot and the Atkinson lot within thirty-five years against Aunt Debby's stiffest opposition; she even refused for a long time to receive the pay. In this opposition, however, she only acted out the Coffin feeling, which could not bear to let a single foot of land go. When Amos White, Esq., (father to the late Judge of the Police Court who deserves a better place,) came to Dover he had hard work to get possession of a bit of land large enough for a house lot. Dr. Greene offered him some on Silver street, but he wanted to build nearer the falls; he tried to buy of the Coffins, but not a foot could he get, until at last discovering by hard research that he was a distant connection somehow by marriage, they offered to lease him a lot for 99 years, "seeing he was in the family;" Mr. White however, built on Main street.

While Aunt Debby and Mrs. Bickford remained on the lot where they were born their brother Eliphalet built the present, or rather late, Coffin house, at the head of Washington street. He had remained however in the old one until the earthquake of 18 Nov. 1755 shook down the chimney and forced him to go to the new one already partially completed but which was then only one story. (Papers of A. A. Tufts Esq.) He married 26 March 1774 Patience Evans and died Au.. 1808. He had children.
— Hannah b. 4 May 1774; Mary b.

10 April 1776; Susanna b. 26 Mar. 1778, mar. Wm. Hodgdon, and d. 30 Jan. 1817; Tristram b. 30 Nov. 1781; Abigail (twin to Tristram) mar. Jonathan Young and died 1810; Betsey b. 13 Feb. 1786.

OLD SERIES NO. 183, JAN. 28, 1858.

THE COFFINS.—Concluded.

The Coffin field bordering upon Central Street, descended, as will be seen by Tristram's will, to Mrs. Bickford, Deborah, and Mrs. Evans. The three all died without issue, Mrs. Bickford first, Mrs. Evans next, and lastly Aunt Debby, who died 29 July 1837. The field which had hitherto been kept untouched now passed to their brothers and sisters (or their heirs). Moses Hodgdon was appointed Deborah's administrator 18 Sept. 1837, but he dying, John S. Durell was appointed 4 Nov. 1840. The field was divided or rather partially so, July 25 1842 Abigail Jenness's children, Jane Colcord's children, and Eliphalet's children, inherited; of which Nathaniel White represented the Jenness's interest, Dr. and Mrs. Cowan, Mary and Elizabeth (daughters of Eliphalet Coffin) and Rufus Flagg who had purchased (with Benjamin Wiggin) the right of Mrs. Gilman who had died in Tamworth, and whose right was sold at auction by Tristram C. her son,—received their shares at this first division; a second one made two or three years after, when the others, with W. A. Marston, who had purchased White's share and that of some other heirs, received the remainder. And thus it was brought into the market. This field had been in the family for near two hundred years. Originally Peter Coffin bought of Elder Starbuck two acres, on these, which were on the north side of Orchard street, near Central, he built his house; to this he added two acres adjoining which he bought of Major Waldorn 6 Aug. 1671. And this was how Coffin field came and went.

Eliphalet's children of course inherited his property. Of these Tristram committed suicide about 1824; the inventory of his estate was entered 20 April 1825, William Hodgdon, his sister Susanna's husband, being appointed 20 Jan. 1825 to administer. When Mrs. Hodgdon and Mrs. Young married they gave quit claims of their father's home farm to Tristram; he dying intestate, the heirs were in 1825, Mary, Elizabeth, Hannah, Susan (Hodgdon,) Abigail (Young). The land was then divided; to Mary and Elizabeth was given the home tract at the corner of Tole End Road, and Washington street; to Hannah eighteen acres on the west side of Tole End road, and twenty more reaching from the north side of Washington street to the river; to Susan (Mrs. Hodgdon,) the next section of 35½ acres from the street to the river, ascending the stream; to Abigail (Mrs. Young) 35½ acres next north of the last mentioned share; to estate of late Tristram, in full 56 acres.

Mary and Elizabeth, daughters of Eliphalet continued to live in single blessedness at the head of Washington street, until their death. Mary died in 1843. She made a will 22 July 1842 (pr. ved 1 Nov. 1843) in which she gave all her property to her sister Elizabeth, who still continued to live at the old house. She died however at last, her inventory was entered 18 Aug. 1853 at a very handsome amount; her estates descended to heirs, the Coffin house was sold in Jan. 1856, to Walcott Hamlin Esq. and the last relic of the Coffin premises went out of the name.

We mentioned Deborah as living to the advanced age of ninety-nine years. Asa A. Tufts, Esq., with his usual kindness, permits us to transcribe some minutes of a conversation he had with her and her sister 21 Mar. 1833, she then being over 94 years old :—

"Aunt Debby told me that she was born on the spot where her ancestors lived, which was close to the place where the Bickford house now stands, which house Debby and Mrs. Bickford built. She says she does not remember the garrison house, but she remembers that in digging the garden they found a sleeper of the garrison house. Their father built the old house near the Coffin house. The present Coffin house was built by her brother Eliphalet. She remembers the killing by the Indians of three persons at Rochester, and remembers seeing Indians in Dover when she was young, and says that when she was a girl they did not go out to milking except a man went with them with a gun, for the fear of the Indians.

"She says she went to meeting for years in the old house at Pine Hill, and described the place where it stood, (see account in the Directory for 1833.) It had no steeple, and the bell hung in the school house near by. She very well remembered Parson Cushing, and said he was a good man, and was a large stout ma..

"She said her own father's name was Tristram, and that he was a lame man and went with a cane for many years and she should think was about 60 years old when he died; her grandfather's name was Tristram and her greatgrandfather was Old Peter.

"Betsey Coffin told me that her father Eliphalet died Aug. 4, 1808, and would have been 66 years old if he had lived until the 11th of Sept., consequently he was born Sept. 11, 1742; she was always told that her father was sixteen years old when his father died.

"John Hanson, further says that the old descendants of Lt. Peter Coffin said that four of his hired men who attempted to put the Indians out of the house were prevented from so doing by the family who thought they could trust the Indians. The Indians murdered the four hired men but spared all the family."

As it is very rare we get a chance to hunt up an Admiral, while we are about it, we will give the pedigree of Admiral Sir Isaac Coffin.

James (3) Coffin, brother to Old Peter of Dover, had as we have shown, among his fourteen children, a son Nathaniel, (4) born about 1670, who mar. 17 Aug. 1692 Damaris Gayer, which Nathaniel and Damaris had nine children one of whom was William (5) b. 1 Dec. 1699 left Nantucket and moved to Boston married 8 Sept. 1722 Anna Holmes and had thirteen children among which were only three sons viz. William b. 11 April 1723, (who had ten children.) Nathaniel b. 16 July 1725 and John b. 19 Aug. 1729 (who had ten children.) Of these sons Nathaniel (6) mar. Elizabeth

Barnes, and also had eleven children; viz. Nathaniel b. 1748 was Collector at St. Christopher's West Indies; William d. in New Brunswick; John d. young; Ann mar. Phillips Collbeck Attorney General at St. John's; John d. a Major General at St. John's; Isaac b. May 1759, stuck to the sea became a Vice Admiral and a Baronet and doubtless helped push his brothers along in the world before he died in 1839; Christian died young; Jonathan was a Councillor at Law in England; Christian mar. in 1785 Richard Bardwell Esq. an East India Nabob; Nathaniel Moriv was M. P. for Derbyshire, and had two children.

NOTE BY JOHN SCALES.

By courtesy of Mrs. James E. Fernald of Farmington the following copy of Tristram Coffin's will is here published; it has never before been published, although Dr. Quint refers to it in his Memoranda. It seems appropriated to appear in this connection.

TRISTRAM COFFIN'S WILL.

In the name of God Amen.

This twenty-seventh day of April Anus Domini One thousand seven hundred and sixty-one. I, Tristram Coffin of Dover in ye Province of New Hampshire, Gentleman, being exercised with great bodily infirmities but of a sound and perfect mind and memory, knowing it is appointed for all men once to die, do make this my last will and testament that is to say. Principally and first of all I recommend my soul into ye hands of God that gave it and my body I commit to ye earth to be buried in a decent Christian manner at ye discretion of my Executor hereafter named & as touching such worldly estate as it hath pleased God to bestow upon me I give demise and dispose of ye same in manner and form following viz.

Imprimis I give and bequeath unto my beloved wife Hannah Coffin the free and full use and improvement of ye Westerly lower room in my dwelling house and ye chamber over it, and also such a privilege in the cellar under sd house as she shall have occasion for to secure her stores & also ye use & improvement of ye one third of my barn, also ye one third of ye Produce Proffit & Income of my homestead land of every kind where I now live likewise the priviledge of fire wood sufficient to support one good fire. All ye for going articles I give to my sd wife during ye time of her continuing my widow. I also give to my sd wife, to her own disposal, one third part of my live stock of cattle sheep & swine & also all my household goods & furniture as beds & bedding &c to her own disposal.

Item. I give unto my son Eliphalet Coffin & to his heirs & assigns for ever all my homestead land where I now live together with my dwelling house & barn & all other buildings standing & being upon ye sd land on both sides of ye road & also ye land on both sides of sd road and also my right in ye common land in sd Dover which is not yet laid out. I also give to my sd Son Eliphalet his heirs & assigns forever all my right & interest in ye falls in Cocheco River at Cocheco so called. But in case my sd son should leave no issue of his body lawfully begotten at his decease, then my will is that my sd wife shall have ye use and improvement of ye one third part of my homestead land which I have herein given to my said son Eliphalet & ye other two thirds of sd land together with all my sd Common right & sd Priviledge in ye afores'd falls & all my said Buildings I give to my Daughters viz. Abigail Gennis, Jean Colcot, Susana, Deborah and Parnel Coffin to be equally divided among them. I also give to my sd son Eliphalet Coffin two thirds of my live stock of cattle sheep & swine, a·d also my Cart and wheels & all other my farming Tackling & utenzils.

Item. I give to my sd Daughters Abigail Gennis & Jean Colcot all my land in Rochester both in ye divided & in ye undivided lands in sd Town to be equally divided between them & to their heirs & assigns forever.

Item I give to my sd Daughters Susanna Deborah & Parnel Coffin & to their heirs & assigns forever all my land lying near the Bridge at Cochecho, where I formerly lived, to be equally divided among them.

Item I give to my son-in-law Joseph Ham five Pounds old tenor. to be paid him by my sd son Eliphalet within ye term of six months after my decease.

Item I give to my sd Daughter Abigail Gennis fifty Pounds old tenor, and to my sd Daughter, Jane Colcot two hundred Pounds of ye like old tenor, to be paid them by my sd three Daugaters viz. Susanna, Deborah & Parnel Coffin in equal proportions within ye term of two years after my decease. And I do hereby constitute make & ordain my sd wife Hannah Coffin to be my Executrix & my sd son Eliphalet Coffin to be my Executor of this my last will & Testament, and also hereby utterly disallow revoke a disannul all & every will or wills, Testament or Testaments in any ways by me heretofore made notifying & confirming this & no other to be my 1 st will & Testament.

In testimony whereof I do hereunto set my hand & seal ye day & year first above written.

      Tristram Coffin.

Signed sealed & Declared by ye sd Tristram Coffin to be his last Will and Testament in presence of us ye subscribers.

    Sam'l Hodge
    Isaac Young
    Benjamin Watson

Rockingham, SS Probate Office.
  At Exeter in said County.
    September 22, 1837.

I certify that the foregoing is a true copy of the last will and testament of Tristram Coffin late of Dover deceased which was proved, approved and allowed on the 26th day of August, A. D 1761, at a Probate Court holden at Portsmouth in and for the then Province of New Hampshire by and before Richard Wibird Esq., Judge of said Court.

  Attest John Kelly,
     Register of Probate

OLD SERIES, NO. 131, FEB. 21, 1854.

TRISTRAM COFFIN'S COMMISSION AS CAPTAIN, 1732.

The following ancient documents, which were found among the papers of the Coffin family the last member of which bearing the name in this town, recently died at an advanced age, are deemed worthy of preservation among our Historical Memoranda.

JONATHAN BELCHER, Esq.;

"Governour and Commander in Chief, in and over His Majesty's Province of New Hampshire in New England, in America.

To Tristram Coffin, Gentleman,—Greeting.

B Y Virtue of the Power and Authority, in and by his Majesty's Royal Commission to Me granted, to be Governour and Commander in Chief, in and over the Province aforesaid: I do by these Presents, (Reposing much Trust and Confidence in your Loyalty, Courage and good Conduct,) constitute and appoint you the said TRISTRAM COFFIN to be Captain of a Troop of Horse, enlisted out of the Towns of Dover and Durham, being the Second Troop in Colo. Gilman's Regiment. Hereby giving and granting unto you, all the Powers and Authorities, Profits, Privileges and Advantages, lawfully appertaining to the Place and Office, of a Captain within the said Province;

TO HOLD the said Place and Office, together with Powers, Authorities, Profits, Privileges and Advantages to the same lawfully belonging, during pleasure; You are therefore carefully and diligently to Lead, Order and Exercise the said Troop in Arms, both Inferiour Officers and Soldiers, Commanding them to Obey you as their Captain, and your Self to observe and follow such Orders and Directions, as you shall from time to time Receive from the Commander in Chief of the said Province for the time being, or other your Superiour Officers, according to Military Rules and Discipline, Pursuant to the Trust reposed in you.

Sealed at Arms, the sixth day of November, Anno Domini 1732, Annoque Regni Regis GEORGI Secundi nunc Mag. Brit. Fran. et Hib. Defen. Fid Sexto. J. BELCHER.

By His Excellency's Command,
R. Waldron, Sec'y.

Having received his Commission, Capt. Coffin, like a good soldier, set about obtaining his uniform, which he did some eight or nine months afterwards, but not without considerable difficulty, as will be seen by the subjoined letter. It may be somewhat galling to the pride of a Bostonian, to learn that their great city one hundred and twenty years ago could not furnish the buttons for the "Coat and breeches" of a New Hampshire Captain of Horse!

Salem, July 30th, 1733.

Capt. Coffin,

Sr I have Sent By the bearer mr Will Stone your Cloaths and ass for the order you Sent me aboute the Buttons I could not gett them in the time for ther was not one sett to be got in Boston. I wish you had Concluded when you were at Salem you wold have bene Sutved by this time. Sr I hope your Cloutes will Pleas you i have don all that Lay in my Power to Serve you. Sr I have Reserved the Bords by Mr Stone and have Sent your acompt

your Coat £19 10 00
your Breches 6 12 6
two yds Orsnebrigs a 3s 00 6 00
—————
£26 8 8

Reserved in full of this acompt

Pr Samll Stone Jur

Sr I think you will not Change your Buttons but if you do I shall be Redy to Serve you the next opertunity with others or any other Request

from your friend and Homble Servant

Samll Stone Jr

THE EVANS FAMILY.

We have but few names of the Evans family, but what we have will serve as the vertebra of a genealogy.

ROBERT EVANS, a husbandman, is said to have come from Wales, which is very probable. But the accommodating story that "three brothers came over," one settling in Dover, one in Salisbury and one in Pennsylvania, is doubtless no more correct now than it ever was.

How be it, Robert settled in Dover about the year 1665. He was "received an inhabitant, 19, 1 mo., 1665—6. Tradition says that he settled not far from the site of the store of John H. Wheeler, on Pleasant street. But records locate him near Bellamy in 1669. He "took the oath of fidelity" 21 June 1669, and was on the Cochecho tax-list until his death,—Bellamy people being reckoned as of Cochecho. He was killed in the massacre of 28 June, 1689; and his son Edward returned an inventory of his estate 4 Nov. 1697. There appears to have been no Will found. Perhaps he would have made one but he died rather suddenly.

Robert's wife was named Elizabeth. He had children. (Fam. 1)—Robert b. 30 Sept. 1665; Edward b. 28 June 1667; Jonathan b. 10 April 1669 Elizabeth, b. 28 June 1671. There was also a John who received a deed of ten acres of land at Cochecho from old Major Walderne 16 March 1672; if he was a son of Robert he was born before the old gentleman came to Dover, but we know nothing else about him. Possibly there was also a Benjamin; for Edward, son of Robert, deeds to brother Benjamin thirty acres in Cochecho. Ash Swamp, 4 Dec. 1709.

ROBERT (2) of Fam. 1, was called "Captain Robert." He lived and died in Dover. A document speaks of him 19 Sept. 1753, as "aged about 88," when he testified that he was one of the committee to run the line between Dover and Rochester. Others testified at the same time, and we may as well insert the testimony, so that there may never be any question about that line:

Capt. Evans said that the "bound tree for the head of Dover was a pitch pine tree and now stands three rods due Southwest from the lower side of the first Cove on the Southwesterly side of Salmon Falls river, that is to say, the Cove adjoining to the uppermost head of the Little falls above all the rifling water and likewise stands fifteen Rods and three feet South Sixty Degrees west from a Large Round Rock at the head of said falls and rifels and near about the Middle of said River and five Rods South thirty-two degrees East Distance from a Large white Burch mare" &c.

Ebenezer Wentworth of Somersworth, Samuel Coarson of Rochester, and James Guppy of Berwick, testify to the same point: and they have often seen letters on said Dry pitch pine and knew them to be the reputed bounds of Dover for thirty years past and upwards.

"Likewise Capt. Timothy Roberts of Rochester, Deacon Gers'm Wentworth of Somersworth, and Richard Hussey of Dover," testify to the preceding, the same day; so does Isaac Hanson affirm the truth of the above "for a number o years."

Capt. Timothy Gerrish, Esq. of Kittery, in the seventieth year of his age, testified that about thirty years ago, he with three gentlemen ran the head line of the town of Dover; they "began at Quamphegan and run up the Salmon Falls river four miles to a certain pitch pine tree," and then S. 42 degrees W. on a straight line to the "six mile tree"— being about 15 miles, which line was accepted then by the Province as the true line; he testified that the tree sworn to that day is to his best belief the boundary point, and that the line as formerly run should be the boundary, and that it ran "through a Vault in the earth commonly known and called by the name of the flopper."

The line was renewed according to these depositions, and the return signed by John Gage, John Tasker, Timothy Roberts, Isaac Libby, Committee.

To return to Robert (2). There was a Robert of Mendon, Mass., who deeded to Israel Hodgdon, land in the Ash Swamp, lying north of the way going to Barbadoes, 13 Aug. 1714. If this was the same Robert then Capt. Robert lived at Mendon for a while.

Capt. Robert's wife was named Ann, and he had children born in Dover, (Fam. 2)—Joseph b June 1682; Sarah b. 9 Nov. 1685; Benjamin b. 9 Feb. 1687; Hannah b. 21 June 1690; Patience b. 5 Sept. 1693.

EDWARD (probably the one of Fam. 1) had wife Dorcas, and children. (Fam. 3),—Eleanor b 3 March 1700; Rachel b 6 April 1703; Joseph b 29 Oct. 1704.

JOSEPH(3) apparently and probably the one who was son of Robert and of Fam. 2 settled in Madbury, on the main road to Barrington by Barbadoes pond; his house stood almost exactly opposite the house of Tobias Evans who inherited part of the farm. Joseph's wife was Marcy, and children,—(Fam. 4)—Robert b 11 Jan. 1704, (who lived for some time in Madbury but afterwards moved to Strafford, above Parker's hill, and died there, leaving children one of whom William had a son Lemuel who now lives in Strafford;) John b 3 Feb. 1705 (who lived and died near where widow Church now lives, in Madbury; when living in Madbury near where Benjamin Two nbly lives in Littleworth the Indians caught him one day, 15 Sept 1725 and scalped him; he was taken up for dead but recovered. He left three children viz. Jonathan, Moses (who went to New Durham) and Abigail who married Benjamin Buzzell of Barrington;) Joseph b 28 March 1708, for whom see below; William b 9 Feb. 1711; Daniel b. 28 June 1715; Marcy b 6 Dec. 1717; Mary b 6 March 1720.

BENJAMIN (3) of Fam. 2, had wife Marcy and was killed by the Indians 15 Sept. 1725, as was also William Evans and Benjamin's son Benjamin. He had children, (Fam. 5)—Benjamin b 18 June 1713; Elizabeth b 19 Jan. 1716; Joseph b 7 March 1719; Jonathan b 17 June 1722; Stephen b 13 Nov. 1724.

Joseph (4) of Fam. 4, lived in Madbury and inherited his father's farm. He married Elizabeth Hanson, and had children, (Fam. 6) Benjamin, of Meaderboro, who left children; Soloman b 8 mo. 1743, for whom see below; Marcy, who married Samuel Hanson and died in Rollinsford; Elizabeth, died unmarried, 1, 11 mo., 1829; Mary, died young.

STEHEPN (4) of Fam. 6, born 18 Nov. 1724, was well known to many of our elders as "old Colonel Evans. He lived in a house which stood a few feet northwest of the present brick "Jenness house" on School street; and faced School street; it was not taken down until it almost fell of itself. His store is still standing; it is the old building on the south corner of Main and School streets* Col. Evans was once a man of wealth, and was busily engaged in trade and shipbuilding; but in later years did not flourish so well. He was a soldier too; served at the capture of Louisburg in the old French war, and was engaged in the taking of Burgoyne in later times. The Colonel was a very active man bodily as well as mentally; the season of his death he walked from Rochester to Dover one morning before breakfast, he being then 84 years old. He was often in public office. He died in Dover.

The Colonel was three times married, and had eight children, (Fam 7.), one of whom, Joseph, who lived on Washington street, where Cocheco block now stands, died 30 Aug. 1797. Others of the family still remain.

SOLOMON (5) of Fam. 6, received the homestead in Madbury. He married Catharine Hanson, who died 13, 7 mo., 1849, at the advanced age of 102 years, wanting 5 days. Solomon died 2, 5 mo., 1832, having had children, (Fam. 8), Tobias b 11, 22, 1770, (who lived on the homestead in Madbury, an esteemed member of the Society of Friends, and recently died; he married Sarah Austin, a sister of the late Elijah Austin, Esq., of Madbury; their only child Hannah, is married to Lorenzo Rollins of Rollins ford) Elizabeth, b 10, 3, 1774; David b 24, 5, 1778; Aaron b 17, 7, 1781; John b 15, 10, 1785. (*Since pulled down.)

COL. STEPHEN EVANS' PEW IN THE FIRST PARISH CHURCH.

(NOTE BY JOHN SCALES.—The following was furnished for publication by Mrs. E. H. Durell of this city; she found it among the papers left by her husband, Judge E. H. Durell, who inherited it from his father Judge Danie M. Durell. It is of special interest in connection with the Evans Family, as it shows where Col. Stephen Evans's pew was in First Parish church, which stood where the present brick church stands, and was taken down in 1829. The pews were large, square boxes with seats on three sides; as Col. Evans was one of the aristocrats of his day his pew was undoubtedly in the most fashionble location in the house. Mrs. Durell says:)

Pews cost as much about one hundred years go as at present. One quarter of the pew of John Wentworth was sold to Daniel M. Durell in 1808 for twenty-three dollars and eighty-six cents.

The following is the Documentary history of the first church pew, or seatings, owned by the late Daniel M. Durell, M. C. from New Hampshire, to United States Tenth Congress at that time.

Copy of the sale bill of same—Know all men by these presents that I John Wentworth of Farmington in the County of Strafford and State of New Hamp shire for and in consideration of the sum of twenty-three dollars eighty six cents to me in hand before the delivery hereof well and duly paid by Daniel M. Durell of Dover in said County, Esquire, the rec'ts whereof I do hereby acknowledge. Have given, granted, bargained and sold and by these presents do give grant, bargain, sell, convey and confirm unto him the said Durell and to his heirs and assigns forever, all my right and share of, in and unto meaning the ¼ part of the pew in the Rev. Mr. Sherman's meeting house in said Dover which lately belonged to my father,s estate or to my mother as the case may be being the same pew which formerly belonged to Colonel Stephen Evans dec'd and is the second body pew from the pulpit on the Easterly side of the broad aisle. To have and to hold the said granted and bargained premises to him the said Durell and to his heirs and assigns hereby covenanting with the said Durell and with his heirs and assigns that the same are free and clear of all and every encumbrance and that I have good right to convey the same in manner aforesaid and do hereby promise to warrant and defend the same against all persons whomsoever. In witness whereof have here unto set my hand and seal the 29th day of October, A. D., 1808.

John Wentworth

OLD SERIES, NO. 181, DEC. 10, 1867.

THE CUSHING FAMILY.

JONATHAN CUSHING tenth minister of Dover, and the successor of Nicholas Sever, was son of Peter and Hannah Cushing of Hingham, Mass., where he was born 20 Dec. 1690. He married Oct. 24, 1717, Elizabeth, dau. of Hon. Thomas Cushing of Boston, Mass. He was settled in Dover, 18 Sept. 1717, on a salary of £90 a year, and remained pastor until his death, although for two years previous to that event he had Rev. Jeremy Belknap for a colleague. Parson Cushing graduated at Harvard College in 1712; he was "a grave, and sound preacher, a kind, peaceable, prudent, and judicious pastor, a wise and faithfu friend". In personal appearance, he is said to have been "a large stout man," grave and dignified. The meeting house in which he preached for the first 41 years stood upon Pine Hill, a little distance northwest of the Cushing tomb; in 1758 however a new church was dedicated on the site of the present church of the First Parish. The Parson's dwelling house stood not far from his church, "about 6 rods north west of the well on land (lately) owned by William Osborne." Parson Cushing's wife Elizabeth, daughter of his uncle Thomas Cushing of Boston, came with him to Dover; she died 3 Dec. 1730, aged 39; he died 25 March 1769, and was buried in the Cushing tomb on Pine Hill. During his ministry (not including the two years of colleague,) 1128 baptisms are recorded in the Church books; 130 persons united with the Church upon profession of faith, and 9 by letter. Parson Cushing's memory deserves to be honored for the full minutes which he kept, and which are the first au hentic records of the First Church. Parson Cushing had five children, viz. (Fam. 1 — Peter b. 9 Oct., 1718; Jonathan b. 24 March 1719-20 (who died unmarried in the old French war, or immediately after his return, from disease contracted in service;) Deborah b. 5 Jan. 1721-2, married Daniel Watson of Dover, (we don't know who he was;) William b. 26 Dec. 1723, (appears to have married Mary, dau. of David Watson, and left no children;) Elizabeth b. 5 Jan. 1725, mar. John Wingate of Madbury, and died Dec. 1811.

PETER, of Fam. 1, lived in Dover; he married Mary Bampton who died 31 uly 1798 of fever, aged 84. He died suddenly in the street, of apoplexy, 24 June 1780; children were (Fam. 2).

— Thomas b. 1745; Hannah b. 5 Jan. 1749-50, mar. Josiah Folsom, and died Jan. 1841; they had two children who left no descendants; Daniel b. 4 June 1752, Mary b. 18 June 1754, died unmarried 1 March 1835; Peter b. 22 Feb. 1757.

THOMAS, of Fam. 2, mar. 12 Feb. 1788, Widow Anna Tuttle; they had children (Fam. 3).

—Jonathan, who died May 5, 1827, mar. Hannah McCauselin (not Casling); William b. April 17, 1781, mar. Nancy Hayes; Mary, b. Dec. 11, 1783, died single Dec. 7, 1837; Nancy r. Mar. 26, 1787, died Aug. 27, 1831; Peter b. Feb. 29, 1790, died Jun 15, 1867 mar. Sarah Austin.

DANIEL, of Fam 2 married, 8 Jan. 1786, Tamson Hayes, dau. of Lieut. Jonathan Hayes of Dover; they lived and died in Dover. Children were (Fam. 4)

—Jonathan H. b. 27 March 1786, died 22 March 1836; Mary H. born 8 Mar. 1789, Lydia W. b. 18 June 1793, mar. 31 Dec. 1818, Daniel Sargent; Peter b. 3 June 1796, our well known and esteemed fellow citizen, now Deacon of the First Church; Robert H. b. 31 July 1798; Samuel W. b. 9 April 1802; Clarisa W. b 3 Sept. 1804.

PETER, of Fam. 2 b. Feb. 22, 1757, mar. 1 April 1784 Hannah, dau. of John Burnham Hanson, born in Durham 11 July 1766; they lived in Rochester. He died in 1804. Children, (Fam. 4.)

—John b. Dec. 25, 1784, died unmarried at New Orleans 1809. Elizabeth b. Nov. 26, 1786 died July 19 1823, mar. Dec. 8, 1811 Jabez Dame, Jr., of Rochester, N. H., and had one child Pamella C. Dame. Jonathan P, born Mar. 12, 1793.

JONATHAN, of Fam. 3, mar. Hannah McCasling, and died 5 May 1827 aged 88; children were (Fam. 5.)

—Eliza b. 3 Dec. 1805; Caroline b. 7 Nov. 1807; Charles b. 2 Oct. 1809, d. 1830; Alexis b. 22 Feb. 1812; Anna b. March 1814, d. 1816.

WILLIAM, of Fam. 3, mar. Nancy Hayes of Dover, and had children (Fam. 6.

—Thomas d. aged about 21; Augustus (mar. Rachel Parker, dau. of Rev. Mr. Parker of York, Me., lives in Great Falls; Jarvis, (resides in Charlestown, Ms.;) Nathan (mar. Miss Prescott of Dover.)

PETER, of Fam. 3, of Dover, mar. Sarah Austin; children (Fam. 7).

—Joseph W.; George W., William, Charles.

SAMUEL W., of Fam. 4 of Dover, mar. Asenath dau. of Jacob Hyde of Tamworth, N H.; children (Fam.8)

—Louisa b. 18 May 1835; Asenath b.

17 Mar. 1837; Samuel b. 25 Mar. 1839: Charles b. 4 May 1842, d. 25 Mar. 1846.

JONATHAN P. of Fam 4 was born in Rochester 12 Mar 1793; in 1804 his father died; in 1806 he became apprentice to a saddler; by extra work he purchased his time, and in 1811 went to Exeter Academy. In Sept. 1815 he entered the Junior class Dartmouth College, and graduated in 1817. His health being feeble he went south; while in the family of Rev. Dr. J. H. Rice of Richmond, Va., he became acquainted with a young man, tutor in Hampden Sidney College, who being in ill health urged Mr. Cushing to occupy his place temporarily; he entered upon the office 1 Nov. 1817, which resulted in his permanent connection with the college.

In Jan 1819 he was elected professor of Chemistry and Natural Philosophy; in 1820 he was chosen President pro tem., and in 1821 was elected President. In time his health failed; in April 1835 he started for Charleston, S. C., for its restoration, but died 25 April 1835, at Raleigh.—He had married Mar. 1827 Lucy Jane dau. of Carter Page, Esq. of Cumberland Co.; and left two daughters.

OLD SERIES, NO. 153, AUG. 9, 1855.

THE DAVIS FAMILY

Davis families of N. E. are numerous now, and must have been so anciently, if we may judge from Farmer's mention of twenty persons bearing that name before 1700, many of whom were heads of families. Doubtless there are several totally distinct families.

The Davises of Dover and vicinity are descended, probably without exception, from JOHN DAVIS, an early resident of Oyster River.

JOHN DAVIS was born, according to a deposition of his, in 1623, and doubtless in England or Wales. He was son of James Davis.

JAMES DAVIS was an early settler of Haverhill, Ms.; was freeman in 1640, Representative in 1660, an died 29 Jan. 1678-9, age about 90. His wife was Sisella—, whom he married in England; she died in Haverhill 28 May 1673. Of their children, were, (Fam. 1)—James; John b. 1623 Judith; Ephraim; Sarah; Samuel; and Joanna.

JAMES made his will 17 Mar. 1675-6; it was proved 5 Nov. 1680. He gave to son John "my third division of land in Haverhill." To James Davis, "son of my son John," one half of "my fourth division of upland in Haverhill." To son Ephraim Davis thirty acres which "he hath built upon joyneing to ye great plaine in Haverhill;" also the east meadow; also such sheep and cattle as were then in his hands; "two Ox Comons and also five Cow Comons." To Stephen and Ephraim, sons of son Ephraim, half of fourth division of upland. To son Samuel "my second division of upland and one Ox Comon and also three Cow Comons all in Haverhill. To daughter Sarah, wife of John Page, Jr., one half of my Pond meadow," and all his goods in possession of her husband "excepting only my warmeing pan." To James Gild, son of Samuel Gild, one half of pond meadow. To son James (executor) all other estate. In a codicil added 22 July 1678, he made Wm. White and Nathaniel Saltonstall both of Haverhill "overseer of this my will" with a special injunction that "If I outlive the Time among (you) I thought to spend, justice, according to proportion in my Will mentioned, may be done to my eldest son James" before any legacies are paid.

The old gentleman's apparent expectations of the need of interposition were not unrealized. The children pretty generally wanted each a thicker slice of the estate. Accompanying papers show that John (who is said to have removed "to Pascataqua above twenty years since," had some altercation regarding land of his own which he had once authorized somebody to sell—that a variety of others claimed land which their father, they knew, always intended to give them, and that one claimed handsome share for taking care of his feeble old mother; these little things however, were settled by a peremptory decision against John, a denial of all "intended" gifts except one to Samuel which was proved clearly enough, and by a merited rebuke to the son who manifested such filial affection to his mother, the affairs were settled in 1680.

The children's names are found also on the Haverhill Records, where we gather also the following facts:—that James Davis, son of James, mar. 1 Dec. 1648, Elizabeth Eaton, and d. 18 July 1694, she dying 21 Jan. 1683, having had children, (Fam. 2) Hannah b. 19 June 1650, d. 8 July 1650; Esther b. 8 Oct. 1651; Elizabeth b. 11 Mar. 1653-4; Ann b. 13 Feb. 1655; Sarah b. 5 Aug. 1658; James b. 3 Oct. 1630; John b. 30 June 1664, killed in Canada in 1690; Daniel b. 19 Sept. 1666, killed at Pemaquid in 1689; Elisha b. 30 Aug. 1670; Constant b. 9 March 1673-4;—we learn that Joanna Davis mar. 26 Oct. 1645, George Corliss, who died 19 Oct. 1686, and had children (Fam. 3) Mary b. 8 Sept. 1646; John b. 4 Mar. 1647-8; Joanna b. 28 April, 1650; Martha b. 2 Jan. 1652 Deborah b. 6 June 1655; Ann b. 8 Nov. 1657; Huldah b. 18 Nov. 1661; Sarah b. 23 Feb. 1663; --that Judith Davis mar. 1 Sept. 1647 Samuel Gild, and had children, (Fam. 4) Samuel b. 30 Aug. 1648, d. Sept. 1675; Judith b. 5 April 1650, d. 28 April 1672; John b. 8 Dec. 1652; Hannah b. 12 Feb. 1654; Sarah b 1 March 1657 8; James b. 27 Aug. 1660; Ephraim b. 21 Mar. 1661-2;—that Ephraim Davis mar. 31 Dec. 1659, Mary Johnson, and died 28 Sept. 1679, having had children (Fam. 5) Ephraim, who died 29 Nov. 1662; Stephen b. 15 July 1663; Ephraim b. 19 July 1665; Mary b 1 Mar. 1666-7; Thomas b. 2 Mar. 1668-9; Jonathan b 8 May 1671, d. of small pox 7 Dec. 1690; Joannah b. 22 Sept. 1673, d. 27 Sept.; Susannah b. 28 Dec. 1674; Hannah b. 15 Feb. 1676;—that Sarah Davis mar. 18 June 1663, John Page, Jr., who lived until 7 June 1714, she dying 7 July 1680;—that Samuel Davis, mar. 17 Dec. 1663, Deborah Barnes (dau. of Wm. Barnes,) who d. 14 Jan. 1718-19, he dying 10 Sept. 1696, having had children, (Fam. 6,) Samuel; Deborah, died 25 Sept. 1669; Joseph b. 3 May 1673; William b. 20 Feb. 1674; Ephraim and Sarah, b. 8 Nov. 1679; Amos b. 18 June 1683, d. 25 April 1686 Mary b. 16 May 1685.

OLD SERIES NO. 154, AUG. 16, 1855.

THE DAVIS FAMILY.

JOHN DAVIS, son of Thomas remained in Haverhill until about 1652 or '3. We should be half induced to think that he spent a year or so at Kittery, where a John Davis, in 1652, was admitted freeman and appointed to keep an ordinary, but that our John was admitted freeman at Dover 22 May 1666; we reserve a judgment however. He was in Dover in 1652 certainly, and in 1656 purchased land at Oyster River, where he was thenceforward a resident. He had afterwards various grants of land, an account of which we defer, as they will be found in the abstracts of all the Dover grants, which are in course of preparation. He was selectman in various years, among which were 1663, 4, 5, 7 and 71; and in 1674 was Ensign.

John married at Haverhill, and had some children born there, whom he probably brought with him to Dover, where his family speedily increased. The Haverhill records say that he married 10 Dec. 1646 Jane Pearley, and had children, (Fam. 6)—Mary b. 6 Nov. 1647; Sarah b. 7 Mar. 1648-9, John b. 22 Aug. 1651; and the N. H. State Records say that after he removed to Dover he had, with commendable regularity six more viz. :—Hannah, b. 24 Dec. 1653; Jane b. 29 Dec. 1655, died 23 Sept. 1656; Moses b. 30 Dec. 1657; Joseph b. 26 Jan. 1659; James b. 23 May 1662; Jane (2)d 15 May 1664; and by his will we learn that he had also Jemima and Judith. He died in 1685 or 86. Here follows his will—

In the name of God, Amen. The first day of April in ye year of our Lord God, One thousand Six hundred Eighty-five I, John Davis of Oyster River, in the Province of New Hampshire, being of perfect memory (blessed be the Lord for it;) and calling to mind the frailty of my nature and the certainty of death, & how soon it shall please God to call me hence, I know not, I do here make my last Will & Testament, revoking & annulling all & every Will or Wills, Testament or Testaments heretofore made, or done either by word or Writing, and this to be taken for my Last will and Testament.

Imprimis, I commit my soul to God who gave it, and my body to ye earth from whence it was taken, & to be decently buried in some convenient place where my Executors hereafter named shall appoint. And as for my temporal, Estate which it hath pleased God to bestow upon me, I do order and dispose of in manner as followeth.

It. my Will is, That all such Debts as I do in reason & conscience ow to any person or persons, be honestly and justly paid in some convenient time after my decease; Then my debts being paid & my funeral charges defraid, what shall remain I do dispose of to wit:

It. I do give to my son John Davis, the Six Score acres of Land which I had by a Town grant, Situate & lying & being at Turtle pond in Oister river; and my best ffeather bed, the ticking and feathers after the decease of my Wife.

It. I do give to my sons Moses Davis & Joseph Davis that Tract of Land situate and lying at Mount Spicket ffalls in the Township of Haverhill, which was while willed to me by the Last Will & Testament of my ffather, being by estimation Two hundred acres, be it more or less, to be equally divided between them.

It. I do give my son Moses Davis Policio meadow, which my ffather did will to me, lying in Haverhill Township.

It. I do give to my son Joseph Davis, the one half of the Marsh which I bought of Mr. Valentine Hill, situate and lying at Greenland.

It. I do give to my three elder Daughters Mary Heath, Sarah Smith, and Hanra Kezar, each of them ffive shillings.

It. I do give to my three younger daughters, Jane Davis & Jemima Davis, and Judith Davis, fifteen pounds each of them, and at or before the ffirst day of April in the year of our Lord God one thousand Six Hundred Eighty Six; to be delivered to each of them one Cow and one Ewe Sheep in part of the said fifteen pounds at such a price as my overseers shall judge of; or as my Executors and they can agree: and the one half of what shall be due to them of the said fifteen pounds a peace, to be paid to each of them at or before that day Twelve months next following; and the remainder of the said fifteen pounds to be paid to each of them at or before that day Twelv month then next following after, and if it do happen that if either one of them, or two of them do dye before, & not being married, that then th ir said Porcons shall remain to ye Survivors, or Survivor of ye three. But if Providence of God should so fall out that they could not — — — out with damage to ye Estate, then my Will is, to stay a year or two longer.

It Whereas I John Hearth my Grandchild, which I have kept and brought up ever since he was two years of age, now, if ye said John Hearth do remain & dwell with my Executors untill he shall accomplish ye age of One & twenty years, that then my Will is that my Executor do give the said John Hearth Twenty pounds.

It I do give to my ffour Sons, my Clothes, & my Guns, & all my Tools, as I shall order them to be divided in a Codicil, or a peace of writing

It Also for my Household Goods which I shall not dispose of by a Codicil or a peace of writing, I do leave them to my wife to dispose of to my Daughters, as she shall see meet.

It I do give unto my son James Davis my Estate of Houses & Lands wth all ye privileges thereunto belonging, wherein I now dwell, after the decease of my wife; and also ye one half of ye Marsh at Greenland;& do also make my beloved Wife Jane Davis & my sd son James Davis to be joint Executors during my Wife's life or widowhood; during which time I give my wife the Leanto, & ye Leanto Garret to her use.

It I do bind my Exectr James Davis not to trouble my brother James Davis ror his Exectrs concerning ye Land wch I had when I did live at Haverhill.

It I desire Mr. John Gerrish of Dover, and Mr. Thomas Edgerly of Oistr river to be my Overseer in trust, to see this my Will performed.

Witness John Evans   John Davis
         John Meader
         Joseph Meader
         May 25th 1686.

That this is the Last Will & Testament of ye herein named John Davis, the sd John Evans, John Meader made oath, & that they were prsent & saw the sd John Davis sign & heard him publish ye same, before me,

    Waltr Barefoot Dep. Govr.

Entred and recorded according to ye Original.

    R. Chamberlain, Secr.

The 7th day of April, 1685.

This Codicell or piece of Writing which is the trew meaning & intent of my Last Will and testament Dated ye first Dy of April 1685 that is to Devide my Cloths my tools & Guns among my fower sons vizt. my son John Davis to have my Cosslet & my best Cloak and one sute of my Coopers tooles, & my son Joseph Davis is to have my best hatt and my Cane and ye Other sett of my Coopers tooles and my son Moses Davis is to have all ye Rest of my waring Clothes & my Brass pistol and my Guns to be devided to Each one as my Exectrs shall see meet; and my son James Davis is to have the Rest of my working tools with all ye Land that I have or ought to have that which is not mentioned in my Will or disposed of to Enabell him my Executor to pay my Honest Debts and this is the true Intent & Maining of my Last will and testament In testimony hereof I have set my hand.

   his May 25, 1686. John Davis.
John X Meader
  mark
John Evans
Joseph Meader

John Evens and John Meader made oath that they saw John Davis sign the afore Cudicill to his Will and ye signed as Evedances before me

  Walter Barefoot, Debety Governor

Entred & Recorded according to ye originall

    R. Chamberlain Secry.

December ye 2d 1727 pr

    Mark Hunking Recordr.

OLD SERIES, NO. 155, AUG. 23, 1855.

THE DAVIS FAMILY.

Continued.

Of the children of John Davis of Oyster River, MARY, the oldest, married 19 July 1671 Josiah Heath of Haverhill, (Fam. 7) Mary b. 8 May 1672; Josiah b. 4 Mar. 1673-4; John b. 2 Mar. 1676, the grandchild whom John of Dover had "kept and brought up ever since he was two years of age;" Jane b. 9 May 1678; Deborah b. 26 Dec. 1680; James b. 25 Mar. 1683; Sarah b. 17 June 1685; Hannah b. 2 Dec. 1688; Judith b. 9 Dec. 1691.

SARAH, second child of John, married James Smith and lived at O. R. falls. She had children as related in No. 52 of these memoranda, John, James, Samuel, Mary, Sarah, and two that died while children. Her husband died "from a surfeit which he got in running to assist Capt. Floyd at Wheelwright's Pond," in 1690. She being with her brother John, was killed by the Indians 18 July 1694, as was also her son Samuel.

JOHN third child of John, lived at O. R. He was called Ensign at the time of the attack on O. R. 16 July 1694, when he, his wife and several children were killed, and two daughters carried captive; one of their daughters afterwards returned, the other enter d a nunnery.

HANNAH, fourth child, mar. 28 Sept. 1677, John Keyzan or Lezan, who lived at Haverhill and was killed by the Indians 15 March 1696-7; children (Fam.8) John b. 6 July 1678; George b. 8 Jan. 1679, killed by Indians with his father; Timothy b. 23 Nov. 1683; Sarah b. 5 Oct. 1686; Mary b. 27 April 1689; Eleazar b. 9 Aug. 1692; Samuel b. 30 Dec 1694; George b. 22 April 1697.

MOSES, fifth child, was probably the Moses Davis who married 16 Jan. 1681, at Haverhill, Reuhamah Dow, and there had children, (Fam. 9) John b. 4 Jar. 1682; Moses b. 2 Nov. 1686; especially as by the Dover Records we find that a Moses and Reuhaman Davis had son Ebenezer b. 10 June 1702. The Dover Moses had also a son Jabez, who supplied Dr. Belknap with some historical information.

Moses was living at O. P. when the attack above mentioned was made; he with his sons escaped, as related in No. 49 of these memoranda; but he, with one son, was killed 10 June 1724.

JOSEPH, sixth child was probably the "Sergeant Davis" who assisted in defending the house of his brother not mentioned on its attack. We know nothing further of him.

JAMES, seventh child lived at O. R. He was Lieutenant in 1691, Captain in 1713, Colonel in 1720. He was a brave and successful officer in the Indian wars, and was a Magistrate. History says however, that he was no favorite with Parson Hugh Adams, of Oyster River, who was once charged with attempting to bribe the Governor and Council, "which," said Mr. Adams, "I abhor, seeing it is written in Job XV. 34, Fire shall consume the tabernacles of bribery." Mr. Adams considered it his duty to administer advice to all at discretion, and reproof to those especially who opposed him, but he found in the Colonel a character he could not conquer; and in recommending to the Governor a couple of men fit to be appointed Justices of the Peace, "who were resolute in duty and willing therein to be admonished," he took the opportunity of expressing his opinion of his neighbor Davis, whom he characterized as "being doting, superannuated, selfish, covetous and partial, being utterly disqualified for such an office any longer, being grown old and foolish that he will not be admonished, as contemptibly characterized in Eccl. IV., 13." The world and the minister thought differently. He was Judge at the time of his death, which was in 1749. Land which he owned in Madbury is still in possession of descendants, but so disputed that says an authority, "as to the boundaries of the tract and the division lines, it would puzzle the Judge himself (could he visit the world again for that very purpose,) to settle them to the satisfaction of the several claimants," He had children (Fam 10.) James b. 10 July 1689; Thomas, who died aged 88; Samuel, who died aged 99; and his widow in 1791 aged 102; Daniel, d, ag. 69; Sarah (Hicks) d. ag. 91; Hannah (Deering) d ag. 77; Elizabeth (Hicks) d. ag. 79; Ephraim d. ag. 87; Phebe (Mathes) d. ag 85.

James Davis of Durham made his will 18 Oct. 1748, "advanced in years," &c. He gave to son Ephraim, wearing apparel. To son James and son Samuel, one hundred acres of land in Dover, where they now dwell, which land was granted to my father John Davis by the town; also twenty acres more on the northwest side of Maharrimetts Hill. To son James, all my right in the first division in Bow. To son Thomas, twenty acres granted me by Dover on the northerly side of Strong's hundred acres, and three-fifths of one hundred acres granted to father John Davis near Lampereel river, and the other two-fifths to go to sons Samuel and Daniel. To son Daniel six acres of Fresh meadow granted by Dover, and seventeen acres granted him in the common land in Durham, adjoining to Cauley's marsh. To son Ephraim, the Homestead where I now live, between Coll. Samuel Smith's and Daniel Meader's with house &c. and that Ephraim shall entail said homestead to which ever of his sons he shall see fit; also twenty-five acres which I purchased of Joseph Sheffield with fifteen more granted my father by Dover. To daughters Sarah Hicks and Phoebe Mathews all my right in Barnstead. To daughter Hannah Deering my first division lot in Rochester; also forty acres in the second division lot in Rochester. To daughter Elizabeth Hicks land in Canterbury. To my five sons James, Thomas, Samuel, Daniel, Ephraim, all remaining right in Rochester. To all the sons but Ephraim all rights in Haverhill and all other remaining estate. To the four daughters above mentioned all moveable estate. James is Executor.—Proved 27 April 1749.

Of JANE, JEMIMA and JUDITH all unmarried and young when their father died we know their names only by their occurrence in their father's will.

JAMES, son of James, as in Fam. 10, mar. (1) 5 Nov. 1728, Ruth Ayer of Haverhill, who d. 28 April 1730, leaving (Fam. 11,) one child, Ruth b. 8 Nov. 1729; he mar. (2) 14 April 1743, Elizabeth Pain of York; their children were James b. 14 Feb. 1744-5: Mary b. 28 March 1746; Daniel b. 7 June 1748, died 27 May 1749; Thomas b. 7 Sept. 1750; John b. 6 July 1754.

Of these families many descendants are living. We have given above three generations quite fully, and a fair start on the fourth, and we would give more if we had it. As it is we recommend the families to trace out their genealogy. As it may be of use we will give them the remaining records of their name in Haverhill prior to 1700

THOMAS DAVIS and his wife Christian, came from England; he is probably the Thomas, who was of Newbury in 1640 and became an early "settler of Haverhill." A child, Joseph, is spoken of as dying 15 Sept. 1670. Thomas died 27 July 1683; his wife 7 April 1668. It may be that some of the preceding families which we have supposed to belong to James Davis, really were children of this Thomas, but we think not.

Robert Hastings and ELIZABETH DAVIS of H. were mar. 31 Oct. 1676; they had children (Fam. 12) Katherine b. 8 Nov. 1677; Elizabeth b. 3 Jan. 1679: Robert b. 4 Mar., 1681-2, Ann b. 15 Oct. 1686; George b. 24 April 1688; John b. 13 Sept. 1691, Esther b. 19 Jan. 1693-4.

Joshua Clark and MARY DAVIS of H. were mar. 18 Aug. 1685; children were (Fam. 19) Hannah b. 29 Oct. 1685; Joseph b. 6 Sept. 1687; Jonathan b. 25 Mar. 1690, d. 20 Nov. 1690; Ephraim b. 18 Aug. 1694; Tabitha b. 1 Dec. 1696; David b. 21 Aug. 1699; Nathaniel b. 25 Feb. 1702-3.

STEHPEN DAVIS of H. was mar. to Mary Tucker 23 Dec. 1685. Children were (Fam. 14) Judith b. 23 July 1687; E enezer b. 3 Nov. 1689; Eleanor b. 13 April 1694; Jemima b. 30 Oct. 1697; Phebe b. 16 Jan. 1699-1700; Jabez b. 24 Feb. 1701-2; Jonathan b. 16 Dec. 1703; Gideon b. 2 June 1704; Dinah b. 24 Mar. 1706-7; Priscilla b. 15 Sept. 1711.

Samuel Emerson and JUDITH DAVIS of H. were mar 14 Dec. 1687. Children (Fam. 15) Samuel b. 21 Aug. 1688; Hannah b. 22 Dec. 1691.

ELISHA DAVIS of H. and Grace Shaw were married 19 June 1694. He died 8 Jan. 1738-9. Children (Fam 16)— James b. 24 June 1695; Daniel b. 2 Dec. 1697; Elizabeth b. 29 Feb. 1699-1700; Abigail b. 11 Mar. 1702-3; Esther b. 1 Oct. 1706; John b. 13 Mar. 1708-9; Susannah b. ——.

There was also a SAMUEL DAVIS who made his will at Amesbury 7 Sept. 1696, which was proved 29 Sept. 1696. He gave to "two sons Samuel and Joseph, land in Amesbury, and "other two sons" William and Ephraim land in Haverhill; wife was Deborah, to "my four daughters" Rachel, Deborah, Sarah and Mary £18 each.

Other settlement of estates are recorded in the Essex Co. books at Salem Mass.,—relating of course to Haverbill Davises.

OLD SERIES NO. 220 APRIL 24, 1862.

WINKLEY FAMILY.

The first Winkley or Winckley as sometimes spelt who emigrated from England to this country, of which we have any ecord, was Samuel Winkley, Esq. All the Winkleys we know of in this country sprang from him. He came from the county of Lancashire in England to Portsmouth, N. H., about the year 1680. The arms used by his family was an Eagle displayed counter-charged Argent and Gules, Motto Spes. He settled first in Kittery Maine where in 1684 he married Sarah, daughter of Thomas Trickey. They lived on the lot of land at Crooked Lane which was granted to the said Trickey by the town of Kittery, in 1656. They afterwards moved to Portsmouth N. H., where he was engaged in trade and commerce. He died in 1736, aged about 70 years. Their children were Samuel b. 20 Oct. 1686, died at sea 1707 or 8. Francis (13 b. 1689, died 23 Apr. 1776, aged 87. Nicholas died a young man not mar. William (1)) mar. and lived in Ports. he died a young man. Sarah mar. Tobias Langdon of Ports.—Elizabeth mar. Samuel Weeks of Boston Mass.—Samuel (2) b. after the death of the 1st son Samuel died a young man not mar.

We find that the Samuel Winkley who came from England made a will dated at Ports. 13 Nov. 1726. Proved 6 May 1736 in which he says:

"Then I give and demise unto my son Thomas Winkley all the now dwelling house and land at Crooked Lane Kittery where he now lives and formerly lived. I having given my said son Francis other things out of my Estate for his preferment already and have made all his brothers and sisters to quitclaim any interest in said Estate to my said son Francis. Then I give unto my son Nicholas Winkley besides what money I have already given him all my right in the new town of Barrington and whatsoever Estate I may be entitled to there as I am an inhabitant of the town of Ports. Also I give unto him my bed I lie on and bolster and two pillows and blanket and one blue rug and bedstead and my Bible that was my fathers and what plate I have assigned him I have given him already. Then I give unto my son William Winkley all that hundred acres of land in the town of Berwick, in the county of York, in New England, which was granted to me by the town of Kittery. Then I give unto him a silver Porringer made by Mr. Drummer and six silver spoons with mine and his mothers name on them and silver whistle and two silver cans with my name on them made by Mr. Tyler and my bed in the kitchen chamber and blankets and bolster and the other blue rug and bedstead. I also give unto my son William two large silver Porringers and one silver can marked S×W and the goldsmith's mark on each I. R.—Then I give unto my daughter Elizabeth Weeks besides what I have already given her, six cain chairs I bought of Capt. Paxton and seven pewter dishes, twelve plates and quilt and blankets and also if it so happens that she should be a widow and desire it I give unto her during her widowhood the use of my corner shop on the place where I now live and the yard before it and my new cellar under my house and about one third part of the garden if she see fit to make use of it. The pewter dishes my daughter Elizabeth have them sent her already.—Then I give unto my son Samuel Winkley all my now dwelling house and land in Portsmouth with all the houses, privileges and appurtenances to the teams belonging, except what I have before given my daughter Elizabeth during her widowhood. I also give unto my said son Samuel the sum of one hundred and seventy-five poundes current paper Bill of Credit to be put at interest on good security for the bringing up of my said son and also one feather bed, my camel curtains, blankets and white rug, bedstead curtain rod, bolster and pillows and he to have his mother's bed and all the furniture belonging to it and my silver tankard made by Mr. Greenough and six silver spoons made by Mr. Curry and seven silver spoons made by Mr. C marked with his mothers former name and a silver cup I bought of Capt. John Hunking and a little two eared silver cup and silver bodkin and silver porringer that is at his sister Weeks in Boston and five gold rings, one of them a seal ring with my name on it, two Moidores of gold and one small piece of gold about six shillings value and the twelve cain chairs and glass in the Hall and the glass in the Hall chamber and the six Turkey worked chairs in the Kitchen chamber and four pewter dishes and six pewter plates. If my son Samuel should die before Marriage or become of age, then all the above Bequest after his funeral charges and lawful debts are paid the remainder to be equally divided amongst my other children or their representative. Then I give unto my Kinds woman Elizabeth Hunking that now lives with me Ten pounds in Money or out of my goods to be paid her by my Executors and one silver spoon made by Daniel Greenorgh. Then whatever is left of my Estate after the gifts and Legacies above expressed and my funeral charges are paid my will is that it shall be equally divided amongst my children or their representatives. My daughter Sarah Langdon to have her part of that, her name not being mentioned before in this will I having paid her proportion already. Then I give unto Mary Grant my old servant a silver spoon made by Daniel Greenough. And I do hereby desire my trusty and well beloved fierds George Jeffrey, Esq., and Mr. Ephraim Dennett both of Portsmouth aforesaid to accept and to be the Executors of this my last Will and Testament and Guardian to my son Samuel until he comes to age. And I do by these presents constitute and appoint the said George Jeffrey and Ephraim Dennett Executors of this my last Will and Testament and Guardian to my son Samuel Winkley until he comes to age I do hereby revoke, disannul and disallow all former or other Wills and Testaments by me made allowing and holding firm and valid this and no other to be my last Will and Testament. Witness whereof I have hereunto set my hand and seal the day and year first above mentioned.

Samu'l Winkley (seal)

Signed, sealed, delivered, declared and pronounced by me the said Samuel Winkley to be my last Will and Testament in presence of

Samuel Shackford
John Shackford
James Jeffery.

OLD SERIES, NO. 221. MAY 1, 1862.

WINKLEY FAMILY.

Francis Winkley (1) son of Samuel (1) lived at Crooked Lane in Kittery, Me. His occupation was that of boatbuilder having learned his trade in Boston Mass. He mar. Mary dau. of Rev. John Emerson of Portsmouth N. H. She died 17 March 1745, aged 41. Their children were John (1) b. 1726, d. 31 Mar. 1811, aged 85. Elizabeth b. 1728 d. at Barrington, 23 Nov. 1806, aged 78. Samuel (8) b. 9 Mar. 1731 d 29 Nov. 1806. Francis (2) b. 1733 d. 9 Oct. 1818. Mary b. 1736 d. at Boston, Mass. 1 Dec. 1776 Emerson b 1738 d Barrington, 17 Sept 1810. Sarah; b. 1740 d. 6 Feb. 1808. The daus. were not married.

John Winkley (1) son of Francis (1) mar. Deborah Cain of Kittery where they lived. She d. 27 Mar. 1829 aged 95. They had chil. Joseph, Francis (3), John (2), Elizabeth, Mary, Sarah, Dorcas, Esther, Dorothy and Martha. Joseph died a young man. Francis (3 mar. Martha Brown of Kittery. They lived in Ports. He died at sea. They had children, John (3) William (4) and Martha M , who mar. Seth Leighton of Dover. John (2) the Clockmaker mar. Lydia Hoit of Newington. He died 18 May 1813, aged 46. They had chil. James who mar. Martha Hicks. He died 13 Sept. 1846, aged 50 He left no chil.

Lydia wife of John (2) and two dau. died with the Shakers at Canterbury N. H. The dau were Charlotte and Clarissa.—Elizabeth dau. of John (1) mar. Mr. Boosby of Limerick, Me. Mary mar. Mr. Stone also of L.—Sarah mar. Wm. Tibbetts of Brookfield N. H. —Dorcas mar. Mr. Wiggin also of B. Esther mar. Joseph Benson of Kittery. Dorothy mar. a Mr. Blaney of Ports. Martha mar. a Mr. Cotton also of P.

Samuel Winkley (3) son of Francis (1) was a joiner by trade, having served his time with Mark Langdon of Ports. He mar. Mary dau. of Samuel Brewster of P. She was b. 13 April 1734 d. 3 Nov. 1816 aged 82. Her mother was Margaret Waterhouse grand dau. of Richard Waterhouse who owned and occupied Pierce Island at Ports. in 1688. Samuel (3) lived and died in Barrington.--Their chil. were Samuel (4) b. 24 Dec. 1756 d. 18 May 1812. Francis (4) the Shaker Elder b. 28 Mar. 1759 d. 20 June 1847. Mehitable b. 10 May 1761 d. 22 Sept. 1824. William (2) b. 31 Aug. 1763, d 29 July 1845. Dea. John (3) b. 17 Nov. 1776, d. 8 Jan. 1843. Elizabeth b. 9 Mar. 1769, d. 29 July 1850. Benjamin b 3 Jan. 1772 d. 30 Sept 1851. Col. David b. 4 July 1775, d. 18 Dec. 1852. Mary b. 3 Aug. 1777.

Samuel Winkley (4) son of Samuel (3) mar. Olive Kingman of Barrington, where they lived. She died 17 Oct. 1822, aged 71. Their children were Elizabeth, who mar. Jona. Drew of Durham.-- They lived in Barrington. Mary mar Richard Furber of Farmington. Mehitable mar. Pierce P. Furber also of F. Olive not mar. Samuel (5) died a young man not mar. Abiah mar. Augustus Rollins, Esq. of Rollinsford.

Francis Winkley (4) son of Samuel (3) mar. Sarah Libby of Dover. They had chil. Samuel (6) and Enoch. Francis (4) and wife joined the Shakers at Canterbury where he become a ruling Elder. Their sons left the Shakers and settled in Amesbury, Mass. Samuel (6) mar. but left no chil. Enoch mar. Mary Locke of Seabrook, chil. were John F., Francis J., Mary S. and Sarah L.

Mehitable Winkley, dau. of Samuel (3) mar. Paul Tasker of Barnstead. They left no children.

William (2) son of Samuel (3) mar. 1st Martha Clark of Barrington;b 25 Feb 1763 d 11 (Oct. 1783. They had one son, Paul. 2d wife Mary dau. of Francis Winkley (2) 3d wife Tamson dau. of Dea. Benjamin Pierce of Dover. She was b 6 June 1780, d 28 Jan. 1858. Paul, son of William (2) b. 5 Oct. 1786, d. 28 Nov. 1820. He mar. Abigail, dau. of Moses Rollins of Loudon. Their chil. were Paul T. who mar. Abigail, dau. of Hon. Job Otis of Strafford. They live in Newbury, Mass , chil. Abbie A, Sarah M., Job O., Mary G., Viola F. and Paul T. Martha M. dau. of Paul died young. William M. died not mar. Benjamin F. mar. Cyntha Kimball. They live in Strafford. Abigail A. mar. Charles Clyde of Derry, chil. Martha J., Maria A , Charles M. and Benjamin F. David and Holman sons of Paul died young.

William (2) chil. by 2d wife were William (3) b. 23 Jan. 1789, Martha b. 3 Jan. 1791, d. 11 Nov. 1818. Mary b. 27 July 1793, Ann b. 27 Jan. 1796, Sarah b. 22 Feb. 1798, Henry b. 9 Nov. 1803, Samuel b. 5 Oct. 1805, Joanna b. 13 Dec. 1810.

OLD SERIES, NO. 247, AUG. 9, 1866.

THE MILLET FAMILY.

To the Editor of the Dover Enquirer.

Dear Sir:—My attention has lately been called to an article published in your paper Sept. 14, 1852, giving some history of Thomas Millet of Dover. It is possible that some of the descendants of Capt. Millet may now be living who would be gratified to learn more than that account gives of that man, and also of his brother John and his descendants. Contrary to the tradition referred to in that article, Capt. Thomas Millet was not born in England, although he had only one brother that lived to manhood and no sister.

Mr. Thomas Millet, the grandfather of Captain Millet, came from Southwark, England, in the ship Elizabeth of London, with Mary (Greenoway) his wife, her sister Ursula and his son Thomas, in the spring of 1635, and settled at Dorchester, Mass. Mr. M. was 30 years of age, his wife 29, and the son 2. He resided in Dorchester till 1655 when he bought of Mr. Wm. Perkins of Gloucester, his real estate. and took his place in the church. The same year he conveyed to his son Thomas, lands lying in Gloucester, rear the old Meeting House plain. Mr. Thomas Millet had four sons and probably three daughters: Thomas, Jonathan, who died in infancy) Nathaniel, Mary, Mehetable, and probably Bethiah. His children all settled in Gloucester except Bethiah who married Moses Ayres of Dorchester, in 1666 and died Feb. 18, 1669, leaving a son. Mr. Millet lived in G. till near the close of his life when he removed to Brookfield. At least he and his wife were at Brookfield June 3, 1665. He also bought land of Goodman Coy and paid for the same in part with two cows, showing that he removed to B. with his effects. The last act of his life on record, indeed the last trace we have of him was June 3, 1665, when he, Thomas Millet, sen., and Mary Millet sen. at B., consented to the sale of some land in Gloucester. In about two months after that time Brookfield was destroyed by the Indians and what became of Mr. Thomas Millet or when he died is unknown. His estate was entered in Essex Probate Court in 1676 and his widow lived with her children in Gloucester till she died in 1682.

Thomas Millet 2d, or Lieut. Thomas Millet as he was sometimes called, eldest son of Mr. Thomas Millet, married Mary, daughter of Sylvester Evelath, May 21, 1685, with whom he lived till July 2 1687, when she died leaving no children. The next year he married Abigail Evelath widow of Isaac Evelath, whose maiden name was Coit and by her he had three sons: Thomas born Dec. 20 1689, John, b. April 19, 1692, and Nathaniel, b. Sept. 27 1694 and died April 2, 1695. The father died June 18, 1707 and gave in his will to his wife "all ye my house and upland about five acres more or less situated and lying in Gloucester in ye county of Essex, near ye mill yt was formerly Mr. John Emersons," and "to my sons Thomas and John who now liveth with me all my estate," lying part in Manchester and part in Gloucester.

In 1721 Thomas Millet, mariner, of Dover, N. H., late Thomas Millet of

Gloucester, and brother of John Millet for the sum of six hundred pounds, conveys to said John Millet all his interest in the estate of his father of which they were joint heirs. His wife, Love Millet, (Love Bunker, her maiden name,) signs the deed, and in the acknowledgement he is called Capt. Thomas Millet. John Millet, the brother of Capt. Thomas, married Eunice Babson, Dec. 24, 1723 and had David, Abigail, Abigail, John, Mary, Solomon, Thomas, Eunice and Eunice. He died before June 1, 1747 as at that time Eunice and John present to Probate Court an account of Administration. All his children, except Capt. John, (who was accidentally killed on board of his vessel in the West Indies) with their families removed to Maine, after the close of the Revolutionary war. David settled in Minot and had several children

The widow of Capt. John went to Maine. Her three sons settled in Norway. Of her daughters Mary married John Coy of Minot, Eunice married Bradbury of Minot, Sarah married Bailey Royal, of New Gloucester, Abigai married Dea. Wm. Parsons, New Gloucester, and Elizabeth married Chandler Freeman. The three sons all married and lived in Norway, where they had large families

Thomas Millet's family were the fourth in the settlement of Leeds He married Eunice Parsons of Gloucester, Mass., where most of his children were born before he joined the Revolutionary army. They were Eunice, Thomas, Zebulon, Parsons, John, Benjamin and Betsy, all of whom settled in Leeds, and all, except Thomas, had large families. The descendants of John Millet, brother of Thomas Millet of Dover, are now living in Maine, Massachusetts, New York, the Southern and Western States, and are the most numerous branch of the Millet family.

Yours respectfully,
ASA MILLET,
Bridgewater, Mass., July 30, 1866.

OLD SERIES, NO. 195, JUNE 16, 1859.

LOCALITIES.

THE GERRISH FAMILY.

Next below the Smith place, on Main street, was a passage to the river. Next below that, where now is vacant lot, was the "Gerrish Place."—This lot was a queer shaped concern as will appear the further on. The land itself was a part of the 52 rod piece prescribed in 1785 when the town voted to sell, as lying above Mr. Allen's store. The whole piece covered also the Ela lot—the Allen store being the one story building which stood where the upper end of the Peirce and Nutter Block is. The upper part, the Gerrish place was sold by the town directly to Capt. Samuel Gerrish, or else to Major Tebbets and by him to Capt. Gerrish. At any rate, Major Tebbets here built a house in 1788, for Capt. Gerrish while the latter was off at sea in the Major's employ. Here lived, when at home, Capt. Gerrish, and here he died. The Gerrishes are descended from Capt. William Gerrish, who came from Bristol, England, to Newbury, about 1640. He mar. Mrs. Joanna Oliver, (says Coffin's

Newbury,) widow of John Oliver, 17 April 1645. In 1678 he moved to Boston, and he died in Salem, 9 Aug 1687, aged 70. His wife Joanna died 14 June 1677. Their children were, John b. 15 May 1646; Abigail b. 10 May 1647; William b. 6 June 1648; Joseph b. 23 March 1650; Benjamin b. 13 Jan. 1652; Elizabeth b. 10 Sept. 1654; Moses b. 9 May 1656; Mary b. 9 May 1658; Anna b. 18 Oct. 1660; and Judith b. 10 Sept. 1662.

John (2) as above, was resident of Dover; he took the oath of fidelity here 21 June 1669. He married Elizabeth, daughter of old Major Waldron, and made a very handsome matter of it,—the Major conveying to him, 1 June 1660, part of the mill at Bellamy where Gerrish lived, a hundred acres of land, and 6 May 1670, a house partly finished. John was Representative of Dover in 1684, a member of the Convention of 1689, and judge. He had children, Richard; John; Paul; Nath'l; Timothy b. 1684.

Richard (5) son of John (2) lived at Portsmouth. "He was Register of Probate," says Hon. John Kelly, "Counsellor, and the same year that he died (1717) was appointed Judge of C. C. P." His will was dated 14 Oct. 1717, proved 22 Nov. 1717. His wife Jane, and only child Robert (of whom we know nothing) survive him. "He was a good penman but wrote his own name so flourishingly and curiously, that his official signature in the Probate records, although very fine, is illegible.

Paul (3), "old Colonel Paul son of John (2) mar. 12 Oct. 1712, Mary dau. of William and Oner Leighton of Kittery, who was born 7 May 1693. His children born before 1719 not appearing in our records of baptisms, it seems probable that he lived elsewhere prior to 1718, when he joined the church here 25 May, as did his wife 3 Oct. 1725. He was Representative of Dover from 1728 to 1740; died 6 June 1743. Their children were,—Paul b. 2 Aug. 1713 Elizabeth b. 13 Nov. 1714; Mary b. 15 Aug. 1719, (mar. Doctor Moses Carr of Somersworth, and had children, John Carr b. 26 Oct. 1741; Paul Carr b. 6 June 1743, and d. 5 Sept. 1753; Mary Carr b. 21 Oct. 1744, mar. John Rollins; Moses Carr, b. 28 May 1746, mar. Hannah Hamilton; James Carr b. 22 April 1748, m. Susanna, dau. of Col. John Wentworth of Somersworth; Betsey Carr b. 26 June 1749, m. James Rollins; Sarah Carr b. 17 Sept. 1751 and d. 4 July 1755: Daniel Carr b. 2 June 1753 and d. 30 June 1753; Hannah Carr b. 9 Dec. 1754, m. Reuben Tibbets; Sarah Carr b. 29 Nov. 1756, m. Dr. Nath. Low of South Berwick, father of Dr. Low of our own city; Paul Carr b. 6 Nov. 1758; and Susan Carr b. 25 Feb. 1761, m. Elijah Clemens;) Samuel (Gerrishes again) b. 30 July 1722; Jonathan, b. 24 May 1726; Lydia b. 26 April 1730, died 12 Aug. 1732, and Benjamin b. 7 Aug. 1732. The baptisms of Mary, Samuel, Susanna, Lydia, and Benjamin, are on our Church records.

Timothy (3) son of John (2) was also a Captain. He mar. Sarah, dau. of Robert Eliot.—From 1717 to 1723 his children's baptisms appear on our church records. Their children were. --Robert Eliot b. 18 Sept. 1708, grad. H. C. 1730, d. in 1784; John b. 1710; Timothy b. 17 Jan. 1712; Sarah b. 26 March 1714-5; Anna b. 4 July 1717; William b. 24 Aug.

1719; Abigail b. 6 June 1721; Andrew b. 4 Aug. 1724; Elizabeth b. 28 May 1727; Benjamin b. 6 June 1728; Jane b. 22 May 1729; Joseph b. 13 Sept. 1732, grad. H. C. 1752, (where his name stands at the head of the class,) d. 1813. Our church records insert also a Nathaniel (after Abigail) baptised 26 May 1723.

Of Col. Paul's (3) descendants, we know only the families of Paul jr. Samuel and Jonathan.

Paul jr. (4) son of Col. Paul, had wife Mary, and children,—Benjamin b. July 1738, bapt. 9 July; Paul bapt. 25 Aug. 1743; Mary bapt. 4 June 1748; Thomas bapt. 7 Nov. 1750; Abigail bapt. 20 Nov. 1754.

Samuel (4) son of Col. Paul, was a Captain.—He married and had children, Elizabeth, bapt. 8 Nov. 1747; Lydia bapt. 10 Dec. 1747, died 17 Sept. 1833; Mary bapt. 2 Feb. 1752; Eleanor bapt. 17 March 1754; Samuel (the Capt. Samuel of the Gerrish place on Main street,) bapt. 11 July 1756; and Sarah bapt. 22 Nov. 1761. The father died in Dover 28 March 1776.

Jonathan (4) son of Col. Paul had children baptised as follows: Molly, Nanny, and Eunice, 18 Sept. 1757; James Toby, 24 Sep. 1758; and Martha, 22 Aug. 1762.

Of Capt. Timothy's (3) children, we have no doubt but John, William, and Andrew, are the ones of those respective names appearing on our church book and other ways as follows:

John mar. Margery Jackson of Kittery; their "intentions" were published 17 Oct. 1734; and their children were,— John b. 5 Sept. 1735; Geo. b. 9 April 1737; Sarah b. 11 April 1740; Margery b. 30 March 1742; Timothy bapt. 15 April 1744 and Dorothy bapt. 21 Dec. 1746.

William had children baptised as follows: Molly, 28 Aug. 1743; Timothy, 13 Oct. 1745; Eunice, 23 Sept. 1750; and Sarah, 27 Oct. 1754.

Andrew of Dover had a wife Hannah, and children Sarah b. 12 July 1748; Elizabeth b. 9 May 1750; Hannah b. 25 April 1752; Joseph b. 6 July 1754; Timothy b. 7 April 1756; and Sarah (again) bapt. 4 June 1758; all these children were baptised in Dover.

OLD SERIES NO. 196, JUNE 23, 1859.

THE GERRISH FAMILY.

It is time to return to Capt. Samuel Gerrish of the Gerrish place on Main street. He was, as a careful reader will discover by our last number, a son of Capt. Samuel Gerrish and a grandson of old Col. Paul Gerrish, and was born in the year 1756. He went to sea while young. Acquainted with an officer of the British navy whom he had met at his father's, he obtained a situation on board of a man of war, of which the officer in question was a Lieutenant. Here he met with savage treatment, notwithstanding the friendship of the Lieutenant. Proving intractable under harsh discipline, he was put in irons. Nearing the coast of Ireland, the daring youth leaped overboard and swam still partially ironed, a mile and was assisted to land by friendly hands. He succeeded in getting to France; found Dr. Franklin, and by his friendly assistance, came home. War had commenced, and fired with ven geance, he started for the seat of hostilities. In course of events, the troops with which he had taken service were hard pressed by the enemy, in Burgoyne times. He, almost dead with small pox, was left behind with two others and a supply of water, and, at his request, a gun. Pursuit slackened, and the next day, sixteen men, of whom the late Benjamin Roberts of Rochester, was one, were sent back for the three. As they approached the place, they heard the click of a gun; a shout from Roberts was just in season to prevent Gerrish from firing. They found that he had drink the water left him, had found his companions dead the next morning and had drank their portion also, and was revived.—He recovered and fought all through the war by land or sea. When peace was declared, still fired with vengeance on account of the unforgotten tyranny, he went to take service with France against England. Dr. Franklin dissuaded him, intimating, it is said, that England could be injured more easily by free trading; in plain English, smuggling. It is also said that he profited by the hint; he also kept store in a building then standing on the same lot north of the house. Whether the tradition is true that he was to have commanded a frigate building at Portsmouth, but died of consumption before its completion, we do not know; but that he did die of consumption, 7 June 1800, is true. He was an impulsive man, a fine sailor, a fearless fighter.

Capt. Gerrish had several children,—two perhaps. John, his first son, was killed at Huckleberry Hill one Sunday; he and somebody had Joseph Smith's horse and yellow chaise for a ride; the horse becoming startled, ran against a stone still lying in the corner of the roads, when the chaise was smashed and John killed. Alphonso, the second of the family, died 15 Nov. 1825; Samuel Gerrish is his son.

Capt. Gerrish's widow, who was a Brewster from Portsmouth, kept tavern, and then married Capt. Samuel Wentworth, who traded opposite, and who also kept tavern in the house. Mr. Ela however, distanced all opposition, and Wentworth proved unsuccessful in business. The place descended to Alphonso Gerrish, who, with Lydia his wife, sold it to the Great Falls Manufacturing Company, 2 April 1824, for $3100, describing it thus: "beginning on the main road or street at the north easterly corner of the house lot belonging to the estate of Joseph Gage decd, thence running by said road north five degrees east as said road runs about ninety-nine feet to the passage way adjoining Joseph Smith's and, thence running by said passage way south sixty nine degrees, west about one hundred and sixty five feet to the river, thence southerly to the river about nineteen feet to said Gage lot south eighty two degrees, east one hundred and fifty two feet to the first mentioned corner by the road."—with the passage way north, saving Smith's right; it is called Capt. Samuel Gerrish's homestead. The Great Falls Company sold the premises, 15 March 1827, to the Dover Mfg. Company; the old house was hauled off to the south east corner of Third and Chestnut streets where it still stands, and the "Gerrish place" disappeared.

OLD SERIES, NO. 243, MAY 11, 1865

THE TWOMBLY FAMILY.

We can only, with our present means, start the Twomblys, and trust to some of the family to continue the record. TIMOTHY RALPH, had land laid out 1656-10 4. He was first taxed in 1657, at Cochecho.

His will was dated 28 Feb., 1684, proved 7, 8, mo. 1686. Elizabeth, his wife, and his son John were executors. If son John live with his mother then they are to occupy the homestead jointly; if not, his wife to have the estate for life, after which John should have one-half. If son Ralph live with his mother till he is twenty-one, then he is to have £10 in money or goods equivalent to money. To son Joseph, a heifer; to daughter Mary (Tebbets), 5s; to each of the children, Elizabeth, Hope, Sarah, Esther, and William, when eighteen years of age, a cow.

Of the children of Ralph Twombly were (Family 1):—
 John;
 Joseph b 1661;
 Mary,   (married Tebbets);
 Ralph,   (he had a son Ralph);
 Elizabeth;
 Hope;
 Sarah:
 Esther:
 William.

JOHN (2) son of Ralph 1, as in (Fam. 1) married Rachel ——. He made his will 18 July, 1724, and gave to his wife Rachel, one-half of the homestead lying on the south side of the road leading down to Joseph Hanson's and so to the Neck. After her decease it was to go to son William;—to son, John 20 acres at Littleworth, as by deed; to sons Joseph and Samuel, certain land, they to pay legacies to their uncles and aunts as provided in the will of their grandmother Elizabeth; to son Benjamin, £5 to William, half of the homestead; to daughters Sarah, Mary, Rachel, Esther and Annah, £5 each; William to support his mother;—wife and son Joseph executors.

Of the children of John, and Rachel were, (Family 2):—
 John;
 Joseph;
 Samuel,   b 10 March, 1699;
 Benjamin;
 William;
 Sarah;
 Mary;
 Rachel;
 Esther;
 Hannah.

SAMUEL (3) son of John 2 and Rachel, as in Fam. 2, married, 26, 9, 1723, Judith Hanson, daughter of Tobias and Ann (Lord) Hanson, born 12, 7, 1703. They were "Friends." He died 9 mo. 1769. She died 23, 6, 1793. Their children were, (Fam. 3):—

Ann, b August 15, 1724; (m. James Nocks);
Samuel, b March 18, 1726;
Jonathan, b Oct. 21, 1727;

315

Tobias, b 24, 10, 1728 died 11, 25, 1809;
Judith, b 5, 7, 1730, (m. Capt. John Gage);
Rebecca, b 31, 3, 1737;
Isaac b 23, 3, 1739, died 8, 1, 1824.

The following families we have not proof enough to connect.

JOHN, married Sarah, born 21 April, 1692, daughter of William and Martha Dame. Their children were, (Fam. 4):

John, b 28 Oct. 1712;
Sarah b 21 Feb. 1714 married Hanson;
Daniel b 18 Jan. 1716;
Martha b 25 Feb 1719;

This JOHN made his will 20 Dec. 1747; it was proved 27 April 1748. It was a joint will of John and his wife Sarah. They mentioned son John, who is executor, daughter Sarah (Hanson) Martha Twombly and daughter-in-law Mary widow of son Daniel now with child.

It is highly probable that this John was son of John 2.

JOHN son of John, as in Fam. 4, lived in Dover. His wife's name was Mary. His will was dated 5 May, 1764. To sons John and David he gave the homestead formerly belonging to my "honored Father and Mother, John Twombly and Sarah Twombly, of Dover, deceased;" both of these sons were then under age; he gave something to daughters Lydia (Runnels,) Anna (Purington,) Sarah Twombly (under 18) to sister Martha, to nephew Daniel Twombly, (under 21), and to wife Patience, who is executor with father-in-law Joseph Bunker. Their children were (Fam 5).

John; David; Lydia; Anna; Sarah.

JOHN, a friend, married 30, 1, 1734, Martha, daughter of Ebenezer Varney and had (Fam. 6); Anna b. 10, 3, 1740.

WILLIAM, probably of family 2, married Mary ———.

He made his will in Dover 14 Sept. 1763; it was proved 9 Oct. 1763; he gave to his son Isaac the homestead in Madbury; to William, land in Madbury, Barrington, &c.; to daughter Elizabeth, wife of Benjamin Pearl, of Barrington, land in Barrington; to Eleanor, wife of Nicholas Ricker, of Dover, land in Barrington something to granddaughter Tamesin, daughter of son John, deceased; to sons Ralph, Isaac, William, and son-in-law Ichabod Hayes, a saw mill; to Ralph, executor, land in Dover, &c.

The children of William were, (Fam. 8)

Ralph, b Sept. 13, d 1713;
Isaac, b Dec. 18, 1715;
William, July 25, 1717;
Mary, b Feb. 25, 1721;
Elizabeth, b Nov. 1, 1723; m. Benj. Pearl);
John b Sept. 19, 1725, was dead in 1763;
Eleanor, b- —, (m. Nicholas Ricker);

It was probable that William was son of Ralph (3), son of Ralph of Fam. 1.

BENJAMIN, probably of Fam. 2, lived in Somersworth; his will was dated 29 Dec., 1761, proved 30 March, 1762; he gave to wife Hannah, half of estate for life; to son Benjamin all of estate except as above, he to pay certain legacies, viz. to daughters Hannah (Haves,) Tamson (Hodgdon,) Abra Woodbridge,) £100 old tenor each; to Ralph (Hayes,) £100; to Abigail, (daughter,) £250, to daughter Sarah and Abigail, one room while single; Benjamin, executor.

Children of Benjamin were, (Fam. 9): Hannah, b May 16, 172?, m.(.——Hayes)

Tamson, m. —— Hodgdon);

Abra, bapt. 28 June, 1728, (m. Woodbridge);

Sarah;

Benjamin;

Rachel, bapt. 25 Sept. 17?6, (m. Hayes).

———

(NOTE BY JOHN SCALES. The above is the end of what Dr. Quint furnished for publication in 1865. Since then Mr. Nathaniel Twombly of this city has collected the following additional memoranda which he permits me to use to complete the data in certain lines.)

———

William Twombly who settled in Madbury, had four sons: he was born 25 July 1717. His children were:—Moses, Nathaniel, Joshua, John 24 Nov. 1755.

The children of the last named John were:—Peter, John, Hurd, Sarah, Mary.

Joshua Twombly, who was born in 1755, married Hannah Willey and settled in Strafford; their children were:—Samuel, Jacob, Polly, Aaron, Joshua, Susan, Sally, Hannah, John, Nathaniel, Abigail, William, Mehitable.

Joshua, b. 1750, died 20 Feb. 1837. His wife d. 6 Jan. 1835, aged 79 years. Samuel (son of Joshua) settled in Vermont; he moved from there to Illinois (probably in 1816. Jacob married Tamsin Hill, she died 24 Jan. 1868, age 96 years, 5 mo. He died 15 Dec. 1852, aged 77. Their children were: Daniel, Sally Samuel, Andrew, John, Susan, William.

Polly, dau. of Joshua, married James Grey and settled in Vermont. Aaron settled in Strafford. His children were: Smith and Sally.

Hannah, dau. of Joshua, b 14 Feb. 1789, b. 14 Feb. 1789, m. William E. Evans, b. 7 Dec. 1786. They lived in Barrington and had children:—John, Rhoda, Samuel, Joseph, Eliza, William, Mary, Sarah.

Nathaniel, son of Joshua, lived in Strafford; his children were Ira, Nathaniel.

Abigail, dau. of Joshua, b. 31 Aug. 1795, m. Peter Hackett and settled in Rochester.

William, the youngest son of Joshua settled in Dover; he had three children; —Mary J. Elizabeth A. and William K.

Mehitable m. Uriah Henderson, and settled in Holderness. Their children were:—Alfred, Richard, Hiram, Warren, Abby, Lydia.

John, Twombly, b. 24 Nov. Nov. 1755; (son of William b. 25 July 1717; son of William; son of John; son of Ralph, the immigrant who settled at Dover Neck about 1636;) married Anna Hurd who was born 24 May 1749. Their children were:—

Mary, b 7 June 1776; Sarah b 3 June 1777; Peter b. 11 Oct. 1778; Anna b. 15 Feb. 1780; Phebe b. March 1782; John b. 19 March, 1787; Hurd, b. 31 Dec. 1789; Mary b 10 Jan. 1791.

Hurd b. 31 Dec. 1789 married Sarah C. Caverno in 1812; she was b. 25 June 1792 and died in Aug. 1827. Their children were—:

John b. 2 Aug. 1813; Mary, b. 9 Feb. 1815; Jeremiah b. 15 Feb. 1817 d. 3 July 1859; Nathaniel, b. 7 March 1819; Benjamin b 15 Jan. 1821; Hannah b. 2 Dec. 1822, d. 26 April 1843, not married Geo. W. K. b. 19 Nov. 1824, d 1 July 1872.

Hurd Twombly's second wife was Mrs. Lavinia Tuttle; she died in Jan. 1881; he died 1 March 1872. Their children were James T. b. 2 Sept. 1829; Sarah C. b. 22 Jan. 1831; Levinla H., b. 1833, William Henry Harrison, b. 16 Oct. 1840

John 7, (son of Hurd 6, John 5, William 4, William 3, John 2, Ralph 1,) m. 1st wife, Susan Colbath, who died 24 Nov. 1839, leaving no children. 2d wife Charlotte Drew b. 8 Oct. 1818, m. 7 Jan. 1842, died 9 Dec. 1859. Their children were:—Herbert A., b. 18 April, 1845; d. Sept. 1848; John Herbert b. 17 Oct. 1848; Charles A. b. 7 Sept. 1859; d. 2 Oct. 1868.

Mary 7, (dau. of Hurd 6, John 5, Wm. 4, Wm. 3, John 2, Ralph 1,) m. Samuel Davis, Jr., 1 Jan. 1837; he was b. 11 Aug. 1799, and d. 11 Jan. 1853. Their children were:—Mary E. b. 1 April 1838, d. 16 June 1842; Samuel C. and Judith A., (twins) b. 15 March 1842; Mary A. b. 28 April 1847; James J. b. 4 Jan. 1851, d. 20 March 1851; Wm. L. b. 24 Sept. 1852.

Jeremiah 7, (son of Hurd 6, John 5, Wm. 4, Wm. 3, John 2, Ralph 1) m. Jane Maltby of Illinois, who died leaving one dau. Martha J. His 2d wife Louisa L. Kembrick. He died 3 July 1859. Their children were:—Benjamin T. b. 19 June 1854; Mary A. 24 Oct. 1857; Katie b. 5 April 1859; Sarah C. b. 24 Dec. 1860.

Nathaniel 7, (son of Hurd 6, John 5, Wm. 4, Wm. 3, John 2, Ralph 1) b. 7 March 1819, m. Martha A. Drew 13 June 1843; she was b. 18 Feb. 1824; d. 2 Aug. 1897. Their children were: Helen F. b. 24 Jan. 1845; d. 30 Oct. 1850; Mary E. b. 26 Oct. 1846; d. 21 Oct. 1853; Frank H. b. 20 Sept. 1851; Mary H. b. 8 Dec. 1853 d. 29 Aug. 1864; Nathaniel A. b. 20 June 1857; Walter J. b. 2 Aug. 1859; Wm. D., b. 3 Feb. 1863; d. 2 Sept 1864; Martha L. b. 4 Dec. 1866; d. 13 March 1874.

Benjamin H. 7, (son of Hurd 6, John 5, Wm. 4, Wm. 3, John 2, Ralph 1) m. Rowena L. Boone 26 May 1852; she died 14 April 1854. He m. 2d wife Augusta A. Kellow 21 Oct. 1855. Their children were:—Alice A. b. 11 May 1859; Benj. H. Jr. b. 7 Dec. 1862.

George W. K. 7 (son of Hurd 6, John 5, Wm. 4, Wm. 3, John 2, Ralph, 1,) m. Mary A. Langley in 1846; she died in 1856; he d. 1 July 1872. Their children were:—Geo. W. b. 15 Dec. 1848; Hurd W. C. 22 Sept. 1852; John C. b. 2 Feb. 1854. His 2d wife was Louisa L. Kembrick m in 1860. Their children were.—William C. b. 10 Dec. 1862, d. 1871. Helen b. 6 June 1869, d. 1871.

James T. 7, son of Hurd 6, John 5, Wm. 4, Wm. 3, John 2, Ralph 1) m. Hattie Raymond. They had one son Charles E. b., 11 May 1878 d. July 2, 1880.

Sarah, C. 7, (dau. of Hurd 6, John 5, Wm. 4, Wm. 3, John 2, Ralph 1, m. Hon. Jacob D. Young; he was b. 28 Dec 1823: —Their children were:—Lillian L., b. July 1858, Edward L., b. 21 June, 1860;

Lewis H. b. Dec. 1863. Esther S., b. 14 May 1868.

Lavinia H. 7, (dau. of Hurd. 6, John 5, etc.,) m. Daniel Drew:—Their children are Rowena L., Nelson U., and Alice.

Wm. H. H. 7, (son of Hurd 6, John 5 Wm. 4, Wm. 3, John 2, Ralph 1, m. Mary Esther Hall, dau. of Gilman Hall, Esq., and sister of Col. Daniel Hall, 4 June 1865:—Their children are Rocsoe R. h. 22 June 1866; Gergie E. b. 24 June 1868; John H. b, 23 May 1870; Gilman H., 18 Feb. 1872; Harry L. b. 10 Dec. 1873; Walter T. b. 7 March 1876, d. 17 Jan. 1884; Lavinia H., b. 13 May 1878; Winfield H., 19 Jan. 1880; Fred C., b. 21 June 1883

OLD SERIES, NO. 191, MAY 12, 1859.

THE WALKER FAMILY.

Returning to the houses which lined the west side of Main street which is called in old records "the main road, and the "Main street,")—two only of the lots were originally in the possession of the Waldrons; these were the "Mark Walker place," and the "Boardman place," which two joined.

The Mark Walker house stood a few feet south of the present site of No. 2 Engine house; as appears by a plan lying before us. This lot was owned and occupied by Mark Walker, who came here from Portsmouth, and who after the death of Thomas W. Waldron, took the "Waldron farm" the piece from the river up to and including the "factory field,") for three years. A brother of Mark's took the grist mill for the same time— Mark brought his lot, directly or ind'rectly, of the Waldrons, and hauled there from the "Plains," above Dover, for a dwelling house, a building which Capt. William Horne had used as a store; Mark's large barn stood back towards the factory yard.—Here Mark lived after measuring vast quantities of lumber, died. He was born in Portsmouth, March 1753; was twice married; 1st, to Mary ——, who died of Palsy 13 April 1825, aged 66; 2d, to Abigail, daughter of Thomas Westbrook Waldron, and widow of David Boardman, born 14 Dec. 1770, died 1858. Mark had two children, (both by his first marriage,) viz., Seth S., born 20 May 1780, and Mark jr., born 18 June 1794. Seth S. married Sarah, daughter of John Smith 3d, of Durham (born 24 Dec. 1736, died 24 May 1791,) and his wife Sarah (born 8 April 1744, died 7 April 1838. Seth S. and Sarah had three children, viz., Mark William b. 12 Jan. 1815, d. 16 Feb. 1832; Emily b. 28 Nov. d. 7 Dec. 1816; and Caroline b. 9 Dec. 1817, d. 6 July 1834. Seth's wife (born 19 May 1780,) died suddenly 23 Feb. 1843 Seth was "a man of more than ordinary mind and considerable intellectual culture in his early manhood he was a shipmaster, in later years employed frequently as a practical surveyor and magistrate; he died suddenly 12 Jan. 1859.—Seth's only brother, Mark Jr., a fine scholar and "one of the most promising young men in Dover, died in the old house, of consumption, 6 Feb. 1812, aged 17. And thus the Mark Walker blood is utterly extinguished.

The Walker family, of which Mark was

a scion, is descended from EDWARD WALKER, a native of England, who emigrated to this country generations ago, with a wife and family, tradition says) and settled at York, Me. Who were his children, save Edward, we are entirely ignorant.

But Edward, jr., (?) was one; he, after his father's death, removed to Wells, and subsequently, for safety in war-times, to Newington, N. H. — He married at Kittery, 6 Sept. 1710, Deliverance Gaskins, so named, it is said, because born at sea and safely landed; she became, in time, mother of nine children, viz.: Edward, who married Eleanor Nutter and lived and died in Newington; Elizabeth, who married a Miller of Newington; and had twelve children, of whom three only survived her; Deliverance, who married Nath'l Grover of Greenland and left three children; Seth who married Nancy Tripe of Portsmouth, lived in Portsmouth (near Newington line,) and had seven children, of whom Mark of Dover was one, and which we will enumerate below: Lydia, who d. in Newington aged 16; Gideon, who married Eleanor Bickford and lived in Newington, with a family of ten children Ebenezer, who died in Newington at the age of 10; Mary, who mar. Jonathan Huntress of Newington, and had nine children; and Martha b. 1735, who mar. William Brastridge, grandfather to the late Sheriff Brasbridge, (officially "late" we mean, as, notwithstanding his head was removed for "the public good" for being on Democratic shoulders, and his office passed to other hands, he still thrives personally and purseonally.)

Seth Walker (3) son of Edward jr., as above married Nancy Tripe of Portsmouth, lived in that ancient town, and raised a family; they had seven children, viz., Mark of Dover, with whom we started; William, who removed to Barnstead, lived and died there; Anna or Nancy, who married Samuel Shackford, of Strafford; Seth, who married Jan. 1777, Temperance Peverly, in Portsmouth; and was Register of Deeds at Exeter; Gideon who mar. Lydia Watson of Dover, and lived in Portsmouth; Lucy b. July 1766, mar. Nathaniel Ham of Portsmouth; and Nicholas, who died young.

Of these children of Seth (3 Mark's (4 family is given above. William (4) lived and died in Barnstead, having a family of eight children, viz. William mar. Dow, lived in Barnstead and had children John, Seth, Ann, m. Davis and Abby m. Davis; John S. mar. Sarah Ham lived, or did recently live, in Portsmouth, had children, William, Mary, Elizabeth who m. John Norton of Portsmouth, Lydia Ann who m. Geo. W. Plummer of Portsmouth, George b. 1829, Samuel, and Lavina, Samuel and John Andrew who are dead; Samuel, mar. Ruth Jenkins, died in Barnstead, having children, Mark (M. D.,) Betsey B., Mary Jane, Samuel, Cleora, and George Ansell; Joseph A. mar. Abigail Murray, lives in Barnstead, and has a family; Mark, o. unmarried, Betsey, Nancy, m. Jenkins, and d. 8 Jan. 1833; Lucy, m. Solomon Young late of Strafford, author of a remarkable Hymn Book.

Anna or Nancy (4 mar. Samuel Shackford, who was born in 1751 and died in 1842. They had two children, viz.: Samuel, and Nancy (who mar. Hen. B.

W. Jenness of Strafford) Samuel b. 1780, mar. Nancy Buzzell (who was b. 1797, and who mar. 2d Capt. John Sherburne of Northwood;) they had children, Eliza, m. Wm. Hale, (and had Thomas, Mathew, Samuel, and Elizabeth;) Susan d. unmarried; Mary; Lucy; Abigail m. Dr. Levi G. Hill, a successful physician in Dover; Samuel m. (!) Martha Susan Hale, (2) Lydia Pendexter, and had (by 1st marriage,) Onslow, Charles, and Martha Susan; John; George m. Mary Ann Stone, and had Charles F. and Geo. W.; Charles Harrison (M. D., a physician at Great Falls;) and Caroline who m. Samuel Hayes of Barrington.

OLD SERIES, NO. 194, JUNE 2, 1859.

THE WHITE FAMILY.

The lot next south of the "Horne place" was a double one. It covered the land occupied by the "White house" and Smith house,"—the latter in part only, perhaps. The whole lot was purchased of the town, 23 Oct. 1786, by Charles Clapham, Gentleman, for £40 The boundaries are thus described: "beginning at the river North 15 degrees west thirteen rods from the northwesterly course of Joseph Allen's store and running north 73 degrees (east) eight rods then north 23 degrees eight rods, then south 65 degrees west to the river, then by said river to where it began, containing fifty-two rods." Charles Clapham was an Englishman by birth, and a lawyer. He commenced practice here, Cogswell says (Am. Quart. Reg. xii:47,) in 1788, and that he left Dover about 1798. In 1789, he and Jonathan Rawson were "elected "attorneys for the town." (Rawson was another Dover lawyer, a native of Yarmouth, Mass., and commenced practice here in 1785 and died 30 May 1794 aged 35.) Clapham lived on the Parson Belknap place, which he bought of the Parson 6 July 1789, giving two notes of £41 each, and mortgaging back for security. A good many deeds to and from this individual are on record in our County office. Very likely his trading operations were like those of two men confined in the same cell once, in a building well secured against fire; one had a jack-knife, and the other a slate pencil, and by shrewd trading, they accumulated a capital, one of three thousand, and the other of forty-five hundred dollars. Mr. Clapham was afterwards an officer in a man-of-war, and died on board. A son of his is, or recently was, in Portsmouth.

The upper part of this lot Clapham sold 21 June 1791, to Amos White, saddler, for £18 "beginning at the corner of the lot lately sold to Joseph Gage, by the road, and running by said road four rods to Capt. William Horne's land, then south sixty-five degrees west. to the river, then by said River to said Joseph Gage's land and from thence by said Gage's land to the first Bound, said line running north seventy-three degrees east." This lot was a cone or sugar-loaf in shape, being a rocky, sharp-pointed hill, which Amos White reduced till he got a good situation for the house which he built and which still stands on its original site. Amos White was a son of Timothy White and was born, it is supposed, in the Major Hodgdon house which stood once (not now) beyond Pine Hill. Amos White early in life travelled collecting furs; built some vessels; traded in the old Gage store which now stands next below Wm. Hale's. In early life he was troubled with raising blood; Dr. Belknap advised him to consult Dr. Rush of Philadelphia, and, especially, to make the journey on horseback; he did so,— the journey probably doing as much good as Dr. Rush; Dr. Rush gave him excellent advice, which he followed, and he recovered to live to a good old age. While in Philadelphia, by the way, Dr. Rush introduced him to Dr. Franklin, who on finding him recommended by Dr. Belknap, regarded him with great favor. The great philosopher spoke in high terms of Dr. Belknap; he declared that to Dr. Belknap as much as to any other man was owing the American Revolution, as the Dr. had incessantly written, over various signatures for newspapers north and south, articles which had powerful effect on the public mind.

Amos White's father, Timothy White, came here from Haverhill; taught school; traded; was Quartermaster in Col. Wingate's regiment; was at the second taking of Louisburg, and at Ticonderoga. He lived at the time in the Freeman house on Silver street,—Parson Belknap's father, who was turned out of Boston in revolutionary times, lived in the other half. He was a son of Timothy White was graduated at Harvard College in 1720 and died in 1765 Amos White lived for many years in the White house; there was born our fellow citizen, John H. White, Esq.—Amos sold the premises to the Dover Factory Company, 25 Oct.

1824, for $4000.

The other half of the original Clapham lot, Clapham sold, about or before 1791, to Joseph Age, trader The deed we are unable to find, but that is of little consequence as the boundaries are all described in the sale by Gage to Joseph Smith, "Baker," very soon after. This was on the 12 March 1794, for £70: "beginning near the river on the north side, north fifteen degrees west thirteen rods from the store late owned by Mr. Joseph Allen and running north seventy-three degrees east eight rods to the road, then north twenty-three degrees west by said road four rods, then on a parallel line with the first line to the river, carrying the breadth of four rods, it being the same land I purchased of Charles Clapham. It will be seen that the description corresponds exactly with that of the lower part of the lot which Clapham bought of the town. To this lot Smith added on its south side, by purchasing of the town, 1 July 1799, for $95, "beginning at the south-east corner of said Smith's land, thence by said river one-half of the distance between said Smiths land and Capt. Samuel Gerrish's land, then through the middle of said land to the road,—being the one half of a Lot or piece of land sold at Vendue the tenth day of June 1799 and bid off by Joseph Smith, containing about ten and a half square rods be the same more or less." This latter lot, that is, the whole of it, was one of the lots whose sale continually agitated the town. It is referred to as early as 1785. After various proposals, in 1791, it was voted to lease it (described as being between Clapham's and Capt. Samuel Gerrish's (to Capt. Isaac

Watson, and we suppose it was so arranged. On the 3 June 1799, the town voted to sell this place which had been reserved as a temporary road to be used in case the lower bridge should again sail off on a freshet, but which the town finally thought needless; t was described as between Joseph Smith's and Captain Samuel Gerrish's and as having been left as a public road to the river. It was under this vote that Smith purchased; the remaining half being left as a passage, whether at the town's expense or that of the abuttors we are ignorant; tradition says the latter.

On this land Joseph Smith, who came from Newburyport, built—we suppose—the house still standing. There, for many years, he carried on baking extensively. On the south side of his land he built up a high stone face wall, on which used to be great piles of wood, under which the passage way already spoken of, led to the river, and then turning southly, come out in the passage way between the Nutter Block and the Jewett store.—Mr. Smith also built, in the rear of his lot, an immense storehouse and bakery, facing the street, two stories in front and four or five on the river where boats brought up the floor. Mr. Smith is of course well remembered. After selling out his premises to the Company, 25 Oct 1824, he built and carried on business on Water street. He died 17 Sept. 1857, aged 85 years and 9 months. Mr Smith was twice married; 1st, to Judith, daughter of Frederick Bell; 2d, to Mary Emerson. Frederick Bell was a son of ——— Bell and Mary, daughter of Benjamin Mordaunt; Benjamin Mordaunt, was a native of either Jersey or Guernsey, of a family of rank; he was a shipmaster and settled at Great Island. He had several children, viz. Margarette, who married Capt. Benjamin Randall and was mother to Elder Benjamin Randall; Mary, who mar. 1st, a Cary who died childless, 2d, Bell, and had two sons and a daughter; Betsy, who married a Lomboard, early became a childless widow, and died in Saco; and Jacob, an only son, a shipmaster, who died at sea young and unmarried. The two sons of Mary, whose second husband was a Bell, were George, who died in Newcastle in Jan. 1849, aged 87 or thereabouts,) and Frederick, the father to Joseph Smith's first wife, and who was killed in the Revolution. Mr. Smith's children were William Jarvis, Elizabeth, and Sarah Fisher, wife of our well known fellow citizen and former excellent Town Clerk, George Piper, Esq.

Our own recollections of the "Smith house" do not go back to its bakery days; they are more vivid in connection with the front projecting basement room of a quarter of a century ago, now retired, where "Dominick Peduzzi jr. and Co." used to dispense eatables and sweets; Dominick's father (an Italian) lived at Portsmouth and furnished the candies. A good many of the copper coins of our country escaped from our grasp into the till of that eminent firm However great may be modern improvements in science and art, the molasses gibralters dispensed at that establishment will never be surpassed.

OLD SERIES, NO. 271, DEC. 2,, 1875.

TIMOTHY WHITE'S SCHOOL IN 1772.

Timothy White came to Dover from Haverhill, Mass. He was son of that Timothy White who, graduating at Harvard in 1720, was long and useful preacher and school-teacher at Nantucket, and who ended his days at Haverhill in 1765.

Timothy, the eldest son, was born on the Island. In Dover he did some trading. He was also Quartermaster of Col. Wingate's regiment, and, by way of episode, was at the second taking of Louisburg, and at Ticonderoga. But mainly he was a teacher. About revolutionary times, he was living in the "old Freeman house" on Silver street, in whose other half dwelt Parson Belknap's father and mother when the Parson got them out of the besieged Boston. Timothy's wife was Lydia, daughter of good old Parson Amos Main, of Rochester; wherefore he named one son Amos; but Amos, it is believed, was born in the "old Major Hodgdon house," which many years ago became too old to stand on its site a little south of Pine Hill. The Amos, whose son, John H. White, Esq, is still on the active list in Dover.

In the house on Silver street, doubtless was kept that School in 1772 whose record we select from those of scattered years from 1769 to 1785. We select it because it is the most complete. The right hand column evidently denotes the name of the head of the family.

Began School June 8th, 1772.

Scholars entered.

Sally Belknap	Mr. Belknap
Joseph Belknap	
Otis Baker	Esq. Baker.
James Baker	
Joseph Pierce	
Betty Pierce	Benj: Pierce
Betty Dodge	Nath'll Balch.
Douglas Stagpole,	Sam'll Stagpole
James Chace	Enoch Chase
Eleanor Waldron	Esq. Waldron
Charles Waldron.	
Nancy Ham	
Moses Ham	Moses Ham
Samuel Ham	Samuel Ham
Hitty Morse	
Wm. Peaslee	Robert Peaslee
Robt. Peaslee	
Nancy Gage	Col. Gage
John Hall	
Hannah Hanson	Jno. Bm. Hanson
Susa: Hanson	
Betty Hanson	Joanne Hanson
Betty Roberts	Ensn. Roberts.
James Roberts	
Benja. Watson	Wm. Watson,
Sally Titcomb	Wildar Titcomb
Susa Varney	
Joshua Varney	Moses Varney
Anna Varney	
Elisa Gage	Jona. Gage
Nancy Gage	Capt. Gage.

Finished School Jany. 16 1773.

Then follows the accounts with each parent, and credits by groceries and all sorts of articles. For example, Benjamin Pierce is credited with a pound of coffee, a pint of rum, two quarts of molasses, one mugg, a Platter, etc., etc.— The charge for schooling was eight shillings a week, save in Parson Belknap's case, where it was seven only. The accounts are kept in pounds, shillings and pence of course.

We feel an interest in the urchins trudging to school into that venerable old house. Let their grandchildren look at that house with respect as they pass by!

We append some notes, assuming, first of all, that it is safe to consider that all who went to school a hundred and three years ago are now dead.

Sally Belknap was born 7 April, 1768, and baptized three days after; baptized by old Parson Cushing, then in his seventy-eighth year,—"being ye last that ever baptiz'd. When Parson Belknap moved to Boston, of course Sally went, and she died single, advanced in years.

Sally was four years old at that school. But just think of Joseph! He was born 2 Dec. 1769, and was but two years and six months old. Lucky it was not far from the Parson's up by the new Belknap school house. Joseph grew up, became a printer, and lived in Boston.

"Esq. Baker" was the Lieut.-Col. Otis Baker of the old Second. He was son of that Christine (Otis) Baker who, when an infant, was carried to Canada by the Indians out of the massacre of 1689.—The Colonel was a very prominent man in Revolutionary times. His house stood a few feet northeast of the Whidden house, on Silver street. Otis, the schoolboy, was born 3 Aug. 1766. He grew up, married, and left descendants. His brother James was four years old then, and now Dr. James H. Wheeler is one of his grandsons. Time flies.

Benjamin Pierce was the good man who was chosen Deacon in 1780, and whose mantle fell on that noble man, his son, Col. Andrew Pierce. His house is still standing on Silver street—the old Pierce house east of Locust street. His son Joseph, born   lived to manhood, but died single, and his body was laid on Pine Hill. Betsey, also, never married, and lived and died in the family of her brother Andrew.

Who Betty Dodge was, defies our search. Nathaniel Balch sent her to school, but beyond the fact that he had several children of his own baptized, we now nothing about him.

Samuel Stagpole, a native of Rollinsford, afterwards was a Lieutenant in the army of the Revolution. Where Locust street now runs north out of Silver street was once a short and narrow lane, and at the head of that lane lived Samuel Stagpole. The boy Douglas (we don't know his age, but he was at school in 1769, was related to the Baker children; his father and they were own cousins.—He was also own cousin to Betty Hanson, and second cousin to Benjamin Watson, who went to school at the same time. He grew up and married Sarah Low, of Berwick, and left plenty of descendants.

James Chace was doubtless the one who eventually lived on a site now covered by "No. 4," just west of the old path which led from Washington street in to the grist mill. He married Betsey, daughter of Moses Gage, and died 14 Sept. 18 V01. He left children. A daughter of his married John B. H. Odiorne, and is living in this city Chace's widow married Capt. Jeremiah Banks.

Eleanor Waldron's father, Thomas Westbrook Waldron, was an important man. He lived in the then Waldron mansion, erected a dozen years before, whose ample lawn and fine garden have long since vanished. A relic or two of his orchard remains,—one tree, over fifty years old in 1832, still stands in the premises of George Quint. The house has been twisted round. Who would think that "the old boarding house" was the elegant mansion of the Waldrons, from which Eleanor, then six years old, trudged to school a hundred and three years ago last June! Eleanor grew up, married James Smith, and had five children.

Charle Waldron was only four years old when Eleanor used to lead him to school. He died of consumption, 18 May 1791, and thus failed to become the heir for which his father's will destined him.

Moses Ham was the son of that Ephraim who was Selectman off and on, and who lived on his grandfather's farm—Moses lived on Main street, was a tailor and had twelve children. He moved off up to Wolfborough, but came back here and died in 1817. The two children who went to School, Nancy and Moses, were his sixth and seventh children. Nancy was born 3 Feb, 1765. She married a Gage. Moses born 14 Nov 1769, married Mehitable Hanson. He moved to Danville, Vt. in 1814, and died there 2 Aug. 1839, having had seven children. One of his sons lived in Boston, and one in Oskosh, Wisconsin.

Samuel Ham married, 1st, Sarah Wingate, 2d, Widow Sarah Morse. He was owner (part at least) and master of "The seven charming Sallies," in which he sailed, on its first voyage, out of Portsmouth in 1788, and was wrecked on Plumb Island in a cold and blinding snow storm, All hands were lost.— Samuel had built, and lived in, the Pendexter house. His son Samuel, who went to school, was born in 1769, baptized 18 June 1769; settled in Portsmouth, lived in the Woodbury mansion when at home; was a sea-captain; married, 1st, Sarah (somebody), 2d, Abigail Boyd. He died about 1820, leaving two children. Hittie Morse was evidently daughter of Samuel Ham's second wife. She married, it is believed, a Crummett, of Berwick. Her mother married, third, a Carr.

Enoch Chase married, 31 Dec. 1767, Joanna Balch, and he lived, or his family did, on Silver street, very near the Dr. Dow house. We found this by a conveyance, 4 April, 1780, by which John Gage conveys to Jonathan Gage ten acres bounded "northerly by road leading to Barrington, westerly by land of Nathaniel Ham, southerly by land of Benjamin Hanson and Moses Hanson, and easterly by lands of Theophilus Dame Esq. and others" "being the premises where Samuel Ham and the family of Enoch Chase now live, and is part of the estate of my late Father deceased," with all the buildings i proved by Ham, but reserving the right to take off within one year, the buildings occupied by the Chase family. Now, Nathaniel Ham lived on Silver street, just opposite the present Pierce house. Capt. John Gage lived in the Dow house before 1780, and before he built the "Robinson house" up above Friend Ham's. Theophilus Dame, a fine old gentleman lived on the spot where Dr. Low once lived, on Pleasant street. It is easy to see that the Chase residence was close to the Dr. Dow house, probably east of it. James Chase was born in 1768; grew up, built a house on a spot now smothered by "No. Four" and died of billious fever, 14 Sept, 1801. His wife. Betsey, was daughter of Moses Gage of Dover Neck, [She afterwards married, 14 Dec. 1807, Capt. Jeremiah Banks. Of Chase's three children—John G. married, 15 Oct. 1823, Lydia Roberts of Somersworth; James was "of Charleston, S. C., in 1820; and the marriage of Abigail G. was 8 June, 1832.

In the above deed it is melancholy to notice how Silver street is designated; "the road leading to Barrington!"

We now return to our list.

But, concerning Robert Peaslee we are still ignorant. There was a widow Peaslee who had divers children, particularly John, (who went to Burlington, Vt., and used to come down here of a winter with a dashing pair of horses), Samuel, (who served his time with Amos White, and also went to Burlington, and who left descendents), Amos (who went to sea, and who had his head shot off in action, on board Decatur's United States, as his uncle Amos likewise is said to have had his head shot off in the Revolution), and Sylvester. There was an Amos Peaslee who married Lydia, daughter of Samuel Ham, in the last century. Later was Nicholas Peaslee, of Back River, many years one of the Selectmen. But none of these touch the case of Robert's little boys, William and Robert, who went to Mr. White's school. Will somebody enlighten us.

Nancy Gage and John Hall were charged to Col. Gage. There are too many John Halls to allow us even to guess who this one was. As to Nancy, it will be seen that the last on the list is also Nancy, charged to Captain Gage. We do not know quite how to settle it.— Captain John Gage was Colonel John Gage's son. We thought that perhaps the Captain was off at sea when school began, and that Nancy's name was repeated when he came home. But, according to rather vague records, Nancy, daughter of the Captain, was born in 1769; whereas a Nancy was in the school of 1769. Perhaps the record of Nancy's age, which is derived solely from her reputed age at death, is not correct, and that the two are one and the same. Certainly, no other Nancy appears in the Gage records.

John Burnham Hanson lived in the Pendexter house. Hannah was born 11 July 1766. She married Peter Cushing Her son, Jonathan P., graduated at Dartmouth in 1817, and died while president of Hampden-Sydney College. Susa was born 25 May 1768. What became of her, we do not succeed in ascertaining. Concerning John Burnham Hanson we shall have more to say in other articles.

Betty Hanson never saw her father. He was Humphrey Hanson, brother to John B. just mentioned, and died in the November before Betty was born 12 May 1767. Her mother was Joanna Watson. Humphrey lived next west of the present house of David L. Drew.

As to Ensign Roberts, he was doubtless Joseph Roberts, who had Elizabeth baptized 15 Sept. 1765, and James baptized 21 August 1768. But what became of them, the Robert's archives have not yet told us.

William Watson lived on the northwest corner of Silver and Locust streets, but the house has long been gone. He died 25 Jan. 1800, aged 67. His wife was Lucy, daughter of Joshua and Lucy (Baker) Stagpole, and so was own cousin to the Baker children. By the father, the boy Benjamin was also related to the Betty Hanson, and by his mother to the Stagpole boy. In fact, this school was pretty much relatives. Benjamin grew up and his son Jeremiah died some years ago in Barrington, leaving children.

Widow Titcomb, again perplexes us a little. There was a widow mentioned in the church records in 1771. Likewise there was John Titcomb who had a daughter Sarah baptized 26 June 1763, the only Sarah possible. So it is likely that this widow was widow of John. John was the Captain John of the old French war, who led a company in Col. Meserve's regiment in 1756—7, and was at Louisburg in 1758, a Major; and when Col Meserve died at that great siege, Titcomb became Lieutenant Colonel. As to Sarah, perhaps she was the Sarah Titcomb who married Richard Waldron, 11 Dec. 1785.

Moses Varney appears clearly to be the one who married Mary Estes. Two of his children are on record corresponding to two at school, viz: Joshua, born in 1767, and Anna born in 1769. This does not account for Susa,—which is our trouble. But his record is not a complete one; and in the next year's school appears Ruth, with by the same Moses Varney, and his record gives us a Ruth, who eventually married James Wiggin. Besides, it has already been seen that the children of this school were generally relatives. Now Moses Varney was a relative; that is to say, first, his father's mother was own cousin to Col. Baker. secondly, he was first cousin to John Burnham Hanson. This must be the Moses. But what became of the Susa, Joshua and Anna?

Eliza Gage (written short for Elizabeth,) was daughter of Jooseph Gage, who kept tavern which swelled into the "Dover Hotel." Jonathan married Rebecca, daughter of John Hanson, and sister to John Burnham Hanson— So Elizabeth was cousin to the Hanson children. She was born 4 June 1768. She lived to grow up, and married Shadrach Hodgdon, grandson of old Deacon Shadrach; and the widow of that noble man, Capt. Moses Paul, is her daughter.

Nancy Gage, last on the list, was daughter of Capt John Gage, who lived in the Dr. Dow house. She is recorded as dying in 1850, aged 81. If so, she was born in 1769. She married Paul R binson. John Paul Robinson, who graduated at Harvard in was one of the finest scholars Dover ever furnished to the world.

The extreme youth of the children of this school is noticeable. We have dates of the births of twenty of them; their average age is but four years and eight months. Of the thirty (if Nancy Gage is but one and not two), we have no knowledge of what became of eleven. In some of these cases, the parents appear to have moved away. But the nineteen of whom we have records, all lived to maturity, and fifteen of these married and had families. They seemed to have turned out well. Nobody knows how much of their good behavior in life was due to Timothy White's School in 1772.

DOVER IN THE REVOLUTION.

The people of Dover took an early part in remonstrating against those aggressions of the British Government which led to the Revolution; and when remonstrances failed, and the cause of liberty was submitted to the stern arbitrament of arms, none exerted themselves more cheerfully, or contributed more in proportion to their means, to render that cause successful. As a record of interest, and one well worthy of reproduction in these "Memoranda," we publish from the Town Records all the proceedings, votes, etc., which we find in reference to the Revolutionary War. The first record which is made is the following.—

At a legal meeting of the qualified voters of the town of Dover this tenth day of January 1774 convened at the Friends Meeting House in said town on purpose to consider of the innovations attempted to be made on American privileges—

Col. Otis Baker was chosen Moderator—

Although we deprecate every thing which in its infant motions tends to alienate the affection which ought to subsist among the subjects of the same King, yet, we cannot longer behold the Arts used to curtail the Privileges purchased with the blood and treasure of British America, and of New England in particular, for their Posterity, without bearing our Testimony against them.

As these Colonies have recognized the Protestant Kings of Great Briain as their Lawful Sovereign, and WE in this Province the Man whom the King has pleased to send us as his Representative—We acknowledge this Representative from our first formation into a Government has had a negative voice on all Bills proposed by Laws in the manner his Majesty has at home.

And as it doth not appear that any Parliaments have been parties to any contracts made with the European Settlers in this once howling Wilderness, now become a pleasant field—We look on our

Rights too dearly bought, to admit them now as Tax masters—Since (by laws as firm as the honor of crowned heads can make them, and which we have no Apprehension so good and gracious a King as we obey, will suffer to be abridged) we have Parliaments of our own—who always with the greatest Cheerfulness furnished his Majesty such Aids as he has been pleased to require from time to time according to the Abilities of the People, and even beyond them, of which, none but themselves could be adequate Judges.

Why the King's Subjects in Great Britain should frame Laws for his Subjects in America, rather than the reverse, we cannot well conceive, as we do not admit it to be drawn from any PACT made by our ancestors, or from the Nature of the British Constitution, which makes Representation essential to Taxation—and this supposed Power of Parliament for taxing America is quite novel, some few instances for the better Regulation of Trade excepted, which no more prove their supposed Right, than the Tortious Entry of a Neighbor into the Infant's field does that of the Intruder—but if Superior Strength be the best plea, how would they relish the Alternative? which if political Arithmetic deceives not advances with Hasty Strides; tho' nothing but downright oppression will ever effect it.

Therefore, Resolved, 1ly, That any attempt to take the Property of any of the King's Subjects for any purpose whatever where they are not represented, is an infraction of the English Constitution; and manifestly tends as well to destroy it, as the subject's private property, of which recent proofs are plenty.

Resolved 2ly, That We and our American Brethren, are the liege People of King George the Third, and therefore have as full, and ample a claim, to all the Privileges and Immunities of Englishmen, as any of his Subjects three thousand miles distant—the Truth of which, our demeanor clearly evinces.

Resolved 3ly, That the Parliament in Britain by suffering the East India Company to send us their Teas subject to a duty on landing, have in a measure testified a Disregard to the Interests o Americans, whose liberal Services ill deserve such ungenerous Treatment.

Resolved 4ly, That we are of opinion that any seeming Supineness of this Province in these very—very interesting matters, hath proceeded from a Consideration of their Smallness among their Brethren, rather than from any insensibility of impending Evils.

Resolved 5ly, That this Town approves the general Exertions, and noble struggles, made by the opulent Colonies through the Continent, for preventing so fatal a Catastrophe as is implied in Taxation without Representation, viz SLAVERY—than which, to a generous Mind, Death is more Eligible.

Resolved 6ly, That We are, and always will be ready in every constitutional Way, to give all the Weight in our Power to avert so dire a Calamity.

Resolved 7ly, That a Dread of being enslaved Ourselves, and of transmitting the Chains to our Posterity (by which we should justly merit their curses) is the principal Inducement to these Measures.

And Whereas, our house of Commons

have a committee for corresponding with the several Colonies on these matters and the Committees of the several Towns of this Government to correspond with each other at the necessary Times may be subservent to the Common Cause;— Therefore resolved that a Committee to consist of five persons be chosen for that purpose.

Voted that Col. Otis Baker, Capt. Caleb Hodgdon, Capt Stevens, Capt. Joshua Wingate and John Wentworth, Jr. or either three of them be the Committee of Correspondence for this Town.

Voted that the proceedings of this meeting be entered in the Records of this Town and that an attested copy thereof be sent to the Committee of Correspondence at Portsmouth, to assure them and all concerned, that our hearts are knit with those, who wish the weal (as it is constituitionally fixed) of our most gracious Sovereign and all of his numerous subjects.

OLD SERIES, NO. 187, OCT. 14, 1858.

DOVER IN THE REVOLUTION.

July 18, 1774. A committee of five was chosen to represent the town at a meeting to be held at Exeter for "appointing Delegates to join in a General Congress of the Provinces for considering of and advising to the most conciliating methods of establishing their rights and harmony among all the subjects of our gracious sovereign, which meeting is proposed to be held on the 1st Sept., at Philadelphia." And £6 10s. were voted as the proportion of Dover towards paying the expenses of the Delegates, which the selectmen were authorized to advance.

Nov. 7, 1774. A town meeting was called to see if the inhabitants would raise anything either "in Money, Fat Cattle or Sheep" for the relief of the Poor in Boston, then suffering from the operations of the Port Bill. And it was voted that the town would "give something"

Dec. 26, 1774. At a town meeting the following preamble and resolutions were adopted:

The Designs of the Continental Congress holden at Philadelphia being so humane and benevolent, the result of their proceeding so salutary and effective as justly to attract notice of the millions of freemen in America, this town on mature consultation are fully convinced that nothing (under Heaven) will so evidently tend to preserve the rights of Americans or frustrate the attempts already made for their destruction as carrying the same into full execution. For which purpose,

Voted, That Messrs. Otis Baker, Shadrach Hodgdon, Stephen Evans, Joshua Wingate, John Waldron 3rd, Caleb Hodgdon, Job Wentworth Jr., John Kielle and John Gage be a committee.

Voted, they have the following instructions, viz.

1st. We expect that to the utmost of your power you carefully intend the preservation of peace and good order In the town so far as the same may be endangered by a discussion of a sentiment relative to political matters.

2nd. We enjoin you that by every lawful means you see the recommendations and proceedings of the Continental Congress strictly complied with by the in habitants of this town so far as we are therein concerned.

3rdly. As examples you are to encourage every kind of Temperance, Frugality Industry and Economy and to discountenance every species of Vice, I - morality and Profaneness. Neither to use any sort of Gaming or unlawful diversions yourselves nor suffer it to be done within your knowledge without intimating your own dislike and the displeasure of the town thereat.

4ly. Whereas Hawkers, Pedlars and Petty Chapmen are continually strolling through the Country with Goods, Wares and Merchandise (much of which was undoubtedly forwarded by the enemies of America) in order to vend the same to the great hurt and decay of trade and in defiance of a good and wholesome law of this Government—You are therefore not knowingly to harbor, conceal or entertain any one of them, nor purchase any of their wares, nor permit any within your knowledge to do it, and in case any Taverner, Innholder, or Retailel within this town, after being duly informed thereof, shall be knowingly guilty of either of the acts in this instruction mentioned—You are to take every legal measures to prevent their ever hereafter being licensed by the Court of Sessions either as Taverners or Retailers.

5ly. Notwithstanding any persons may be so daring and hardy as to counteract the sense of the town expressed in these instructions, you are by no means to suffer any insult or abuse to be offered to either their persons or estates, but use your utmost endeavor to prevent the same.

6ly. Of all breaches of these instructions you are as soon as may be to inform your neighbors and the Selectmen of the town that whenever it may be necessary the town may be convened in order to consult and advise thereon.

July 13, 1776. Voted that forty two shillings be given by the town to each of the soldiers entisted and that shall enlist since the 11th inst. and proceed in the present expedition to Canada, not exceeding fifteen or sixteen men, and that the Selectmen hire the money (and pay the same) in the best manner they can immediately on the town's account.

May 5, 1777. Voted that Col. Otis Baker, Capt. Thomas Young and Capt. John Hayes be empowered to enlist what men is wanted to make this town's quota of men for completing the Battalions to be raised in this State, on the best terms they can.

Voted that the Selectmen furnish the Committee with money to hire said men and raise the same in the next tax bill.

May 15, 1777. Voted that the Alarm and Train Band Lists have three shillings a day and one shilling and sixpence a half day allowed them by the town for each day they train in a year more than the law requires.

Sept. 10, 1777. It was "voted that thirty dollars be given to each soldier who enlists for the Continental Service until the last of November next, and that the Selectmen pay each soldier the said sum when mustered."

March 30' 1778. It was voted that a committee of two persons be chosen to inquire into the state of our quota of Continental troops, and if we are found lacking to take the most effectual measures for filling up the same.

June 15, 1778. It was voted that Mr. John Bm. Hanson, Col. Joshua Wingate and Maj, Caleb Hodgdon be a committee to hire six men as soldiers to go to Rhode Island to reinforce General Sullivan's Division.

May 10, 1779. It was voted that the Selectmen advance the Continental and State bounty agreeable to a request of the Committee of Safety if they have it in stock, and if not the Selectmen are empowered to hire money for said purpose.

July 5, 1779. It was voted that the Selectmen advance the Continental bounty being £60 and State bounty of £30 and travel for five men, and if they have it not in hand that they hire the same and have power to raise it in the next year's tax.

Voted that a committee be chosen to hire eight men for the Continental Army one year and five men for the service of Rhode Island six months.

Aug. 30, 1779. It was voted that a hundred dollars a month be given nine men to serve as soldiers at Portsmouth, &c., including what the State is to pay them.

June 26, 1780. It was voted that the Selectmen be a committee for the purpose of getting eight men for the Continental Service on the best terms they can.

July 4, 1780. It was voted that the Selectmen with the two Captains of the Companies in Dover be a committee to get our quota of militia men for the Continental Service.

January 22, 1781. It was voted that Mr. Andrew Torr, Capt. John Gage, and Maj. Benja Titcomb be a committee to get the proportion of men wanting from this town to fill up and complete the Continental Army in the cheapest and most expeditious manner possible.

March 5, 1781. It was voted that each Recruit from this town as their quota of men completing the Continental Army have and receive as wages fourteen bushels of Indian Corn per month during their stay in service and that the Selectmen give their security as payment of the same accordingly.

July 16, 1781. On the petition of Capt Thomas Young and Capt. James Calef, stating that they had been "ordered by Col. Stephen Evans without loss of time to enlist or draft fourteen able bodied effective men to serve three months if not sooner discharged, wherever the Commander in Chief shall order as soldiers, it was voted that Capt. Young and Capt Calef be a committee to raise the 14 men required and that they give 30 shillings silver money to each man that enlists, which they shall have whether called on to go into service or not and when they march each man shall receive thirty shillings more like money.

Sept 19, 1781. At a town meeting held for raising soldiers, it was voted that nine men now to be raised for three months be given ten silver dollars each as bounty and paid 14 bushels of merchantable Indian corn per month by the town in Jan. 1782.

After this date we find no record of any further proceedings in relation the war.

OLD SERIES,. NO 163, SEPT. 18, 1858.

The following letter was written by Rev. Hanserd Knollys in 1690, he being then over ninety years old, to a church in London, of which he died the pastor. We have copied it from a rare work containing the autobiography of Mr. Knolleys, believing that it will be of interest to the members of the First Church in this town, of which Hanserd Koollys, a good, earnest' noble hearted man, was the first pastor. Under him the First Church was organized in December 1638 he left the place in the last of the Spring or early part of summer in 1641; was in Long Island in September and reached England 24 Dec. 1641; he was a prominent Baptist there, being still honored by that denomination then, and died revered for ability, learning and piety, 19 Sept. 1691.

MR. KNOLLYS S LAST LEGACY TO THE CHURCH.

Written a little before his death.

To the Church whereof I am Pastor, Grace, Love and Peace, by Jesus Christ our Lord and Savior, Amen.

Holy Bretheren, partakers of the heavenly calling' I not being able to preach any more unto you, do take liberty by writing to give you this as my last counsel; and I hope the whole church will seriously consider what I have written, as the last words of your aged Pastor, whose departure, as I hope, is at hand.

First of all, I do humbly beseech my reverend and beloved brother Steed, for Christ's sake, that the fervent love to the church, and the watchful care over the particular members of it, expressed and published in his little epistle touching singing, may be revived; and also that the brotherly love of the ministering bretheren and likewise of all my beloved bretheren who are helps in government, may be stirred up to help, to assist, to provoke the rest unto good works. Gal. iv. 18.

Now I do unfeignedly, and without vain boasting, commend many of you my beloved brethren and sisters, for continuing in the Apstle's doctrine and fellowship, in breaking of bread, and in prayer.(but as for the rest, who forsake the assembling of themselves with the church on the Lord's day, I commend them not,)especially not only in this time of liberty, but when it was a time of violent persecution, when I was shut up a year and four months, (blessed be God for prison mercies,) in New Prison and having mentioned that time of persecution, can I pass it withou commending the constant assembling of our brethren, and sisters all that time, every Lord's day to worship God? And may I not with great comfort, commend the labour of love of our ministering bretheren in the work and doctine of the gospel, without ceasing, (as you well know,) and among whom they still labor and faint not? And now some of our younger brethren begin to improve their gifts and talents for the glory of God,and the edification of the Church, whom I desire may be encouraged. Another thing very commendable in this church is, the charity which they have added to their brotherly kindness. 2 Pet. 1. 7. It was great brotherly kindness which was manifested at the church. by those brethern who looked out our Meeting House; and prepared it f r us as it now is; and unto this, many of our brethren and sisters have added their charity, in a free and very liberal collection and contribution, given into the Trustees of the fund; and I hope they will be ready to do the like again, when the like necessities call for it. Read I pray you the eighth and ninth chapters of the second epistle unto the church of Corinth; all this and much more are the riches of grace, which God hath freely given by our Lord Jesus Christ unto this Church, for his own glory. Nevertheless, I must in love and faithfulness to your precious and gracious souls, holy and beloved, tell you of some things not to shame you, (for I myself also found guilty as well as you, and more than some of you,) but to warn you and to counsel you, as a father doth his children; and they are these. First, that several of us are fallen in some degree from our first love, cooled in our spiritual affections to Jesus Christ and the saints. Must not you and I confess that it is not with us now as it was in the day of our first espousal? God the Father, the Word and the Holy Spirit remember it, Jerem. II. 1, 2; and we should remember from whence we are fallen, and should say, "I will go and return to my first husband, for then was it better with me than now," Hos. II. 7: Rev. II. 4, 5, Now the first part of my counsel, which I desire to take and receive from Christ and give unto you, my dearly beloved brethern and sisters, who are convinced, and have confessed it before the Lord on several days of fasting and prayer, is this:—First I do counsel you to repent, Rev. II. 5: and I must tell you, beloved, that our assembling once in four weeks, and sounding four hours, from eleven to three, in prayer and preaching as we have often done, is not such a fast that will make our voice be heard on high, Isai. LVIII. 3, 4. Several things are essentially necessary to evangelical repentance that it may be acceptable unto God by Jesus Christ, namely godly sorrow, which worketh repentance never to be repented of, 2 Cor. VII. 9, 10. A broken, contrite spirit. Read the Scriptures, "The sacrifices of God are a broken spirit; a broken and a contrite heart, O God, thou wilt not despise.") Psal. II. 17, Be afflicted and mourn, and weep; let your laughter be turned to mourning, and your joy to heaviness. Humble yourselves in the sight of the Lord, and he shall lift you up." James IV. 9, 10. "But to this man will I look, even to him that is poor, and of a contrite spirit, and trembleth at my word," Isai. LXVI- 2. "For thus saith the high and lofty One that inhabiteth eternity, whose name is Holy, I dwell in the high and holy place; with him also that is of a contrite and humble spirit, to revive the spirit of the humble, and to revive the heart of the contrite ones," Isai. LVII. 15. And I will pour upon the house of David, and upon the inhabitants of Jerusalem, the spirit of grace and of supplications, and they shall look upon me whom they have pierced' and they shall mourn for him, as one mourneth for his only son, and shall be in bitterness for him, as one that is in bitterness for his first-born. In that day shall there be a great mourning in Jerusalem, as the mourning of Hadadrimmon in the valley of Myiddou, Zech. XII. 10, 11. Alas, where are our tears of godly sorrow, our broken hearts and our afflicted souls? Reformation after humiliation! "Repent and do the first works," Rev. II. 6. O holy brethren, let us do so, let you and I beg grace that we may both mourn and turn from all our sins to the Lord, with all our hearts We have cause to repent of our formality and Laodicean lukewarmness, especially for want of zeal for the house of God, Psal. LXIX. 9, " For the zeal of thine house hath eaten me up." "As many as I love I rebuke and chasten; be zealous therefore and repent," Rev. III. 19: John II. 17. Secondly, I counsel you to be zealous; zeal is a fervent and constant affection of a gracious soul in a good thing, managed with discretion, Gal. IV. 18. If our zeal be not fixed upon a right object, and good matter, it may be hot and great, but it cannot be too good. Compare the zeal of Paul,

Phill. III. 6; with the zeal of Epaphras, Col. IV. 12, 13. To guide our zeal aright, two things especially ought to accompany it. First, the light of knowledge: "Brethren, my heart's desire and prayer to God for Israel, that they might be saved. For I bear them record, that they have a zeal of God, but not according to knowledge. For they being ignorant of God's righteouness, and going about to establish their own righteousness, have not submitted themselves unto the righteousnes of God." Read the words again and again, and as often as you read this paper. Many professors of the law then were very zealous of establishing their own legal righteousness and not Christ's. Oh! say some, if I could pray so, mourn so as others do; if I were so holy and so humble, &c., then I would believe. Oh! say others, if I could get power over my corruptions and strength against satan's temptions and victory over the allurements of this present evil world, then I would believe but I have a heart so full of vile affections, vain thoughts, and doubts that I cannot believe. Consider, are praying, mourning, humbling our souls, gospel duties?

Even so is believing a gospel duty, which God commands; "And this is his commandment, that we should believe in the name of his Son Jesus Christ," 1 John III. 23; and he threatens to damn those that hear the gospel preached and will not believe, Mark XVI. 16. Secondly, the aim and end of our zeal must always be the glory of God, and guided as I said by discretion, wise as well as warm; greatest zeal in greatest matters, and lesser zeal in lesser matters. Compare, Gal. V 11, 13; with 1 Cor. XI 13, 16; and Prov. XIX 11. My counsel also is, and I humbly beseech our honored and beloved Elder, and entreat our ministering brethren who are helps in government, to join together to set in order these things. I mean no other things than those holy administrations which Christ, his Apostles and Disciples practised in the beginning. Search the Scriptures, 1 Pet. II 21; Phil. III. 17; Luke XIV 16, 22; Acts XXVIII 23, 24, 28, 31,; 1 Co. XIV 13, 23, 24, 24, 29; 1 Tim. IV 13; Col. IV 16; 1 Thes. V 27; Rev. I 3 Consider, holy brethren, that as reading and expounding are two different administrations, so are prophesying and preaching, yet both gospel ordinances, Rom. XII 6, 7. Fourthly, and lastly, my counsel to the church is, that you will look out a minister of Jesus Christ, whom he hath in some competant measure qualified with such minister ial gifts and graces, as may make him worthy of so great honor as is due to a Pastor, and Elder of the Church of God; yea, of double honour, 1 Tim. V 17; both of maintainence and obedience, Heb. XIII 17. And now my dearly beloved, brethren and sisters, I commit you all to the word of his grace, which is able to build you up, and to give you an inheritance among them which are sanctified. So I remain, while in this tabernacle,

Your brother in the Lord,
HANSERD KNOLLYS.

OLD SERIES, NO. 172.

HANSERD KNOLLYS' LAST CHURCH

His first church was in Humberstone, England, to which he was appointed by the Bishop of Lincoln, in 1629, or thereabouts. His second was our First church of Dover, which was organized under his care in Dec. 1638. His third (for we do not think he was settled between) was at Broken Wharf, Thames Street, London, which Jones' "Bunhill Memorials" says was founded in 1664; and there he died.

He was an active man especially as to preaching When settled at Humberstone, he often preached four times on the Sabbath, viz. 7 a. m. at Holt n, 9 a. m. at Humberstone, 11 a. m. at Scartho, and at 3 p. m. again at Humberstone. After returning to England, he preached in parish churches till forbidden; then set up meetings as fast as the authorities stopped them; preached at a distance as in Suffolk, Rotterdam and other places, when he could not stay at home; not allowed churches, he preached in grave-yards; keeping school for a living he preached Sundays; connected with the army he preached to the soldiers; put in Jail he preached to the prisoners; so we can believe what one writer says of him, that he "continued in his work as long as he had strength to perform it; often entering the pulpit when he could scarcely stand and his voice so low as hardly to be heard, but such an effection had he for the work, that he was unwilling to leave it." It is said on apparantly good authority, that he was admitted to converse with Charles I, when that monarch was under sentence of death. He died 19 Sept., 1691, aged 92, a d was buried in Bunhill Fields.

To the church of which Knollys died the pastor succeeded Robert Steed. John Skepp, the latters successor, says to this church, "your foundation, as to gospel order, was skilfully laid in the very beginning of troublesome times, by the indefatigable pains and care of that eminent servant of, and sufferer for, Christ, Mr. Hanserd Knolleys, and your walls were beautified by the labors of that evangelical son of consolation, Mr. Robert Steed." But of Mr. Steed we are unable to find any other account.

He was succeeded by John Skepp. This minister born in 1676, was in early life a member of the Independent church at Cambridge, but became a Baptist, a d before 1715' was chosen pastor of this church, (then called "Currier's Hall Cripple gate.") Though not educated at college, he was a good scholar, especially skilled in Hebrew and Rabinnical lore. When the famous Dr, Gill was ordained, Mr. Skepp preached the sermon, and his library passed after his death, to the Dr. who made use of it in his voluminous writings. Mr. Skepp died 1 Dec. 1721, and was buried in Bunhill Fields. Dr. Gill says of him (in a preface to the second and posthumous edition of the only work Mr. Skepp published, viz. "Divine Energy, &c.") "the worthy author was personally and intimately known by me, and his memory is precious to me. He was a man of singular habits and abilities of very quick, strong, natural parts, of great diligence and industry in acquiring useful knowledge, a warm and lively preacher of the gospel, a zealous defender of the peculiar doctrines of it."

He was succeeded by William Morton, of who we know nothing.

In 1730, John Brine succeeded. Born at Kettering in 1702, he was for a few years minister at Coventry, before he succeeded Mr. Morton. He was a leading man in his denomination and published numerous works. He died 21 of Feb. 1765, and was buried at Bunhill Fi lds.

John Reynolds succeeded him. He was born 5 Jan. 1730, in the parish of Farmington, near North Leech, Gloucestershire, was ordained pastor of this church in October, 1776 and died after a faithful ministry, 5 of Feb. 1792. He received, in 1770, the degree of M. A. from the University of R. I. His grave is in Bunhill Fields.

Whether a pastor was immediately settled we cannot ascertain. But we think not. It removed in 1779 to Redcross street. Its numbers became reduced, and was well nigh extinct, when in 1808, another society joined it, coming from Chapel street, Mile End, and bringing with them their minister, Jonathan Franklin, who labored faithfully until his death in 1833. He too, sleeps n Bunhill Fields.

What is the present condition of this ancient church, we have no means of knowing. We hope it is flourishing for the sake of Hanserd Knollys' memory.

OLD SERIES, NO. 306.

TOWN RECORDS.

Pages 22 to 30 are filled with land grants. Page 31 has the following.
the 14: 11: 56.
It is ordered that william Pomfret shall haue eight pounds for his serues for the Towne for the time past to this daye. . . yeir.
By the Selectmen 5: 10 mo. (52.
Ordered that william ffurber shall be the steward of the Towne for this yeare till the last of October next to receive all such Rents as is due to the said Towne; in case that any refuse to pay him upon demand that hee hath hereby full power to take all such sunm by Distress, & to be accountaale for what hee shall receiue when the Townsmen shall call him thereunto; The dayes of all Rents to be paid is the last of March & the last of September' & likewise the stewart of the yeare hath such power to giue discharges for all such summes as he shall Receive.
By the Selectmen 5: 10 m (52.
It is ordered that the Clarke of the Towne shall not give any Coppy of any sawmill Grant without a note from the stewart of the Towne, & that the steward shall take pay for what charges is laid out in diuiding of the Grants of the Mills, which is three pounds p Mill, before hee giueth a note to the Clarke.
Pages 32 to 35 are filled with land grants.
Page 36 has this:
5, 10 mo. 1652. Ordered that the Inhabitants of Douer Necke shall haue the land that lyeth wast on the west side of the necke to make them a calves Pasture from the Lott of John Hall & Philip Lewis to the water side, to be ferced in by the Inhabitants.
Page 27 has this:
5, 10th mo. 1653. Ordered that the Inhabitants of the Necke of Land of Dover shall have all the necke of Land below the Towne which is called the Swampe, and so to Hilton's Point to make an Ox Pasture.
Page 38 has:
By the Selectmen the 5: 10 mo. 52.
It is ordered that all Grants' that hath formerly bi granted to any Person or Persons for the accommodations of saw Mills, or what shall hereafter be granted or made to any of the same nature, that all the Inhabitants shall haue free Liberty & Priuileadge to fall Timber f r Staues & Boults & for cannowe Trees & likewise Timber to saw by hand, Liberty to fall Timber also for buildinge fenceinge & firewood in any of the aforesaid Grants without any Molestation of any that it may concerne. Provided that no Inhabitant shall fall aboue flue T pipe staus Boults or Sawinge by hand at one time till they be wrought up, & in case they fall above flue at once, to pay for euery defect tenn shillings upon euery Tree.
It is ordered that whereas there are seuerall oiders about the Grants of tenn Trees to perticular men both of mast Trees & Clapboard Trees & Pipestaue Trees, that all such orders & Grants are made voyd & of none effect, and likewise that all the Inhabitants are to attend the Order made about Trees the 5: 10 mo. 52.
Ordered that all such masts as shall be cutt by any of such as shall be interested in Saw Mill Grants shall pay tenn shillings p mast f r the use of the Towne, for all such Masts as they shall cutt in their Limits Prouided the be aboue twenty foure Inches through, except the Masst granted & s uld to Mr. Walderne formerly
Page 39 has this:
At a Publique Towne meetinge this 15 of the 2nd month 1655, it is agreed upon as f lloweth:

first It is agreed upon concerning the setlinge of comfortable maintenance for the ministry of Douer and Oyster Riuer, yt all the Rents of the sawmills shall be sett aparte into a Towne stocke, wth two pence upon the pound to be rated upon the estates of all the Inhabitants, and all such estates so appointed are to be put into the hands of any that are to be chosen Treasurers by the said Towne to receive the same wch summ, that hath respect to the Rate, is to be paid in money, Beaver, Beife, Parke, wheat Pease, Mault, Butter, cheese, in one or any of these; this order to take place the 25th of June next, & to continue one whole yeare; one quarter part of the rate to be paid by the 25th of July next, & the rest to bee paid in October next; The Tresurers chosen are Captaine Walderne william ffollett, who are hereby invested with power from the said Towne, not onely to receiue the rents and Rates, but likewise to straine upon the estate of any that shall be delinquent, & for the rents already due, you have at present the like pow r, & for all such estates, as you receiue into your hands; you are to improue the same the best you can, for the ends intended & likewise to give accompt to the selectmen, when they shall require it, & also to attend to the Order for the payments of any ingagements yt concerne the said Towne otherwise; & also they haue power to giue the warrant to the constable to straine, where need require.

Mr. Val Hill his acco: 16, 1 56-57 for Debts yes Charges.

	£	s	d
for hir selfe, 7 times 21 weikes to the General Cort.	21	00	00
for his Charges in goeing to and againe 2 times in the spring,	6	00	00
for 6 ties at the fall	4	10	00
for his 7 voyges	7	00	00
for his horse Charges at the spring		14	00
for his horse Charges at the fall	1	04	06
for his Charges in going three times about or flecher	3	00	00
for Charges about him and his bringeing	2	00	00
far extreordenarey Charges in Expense in Boston yehole time	4	00	00
for charges in Raesin ye mieting hous at oyster Riuer		2	00
for mens hier for underpeining tne meeting house	10	05	00

NUMBER 308.

TOWN RECORDS: OLDEST BOOK,
Page 40 has:

At a towne meiting holden the 6th of the 8 mo,(56.

Voted the former Acktes of the towne Cnserning the maintainance of the ministrey is ferder Confermed and continewed.

At the same towne meiting william fferber Chosen in william fooletts Room Inhaitant this Day Being ye 16th of July 1990

(Page 79 is land Grants.)
(Page 80)

At A meiting of ye freemen the 29th 1: 61.

Capt Waldern Chosen Debary for this yeir for ye Generall Court hose order ar as followeth.

1 ly. th t he shall not ackt nothing that may tend to the infringement of ye towne but shall stand to maintayne the same with all the immunities thear to belonging.

2 ly. Thet he shall Iedeuer ye the Charge wich was imposed npon yt towne of D uer by ye generall Courtt by menes of Capt Pendl ton about a non rescient man thet was taken up frosen with in the County of York may be taken of.

3 ly yt he shell acording to his discrishon as he shell see Case prefer and anega petesh m or Petitions in ye behalf of ye town of Douer.

(iage 81)

At apublek towne meiting holden the 31; 5, 61. (no further record)

At A Publick Towne meiting holden in the yeir 1646. Ordred thet ho esoeuer of our Inhabetants shall haue A

lott Grannted unt/ him and doeth not Buelld on it or fencel it In with In six uonthes shell forfeitt the same againe the T wne.
(In the margin is) See old book paGes 45. (This "old book" is unknown during the last hundred years at least."

NUMBER 309.
TOWN RECORDS: OLD BOOK

Page 49:
30: 1: 55 At a towne mettin g holden the 30th of the first moenth voeted that th ar shall be a house at oyster R Billd meier the meting house f r the use of the menester the the demensions as followeth that is to say 36 feet long 18 fooett Broed 15 fo et in the wall with too chemneys and to be s utabley feneshed

At A Publick towne mieting h lden the 27th 4 mo 57 Ord r d that the Selecktn en that ar to be chos n to order the Afaire of the towne theay shall be chosen the first second day f the s cond moenth yerly and tkat theay and All oeth r offecers shall Bri g in and Give up thear acompts to the T wne on such as shall Be Chosen uppon the same day to Report them to the towne.

Ye 17: 4 57. At the sa e day mr flecher and the towne haueing had som discorse when he wold leaue them, he willingly manefosted that he was not mind d to stay any l nger but to Prepaer him selfe for old Eingland and Cold not Justly lay Aney Blame Apon the Towne.

17: 4 57. will ffurber Petter Coffin to Procu r An Arties to B und Towneshep aud to take what men they shall thinke flett (Added in a later ink) this is nud the 11: 10 mo 58.

17 :4 57. John Woodman James Grant Ezsepte in to the towne as tInhabetants. Pae 45.

At A Public towne meting h lden the 30th of the first moehth 57.

It is ordred that the debetey that shall be Chosen for to goe to the generall Cortt shall haue theirty shillings for his goeing taud Coming and his diet borne by the towne all the time -of his attebance at he generall C rt and 2s 6d p day all the time of his atendance at the Cort and this to stand tell the towne see ferder case to allter it.

At sam time Joseph f Astin and william willyames Chosen Constabells for Douer.

at the sam time Capt wallden mr Vallintin Hill Chosen Debetys for Douer.

At the sam ti e will Pomfrett Chosen to be Clarke of the writes and likewise nomenated to be Recorded of the Certt.

At tne same towne meting Ordred that John Hall decon Tho footn an Petter Coffin haue power to Call the t wnsmen belonging to the towne to acompt for all Compts belonging to towne for the time past and to stand tell new be Chosen and that theay shall Publickely declaer them to the inhabetants at a Publick town meeting.

Ae the same town meeting.

tewnsmen Chosen Mr Vall Hill Elder wenford Cpt Hall will fferbur.

will Storey Chosen Co esheoner.

at the sam tim Capt Wallden mr Hill will Pomfrett Coutenewed Comesheners for small Cases.

17: 4 57. Ordred that if Aney of our Inhabetants shall fall aney Pine Trees for mastes Apcn the Co a es of this towuesh shall paye for Euery maste from 24 Inches to 36: 10,s ahd from 14 to 18: 6s' and from 18 to 24: 8s.

Page 46.
The Proposetions of r Raner in hes writing Bearing date the 18th of the 4th mo 1657 Conser ing his yearly Alowancd from the towne is granted and Exsepted upp n the farmes th arin hee haeth Expressed himselfe. voeted at a Publick towne meiting the last ot August 1657,

voted this last of August 1657 that all tradesmen shall be fr e from paying Rates for thear trades for this Raete owe past.

At A Publicke towne meiting hilled the last of August (1656)Charles Bnckher Chosen by voet A Schoellmaster for this towne.

At A Pu lick towne wetting holden

the 9: 9 57.

Ordred that all Grants of land formerly made shall Be Confermed Ether by the Selleckt men or such as the Towne shall depute to do it soe f r foerth as theay Can be maed apeier By Coeppies ore Euedence moerouer wherea The Mowne is Debared from making Grants of land: It is now we ordred that the felecktmen ro such as the Towne shall depute shall haue power to Graut land Acording as occesion hall Requier the last of narch (A later entry continues) at a metiug ye 21 th 10 mo 57 the time afermenshented conferning is delayed tell ye 21 of June 58.

At the same time (9, 9,1657) the selleckt men Chosen to Oonferme the Grants hoe are nowe in Being.

layers out of land at Oyster Riuer shusen ar Einsine John Daues Robert Bernan for Doue neck Coechechae Bl edy poynt Ar Chosen Elder wentwoerth Cpt Hall John Hall Decon.

21 I . 57 Aa a Publick meitinge Ordered that from henceforth All our Inhabitants shall haue A Respeckte to the order n ayd conserning falling of te ober which is that no n an shall fall ab ue flue tgees for Clab rd or Pipestaues befoer hee haeth (wrought?) up the flue trees and hoesouer shall soe d in Contreary to the former order shall be liabell to the Penealtie thear in spesefied and f r the moer streck ter obseruation of this order the towne haeth chosen Joseuhfe Astien for this part of the towneship and Thomes flootman for Oyster Ceiuer hoe ar Al wed one halfe of the fines of all such delinkquents as theay shall find and lik wise if aney other inhabetant shall inforre and prue it hee shall haue the like part of the fines

the selekt men thei ar nows in being haue pow r to grant land to the inhabetants ye 15: 1 m 57-58.

NUMBER 311.
TOWN RECORDS. OLD BOOK.
Page 54.
At a meitinge of the Selectmen ye 26: 2 mo 58.

It is greed upon that the Rate that was last made for the Cleeringe of the Towne debts shall goe forthwith to be leuied & ga h red in by the Constables, or whome the selectmen shall depute.

2ndly. that if in cas it doth aappeae ye orty pounds wch is to be paid for the agreemen wth the owners be made appear to belonge to the propriators of the Marshes, although it now be paid by the whole T wne, thet then the propriators of the Marshes shell pay the said forty pou ds back to the Towne.

3dly, that Wes the Selectmen do make Choyce of Leiftenant Hall, & Robert Burnam to put up a petition to the next Couete at Poachmouh for th ir Solution C ncerning Rateinge and Saw Mills, & other visible estates belonginge thereunto.

4thly. If any of the Inhabitants doe finde the marshes to be over Rated, they may reraire to the present selectmen, or any three of them, upon ju t Cause th y shall haue Relief, & likewise If it be found that any of our Inhabitants be not Rated according to their Real & visible estates, as they were at the makeige of the Rates, they are to be brought into the Rate now, and that the persons whome this Order Co cerneth shell appear at D uer at Leifenant Halls house upon ye 10th day of May at uine of the clock in the morninge.

At the same ti e granted unto Thomas Turn r & Willia n Hilton Liberty to gath r seaue ty Loade of rine knotts upon the Commons upon the Neck of Land beteweene Oyster & the Bache River provide i they co ne n t into any mans grants, & in consid-ration of the said Grant the foresaid Thomas and Willia u haue Ingaged then selves to pay unto Thomas Canny the summ of three pon ds t nn shillings between the date hereof & nine and twentyeth of September next.

At the sare time giuen Lieftnant Hall order to receiue the Rents of the Mills, & the Arrearages of Mists due to the Towne, & to pay where, the Towne is Indebted.

Page 57.

At a publick Towne Meitinge held the 10th of ye 11mo 58.

It is this day vo'ed that the Charges of the fitting up of the two Meetinge houses of Dour & Oyster shall be carried on Distinkley by tne Neighborhood, or Inhabitants of each place that is to say the Charges of Douer Meeti ge house by the Neighborhood of that, & the Charges of Oyster River Meetinge house by the Neighborhood of Oyster Riuer.

At the same ti e voted, that the former concerninge Runninge of the line at the head of our Townshipp, given by Order of our Towne to william ffurber, & Peter Coffin, nulled.

At the same time voted that Lieftenant Hall, Deacon Hall Robert Burnham shell Lay out forihwith the bounds of the Towne betweene Lampriell Riuer, & Nichewannicke Riuer as also the head Line at our utmost boundes.

Page 58

At a publicke Towne Meetinge held 10tn 11m 58.

It is ordered that Elder Nutter Lhomas Lay on John Dam sen; William Story, Lieftenant Hall to J yne wth them to Lay out & bound the twenty Acre Lotts ouer the Backe Riuer accordinge to the first grant (James Nute- Lott excepted).

At ye same time Thomas Lundall, Richard Hubbarde, Henery Browne, Patriarck Jameson, Edward Erwin, (it seems Erwin, but blotted), Walter Packson, James Murry, Thomas Dowty, James Air, James Middleton, all these Receuied Inhabitants the day aboue said.

At A meting of the Selecktmen the 10th 3mo 58 Ordered that all Comedeg that is being on Blo poynt sied not yet granted out shell be for Comenedg unto the inhabetantes and that noe grant shall be maed with out the Consent of the Inhabetantes thearof.

At A meitting of the Sellecktmen the 28th of the first mo 58-59 Ordered that Douer neckt Oyster Riuer Cocechauew haue the same lebeter for thear Comenedge as was granted to Blode poynt.

At a Publicke Town Meeting holden the 6:4:59.

Ordered that the Present Selleckt-men haue Power with the maiore Part of all our inhabetants in Euerie of our Respecktiue Places *to grant lands as thear (they) see fiett with the Consent of the majoer Part of our Inhabetants in Euerie of our seuerall Respecktiue places and ferder that the Present Sellecktmen haue Power to order all Prudentiall afaieres Conserning the Towene, and likwise the present selecktmen haue power to fenish the Townes house that mr Reaner liueth in according to Covenant and to sell the sayd house to mr Reaner or Aney other man as theay se cause.

Page 59.

Wee howse names ar under writen do Propounde this to your Consideration whether by a unanimus Consent we weaer legaly Chosen as formerly other townsmen wear befoer us and that all our legall ackts shall be Ratified and Conferme and that you loke at us as legall selecktmen for the Towne of Douer as being for the year 1658. This is voted by the maier part of the Towne to pas for acke. (No names were under-written.)

At A Towne meeting holden by the Publicke Inhabetance the 6:4:59. Voted that All the Inhabetance of this townshep of Douer that haue taken thear oeth of fidellity haue thear free voet in C(h)oies of thear Sellecktmen and all other offesers Consarning the Towne afaieres and that the former Ackt of the Sellecktmen made the 17th 4th mo in poynt of time is nullefied and of noe Efeck.

At the same time selleckmen Chosen left Ralphf Hall James nutt Richard Otes Robert Burnum Henry lankster, John Hall Deacon Chosen for Comeshner these are to stand for one hole year or untell new be Chosen. Elder nutter Chosen Moderator.

At the same time Ordred that the

Present selecktmen haue power to Receue the Towne Bookes from the Towne Clarke now in being and to sett unto them soe maney of inhabetants as theay shall see flett to vew the book and order such defeckts as theay shall mett to be done and to Giue a diachars under thear Hands to the sayd Towne Clark and likewise to deliuer the sayd Bokes to the new Towne Clark After he hath taken his oeth.

At the same time John Hall Deacon Chosen Town Clarke. (In a later ink is the rollowing:) this Cold not be don by reason the Courtt would not give the then Chosen Clark his oeth.

At the same time Job Clemant Chosee Constabelle John Bickford seiner.

Page 60.

At A Publeck Towne meeting holden the 6: 4: 59.

Ordred that whear as thear heath bein diuers and seuerall Grants of land maed by sererall of our inhabetants thet all these inhabetants wich haue Grants of land shell Bring them into the Present sellecktmen hoe haue power to Confer me them unto them wich Grants are to be Brought unto the selecktmen betweinn this present moenth and the 20th of the first moenth next inseuing.

(The remainder of this page is land grants.)

OLD SERIES NO 312

A publick Towne meiting holden the 13: 4 1660. Voted that the Present selecktmen haue Power from the Towne with Elder nutter Cpt. Hall Richard Otes to treet with Mr. Broughten and make a finall deternation of the defenc betwein the Towne and him Conserning the grant of the saman fsll.

Page 62.

At A Publick Townes Meitting holdeu the 11th of March 1666. Voted that whearas seuerall of our Grants made to our Inhabetants Run to them and theare heies and Assignes other Grants Run to such a pertickler parson. Nowe That All our Inhabetants mey haue and Injoye Proprieties Alike in and Euerry pertickler Grant maed unto them Wee order thet all grants thet Run to Anie Pertickeler parson his wrighte shell be as good as these thet Run to the u thear heires And Assignes.

(Pages 63 – 68 are all land grants.)

(Page 69.)

At A Publicke Towne meiting h ld en the 6: 4 59. Mr. Daued lesudecoes Ed line John Hance Humfrey Varney, these taken in to the Towne Inhabetants.

(Page 70 is land grants.)

At A Publicke Towne meting h l the 7th of the 9th no 59. the Iuhaberance of Oyster Riuer d denie to uius in a lest of thear Estaetes for the provetion Raett as formerly theay haue doen.

(Gift of dwelling house to Rev. Mr Reyner, with conditions was printed in N). 32 of these Memoranda.)

7: 9 59. At a publick Towne meiting sur uairs chosen for making and mending hiewayes belonging to the Towne of Douer henrey lankster John heared John Roberts william willyames siny h e haue Power Given them to Call and set to worke all the inhabetance Pers ns and oxen for the making and mending all the hiewayes belonging to the townshep of Douer as theay in thear wisdomes in thear seue all places shell se meitt for the Publick good to be Dou giueing unto

Eurey Parson six days warning to Provide themselfs for thet sarues, and if in Case anieshall Refuse or n ckleckt to Com after warning given him he shal pay to the Towne flue shilling for Eurey day that he doeth not Com and this to be taken by destres.

(Page 72.)

At A Publicke Towne meitting holden the 16: 1 mo 60.

voted thet the Townsmen should make destres Apon the Inhabetants of Oyster Riuer for the Rents and Reunews and Rates Dew to the towne since mr flecher went awaye and the Towne is to bear them out.

At A Publicke metting of the freemen holden the last of the first mo 60 Cant wallderre Chosen Debety for the Genarall Court for this yeare insuinge,

At A publick Town meitting holden the 16: 1,60.

Ordred that the present sell cktmen shall Giue Capt waldern our Present Debety His Instrucktions Conserving the afayers of the town to the Genarall Courtt.

At A meitting of the sellcktmen holden the 25: 3, 60 to giue our Debete orders or instrucktions Consarning th afaiers of the towne to the Genaral Courtt as followeth.

1 ly That you Indeuer to procuer us Cometione Courett as hie as Porchmoueth.

2 ly That you take Caer to Reuers the order thet Capt Penbellton haeth from the Generall Court Conserning the frosen (?)man.

3 ly That you wold stand to maintayne our Preueleges Consaruing Melleterria afayers thet we may not be Drawne out of our County of Douer an Porchmoueth acording to our first agre ment.

4 ly That you wold desier the solution of the Generall Court Conserning the Chayse of Towne offesers Whet or noe all that haue takeu the oeth or fideillity haue liberty to Choese.

5 ly That you wold stand to maintayne our Preuelledges by vartu o ou Artickells of a Grement and to bring the Proseidings of the Court thet Consarnes us in writing.

By the selleckt men the 5th 10th mo 59.

Ordered that the Plase Called huckell berey Hill was layd out for a shep Pastuer all thet sayd shep Pastuer is ordred for A Publicke training Plase for the Towneshep of Douer.

At A meting of the selleckt men the 15th 3mo 60.

Acompted with Capt walderne for all Rents and Rates to this day for him self and Companie and thar Rest dew o him tweinty six pounds fiue shillings three pense as doe apereth by the per_tickler Acompt except the tho Rates deue in 59.

(On the same page is a receipt from Mr. Reyner, 12, 4 mo. 1666, printed in No. 32 of these Memoraudа.)

(Page 74.)

At A Publick Towne metting holden the 13th f the 4 mo 1660. Voted tha for time to Com in the Chois of Prudential men thear shell be too Chosen upon the neck of land and one iu Eurey Respective place of the towne.

At A Towne Meiting holden the 13: 4. 60. Prudentiall n ea Chosen Elder went ord Petter Coffin Deacon Hall Wils liam Beard Roberd Burnum. These ar to stand for one hole yier or untell new be Chosen.

We the Inhabetants of Oyster Riuer Doe Protest Against the Ackt maed the 13th, 4, 60 at Douer of being Confined to Chouse too Townsmen on the neck of Douer and soe in Euery Respecktive place of the Towne one we hoe protest haue set our hands.

Roberd Burnum   Tho Steuson
John Daues   Will Beard
John Godder   Edward Patterson
John Martin   Will Willyames
John Bickford   Phelep Chesley
Richard Yorke   Thomas Johnson,
William Roberds

Isaac Stokes, John Wengett, receiued inhabetants the same day (13, 4 mo. 1660.)

The same day Elder Nutter will Por frett Richard Otes Chosen Come-h-

The same day Capt wallden mr Ell Chosen asoetiates for the Cortt.

(Page 75 is land grants.)

OLD SERIES NUMBER 315

The notes upon the Dover soldiers at Louisburg, 1745, we defer until some expected information is received.

(Pages 82 and 83 are land grants.)
(Page 84 contains agreement as to Oyster River, printed in No. 33 of these Memoranda.)
(Pages 85 to 94 are land grants.)
(Page 95.)

At A Publick Towne meitting holden the 28: 2, 64. Ordred thet Cpt Ralphs hall and John hall Deacon shell Lay out a hiegh aye from Lamprill Riuer fall to the waters side in the great bay haue according to order layd it out as followeth thet is to say from the fall aboue sayd to Goe as the old way goeth tell it Cometh to a great Roke with a tree groeing on the top thear of on the left hand of the old waye goeing from the said fall to John Godders neir to wich Roke are too trees marked with H thus betweine wich trees the way is to goo straite Downe to A letell freshett and over it strait to another and over it and soe betwixt two trees marked with H lik the former two trees and soe betwixt a letell swampe and the Rokey hill side thet lieth behind John Martins house and soe strait to the laen thet is batwixt John Godders fence and John martins fence of the Corn fillds that now lieth befoer thear doers or houses tell it cometh to the lower Corner of John martins fence next the foer menshened lean and thear to turne and goe as the old way goeth at the present to the usuall lauding plase tell John martin mak a way from the sayd Corner of his fence lower downe toward the water side then the way goeth att the Present. The way is to be fower poll wied all the way saueing betwen the too foer mentioned ferces and to be Conteneued thear soe wide as the Distance is betwixt the too foer mentioned fences John martin Is to make the way soe as shall be to the Towns Content belowe his feilld befoer it be Altered.

(Pages 96 to 105 areall grants.
(Page 106.)

At A Publick Towne mitteing holden the 50th may 1671 whearas the Towne gaue and granted to old mr Rayner the house he leued in with the Apertenances thear unto longing as by the Orde

Bearing date 7, 9, 1659, for ferder Explanation of the aforesayd order in Reference to the Apertenanoesr thet the Acker of land whear the house standeth Apou and no more was giuen to him and his hieres foreuer as well as the house

At A Publick Towne meting holden the 29th may 1671.

Ordred thet the sellecktmenhaue full power to make a Rate for the 70 lb ordred to mr Rayner if the Townsmen and he do agree.

(Pages 107 to 147 are all land or bounds to individuals.)

(Page 148.)

Att a Proprietors metting held att the old metting houes on Douer Neck ye 16th Day of Aprill 1672.

Vouted thet the swamp According to the Graut giuen by the Sellecktmen in the year 52 to the Iuhabetance of Douer Neck shell be fenced in Generall for the use of the Propriaters that haue Right thearto and thet Euery Propriator shall haue Liberty to Putt in Creturs in Propotion to thear Rights.

att ye same metting votted thet the Calues Paster be all measurered ouer and those Persones thet haued fe ced in a grate Part of sd Laud shell hold there Prosestions Prouided thet they haue not fenced in more than they can show Rights for and if they haue they must turn it out again.

men chosen to mesuer the Land is Capt Thomas Tebbets Ltt Robert s Ltt Beard.

Test Thomas Tebbets Town Clerk
(.Page 149, land Grants.)
(Page 150)

The grant of Land for ye use of ye minestry att Oyster Rinuer which was granted by the selectmen of Douer ye 20th of September 1668 it Apeareth to bee Sixty Acres for the meeting house and burying place is layd out aud bounded for the End aboue said and Accordiug to ye order it Runes from ye water side next to Wiliam Williams sener his Lot and it Runs thear along the highway from the water side south west 324 Rods to a whit oak tree marked on both Sids aud from the tree it Rnues south east 35 Rods to A pitch Pine with 4 Rod alowed ye Leugth for a high way and from thet tree it Runs northeast to John Palles Lot and soe by it to the water side by the same point and wee haue alowed fowar Rod in the Length of it for A high way to go acros the lot this is the towne Lott only exsempting Joseph Fields marsh which is in som Part of the frout of it.

J hn Dauis
Robert Buruum
William Follet

(Page 151, land grants.)
(Page 152.)

Whearas thear was a former high way Rerarued and Laid out by the Lot Layers in the year 56 betweeu Decon John Halls Land and Henry Magouns Laudfrom the water Side up into the wood aud wee whose rames are und r Written by and at the Request of some of the Inhabetance of Douer which we are Impowered by Law to Lay out Publick and Priuet hIghwayes haue Layd out and Renewed the Bounds of th aboue said highway begining at th upper northwest Corner b und mark tree of John Halls Land and on a straight Cors Downe to the weter side Betwen the sd Hall rnd Henry Magouns Land have Layd it out fower Pole wide Joyning to sd Halls Land as witness our Land in the year 1721.

upper northwest Corner bound mark tree of John Halls Land and on a straight Cors Downe to the water side Betwen the sd Hall and Henry Magouns Land have Layd it out fower Pole wide Joyning to sd Halls Land as witness our hand in the year 1721.

    Joseph Robards } Selectmen.
    Timothy Roberson }

(Page 153 is blank.
(Pages 154, 155 156, 157,158, lands)
(Page 159.)

By virtu of an order of the Towne of Douer at a Publick Towne meeaing the 28 of May 1716 for the commite to day out a highway on the south side of Oyster Riuer freshet in answer to the petishon of the inhabitance their use the subscribers being called their for that sarvice haue Laid it out as followeth Viz: Beginning at the End of a highway f r_merly Laid out to Chesley's mill on the south side of sd River the way to be fooer Rods wide along the old way Leaving Moses Davis Junr his forty acre Lott on the south & Barthoma Steaveson his ten acre Lott on the north & so along the Comons Leuing Daniel Missavarue his Thirty acre Lott on the Northwest and so on the Comons Leuing Moses Dauis senr his fowr score acre Lott and Thomes Stephsons Three score acre Lott on the west and so on the comons to William folletts hundred acre Lott at Maharanuts March to two Trees maked H fower Rods Distance. This way Laid out by us the thurteenth Day of June 1719.

          James Davis·
          Thomas Tibbetts.

(Page 160—2, lands.)
(Page 163.)

      Dover, Aprill 4th 1753.

Then Recd of Moses Winget three Pounds in money old Tenor in full of all accounts Debts Dues Notes and Demands from the Begining of the world till the Day & year aforesaid as witness my hand.

          Tho: Varney-
£3: 0: old Telr
Witnes Ephm Hanson.
Brot to Record April 5th 1753. P Jos: Hanson Town Cler.

OLD SERIES NUMBER 316
(Page 164.)

The Deposition of Capt Robert Evens of Dover aged about eighty and eight years Testifieth and Saith thet he was one of the Committee to Lay out the towne of Rochester & he was then Informed by Colo John Davis a Committe man for the Town of R chester which was the bound marked tree for the head of Dover which tree was a pitchpine tree & now Stands three Rods due Southwest from the Lower side of the first cove on the southwesterly side of Salmon fall riuer thet is to say the Cove adjoyning to the upper most head of the Little falls aboue all the rifling water and likewise Stands fifteen Rods & three feet south Sixty Degrees west from a Large Round R ck at the head of said falls and refels and near about the middle of sd River and five Rods South thirty two Degrees East Distance from a Large white Burch markt and standing by said river, and further saith not.

Province of New Hampshire, Septemr 19th: 1753.

Then the above named Robert Evens appeared on the spot where (the) tree Mentioned in the above Deposition by him signed before us the Subscribers two of his Majesty's Justice of the peace for said Province unus Quoram in perpetuam Re memoriam.

Joseph Timpson·
Jos. Newmarch.

Record according to the origual.
Test Jos: Hanson, Town Cler.
(Pages 164—6.)

The Deposition (of) messrs Ebenezer Wentworth of Somersworth Samnel Courson of Rochester and James Guppy of Berwick all of Lawful age.

T·stifieth & saith thet the markt Dry pitch pine Standing three Rods due Southwest from the Lower side of a Certain Cove being the Cove next aqjacent to the uppermost of the Little falls so Calld and above the head of the Rifling of the water and fifteen Rods & three feet South Sixty Degrees west from a Large Round Rock near the middle of the Rivers at the head of said falls and Rifels and flue Rods Due South thirty two Degrees East from a large white Burch standing by said Rivers which Dry pitch piae we the Deponants have after seeu the Letters thereon and have known it to be the reputed Bounds of Dover head line at the South westerly side of said River for thirty years past and upwards and further saith not. Septemr: 19th, 1753. Witness our hands.

Ebenezr Wentworth
his
Sam: O Courson
mark
his
James X Guppy
mark

LikeWise Capt: Timothy Roberts of Rochester Deacon Gersm: Wentworth of Somersworth & Richard Hussey of Dover Testifie to the truth of whats above written tho all of them not tne same number of years & further saith not. Septemr 19th 1753, their hands.

Timo: Roberts
Ges: Wentworth
his
Richd R Hussey
mark

Isaac Hanson of Somersworth affirms to the truth of the above Deposition for a number of years witness his hand ye 19th Septemr 1753.

Isaac Hanson

The Deposition of Colo Timothy Gerrish Esqr or Kittery in the seventieth year of his age. Testifieth & saieth thet on or above thirty years last past from this Date he with some other Gentlemen of the Province of New Hampshire chosen to Run the head lines of the Town of Dover and they then began at Quomphegan and run up the Salmon falls river four miles to a certain pitch pine tree then there standing and from said tree run South forty two Degrees west to the best of their skill on a strait line to a tree called the Six miles tree being absut fifteen miles which line was then and there Received and accepted by the Province for the head bounds of the Town of Dover and the said Deponant has this Day been at the Renewel of the said Dover Bounds at Salmon falls river from the pitch pine tree which hath been this Day sworn to by a number of Evidances, and which he judges by what appeared to be the true bound tree & saith the true Course according to the best of his act & judgment is South forty two Degrees west to a tree called the Six miles tree which Course Leads through a vault in the Earth commonly known and called by the name of Hopper & is the true head bounds of the said Town of Dover and further Saith not from his hand this 19th Day of Septemr 1753.

    Timo Gerrish.

Province of New Hamp: Septemr- 19th 1753. Then the above named Ebenezer Wentworth Samuel Courson James Guppy Isaac Hanson & Timo Gerrish Esqr having been on the spot made oath to the truth of the above Depositions by them Respectively signed, taken in perpetuam Rei memoriam.

Coram Joseph Simpson } Jus: Peace
  Joseph Newmarch } unus Quorum
Recieved according to the original,

    Test Jos: Hanson Town Cler.

November ye 10th: 1753. Pursuant to the Power (given) us the subscribers by the votes of the Towns of Dover and Rochester Pursuant to thm. ee sae Wthe subscribers have preambulated the line between Dover and R chester as followeth thet is to say begining at a Dry pitch pine Standing at a place now known by the name of Mast point by Salmon falls river the said Dry pitch tree standing three Rods Due south west from the Lower side of a Certain Cove next adjacent to the uppermost head of the Little falls (so calld) and above the head ofs the Rifling of the water and fifteen Rodt and three feet South Sixty Degrs Wes-

from a Large Round Rock near the middle of the River at the head of said fall and Rifels and five Rods Due South Thirty two Degrees East from a Large white Burch standing by said River, which Dry pitch pine tree was proved by a Number of Evidances to be the original head bounds of Dover. We began at said tree and Run South about forty two Degrees west and spotted above the old spotted tree which was in the course, which Course Leads through a Vault in the Earth Commonly known and called by the name of the Hopper on the Westerly Side of Cochecho River to the Edge of the hill on the westerly side of the said Vault the line Ending between two pitch pine trees which is marked a number of Letters and the Date of the Year marked on said trees.

  Preambulated by us
    John Gage   ⎫
    John Tasker ⎬ Committee.
    Timo Roberts ⎪
    Isa Libby   ⎭

Recorded accorded (sic) according to the original.

    attest Jos: Hanson Towne Cler.

—With page 166 ends the records in this volume from page 1; but the volume was renewed, and the records continued at the other end, which we shall present.

OLD SERIES, NO. 317, APR. 25, 1878

DOVER OLD BOOK OF RECORDS.

The town clerk made each end of his book a beginning. He wrote on from the first page; likewise he turned the book over, and wrote on from that end, apparently mainly of matters not town action or land grants. We shall give these records.

The first is on a leaf badly torn and extremely hard to decipher. The record is a table of rents payable by the saw mill proprietors for timber, and should probably be dated in 1653. There was a great rush into improving the various falls on the river in 1652, corresponding with great increase in exporting lumber.

We give the lines in the shape of the record, except that we make a separate line of the amounts of money, and inserting dots in torn places, or placing in brackets words we know ought to be there. Ambrose Gibbons's "gran" mill was of course a grain mill.

nechewaneck Rent——Capt weggen and mr Bradstreet .... the foist of 10th July 1650 10lb p annum ye upper fall of Cocchechae Capt Wigin Edward Starbuck Rent begain the first Fey 51	10lb	0 0
Capt wallden Rent begin the 24th 50p annum	12	00 0
Joseph Asttine for his quarter part of the old mill	2	0 0
fresh creick began the first of march 53	6	0 0
Capt wallden grants ye second fall Cochechae ye first of march Joseph Astine grant lettell Johns	4	0 0
Creek & mark the first Ambrose gibins his gran mill	6	0 0
	4	0 0
Valentine Hill for his mill at oyster ......the first of mo 50	10	0 0
Elder Nutter his grant at ....Reuer	20	0 0
........his mast ye first	32 mast	
........er 20 mast		
........ster 20 mast		
........20 mast		

The next record appears, by subsequent conveyances from some of the parties, to assign lots in Cochecho Marsh; but where said Marsh was, we have never quite made up our opinion. The lottes w........
written ye 18 day........1648
1 Antony Emery, 12 yeckeres
2 blank
*3 for Mr Belley, 6 yeckeres
4 George wallton, 6 yeckeres
5 Ye church   12 yeckeres
6 blank
7 John Hall, 6 yeckeres
8 John Hard, 6 yeckeres
9 Henry Becke, 6 yeckeres
10 William Walldon, 6 yeckeres
11 Mr Nutter, 6 yeckeres   In later hand is written: This 11th lot is Exchanged with Edward Colcord for his 6 accer lote of marsh in the Great Bay
12 John newgrove, 6 yeckeres
13 Henery Lanstate, 6 yeckeres
14 John goddere, 6 yeckeres
15 James Newett, 6 yeckeres
16 Robert Hurkenes 6 yeckeres
17 aJmes Rallenes, 6 yeckeres
18 William Ferbusre, 16 yeckeres
19 Richard Walldone, 6 yeckeres
20 John Backer, 6 yeckeres

next joining to yes lottes yer is 10 yeckeres gieuing to John Backer & ye rest of ye marsh (?) given to Richard

349

Wallon by A towne metten & ....
all ye marsh (?) is defided
(signed) Hatevill Nutter
Richard Walden
John Becker
John Hall H his marke
John Goddar
Jmaes Newth

Raett maed ye (torn) of ye 10th mo
1650 for the (torn) ering. Publiek
Charges of the towne.

	£ s d
Thomas Roberds	Rated 1 00 6
Ralf Hall	Rated 1 2 6
Thomas Beard	Rated 00 13 0
A Emery his house & land	00 6 0
John Tuttell	Rated 00 19 4
William Storey	Rated 10 00 6
John Hall sinyey	Rated 1 4 6
Ellder Nutter	Rated 1 15 0
John Roberds	Rated 00 13 8
Antoney Nutter	Rated 00 14 6
James Newett	Rated 10 00 8
William ferber	Rated 1 14 0
Thomas Caney	Rated 1 7 6
Henry Tebbets	Rated 1 11 2
Isaek Naesh	Rated 00 10 0
Thomas Clayton	Rated 00 10 6
Risse Hoewell	Rated 00 00 0
John Dam	Rated 1 14 8
Thomas layton	Rated 2 12 5
William Pomfrett	Rated 1 2 2
Henrey lankster	Rated 1 3 4
Tnoer Trieckey	Rated 1 11 0
John Martin	Rated 00 17 0
John Hall Juner	Rated 00 12 6
John laues	Rated 00 14(torn)
Richard keateer	Rated 1o 5 4
James Raellines	Rated 00 17
William Wentwoerth	Raeed 1 2 2
Joseph Astien	Rated 1 17
Mr Riechard Wallden	Rated 3 2 (torn)
Abraham Raedfoerd	Rated 00 10 (torn)
Petter Coeffin	Raced 00 10
mr Vallentine Hill	Rated 2 2 0

William Beard	Rated 1 4 6
Phellep Cheslv	Rated 1 2 6
Thomas Jonson	Pated 00 14 0
John Hall	Rated 00 10 10
Ambroes Gibbeines	Rated 1 4 0
William Roberds	Rated 00 17 0
Thoes Steunson	Rated 00 16 02
Willam Drew	Rated *1 12 0
Mathew Gielles	Rated 2 00 28
Oleuer kentt	Rated 00 13 0
Charell Adames	Rated 1 00 1¼
mrs matheyes	Rated 10 00 00
James Bines	Rated 00 14 4
John Blckfoerd	Rated 1 17 4
Thomas Welley	Rated 1 13 0
John Allt	Rated 1 3 4
Gorge Webes Hous and land	Rated 00 3 4
Gorge Branson	Rated 00 10 0
Phellep Lewes	Rated 00 18 8
William follet	Rated 00 10 08
Thomas foewettman	Rated 00 12
Richard Yoerke	Rated 1 00
John Gooedard	Rated 1 00
John Hill	Rated 00 10 0
Goodie feilld	Rated 1 00 0q

61 12 1

OLD SERIES NUMBER 315
DOVER OLD BOOK OF RECORDS
The west sied of ye Back Reuer or ouer ye back Reuer.

A Record of the 20 Acker loetes as theay waer in Order Giuen and layd out to the inhabetance hoes names are here under menshened, with the nomber of the loet to each pertickler man: As it was found Recorded by William Wallden in a Pese of paper in the year (16)42 which lots ar in Breadth at the waterside 40 poell and in lenketh 80 Pole up in the woods.

Nam. Thomes Roberds	1
Richard Roggers	2
Henrey Tebbets	3
Mr larkham	4
Edward Colcord	5
George Webe	6
J hn Tuttle	7
William Storey	8
Barthey Smey	9
John Ugroue	10
John Dam	11
Wm Pompfrett	12

(In later hand) this 12th lott is exchauged wth deacon Dam for the Seuenteenth Lott

William Hilton Sin	13
("Sin" is in later hand.)	
Edward Starbuck	14
Samewell Haynes	15

(In later hand), this 15th lott was resined to John Hill and by him sold unto William Follett as was aknowledge

Robert Huggins	16
John C esse	17

(In later hand), this 17th Lott is exchange by Jno Dam wth Lt Pomfret ffor the 12th Lott

Tho layton	18
John Hall	19
Hatabell Nutter	20
Henrey Becke	21
John Westell	22
(Blank)	23
Richard Pinkom	24

At A Gennerall Courtt held in Boston the 8th of the 7 mo 1652

The Inhabitants of northam uppon their petitiou are Granted the Liberties which other townes haue and mr Samuel Dudley mr William Payne Mr Winslows mathew Boyse are to settle their lemytes this is a true Copey of the Courtt Order.

Edward Rason
Secretary.

Wee hose names are under writtens Being apoynted by the Gennerall Conrt to lay out the Bounds of Douer haue thu agreed

That the utmost Bound on the wese is a Creeke on tht East sied of Lamprill Reuiuer the next Creeke in ye Riuer and from the End of that Creeke to Lampril Riuer first fall and soe from the first fall on a west and by north line of six miles from Newchannick first fall one A north and see h line fower miles from a Creeke next Blowe Thomas Canne his house to A Cartaine Coue near the mouth of the Great Bay Called the hogstey Coue and all the marsh and meadowe Ground lyning and butting on the Great Bay with Couuenynte upland to sett thear hay

William Payne
Samen Winslow
Mathew Boyes

At A Gennerell Court held at Boston the 19th of october 1652 it is ordred that the northerne bounds of Dover shall extend from the first fall of newichewnicke Reeuer uppon a north and by west line fower miles

---

At a Generall Court held at Boston the 19 of october 1652 in answer to a petition from the Inhabitants of Exeter for A finall determination of the Case between Douer & Exeter Concerninge the bounds Aboute Lampril Riuer It is orderd that Mr William Paine Mr Samuell Winslow & Mr Matthew Boyse or the maior pts of them shall upon the place appointe & lay out the bounds betweene them & certifie this Courte & the two towns under ther hands what they shall determine this is A true Coppy of the Courte Order

     Edward Rauson Secret.

Wee whose names are underwretten beinge ordered by the generall Courte to settle the bounds betweene the townes of Douer and Exeter we haue thus determined and Agreed thet the line formerly laid out shall stand thay takeing the pointe from the middle of the bridge one the first fall one Lamprill Riuer and so and so to Runne Six miles west & by north butt the Land betweene the line & the Riuer shall belonge to Exeter thay nott haueinge Liberty to set t up any mills Excenting ther right specified one the first fall but the tembr betwixt the line & the Riuer shall belonge to Douer in snch time as they shall see meete to make use of the same to ther best advantage provided thet both the townes shall have free liberty to make use of the Riuer upon all Ocasions also Exeter hath liberty to make use of all the tembr halfe A mile betweene the line and Lamprill Riuer towards the bridge one mile betweene the line & the said riuer toward the second fall & further Mr Edward Hilton is to haue belonging to his mill all the timbr within Compass of one mile & A halfe square of it be to be had betwixt the line & the Riuer Lamprill this beinge our full determination the 19th of the first month 53,

    William Paine
    Samuell Winselow
    Matthew Boyse

Att A Generall courte held At Bosthorne the 19th of Octobr 52

Whereas upod the submission of the Inhabitants upon the riuer of Piscattaqua to this Jurisdiction this Courte did graunte them Amongst their priuilidges to send two Deputies from the said riuer & wheras the free men of Douer are Increased to that numbr thet by Another law they haue liberty to send two Deputies to this Courte; this Court e (do*)the Order & declare that the said towne of Douer shall henceforth Injoy thear liberty to send two Deputyes Accordinge to law & that Strawberrybanek shall haue liberty to send one According to f rmeir Agreement, And this is A true Coppy
     Edward Rauson

*Apparent omission

OLD SERIES NUMBER 319.

DOVER OLD BOOK OF RECORDS.

Dover The Towne Rate, Made the 19th : 10 mo (16)48

	£	s	d
Imprs George Smith:			
Rated at	0032	08	00
and to pay 4d P lb is	0000	10	09
George Webb Rated	46	00	00
and to pay 4d P lb is		12	08
John Goddard Rated	129	10	00
and t pay 4d P lb is	2	2	2
Tho: Layton Rated	156	10	00
and to pyy 4d P lb is	2	12	00
John damme Rated	104	10	00
and to pay 4d P lb is	1	14	10
George Walton Rated	84	00	00
and to pay 4d P lb is	1	7	4
William Pomfret Rated	71	00	00

	£	s	d		£	s	d
and to pay 4d P lb is	1	3	8	and to pay 4d P lb is	1	3	0
Richard Yorke Rated	72	8	00	Darby Feild Rated	81	0	0
and to pay 4d P lb is	1	4	00	and to pay 4d P lb is	1	7	0
Hatevill Nutter Rated	78	16	00	Oliver Kent Rated	70	10	0
and to pay 4d P lb is	1	6	3	and to pay 4d P lb is	1	00	10
William Storey Rated	66	4	00	Tho: Johnon Rated	40	00	00
and to pay 4d P lb is	1	2	1	and to pay 4d P lb is		13	4
Joseph Austin Rated	91	10	0	John Baker Rated	92	10	0
and to pay 4d P lb is	1	11	2	and to pay 3d P lb is	1	1o	1o
Tho: Canny Rated	84	0	0	Francis Ltttlefeild Rated	6o	15	o
and to pay 4d P lb is	1	8	0	and to pay 3d P lb is	1	o	3
Samuel Haines Rated	65	10	0	Rich: Walderne Rated	131	o	o
and to day 4d P lb	1	1	10	and to pay 3d P lb is	2	3	3
John Turc Rated	35	0	0	more to pay		3	3
and to pay 4d P lb is		1	8	Thomas Trickett Rated	1o3	1o	o
Jo: Hall Rated	79	12	0	and to pay 3d P lb is	1	8	3
and to pay 4d P lb is	1	6	8	Henry Longstaff Rated	175	0	0
William Furber Rated	81	10	(?)	and to pay 3d P lb is	1	5	0
and to pay 4d P lb is	1	7	2	Geo. Branson Rated	3o	o	o
He ry Tibbetts Rated	87	0	0	and to pry 3d P lb is	o	1o	o
and to pay 4d P lb is	2	9	2	Henry Beck Rated	40	16	o
John Tuttle Rated	69	0	0	and to pay 3d P lb ir		13	7
and to day 4d P lb is	1	3	0	John Hillton Rated	46	o	o
James Newte Rated	83	0	0	and to pay 3d P ld is		15	8
and to pay 4d P lb is	1	7	8	Willm. Roberts Rat d	46	1	o
Mr Roberts Rated	69	10	0	and to pay 3d P lb is		15	2
a d to pay 4d P lb is	1	3	2	Tho: Footman Rated	6o	0	0
Edw: Starbuck Rated	45	0	0	and to bay 3d P lb is	1	o	o
and to pay 4d P lbs		15	4	James Rawlins Rated	60	o	o
Ambrose Gibbons Rated	86	0	0	and to pay 3d P lb	1	o	o
and to pay 4d P lb is	1	8	0	Mr Seeleys house Rated	8	o	o
William Beard Rated	76	10	0	and to pay 3b P lb is		2	8
a d to pay 4d P lb is	1	5	6	Tho: Fursen Rated	16	o	o
Tho: Stephenson Rated	50	0	0	and to pay 3d P lb is		5	o
and to pay 4d P lb is		16	0	Francis Small Rated	1o	o	o
William Drue Rated	70	0	0	and to pay 3d P lb is		3	4
and to pay 4d P lb is	1	3	4	Jeff ry Raggs house	4	o	o
Matthew Gyles Rated	194	10	0	and to pay 3d P lb is		1	3
and to pay 4d P lb is	3	3	2	Thomsons point house	4	o	o
Mrs Matthews Rated	139	10	0	and to pap 3d P lb is		1	3
and to pay 4d P lb is	2	3	2	Robt: Hethersey Rated	6o	0	0
Jonas Binns Rated	42	0	0	and to pay 3d P lb is	1	o	o
and to pay 4d P lb is		14	0	Tho: Beard Rated	62	0	0
Charles Adams Rated	31	0	0	and to pay 3d P lb is	1	o	8
and to pay 4d P lb is	0	5	14	J hn Hall Rated	42	0	0
John Bickford Rated	115	10	0	and to pay 3d P lb is		14	o
and to pay 4d P lb is	1	18	6	John Martin Rated	41	1o	o
Philip Chaseley Rated	78	10	0	and to pay 3d P lb is		13	1o
and to pay 4d P lb is	1	6	6	Antho: Emery Rated	1o8	1o	o
Tho: Willey Rated	71	10	0	and to pay 3d P lb is	1	16	o
and to pay 4d P lb	1	3	6				
John Allt Rated	69	0	0				

353

more to pay for a bull $\begin{cases} 2\ 10\ 0 \\ 0\ 0\ 10 \end{cases}$

This Rate within specified Is to bee paid in such comodities, time and place as follweth, viz•

One fourth part in Corne, to bee pd, and brought in at the rates as followes rt: Ijdian Corne at 4s p bushell' wheat & pease at 5s p bushell, and to bee paid by the 10o day of the next mo at the house of Wm Pomfrett, & ye rest of thee rate to bee pd in by the 10o day of March next ensueing, At the saw pitt below Tho. Cannys for ohe place of receipt for part of the said rate, and ye other to be paid in at the back Coue, to the Cons able or his Assignes. All pipe staues are to bee delivred in at the rate of 3. 10. 0. and hhstaue at 02 05. 0. And for default of paymt in either or any of the s id paymts in pt or in all contrary to the forme aforesaid Wee doe hereby authorize and giue unto the Constable full powr to arrest & attach the goods of 'such pson or psons as shall make denyall. Witnes or hands this 19th day of ye 10o mo 48

    Ambrose Gibbons
    Hateuill Nutter
    William Pomfrett
    Antho Emerey
    Tho: Layton

(In the amounts given ciphers are always prefixd to pounds sufficiently to make four figures, shillings and pence two figures each)

OLD SERIES NUMBER 320.
DOVER OLD BOOK OF RECORDS.
 A Rate made the 8th of 10mo (16)39 for the Discharging the Corte Charges and Elde(r) Nickles hickmans Diaet and the charges within (?) for cloething and likewise for satisfieing mr Coelcoerd hio Exseqtion and other Charges wich the towne is Dpt.

	lb		
Imprimis mr George Smith *Rated	3o	0	0
and to pay 4d p lb	00	10	0
George Webb Rated	45	00	0
and to pay 4dp lb	00	13	
Mr Roberds Rated	66	0	0
and to pay 4d p lb	1	2	0
Thom Beard Rated	38	00	00
and to pay 4d p lb	00	12	8
Antoney Emrey his houes Rated	22	0	0
and to pay 4d p lp	00	7	8
Elder Starbuck Rated	55	1o	0
and to pay 4d p lb	00	16	1o
John Tutell Rated	52	1o	0
and to pay 4d p lb	00	1o	
John hill Rated	3o	0	0
and to pay4d p lb	00	1o	0
William Storey Rated	68	00	0
and to pay 4d p lb	01	2	8
Elder Nutter Rated	40	0	0
and to pay 4d p lb	00	13	4
James Newtt Rated	55	1o	0
and to pay 4d p lb	0c	16	1o
William ferber Rated	77	00	00
and to pay 4d p lb	1	5	8
Samewell Astin Rated	35	0	0
and to pay 4d p lb	00	15	0
Tho Camer Rated	82	00	0
and to pay 4d p lb	1	7	2
James Orderway Rated	55	1o	0
and to pay (blank) p lb	0	16	1o
Henry Teubtes Rated	92	4	0
and to pay 4d p lb	1	1o	0
Richard Yrke Rated	71	0	0
and to pay 4d p lb	1	3	8
John Dam Rated	12o	1o	0
and to pay 4d p lb	2	0	2

Name	£	s	d
Tho as layton Rated	155	0	0
and to pay 4d p lb	2	11	8
Mr Richard Walldern Rated	72	0	0
and to pay 4d p lb	1	4	0
leftenant Baker Rated	99	10	0
and to pay 4d p lb	1	10	0
Josef Asten Rated	87	0	0
and to pay 4d p lb	1	9	0
Mr Ambroes Gibbins Rated	104	10	0
and to pay 4d p lb	1	4	10
William Heard Rated	65	0	0
and to pay 4d p ld	1	1	8
Phelipe Chesley Rated	69	0	0
and to pay 4d p lb	1	3	0
Thomas Jonson Rated	45	0	0
and to pay 4d p lb	0	15	0
William Roterds Rated	46	10	0
and to pay 4d p lb	0	15	12
Thomas Stuenson Rated	50	0	0
and to pay 4d p lb	00	16	8
William Drue Rated	77	0	0
and to pay 4d p lb	01	5	8
Mathew Gilles Rated	121	10	0
and to pay 4d p lb	2	00	6
Mrs Mathes Rated	126	10	0
and to pay p ld	2	2	2
Charles Adams Rated	31	10	00
and to pay p lb	0	11	2
Jonas Bines Rated	43	0	0
and to pay p lb	00	14	4
Olluer kent Rated	65	01	0
and to yay p lb	1	1	8
John Bickford Rated	105	10	0
and to pay p lb	1	15	2
Thomas Welley Rateq	80	10	0
and to pay p lb	1	6	10
John Allt Rated	72	0	0
and to pay p lb	2	4	0
Robert hethersay Rated	41	0	0
and to pay bl	00	13	4
John Godder Rated	102	0	0
and to pay p lb	1	14	0
Henry lankster Rated	74	10	0
and to pay p lp	0	4	10
John martten Rated	42	10	0
and to pay p lb	00	14	2
To Trieckey Rated	107	0	0
and to pay p lb	1	15	8
J. hn haell Rated	42	0	0
and to pay p lb	00	14	0
James Ralleins Rated	61	10	0
aud to pay p lb	1	0	6
John Buesley Rated	43	0	0
and o pay p lp	00	14	4
frances Treickey Rated	30	0	0
and to pay p lb	00	10	0
Phelep leWes Rated	67	10	0
and to pay b lb	1	2	6
William follet Rated	60	0	0
and to pay p lb	1	0	0
To futtman Rated	97	10	0
and to pay p lb	1	12	6
Georg Bransen Rated	30	0	0
and to pay p lb	0	10	0
Antoney nutter Rated	30	0	0
and to pay p lb	00	10	0
John R berds Rated	30	0	0
and to pay p lb	00	10	0
Richard Catter Rated	67	0	0
and to pay p lb	1	2	4
Darbey feilld Rated	91	0	0
and to pay n lb	1	10	4
Robert Naney Rated	30	0	0
and to pay p lb	00	10	0
John laues (or loues?) at blodey point for his house	00	2	8
James wall for hi 3 quarters of a saw mill and a honse Rated	125	0	0
and to pay 4d p lb	1	1	8
Jo Hall Rated	79	12	0
and to pay 4d p lb	1	6	4
Samwell haynes	64	10	0
and to pay 4d p lb	1	00	10

This Rat is to be paid in pipestaues

and Indian Corn pease or Wheat the
pipestaues 4ld o thousan indan Corne 4s
p bushell pease at 4s 6d wheat at 5s p
bushell
The places wheare these pipataues ar to
to be broft is
    for Oyster Riuer to John Bickfords
    poynt for Douer to the back Coue
    For Cocehee at or obowt Richard Na-
sones or the golfe
    for blode poynt at the point.

———

    *George Smith's figures have a line
drawn across.

OLD SERIES NUMBER 321.
DOVER OLD BOOK OF RECORDS.

A Rate this 21th of July 1657

By the sellekt men of Douer for six pence uppon the pound to be payd in prouitions marchantabell Pipstaues and hogshead staues Boaods and fatt Cattell which is for the Clearing of all the Ingagements of the Towne and this to bee Performed by the first of September next at the prices following Pipestaues 4lb p th usau hogsnad staues 2lb 10s 0 p thousan (.) bords at 50s Wheat at 5s p bosh Pease at 4s p boshell beeff at 2d 1-2 p lb porke at 3d 1-2 p lb Indian Corne at 4s p buseell, and where any man is defeckive the Constabell haeth Power to take it by destrea and these Goods to be delivered at Bloody poynt sandy poyntt and the back Cove and at John Bickfords at Oyster Ruer

Henry Tebites	2	10	09
John Hall Deacon	2	14	00
Tho Layton	8	13	9
Tho Beard	5	0	3
Rafe Hall	2	5	6
J hn Tuttell	1	18	0
John Roberds	4	16	6
Jermey Tibbittes	1	14	9
Tho Canny	6	5	0
Josephfe Astin	5	9	6
James Nutt	2	11	3
Isake Nash	1	4	9
Wm Storey	2	11	9
mr Roberds	1	7	0
Wm Pomfreet	2	1o	7
Rafe Twambly	1	12	3
Jedediah Andres	o	15	0
John Hilton	1	4	6
Tho Downes	1	13	9
Tho nock	1	4	6
Capt wallden	9	15	6
nathell wise		15	0
John hance		15	0
Tho hanson	1	17	9
Ed Patterson		15	0
Rob Joanes	3	12	0
James kid		17	9
John heard	4	17	0
Joh louering		16	9
will hackett		18	6
Rich Oettes	2	1	3
Job Clemont	3	15	0
Petter Coffin	6	1	9
Rich Sloper		4	6
Phelep Cromwell		15	0
will Pylle	1	3	6
John key		15	0
will Sheffilld to his mds (merchandise?)	2	15	0
will Sheffilld			0
John meader	1	11	6
Elder Starbuck	2	12	0
nathell Starbuck		19	3
Capt wiggins and Mr Brogton		17	0
for henry hobes		15	c
henry magoune		16	0
John Cernicle		15	
James Grant	1	7	6

Patrick the s....ett		3	o	John woodman		1	3	9
John Dam	6	13	6	Joseph field		1	1	0
wm Tomsom		15	o	Mr Pitman his (......)				
Sargant Hall	2	o	9	& land 40 lb		1	0	0
Sargant ffurber	3	6	6	these Rats are to (wad omitted ?)				
Antoney Nutter	3	5	3	doeth wis to be receued of the non in				
Tho Roberds Juner	1	13	9	habetance				
henrey lankster	5	o	9					
Tho Trickey	3	1	6	A Rate mad the 10: 9 (16)57 for pro-				
John Hall	1	3	o	uetion for Douer necke Cochechae and				
John Bickford	1	10	o	bloodey poynt.				
Richard Caetter	3	5	o	Henrey Tebbets			15	9
Jomes Rallines	1	15	3	John Hall Decon			19	0
Richard Carell	1	1	0	Tho layton		2	4	5
vall Hill	12	14	3	Tho Beard		1	13	2
wm Beard	6	8	3	Lft Hall			13	9
Rob Bernam	4	0	0	Jo Tuttell			13	2
wm Roberts	2	7	6	Jo Roberds		1	11	8
will willyams	4	6	o	Jr Tebeets			10	1
James Bunker	1	9	o	Tho Caney		2	0	4
wm follett	3	8	9	Josf Astine		1	14	8
Tho Johnson	2	14	6	Jam nutte			16	6
Rice Howell	1	1	o	Isak nash			11	11
Rob Junkins	1	7	3	wm Storey			16	9
Phelleps Chesley	5	19	9	mr Roberds			7	2
Tho Steuenson	1	18	o	wm Pomprett			12	4
mathew Gilles	4	3	6	Ralf Twambly			10	0
mathew willyams		16	6	John Hillton			7	2
wm drew	1	17	9	Tho Downes				1
Charells Adames	1	18	3	Tho nock			8	0
Oleuer keintt	2	1	6	wm Tomson			5	0
mrs mathewes	4	9	6	Elder nutter		1	7	2
John Bickford	(?)	4	3	John Carter			5	0
Tho Welley	3	3	9	Chas Buckner			5	0
John Allt	2	19	5	Anto Caraway			5	0
Richard Bray	1	3	3	Capt wallden		4	9	9
John Hill		19	6	John Hance			5	0
John Daues	2	6	0	Tho Hanson			12	4
Tho ffootman	3	14	6	Ed Paterson			5	0
Richard yorke	3	6	9	Robert Jones		1	2	0
John martine	2	11	0	James kied			5	10
Jahn Godder	7	0	6	John Hard		1	0	01

John Louring		5	7	wm willyams	1	7 4
wm Hakett			5	James Bonker		8 4
Ric Otes		13	4	wm follett	1	16 3
Job Clamant	1	0	10	Tho Johnson		16 2
Peter Coffin		9	2	Risse Howell		5 0
Richard Sloper		7	0	Roberd Jongkin		12 8
Phel Cromwell		5	0	Phelep chesley	1	14 7
wm Pille		7	10	Tho Steunson		12 8
wm Shefd mder (mercandise?)		13	4	mathew Gills	1	7 10
wm Shefeld		5	4	mathew willyams		5 10
John meader		11	6	wm Drew		15 7
Ed Starduck		17	1	Charles Addams		12 9
nat Starbuck		6	6	Oleuer kent		8 6
Capt wiggin & mr Broughton		5	8	mrs matthewes	1	7 10
Hen hobes		5	0	John Bickford	1	16 1
Hen magoune		5	0	Tho well-y	1	1 2
Jams Grant		7	2	John Allt		19 10
John Dam	2	3	4	Richard Bray		7 9
Elder wentworth	1	6	0	John Hill		6 9
John Hall of Grineland			13	John Daues		15 4
wm furber	1	3	6	Tho ffootmnn		19 10
Antony outer	1	3	7	Richard Yorke		19 7
Tho Roberds		14	1	John martin		15 0
Hen lankster	1	14	1	John Godder	1	10 2
Tho Trickey	1	0	4	Josephf fleld		5 0
John Hall		7	8	John woodman		7 11
John Bickford		10	3	will Pittman		8 0
Richa Catter	1	0	3	will willyams juner		5 0
James Rollins		11	9			
Ric Carell		6	8		31	15 10

49 16 4

A Ratte mayd the 10th 9mo (16)57 for the inhabetauce of oyster Reuer fo the Prouetion being Rated at 2d the pound.

u r Hill	4	4	6
wm Beard	2	2	4
Roberd Burnum	1	6	8
wm Roberds		15	2

These Prouetious are to be Brought into John Bickfords house anei man be deflektife we giue the Constabell Power to stayne this Rat is to be payd in Beffe at 2d 1-2 p lb boull beff at 5d p lb Porke at 3d 1-2 p lb wheat, Barley and malt a 5s p boshell Pease at 4s p boshell Butter and Chese at prise currant.

OLD SERIES NUMBER 322.

THE REYNERS

In Nos. 62 and 77 Hist. Mem., accounts

were given of the Reyner ministers of Dover, father and son. Regarding each we add something,—that as to the father, argely from papers of William H. Whitemore, Esq.

John Reyner, sen., was born at Gildersome, parish of Batly, Co. York, Eng death, which lands he disposed of by will He graduated at Emanuel College in 1625. Doubtless he was ordained in England but we have no record. He came to this country in or near 1635: settled as pastor at Plymouth, Mass., in 1636, and there remained until Nov. 1654; thence he came to Boston and spent the winter, and in 1655 was settled as pastor of our Dover First church, in which office he remained until his death. He died April 20, 1669; to says Hull's Diary, which is corclusive, Mr. Reyner's will being made April 19·

Mr. Reyner married, 1st,——Boys, probably in England; 2d, before 1642, Frances Clarke, of Boston. She, then his wife, was dismissed from the Boston church to that in Plymouth, 18 Sept. 1642. The second wife survived him.

Mr. Reyner clearly had the following children:

By his first wife,

1. Jachin, of whom see below.

2. Hannah, married Job Lane, of Billerica.

By his second wife:

3. John, born in 1643, of whom see below.

4. Elizabeth.

5. Dorothy, probably the one whose date of birth is given (without name) as 26 Dec. 1647.

6. Joseph, born 15 Aug 1650' died 23 Nov. 1652.

7. Abigail, appears to have married George Broughton.

8. Judith, born in 1656; she m, rr st, Rev. Jabez Fox, of Woburn; he was ordained 5 Sept 1679, and died 28 Feb. 1703, aged 56, having had 5 children. Judith married, 2d, Col. Jonathan Tyn of Dunstable, who was of the Royal Council 1686-7. She was his third wife, —his second wife having died in 1714. Judith survived him, a d died 5 Jun, 1756, in her 99th year. Savage erroneously calls her daughte of the second John Reyner.

An Elizabeth Reyner, of Plymouth married, 1 Sept. 1641, Capt. Thomas Southworth. Baylies's New Plymouth calls her "daughter of Rev- John Reyener," but if so, she must have been born before Rev. John left college, which is not likely. Moreover she left issue living in 1669, and either she or her issue would have been mentioned in Rev. John's will. More likely she was a sister, but we are open to conviction.

All the above children, except Joseph who died in infancy, are mentioned in Rev. John's will, the first two being referred to as of another mother than his then wife. The will is printed in full in N ·. 66, Hist. Mem. The four daughters of the second wife were then, 166 4, unmarried.

Jachin, son of Rev. John, as above, lived in Rowley. He married 12 Nov. 1662, Elizabeth Denison. Either he or she died 8 July 1708, but the records are mixed. He had:

1. Edward, born 6 July 1671.

2. Jachin, born 31 Jan. 1673-4.

3. Anna, born 22 July 1678.

4. Jachin, born 20 Jan. 1681-2.

Rev. John, Jr.., son of Rev. John as

above, graduated at Harvard College in 1663; about 1667 he became assistant to his father in Dover Immediately upon his father's death he was invited (22 July 1669) to officiate for one year. He accepted the position, and appears to have con- in red in the same service but was not regularly settled until 12 July 1671. He married Judith, daughter of Edmund and Joanna Quincy, of Braintree- Her father was the second Edmund Quincy, and she was born 25 June 1655. She outlived her husband, but died y ung. Her tombstone at Quincy says: "Judith Reyner, daughter to Edmund and Jaonna Quincy, Relic of the Reverend John Reyn r' late Minister of Dover, aged 23 years."

Rev. John, Jr., died 21 Dec. 1676, evidently in Dover; and his mother administered on his estate, He was buried, Sewell says, 28 Dec.

Judith (Quidcy) wtfe of John, was cousin to the wife of Judge Samuel Sewall, who kept a minute diary. Judge Sewall married Hannah, daughter of Capt. Hull, the famous mint-master, by his wife Judith, sister to the second Edmund Quincy, and aunt to Mr. Reyner's wife. Capt. Hull likewise kept a diary. Fro n the two we get various items.

Hull says, 21 Dec 1676: "Mr. John Reyner, Minster of Dover, died of a cold and f ver that he took in the field among the soldiers." This time it will be seen, corresponds with the expedition of Capts. Syll and Hawthorne, who went eastward, stopping at Dover on their way, where they were joined by a force under command of Major Richard Waldr n. The Massachusetts forces reached Dover 6 Sept. 1676. The sham fight, given in history, took place on the next day, in which two hundred Indians were seized. The expedition then went on to the east, but with little result.

Hull says: "Mr. Reyner of Sept. 25 saith that their Indian Messengers returned the night before, and informed they saw two indians dead' their Scalp taken off: one of them was Canonicus hi Captain. 'Tis judged that Canonicus himself is also killed or taken by the same Hand, viz, of the Mohawks."

"Mr. Reyner, in a letter dated at Salisbury, Sept. 21 '76, hath these pas, sages: "God still is at work for us. Oneey'd John, with about 45 of your Southern Indians, have been apprehended since the Soldiers went East ward. They we judge them All of our Southern Indians. And nothing yet heard of damage in the Eastern parts. A sagamore of Quapaug is one of the Indians taken and sent Canonicus we believe was killed by the Mohawks when his Captain was slain. N. B. We have in our Business here great discoveries of our shameful Natures. Pray that the Sanctification an Reconciliation by Xt. may prevail to his honour."

"Vae malum. Dec. 21, being Thursday Worthy Mr. Reyner fell asleep: was taken with a violent vomiting the Friday before, Sightheaded by Saturday, Lay speechless 24 hours, and then died on Thursday even. We heard not that he was sick till Friday about nine at night: on the Sabbath morn comes William Furbur and brings news of Death. After last Exercise (public worship) Father dispatches Tim to Braintry. Monday morn, Uncle (probably Edmund Quincy, Mrs. Reyner's father) and Tim come back. Uncle concluded from the Winter, his own infirmity and my cousins indisposedness, to dispatch away Wm. Furbur with letters onely. O how earnestly did I expect his coming hether, and say with myself, what makes him stay so long? I might have seen him when I went to Sandwich, but God hath appointed I sh uld see him no more. The Lord that lives forever, grant us a comfortable joyous meeting at Christ's appearance. Note. Many of us saw Mr. Reyner Oct.15 for he posted to Braintrey in the night and he went back when I was at Sandwich

I suppose the last time that I saw and disc ursed him was (black) He was here with Mr. Broughton earnestly urging to make sure Lands of Mr. Broughton at Dover to my Father, and so take him Paymaster for the Annuity laid on it. Mr. Broughton with stood, and Mr. Reyner feared it was b cause he would not let it go out of his hands, though he pretended other things and seemed to reflec on Mr. Reyner. Note. Mr. Reyney and I discus-ed of it in the orchard, and he professed his integrity in it, and that he thought that Father (Hull) would never have it sure, if not that way. Advised me not to keep overmuch within, but goe among men, and that thereby I should advantage myself."

This turns us to the Broughtons; what had Mr. Reyner to do with their affairs? This, about 1656 (we do not find the record), Mr. Thomas Broughton had a grant of 200 acres on our bank of the Newichawannock river, and was taxed on it 1657 to 1663, when tax-lists disappear. He was of Watertown, a man of pr perey and great business. His land was at the head of the ten lots (1656 and Cove up the river, as described in Mem

273-4 which carried his lands up to Quamphegan or even Salmon falls. He appears to have had saw mills there Sewall's diary says: "Sept. 18, 1676, Mr. Broghton and his son George being here, said Mr. George agreed to deliver up his writings of the Mills, and give up the management of it to Father Hull." It should be remembered that Father Hull had made enormous profits in the coinage business.

Savage says that George Broughton was "perhaps son of Thomas,"—and he certainly was, and "probably married Abigail, daughter of Rev. J h Reyner;" and was "perhaps" the one mentioned by Hubbard as of Salmon Falls in 1675, and was captain in Kittery in 1682. But it was all Kittery then on that side.

Now, later, Sewall says, Sept. 1, 1687 "This day we received a Sloop Load o Boards from the Salmon Falls Saw-Mill, and the same day, I think by the sam Boat, I received a Copy of a Writt o Ejection which Mr. Mason has caus'd to be serv'd on John Broughton respecting the said Mill."

So on Sept. 9, "Mr. Cook and I" set out for Portsmouth. Sewall tells where they lodged and where dined, and whom they heard preach on Sunday. On th 13th he went to Bloody Point, and crossed to Hilton's Point by the ferry; called at Parson Pikes, but the parson was absent, and they saw Mrs. Pike and two sons; called at Major Waldren's where Cook stopped, but Sewall went over to Salmon Falls, George Broughton, who happened to be in at Otis's being guide. On the 14th, he saw the Mill, and "visit Mrs. Rainer and her daughter Broughton." On the 16th "stay a little at George and Jno Broughton's." And so on.

By which it appears clear enough that Abigail, sister of the second John Reyner, did marry George Broughton, and probably the widow of he first parson Reyner,—her only son also being dead, was living with her daughter Abigail, and when John Reyner, Jr., came down to Boston with George Broughton, it was with his sister's husband, and perhaps interested in that his sister Abigail had a good property somewhere from her father's estate.

OLD SERIES NUMBER 323.

DOVER OLD BOOK OF RECORDS.

By the Selecktten en ye 14 of 11th mo 1655.

Ordered that wheras thear is Grants maide of Seuerall Saw mills to seuerell Persons as Apeireth by thear dates to begein thear Rents the first of march it is ordered that from all such mills thear is to be payd acordinge to thear seuerall ingagements the first of Aprill next 1656 Rents for two years past dew from such mills.

2ly it (is) ordred for the cleareing of the accompts of the towne fro year to year if anie such parsone or parsons that shall charge the sayd towne theay are to Giue in thear perticklers of thear charge and that the same is to be Intred upon Record.

3ly Its ordred to mr Vallintin Hill or his Assinges free liberty to Cutt through our Comans for drawings Parte of the water of lamprelle Riuer into oyster Riuer for the supply of his mills thear Prouided that the sayd Hill or his Assinges in soe doeinge doe not Preiudice any former Grants by water or by land and that in Case the sayd Hill or Assinges shall see Cause too Through up the Grant of lamprieell Riuer that then the water Course thet hee or his Assinges cut it shall sease and Run in its former Course as allsoe that in Case thay Cut through any hie wayes then theay are to make suffysiunt Bridges (sic) or Bridges for foot and horse and to maintayne the same soe long as theay make use of the sayd water Course As allsoe theay ar to stopp up the sayd watter Corse at thear owne Proper charge in Case theay Cast up the sayd Grant of lampreele Riuer.

4: 1: (16)56 At A Publick meiting of the Inhabetants now Agreed that mr vallintine Hill of oyster Riuer for the Cleiring of the bound line Betwin the towne of Douer and Exeter and also the bounds of the grant of the sayd towne of douer mayde to the sayd hill of lamprell Riuer and acomedations for timber to the sayd Riuer belonging for Erieckting of a sawmill that the sayd vallintine Hill sholde heirby be Atoriesed to take one or omoer of the inhabetants of the sayd Doner with him to Appoynt some of the towne of Exeter to giue the a meiting for the seiteng forth the line always provided that the sayd vallintine Hill shall neglecte to performe this order sumetime betwext the Date of these prences (presents?) and the nexte sessions of Genarall Corte at Boston that the sayd Hill shall for euer after be dischaged from laying any clame to the sayd Grant of lamprell Reuer and appertenances.

The Adjierment of the Genarril Towne meting to the 22th cf 12th mo 1656

1. Whearas thear is a clase in such an order dated 10: 1: 55-56 that thear shall be noe moer grants of land made to anie of the present Inhabetants or to anie other untell all the grants thet ar made allredie be layd out and bounded this order is heirby Repealled in poynt of time.

1ly. That all new Grants are not to take place untell thee last of november 1657 and that whearas thear is ani old grants voyade of men to lay them out thear is apoyntid for Douer Neck and the back Riuer Raphe Hall and Tho layton (.) for Cochechie Capt walldern william wentworth (,) for Blodi point william ffurbur and henrey lankster (.) for oyster Reuer Tho footman and John Bickforp (,) and all soe the old grants ar to be layd out in the time mentined and apon the defeckt thear f the new grants mayde since haue power to take place to be layd foerth and in Cass the men apoynted neglect thear office tell one moenth of the time prefixted theu the parties Concerned haue power to Call for Relefe from the flue men appoynted by the towne or anie three of them wich ar upon thear oath.

— — .. —

A Rate maed the 12th 8th (16)58 for mr Reyner his preuetione

Isake Nash	0	12	3	
Tho Downes	0	8	11	
Job Clemants	1	9	1	
Mr Roberds	0	7	1	1-2
William Pomfrett	0	8	9	
Tho Beard	1	12	8	
Tho loyton	2	12	6	
John Hall Decon	0	16	0	
John Dam Sinyer	1	11	3	1-2
John Tuttell	0	11	9	
John Dam Juner		011	1	
William Storey	0	16	9	
Elder nutter	1	8	1	1-2
J. s phf Astin	1	5	11	
John Roberds	1	10	10	
John Hillton	0	7	2	
Ralphf Twombly	0	9	4	
James Nutt	0	12	6	
Jeremy Tebetts	0	12	0	1-2
Henrey Tebetts	0	16	2	
Tho nocke	0	8	7	
William Tomson	0	5	0	
Blo. Poynt				
James Rallins	0	12	6	
Richard Catter	1	1	6	
Thr Trickey	1	0	4	
John Bickford	0	13	10	
Henrey lankster	1	11	6	
William ffurber	1	4	11	1-2
Ant ney nutter	1	5	1	
Th) Roberds	0	12	6	
Michi-ll Brane Cochechae	0	6	0	
Edward Starbuck	1	3	5	1-2
Capt Wiggin	1	16	8	
Petter Coffiin	0	11	8	
Mr Broughton	0	16	8	
Henrey hobes	0	5	0	
Phelep Crow well	0	6	4	
Richard Sloper	0	1	8	
Nathanell Starbuck	0	6	8	
Th) Hanson	0	17	6	
Edward Paterson	0	5	0	
Ickaebod Shiffild	0	5	0	
William Shiffild	0	9	0	
Roberd Jones	0	19	8	
Campt Walldern	3	3	4	
Charll Buckner	0	5	0	
George Goldwier	1	5	2	

363

	£	s	d				£	s	d	£	s	d
John heard	1	9	4 1-2		Thomes Dowty		0	10	0	1	0	0
paid in bef	1	8	11 1-2		James Oer		0	10	0	1	0	0
Richard Otes	0	15	2		James medell-man		0	10	0	1	0	0
John Curtes	0	5	2		Edward Arwin		0	10	0	1	0	0
John louring	0	5	0		John Barber		0	5	0	0	10	0
William hoket	0	5	0		Edward Patterson		0	10	0	1	0	0
Elder Wentworth	1	4	10		Roberd Bernom		1	6	8	2	13	4
William loue	0	5	4		william Pitman		0	10	0	1	0	0
James Grant	0	8	4		Williar R berds		0	10	0	1	0	0
henrey Magoune	0	5	2		William Willyams sin		1	5	8	2	11	4
Barthellme lippincott	0	5	0		Thomes Steuenson		0	13	4	1	6	8
William ffollett	9	3	4		William Drew		0	11	8	1	4	4
					Rice howell		0	5	0	0	10	0
					Joseph filld		0	8	4	0	16	8
	48	19	10 1-2		Mathew Gills		1	6	8	2	13	4
							24	1	6	47	6	0

OLD SERIES NUMBER 324.

DOVER OLD BOOK OF RECORDS.

Oyster Riuer Prouition Rate used the 22: 9: (16)59.

				the great Rat				
	£	s	d	£	s	d		
Mr Hill	2	12	8	5	5	4		
Thomes u firie the stiller	0	8	4	0	16	8		
John meader	0	13	4	1	7	4		
William Graues	0	5	0	0	10			
Einsin Iohn Daues	0	15	0	1	0			
Juner William willyams		8	0	0	16	0		
James Bunker	0	8	0	0	16	0		
Will fullett	1	0	0	2	0	0		
Thomes Jonson	0	13	4	1	6	8		
Phellep Chesley	1	12	8	3	5	4		
Roberd Junkes	0	8	4	0	16	8		
James Jackson	0	5	0	0	10	0		
Walter Jackson	0	5	0	0	10	4		
Willia n Beard	2	7	8	4	15	0		
John Woodman	0	15	0	1	10	0		
Patrick Jemeson	0	15	0	0	10	0		
Henrey Browne	0	10	0	1	0	0		
mathew willyams	0	10	6	1	1	0		
Beniamen mathews	1	5	0	2	10	0		
Charlls Adames	0	13	0	1	6	4		
John Bickford	1	6	8	2	13	8		
Thomes weily	0	18	4	1	16	3		
John Alllt	0	19	10	1	19	8		
Richard Braye	0	6	10	0	13	8		
John Hil	0	6	8	0	13	4		
Thomas footman	0	3	4	2	6	8		
Richard yorke	0	19	4	1	18	8		
John martin	0	18	0	1	16	0		
John Godder	1	14	8	3	9	4		
Beniamen Hull	0	8	4	0	16	8		
John Hillton	0	6	8	0	13	4		
James Nutt Juner	0	5	0	0	10	0		
Olleuer Kent	0	8	4	0	16	8		
John hance	0	5	0	0	10	0		
John Dauill	0	5	0	0	10	0		
Roberd Hussy	0	5	0	0	10	0		
William Risbey (Risley?)	0	5	0	0	10	0		
Thomas Ginn (Green?)	0	5	0	0	10	0		
Steuen ye (westinman?)	0	5	0	0	10	0		
will Jones	0	5	0	0	10	0		
	14	0	2	28	11	4		

By the Generall Courtt

It is now ordred By the Generall Court holden at Boston the 9th of the 8 th mo 1641 and with the Consent of the Inhabitants of the (omission?) of Psu-

ataway as followeth
Inprimes that from henceforth the sayd People Inhabiting thear ar and shall Be Accepted and Reputed under the gouerment of the Massachusetts as the Rest of the Inhabetants within the sayd Jureisdiction and also that they shall haue the same order and way of Administration of Justice and way of kipping of Courts as is Established at Ipswich and Sallem Also they shall Be Exempted from all publicke Charges other then those that shall arise Among themself or from any occasion or Course that may be taken to pramote thear owne proper good or benifitt Also theay shall injoy all such lafull liberties of fishing Planting falling timber as formerly thay haue Injoyed in the sayd Riuer

Mr Symion Bradstret mr Israll Stoughton mr Samewell Simones mr william Tings mr Frances willyames and mr Edward hillton or anie fower of them whea of mr Bradstreet or mr Stoughton to be one these shall haue the same power that the quarter Courts at Salem and Ipswioh haue Also the Inhabetants thear ar alowed to send too depeties from the hole Riuer to the Court at Boston also mr Bradstreet mr Stoughton and they of the Commissioners shall haue power at the Courtt at Puscataway to acynt tec or three to Jeyne with mr willyams and mr hillton to govern the people as the magistrates heir tell the next Cenerall Court take ferder order.

OLD SERIES NUMBER 325.

DOVER OLD BOOK OF RECORDS.

A Raet md for mr Raners Prouition at 2d in the pound for Douer the 22: 9; (16)59
the great Rnte

Name	£	s	d	£	s	d
Tho layton	2	10	0	5	2	0
John Dammsinyer	1	10	0	3	0	0
John Hall devon	0	18	2	1	17	0
will Pumfrett	0	12	0	1	4	0
mr Roberde	0	6	7	0	13	2
Tho Downes	0	9	0	0	18	0
mr Cimball	0	10	0	1	0	0
mr Edward Buhnall	2	3	4	4	6	8
Mr Chadwell	0	5	0	0	10	0
moses Chadwell	0	5	0	0	10	0
Benjamin Chadwell	0	5	0	0	10	08
John Sathom	0	5	0	0	10	0
Richard Knight	0	5	0	0	10	04
tor Clements	0	6	8	1	13	
mr Reaner	0	7	4	8	14	2
William Junes	0	5	0	0	10	0
Tho Beard	1	12	4	3	14	8
william hakett	0	5	0	0	10	0
John Tuttell	0	5	4	0	10	0
left Hall	0	13	3	1	6	8
wedge storey	0	8	3	0	16	6
Elder nutter	1	5	0	2	10	6
Tho Caney	1	14	4	3	9	0
Tho R berds	0	14	8	1	9	8
John Roberds	1	6	8	2	13	4
mr ludecues Edlin	0	5	0	0	10	4
James nutt sinyer	0	12	7	1	5	0
Jeremie Tebutt	0	13	0	1	6	2
Henry Tebute	0	14	4	1	8	8
Thnocke	0	8	0	0	16	0
Jonethan Hillton	0	5	0	0	10	0
Isake Stokes	0	5	0	0	10	0
Mr Buckner	0	8	4	0	16	80
Ralf Thwamly	0	11	6	1	3	
Thoes Hansn	1	5	4	2	10	8
william ferbush	0	5	0	0	10	0
Eider Starbuck	1	13	0	3	6	8
nathanell Starbuck	0	10	0	1	0	0
Roberd J nes	1	11	8	3	3	4
John Ash	0	5	0	0	10	0
Petter Coffin	1	5	0	2	10	0
mican (blank)	0	5	0	0	10	0
Cristin Dalak	0	5	0	0	10	0
wesh James Grant	0	8	6	0	17	0
Petter Grant	0	5	0	0	10	0
mr Tho wiggin	0	9	2	1	18	4
Gorge Wedon	0	5	0	0	10	0
Jere Li marcom	0	5	0	0	10	0
Phelep Crowell	0	9	6	0	19	0
Richard Otes	0	19	2	1	18	4
Joseph Astin	1	13	9	3	7	6
John Hard	1	10	6	3	3	0
mr Goldwir	1	13	4	3	6	8
his man	0	5	0	0	10	0
Capt wallden	4	11	2	9	2	4
mr George wallden	0	5	2	0	10	4

Samuel wentworth	0	5	0	0 10 0	
	45	10	7	97 1 2	
Umfrey Varney	0	5	0	0 10 0	
John louring	0	6	8	1 13 4	
Will Horne	0	6	2	0 12 4	
Josephf Sanders	0	5	0	0 10 0	
William Sheffild	0	10	4	1 0 8	
Tho Payne	0	5	2	0 10 4	
Richard Morgin	0	6	8	0 13 4	
Sargant Hall	2	3	4	4 6 8	
William ffurber	1	4	8	2 9 4	
Antoney uutter	1	8	3	2 16 6	
John Dam Juner	0	12	0	1 4 0	
Richard Rooe	0	8	0	0 16 0	
Thomas Tredick	0	15	8	1 11 4	
michikell Brane	0	9	4	0 18 8	
James Ralliens	0	17	0	1 14 0	
Richard Keater	1	4	4	2 8 8	
John Bickford	0	14	0	1 9 8	
henry lankster	1	9	2	2 18 0	
henry hobes	0	19	4	18 0	
Richard Toser	0	6	0	0 12 0	
mr Andrew wiggin	1	0	0	2 0 0	
mr Broghton	0	16	8	2 13 4	
Gorge vesey	0	5	0	0 10 8	
wiiliam Smeth	0	5	0	0 10 0	
niuin (ninin?)the scot	0	5	0	0 10 0	
James keid	0	5	0	0 10 0	
laserres Permet	0	5	0	0 10 4	
William Tomson	0	4	0	0 10 0	
Jedediae Andres	0	9	4	0 18 8	
	20	6	9	40 13 7	

The prices of the prouetions
Bef at 3d p lb
pork at 4d lb
Wheat 5s p boshel
Pease 4s p boo
malt 6s p bosh
Barle 5s p bosh
Buter 6d p lb
Chese at price corant

These prouetions are to be brought in to mr Reaners forthwith after demaud heir of and apon non performance heir of we give our Constabell full Power to straine upon eurey Delinquent fr thear efeckt.

Att A meeting of the major part of the Inhabitants of douer neck it is apon that the swamp according The grant that was giuen by the selectmen to the Inhabitants of the neck of douer for an ox pasture in the year 52 shall be Equally deuided unto Euery settled Inhabitant now in being proportinably unto Euery person that hath Right there to men Chosen to measure the Land is John Hall Ltt Hall John dam Will Pomfret.

A List of the names of the Inhabitants of Douer neck that haue Right to the Comminage of the ox Pasture and the Calues Pasture taken the 13th of the 7th mo 1661

Mr Thomas Cimball
Job Celmants
Thomas dounes
Thomas Robards senr
The ministers house
Charles buckner
william Pomfret
Thomas Beard
Ino Tuttle senr
John Hall deacon
Thomas Leighton
Jno Dam senr — Jeremiah Tebbets
Ltt Ralph Hall — Humphry Varney
Elder nutter — James Nute
Joseph Austin — Richard Pinkham
Philip Cromwell
william ffurber
Thomas Canny
Sargt Jno Robards
Thomas Robards Junr
Jedediah Andros
Henry Tebets
Thomas nock

OLD SERIES NUMBER 134.

Items regarding Dover Settlers.

From Old Norfork Records (Salisbury, 24, 2, 1649.)

Edward Colcord plaintiff agt the Towne of Douer for a debt of 50 lb wich was some time due to mr Burditt. The Jury finde for the plaintiff 20 lb debt

hee would take his oathe that mr Colcord was really payd the debt of 20 lb to mr Burditt now in question.

This had no effect: but the next year the decision was reversed as follows: (9, 2, 1650.)

Mr Richard Walderne, Jno Baker, Willi Storie & Willi ffurbur plaintifis in behalfe of The Towne Douer agt Edward Colcord defend in an acton of reuieue of of an acton of debt wich ye sayd Edward Colcord recovered agt ye sayd towne att ye Court held att Salisbury ye 24th of ye (2) mo. 1649: the Jurie gives in a speciall verdit the court finde for ye plaintiff costs of court & damages 43, 10, 2.

Edward Colcord, aged 43, depuses 13 uly 1659, that he was at "Tiugmouth i Devon," England, in 1646. (Rockingham Registry of Deeds.)

Edward Colcord was sued, 30 Mar. 1678, as administrator on the estate of his son Edward late deceased, for a debt contracted in 1674. (Old Norfolk Files)

2,9, 1649: The town of Hampton ordered to "make their pt of the highway to Dover sufficient by the last of ye 1s mo. next ensuing uppon the penalty of b5 (Norfolk Co. Records.)

James Morry was killed by fall of a tree, as by coroner's verdict dated 11 Nov.165-. (Rck.Records.)

"To the Honord Court. (Mass. Archives.)

The inhabitants of Dover desire Mr Ambrose Gibbons to be a Comisionr to sit in Court with our honord Magistrats.   William Waldern,
in behalfe of the towne.
The petition was granted.

John Waldron, sen
Will dated 12 May 1740, he being "very sick;" proved 30 July 1740. Wife Mary to have one half of homestead, which should go to son Richard after her decease; to John Waldron Jr. (beside the 100 acres where he lives) land in Rochester "which I bought of the Twomblys" & "all my wearing apparrel;" to dau. Elizabeth Kimball, wife Ezra Kimball, 30 acres wh. were bought 'of Reyner,' and £30; to dau. Anne Roberts, wife of Timothy, 70 acres in Rochester, 40 of which joins land which Dea. Gershom Wentworth bought of Esqr Atkinson; to dau. Mehitable Chesley, wife of James, 30 acres in Dover, 'purchased of Reyner,' and 30lb: to dau Sarah Libbey, wife of Isaac, same as to Mehitable; to grandsons John Waldron, Richard Kimball, John Roberts and Samuel Libbey, land in Rochester; to son Richard (executor) all other property. (Rock. Records.)

Isaac Waldern of Boston, complains, 15 Oct. 1679, of William Henderson of Dover for not working on a ship according to agreement, he having paid said Henderson in advance. (Mass. Archives)

"William Walderne of Dover in Pascatq river mortgaged his house & land in dover unto Richard Walderne for his security to save him harmles from a bill wherein the said Richard stands bound wch give for payment of thirty pounds unto mr wm Whiteing &c." 2 oc 1645.

"William Walderne & Richard Walderne of dover gave joyntly theire bill unto wm Whiteing of Connecticut for the summe of thirty p unds fifteen shillings due to him and the other Adventures, to be paid in sterling money, to wit, seven pound eight shillings four pence uppon the 11th June next ensueing the date thereof for the use of hi uselfe and the other Adventures in Piscataq River & twenty foure pounds six shillings eight pence to be paid the 12th of June 1648, for the use of the Srewsbury mens ——unto the pformance whereof they bind them shlves theire heirs & administrrs. And william waldern in speciall did bind his house & land situat in dov r to the pfor rance of the the ——. As by theire deed dated 12th June 1645 doth appeare.

2 hands & seales.

'Richard Waldern of Quechecho in the Pascataq river conveyed to James Wall of Exeter Carpenter all his right for erecting a sawmill at Quechecho together With 60 Acres of land at the falls of Quechecho & fifteen hundred of trees." 2 (8) 1649. (Mass. Archives)

John Phillips of Dover was dead in 1642. Hatevil Nutarbuck aSadernttpp.. admn 28, 5, 1642, inventory entered 20 Mar. 1641, when property amouuted to 17lb, 0, 2' ad debts to 17,14, 4; no relations (Rock. Rec. as also the following.)

William Bellow sold, 5 Sept. 1644, his house in Dover, with 20 acres of land in the back River ' to Christopher Lawson

In 1647, 'John Redman of Dover' Joanna, dan. of John Bickford of O. R.

26, 6, 1647. 'ordered that John See at the Ile of Sholes take the oathe of a Constable before mr Smyth.'

Joseph miller of Dover' sells to John Goddard 22,Sept. 1647, house where he dwelt; also 20 acres given by Dover to Thomas Larkham on the west side of Back River; also 30 acres of Marsh similarly given on the west side of Great Bay near the 'great Cove,' also 100 acres similarly laid out west of said mars

At the Courte holden at dover t 10th day of the 7 mo. 45, whereas upp the complaint of John Awite & Remembrance his wiefe against Captaine Thoma wiggin f r wages due to his weife before she came to pascattquacke new Englande, beinge on the 14th december 1632, and for as much as it was proued by the oath of henry Tybbets that her time of servece did begine the firste of march before she came to new England, yt was therefors ordered by the saide Courte that the said Remembrance shall have such wagis due unto her from ths saide firste of march untill the said 14 of december.

ODD SERIES NUMBER 136.

Newichwannock.

Newichwannock, or Salmon Falls was originally part of the plantation of Pascataqua and subject to the local governm ent which had its head quarter at Portsmouth The territory on the Somersworth side of the river was, however, within the limits of Dover when the boundaries were actually defined. As such it comes under our notice.

The settlement at Newichwannock was made entirely for the purposes of gain, and under the ownsrship and direction of English proprietaries, and of course was not prosperous until the title of the English owners to the soil was practically annulled. In fact the tenant system in every instance proved a failure, with its whole array of manors, lords and rristocratic privileges, and for obvious reasons. It was so in Mainie, in New Hampshire, in Pennsylvania, in Virginia and the Carolinas, in all of which the absence of that spirit of enterprise which ownership by cccupants creatts would proved fatal but for the entrance of contrary and generally forbidden elements. The "Cauncil at Plymouth" claimed to posssss by virtue of Royal Charter, the title and right af government to the lands in America between the fortieth and forty-eighth degrees of north latitude. Among their confused and confusing grants, was one dated 19 Jan. 1619, conveying to Capt. John Mason, all the lands between the Merrmack and the Piscataqua. It was followed by a second, dated made to Sir Ferdinando Gorges and Capt. John Mason, who received partners and formed a company takng the name given to this tract viz, Laconia. By this company Portsmouth and Dover were settled in 1623, and some parts of Maine soon after. Most of the partners became discouraged by the absence of the anticipated income, and formerly or virtually gave all into the hands of Gorges and Mason. who, in 1633 or 1634 divided the territories, making, we thihk, only a formal and legal act of what had for some time been their understood purpose and which had really cousidered Gorges for four years forbearance 6 lb, 6, 8, & costs of Court 4lb, 9, 8.

On this trial, John Baker of Dover affirmed in Court yt Rich Walding sayd the proprietor of Maine, and Mason that of New Hampshire for several years. Gorges sold Mason, however, a strip three miles in width bordering the Pascataqua and Newichwannock for their whole extent, so thas finally Mason was the owner of the whole river.

It was under either the joint cou pancy or the implied division, but certainly before the formal purchase that Newichwannock was settled. Ambrose Gibbons was sent there as "factor" or agent, soon after the settlement at Portsmouth. A writer in the Geneal. Register, III, 250, states that in 1624, a saw mill and a palisadoed house were erected there and that Gibbons was placed in charge. Unless there is very positive authority for this statement, we are inclin·d to reject it. That h· occupied a house there early is true, as letters dated 1630 prove; but that he had been there six years is doubtful.— That his house was a trading post with Indian, whose chief commodity was fur, is evident, but that a saw mill was there seems inconsistent with a letter from the proprietors to him dated "last of May 1631" to the effect that there was soon to be sent "the moddell of a saw mill that you may have one going," and with the engagement made with other individuals which is given below. Belknap speaks of the sale of the mill there upon the three mile purchase by Mason, but he dates it Sept. 1635; one letter speaks of "boards" with which a vessel was to be loaded, but another explains by the words "clove boards."

This however is certain that between 1624 and 1630, Ambrose Gibbons was placed at Newichwannock partly to trad with the Indians, (of whom he says he sometimes had a hnundred with him and partly to explore the country for mines, &c; at one time he attempted the culture of the vine there, but the soil rebelled. Letters passing between him and the owners are extent which tell of the attempts to make the estate there profitable and of their failure. In 1631 there is no mention of any being with him except his wife and child, and Roger Knight and wife, but probably there were others as workmen, as there were 13 July 1633 when he mentions as such Charles Kneil, Thomas Clark, Steven Kidder, and Thomas Crockett.

When the joint proprietorship ceased the enterprise received a little life from Mason's energy— Gibbons was informed by Gorges and Mason in a letter dated 5 May 1634, of the division already mentioned, andthat other men were already shipped either to reinforce or to super sede him. A letter came at the same tim rom Mason stating that the person "now sent with Mr. Joselyne are to sett upp two mills upon my own division o lands;" the servants were to be paid out of the stock of beaver on hand and to be discharged. An inventory was to be taken and division made. The pers n alluded to were bound by contract as follows, in which it appears that Belknap either substitutes Humphrey for William Chadburne, or else that Bot were there.

In the Mass. Archives are these Articles of agreement between John Mason on the one hand and James Wall, William Chadbour e, and John Goddard on the other: they are written on parchment, dated 14 March 1633, and though of a peculiar handwriting are remarkably legible. The document represents that John Mason owns certain lands in New England and especially an "estate and interest called Newichewannock lying upon and neer to the Ryver there Called the Pascataway," that he intends "by Gods permission by the first and next Couenyent shiping to send to his said lands and there to place and settel servanntts and others." that he has agreed with the three individuals above na med that they are "to goe over unto the said lands" and to stay there for five years, in which time they are to cut timber, build dwelling houses, erect two mills, "and pfor ne such other work" a the said John wants done; John agre s als for the sake of their haviug "victuell and other provissions," to send over "certen Cowes goates swyne and other things," to the amount of 40lbs, and to pay the expense of transporting the men and articles; and in return, the three men are to have three-fourths of the profits of the mills' own three fourths of the houses, and receive three fourths of money for which houses, frame or timber shall be sold. Mason agrees also to furnish within thirty days after their landing "Three Cowes ffoure goats and floure eowes" for which they will pay yearly 6lb, 13s 4d, in money and half in the yearly increase of said live stock, and which they covenent to make good at the end of five years. Mason also promises that within forty days after their landing, there shall be allotted to each, ten acres of land for their paesent use for planting corn, grazing, and as house lots, for which each shall pay him yearly "at the feast of Saint Michaell The archungell" ne bushel of corn and at the end of five years the said amount of ten acres with forty more shall be leas d to each of them for three years, the yearly rent f which to be thre bushels of corn. And for the fulfillment of these conditions on their part, the emigrants are bound, jointly and severally in the sum of £100

I appears probable that these persons came over in the "Pide-Cow," the same ship which brought the letters to Gibb ns, and which arrived at Portsmouth 8 July 1634, casting anchor half a mile below the lower falls at Quam phegan on the 13th; the ship was com pletely unladen on the 18th, and the carpenters began their work for the erection of the mill on the 22d. That the came according to agree ent is absolutely pr ved by the testimony of Wall, 21, 3, 1652, when he says that he, William Chadbourne and Jonn Goddard "came over" about 1634 "for themselvet and as agents" and were placed at Newichnwan n ck, and they there "built a sawmill" and a "sta nping ill for corne" and bought upland of the Indians, that they held this land for three or four years and then conveyed in to Thomas Spencer (s n-in-law to said James Wall) who then, 1652, lived upon it.

OLD SERIES NUMBER 137.

NEWICHWANNOCK.

(concluded)

The inventory ordered by Mason doesnot appear to have been made unill July 1635, when the following was ound to be the account of goods at Newichwannock:

Arms and Ammunition.
2 Robenets, 2 Murthers, 2 Chambers 9 Harquebusses, 47 Muskets & Bandeleers, 28 ffowling pieces, 33 Carbins,

Case Pistols, 56 Swords & Belts, 6 Bar Pwder, 57 Bullets, 1 firkin lead Bullets Bar. Matdh, 1 Drum, 204 S all Shot Stores.

31 Cloth Cassocks & Breeches, 35 Canvas Cassocks, 55 Stuff Coats & Breeches, 67 Shirts, 43 Hats, 191 pr. Shoes, 152 pair of Stockings' 28 Monmouth Caps, 42 lined Coats, 32 Red West Coats 6 ps. Bays, 4 Bolts Canvas, 14 ct w Lead, 793 pewter, 594 ct Brass, 482 of, Copper, 3 Bar Nails, 90 Bars Iron, 14 Bars Steal, all sorts of Smith's, Carpenters, Masons, Coopers Tools, 2 Scaws, 345 pine planks, 1073 Boards.

Pronisions

192 Bushells Corn, 5 Bar, Oatmeal. 4 Bar. Meal, 12 Buts Malt, 9 Baca Pease, 97c Candles, 390 Tobacco, 370, Sugar, 2 Pips Wine, 240 Galls. Aqur vita, 1 Chirurgons Chest.

Cattle.

24 Cows, 2 Bulls, 22 Steers & heifers, 10 Calves, 92 Sheep & Lambs, 27 Goats, 64 Hogs old and young, 13 Mares and horses, 9 Colts.

This was certified as being a true inventory by Ambaose Gibbins and Thomas Wenerton, of the goods delivered to Mr. Joselyn.

It is possible that Mason's energy might have caused the settlement to flourish, but his unexpected death, in 1635, was fatal to his family interests. Some time after his death, Mrs. Mason, Widow and Executrix, sent over Francis Norton, as her agent to manage the business of the estate at Portsmouth and Newichwannock: but the expenses excedrd the income, the servants grew impatient of arrears for wages, and Mrs. Mason was forced to abandon the working of the plantation, telling the servants t take care of themselves, which they did by dividing the goods and cattle, scme of the settlers abandoned the Masonian estates, others remained and finally claimed the improvements as their own; before 1644 the hauses at Newichwannock were burned, and in both that place and Portsmouth Mason's property was ruined. An effort was made aso had right by purchase of the Indians, as also by possession and improvement," and the government rdered "a quantity of land proprionable to his disbursements with the privilege of the river, to be laid out to his heirs."—Inasmuch as Mason claimed the whole territory, this decision was unsatisfac or, and he returned to England without further effort. This was the last special attempt to recover the title; it is probably true that the title to the soil of part of Mason's estate was claimed and used by the town.

The firs actual settlers of Salmon Falls, were, as already stated, Ambrose Gibbons, James Wall, W. Chadbourne, and John Goddard.

Ambrose Gibbons, removed to Sander's Poin, a tract given him by the proprietors, in 1632, on account of his faithful services. e was a magistrate of Dover at a subsequent period, had grants of land, &c as in 1652, when he received land joining his marsh from "the creek between his land a d William Roberts'" to the "westarn creek," and in 1654, 200 acres near his house which was laid out 9, 9, 1651, to Robert Burnum, success r to Henry Sherburne his son-in-aw. His will was dated at Oyster River 11 July 1656, proved 9 May 1656. Samuel, his grandson, son of Henry Sherburne and his wife Rebeckah Gibbons, to be his heir, he paying certain sums to brothers and sisters (all under age) viz, Elizabeth, Mary, Henry, John, Ambrose, Sarah, Rebeckah.

James Wall, appears to have a had son-in-law of Thomas Spencer, and to have witnessed the Indian deed to Wheelwright in April 1638, he was one of the signers to he "combination" in Exeter 4, 8, 1639, was selectman in 1649, and 150. He resided in Exeter but further information (published in Exeter News Letter) is not now within our reach.

William Chadbourne, may have had decendants at Newichwannock, or they may have come from Humphrey Chadbourne. He had one son, who came here with him, William, Jr. who was o

Kittery 1652. William Sen. may have b en the William of Boston 1644.

John Goddard, became a settler of Dover Neck, where he was in 1648; was a carpenter; was freeman in 1653: went early to Oyster River, where in 1659 he, sold land to William Williams. He resided near Gr at Bay, where "Goddard's Creek" immortalizes his memory. He died about 1659-60; inventory entered 15 Nov. 1660; His wife Welthea, was born in 1621, survived him and afterward mar.—Simmons. She was alive 27 July 1705, but incapable of business; at that date she gave her farm to her grandson which caused a lawsuit, in which John Woodman testified as to her incapacity. John had children, John B. b. 1942; Benjamin; daughter, who mar. John Gilman; daughter, who married Arthur Bennet; daughter, who mar. James Thomas. John 2 lived at Oyster River. His will was dated 2 July 1672 some time between 1674 and 1677 he came to an "untimely death:" in his will he gave property to bro. Benjamin, to sons of his three sisters, viz. John Gilman John Bennet, and James Thomas, jr. and Martha Welthea Simmons.

Other men succeeded these at Newichwannock; who they were we have no means just now of stating. When the claim of Mason became imperative, other settlers took possession and the place flourished. The falls came, before 1700, partly into the hands of Judge John Tuttle, who also owned large tracts adjoining; other men purchased land in that vicinity as recorded in Dover Records; but our present purpose is accomplished in narrating the circumstances of the settlement.

OLD SERIES, NO. 139.

DEEDS.

To or from Dover men: taken from the Registry at Exeter.

These abstracts, uninteresting as they may appear to the General reader, are in fact of importance to all interested in Dover history, and invaluable to those who are investigating the genealogy of their families. We preserve spelling, localities, boundaries and names, verbatim.

From Vol. 1—complete.

Joseph Miller of Dover to John Goddard of Dover; house, &c. where "Miller now dwelleth, and five acres of land;" also 20 acres of land given by the town of Dover to Thomas Larkham, "lyenge on the west side of backe River;" also 30 acres of "meadow ground" given to Larkham by the town, lying on the westerlie side of the greate baye neere unto a Cove called the greate Cove," excepting 10 acres given to "John Aulte by the saide Thomas Larkham, also 100 acres "of grounde lyenge on the Esterlie side of the saide marshe groudde also given by" Dover to said Larkham; dated 20 Sept. 1647.

Richard Cater "sometime dwelling in Pascataway" to "my trustie and well beloved friend Mathew Giles dwelling in Oyster River;" "messuage and Tenemente lyeinge & beinge in Pascataway river, lyeinge upon pine point;"—24 June 1648.

Edward Colcord of Hampton to Edward Starbucke: the "Island called or knowne as Umbunbacke or Edward Colcorde I lande lying or being or neer adioyninge unto the northerlie side of Lampreye River."—3, 6, 1648.

Valentine Hill of Boston, give bonds to Thomas Cobbit of Linne for Estate of Jane Skipper which was in his possession, pledging his right in "three quarters of Oystor River" and in "three quarters of the mill worke erected there at psent or in its best psertion."—18 Nov. 1650.

Samuel Austin to William ffurbur of Dover; "huuse and two lotts with all the boards aboute saide house," he professing himself satisfied except "three pounds to be paid to Goodman hearde, by nexte michalmas, in pease or wheat, or goodes price currante."—Dec. 1650.

William Pomfret of Dover to Hatevillo Nutter; "all that messuage or Tenemente in Dover now in the Tenure or occupation of me the saide William Pomfrett, lyeinge & being neer the backe Cove in Dover, with a barn and garden thereunto belonginge;" also 5 acres on the easterly side of said premisses; alst marsh on the north east side of great bay "at the great Cove there ab ve longe pointe between the marsh of John Dam of the one side and the marsh of Thomas Layton on the other side."—20, 6, 1651.

John Aulte of Oyseer River to Charles Adams, for £20; "mesuage or tenemeute" at Oyster River; also "so much marsh ground as will keep three Cows in the winter time.—10 April 1645.

John Lavis (Davis ?) of "bloodye pointe" to Michael Brown; premises formerly in possession of Thomas ffurber.—30 June 1651.

Anthony Emery " of Coleharberte in the province of mayne," to William Pomfrett; "two houses in Dover late in" Emery's occupation, with garden and land adjoining.—1, 6, 1651.

William Pomfrett of Dover, planter to William ffollett, Phillipp Lewis, for 4 lbs two thirds of the "accomedation of a saw mill given to me at bellemies banke fall by the Towne of dover."—16, 5, 1651.

Thomas Johnson of pascataway, planter to Nicholas ffollett, for 80 lbs. house, marsh, goods, cattle &c. 6 Sept. 1652.

William Bearde to ffrancis mathews; for 35 lbs.—10s; premises in O. R. joining lands of Darby Field.—June 1640.

William Hilton of Dover to francis mathews; 88 acres of land on the north side af O. R. which was given him by Dover; also "marsh in a Creeke thereunto adioyning." 7 July 1641,

Edward Starbuck & wife Kathren to Peter Coffin of Dover; "Cochecho upper ffalls granted to him" by town of Dover 6 Dec. 1650, with all "accomedations of water & timber." 20, 5, 1652.

George Smyth of Dover to Denys Downinge of Kittery; "messuage" &c. in Kittery. Dec. 1656.

From Vol. 2.

Richard Waldern of Cuchichoe to Joseph Austin; one fourth "of a sawmill which is Erected & set upp at or upon Cuchechoe falls," for 25 lbs. 20 Dec. 1649.

John Herd "of the River Pascata. quacke planter" to "george walton of the same place Taylor on(e) neck of Land Called muskito liinge on the great Island." 1 March 1649.

Henry Tibbatts of Dover, planter, to John Tuttle on the west, & the lott of Thomas Bearde on the South." 1 June 1657.

William furber of Dover to Thomas Noke of Dover; 20 acres of upland on "the north side of kerchechqcha river at a place called by the name of the golfe granted to the said furber by the towne of Dover." 2 July 1657

James Rawlins of Pascattaquacke planter to Richard Cater; marsh "lyenge in the bottom of the great bay;" also 33 acres of upland for 20 lbs. 14 July 1657.

John Godard of Dover, Carpenter, to William Williams of Dover, planter; 40 acres "which was John Hilon's with ye Necke of land wch lyes betweene Stouey Brooke & the Meeting house Lott;" 6, 4 1659,

Richard Walderne of Cochecho in presincts of Dover in pascattaquack River now resident in Boston in New England mecht & ann his wife" to Richard Russel of Charlestown; for 120 lbs., one-fourth of saw mill "at Bellemyes banke River in ye Limits & bounds of Dover wch he lately purchased of phillip Lewis, Thomas Bird and Thomas Scruton all of Dover aforesaid," with timber &c. 13 April 1660.

Thomas Broughton to Capt Thomas Clarke of Boston ; one fourth of the sawmill at the second falls which he purchased of Edward Starbuck; also the "house yt Goodwife Starbuck lives in." 4 April 1659.

OLD SERIES, NO. 140.

DEEDS

to or from Dover men: taken from the Registry at Exeter.

Vol. 2—Continued.

"Valentine Hill of Dover in Piscataq. Riuer in New England archt & Mary my wife for 230 lbs. to Nathaliel Micklethayte of London 300 acres in New Haven, formerly in possesion of Mr. Theophilus Eaton, Esq. gouernor of New Haven Given by him as a Legacie to Mary my wife." dated 2 Nov. 1660,

Richard Walderne of Quochecho resigns unto Capt. John Sealy his right to land which they had jointly brought of Ronald Fernald deceased. 15 Nov. 1660. (Capt, Sealey was Commander of the ship Called the Dolphin of London.")-

Thomas Willey of Oyster Riuer & Margaret Willey Wife of &c for 87 lbs. sells to John Cutt of Portsmouth, house and lands marsh, cow, calves, bull &c. 27 June 1660.

"James Rawlins of Douer yeoman," for 4 M white oake pipestaves to Capt. Bryan Pendleton "Land att Cannyer Cove we I bought of John Sealey and did formerly belong to Thomas Canny of Dover." 20 Jany 1661.

"Edward Starbuck of Cochecha," to "my sonn in law peter Coffin all my houses & Lands marsh & Meadows Scituate and Lying within the jurisdicktion of Dover, with all the appurtinances thereunto belonging & also all my house holdg ods or implements within doors lor without to him the sd Peter &c.;" also "all my Cattle and beasts of all sort;" 9 Mar. 1659-60,

6 March, 1659-60, a dwelling house "scituate & being in New worke in Douer," and 25 acres of land; the house he had lately dwelt in.

Valentine Hill of Dover for 45 lbs sells "to Patrick Ginison ofthe same towne" all my land on the North side of Oyster Riuer adjoyning to my land at my mills there. 11 May 1659.

Valentine Hill of Dover, to "Capt. Clark & Mr. Wm Paddy of , " my far e caled Greenland lying in ye batt of the greate bay in ye Riuer Pascataqua," 21 Oct, 1658,

"Wher as Capt. Jno Mason of London, as at his death sized & pessest of Certaine Land at Pascataway in New England as Namely the great house upland & marshes," and had servants and cattle there, and "did Intrust one Ralph Gee a servant of his more pticiler to Lo ke unto ye sd Cattle & did furnish him with a plautation were adjoyning," now Joseph Mason, Kinsman of said John, in behalf of Ann, Widow and Adinin'x of said Joh , finding that said Ralph Gee is deceased & dyed in ye yeere 1645," and that said Gee was much indebted at ye time of hi decease unto Wm. Seavey the Eldr," and that said Seavey had taken possession of the abovementioned plantatlou (appraised however only at £18 towards a debt of 52lbs,) he, the said Mason, quit claims said plantation to Wm. Seavey. 30 March 1660.

Samuel Hall, witness—p. 61 - of Portsmouth,

"Phillip Chesly of oyster riuer in Douer of piscattaq in New Engladd husbandman," conveys to wife and children "house & Land & all my Cattle namely horses oxen Cowes & you N cattle sheepe & Swine & all my pirestaues & hhd staues & barll staues & all my movable goods except a bed," — to wife one third and to children two thirds; and considering "my children are in theire nynoritie or nonage & my wife a Weake Woman," Thomas Wiggin of Quamscott is to be guardian. 28 June 1661.

Jeremy Tibqetts, for 7 lbs, 4s. conveys to Job Clements "ffive score acres of Land" which had been granted him by the selectmen in 1658, and laid out 22, 2. 1662, "lying and being at ye head of ye Lower range of Lotts wch are Laid out by Nechewannuch Riuer side betwixt St. Albanes Cove & Quamphegin fall and bounded as ffull wth, that is to say on the North East by Thomas Hansons hundred acres of Land Lade out at the same time whn this was, on ye South East by some of ye Lower Range of Lotts, on the Southwest part by ye Comm n & par ly by Eldr Wentworthes Land wch he bought of Anthony E ery, on ye North West by the sd Mr. Clemants his five scoore acres of Land Laid out at ye same time alsoe." Signed by Jer. Tibbetts (his mark,) 23, 2, 1662; witnessed by Charles and Mary Buckner.

John Hall "of Douer in pascattaq, in New England, planter," conveys to Job Clements of the same place tannir," "flvs score acres of Land wch Was granted to be sd Hall by ye selectmen" 11, 11, 1648, "which lyeth betwixt Cohecho & Salmon fall bordering on ye North North west on ye Comon on the south west upon five score acres of land which was granted to ye sd Clements at the same time when this Land was granted to ye sd Clements at the same time when this Land was granted, on the south scuth east ptly by Tho Hansons Land & partly by Ralph Twomblys Land, on the North east by Mr. Tho Broughtons Land;" 21, 4, 1664. Acknowledged by John Hall and wife 23, 4, 1665. Witness, Wm. Pomfret, Charles Buckner.

James Rawlings, for 40 lbs, 16s. 9d. mortgages to Brian Pendleton of Portsmouth "An hundred Acres of Land" Lying in ye Long reach fro Cannye Coua upward nyntie cd pole by ye water side & soe up into the Woods, together with the Land wch is in Tilledg with ye Corn upon it & my New Dwelling house, with two Ccwes," &c; 25 Aug. 1662; witnessed by Christopher Banfield, Robert Taprill.

Joseph Austin's will lrcght ino Court 30 June 1663, by his wiw Sarah Austin.

"Whereas Hatevell Nutter of Douer & Tho Layton of Dover at ye request of John Godard of Douer aforesd & for his jointly & seuerally standeth bound with ye sd Jno Godard unto Joseph Miller of Dover aforesd for ye payment and delivery of 16500 of mert pipe staues made of white oake at ar before ye 24th day of June wch shall in ye yeer of our Ld God 1649 at high water marke where a boate of 10 tunn may conveniently come to Laye yu with ye precincts of Dover as by a Certaine writing undr ye hands & seales more at large appeareth bearing date ye 21 day of Septemb 1647." Now John Goddard binds his lands &c. to the said Nutter and Layton for securty, 21 Sept 1647: Gorge Smith witness.

Philip Chesley of Oyster Riuer quitclaims to Joseph Austin, of Dover, planter, right 20 acres of upland at Cchecho joining land of John Godd, Jno Goddard given him by the town of Dover in the year 1644: 7 Aug. 1661; signed by Phillip Chesley and Elizebeth Chesley; witnesses, Charles Buckner, Ralp Twamley (his mark.)

Richard York of Dover, planier, quitclaims to Joseph Austin, right to marsh at iLttle John's Creek, sold to him by Mr. Hilton and which was given by the town to Hilton; 7 Aug. 1661. Signed Rrchard York (his mark) and Elizabeth York; witnesses, St phen Robinson, Jno Wood an.

John Roberts conveys to Joseph Austin "all my uplaed" "commonly called & knowu by the name of Cchecho poynt in Piscattaq Riuer; 7 July 1658. witnesses, Ralph Hall, Charies Buckner.

Willm ffurber, for 22 los, 10s. conveys to Josph Austin, "the Quarter part of a saw mill grant, Granted to me ye sd Wm ffurber by the town of Dover," "Scituate lying & being betwene fresh Creeke Newichwannuck River;" 2 July 1662; witnesses, Thomas Beard, Charles Buckner. Elizabeth Furber wife surrendered right 3 July.

Wm. ffurber, for 45 lbs, conveys to Joseph Austin, reserving one quarter acre, " y dwelling house & Lott granted to me ye sd Wm, Furber by the town of Dover," "on ye Neck of Dover," with two other Lotts purchased of Thomas Beard & Samuel Austin, all of which, consitute 10 acres or thereabouts were bounded N by lot of John Heard of Cchecho, E. by "fore Riuer," S. by "the Layne," W. by " he strcete." 12 July 1662 Elizabeth Jones, Thomas Beard and Charles Buckner, witnesses

Richard Walderne of Cochecho sells to Joseph Austin, one fourth part of "Saw-will wch is erected & set up at or upon Cochecho ffalls" with liberty of passage &c.; 20 Dec. 1649. Witnesses, Jonan Coventry, Edward Starbuck, John Poor.

Whereas Massachusetts in 1656 "granted a Deuision of the pattent of Quamscot" by which the lands of "Nathaniell Gardner, Thomas Lake & ptners fell iu the bounds of Strabery banke" & Capt Richard Walderne here purchased an interest, and Lake had sold to Strawberry Bank, lands, reserving 450 acres for the far s of Goodman Haynes, Jno Hall & Wm. flurber. Waldron and Lake sell to John Hall 170 acres of upland "nere adjoyning to his house & ten acres more on the North side of Jno Roberts his Creeks in twentie Acres of marsh in the ffrsh meadow we'le ye sd Jno Hall has possessed seuerall years." 24 Mar. 1657, Witnesses Edward C lcurd, William Po fret, Chares Buckner.1

Peter Coffin sells to Jno Hall of Greenland upland "formerly the Land of Edward Starbuck granted" by Dover, on the S. E. ide of Great Bay. 15 Dec. 1662. Witnesses, Tho. Bradbury, Willi Sargent. Possession given "wth twigg aud turfe," 25,10, 1662, in presence of Nat. Nutter, Thomas Roberts, Joseph Hall.

OLD SERIES, Number 141.
DEEDS.

To or from Dover men: taken from the Registry at Exeter.

Volume 2—Continued.

"Olliuer Winget of Bridgtowne In the Countie of Deun in Old England being lately cast away at ye Isles of Sholes, & dying intestate, It is granted unto Edward Holland his kinsman pow er of Administration in sd Olliuer Winget his estate. And sd Edward is Injoyned to bring in an Inventory of his estate to the Next Court held at Portsmouth the 28th of this Instant June 13, 4, 1664.

"Mrs Ludeces of dover" having died intestate, James Middleton appointed Administrator and serves. 28 June 1664.

Oliver Wingate left a widow, as appears by record of 28 June 1664; his estate was valued at 60 lbs-, 11s. 2d.

Richard Walderne lets to Phillip Cromwell three rths of sawr ill at Bellymyes Bank for four years, promising and keep it in repair, as also a medow at Sandy point in Great Boy; 26 N.M. 1660. John Heard (his mark,) Joseph Sanders (his mark) and Timothy Walderne, wit esses.

By the next paper, releases, for cor siderations, the pledge to finish and keep in repair Sa e date, same witnesses.

Richard Walderne conveys to Richard Russell of Charlestown, a certain part of the sawmill last mentioned; Boston 20 Dec. 1660.

James Rawlings mortgages to Arian Pendleton 100 acres at Long reach: July 1663.

John Robberts having sold to Lieut. Ralph Hall, in 1663, five acres of land, dw ng house, &c. on Dover Neck, bounded N. by lot formerly Wm. Story's now Philip Cromwells, E by the fore River, S. by "a Layue Running fro the street to ye f r d Riuer towards ye bottom turning first Southward then againe Eastward to ye Riuer," W. by ho street, c nfirms the sale 18 Oct. 1664: Abigail, his wife made her mark. Walter Barefoote, Job Clements, witnesses.

Ralph Hall and Mary his Wife sell for 45 lbs., to "Mr. John Reyner senior Teacher of the Church of the sd Douer," "my dwelling house & Lott" on Dover Neck, bounded as the preceding; Oct. 19, 1664. Ralfe and Mary sign. Witnesses, Richard Walderne, Elias Stileman.

Thomas Beard and Mary his wife, for 80lbs Mr. John Reyner, land "being a part of my Lott, Lying on the East side of Doyer Neck, ' next north of Mr. Reyner's. 3 Feb. 1664. Mary his wife made her mark. John Hall senr. John Hall jr (his mark) witnesses.

Nathaniel Starbuck sells to William Horne, land "Scituate in Dover, aforesd betweene Cocchecho & Tole end, 240 acres; 20 Sept. 1661 Ralfe Hall, Abraham Corbett, Witnesses.

Thomas Payne sells to Job Clements 60 a. given by Douer 21, 9, 1659, lying and being at the N rhern end of Richard Oatis his hundred acres of Land being North East fro cochecho marsh and was formerly granted & Layd out to him the sd Otis," bounded S. W. by Joseph Austin's land, N. E. by the common and Job Clements; acknowledged 29, 4, 1665. John Hall, John Brady (his mark,) witnesses.

Patrick Denmark had wife Ann. W... Pitman had wife Ann.

"James Paquamehood of Tollend," sells to James Rawlings of Long Reach for 20 lbs "land, upland& marsh, hills & ponds comonly called and knowne the seurall names hereafter named (viz.) one hill called by ye name of piscosauak, e second h ll called by ye name o Munsacko, the Third hill called by ye name of Pinnische, the first pond called by the name of Sinquamosey, ye Second pond called by the name of Westsac ack & ye third pond by the name of Pumbassamod, wch sayd hills & ponds do encon pass & make the bounds of the sd Lands and also all & singular wayes, rathes, passages, Trees, wood & underwoods, Waters and Water courses, comons, Comma (?) of pasture on the Waits & woods there, & all easements, & 'fitts conudities" &c. &c ; 20 Oct. 1665. Witnesses: Henry Longstaffe Walter Barefoote, Anthony Nutter, Abram Corbett.

John Roberts "of the Town" of Dover in the County of Norfolke, Masachusetts," planter, and wife Abigail, sell to Joseph Hall of Greenland planter, certain upland, 18 acres, being part of the 400 a. given by Mass. General Court to town of Dover, bounded W on Great Bay, E. upon the "Countrie highway Leading to a place called bloody poynt," N. upon land of "John Hall father to ye d Joseph Hall;" 29 June 1665. Job Clements sen. John Redman, sen., witnesses.

James Ordway of Newbury, sells to Jno Heard of Cochecho, 70 acres formerly granted him by the town," being on the further side of the half wayes Swa p going to the marsh of "cochecho;" 10 Mar. 1662. Signed by James (his mark) and Ann Ordway (her mark) Witnesses, Peter Coffin, Richard Oatis (his mark.)

Anthony nutter, and Sarah, conveys to John Roberts Jr, land lying on "Harrod's Coue" in Great Bay, in exchange, for marsh at "Welchman's Coue"' 25 June 1664. Sarah made her mark. Hatevil Nutter, Ralph Hall, witnesses.

Thomas Roberts Jr., and wife Mary' give papers corresponding to last mentioned; same day same witnesses. Thomas and wife made their marks.

Thomas Willey, of O. R. sells to William Parkesin of O. R. a lot lyg between land lately Henry Hollwells and another lot of Willeys; 4 Aug. 1666 Thomas made his mark. Witnesses Phillip Russell (his mark,) Steeven Willey (his mark,) Rich. Stileman Sen.

John Allt, for the "father affection I bear to my son Thomas and daughter Rebecca Edgerly," conveys Lands bought of Tho Seabrooke, "Lying in the Little Bay in ye South west side of yt brooke wch runneth betweene ye Lott of Rich. Bray & Tho Humphreys with ten acres adjoyning;" John and wife Remembrance made their marks; 17 June 1667. Witnesses, Hatevil Nutter, John Reyner.

"Goodman Kirke of Dover" licensed to keed house of entertainment. 25 June 1667.

George Walton of Portsmouth, conveys to John Haunce of O. R. carpenter land on Great Island; 24 May 1665.

Widow Goddard bought in valuation of estate of her late husband, at £554 2s; 17 Sept. 1667.

Report of Jury on "untimely death of Simon Buzie of O. R.; 17 Sept. 1667.

"Thomas Doutie now Resident at oister Riuer," sells to Jno Cutt of Portsmouth, land, marsh &c. dwelling house, &c, now in occupation of Wm. Roberts of O. R. and purchased of him; Oct. 1657. Thomas made his mark. William ffollet, Wm. Roberts, Wm. Williams Sen.

OLD SERIES Number 142-

DEEDS·

To or From Dover men: taken from the Registry at Exeter.

Vol. 2—Continued.

Charles Buckner and wife Mary of Boston, sell to Job Clements senr. four acres of land bounded E. on fore River, N. by common, W. by highway, S. by "Mr. David Ludecas Edling his Lott formerly soe called;" 12 April 1668- Witness, Samuel Peacock, Ebenezer Hagden.

Oliver Kent of O. R. having died intestate, Widow Dorothy, and John Bickford appointed to administer. 3 July 1669.

Will and inventory of Thomas Leigton brought into Court by Jno Reyner and Thomas Boberts. 25 June 1672.

Wm. Durgin having married the Relict of Thomas Footman, petitions the Court to divide the property of said relict so that he be paid for their support, which was done; children under age: 25 June 1675

Hatevill Nutter to son Anthony Nutter of Welchman's Cove, planter, gives to Anthony and after Anthony's decease to grandson John, land given him by Dover in 1663 at or near La uperele River: as also right in Lamperle lower falls; 10 April 1669. John Roberts, Job Clements, witnesses.

From Vol. 3-

John Ault "of ye Little Bay in ye township of Dover yeoman" and Remembrance, sell to Wm. Perkinson of ye same place yeoman, land on Gopard's Creek in Dover, between land of Charles Adams and Nicholas Dowe; 8 June 1669.

Ralph Twamley of Dover, and wife Elizabeth, for 8 lbs. sell to Ralph Hall of Dover right to 16 acres given by Dover, lying between St. Alban's Cove and Quamphegan, bounded N. E. by Mr. Broughton's 200 acres, N. W. by the common, S. W. by Thomas Hanson's, S. E. by John Dam and Henry Tebbetts: Ralph made his mark; 1 Mar. 1659. Thomas Kemble, Thomas Robards, witnesses.

Thomas Canney sen. "for natural affection" &c. gives, with slight reservations, all his property to his son Joseph, for an annuity of 18 lbs; Thomas made his mark. 3 Dec. 1669. William Pomfrett, Job Clements Junr. witnesses.

Isaac Gardner attorney of his brother Nathaniel Gardner who "sometime since Lyuing in New Fngland" owned a moiety "or halfe part of Twelve shares in ye two pattents of Swamscott & Dover" as by deed from Thomas Lake of Boston 2 Nov. 1649, and had sold one third of his right to "Henry Barkley of London mcht,"—conveys the remaining right of said Nathaniel to Thomas Lake of Boston and Richard Walderne of Dover; 4 June 1670.

Joseph Sanders "of Dover in ye Countie of Dover & Ports,o" sells to John Heard 30 acres on Dover Neck neere Cochecho, right up from Campons Rockes," joining Tobias Hanson's land and the common; 25 Oct. 1669 Joseph made his mark. Witnesses, William Keene, John Gatting-ly (eis mark).

Samuel Wentworth of Portsmouth and wife Mary, sell to Job Clements tanner, 20 acres between Nechewannucn & Cochecho, bounded E. by land of Clements, N, by Richar Oates, W. by Joseph Banney, S. by Peter Coffin, 4 Aug. 1670.

Richard Waldren of Dover, sells to Robert Evens, husbandman, 5 acres at Bellerman's tanke, next to land where said Evans' dwelling house stands; 8 Dec. 1669. Peter Coffin, Tho Pinckhav witnesses.

Henry Brown of O. R. for 30 lbs. sells to Teige Riall of O. R. four and one half acres "with housen fences" &c. next land of Edward Leathers and of Edward Patrison, at O. Rr Henry made his mark. 8 Aug. 1667. Witnesses, J hn Woodman, Patrick Jemmesou (his mark.) Same land, Teige Riall conveys to James Smith, "Talour." of O. R. 28 Mar 1670. Thomas Michell, Thomas Edgerly, witnesses.

Ralph Twamley sells to J dedioh An drews, "my hou-e and land c ntaining three acres" being in Dover in the south side of Mr John Reyner's land;" 20 Mar 1628-9. Ralph made his ark. Charles Buckner, Sames Newte, witnesses.

Thomas Downes, shoemaker sells to Jediah Andrews of Salisbury Mass. carpenter "my late dwelling house and Lott" east side of the neck, bounded E. by fore River, S. by Mr. Reyner's land' N. W. by common; 17 May 1670. Hatevil utter, Thomas Layton, witnesses.

Jedediah Andrews of Salisbury and wife Mary sell to Mr. John Reyner Minister, "y house & La d;" the 1 t being granted him by Dover 17 Mar. 1659: bounded E· by highway which "goeth between it and ye land of ye sd Reyner," N. by Mr. Reyner's upper lot, W. by Sheep pasture, S by Mr. Rob erts lot, also 3 a. laid out to Ralph Twa ley at "Clay poynt between the house lot of Thomas Roberts & the Land of ye sd John Reyner above sd below ye highway above menconed wch was given to & possessed by ye sd T vanley as a house Lott." Also a house Lott "granted to & laid to & possessed formerly by Thoras Downes," joining lot of Mr. Reyner on ye South. Also 66 acres granted to said Andrews by Dover in 1656 on "the north rly side of cochecho Riur" bounded N. E by common, S. E. by 60 acres laid out John Hilton, S. W. by "Cochecho River ffreshett," N. W. by 50 acres granted to Thomas Downes;" 5 Jan. 1669. Jediah made his mark. Hatevill Nutter, Thomas Layton (his mark) witnesses. Thomas Canney renews deed of property to son Joseph; my late dwelling house and land, bounded E. by fure river, N. by a Cove, W. by "ye Great Streete on Dover Neck," S. by land lately Joseph Austin's; also lot on D, N. bounded N. by John Roberts, W. by a Cove, S. by land lately Richard Pinckam's; also 4 a. on D. N. bounded N. by common also 30 acres west Great Bay, except 3 acres of marsh already laid out to son Thomas; also 80 acres on north side of Cochecho narsh; also one eighth of Cochecho poynt, bound d (undivided) by "Cochecho Riuer, Nechewannick Riuer & Nechewanick path from fresh creek to St. Albans Coue;" acknowledged 6 Oct. 1670. Jabez F e, Hatevell Nutter, Job Dlements, sen, Witnesses.

OLD SERIES Number 144

A careful search hrough old Norfolk Co. Deeds, has given us several items regarding Dover people or their relatives, which we deem worthy of preservation.

Edward Colcord, as usual, occupies a large share of space, He was a Hampton man a Dover man, an Exeter man, now in Massachusets, then in England, n several sides in every quarrel and quareling on every side himself, The first extract is of course about him:—

Edward Colcord sold, 15, 12, 1646, to Thomas Chase three and a half acres of meadow n Hampton.

We might as well follow him up perhaps:

Edward Colcord bought of John L gate of Exeter ten acres of marsh, 1, 1, 164 - 50.

Edward Colcord mortgaged to Richard Oliver of Hampton' land, 10, Aug. 166., fo 50 lbs.

Edward Colcord of Hampton settles an execution for debt due to Thomas Kimball of Ipswich by deeding him land 28, 9, 1666.

Edward Colcord discharged Francis Swain's estate of a debt of 3000 pipstaves assigned him 16 Jan. 1657 by Henry Green f Hampton, 3, 12, 1667,

Edward Colcord was attorney for Geo. Peirson of Boston to collect a debt of Samuel Leavitt of Exeter, 19 Mar, 1672.

Edward Colcord "in consideratfon of ye great care, love and respect wch my brother Robert Page, Decon of ye Church of Hampton hath manifested to mee, my wif and childre in securing my est e of housing & lands in Hampton & makeing severall disburs mts for my wife & children in my absence & now at ye as resigning up ye sd nousing & and n Hampton unto mee wife and children forever without any foerther co s'e ation but ye paymt of ye sum of twenty pound wc my sd deare brother Deacon Page doth gi e as a t en o his love unto six of my children," viz, to Sarah Hobbs 4 lbs. to Mary ffifeild 4 lbs. to be paid 1 year after the Deacon's decease & to "my fouer children at home viz. Mehitaball, Samuell, Shuah & Deborah, 3 lbs. apiece as they come of age.

While we are on this matter we might as well finish up Edward; we wrote a little about him once, but other facts, which corroborate all we said of him, give us more light. Edward was born in 1614 or 1615; we dont believe Hubbard wh n he says that Edward was once Governor of Dover, but he was in Dover in 1642. He was in Hampton as early as 1645 and lived where the old north school house now stands. He was perhaps in Exeter by and by, and certainly in lawsuits pretty much all the time. He was a very busy man indeed, was in bad repute with all parties, was now and then indicted for quarrelsomeness, but was liked by various very respectable people. He died in Hampton 10 Feb. 1681-2. He had wife Anne, and children, Jonathan b.— d. 31, 6, 1661; Mary b. 14, 8, 1649, mar. 28, 10, 1670, Benjamin Fifield; Edward b. 2, 12, 1651, killed by the Indians 13 June 1677, undoubledly the one referred to by Belknap, "whose death was very much regretted," and whose inventory was entered 9, 8, 1677; Hannah b.—mar. 28, 10, 1665, Thomas Dearborn; Sarah b.—mar. 30, 10, 1668, John Hobbs; Shuah b. 12, 4, 1660; Deborah b. 21, 3, 1664; Abigail b. 23, 5, 1667; Mehitable b.— mar. 20, 10, 1697 Nathanielel Stevens of Dover. We think that there was another son, Samuel, who had wife Mary, and ch. Jonathan b. 4 Mar. 1683-4; Elizabeth b 26, Dec. 1686. Regarding the doubt whether is was Abraham or Edward who was killed 13 June 1677, we can add that Abraham Jr. implies an Abraham senior who hasn't yet turned up, and we think never will.

JAMES WALL, carpenter, f Hampton, deeds land, 18, 5, 1654 to Wald on and others in trust for his unmarried daughters Elizabeth and Sarah, when they marry. James Wall and Mary his wife, had children born in Hampton, Mary b. 8, 11, 1655; Hannah b, 17, 1, 1658;. He sold dwelling in Exeter to Nicholas S ith 8 Sept 1658. And died 8, 1659.

This Wall was the James whom Mason sent over in 1643 to Settle Salmon Falls. We didn't know what became of him, till we stumbled on his name in Old Norfolk Co.

THOMAS KEMBLE (who had bought of Valentine Hill on the 22 Oct. 1655. one quarter of his interest in Sawmill, land, &c. at Oyster River,) sold the same for 300lbs. to Randall Nichols of Charlestown, 20 Feb. 1653-4. We believe he is the individual afterwards taxed in Dover in 1650; very likely he is the ancester of the Dover Kimballs. but we dont know.

HUMPHREY VARNEY, was a witness in Salisbury 4 Nov. 1658. He was doubtless son of Bridget Varney of Gloucester, who had also a son Jeffrey Parsons, a daughter Rachel (wife of Vinson;) and a son Thomas. A. William Varney, of Ipswich, whose inventory was entered in 1654, may have been the father. Bridget d. 26 Nct, 1672. we have no doubt that Humphrey was our Humphrey, the ancester to a race of indefinite numbers.

The following is a curiosity for dealers in live steck.

A stray horse taken upp att Haverhill by Robert and Thomas Eyere it wan tkne u⸝ in ffebruarie 1660 the color of the horse ps much like that of the Spannish Cattell which were formerly in this couatrey. hee has white feet and legs, a white face with wall eyes butt no flesh mark about him that we can finde. It was priced by Bartholemew Heath and Abraha n Tiler at eleven pound price."

EDWARD HILTON conveys to Wm. Payne of Booton 3 Oct. 1669, a grant which Eqeter had made him in consideration of 5 lbs. rent, of "ye whole river (of Puscassic) to ye extent of one mile and a quarter upon a straight line," and a mile and a quarter in width: "beginning a quarter of a mile beloo Mr. Hilton's now spent saw mill standing upon ye sd rivtr taking in a stone throw of a man on ye westermost side of ye say'd river," &c.

Where was Puscassick re respectfully ask some Exeter reader to inform u

GEO. WALTON of Portsmouth, vintner, sold premises at Great Island to Henry Robie, including dwelling, 1 Aug. 1662. This man was the father to Shadrack Walton, who acted his part on th political stage a hundred and fifty years ago, being Councilor for many years, acting President of N. H., Chief Justice, Colonel in the attack on Louisburg, &c. Concerning George himself, (though his wife Alice was an excellent woman,) little can be said. He was a little loose about some things, Sunday for instance, and was now and then fined by our Puritan rncestry. The writer of this note traces his lineago to George who was indicted and to one of the Jury who fined.

OLD SERIES Number 144.

Will: Pile of Dover sold to Richard Swain of Nantucket right in Nantucket 2 July 1663, for 40 lbs. We dont know who Pile was.

Hutchins is a name not unknown to us John and Joseph Hutchins, yeomen were of Haverhill 6 April 1664.

John Clough Salisbury, carpenter sells for 700 lbs. sterling, to Wm, Horne of Dover "my whole estate in Salisbury in land & cattle, houses & Swine." 7 Nov. 1665.

As to the Hornes, we have not made up our mind where they came from There were Hornes in Salem in early time; Old Deacon Horne was in office a great many years. About this time also a Wm. had a wife Elizabeth and was o Salisbury.

John Warrin of Exeter conveys to John ffoss of Sandy Beach, 29 Sept. 1668, a dwelling house and 100 acres "situate upon Shrewsbury pattent upon ye westerly part of ye same," provided that if the Shrewsbury patent ever make claim, Foss shall pay then their legal dues.

Sandy Beach was Rye and is Ry now. But who John Foss was is a different question. The origin of the family in this oouutry is a little in the fog also. Records find the Fosses at Rye early; but tradition says that a hundred years ago a Foss ran away from a British man-of-War in which he was midshipman, as the vessel was on our coast and that he settled in Rye. Still other additions make the name originally Faust, pronounced Foust, and testify to a gradual corruption into Foss; this tradition is bourne out by the facts, inasmuch as John Fost was received an inhabitant in Dover 1, 1, 1665-6; the same who was taxed at Cochecho from 1665 onward. The John who bought of Warren, sold again in 1671, and we rather think it was our John. But such a variety of Johns exist that they puzzle us. Whether, however, the ancester was a midshipman, or a relation of the hero of the old story of "Faust and the Devil," there is no doubt now that the name will last forever.

John Hugging of Haverhill made his will 31 Mar. 1670. He mentions son John, and had other children.

Robert Tuck of Gorlton, near Yarmouth, Suffolk Co, England, son and heir of Robert Tuck late of Salem dec. -makes his son William Tuck his attorney to settle Robert Tuck's estate; 13 Mar. 1670. Said William was aged twenty four and was about(13 Mar. 1770) to embark in the "Bilboa merchant of Yarmouth." John Tuck of Hampton, carpenter, receipts to "my uncle John Sanborne administrator" to estate of Robert Tuck of Hampton dec. for one half off his grandfathers estate, 26 Feb. 1673 — Ancestry of the Hon. Amos Tuck.

John Warren of Boston sold to Peter Coffin of Dover 10 May 1673, one eighth of Sawmill at Exeter Lower Falls Peter was shrewd in trade. Some day we may look him up

Peter Coffyne of "Cochecho upon ye river of Pascataquack" purchases of George Goldwier of Salisbury land in Salisbury 4 May 1678.

George Goldwier conveys to Rob Downer land in Salisbury for 30 lbs. paid by Downer to Major Richard Waldern of Quochecho; 20 April 1678.

Thomas King of Exeter mentions in will 21 Mar. 1666-7 "my cousin Christia Dolhyrt."

Richard Dole, attorney for John Sander "of Weeks in ye parish of Donuton within ye County f Willts in Old England," sells land of said Sanders In Salisbury (the letter of attorney was dated 9 May 1674,) to Philip Grele land including an island called "R lfs Island," 6 Mar. 1676: also other property 25 July 1677. Sanders is a name not uncommon here,

The land mentioned in the lawsuit in which Robert Smart, son of Good van John Smart, was engaged in about the meadow in the south west side of John Goddard's Creek, is less valuable than the depositions put in on that occasion. Considering that we should never have had the said papers, if Robert had no been forced to go to law, we are rather glad they tried to cheat him. Here they are:

John Alt, "aged about seventy three years" deposed that "John Sart did own & possess all ye meadow in ye S. west side of John Goddard's Creek and ye said Smart did possess it twelve years before Douer was a township & he did possess it sixteen years together peaceably & no man did molest him to my knowledge." 2 Mar. 1677-8.

W. Perksns "aged about thirty-nine years" deposed that "Rob. Smart possessed the above 16 years, without hindrance; & "yt hee did see John Meder & Eohn Davis to mow ye thatch of ye flatts against ye said meadow & carie it away. 2 Mar. 1677-8.

William Durgin "aged thirty five or thereabouts" says that Rob. Smart did mow & possess 16 years the two marsh. S. W. side of "ye cove of John Goddard;" & that Said Meder sen. & John Davis, jun. mowed the thatch &c. & carried i "& load it on ye Canoas last hay tyme." 12 Mar. 1677-8.

Benj. Yorke "aged about twenty three years," said that Smart had mowed, &c 10 years, & that "my father mowed ye marsh of Robert Smart about ten years agoe with ye leave of ye sd Robert Smart," & that Meder & Davis, &c. last hay time. 12 Mar. 1677-8.

Edward Hilton "aged about forty eight years," & Wm. Hilton "aged about 46 years," testified that "old Goodman Smart deceased did mow and carry away ye hay from yeare to yeare peaceably severall years before fifty two & yt his sonns John and Robert successively after their father's decease," did the same, "tillt so or three of these later years they have been molested." This meadow "in controversee lieth in ye neck of land betwixt Godders Cove and Lampeele River." 39 Mar. 1678.

OLD SERIES Number 148.
DATES.

The indefinateness which exists as to the times of transactions in and around Dover for the first twenty five years of its history, has induced us to examine minutely and compare all desirable authorities, printed or written, so as to fix as well as may be the dates of each. The labor has not been slight; its imperfect results we give in this article.

The settlement at Dover Point by Edward and William Hilton was "in the spring of 1623;" to this uniform statement of all reliable authorities, a careful scrutiny can add nothing beyond conjecture. Winslow says "that spring begun a plantation 25 leagues N. E. from us at Pascataquack." "No English ship is mentioned as coming upon our coast" (fishing vessels always out of the question.) says a learned antiquary "before" that commanded by Capt. Francis West, who came over, with a Commission as admiral, to prevent illegal fishing; he arrived at Plymouth in June, and the antiquary alluded to thinks that he had first gone to Pascataquack with his passengers Thompson and the Hiltons; if so he landed them late in May or early in June. In September, Standish returned to Plymouth from Pascataquack, whether he had been to buy provisions which the first settlers brought over. We cannot find that others than the two Hiltons settled then at Dover. "Possibly others might be sent after them in the years following, 1624 and 1625."—Hubbard.

AMBROSE GIBBONS probably came from Newichwaunock in the year 1630 in the bark Warwick which arrived late in May that year. The camparison of the first letters in the appendix to Belknap which Hon. James Savage makes in Winthrop I. indicates though it does not prove it.

Edward Hilton obtained a patent from the Council at Plymouth, commonly called the Squamscot Patent, comprising Hilton's Point, &c. according to Belknap (p. 9) "in the following spring" after a grant to Mason dated according to Mass. Records, 7 Nov. 1629, which places Hilton's grant in the spring of 1630; but the memorial of Allen, Shaleigh and Lake(badly printed in Belknap p. 435,) says that Hilton had possession about 1628. Hilton sold this land to some merchants of Bristol in 1630. The sending over of Capt. Thos Wiggans by the Bristol owners was in 1631, who appointed him to look after their interests; he found but three houses around that part of the Pascataqua; In 1632 he returned to England to procure men and means for the settlement; two letters of his are extant written while he was waiting in England, dated "Bristol, last of Aug. 1632." He found that his employees the British owners, had, in his absence, after two years possession sold their title (in 1632) to Lord Say and others for 2150 lbs; the new proprietor continuing him in the agency, procured families to emigrate; he, with about "about thirty," including Rev. William Leveredge, came over in the ship James, Capt. Grant, which arrived at Salem Ms. 10 Oct. 1633, having been "eight weeks between Gravesend and Salem;" they immediately came to Dover, Capt. Wiggans writing from that piace in November. Belknap says that at the expiration of seven years, i. e. in 1639, the interest was sold to Wiggans for 600 lbs; his statement, therefore, that, at the union with Massachusetts in 1641 one third of the patent of Dover was reserved to the proprietors must refer to the one third which the Shrewsbury men held.

The church may have been built on Dover Neck in 1633, but there is no early positive statement to fhat effect; Belknap dates its erection about that time, but as it is pretty probable that the new emigrants had enough to do after October to build their own houses, it is most likely that the church was left till the next spring.

Rev. Mr. Leueridge left Dover in the summer of 1635; went to Boston and was admitted member of the church there 9 August 1635.

Rev. GFORGE BURDETT had been appointed "lecturer" at Yarmouth, Eng. in or near March 1633; left that place and the country in April 1635 and came to Salem; was admitted member of the First Church, was freeman 2 September 1635, received a grant of land in Salem 5 July 1637 and probabley came to Dover in 1637. When Gov. Winthrop wrote to him and Wiggans by order of the General Court which met 7 mo. 1638, he had been sometime Governor of Dover, having "thrust out Capt. Wiggans," but was already in danger of being similarly treated by Capt. Underhill, who removed to Dover just after 7 mo. 1638, and who was actually elected Governor previous to 13, 10 mo. 1638 when Winthrop wrote to Hilton;

The First Church was organized immediately after the letter just mentioned as dated 13 Dec. 1638, Hanserd Knolles being its pastor, though Burdett was still in Dover.

HANSERD KNOLLES came from England in a ship commanded by Capt. Goodlad, which left Gravesend 26 April 1638 and arrived in Boston about 20 July 1638. (We had almost despaired of ascertaining the precise time of his coming over when we found it in Drake' History of Boston, now publishing in numbers, whose indefatigable author had ascertained the time by careful and ingenius comparisons; that work is full of similar and more important facts, and is well worthy the attention of both historical and general readers.) He came to Dover within a few weeks, probably about the last of August. Burdett forbade him to preach, but Underhill, who succeeded, had him made pastor of the church then formed; and he was preaching in 1638-9.

Before 3 mo. 1639, Burdett's correspondence with Archbishop Laud was discovered, he being still in Dover.

In 5 mo. 1649, there came to Gov. Winthrop a copy of a letter written to England by Mr. Knolles against the Mass. Government. Knolles went to Boston and confessed the offence which further consideration showed him he had committed, 20, 12 mo. 1939, that is 26 Feb. 1640. Before this date Burdett had gone to Agamenticus, and before 5 mo. 1640, (July) he had returned to England.

The name of Dover was adopted in the fall of 1639. At the general Court held ——a part of the inhabitants offered to place themselves under the Mass. Government; by request of the latter three deputies appeared from Dover 4, 7 mo. 1639, to treat concerning terms. We think that this was the result of Underhill's management (Belknap p 26;) it was opposed by a paper dated 4, 1 mo (1651,) signed by Larkham, Waldern, Roberts, Layton, Hall and other leading men, numbering twenty-five names in all, addressed to the General Court and disclaiming any such intention. This paper will be printed at some future time,

Underhill's pretended repentance he made public at Boston, 5, 1 mo. 1639-40, that is 5 Mar. 1640. His second and true one was avowed 3, 7 mo. 1640. In 7 mo. 1641, Underhill removed to Boston.

Knolles was in Dover 4 Mar. 1640, as on that day he commenced an action against Edward Starbuck for slander.

THOMAS LARKHAM came to Dover in the latter part of 1639 or the first of 1640; the people admiring his talents determined to cast off Knolles and receive Larkham as Pastor. The "more religious" however adhered to Knolles; troubles arose which were compromised under the direction of Mr. Bradstreet, Rev. Hugh Peter and Rev. Timothy Dalton, in April 1641: a second visit of Peters was needed soon after for a similar work which resulted in judicial proceedings in which Knolles and his party were defeated. Knolles departed very soon, probably in April. A protest of James Farret against the occupation of some part of Long Island by "Hanserd Knolles" and two others, dated 28, 7 mo. 1641, would indicate that he spent a little time there; but he reached England 24 Dec. 1641.

The town received the name of Northam before 4, 1 mo. 1641; the name of Dover was again in use 10, 3 mo. 1643.

The proprietors of this plantation ceded the right of jurisdiction to Mass. 14, 4 mo 1641. The act receiving the town was passed 9 8, mo. 1641. The Dover deputies took the oaths at Boston 3 mo, 1642.

Larkham had a controversy with Richard Gibbons, a minister at the Isles of Shoals 3 mo. 1642; he was "Pastor of the church in Northam" 13 Sept. 1642 in the 9 mo. 1642 (Nov. 1642) he left Dover suddenly, but he had an action in court 10, 9 mo. 1642, against J hn Richardson. None of these dates however harmonize with the town note of 1, 6 mo 1642, in which Mr. Maud, (and his wife) who we are told did not come to Dover until after Larkham's departure, received a grant of "the house they now dwell in." The difficulties here are however but specimens of the contradictory dates given by different and even by the same authors, reagrding transactions of that time in Dover. The others we believe we have settled, but this one puzzles us.

DANIEL MAUD graduated at Emanual Coll ge, Cambridge, Eng. receiving his degrees in 1606 and 1610; he came to America in 1635; was admitted to the Boston Church 25 Oct. 1635. was freeman 25 May 1636; Mary Bonner his wife was dismissed from the First Boston Cnurch to the Church in Dover 18 Aug. 1644; His will was dated 17, 11 1654, proved 26 June 1655.

For the preceeding dates we have, searched and compared the Mass. Records of Dover, of the First Church, of Massachusetts State Archives, of Rocking. Co. and the Mass. Hist. Coll, N. H. Hist. Coll, N. E. Hist. Gen. Register, Drake's Boston, Farmer and Moore's Hist. Call, Boston Ch. Records, Feli's Salom, Aut biography of Hanserd Knolles, Belknap's N. H Hubbard's N. E., Brook's Puritans, Calayn's Nonconformists, Hist. of Norfolk Co. England and Winthrop's Journal.

OLD SERIES Number 157.

News from the Boston Papers.--No 1.

"The first newspaper published in North A erica," says Hon. J. T. Buckingham, "was the Boston News Letter, the first nu ber of which appeared on Monday, April 25, 1704." The size of this early specimen was half a sheet of paper, about twelve inches by eight; in process of ti ne it enlarged somewhat in length and breadth, aud doubled itself into a folio. A file of that paper, more or less defective however, is in the Massachusetts Historical Society's Library, and we learn from it that it was "Sold by Nicholas Boone, at his Shop near the Old Meeting House." The paper was princi ally made up of foreign news but occasional information was received about home and we have thought i worth while to glean such "news" as c ncerns D ver for our own readers. The instalment of this week will be folowed by others by and by.

The first item which we find appropriate is the following, from the paper, dated May 8 - 15, 1704: -

Pascataqua. May 6. Letters thet c9 say no certain Inteligence of any Indias seen a Mr. Waldron's since last Week only some wer j track about three miles, above Nitchewanock, in a Swamp where were Cranberries, and 'tis believ'd they saw our Scouts. and narrowly escap'd them; the tracts seeming very new. They are making what preparations they can to fortifie the place, in case of any attack oy the French and Indians."

This was in Queen Anne's war; and the above date was in the week follow. ng the alarm given by Than in Mesarvey, Mr. Waldern's servant, about whom it is doubtful whether she was actually knocked down by the Indians on the particular 28th of April, or whether she chatted too long with her lover; the allusion to last week above refers to that alarm.

Further information, though with admirable independence as to punctuation, came as follows—

June 1. On Sabbath last, some of the sculking Enemy lay in an bush for people at Cochecho, going to Publick Worship, & narrowly escap't being on Horseback, ran safely by them, scouts went out immediately after them, & found some dryed Beef, & pewter bullets in the Thicket where they lay.

Belknap says nothing of the above; though he is quite full in reference to this war, which lasted until 1713.

No furthur items regarding Dover or Dover people until 1715. In the paper of March 25, 1715, under the head of "Pascataqua," appears this obituary, and the interesting piece of information therewith connected:—

On Monday the 21st Currant, Dyed at Exeter the Honourable Peter Coffin, Esq; in the 85th Year of his Age, who was late Judge of his Majesty's Superiour Court of Judicature, and First Member of his Majesty's Council of this Province; a Gentleman very Serviceable both in Church and State. We have now a Severe Storm of Snow.

The Honorable Peter Coffin, Esq, was an early resident of Dover. We will by and by give some account of him and his family.

Under date of July 22, 1715, at Pascataqua, we are informed that—

Jethro Furber is arrived here from Jamaica, but last from Turks-Island Loaden with Salt.

Jethro was doubtless one of the Newington Furbers, though we didn't know that before that he went to sea. WILLIAM FURBER, the first of the name we know anything about, was born in 1614 or 15: 1 Dec. 1676, he testifies (aged 62 or thereabouts,) that he came here in the ship Angel Gabriel, which was wrecked at Pemaquid in Aug. 1636: that in Nov. 1636 he went to Ipswich and hired himself for one year to John Cogswell, who with his three sons (William aged 14 in 1635, John aged 12, and Edward aged 6) came out with him. He came from London: was at Dover in 1637; was freeman in 1653; was taxed in 1648, and at Bloody Point where he lived from 1666 to 1671; in 1642 he was living at Welchman's Cove, on Newington side: he was alive 1 Dec. 1696, but dead 1699, intestate. William had a grant sometime bout 1610 of "Two houses Lotts" on the E. side of Dover Neck, bordering on the "fore river' (Newichwannock) and lying west of Joseph Austin's. At the same time he received marsh in the Great Bay and some where near "Turney Point." Also, 19, 8, 1657, he received 30 acres of the 400 reserved to the town of Dover on Newington side' when Dover went under Massachusetts government; 20 of it "on the same side John Tuttell is on the northwest side and tenn accers on the other sied of Creeke wich is the Soueth sied," This, like all tho 30 acre lots on Great Bay, was laid out in pursuance of town vote by "Elder Nutter, William Storey, willliam flurber, henrey lanklster." William was a lieutnant. He had a wife, Elizabeth, and five children, viz: William the eldest, born 1646; Jethro; Susan a C. 5 May, 1664, mar. John Bickford; Elizabeth, mar. John Dam; Bridget, mar. Thomas Bickford. John and Thomas Bickford were probably brothers; where John lived we do not know' but he had nine children; Thomas lived at Oyster River, and successfully defended his garrison home in 1694, and had four children.—Jethro, son of William, had a deed of land from his father at Longpoint, 19 Feb. 1677. We do not think he was the sailor, as at that time our Jethro came here from Turks Island he would have been seventy years old. But Capt. Jethro was doubtless either a son or a nephew of the other Jethro.

The first Furber had not a very large family having only two sons, but the descendants remedied the difficulty. The first Furber's grandson, William for instance, who was born in 1672, and died 20 March, 1757, who lived in Newington, and married Sarah somebody, (born 1675, died 28 April, 1772) had a variety of children, one of whom, Nehemiah, born 21 Jan. 1710, had a wife Abigail (born 14 June, 1710) had nine children, viz: Elizabeth, b. 26 April, 1733; Mary, b. 5 May 1735, d. 18 April, 1736; Jerusha, b. 6 Jan. 1738; Abigail, b. 11 June, 1740; Deborah, b. 19 April, 1743; Sarah, b. March, 1745, Nehemiah. b. 24 April, 1748, died 23 Feb. 1754; Levi, b. 16 May, 1751; Fabyan, b. 14 June, 1752, died 13 Feb. 1802; this last had thirteen children himself. The family proceeded to increase and multiply;—their exact relation to Furber's Corner we have no means of tracing.

The indefatigable correspondent at Pascataqua writes under the date of June 1, 1716:—

Our People up the River are afraid of the Indians breaking out into a war. They didn't however for seven years. The next winter was a very hard winter. On the 1st of March, 1717, horses could not pass and persons travelled only on snow shoes. The winter after had more snow also; on the 24th of January, 1718, the snow was three and a half feet deep on a level.

In connection with the weather occurred the following:—

Mar. 7, 1718. We are Informed from Dover that the snow lies two Foot deep on the Ground, and that several parts are bare on the Neck.

OLD SERIES Number 158.

News from the Boston Papers.--No 2.

In 1718 appears the following:

At Oyster River—Parish in Dover, March 26th. This day (through the smiles of Heaven upon us) we had a Church gathered here. in the Decency and Order of the Gospel, and our Teacher the Reverend Mr. Hugh Adams was then consecrated and Established the Pastor thereof: Who then preached from that Text in Cant 3, 11. We being then favoured with the Presence and Approbation of some Reverend Pastors of the next Neighbouring Churches, with the Honoured Messengers thereof; at the said Solemnity, in our New-Meeting-House, wherein they gave the Right Hand of Fellowship.

As Witness our Hands,
Nathaniel Hill
Stephen Jones.

As to the signers to this letter we know but little, and that little is easily told. Nathaniel Hill was doubtless the Nathaniel who was son of Valentine Hill. Valentine was of Boston in 1638, a freeman there in 1640; a mercer, a man of note, and a member of Ancient and Hororable Artillery Company; he was of Boston as late as 1643, but soon after, he came to Oyster River, his residence was hardly defined in 1650; what became of him we don't know, but he went into business pretty extensively, especially in saw mills and politics. The first deed on record of his business transactions was of his pledging three fourths of O. R. mills, and mil privilege as bonds for estate of Jane Skipper then in his possession Various bargains of his are thenceforward recorded, needless here to specify. His grants from the town of Dover were as follows:

5, 5, 1643, Valentine Hill "of Boston" has a grant of "land from a Creeke over against Thomas Stephenson At Oyster River that hath an Island in the mouth of it, to the head of that Creeke in Royalls Cove to ye part of the North east of mr. Roberts his Marsh reserving to Mr. Roberts Marsh and 20 acres of upland, all the rest of that Neck wee give to mr Hill, & one hundred acres more up in the Country"

Granted to Valentine Hill and Thomas Beard, 19, 9, 1649, "the fall of Oyster Rive.," "for the Erickting and setting up of a sawe mill and A Comedatine for the mill of Timber for the Imployment of the mill and Consideration of this Grant the Above named Vallantine and Thomas or thear Eares or a sines are to paye yearly to the towne of Dover the sum of ten pownd p annum the time of the Intrey or beginning of the Rent afoersayd is to begin the first of September next inseuing and so to contenew the sayd yearly Rent soe long as theay shall hold the propertie of the plas and If the mill b(eg)in to worke befoer the above menshened tim that then the vear is to begine."

14, 5, 1651, he received 500 acres of land adjacent to his mill at O. R. for a farm; its N. E. side was bounded by the river.

7, 5 1652, he had a grant of the mill privilege in Lamprey river with timber corresponding for which he was to pay £20. On the 5, 10, 1652, he had 100 acres of upland for the accommodation of the Lamprey river mill site; and on the same date at Oyster River 20 acres of upland "Eastward of Thomas Johnson his Creeke betwixt William Storyes lott & the Swampe;" this grant was laid out and bounded 2 Dec., 1709, to the Nathaniel with whom we started "the only sonn of the sd Vallentine," when its eastern corner was the "ancient nor west Corner bound mark of William Stories hundred acre lot" and the lines ran S. E., E. N. E., N W. and W.

It may not be known, but we are inclined to think that Mr. Hill projected the first canal or at least feeder in New England; for, on the 14, 11, 1655, he had "free leberty to Cutt through our Comans for drawinge Part of the water of Lamperelle River into Oyster River for the supply of his mill," provided he injure no other grants of land or water, and provided also that if Mr. Hill "throw up" the grant of Lamperel river, than this water course to cease, and provided also that he build bridges whenever his new feeder interfere with the "hieways".

The Lamprey river grants got into trouble by reason of the disputed claims of Exeter and Dover; so to settle the latter difficulties, and also Mr. Hill's claims, Dover voted 4, 1, 1656, that Hill and a committee shall meet a committee from Exeter to arrange the matter; and if he didn't attend to it before next session of the General Court, then he was to lose all title to Lamprell river. How it ended we suppose is seen in the fact that next April (14th) 1657, Hill, Edward Hilton, John Bickford, sen. John Gilman and William Furber, reported a settlement of the boundaries, which, as it was printed in No. 20 of these memoranda, need not be repeated, but which seems to give Valentine a good title.

Valentine must also have had other grants; one at least, "of all the meddow att the head of Oyster River at the pond & with in a mile square on both sides of the River," was laid to our friend Capt. Nathaniel 1 Aug. 1713, beginning at the west side of the head of the river at the pond running W. by N., N. by E., E. by S., and to the first bound. Five acres granted to him in 1652 were laid out apparently in 1663 to "henrey Browne and James Ore;" which land lay on the west side of land granted to Hudson and then in possession of Edward Patterson, and bounded, beginning at "the freshett at a letell Cove that doeth com in to the freshett" and so to a red oak by a "lettell spring neir the house."

These are all the grants to Mr. Hill recorded in our first volumes of records; there is however a quitclaim of his, and in the Exeter deeds office are records of various other transactions.

Mr. Hill had been a merchant in Boston. On the 7 Mar. 1643-4, he and others were incorporated as a trading company. A suit in reference to the Ship Planter in which he was concerned is also recorded at Boston. He was also engaged in iron works.— In fact he had a variety of irons in the fire, and at the time of his death some of them had got scorched. He was a member of the church also; in the Boston church he was "by ye laying one of ye hands of ye presbytery, ordeyned to ye office of deacon, 17 May 1640; and he was dismissed to the church in Dover when he moved.

Mr. Hill was also in office. He was selectman in Dover in 1651 and '7, and probably most of the intermediate years. He was Deputy from Dover to Mass. Gen Court in 1652-5, (and probably 1656,) and 1657. He was "associate" in 1657 and 3.

When in 1659 the Gen. Court found that there was "many complaints of the great suffering of the familyes of diverse revend ministers of God's word," and appointed commissioners to look into it, Mr. Hill was selected for Norfolk, our county. Once or twice he settled troubles down in York, and tried to settle some for the Gen. Court about a sawmill at Exeter, which James Wall was mixed in somehow.

Mr. Hill died in 1661. As intimated his affairs were in confusion. The Mass. Gen. Court appointed three administrators 22 May 1661. Affairs proved complicated; after two years of labor, the administrators petitioned the Court to appoint men to sell the estate that the creditors might have their shares and they might get rid "of so troublesome a business;" men were appointed. Still the debts due the estate were not paid, and in 1672, three men were appointed to sue in behalf of Valentine Hill's estate "for three years next coming." What was the final result we do not know; but the town found it desirable to obtain a quitclaim from Nathaniel to the Oyster River mill sites so late as 13 Sept 1697. His inventory was entered in 1699.

This Nathaniel, the one with whom we started as a member of the Durham church, was born "last of March 1659 60," and was Valentine's only son. Valentine's wife was Mary, daughter of Theophilus Eaton, Governor at New Haven, by whom he inherited property to the amount of 300 acres in New Haven, which they sold 2 Nov 1660 for £230 to Nathaniel Mickelthays of London.

That Nathaniel was a resident of Durham and a member of the church at its organiation and wrote for the newspapers, the extract which we started with, shows. More about him we know not at present

OLD SERIES, NO. 159.

NEWS FROM THE BOSTON PAPERS—NO. 3.

Of Stephen Jones, the other signer of the letter, we have less to say. If he was a wise child he knew his own father, and we wish he had left the information on record. We should not be surprised if he turned out to be son of Stephen who was received an inhabitant by vote 19, 1, 1665-6, took the freeman s oath 15 May 1672, was Ensign in 1691 and in '94 commander-in-chief of his garrison house at O. R. which he defended like a Trojan only with better success. He and William owned the lower mill privilege at O. R. which had once belonged to Valentine Hill. And it may be that both of them were sons of the William who was of Portsmouth 1640, of Dover 1644, and gone in 1648. This Stephen was married by Maj. Waldern 29 Jan. 1663 to Elizabeth Field.

There were other Joneses about. Robert lived near Cochecho, or more particularly near Bellamy where he had land from the town; he was taxed in 1657 and in 1662 The grant to him is the only Jones grant on our first book, and was made 21, 9, 1659, being of "ten acres of upland bordering on Ralpfe Twamlys 14 acers neir Bellimies bank," on the N. W. side of the "Brooke that Runeth from Ralpfe Twamly his house to Bellemies Banke on the Right hand of the paeth as on goeth from Dover to Cochecboe." There was also a Jenkin Jones, taxed 1667 to 1672, who married Abigail, daughter of old Master John Heard of Garrison Hill, and a Mary Jones who was killed at O. R. 22 July 1696. And later still, William Jones, married Hannah Ricker 23 July 1720, and had children, Eleanor b. 3 April 1723, William b. 7 July 1725. This includes about all we know of the Joneses.

Undoubtedly Oyster River was settled very soon after Dover Neck, perhaps as early as 1631 or '3, it ran pretty close after its neighbor; some of its territory was in dispute between Exeter and Dover, and some of its inhabitants considered themselves Exeter people. It came under Dover jurisdiction at last, and its residents went over to Dover Neck to meeting from Parson Leveridge's time twenty years, in fact, till about Parson Maud's death. They were restless, however, about it sometime before, and in 1651 the town agreed to raise £100 a year and employ two ministers, one for Dover Neck, the other for Oyster river, they to have £50 apiece and to exchange whenever they wished, and no grumbling. Large bodies move slow; and it was not until 1655 that the promised meeting house was built at Oyster River; next year they built a parsonage near it "for the use of the menestrey, the demenshens as followeth, that is to say, 36 feet long, 10 fooett Broed, 12 fooet in the wall, with too chemeneys and to be seutably feneshed;" "long and flat, like Franklin plain," as a venerable Doctor of Divinity told an ambitious young pulpit orator his sermon was. The same year they got a minister, Rev. Mr. Fletcher; but difficulties arose and he stayed only one year. telling them he was minded "to Prepaer himself for old England," whence if he went at all, he soon returned to America.

After Mr. Fletcher's departure, the town did not hurry themselves about another minister for Oyster River. Parson Reyner who preached at Dover Neck, was an excellent man, and the Durham people couldn't do better. Besides, as taxes were just half as much if the vacancy at Durham was not filled, the inducement was rather against exerting themselves anxious'y. This calculation however was overset by the obstinate refusal of the Oyster River people to pay taxes for the ministry until they had a minister of their own. It was a good ways to go to meeting, and besides when Mr. Fletcher left Durham had thirty two polls, and the Neck, Cochecho, and Newington, united, had only sixty. while the Neck had doubtless less than Durham. Still the town endeavored to collect by law, the taxes, with the result which always appear when public sentiment is not decidedly in its favor, as our temperance friends, can testify. Various treaties were tried, but in vain The aggrieved people, numbering 220 souls, endeavored in 1669 to get a division of the town, but without success. In 1675 however, they obtained an act allowing them to elect their selectmen annually for the specific purpose of assessing their ministerial taxes distinct from the other part of the town. — The people had, it seems, obtained a minister the year before, who was always considered their minister, though not formally installed. John Buss, both physician and minister, stated in a petition to Gov. Shute in 1718 that he had been laboring at Oyster River forty five years, and was then seventy eight years old; he was therefore born about 1640. We suppose him to have been a native of Concord, Mass., where the Buss family resided, and to have been a son of William Busse, who took the freeman's oath in Concord 14 Mar. 1638-9, and who had children, Richard b. 6, 5, 1640; Anne b. 18, 12, 1641; there was also a Jospeh Buss there, a tythingman in 1679. A John Buss, whom we suppose to be Durham John, married 12 May 1673, Elizabeth, daughter of Thomas Bradbury of Salisbury, who was born 7, 9, 1651. John came to Durham in 1674 from Wells, Me. Whether Joseph Buss and William Buss, who were killed 28 June 1689, and John Jr., who had a grant of land 25 June 1701, were his children or relatives, the reader can guess as well as we.

OLD SERIES, NO. 160.

NEWS FROM THE BOSTON PAPERS.—NO. 4.

This organization of a church, at Durham, evidently took place in connection with the parish which was constituted as distinct from Dover town 4 May 1716. Mr. Hugh Adams, who was ordained 26 March 1718, had commenced preaching there in 1716. He was born in 1676, graduated at Harvard College in 1697, was ordained in the 2d parish of Braintree, 10 Sept. 1707, was settled till 1716 in Chatham, Mass. Mr. Adams was a good and pious man, tradition tells us, but knew a thousand times more about scripture than human nature This, with the peculiar habits of the people as to harmony, caused him no little difficulty during his ministry and finally brought it to an abrupt termination. A curious petition of his to the General Assembly in 1738, complaining of the delinquencies of his people, is still preserved; in this he represents Durham "as an Achan in the camp; and as the seven sons of Saul in the days of King David; and as Jonah in the ship of the Commonwealth of the Province;" he prays for justice to himself and also that neglect to pay a minister may be made penal as in Massachusetts, which he considered the principal reason why that Province had been "proportionately spared from the throat pestilence, and other impovishing, more than New Hampshire." He informed the assembly also of his power in prayer, specifying how that being provoked by the injustice of his people and their robbing him of £50 addition to his salary, he prayed three months before harvest, that it might not rain; and it did not rain for three months, when he was coaxed out of his position and "appointed and conscientiously sanctified a church fast from evening to evening and abstained three meals from eating, drinking, and smoaking anything." And the rain came and they had, in answer, considerable of a harvest after all. He wound up by begging for justice; expressing his poor conviction that after he had got it, God would be entreated for New Hampshire.

In another petition requesting the appointment of Joseph Drew of Durham and Captain Edward Hall of New Market as Justices, they being "able in estate and understanding in the law, in writing a good hand, fearing God," &c; he gives us a descripiton of Durham by no means flattering: "The said town and parish being (too long time) the majority of the inhabitants of each sadly grown exceedingly vicious, disorderly and unruly;" he said they lacked a justice badly, "Col. Davis in our Town being now doting, superannuated, selfish, covetous, and partial utterly unqualified for such an office any longer; being grown so old and foolish that he will be no more admonished; as contemptably characterized in Eccle. iv. 13 " The parson's contemporaries however agreed with him neither as to Col. Davis nor himself.

Mr Adams obtained a judgment against his parish in 1738 as another curious letter to Secretary Waldron dated 11 April 1739, informs us. In this he alludes also to a charge of bribery brought against him; it seems that in a memorial to the Governor and Council who were to determine "the case of said Minister Appellant, already passed through the other two Courts of the Law," he declared that he considered it his duty, in case they decided rightly to divide one fifth of the £1858 which he claimed, among those who voted right, i. e., £200 to the Governor, £40 to the Secretary, and £20 to each Counsellor on his side,—which with fees made the fifth. Now this "Bond," he says, "was not intended for A Bribe which I abhor in any Profferer or Receiver; seeing it is Written in Job xv. 34— Fire shall consume the tabernacles of bribery, which I have Remarked in Sundry instances fulfilled. But I Deliver'd said Bond Conscientiously In Obedience unto That Sacred Law in Gen. xl ii. 27, and Rom. xiii. 4, 6, 7, For A Gratefull Tribute intended for the Rulers, which should in Justice and Equity Overrule the letter, rigour, and perverting tricks of human laws, to Defend the poor, afflicted and neady."

Notwithstanding his success in the suit, an ecclesiastical council assembled 23 Jan 1739 and dismissed him; they censured him for the petition alluded to above, protested against "his great presumption in pretending to imprecate the Divine vengeance and that the calamities that had befallen sundry persons were the effect of his prayers; and "considering to what a height the disaffection of great numbers of his people had arrived," they were "of opinion that it would not be for the honor of Christ or the interest of religion nor any way answer to the great ends of his ministry in this place for him to continue any longer in it." He remained in Durham though dismissed from the ministry and he retained the confidence and affection of many of his people and a good deal of influence in the town. He lived through the ministry of his successor, saw his nephew ordained by his own friends and died in 1750. His wife was a Winburne and they left descendants.

On the 3 March 1742 Nicholas Gilman was ordained successor to Parson Adams. He was a son of the Nicholas Gilman of Exeter who was grand father to John Taylor Gilman the Governor; he was born 18 Jan. 1707-8 grad. H. C. 1724 was ordained as said above and remained at Durham till his death 13 April 1748. He was a man of piety and an "evangelical" preacher but was deluded by a fanatic named Woodbury from Rowley who went about to examine the state of the churches and who obtained complete ascendency over him; Woodbury would call him from bed at midnight and lead him into woods and swamps to spend the night in prayer; under his influence Gilman declined to preach, and a Mr. Wooster was employed in his place. A committee of the State Ecclesiastical Convention visited Durham in 1747, who reported that a "considerable number of communicants and others of their congregation had separated from them (the church) and held a separate meeting in a private house in the town on the Lord's day, and at other times. And the said committee was further informed by divers of said church, that at said separate meetings, there were very disorderly, vile and absurd things practiced, (such as profane singing and dancing, damning the Devil, spitting in person's faces whom they apprehended not to be of their society," &c.) They had found, however, that the Durham people didn't want any advice and they dropped the matter.

Under these painful delusions to which he was subject Gilman's health declined and he died of consumption. He was buried at Exeter, regretted for his excellencies of character and disposition, and greatly beloved, notwithstanding the difficulties. His wife was Mary, daughter of Bartholomew Thing, whom he married 22 Oct. 1730 she survived him and died 22 February 1789. They had five children, viz: Bartholomew, b. 26 Aug. 1731; Nicholas b 13 June 1733; Tristram b. 24 Nov. 1735, of H. C. 1757, (minister at North Yarmouth until his death, marrying Elizabeth Sawyer of Wells, and having seven children, of whom Elizabeth, the youngest, mar Rev. Dr. Francis Brown who was President of Dartmouth College from 1815 to his death 20 July 1820, and was father to Prof. Samuel G. Brown, who was b. 4 Jan. 1813 and is now of Dart Coll) Joseph b. 5 May 1738, a Judge in Ohio, where he died 14 May 1806, having had two children; Josiah b. 2 Sept. 1740, m. Sarah, daughter of Samuel Gilman and died 8 Feb. 1801 and had nine children.

OLD SERIES, NO. 161.

NEWS FROM THE BOSTON PAPERS—NO. 5.

We omitted to state in the proper

place that in 1662 or 3 Rev. Mr. Hull was minister at Durham; we suppose he was Benjamin and father to Elizabeth, wife of John Heard of Dover; if so he was a "godly man."

After Mr. Gilman's burial at Exeter whither he was carried in procession by the young men of the town, he was succeeded in the ministry at Durham by John Adams, who came in 1748. He was a son of Matthew Adams of Boston, born 19 June 1725, and was a nephew of Parson Hugh Adams of whom we have spoken already. This Adams family was distinct from that of the Presidents', and therefore not related to Parson Joseph Adams of Newington or Reformation John Adams. There were three brothers of them, all distinguished men, viz. John, Matthew and Hugh. About Hugh we have already said all we care to; John (Hon.) was of Nova Scotia; his son, Rev. John, graduated H. C. 1722 and died at Cambridge in 1740 aged 36, distinguishd as a writer; preacher and poet. Matthew, father of the Parson John of Durham, and brother to Hugh, is spoken of in Franklin's autobiography (Sparks Ed. p. 16;) "a merchant, an ingenious, sensible man who had a pretty collection of books, frequented our printing office, took notice of me, and invited me to see his library, and very kindly proposed to lend me such books as I chose to read." He married (1) 7 Nov. 1715 Katherine Brigden, (2) 10 June 1734, Meriel Cotton he died in 1753; his children, all by his first wife, were Matthew, Katherine, John (our John of Durham) b. 19 June 1725, and Nathaniel b. 1726. John grad. H. C. 1745, and as we have said was ordained in 1748. The old quarrel had not been made up; at the time of his settlement the church had about forty male members, of whom several opposed his settlement, and about half did not attend his meeting; these complained to the Ecclesiastical Convention that he was settled by old Mr. Adams's party "who had for a long time been separated and were a distinct body by themselves," and that "a controversy was then subsisting whether they ought to be acknowledged as belonging by right to the standing church." The Convention recommended a mutual Council but nothing came of their advice; gradually the opposition subsided and Mr. Adams remained at Durham about thirty years; new difficulties then arose and he was dismissed. It is said of him "when out of the pulpit he appeared as if he ought never to enter it; and in it he appeared as though he ought never to go out of it" He moved to Newfield, Me., where he had a grant of 400 acres of land preached and practiced medicine in three or four towns until his death, 4 June 1792.

Mr. Adams' wife was Hannah Chesley, who died in 1814; they had fourteen children viz., Sarah, Catharine, John, Deborah, John, Nathaniel, Thomas b 11 Sept. 1769, Hannah, William, Dart. Coll 1799, Abigail, Ebenezer, Samuel, b. 19 Sept. 1777, Eliza and Amos Chase. Two of the daughters married and settled in Parsonsfield, the one a Morrill, the other an

Allen, Samuel mar. Betsey, dau. of Hon. John Prentice, of Londonderry, and d. 1815. Thomas (who is still living) married Mar 1803, Sally Wilson, and has several children, one of whom Samuel Chesley Adams, Esq , of Newfield was b. 11 Oct. 1807 and mar. 11 Oct, 1833, Theodate Drake Page.

Parson John's brother Nathaniel was a merchant, and settled in Portsmouth, N H., he married twice; in 1752, Deborah Knight who d. in 1754 at the birth of a daughter, Elizabeth, who lived, married John Raynes of Portsmouth and d. without issue in 1834; Nath'l m. (2) in 1755, Elizabeth dau. of Hon. Wm. Parker, of Portsmouth, who was a sister to Bishop Samuel Parker of Boston, (father to Richard G Parker, Esq. known as author of various school books,) to Sheriff John Parker at Portsmouth, &c. &c. —and to Lydia, mother of Hon. Parker Hale of Rochester and grandmother to John P. Hale, our eminent townsman Nathaniel's second wife was sister also to Sarah, wife of Col. Toppan of Hampton, the mother of Mrs. Charles H. Atherton, Nathaniel died in 1766; his wife Elizabeth died Nov 1814 aged 80; they had six children, viz. Nathaniel b. 1756, Mary, b 1758, Deborah b. 1759, John b. 1761, Anne b. 1763, William b. 1765.—Of these children, Nathaniel grad. H. C. 1775, and is well known as for fifty years clerk in various N. H. Courts, Reporter of the Vol I, N. H. Decisions, author of Annals of Portsmouth, &c. he twice married, (1) in 1784, Eunice Woodward and had three children, (2) Oct. 1795, Martha Church, and had five more. Mary, the second child, mar. Dr. Abiel Pierson of Andover and had four children; Deborah, third child, mar. (1) 1786 Nathaniel Sparhawk of Kittery, grandson and heir of Sir William Pepperell, and (2) Dr. Abiel Pierson. John, third child, mar. Elizabeth, dau. of Rev. Dr. Haven, and had one child, Ann Hall, b. 1794, m 1814, William Appleton of Quincy, and d. aving children. Anna, fifth child, mar. Hon Joseph Hall, late Sheriff and Judge of Probate for Suffolk Co. and d. 1793, leaving one son, the late Joseph Hall, Esq. of the Hamilton Bank. William, the youngest; mar. 1784, Hannah Hubbard, of Middletown, Conn., and d. Nov 1790, leaving three daughters and one son; of the daughters, Eliza b. 16 May 1788, mar. Gen. Timothy Upham, a gallant soldier in the war of 1812 15. Collector at Portsmouth from 1816 to 1829, Navy Agent at Portsmouth in Gen. Harrison's presidency, and who d. 2 Nov. 1855, and was buried at Portsmouth, his wife having died 18 Mar. 1354; Anna Maria b. 23 Mar 1787, m. Nov. 1813, Rev. Wm. A. Thompson of South Berwick, and d. 1835; Sarah b. 22 May 1789, m. 14 Sept. 1817, Hon. Timothy Farrar; William, the son, b. 29 Feb. 1791, died young, unmarried.

When, by the way, Parson John Adams preached his farewell sermon at Durham, he read in closing, and requested the people to sing to the glory of God and their own e ification,' the first three verses of the 120th Psalm, as follows:

Thou God of love, thou ever blest,
 Pity my suffering state;
When wilt thou set my soul at rest,
 From lips that love deceit.

Hard lot of mine! my days are cast
 Among the sons of strife.
Whose never ceasing brawlings waste
 My golden hours of life.

Oh might I fly to change my place,
 How would I choose to dwell
In some wide lonesome wilderness
 And leave these gates of hell.

The remaining facts pertaining to the Durham church, so far as we think best to give them, will take but little room.

Rev. Curtis Coe was ordained 1 Nov. 1780; born at Middletown, Ct., 21 July 1750, grad. Brown Un. 1776; was minister at Durham until 1 May 1806; he died 7 June 1829. During his ministry in 1792 was erected the immense church with which our readers are familiar, and which stood until 1848. The earliest Durham church stood somewhere between the falls and Durham Point, where the people lived then. The fourth and present edifice, which is a model for a country village church, was dedicated 13 Sept 1849.

For ten years after Mr. Coe left, no minister was settled; he was the last one settled by the town as such. On the 18 June 1817, Federal Burt was ordained; the church then had but two acting male members and one of these was almost superannuated. He died 9 Feb 1828, having been born in Southampton, Ms 4 Mar. 1789, which was why he was called "Federal" 3 Dec. 1828, Robert Page was installed; he was dismissed 31 Mar. 1831.

Alvah Tobey, born in Wilmington' Vt. 1 April 1808, grad Amherst 1828, Andover 1831, came in 1831 to Durham, and was ordained 20 Nov. 1833; our readers need no words of commendation for one to whom the town owes so much, as to the present minister of Durham.

OLD SERIES, NO. 162.

NEWS FROM THE BOSTON PAPERS.—NO. 6.

In the News-letter of 10 April 1723, we find a record of "Mr. Hall's Coffee House in Boston;" whether he was a relative of Dover Halls we do not know.

We are sorry to learn under date of 26 April 1723, that "John Cromwell of Dover of Col. Westbrook's Company," was with others advertised as a Deserter from the force sent to the Eastward. There were Cromwells in Dover quite early. Phillip had a wife Elizabeth, and a child Ann b. 19 Aug. 1674—unless he had a son Phillip to be father of Ann, which is possible considering that he was taxed as early as 1657 and 8 at Cochecho, and a Philip Cromwell is taxed at O. R. 1664 to 1672. There was a Philip Cromwell at Salem, whose wife Dorothy died 28 Sept. 1673, and he married widow Mary Lemon 19 Nov. 1674. There was here a Joshua who had land granted him in 1693-4.—There was a Samuel Cromwell also in Dover who had a wife Rachel, and children. Dorothy b. 13 May, 1713, Eliphalet, b. 12 Nov 1716; and a Samuel who mar-

4 Dec. 1727, Betty Pinkham.—There was also a John Cromwell in Dover who married 26 Dec. 1720, Mary Riddley.

Under date of Aug. 1723, we are informed, "a man was killed at Cochecho on Saturday," Aug. 24, 1723. Several were killed about that time, but Belknap mentions none.

"On the 27th of Aug. last, (1724), the Indians came upon the House of John Handson, a Quaker at Dover, who lived in a very exposed place (he then being at meeting) and took his faimly, kill'd two children and Scalpt them, and carried away his Wife, Maid and four Children into Captivity."

This Hanson was a son of Thomas Hanson, and a grandson of Thomas the first settler of whose descendants we shall by and by give some account in detail; John lived at Nock's Marsh on the place where Samuel Hanson now lives Being a Friend, he refused to leave his exposed position; and his house was marked for an attack Thirteen Indians and French Mohawks, lay for several days near it in ambush, waiting until Hanson and his men were away, for the Indians were a cowardly set of villains; and when he had gone to the week-day meeting and two sons were at work at some distance, the Indians entered the house; Mrs. Hanson, a servant, and four children, were in the house, of which, one child the Indians immediately killed to terrify the others; two other children were at play in the orchard, and would have escaped but that just as the Indians had finished rifling the house, the two came in and made such a noise that the Indians killed the youngest boy to stop an alarm They then started for Canada, with Mrs Hanson (who had been confined but fourteen days prior,) her babe, a boy of six years and two daughters, one fourteen years old, the other sixteen, and the servant girl. All reached Canada, but the party was repeatedly subdivided during the journey.

The first person who discovered the tragedy was Hanson's eldest daughter on her return from meeting. Seeing the children dead she gave a shriek which was distinctly heard by her mother in the hands of the enemy and by her brothers at work. Pursuit was instantly made but the Indians avoided all paths and escaped undiscovered. After this disaster Hanson removed the remainder of his family to the house of his brother "who" says Belknap "though of the same religious persuasion yet had a number of lusty sons and always kept his fire-arms in good order for the purpose of shooting game"

An account of Mrs Hanson's capture was printed in 1780; a new one was issued here by John Mann in 1824 and is very interesting.

Mr. Hanson soon after the attack went to Canada to ransom the family; the following item from the News-Letter of 1725 is of interest in that connection:

Newport. Aug. 27th, (1725.) On Tuesday last, (Aug. 24) arrived here, Mr. John Handson, of Dover, Piscataqua, and about a Month's time from Canada, but last from New York, with his Wife & three children and a Servant Woman; as also one Ebenezer Downs, having a Wife & five children at Pascataqua; also one Miles Thomson, a Boy, who were all taken Captives about Twelve Months since, by the Enemy Indians, and carried to Canada, except the abovesaid Handson; who at the same time lost Two of his Sons by the Indians; & now it hath cost him about £700 for their Ransom, including his other necessary charges. He likewise informs, That another of his children, a Young Woman of about Seventeen Years of Age was carried Captive at the same time with the rest of his Family, with whom he convers'd for several Hours, but could not obtain her Ransom: for the Indians would not consent to part with her on any terms, so he was obliged to leave her.

Mr. Hanson got home 1 Sept. 1725, but he could not content himself while his daughter Sarah was in Canada; and about the 19th April 1727, started in company with a kinsman who with his wife was bound on a similarly sad errand to redeem children; but he was taken sick on the journey and died about half way between Albany and Canada. The daughter married a Frenchman and never returned.

So far as records are obtained, John Hanson's family was as follows; he married 23, 5, 1703, Elizabeth —; children were, Hannah b. 11 June 1705, (married Samuel Hodgdon, the record says, but we have no doubts he mar. Israel Hodgdon, whose dau (Sarah mar. Elijah Estes;) Sarah b. 13 Nov. 1708, who married in Canada; Elizabeth b. 13, 9, 1710, mar. Ebenezer Varney, who was son of Mary Otis who was neice to Christine Otis, who was captived in 1689 and mar. a Frenchman in Canada, but afterwards Junn· toherred; b. 17, 1, 1712, m. (1) Phebe Austin, (2) Sarah Tuttle; Isaa b. 25, 12, 1714, mar. Sarah Horne; Daniel b. 26, 1, 1717; Ebenezer b. 27, 12, 1718; Caleb b. 8 Feb. 1721 (N. S.) Daughter b. 13 June 1724. Perhaps we will attend to their descendants some day.

OLD SERIES, NO 170.

WADLEIGH'S FALLS.

In the mutations of one local history, one landmark (if that is not a misnomer,) has had its name one hundred and seventy five years. Wadleigh's Falls are as well known by that title now as when in the seventeenth century, Robert Wadleigh made their waters saw his logs.

We propose to give a little account touching their early ownership These Falls were first reclaimed from idleness by Mr. Samuel Symonds, who in the year 1657, on the third day of June, took possession of "six hundred and forty acres of ground granted to him by the honoured General Court, in the presence and with the consent of Mohermite, sagamore of these parts." This sagamore, by the way, we suppose had his principal country residence in Madbury, on what is now called "Hick's Hill," but which bore the Indian's name even in the memory of persons now living; a marsh somewhere in that vicinity had the same title. Mr. Symonds was a resident of Ipswich, a gentleman of good English descent, a man of property, and one who did the State some service When Dover was received under Massachusetts jurisdic tion. he was one of the judges appointed to hold courts here; he was Assistant for thirty years; five years he went to General Court; once he was Recorder for Ipswich; and from 1673 to 1678 he was Deputy Governor of Massachusetts He died in Oct 1678, having had three sons, viz, Samuel, William who lived at Wells, ud Harlackenden. and seven daughters, all of whom married and we believe, did tolerably well.

The General Court, grateful to Mr. Symonds for various services, on the 14th of Oct. 1651, made him a grant of three hundred acres of land anywhere north of the Merrimack river in the power of the General Court, provided "he. or his assignes set up a saw mill within the space of seven years." And for services rendered in "York and Kettery," he received, 14th Sept., 1653 five hundred acres more to be located at his own choice. On the 15th of May, 1654, the General Court appointed John Gage, Robert Lord, John Dane and Daniel Epps, in view of both these grants, "to lay out ye same in some free place beyond the River of Merrimacke, provided no pt ther of shall be within five miles of the meeting house of Exeter " The Court at the same time took off th proviso requiring the erection of a saw mill

It was under these grants that six hundred and forty of these eight hundred acres, were laid out by John Gage and Daniel Epps 3 June 1657 to Mr. Symonds, who then, by the consent of the Sagamore and the General Court became the first white owner of the premises. "The place and farm," say the committee, "is now called the Island Falls; there is a tree close by that falls marked with two S S, and a little island in the river by the falls there douneward, conteying in length one mile from the lower end of that little island aforesayd, up the river, and half a mile in breadth on each side of the sayd river, wch river is called Lamper Eele River. That place or part of the Lamper Ele River, is between the townes of Dover and Exeter up into the 'cor trje, beyond the bounds of either of those towns in that place, and about sixe miles douneward by land to the mouth of the sayd Lamper Ele River, which emptjeth itself there in o the great bay." As to the truth of the statement about the bounds of Dover and Exeter, there is a little chance for doubt; Symonds, at any rate, fortified his title by a quitclaim from Exeter, which pretended to own as far as Oyster River but never got beyond Lamprey River and Dover, by and by granted all their right over these premises to a subsequent occupant.

Nothing appears to show whether Mr Symonds did anything with his farm and fall; until on the 12 Sept. 1664. he conveys to his son Harlackenden one half of the premises, reciting that "whereas ye genll Court hath granted unto mee a farme containing six hundred and forty acres of ground att Lampeele River," "the town of Exeter having had ye interest with ye rest of ye land northward as far as the Oyster river before the government of Massachusetts did acctually possess ye same from ye Sagamores and Indians Inhabiting there) haveing granted and confirmed also unto mee my sd farme. This I say doth witness, That I Samuell Symonds of Ipswich in ye County of Essex gent. have allreadie granted unto my Soune Harlackenden Symonds ye one halfe of ye sd farme" &c. The old gentleman now owned one half, and Harlackenden the other.

Harlackenden, who was admitted a freeman in 1655, sold his half, 12 Sept. 1664, to Capt Walter Barefoot, a man famous in New Hampshire annals as Counsellor, Deputy Governor and Rogue —Samuel Symonds sen., and Barefoot now owned together: but on the 11 May 1666, Barefoot sold (warrantee,) to "Robert Wadley (then of Kittery,) one half of six hundred and forty acres of land wch I bought of mr Harlackentone Simons lying and being in Lamprll River," as described in deed of Samuel Symonds of 12 Sept. 1664, by which Robert Wadleigh came into possession of the one half, and Mr. Symonds retaining the other.

On the 9 May 1667 Wadleigh sold half of his share. He "liveing and residing at Lampariell River at Mr Symons falls in ye township of Exeter according to ye purchase of ye Indians," conveys to Nicholas Lissen of Exeter a certain pcell of land lying at or near ye river called lamprill river," it being "halfe of three hundred and twenty acres wch I ye sd Rob. Wadly formerly bought of left Walter Barefoot ye wch 320 acres was one moyety of 640 acres of land granted by ye honored genll court unto ye worsipll Mr. Sam Symons sen: ye one half wrof being by mee ye abovsd Rob. Wadly purchased of Capt. Barefoot." Now Mr Symonds owned one half and Robert Wadleigh and N cholas Lissen each a fou th

The next deeds disagree with previous papers; in the first Mr. Symonds re conveys the one half which had been traded round: it recites that whereas the General Court confirmed to Mr Samuel Symonds of Ipswich "all yt farme by some called ye Iland falls, containing six huurded and forty acres of land lying on both sides of ye river called Lamperell River wch, emptieth itselfe into ye great bay wch is between ye meeting houses of Exeter and Dover wch farme containeth one mile square: and whereas also ye town of Exeter haveing bought ye said pcell of land amongst other lands) of ye Sachem or Sachems and Indians Inhabiting these pts before yt Exeter was actually under ye government of Massachusetts have granted unto me" all its "title and interest," upon wch farme and River at my Iland there is a saw mill lately built," and whereas he gave one half to Harlackenden years ago but the deed was never recorded and ould not be found, he the said Samuel (who says in the deed that he was a "Gentleman,") now re-conveys to him the one half in question; this was on the 21 April 1668. And on the next day Harlackenden Symons of Gloucester sold the above to his brother Samuel, of Ipswich.—This paper secures three results: first, it settles the date of the saw mill; secondly, it introduces to us Samuel Symons, Jr., and thirdly it opens a chance for a lawsuit. As to the saw mill, it was there as early as 1668. As to Sam. Symons, Jr., Farmer says he died about 1655; but inasmuch as he purchased a share of Wadleigh's Falls as late as 1668, and signed his name to a quitclaim in 1670, it is hardly probable that he was dead. The chance for a lawsuit was profited by: the half which Barefoot sold to Wadleigh and the half of that to Lissen was claimed by Samuel Symons, Jr. On the 4th May 1669, Samuel Symons, sen., sold the other half to his son William, "being possessed of ye farme att Lamperele River" &c., which land was given him by General Court in 1654, (wch date were formerly mistaken by mee,") and whereas reserving one half, he had formerly given to son Harlackenden the other, he now gives to son William the remaining half. And so they got ready for a lawsuit

OLD SERIES, NO 171.

WADLEIGH'S FALLS.

Samuel Symons, jr and William, now claiming to own the whole, brought a suit for trespass against Nicholas Lissen, and in the lower court succeeded: the case was tried at Salisbury, in the court held 14, 2, 1668: and Harlackenden (who suddenly turns up owner again), and William, obtain a "judgment" of 50 shillings damage against Nicholas Lissen in an action "for trespass done in their farme and land in and near Exeter or Dover in entering upon y$_e$ farme and selling tymber there, &c.- as also for his disparaging their o either of their right and title unto ye said farme." In addition to levying the fine, the marshal was ordered 13, 8, 1668 to put the Symons brothers in possession. The marshal did attempt it turned Wadleigh's family out of doors, (they lived at the Falls,) and his and Lissen's workmen out of the mill, and notified Wadleigh of this by writing still preserved, 30 Oct. 1668. But Wadleigh wouldn't stay turned out; and the marshal, Abraham Drake, rather puzzled as to what wa safe, applied to the General Court at Boston in November, "for advice;" he says "the defendant with his abettors still hold possession, and vpon demand, after judgment given for the plaintiffe refused to surrender;" so Abraham wants to know as he finds "it a case rarely in vse," whether he shall use force, and, says he, "that I may more fully be vnderstood by abettors I intend Robt. Wadleigh, of whom the defendant (Lissen) holds, (who, wth the defendt have carried on the worke and milne vpon the plaintiffs farme,) their workmen or any one else holding by the same reputed title." The court advised him to go ahead. He did so, by no means to the satisfaction of Wadleigh, who, in the spring, (22 May 1669) petitioned to the General Court on appeal from the lower court. This petition is as follows:

Robert Wadleigh, &c., &c.

"Humbly Sheweth, that he your petisioner some years past having some incuridgment therto, did adventure upon the setting up of a saw mill upon Lamprill River nigh Dover and did there disburss a great esstate viz many hundred pounds and was in quiet possession thereof for some years and did also dispose of a pt thereof unto Nicholas Lissen. But now of late there hath binn an action against the sayd Lesson, and a judgment gained against him to the value of about 50 shillings and execution upon that sd judgment: But besides the sayd Lessens esstate, thee offiser cam and seased upon your supplyants esstate, which was never sued nor had any judgment against him, and tooke away from him his sayd mill, housen and all esstate; to his utter ruin in poynt of subsistance: except this honored court doth help and releave the oppressed. Therefore your poore supplyant doth humbly begg the honored court favour, to take cognisance thereof, that he may be relieved in great straight and pinching necessity; wh- - have not wherewith to wage law with the mighty, nor contend with a potent advasary. This is that your poor supplyant doe entreat that he may possess & injoy his great esstate thus taken away from him as he suppose without law (and if s)e then) contro-dictory to law, that his poore ffamilie may not still r main in a perpetual way of suffering, not further to presume but your said supplyant doth humbly leave himself and his cause to the wisdom and justice of this honored Court upon whose determination he shall acquiesce and remaine.

Yours in all humility,
Rob: Wadleigh."

He was granted leave to present his case, and did so 19 May 1669. The papers laid before the court are still on file in the Mass. archives, from which he appears to have made two points.—(1) that he and Lissen had d.vided, and instead of holding jointly, each held a separate side of the fall, (which he proved by affidavit of Antipas Maverick then 50 years old and other workmen.) execution in his premises was illegal based on a verdict against Lissen: and (2) that Lissen himself was not guilty, inasmuch as the title which he, Wadleigh, had given him, was valid. With all their faults our Massachusetts settlers were just between man and man, following equity rather than anything else and on the 21 Oct. 1669, they decided "that the petitioner hath binn illegally dispossessed, and order, that he be repossessed in the sayd estate, and have the costs of this court, fifty fower shillings, besides ye charge of ye Court." Wadleigh was then on the premises, he and Symons having had sense enough to see that the mill was going to ruin, and having agreed 3 Nov. 1668, that Wadleigh should own the house and mill, putting the latter again into repair, he paying part of the lumber proceeds to Symons, and neither party's title to be prejudiced thereby.

Wadleigh had also sued Barefoot, whose rascality was doubtless at the bottom of the whole affair; and at the Court of 19 May 1669, it was decided that Barefoot should give a legal conveyance to Wadleigh with warranty against the Symmonses, by the 10th of June following, or else to pay £400 and costs. This was adjudged, 21 Oct. '69, to have been done.

On the 15th of April, 1670, Samuel, jr. and William Symons quitclaim to Robert Wadleigh and Jonathan Thing (to which two Lissen conveys same day,) one half of the farm, and one half of saw mill, the latter two acknowledge themselves holden for half of cost of dams, mills, utensils, &c And on the next day, 16 April, 1670, Wadleigh conveyed to Samuel, jr. and William Symons each a quarter, half a grant of standing timber he had obtained from Dover, they paying a proportionate share of the rent. This grant from Dover, as appears on our records, had been obtained 3, 3, 1669, when there was granted to him, "An accommodation for the erecting and setting up of a saw mill or Mills at the uppermost fall, upper Lampereele river, commonly called by the name of ye Ileland falls;" he received "all ye timber on ye south side above ye sd falls as far as ye towne bounds doth goe, and on ye north side all ye timber that is within one Mile of ye River above ye sd falls as farr as the towne bounds doth goe, with one hundred acres of land on ye south side of ye said River and twenty acres of land on ye north side of ye river. Adjacent unto the said falls one both sides; for which Wadleigh is to pay £10 per annum "in Merchantable pine boards at price current at the ordinary landing place by Lampereele river lower falls," rent to begin the last of August next insuing: if the grant covers any former grant the rent is to be proportionably diminished From this grant Hatevill Nutter entered his dissent in writing, on the same day.

Wadleigh owned other property; he had made a purchase of John Gilman of Exeter of 30 acres of land "lying and being on both sides of the high- way wch goeth from Pusscascock bridg unto Lampereel river landing place," the consideration being "one horse in hand received," &c., 1 Oct. 1668, which last phase is probably metaphorical The Symonses also had the rest of their 80 acre grant, part "fr m Lamperill river mill falls about north and by west; some where about a brook, which, uniting with another brook running out of "Triangle Pond" hard by, emptied into Lamprey river, the land lying near what the state, commissioners concluded to call "Randevow Hill:" some more of it was about five miles from the falls; some more "with all the corners and nookes being very brushy and bushy," a mile from the last; some more joining his farm there; and the residue a piece of meadow attached

Something about Wadleigh's Falls and Robert Wadleigh we expect to say by and by

OLD SERIES, NO 178

THE WALDRONS—NO. 4.

Thomas Westbrook Waldron (7) of Fam. 12, born 26 July 1721, inherited the homestead, mill privileges, &c., purchasing the rights of his brother George. He was a man of large property and extensive influence, although not so much in public office as his father, grandfather, or great-grandfather Our town records show him to have been frequently moderator of our town meetings (1754, '6, '7, '9, '60, '62 to '69, '71 to '75; a selectman in 1751, '3, '4, '6, '8 to '61. Townclerk from 1771 to 1785, Representative in 1756, '62 to '65, '68.

He lived on the old property and in the Waldron house, which is now called, as for many years, the "Old Boarding House," and died there 3 April 1785 he was buried in the burial ground west of the Methodist Church; after his death, the children were carried to Portsmouth where they remained for several years.

Thomas Westbrook married Constant Davis of Dover, who was born 16 March 1734-5 and died 25 Sept. 1783; they had children, (Fam. 14,) William b. 8 June 1756, d. 18 Sept. 1793; Elizabeth b. 3 Jan. 1761, (mar. Joseph Evans of Dover and died 8 Dec. 1820, having had children, Elizabeth, Joseph, Stephen, Vesta, and Abigail;) Richard b. 27 April 1762, d. 15 Oct 1787; Samuel b. 17 Nov 1764, d. 29 July 1765; Eleanor b. 28 May 1766, (mar. James Smith, a native of Durham, but who lived in Dover where he d. in July 1811, having had children, Thomas W. of Augusta, Me., Mary, James, and Daniel, besides others by a second wife: Charles b. 26 Feb. 1768, d. 18 May 1791 of consumption; Twins (girls) b. and d. Dec 1769; Abigail b. 14 Dec 1770) mar (1) David Boardman, and had children, Ann (Riley,) Benjamin (late deceased,) Olive, Harriet, and Thomas; mar. (2) Mark Walker, now deceased, and lives in Dover with her daughter Mrs. John Riley;) Daniel b. 9 Nov. 1776.

Thomas Westbrook Waldon made his will 7 Aug. 1779; it is long, occupying six large foolscap pages closely written over, thirty six lines to a page; in it he mentions his wife Constant, to whom he gave the use of one third of all his real estate in Dover and Portsmouth for life, together with his negro Dinah and her two children Chloe and Plato also one half of his live stock, his riding "chair" and harness, sleigh runners, one third of all his notes of hand, bonds, moneys, and plate, and one third of all his household goods, wool, flax, cloth and yarn; he mentions son William, son Richard, son Charles, son Daniel, daughters, Elizabeth, Eleanor and Abigail, also Jonathan, Mary, and Anne, children of his deceased brother George; also Rev. Jeremy Belknap. He owned enormous quantities of land; in addition to the Dover property he owned lands in Rochester, Barrington, Gilmanton, Grafton County. Lebanon, Chichester, Canaan, Kilkenny, and the Globe Tavern, the Square and the Training field in Portsmouth; two mill privileges in Portsmouth, and part of our lower falls; these quantities of real estate were divided among his children, Charles and Daniel inheriting the Dover property he disposes; also of his "English gun," his brass mounted surveying compass, gunter's chain, share in Dover Library, writing desk, "letter'd case," French gun, share in Portsmouth Library, silver hilted sword, blue suit of clothing, black suit of clothing, pews in Dover and Portsmouth Meeting houses, Theodolite, case of surveying instruments, French gun with a silver sight and thumb piece, silver watch, Library, his father's desk, a large chest of papers not to e opened till Daniel was twenty one, or dead. This will was witnessed by Thomas Shannon, Michael Reade, and Samuel Mills proved 8 June 1785

George Waldron (7) of Fam. 12, brother to Thomas Westbrook Waldron, lived in Dover, was married and had children, of whom we have no accurate account. There were however (Fam. 15.) Mary, Anne, and a son Jonathan; it is believed that these comprised the whole family One of the daughters married Dr. Wigglesworth, formerly of Dover, who lived in the Durell house on Central street Jonathan, George's son, lived in Rye

Of the sons of Thomas Westbrook Waldron, (the daughters we have already mentioned) —

William (8) of Fam 14, died 18 Sept. 1793; he left two children, (Fam. 16) one of whom a daughter married a Ham.

Richard (8) died at Portsmouth 15 Oct. 1787; he was married but left no issue.

Samuel (8) died 29 July 1765.

Charles (8) whom his father made joint heir with Daniel, died of consumption 18 May 1791.

Daniel (8) is still well remembered. By the death of his brother Charles he became, under the terms of their father's will, sole owner of the bulk of the Dover property. Part of his life he was in business in Portsmouth; the other part he resided in Dover the last Waldron occupant of the old house; he came to Dover 11 Nov. 1811.

Daniel married 5 June 1802, Olive Rindge Sheafe, who was born 24 May 1777 and who died Sept 1845. Their children were (Fam 17.)

Richard Russell, who was a Purser in the Navy, and died unmarried; Nathaniel Sheafe b 10 Oct. 1804, mar. Virginia Riggs of Baltimore, and died in Portsmouth 21 Feb. 1857, leaving two sons, and being Brevet Major in the U. S. Marine Corps; Charles lives in Cleveland, O io, married and having children; Mary Constantia is wife of Justin Dimmick, a Major in the U. S Army, and has children; Daniel married Susan Wingate, and is resident of Augusta, Me, Olive b 3 July 1811, d. 1 Aug. 1811; Edmund b. 6 July 1812, is a Catholic Priest, and now resides in Philadelphia; Thomas W. b. 21 May 1814, died at Hong Kong.

Daniel was the last owner of the extensive Waldron real estate in Dover. It probably came into the family in 1642, when the mill privilege in the centre of our city was granted to Major Richard Waldron, from whom it descended to his son Colonel Richard Walrdon in 1689; who bequeathed it to his son Secretary Richard Waldron in 1730, from whom it descended in 1753 to his son Thomas Westbrook Waldron (he purchasing certain rights of his brother George,) who bequeathed it to Daniel Waldron by will proved in 1785. The property at the present time is immensely valuable but its value has been mainly created by the manufacturing establishments erected upon it. When the eyes of some manufacturers were bent upon the water power, they obtained possession of th-bulk of the estate, which passed out of the hands of Daniel Waldron 31 January 1820. Upon that day an uninterrupted family ownership of one hundred and seventy-eight years terminated. With the disappearance of an old and illustrious family, the release of a third of our central territory to the uses of a new population and the whirl of machinery, old Dover passed away and new Dover began its life.

OLD SERIES, NO. 179.

DEEDS

To or from Dover men; taken from the Registry at Exeter, Vol. 3, continued from No. 142.

Hatevil Nutter to John Wingate his "son-in-law" husband of daughter Mary, two twenty acre lots, bounded E. by Back river, N. and S. by land of Thomas Layton sen., W. by the common. 13 Feb. 1670.

Thomas Layton sen., to John Wingett, a twenty acre lot bounded E. by marsh or flats of river, N. by land late Elder Nutter's, W. by land of said Wingett, S. by land of John Damesen., with half the marsh attached. 16 March 1671.

Hatevil Nutter and wife Ann convey to John Wingett his marsh on the E. side of Back river between Little John's Creek mouth and Bellamy's bank, also the marsh appertaining to the twenty acre lotts on the W. side of Back river, for which Wingett is to furnish a certain amount of fodder yearly during their lives. 1 March 1670-1.

Peter Coffin of Dover to John Church, one quarter of a tract near Cocheco containing 75 acres, bounded E. and S. E. by Thomas Downes, W. by Thomlenson's Swamp, for £31 1 Jan. 1668.

Thomas Roberts sen, to Zacharias ffield, 20 acres granted by the Town of Dover to said Roberts, lying in the "bottom of Ryall's cove on ye west side of Back river, knowne by the name of the first twentie acre Lott." 12 May 1671.

Richard Pincom to son John Pincom his 3½ acre lot with orchard, bounded E and S. W. and N. W. by highway, and N. E. by Joseph Canney's, for £12. 22 June 1671.

Richard Pincom to John Pincom, his house, lands, meadow, orchard household goods, cattle &c, for which John agrees to support his father "in a christian way" and give him every year 4£. 12 June 1671.

Elizabeth Drew, adm of estate of Wm. Drew of Oyster river deceased, gives bonds to pay £70 due Thomas Drew from said estate, mortgaging Wm's house and land. 8 July 1671.

Brian Pendleton of Winter harbor to Richard Waldron of Dover adm. of estate of John Webster late of Portsmouth Webster's house near Portsmouth meeting house. 7 July 1670.

Thomas Roberts sen, to his sons John and Thomas Jr. half his marsh at the mouth of Winnicott river on its west side at the bottom of Great Bay; also 30 acres which was his part of the 400 granted to Dover by Mass Court 16 Jan. 1670.

Henry Tippett and Thomas Nock

agree with Philip Lewis about land and marsh on the north side of Winnicott river then occupied by said Lewis. 1 April 1662.

Richard Cator of Dover makes marriage settlement with Mary Ricord whom he is to marry.—Cator then had a grandchild John Bickford. 16 Aug. 1672.

Hatevil Nutter to son-in-law Thomas Layton Jr. who married daughter Elizabeth, one 40 acre lot between Oyster river and Back river, bounded S. by land lately held by Thomas Layton sen., W. by land of John Meader, N. by land of Job Clements, E. by head of 20 acre lot. 13 Feb. 1670.

Thomas Layton, sen., to son Thomas, the dwelling house then in possession of Thomas Jr., bounded S. by Riall's Cove, E by Back river, N. by a lot lately Elder Nutter's W. by John Meader's and Joseph Field's 13 Feb 1670.

Ralph Hall of Exeter to John Wingett of Dover, 20 acres "laid out the seventeenth of this month," being on the W. of Back river at the head of the 20 acre lott, bounded N. W. by John Wingitt's 20 acre lot, S. W. and S. E. by the common, N. E. by one of the old 20 acre lots. 9 May 1672

Richard Waldron, having given to John Gerrish 20 acres at Bellamy, releases Gerrish also from cost of disbursements which Waldron had made for Gerrish's house there built 6 May 1670.

Richard Waldron to son-in-law John Gerrish a quarter of saw mill at Bellamy bought of Wm. Fuller, and 100 acres of land. 1 June 1668.

Andrew Wiggin of Quamscook to Thomas Wiggin of Dover, land at Sandy point. 1 Aug. 1666.

James Nute of Dover to son James, land W. side of Back river which he bought "many years since" of John Newgrove then of Dover; also 40 acres granted by town in 1656. 15 Feb. 1671.

John Partridge and wife Mary of Portsmouth, to Job Clements sen., dwelling house and landd in Portsmouth sometime the dwelling of Rennald ffernald. 21 Aug 1762.

Philip Chesley to son Thomas Chesley, half of house, barn, land &c., Thomas being about to marry Elizabeth Thines. 12 Aug. 1663

Philip Chesley of O. R. to youngest son Philip Chesley, the whole "neck of land" upon which he lived, excepting the ha'f already given to son Thomas. 29 Nov. 1664.

"Whereas ye Generall Court holden in May 1656 settled the Division's of ye Pattents of Dover & Quamscott in wch order ye sd Court did give full powr unto me ye sd Waldron to dispose of fiftie acres of land neer the Great Bay,"—Richard conveys the 50 acres to John Hall, planter, to be laid out as convenient as may be to Hall's dwelling. 9 Oct. 1666.

Samuel Whidon of Portsmouth to John Hall of P a piece of land joining Nehemiah Partridges. 29 June 1672.

James Kid of Exeter to Job Clements, tanner, land in Dover bought of Meader formerly occupied by Richard Nason at Cochecho. Also land (6 acres) by the river's side below the gulf; also 20 acres bought of Peter Coffin on N. W. side of Great Pond at Cochecho; also 20 acres N. side of Cochecho river. 27 June 1671.

Peter Coffin of Dover to brother James Coffin, half of 60 acre tract near Cochecho, bounded E. by Thomas Downes, W. or N. W. by Plumpudding hill N. by highway, lying next lands of Capt. Richard Wa'dron 6 May 1669.

Richard Waldron to Peter Coffin one quarter of sawmill on south side of lower falls, and of all its privileges also half of mill grant from Dover at "Towle end;" also half of 200 acres bought of Edward Rawson to be laid out to Coffin's, up or near adjoining the river; also half of 600 acres bought of Emanuel Downing of Salem; also 6 acres on the south side of Cochecho river joining 2 acres "upon part whereof ye said peter Coffins house now stands the wch he ye sd peter Coffin formerly bought of his father in Law Edward Starbuck," £300. 27 May 1671.

Richard Waldron to John Evans, 2 acres at Cochecho whereon Evans' house stands, bounded S by cartway, W. by land of Nathaniel Stephens, E. and N. by land of Walrdon, for 20s 6 March 1672.

Richard Waldron to James Coffin, 2 acres at Cochecho whereon Coffin's house stands, bounded S. by Cartway, near a spring, for 20 shillings. 1 Feb. 1672.

Richard Waldron to Nathaniel Stephens, for 20 shillings, 2 acres whereon Stephen's house stands, bounded N and E by land of Waldron. 20 Feb. 1672.

James Nute to son Abraham, land at N. W. end of Dover, about 12 acres, E. of Back river, with house &c, after decease of said James and his wife Sarah. 15 Feb. 1671.

OLD SERIES. NO. 210.

Deeds to and from Dover Men, as Recorded at Exeter, Vol. 3.

Laid out to John Hall, 12, 10mo. 1658, by William Furber, 250 acres of land and marsh according to deed from Capt. Waldern and Thomas Lake, dated 24 Mar. 1657, bounded n. by freshet running into John Roberts' creek and coming out of the Great Swamp, s. by freshet coming out of John Hall's fresh marsh, e. by Strawberry Bank Common, and near New-found Marsh.

Mrs. Frances Rayner, widow of Rev. John, to her son John, 27 Sept 1671, her life use of dwelling house orchard, &c. and the two acres on which situated, for "two pepercones as ye only rent."

John Rayner to Job Clements, sen tanner, 4 Jan. 1672-3, for £102 10s. the two acre homestead as above, bounded w. by the street, n. and e. by land of Thomas Beard, s. by land in possession of Capt. Richard Waldron.

Peter Coffin of "Cochecha" to Mark Giles of C. "in consideration of affection," 6 a near Cochecha "where ye new dwelling house of ye sd Marke Giles now standeth," at "plumpuding hill," bounded n. by "great mast way going to ye swamp," e. and s by land of Peter Coffin, being part of land granted by town for his (Peter's) charges to John Church "as concerning the child of Naomi Hull," as by record 5 Mar. 1667 also all claims whatever upon Mark: 1 April 1673

Peter Coffin of Cochecha. to Nath. Stevens for £20 1 April 1673, a quarter part of land near Cochecha, bounded n. by road going from Muchadoe to Plumpuding hill, e. by land in possession of Tho's Downes, and towards "Trumbelow swapme," s. by said swamp.

Wm. Winford (Wentworth) of Dover, with wife Elizabeth, for a "valuable sum," to Peter Coffin, all his title in a piece of marsh about 16 acres as granted to John Baker of Dover in Cochecha marsh; and in a tract granted to Winford by Dover on the further side of Cochecha marsh, being six score acres more or less, excepting 20 a. given to son Samuel next to Richard Oates' land; b. e. and n. by common; s. by Emery's farm; w. by Oates' land and Emerys' meadow, as granted by Dover in 1658; 18 November 1667.

Thomas Canny sen. and Joseph his son, of Dover, make void all previous contracts, and agree again, 28 June 1673; Thomas conveys to Joseph 7 acres on Dover Neck, with house, &c —3½ a. purchased by Thomas of Wm Thomson, 30 a in Great Bay, joining to Thomas Canny's marsh, excepting 3 a formerly given to son Thomas,—80 a. on n. e. side of "Cochecho" marsh, —one eighth of neck lying between "Nechewannuck" river and Fresh Marsh.—with all houses cattle, gardens, orchards, tools, furniture, and utensils whatever, and all cattle, horses, and other creatures belonging to Thomas; only, all the cattle and goods which said Thomas brought "from Yorkcare" are reserved.

Thomas Wiggins of Squamscot, and Thomas, jr of Dover, for £400, to Capt. Walter Barefoot of Dover, 1-2 of sawmill on "Cochecho" river, with half of all buildings, grants, &c. connected therewith, half of 600 acres granted by Dover; also half of 200 a. grant to Thomas sen. from Mass. government; also 20 a of salt marsh near Sandy Point in Exeter; also one half of ten mares, one colt three oxen, and three cows, (half of each.) 21 Ap. 1662 Ralph Hall and others afterwards testified that they were present &c.

John Alt of Oyster River, and wife Remembrance, to John Cutt of Portsmouth, 18 Aug. 1670 for valuable consideration 80 acre piece in "Veedum's" cove Great Bay. Accompanying is copy of grant from town 10 8 mo. 1653.

Thomas Payne of Dover to Ginking Jones of Dover, for £18, 20 acres at "Cochecha" near the Great Hill, being part of 50 acres granted to William Wentworth 1, 10 mo. 1652, and bought of him in 1666. b. "to begin at a Gutt at ye Lower end ye sd Great hill & soe to run by ye Cart way untill it come to ye marked tree W. W. and so by that width "along by ye Commons N. W. till 20 acres are measured." 9 July 1673.

William Furber, husbandman, to Thomas Nock 20 acres at the place "called the Gulfe" on the north side of "Cochecho" river granted to F. by the town 2 July 1657.

John Alt of O. R. to son-in-law John Rand and dau. Remembrance Rand's wife "ali ye place or plantation whereon I now live," at O. R., —after decease of Alt and wife.,—the premises to go to Remembrance after Rand's death. 21 April 1674

Ralph Hall of Exeter mortgages to John Hunking of Pascataqua for 17 m. of pine boards, land in the s. e. of Dover abutting on the first range of lots "that buts on Nechewannick River, joining Thomas Broughton's (formerly Ralph Twombly's) Isaac Hanson, the Common, and Job Clements (formerly Twombly's.) 30 June 1674.

John Alt of O. R. to son 'n law Thomas Edgerly of O. R. weaver, a fourth of acre at west end of field called "Stilliard's" (Hilliard's) and joining Edgerly's land. 3 April 1674.

Thomas Roberts sen. of Dover, to son in law Richard Rich and wife Sarah, for natural affection, one half of goods, lands, chattels, household stuff, houses, orchards, &c. &c.—this immediate; and the other half after his decease; with half of all real and personal estate 29 2 mo. 1671. Job Clements, Thomas Watkins witnesses. Inventory follows—: 3 acre lot, house, 3 and one half lot near swamp, 6 a. on south side of bottom of Great Bay, 2 cows, 2 heifers, and some 'small household stuff.'

James Rendle (of N C.) from Moses Pacheco, a bond for 6 and 1-2 barrels of molasses for a horse delivered in Barbadoes. 12 Nov 1668.

John Cutt calls Reuben Hull "my kinsman," 24 Dec. 1674.

Hatevil Nutter, t Sergeant John Hall, 23 Oct. 1649, by way of exchange. 30 a with 6 a. of marsh, and with adjoining flats, at Greenland in Dover, near Capt Champernoon's farm—south by country highway running between Bloody Point and Hampton n. by John Roberts, w. by Gt. Bay; also, all his right in a piece of "fresh marsh lying about a mile south east from sd Land."

OLD SERIES, NO. 188

THE RIVER AND FALLS.

The section of territory which contains the industrial operations with whose success the prosperity of Dover seems to be identified, (or did, till new business has arisen,) viz. "The Factory Square," bounded by Main, Washington, and Central streets, is now owned entire, with the exception of Nutter's Block, the store next the bridge, and the Dover Bank building, by the Cochero Manufacturing Company. This immense property, however, has been consolidated only by degrees.

Two hundred and eighteen years ago, (from 1859) this tract was a wilderness. Indian trails connected the falls, a favorite camping place, with Dover Neck in one direction, and Salmon Falls (the seat of a tribe) in the other and the river furnished a convenient highway for canoes It was by the river, doubtless, that Major Waldern, in 1640, ascended to the spot where he located, quitting Dover

Neck where he had lived for a few years. No doubt a path was soon cut from the Neck to Cochecho, and it followed, or rather preceded, nearly or quite the present Main road, coming down Pleasant street, winding along the brow of the ridge now Central street, and striking the river where the upper bridge stands. This became the travelled road and a hundred and fifty years it glittered with the finery of many a gay party of provincial dignity or pleasure on its way to the Waldrons. Such a party, coming from the Corner, would cross, in front of the City Hall, a gully, and in it a large brook which still runs under ground across Central square and down in front of Cochecho Block; would ascend, in front of Varney's Block, a rise as high as the second stories of the buildings now lining the street, and which was a continuation of the hill which stood where Varney's Block now is; and would, if a hundred and fifty years ago, have crossed a "boom" of logs which then answered the purpose of a bridge over the far greater waters which are now subdued to a quiet stream; or, a hundred years ago, would have found a bridge, destined to be carried away in the great freshet of 1785, or, after that period, would have travelled, sobered into republican simplicity, down by the present Cochecho Block, across the present lower bridge, and up Main street.

The matter of Bridges had excited a great deal of feeling in Dover The old bridge, in continuation of the town main road, where the upper bridge now stands, in process of time grew old, and it was evident that something must be done. So, on the 26th March 1759, the town voted that "Col. John Gage, Capt. Howard Henderson, & Lt. Dudley Watson, be a Committee to Petition to the General Court for Liberty to raise money by Lottery for the Carrying on the Charge of Building a Bridge over Cochecho River." Whether the desired petition was granted or not, we are entirely ignorant; nothing further appears about it on the records. But on the 17th Aug. 1761, the town voted "That a new Bridge be Built over Cochecho River." And also, "That a Committee be chosen to View the old Bridge to see where it be proper to Repair it so as to be passable for man & horse until next spring or Longer until the Town may more Conveniently Build a New one" The Committee reported, 2 Aug. 1761, that no repairs would make the bridge passable. So the town set itself seriously about the matter, and at the same same meeting voted "That the New Bridge to be Built be built over the upper Ware so called" It also voted "That the sd Bridge be built by Labour at the Discretion of a Committee to be chosen for ye Carrying on the Building said Bridge" Capt. T. W. Waldron, John Hanson, and Lt. Joshua Winget, were appointed Committee, and James Place of Rochester was selected to plan the bridge; the "upper ware" was where the lower bridge now stands; the "lower ware" was against the "Young tanyard"

The friends of the old site were

not contented; and at an adjourned meeting held 27 Aug., the record says "There being a Debate in sd meeting about Reconsidering ye vote past for ye Building the new Bridge over the upper Ware so call'd, nothing voted thereon."—But at still another adjourned meeting, held 31 Aug., the vote locating the bridge, at the "upper ware" was reconsidered, and the proposition lost, and a vote passed "that the new Bridge voted to be Built be Built where the old Bridge now is or near thereto as it may be thought best." So the friends of the upper site prevailed and the bridge was built—with "pitch pine piers"— where the upper bridge now is, in 1761-2, at an expense of £3000 old tenor.

The friends of the lower site were not idle. Quite an interest had grown up—through navigation and in other ways—about the Landing. A controversy sprung up which caused a good deal of bitterness, ended at last by a vote 22 Jan. 1770, "that a new Bridge be built over Cochecho River,"—a vote which was the result, as tradition tells us, of pledges of private subscriptions towards part of the cost. It was voted that it "be built over the upper Ware so called;" that the string pieces should be of "timber pine" and white oak, and that the piers should be white oak; and on the 26 Feb the town voted "not to re consider." So the bridge was built.

At a meeting held 9 Oct. 1784, the matter of bridges came up again. Repairs had been made, it was stated, by individuals, on the lower bridge, but by a "late accident," it was rendered entirely impossible. The town voted £15 for repairs. What was done, however, was of little use; as in October 1785, all the bridges were carried away by "the greatest freshet that ever was." The town came together 31 Oct. 1785, and voted to rebuild the lower bridge; the tables were now turned; the upper site was abandoned, and so remained; a boat took across the few who had business that way; a fence was built in a curved line from the Dover Bank corner to the City Hall corner, in which a pair of bars could be taken down to admit such as wished to go in, by a cart path, to the mills. When the Factory Company commenced operations they laid a floating bridge; the town voted not to build, and the Company built and asked their acceptance of the bridge in 1824, which the town refused; it was not for several years after that the bridge was made the town's.

The bridge of 1785, although an abutment was built at the west end in 1795, was pronounced dangerous in 1796; the town therefore voted, on the 5 Oct 1796, to rebuild the next summer. A new bridge was accordingly built, of which Richard Tripe as the constructor. This was the first bridge hereabouts with pile peers; hitherto a frame had been constructed which rested on the bottom and was loaded with rocks to keep it in place. This was also the first bridge which had a railing, of which the immediate cause was this: Major Tebbets' store, which stood where Wm. Hale's now does, was replaced on the site whence a freshet had swept it; on that occasion, the Major "did the handsome thing;" going home in the dark, one of the company, Daniel Plumer, walked off the bridge and perished wherefore the citizens of this old rum loving town, feeling that it was a matter of personal concern to most of them, held a town meeting 18 Sept. 1797, and voted instanter to have a railing.

Main street, which from 1785 to 1830 or thereabouts, was the only street, had a much sharper pitch than now. School boys of twenty years ago remember the blasting of rocks in front of the Michael Reade place, when the road was considerably lowered.

At the time of the revolution and a little later, the only buildings about the falls, except mills, were these: the Durell house, still standing, on Central street the late Bickford house, on the present site of Varney's Brook, though thirty feet higher in the air the Col. Evans house, a large dwelling which stood on the site of Dea. Jenness' brick house on School street; the Andrew French house, which stood where Nath'l Tibbett's store is; a small building of Waldron's which stood near or upon the site of the American House, used for many years as an office and afterwards hauled away to the turnpike; the Waldron mansion; the Shannon tavern and the mill-house, inside the factory yard, north of the river, and Friend Ham's house, up on the brow of the hill, still standing. This state of things continued until the lower bridge was built and the town threw into the market their lots on Washington and Main streets. After that event, houses lined the street from Dover Bank corner, around the landing corner and up Main street to the old Mark Walker place. These the Facto ry Company found when it commenced here, and most of them or the lots on which they stood are now included in its capacious grasp.

OLD SERIES, NO. 189.

THE MILL PRIVILEGES.

Up to the year 1642, the falls had run undisturbed. In that year, the first in which we have any notice of them, we find, 1, 6mo. 1642, that the town by grant of that date, and again by subsequent grants, 30, 6mo. 1643, conveyed to Richard Walderne, who had come here to seek his fortune, the falls, fifty acres of land on the north side, and sixty acres on the south. Here the Major built a mill In all probability he built mills on both sides of the river; he certainly built a sawmill on the south side, and mills existed on the other shore "beyond the memory of the oldest inhabitant." —On the 20 Dec. 1649, the Major sold to Joseph Austin, the ancestor of all the Austins hereabouts, for £25, one quarter part of the sawmill on the south side, with all appurtenances. The remainder he held until 27 May 1671, when he sold to Peter Coffin another quarter of the south-side privilege.

Of the Major himself everybody knows. He lived about where the north side of Central avenue is, a few rods, perhaps, from Central street No other house or buildings, save his out-buildings, stood on the west side of Central and Franklin streets, from the river to Otis's garrison, just above Brick street, for perhaps two hundred years. That property together with the whole of the north side mill privilege and the half of the south side, on the old Major's violent death in 1689, descended to his only son Richard; Richard lived here a portion of his life, but by and by moved to Portsmouth.—He devised the property, by will, April 6, 1730, to his son Richard, the Secretary of the Province, at whose death Aug. 23, 1753, it descended to the Secretary's sons Thomas Westbrook and George.—Thomas W. lived in the mansion built on the old property and which stood exactly back of Morrill's Block, a few feet west, with the end lapping over the line into Second street

A handsome yard was in front, as it faced the east, and its garden ran down to the river; the old house still stands near by. Thomas W. bought out his brother George's right to the mill and homestead 21 Nov. 1758, and by will dated 7 Aug. 1779, (proved 8 June 1785,) devised it to his two sons Daniel and Charles, or to either survivor in ase the other died, without lawful issue before attaining the age of 21. Charles did so die, and Daniel came into possession. Daniel lived in the old house. He mortgaged, by deeds dated 29 April 1811, and 18 Dec. 1815 the falls and all the land on the north side of the river, excepting the small lot then in possession of Abigail Boardman (next below the Mark Walker lot,) to the New Hampshire Strafford Bank; the Bank came into possession 31 Jan, 1820, and conveyed the whole to William Payne of Boston 23 April 1821, who obtained released of dower the same day. Thus passed out of the Waldron possession the lands lying north of the river and west of Main street, a tract bounded on the south by a line striking from Main street to the river as the north boundary of the "Horne lot" goes, then following up the river half the way to Whittier's fall till it met the Horne property, then running a little east of north till it met the John Waldron property, thence east to the road, and so down the road to the west side of Main street again This did not include their property on the east of Main street, nor south of the river.

So far as is now known, no buildings stood on the north side of the falls in the "Factory Square," except mills, for a great many years Over a hundred years ago, the Waldrons erected a building which was used as a tavern by Capt. Thomas Shannon; this stood near the present gate, but a little nearer the river, and faced Central street. Capt Shannon left it, however, about 1796, and went to Rochester Plains, continuing in the same business; it was afterwards occupied by tenants; Samuel Ricker and his family, and his brother William Ricker and his family occupied it once; other tenants succeeded, but its dilapidated condition rendered it a poor residence. A "mill house," built probably earlier than the Shannon house, stood a rod or two east of the north end of that building; it was a structure of logs and in later days was inaccurately known as the "garrison house;" it had been used for millers families. These with the grist and sawmills, were all which the Company found on the northern side of the mill property.

The Company took these away, and placed their "counting room" about where the gate now is, north of the river; they built a blacksmith shop running from near the "counting room" (a gate between) almost to the river. These are now all gone; but the shed running north from the gate, which was built at an early date, still remains. The nail factory, the first substantial building in the new regime, still standing and occupied for shops, was erected in 1821; the business proved unprofitable and was abandoned in 1826. The machine shop was a more modern affair, and the present "wood shop" replaced the old one at too recent a date to be worth attending to.

The brick store now occupied (1859) by the enterprising firm of Whitney & Rand, was built by the old Factory Company, and occupied on their account by John B H. Odiorne as a general variety store; here they disposed of their own goods in par, and did a general business with up country as was the custom in the early history of manufacturing As experience showed the inconveniences of this system, and especially after the company had sunk a fortune in the business, the trade was given up.— Odiorne and his brother in-law Sam'l W. Carr, as Odiorne & Carr, went on, on their own account, but probably with no great success. After they gave up business, the building was used for many years as the storehouse of the company's goods, sometimes an office or two being let and sometimes not. By and by, Benjamin Barker, who came from Rochester, hired it; since his return thither it has had various tenants, but it is only within a few years that the enterprise of its present occupants has given it a lively apppearance.

OLD SERIES, NO. 190.

THE MILL PRIVILEGE.

We last week traced the title and buildings of that portion of the north side of the Factory Square which came into the possession of the Company from the Waldron property. That property covered originally all the Square on the north side of the river as far south as to the Horne lot, but it had sold the Mark Walker lot and the Boardman lot before the purchase by the Company —The territory commencing with the Horne lot and running down, between Main street and the river to the lower bridge, the town claimed, and in spite of the remonstrances of the Waldrons, succeeded, in the latter part of the last century, in retaining, and finally in selling. To these lots we will attend by and by. At present, we pass to that part of the Square bounded by the river north and east, by Central street west, and by Washington street, south; that is, the tracts where the factories stand.

This land was not all Waldron property. Striking a line from the counting room gate or a little south on Central street, about east to the river, and you have two sections; the upper one was the Waldron privilege; the lower was the town's and after the opening of Washington street and the building of the lower bridge, was cut, and sold as house lots; to this, by and by.

Of that part of the Waldron grant which lay on the south side of the river, as just described, Major Waldron sold one quarter to Joseph Austin 20 Dec. 1649. This quarter descended by inheritance to his son Thomas Austin; Thomas conveyed it, 14 May 1719, by deed, to son Joseph; from him, either by a daughter's marriage or some other way not recorded, it passed to the hands of Tristram Coffin of Dover, who by will dated 27 April 1761 and proved 26 Aug. 1761, devised it to his son Eliphalet (brother to aunt Debby and Mrs. Bickford;) he sold it, 3 Nov. 1795, to Jacob Currier.

Another quarter was sold by Major Waldron to old Peter Coffin 27 May 1671. Old Peter (we beg his pardon, —Hon. Peter,) conveyed it, 24 Nov. 1714, to his grandson Eliphalet Coffin of Exeter, who by will proved 13 Sept. 1736, devised the said interest to his son Rev. Peter Coffin of Kingston, who, 21 Oct 1741, conveyed the said part together with his share of what was saved out of the mill "that was lately carried away" to John Gage of Dover.—John Gage having died, his estate was divided, 18 Nov. 1794, between Capt. John Gage, Jonathan Gage, Moses Gage, and Sarah wife of Nathan Horne; the quarter of the mill privilege fell to Capt. John and Jonathan jointly; in a further division between the two, made 17 Mar. 1795, the "quarter" was released to John. John sold it, 25 July 1795, for £50, to John Philips Gilman of Dover, so that at the beginning of the year 1796, the south side was owned, half by the heirs of Thos. W. Waldron, a quarter by John P. Gilman, and a quarter by Jacob Currier.

On the 14 May 1796, the property was divided. Daniel Waldron's half was next to Central street, running ten or twelve rods on that street and about nine down the river. Currier and Gilman took the other half, almost where the Factory bridge stands, having also a right of way through Waldron's land, and a right to build flumes from the dam. On the 6 May 1797, Currier and Gilman also divided, in a way impossible to be made intelligible, and of no sort of use now if it could be.

Gilman sold a part of his share, 24 Aug. 1798 to Samuel Gerrish jr.; on Gerrish's death it descends to his children John and Alphonso, and is sold by virtue of license, 29 April 1811, to Daniel L. Currier, an oil mill then standing there. Currier conveyed it, by deed 24 March 1821, to John Williams of Boston and Isaac Wendell of Dover, who conveyed it 28 April 1821, to William Payne of Boston. Gilman conveyed the residue of his share to Joseph Gage, 21 Aug. 1798, whose daughter Mary Wingate Gage inherited it, on whose account it was sold by license to Jacob M. Currier, who included it in his sale 26 March 1821, as below

Jacob Currier conveyed out of his share, 31 Oct 1801, to Daniel L. Currier, a privilege for a fulling mill, who conveyed it to Ephraim Foss jr., who seems to have conveyed it to Jacob M. Currier subject to lease expired 1 Feb 1824 On the 20 May 1815, Jacob Currier sold to William Currier, a quarter of an oil mill standing on the premises, which said William conveyed, 25 May 1820, to Jacob M. Currier; Jacob Currier also had conveyed all his remaining interest, 28 Jan. 1818, to Jacob M. Currier, who thus owned the whole quarter, and who conveyed said quarter to Wm. Payne 26 March 1821.

The upper part of the south side, which, in the division of 14 May 1796 was assigned to Daniel Waldron, he sold 21 Jan. 1819, to Jonathan Locke, the tavern keeper. Locke sold it, 30 April 1821 to William Payne. Thus the whole mill property came into the hands of William Payne, who was a wealthy citizen of Boston, and the first President of the Dover Factory Company, and who conveyed the whole to the Company, with other lands hereabouts, 27 April 1822. And thus the water of Major Waldron's mill privilege was set to turning spindles.

As to the buildings which have stood on this south side tract, prior to its occupation for cotton factories, it is hard to be very specific. There can be traced an "old" sawmill there in 1649; a sawmill in 1671, in 1719, and in 1735; an oil mill in 1798, 1806, 1811, 1815, and 1818; a grist mill in 1798 and 1818; a carding machine "in the building containing and covering said grist mill and oil mill" on Jacob Currier's part, in 1818; Jeremiah Stickney also had a card factory there somewhere between 1810 and 1820, and Ephraim Foss jr. had a fulling mill about where No 3 picker stands, from 1821 (and doubtless earlier) to 1 Feb. 1824.

The "Dover Cotton Factory" was incorporated 15 Dec. 1812, with a capital of $50 000, which built in 1815 the No. One Factory at "upper Factory" Village; it was a wooden structure, and has long since disappeared. The Company had its capital enlarged, 21 June 1821, to $500,000, about the time when it bought up the titles of the lower falls as described above. The capital was enlarged 17 June 1823, to $1,000,000, and the name changed to "Dover Manufacturing Company." The capital was again enlarged, 20 June 1826, to $1,500,000, but the Company did not succeed; and a new Company, the present one, the "Cocheco Manufacturing Company" was incorporated 27 June 1827, with a capital of $1,500,000 which purchased of the old Company all their works and personal property. The chief fault of the present Company is their barbarous spelling of "Cocheco" instead of "Cochecho," for which no possible excuse exists.

No. Two was built in 1822; No. Three in 1823; No. Four in 1825; and No. Five in its present form (which replaced the old Printery,) in 1850

OLD SERIES, NO. 227.

AUNT NABBY BELKNAP

In detailing, in a former number, the origin and history of the "White house." (not the one on Pennsylvania Avenue, but that which was the home of Amos White, Esq., Main street, Dover, N. H.,) we omitted all account of one of its principal inmates, the venerable female whose name heads this article. This intended omission we now proceed to repair

Sister to the Reverend Jeremy Belknap, she was daughter of Joseph Belknap of Boston. Joseph was born 12 Feb., 1717, married, 30 July, 1741, Sarah Byles, niece of the gifted but excentric Mather Byles, and well supported his family by his trade of leather dresser and dealer in furs and skins, which he carried on in the shop in the front part of his house in Ann street, Boston.—Nabby and Jeremy were the only children who lived to mature age. Nabby lived with her parents; but Jeremy graduated at Harvard College, passed through the office of school master with credit, entered that of the ministry, and settled down in Dover. When the revolution came on, Jeremy got his parents out of Boston and into Dover, and Nabby, of course, came with them. The parents stayed so long that their visit ended with the burial upon Pine Hill of all about them that was mortal. By-and-by Jeremy's parochial troubles terminated by his removal to Boston.—Nabby accompanied her brother in his change, but her mind turned with lingering wishes to Dover; and when she heard that Amos White was preparing to build a house, she wrote immediately an earnest request that a room might be finished off for her. Her request was acceded to. In due time Nabby was installed therein; and there she passed the remainder of her days

The room in which she lived was the southwest corner one, on the first floor. Considering her single blessedness, she had very comfortable quarters. Her home was sunny and cheerful. She met with unvarying kindness from the inmates of the house, and enjoyed the respect of the community at large. Her fireplace was one of the master pieces of that Simon Jenks who was the Pnidias of his business. It was not merely that his chimnies had a better draught, that his jambs were a little more flaring, and that his mantels were a little higher;—but that his genius combined these merits into a harmony unapproachable by any of his competitors; and had it not been for the old Dover curse, he had not left his house (the Neal house on the corner of School street,) for a lodging in the ground as early as 1810

Aunt Nabby's room was her kitchen, her parlor, her bedroom, and her warehouse. By the capacious fireplace she cooked such frugal meals as she ate when not sitting at the family table, and doubtless with a flavor now lost since hideous stoves have spoiled cookery. At the same fireplace she once or twice a year made candy for the children, though unfortunately she always burnt it. Her bed, only a foot or so from the floor, because coming rheumatism disliked her climbing, occupied a corner. In a large trunk was her stock in trade,--for she was a trader —consisting of the best needles, the nicest silk, and the finest cultery then to be found in these parts. And by the windows stood her high backed chair and he little round table, where most of her life was spent; here she watched the blooming of apple trees, the peeping up of parsnips and cabbages, the dawning of beans and corn, the growing ruddiness of fruits and grain. Here she noted down rains and snows, and the freezing and opening of the river, and freaks of lightning, and when she sowed her sweet marjoram, and other wonderful occurrences. Here she saw the teamsters going past and speculated on the sleding or wheeling. Now & then Aunt Nabby went a visiting to Sandwich or Lebanon, or Portsmouth. But the great occasion recurred twice a year, when she went to Boston to replenish her stock in trade. For two or three days previous to her well known journey, letters poured in to be kindly delivered by her careful hands. On the appointed morning the stage coach drove up with that pomp and parade which alas have passed away; Aunt Nabby entered and wended her envied way through Portsmouth by the then only route to the famous town of Boston. For two or three days after her return people hastened to see and diminish her admired stock, which however they must not take into their own hands lest the bright steel and fine silk should be tarnished. Thus she drove a brisk trade in a small way, and spent her days in ease and plenty. In process of time, however, she abandoned her sales as other stores came besides those whose staples had been, almost exclusively, rum and salt fish; and especially when the late Mr. George Andrews, with his scrupulous honesty and old fashioned courtesy, commenced a new era in Dover trade.

Aunt Nabby had other occupations however.—She was kind to the sick. She visited the old. Decrepid people came to her for alms, and did not go away empty. The black and white were all the same to her benevolence. She was thoroughly orthodox, a member of the First Church, and was fond of theologic as well as practical religion. Now and then, as Dr. Channing, her brother's successor at Boston, issued those successive sermons which made such a stir in the controversies of a generation ago, her nephew, John Belknap of Boston, used to send them to her; she read them, but it was always, to say "that isn't such doctrine as my father preached," and she clung to the old ways. She used also to discuss matters with old Mr Nason of Dover Neck, who sold fresh oysters from down the river at town meeting times, and who annually brought Aunt Nabby a peck or so, on which occasion she and Mr Nason, who, with a prodigious memory, had the Bible almost by heart, talked to their heart's content.

But Aunt Nabby grew old. Her rheumatism gained upon her She hobbled about with a cane; rather short and somewhat fleshy, and in these respects, much like her brother, as she also was in feature, it came harder and harder for her to move about. She used to watch her camphor bottle barometer, which foretells the weather on the scientific principle that when foul weather is approaching, the camphor will be clear or cloudy,—we could never exactly discern which, although we have faithfully experimented. When too lame to walk out, she bought a chaise, which, with Mr White's horse, saw a great deal of service. She amused herself, if it is not to be rather considered business, with keeping her record of deaths, (whih we have transcribed and will insert by-and-by,) and of changeable weather, and remarkable snows.

When Aunt Nabby's last sickness came Dr. Jonathan Flagg attended her. He was a skilful physician, and obtained a tolerable good pratice although laboring under the great disadvantage that he studied instead of driving about guzzling rum; but he went to Boston somewhere about 1817, where he built up a successful business as a dentist, which his excellent reputation for tooth drawing showed h m well qualified. He w s in Dover when Aunt Nabby was taken sick, and did his best for her But his skill was all in vain, for the house-dog, Pero by name, howled under the window, and Aunt Nabby then knew she was to die. What good could science do, when the howling of the dog had settled the question? So Aunt Nabby, in 1815, died in peace, and joined the silent company at Pine Hill.

John Belknap administered on Aunt Nabby's estate. On the 14th of June 1816, he gave an account of his stewardship, in which she exhibited receipts from Sarah Belknap, Elizabeth Belknap, and A. E Belknap, to each of whom he had paid $342,04; which with his own share made the sum total of $1368,16, the net proceeds of Aunt Nabby's worldly possessions.

As an authoress, Aunt Nabby's productions were chiefly confined to matters of fact She seldom indulged in sentiment,—rarely abandoned herself to flights of imagination Upon these and other points, however, we shall leave our readers to judge· and to give the requisite means of information, shall commence the publication of at least a part,—allowing ourselves no editorial liberties save the insertion of punctuation marks and the capitalizing of the letters which begin sentences.

OLD SERIES, NO. 197, July 7, 1859.

HOW DOVER CAME UNDER THE MASSACHUSETTS GOVERNMENT.

Dover was a part of Massachusetts from 1641, to 1680. How it came to be so, and again not so, was after the manner following. For ten years after its settlement Dover had no government whatever; every man did what was right in his own eyes, perhaps. When new accessions to the colony came over in 1633, Capt. Thomas Wiggin was authorized by the patentees in England to act as Governor. But these patentees Lords Say and Brook, and others, had themselves no right of government; nor had the Bristol men whose right these patentees had purchased, any power of government; nor did Hilton and others who had sold to the Bristol men their Dover and Squamscott patent have any power of government; nor had the "Council at Plymouth" in England who in 1631 gave these patents to Hilton and his associates; neither had Capt. John Mason, whose grants covered the same territory, for, as the English Courts say in 1677, "as to Mr. Mason's right of government within the soil he claimed, their Lordships and indeed his own counsel, agreed he had none; the great Council of Plymouth, under whom he claimed, having no power to transfer government to any " Whatever civil power, therefore, Capt. Wiggin possessed, was a clear case of "squatter sovereignty." And what there was, was of a very weak kind, never extending to anything very serious. Wiggin himself was aware how doubtful his authority was; for in November 1633, on occasion of one of his people stabbing another, he wrote to Gov. Winthrop, desiring that if the wounded man died, the offender should be tried in Massachusetts, to which the Governor responded shrewdly and cautiously, that if Piscataqua, lay in heir limits (as they claimed,) they would try him. So again in February 1634, he wrote as "Governour of Pascataquach under the Lords Say and Brook," to Winthrop, making the same request in regard to another criminal, but it was declined. These things plainly imply a defect of criminal jurisdiction in Wiggin's authority.

That authority itself was soon transferred.—Wiggin was superseded in 1637 or early in 1638, by Rev George Burdett, who succeeded in obtaining a vote of the people to that effect. The fact is generally overlooked, that in the early settlement of Dover, two antagonistic principles were side by side; even Belknap hardly hints at the true cause of "strange confusions" into which the colony fell. The first settlers appear to have been Episcopalian; William Hilton certainly was, as in 1621 he was the occasion of great disturbance at Plymouth by having his child baptized in the Episcopal form; Mason was an Episcopalian; the "Council at Plymouth" mainly Episcopalian. But when the two subordinate patents of Swamscott and Dover passed into

Puritan hands, men of that stamp came over; and the two irreconcilable elements broke out in open hostility. Now it was by appealing to the Episcopal sentiment that Burdett rode into office; and while in power he corresponded with Archibishop Laud freely, entered into all the plans of that tyrant regarding the Colonies, and exhibited in various ways his dislike to the Massachusetts power, the especial hope of the Puritans. It is not a little strange that the accomplished editor of Winthrop's Journal (Hon. James Savage,) should say (p. 332 new ed.,) "I marvel at the charge by Winthrop that he had intelligence with the prelatical party at home;" when Winthrop states the well-known fact (p 358-9,) that a copy of Burdett's letter to Archibishop Laud was found in his study, and that letters from the Archibishop and Lord Commissioners to Burdett were opened and read at Boston.

Burdett was himself dispossessed, in or about 1638 by Capt. John Underhill, a man whose varied attainments in rascality equalled those of Burdett without the latter's subtilty. Banished from Massachusetts, he was still a professed Congregationalist, but he doubtless obtained power through his military abilities. Prior to his election Winthrop had written to Burdett, Wiggin and others, by direction of the General Court, protesting against their advancing of those who had been "cast out" of Massachesetts, meaning Underhill thereby, and hinting strongly that Massachesetts intended to survey their utmost limits and use them, which would, according to their claim, have covered Dover; Burdett returned a scornful answer, for which Winthrop seriously thought of summoning him to appear and answer for contempt, he having taken the oath of allegiance to the Massachusetts government while there, at Salem. The Governor however thought better of it and wrote to Edward Hilton, a man of character and judgment, declaring the state of the case and warning them against Burdett, and against "advancing" Underhill But before the letter came, Underhill had not only been "advanced," but had overthrown Burdett also; besides, Hilton never got the letter.

Once installed Underhill proceeded to exhibit his indignation towards the Massachusetts government. They had not only expelled him from their jurisdiction, but they had warned the people against him, and also informed them of his misdoings in Massachusetts, sending, moreover, to the chief inhabitants, copies of his own abusive letters, in which he "professed himself to be an instrument of God or their (Massachusetts') ruin."—This well nigh destroyed his influence here, although he retained power for sometime longer

Tired however of their endless confusions in church and state, many of the people, more especially the Puritan portion. determined to place the town, if possible, under the jurisdiction of Massachusetts They wrote upon this matter to the Governor, who answered them that "if they sent two or three of their company with full commission," it was probable the General Court would treat with them. They did so; three commissioners appeared at the session held in September 1639, with proposals of union; their terms not being acceptable, they finally admitted that they had full power to conclude any arrangement that might seem proper for them. Whereupn the Deputy Governor, with Mr. Emanuel Downing and Capt. Edward Gibbons for the General Court, agreed with the Committee of Dover upon a union in which Dover was to "be as Ipswich and Salem, and have courts there, etc." the treaty being dependent however upon the ratification of the people of Dover. The people, through the influence of Underhill refused their assent; perhaps Knollys assisted him, as he had no very pleasant recollections of Massachusetts authority.

Underhill was not long suffered to retain his authority. Ashamed of being governed by a man guilty of the crimes which he had at last confessed, as well as disapproving of his opposition to Massachusetts, the people were preparing to dismiss him, when he hastened their decision by rescuing out of the officers' hands a prisoner at Exeter, thus to ingratiate himself with the prelatical party at Portsmouth. He was immediatley removed from the government, and Thomas Roberts (ancestor of all our Roberts's,) was elected to succeed him, in the summer of 1640.

In the fall of the same year, finding the necessity of some more regular government than they then enjoyed, the people of Dover, or rather a majority of them, entered into a "Combination" for government; this was done 22 October 1640, and was signed by Thomas Larkham (the minister who dispossessed Knollys,) Richard Walderne, William Walderne, and thirty-eight others whose names are lost. We have no doubt but that this was done in opposition to the Massachusetts interest, inasmuch as Larkham was himself opposed to their doctrine and discipline; he was a wealthy man and part owner in the plantation, and from this and his ministerial position, possessed of great influence. The form of this combination, being printed in No. 16 of these memoranda, it is unnecessary to repeat.

The government thus established proved itself inefficient. The parties among the people were unreconciled. Larkham and Knolles were sternly opposed to each other; the former sustained by the Waldrons, Layton, Hall, and others, embracing the original Episcopal sentiment; the latter by Underhill and others, who now favored the Massachusetts Government. Underhill endeavored to persuade the people to renew their application to be received under the latter, and succeeded in obtaining a respectable part, for that purpose. The application, on the other hand, was opposed by the adherents of Larkham in a paper a copy of which we will give in our next No.

INDEX OF PERSONS.

INDEX OF PERSONS.

Roman notation refers to the Memoranda in Scrap Books.

Abbott, Joseph, 163, xli.
Adams, Abigail, 397.
   Alexander, 70, 280.
   Amos Chase, 397.
   Ann, 396, 397.
   Benjamin, 80, xxi.
   Catherine, 397.
   Charles, 58, 66, 77, 79, 80, 116, 141, 193, 219, 275, 349, 352, 354, 356, 357, 363, 372, 377, xv, xvii, xx, xxi, xxix, xxxvi, xlix, lv, lxviii, lxxxviii, xc, xci, xcii, xcv, xcvii.
   Deborah, 396, 397.
   Ebenezer, 397.
   Eliza, 397.
   Hannah, 397.
   Hugh, Rev., 303, 388, 393, 394, 395, lxxvi.
   John, 79, 80, 395, 396, 397, xx, xxi.
   John P., 14, iv.
   Joseph, Rev., 395.
   Martha, 80, xxi.
   Mary, 396.
   Matthew, 395.
   Nathaniel, 396, 397.
   Rebecca, 178, xlv.
   Samuel, 77, 79, 84, 265, 275, 277, 397, xx, xxii, lxvi, lxviii, lxix.
   Samuel Chesley, 396.
   Sarah, 79, 80, 397, xx, xxi.
   Tamson, 80, xxi.
   Temperance, 80, xxi.
   Thomas, 397.
   Walter, 80, xxi.
   William, 396, 397.
   Winborn, 77, 79, 265, xx, lxvi.
Addington, Isaac, 221, 246, lvi, lxii.
Alden, Thomas, 61, xvi.
   William H., 102, xxvi.
Allen, Catherine, 260, lxv.
   Dorcas, 260, lxv.
   Edward, 63, 140, 160, xvi, xxxv, xl.
   Eliza, 230, lvii.
   Isaac, 260, lxv.
   Joseph, 104, 320, 321, xxvii, lxxx.

Allen, Mary, 260, lxv.
   Samuel, 63, 242, xvi, lx.
   Sarah, 260, lxv.
   William, 63, xvi.
Alley, Samuel, 61, xvi.
Alt or Ault, John, 37, 69, 75, 122, 138, 140, 190, 349, 352, 354, 356, 359, 363, 372, 377, 382, 411, 412, x, xviii, xix, xxxi, xxxv, xlviii, lxxxviii, xc, xci, xcii, xcv, xcvii.
   Remembrance, 411, 412.
   Thomas, 377, xcvii.
Ambler, John, 4, 161, 186, 250, i, xli, xlvii, lxii.
Ambrose, Alice, 168, 169, 173, xlii, xliii, xliv.
Andrews, George, 104, 421, xxvii.
   Jedediah, 66, 69, 355, 378, xvii, xviii, xc, xcvii.
   William, 14, iv.
Andros, Jedediah, 65, xciii.
Anthony, Emery, 20, v.
   John, 279, lxix.
Appleton, Major Samuel, 247, 248, lxii.
   William, 397.
Arms, William, 243, lx.
Arwin, Edward, 363, xcii.
Ash, John, 364, xcii.
   Thomas, 237, lix.
Atherton, Mrs. Charles H., 396.
Atkinson, Sarah, 281, lxx.
   Theodore, 128, xxxiii.
   William, 14, 106, iv, xxvii.
Austin, Benjamin, 62, 130, 146, xvi, xxxiii, xxxvii.
   Deborah, 281, lxx.
   Elijah, 24, 104, vi, xxvii.
   James, 10, iii.
   Joseph, 5, 24, 25, 40, 41, 49, 66, 130, 136, 200, 201, 338, 348, 349, 354, 355, 356, 362, 365, 372, 374, 376, 379, 387, 415, ii, vi, vii, x, xi, xiii, xvii, xxxiii, xxxiv, l, li, lxxxv, lxxxvii, lxxxviii, xc, xcii, xciii, xcv, xcvi.
   Phebe, 400.
   Rose, 136, xxxiv.
   Samuel, 62, 353, 371, 374, vi, xc, xcv, xcvi.

Austin, Sarah, 295, lxxiii.
    Thomas, 140, 418, xxxvii.
Awite, John, 367, xciii.
Ayer, James, 346, lxxxv.
    Ruth, 304, lxxvi.
Ayers, Moses, 309, lxxvii.
    Tamson, 263, lxv.

Baker, Christine, 101, 102, 251, 324, xxvi, lxii, lxxx.
    Ebenezer, 231, lviii.
    Hannah, 231, lviii.
    James, 323, lxxxi.
    John, 8, 36, 128, 230, 231, 352, 366, 411, ii, ix, xxxiii, l, lviii, lxxxviii, xciii.
    Lydia, 231, lviii.
    Mehitable, 231, lviii.
    Otis, 6, 11, 12, 101, 231, 323, 329, ii, iii, xxvi, lviii, lxxxi, lxxxiii.
    Otis, Col., 327, lxxxii.
    Sharonton, 7, 103, 231, ii, xxvi, lviii.
    Thomas, 231, 251, lviii, lxii.
Balch, Joanna, 325, lxxxii.
    Nathaniel, 323, lxxxi.
Ball, Peter, 262, lxv.
Bampton, 11, 13, iii, iv.
Banfield, Christie, 374, xcvi.
    Joshua, 7, ii.
Bangs, Cyrus, 74, xix.
Banks, Capt. Jeremiah, 324, 325, lxxxi, lxxxii.
Barber, John, 363, xcii.
Bardwell, Richard, 290, lxxii.
Barefoot, Governor, 120, 302, xxx, lxxv.
    Walter, Capt., 66, 141, 376, 402, 404, 411, xvii, xxxvi, xcvi.
Barkard, 130, xxxiii.
Barker, Benjamin, 417.
Barnes, Elizabeth, 290, lxxii.
Bartlett, Israel, 265, lxvi.
    James, 9, 14, iii, iv.
    Josiah, 265, 266, lxvi.
    Mary, 265, lxvi.
    Sarah, 265, lxvi.
    Thomas, 265, lxvi.
Batchelder, Charles, 77.
Bean, Peniel, 260, lxv.
Beard, Hannah, 250, lxii.
    John, 67, xvii.
    Joseph, 195, 199, 236, 275, xlix, lv, lix, lxviii.
    Thomas, 3, 35, 65, 75, 115, 137, 141, 343, 349, 353, 362, 365, 374, 376, 389, 410, i, ix, xvii, xix, xxix, xxxv, xxxvi, lxxxvi, lxxxviii, xc, xcii, xciii, xcvi.

Beard, William, 3, 53, 58, 69, 115, 138, 193, 349, 354, 357, 363, 372, i, xiv, xv, xviii, xxix, xxxv, xlix, lxxxviii, xc, xci, xcii, xcv.
Beck, Henry, 20, 200, 348, 350, 352, v, l, lxxxvii, lxxxviii.
Becker, John, 348, lxxxvii.
Belcher, Governor, 228, 292, lviii, lxxii.
Belknap, A. E., 422.
    Elizabeth, 422.
    Jeremy, Rev. Dr., 28, 81, 86, 102, 104, 184, 296, 303, 321, 323, 420, vii, xxi, xxii, xxvi, xxvii, xlvi, lxxiv, lxxv, lxxxiii.
    John, 421, 422.
    Joseph, 323, 420, lxxx.
    Nabby, 420.
    Sally, 323, lxxx.
Bellow, William, 348, 367, lxxxvii, xciii.
Bell, Frederick, 323, lxxxi.
    George, 323, lxxxi.
    Judith, 323, lxxxi.
Benick, Abraham, 156, 196, xxxix, xlix.
Benmore, Philip, 139, 140, xxxv.
Benson, Joseph, 308, lxxvii.
Bennett, Abraham, 160, 194, xl, xlix.
    Arthur, 371, xcv.
    James, 10, iii.
    John, 78, 80, xx, xxi.
    Eleazer, 78, xx.
    Henry, 127, xxxii.
Berry, Abigail, 264, lxvi.
    Ann, 253, lxiii.
    Benjamin, 264, lxvi.
    George, 264, lxvi.
    Isaac, 264, lxvi.
    Sarah A., lxxvii.
    Susan, 264, lxvi.
    William, 263, lxv.
Bickford, Benjamin, 127, 156, 162, 195, xxxii, xxxix, xli, xlix.
    Bridget, 388.
    Eleazer, 198, 319, li, lxxx.
    George, 121, xxxi.
    Henry, 63, xvi.
    Jethro, 127, xxxii.
    John, 2, 12, 46, 53, 58, 66, 94, 127, 141, 145, 152, 154, 162, 193, 341, 349, 354, 357, 362, 365, 377, 388, 390, 409, i, iii, xii, xiv, xv, xvii, xxix, xxxii, xxxvi, xxxvii, xxxviii, xxxix, xli, xlix, lxxxvi, lxxxviii, xc, xci, xcii, xciii, xcvii.
    Jonathan, 93, xv.
    Joseph, 141, xxxvi.
    Lemuel, 286, lxxi.

Bickford, Thomas, 356, 388, xc.
Bines, James, 349, 354, lxxxviii, xc.
Bird, Bishop of Lincolin, 334, lxxxiv.
    Thomas, 372, xcv.
Boardman, Abigail, 416.
    Ann Riley, 406.
    Benjamin, 406.
    David, 406.
    Harriet, 406.
    Olive, 406.
    Thomas, 406.
Blake, William, 13, iv.
Blaney, Mr., 308, lxxvii.
Blind Will, Indian Chief, 213, liv.
Blydenburgh, John, 89, xxiv.
Boardman, Benjamin, 14, iv.
    David, 318, lxxx.
Bockham, Mr., 241, lx.
Bodge, Benjamin, 265, lxvi.
Bonner, Mary, 386.
    Nicholas, 386.
Bonsell, Mr., 192, xlviii.
Boody, Azariah, 63, xvi.
Boom, Rowena, 317, lxxx.
Boosby, Mr., 308, lxxvii.
Borden, William, 142, xxxvi.
Bowden, William, 20, v.
Boyd, Abigail, 325, lxxxii.
Boyse, Matthew, 40, 350, x, lxxxviii.
Brackenbury, William, 258, lxvi.
Brackett, Abigail, 279, lxix.
    Cisca, 279, lxix.
Bradford, Abraham, 349, lxxxviii.
Brady, John, 376, xcvi.
Bradbury, Elizabeth, 393.
    Thomas, 188, 375, 393, xlvii, xcvi.
Bradstreet, Simon, 29, 40, 41, 164, 246, 348, 364, 385, viii, x, xi, xli, lxi, lxxxvii, xcii.
Bragg, Samuel, 101, xxvi.
Brane, Michael, 362, 365, 372, xcii, xciii, xcv.
Branson, George, 349, 354, lxxxviii, xc.
Braye, Richard, 145, 356, 357, 363, 377, xxxvii, xc, xci, xcii, xciii.
Brewster, Charles, 285, lxxi.
    Mary, 308, lxxvii.
    Paul, 11, iii.
    Samuel, 308, lxxvii.
Brigdon, Katherine, 395.
Brine, John, 335, lxxxiv.
Brock, Betsey, 260, lxv.
    Ezra, 260, lxv.
    Isaac, 260, lxv.

Brock, John, 260, lxv.
    Keziah, 108, lxxvii.
    Nicholas, 260, lxv.
    Ralph, 260, lxv.
    Susan, 260, lxv.
Broks, Samuel, 266, lxvi.
Brook, Lord, 17, 23, 192, v, vi, xlviii.
Broughton, George, 358, 361, xci.
    John, 361, xci.
    Mr., 53, 341, 355, 360, 362, 365, 378, xiv, lxxxvi, xc, xci, xcii, xciii, xcvii.
    Thomas, 360, 372, 374, 412, xci, xcv, xcvi.
Brown, Benjamin, 80, xxi.
    Francis, Rev. Dr., 395.
    Francis, 80, xxi.
    Henry, 145, 340, 363, 378, 390, xxxvii, lxxxv, xcii, xcvii.
    John, 187, xlvii.
    Martha, 307, lxxvi.
    Robert, 74, xix.
    Samuel, 80, xxi.
    Samuel, Prof. Gilman, 395.
    Susanna, 80, xxi.
    Walter, 80, xxi.
Bruen, Obediah, 190, xlviii.
Buckingham, Hon. J. T., 386.
Buckner, Charles, 49, 66, 356, 362, 365, 373, 377, xiii, xvii, xc, xcii, xciii, xcvi, xcvii.
    Mary, 373, xcvi.
Buesley, John, 354, xc.
Bunker, Ephraim, 86, xxii,
    James, 59, 158, 195, 276, 356, 357, 363, xv, xl, xlix, lxix, xc, xci, xcii.
    John, 267, lxvi.
    Joseph, 59, 315, xv, lxxix.
    Love, 310, lxxviii.
    Mary, 381, lxx.
Burdett, Rev. George, 17, 25, 36, 73, 164, 365, 384, 423, vi, vii, ix, xix, xli, xciii.
Burgin, Hall, 261, lxv.
    John, 261, lxv.
Burleigh, Deborah, 261, lxv.
    John, 179, 261, xlv, lxv.
    Rebecca, 261, lxv.
    Sarah, 261, lxv.
    Thomas, 262, lxiii.
Burnet, William, 61, xv.
Burnham, Elizabeth, 252, lxiii
    James, 238, lix.
    Jeremiah, 3, 59, 79, 156, 158, 199, 202, i, xv, xx, xxxix, xl, l, li.
Jetem, 159, xl.

Burnham, John, 137, xxxv.
　Robert, 2, 38, 49, 53, 58, 65, 70, 74, 89, 114, 121, 132, 141, 146, 150, 339, 343, 356, 357, 363, 370, i, x, xiii, xiv, xv, xvii, xviii, xix, xxiv, xxix, xxxi, xxxiv, xxxvi, xxxvii, xxxviii, lxxxv, lxxxvi, xc, xci, xcii, xcv.
　Susan, 105, xxvii.
　Samuel, 152, xxxviii.
Bushee, William, 61, xvi.
Bushnell, Mr., 364, xcii.
Buss, Ann, 393.
　Dr., 88, xxiii.
　Elizabeth, 88, xxiii.
　John, Rev., 39, 274, 393, x, lxviii.
　Joseph, 243, 393, lx.
　Richard, 393.
　William, 243, 393, lx.
Bulter, William, 280, lxix.
Burt, Rev. Federal, 398.
Byles, Rev. Mather, 420.
　Sarah, 420.

Cain, Deborah, 307, lxxvi.
Calef, James, 11, 104, iii, xxvii.
　James, Capt., 31, lxxxiii.
Camer, Thomas, 353, xc.
Camond, Abel, 20, v.
Canney, James, 62, 268, xvi, lxvii.
　John, 5, 139, 198, ii, xxxv, l.
　Joseph, 132, 137, 378, 379, 408, 411, xxxiv, xxxv, xcvii.
　Richard, 100, xxvii.
　Susanna, 136, xxxiv.
　Thomas, 2, 20, 38, 41, 55, 76, 77, 93, 116, 122, 132, 137, 145, 163, 172, 193, 339, 349, 355, 364, 373, 411, i, v, x, xi, xiv, xx, xxv, xxix, xxxi, xxxiv, xxxv, xxxvii, xli, xliii, xlix, lxxxv, lxxxviii, xc, xcii, xcvi.
　Thomas J., 233, 269, 365, 378, lviii, lxvii, xciii, xcvii.
Canning, Thomas, 20, v.
Caraway, Anto, 356, xc.
Carnicle, John, 356, xc.
Carr, Betsey, 311, lxxviii.
　Daniel, 311, lxxviii.
　Hannah, 311, lxxviii.
　John, 311, lxxviii.
　Moses, 5, 311, ii, lxxviii.
　Paul, 311, lxxviii.
　Robert, 204, li.
　Samuel W., 9, 14, 417, iii, iv.
　Sarah, 311, lxxviii.
　Susan, 311, lxxviii.
Clapham, Charles, 320, lxxx.
Carroll, Richard, 356, 357, xc, xci.
Carter, John, 356, xc.
Cartland, John, 63, xvi.
Cason, Samuel, 61, xvi.
Caswell, Israel, 263, lxv.
Cate, Sarah, 108, lxxvii.
Cater, John, 127, xxxii.
　Mary, 107, lxxvii.
　Richard, 66, 69, 96, 122, 193, 349, 354, 357, 362, 365, 371, 372, 409, xvii, xviii, xxv, xxxi, xlix, lxxxviii, xc, xci, xcii, xciii, xcv.
Caverry, Betsey, 262, lxv.
Chace, Enoch, 323, 325, lxxxi, lxxxii.
　James, 323, 325, lxxxi, lxxxii.
　John, 325, lxxxii.
Chadwell, Benjamin, 364, xcii.
　Moses, 364, xcii.
　Mr., 364, xcii.
Chadburne, Humphrey, 240, 369, lx, xcv.
　John, 13, iv.
　William, 191, 369, xlviii, xcv.
Chadwick, William, 63, xvi.
Chamberlain, R., 217, 241, 302, lv, lx, lxxv.
Champernoon, 20, 215, v, liv.
Channing, George, 421.
Chandler, Philemon, 99, xxvi.
Channel, William P., 85, xxii.
Charles I, King of England, 335, lxxxiv.
Chase, Joseph, 86, 243, xxii, lx.
　Thomas, 379, xcvii.
Chesley, Alpheus, 78, xx.
　Deborah, 88, xxiii.
　Deliverance, 86, xxii.
　Ebenezer, 85, xxii.
　Elizabeth, 85, xxii.
　Eliza, 107, lxxvii.
　Esther, 259, lxiv.
　George, 59, 86, 160, xv, xxii, xl.
　Hannah, 85, 397, xxii.
　James, 231, 366, lvii, xciii.
　Joanna, 85, xxii.
　Jonathan, 78, xxviii.
　Joseph, 86, xxii.
　Mary, 85, xxii.
　Mehitable, 366, xciii.
　Paul, 64, xvi.
　Philip, 36, 53, 58, 68, 71, 85, 140, 156, 160, 161, 218, 237, 259, 343, 349, 354, 357, 363, 373, 374, 409, ix, xiv, xv, xvii, xviii, xxii, xxxvi, xxxix, xl, xli, lv, lix, lxiv, lxxxvi, lxxxviii, xc, xci, xcii, xcvi.

Chesley, Reuben, 63, xvi.
  Samuel, 4, 63, 79, 85, 135, i, xvi, xx, xxii, xxxiv.
  Sarah, 231, lvii.
  Tamson, 231, lvii.
  Thomas, 3, 59, 79, 85, 88, 89, 96, 139, 153, 218, 259, 409, i, xv, xx, xxii, xxiii, xxiv, xxvi, xxxv, xxxix, lv, lxiv.
Choat, Eliza, 107, lxxvii.
Church, Benjamin, 11, 12, 279, iii, iv, lxix.
  John, 96, 98, 147, 150, 153, 243, 279, 410, 72, 140, 193, 408, xxv, xxvi, xxxvii, xxxviii, xxxix, lx, lxix, xviii, xxxv, xlix.
  Martha, 396.
Christie, Daniel M., 9, 14, iii, iv.
Clark, Abraham, 155, 158, 197, xxxix, xl, l.
  Abram, 63, 161, xvi, xli.
  David, 305, lxxvi.
  Ephraim, 305, lxxvi.
  Francis, 358, xci.
  Hannah, 262, 305, lxv, lxxvi.
  Horace, 10, iii.
  Jacob, 232, lviii.
  Jonathan, 262, 305, lxv, lxxvi.
  Joseph, 305, lxxvi.
  Joshua, 305, lxxvi.
  Josiah, 61, xvi.
  John, 263, lxv.
  Lois, 262, lxv.
  Mary, 262, lxv.
  Martha, 308, lxxvii.
  Nathaniel, 285, 305, lxxi, lxxvi.
  Peter, 63, xvi.
  Rhoda, 262, lxv.
  Samuel, 7, ii.
  Sarah, 89, xxiv.
  Tabitha, 305, lxxvi.
  Capt. Thomas, 368, 372, 373, xciii, xcv, xcvi.
Clay, Samuel, 262, lxv.
Clayton, Thomas, 349, lxxxviii.
Clements, Charles, 233, lviii.
  Elijah, 233, 311, lviii, lxxviii.
  James, 62, xvi.
  Job, 2, 10, 44, 61, 66, 70, 74, 95, 97, 115, 122, 132, 140, 141, 148, 150, 153, 157, 233, 341, 354, 357, 362, 365, 373, 377, 409, 412, i, iii, xi, xvi, xvii, xviii, xix, xxv, xxvi, xxix, xxxi, xxxiv, xxxv, xxxvi, xxxvii, xxxviii, xxxix, xl, lviii, lxxxvi, xc, xci, xcii, xciii, xcvi, xcvii.
  John, 7, 114, ii, xxix.
Clough, Elizabeth, 264, lxvi.

Clough, John, 381.
  Mary, 223, lvi.
Clyde, Benjamin F., 308, lxxvii.
  Charles, 308, lxxvii.
  Charles M., 308, lxxvii.
  Maria, 308, lxxvii.
  Martha, 308, lxxvii.
Coffin, Abigail, 131, 284, 288, xxxiii, lxxi, lxxii.
  Ann, 290, lxxii.
  Apphia, 281, lxx.
  Barnabas, 284, lxxi.
  Bartholomew, 285, lxxi.
  Betsey, 288, 289, lxxi, lxxii.
  Brockelbank, 281, lxx.
  Christian, 290, lxxii.
  Daniel, 281, lxx.
  Deborah, 107, 284, 280, 289, xxvii, lxx, lxxi, lxxii.
  Dinah, 131, 281, xxxiii, lxx.
  Edmund, 281, lxx.
  Edward, 131, 284, xxxiii, lxxi.
  Eleanor, 281, 285, lxx, lxxi.
  Elizabeth, 131, 280, 284, 289, xxxiii, lxx, lxxi, lxxii.
  Elizabeth Green, 286, lxxi.
  Eliphalet, 102, 131, 285, 290, xxvi, xxxiii, lxxi, lxxii.
  Eno, 281, lxx.
  Enoch, 280, lxx.
  Eunice, 280, lxx.
  Hannah, 281, 286, 290, lxx, lxxi, lxxii.
  Isaac, 130, 290, xxxiii, lxxii.
  Sir Isaac, 281, 289, lxx, lxxii.
  James, 72, 96, 115, 129, 141, 149, 280, 289, 400, 410, xviii, xxvi, xxix, xxxiii, xxxv, xxxviii, lxx, lxxii.
  Jane, 281, 286, lxx, lxxi.
  Jethro, 131, 285, xxxiii, lxxi.
  Joanna, 281, 286, lxx.
  John, 280, 284, 289, lxx, lxxi, lxxii.
  Jonathan, 290, lxxii.
  Joseph, 281, lxx.
  Joshua, 285, lxxi.
  Josiah, 285, lxxi.
  Judith, 281, 284, lxx, lxxi.
  Lydia, 281, lxx.
  Mary, 131, 280, 287, xxxiii, lxx, lxxi.
  Nathaniel, 131, 280, 284, 289, xxxiii, lxx, lxxi, lxxii.
  Parnel, 285, 291, lxxi, lxxii.
  Rev. Peter, 286, 418, lxxi.

Coffin, Hon. Peter, 281, 284, 288, 387, 408, 409, 411, 415, 418, lxx, lxxi, lxxii.
  Peter, 3, 8, 10, 47, 65, 69, 74, 102, 108, 130, 137, 142, 147, 149, 173, 191, 202, 221, 280, 285, 338, 343, 349, 355, 357, 362, 373, 374, 378, i, ii, iii, xii, xvii, xviii, xix, xxvi, xxvii, xxxiii, xxxv, xxxvi, xxxvii, xxxviii, xliv, xlviii, li, lvi, lxx, lxxi, lxxxv, lxxxvi, lxxxviii, xc, xci, xcii, xcv, xcvi, xcvii.
  Priscilla, 281, 285, lxx, lxxi.
  Richmond, 281, lxx.
  Robert, 131, xxxiii.
  Samuel, 281, 284, lxx, lxxi.
  Sarah, 281, lxx.
  Stephen, 281, lxx.
  Susanna, 285, 291, lxxi, lxxii.
  Tristram, 3, 5, 102, 108, 130, 281, 284, 288, 291, 418, i, ii, xxvi, xxvii, xxxiii, lxx, lxxi, lxxii.
  William, 289, 290, lxxii.
Colcord, Abigail, 380, xcvii.
  Ann, 380, xcvii.
  Deborah, 380, xcvii.
  Elizabeth, 380, xcvii.
  Hannah, 380, xcvii.
  Jane, 380, xcvii.
  John, 380, xcvii.
  Jonathan, 380, xcvii.
  Mary, 380, xcvii.
  Mehitable, 380, xcvii.
  Samuel, 380, xcvii.
  Sarah, 380, xcvii.
  Shuah, 380, xcvii.
  Edward, 20, 36, 90, 128, 186, 188, 348, 350, 365, 371, 375, 379, 380, v, ix, xxiv, xxxiii, xlvi, xlviii, lxxxvii, lxxxviii, xciii, xcv, xcvi, xcvii.
Coe, Rev. Curtis, 398.
  Ebenezer, 90, xxiv.
Cogswell, Amos, 9, 12, 101, 105, 231, iii, iv, xxvi, xxvii, lvii.
  Edward, 387.
  John, 387.
  William, 285, 387, lxxi.
Cogan, Stephen, 79, xx.
Colbeck, Philip, 290, lxxii.
Cole, Robert, 62, xvi.
Coleman, Ann, 170, 176, xliii, xliv.
  Calvin, 165, xlii.
  Ebenezer, 195, xlix.
  Isaac, 129, 280, xxxiii, lx.
  James, 14, iv.

Coleman, Thomas, 187, xlvi.
Connel Samuel, 238, lix.
Connor, Hugh, 61, xvi.
Cook, Richard, 8, 150, 360, ii, xxxviii, xci.
Coombs, Elizabeth, 180, xlv.
Cooper, Nathaniel, 2, 11, 104, i, iii, xxvi.
  Patty, 104, xxvi.
  Rev. Dr., 229, lvii.
  Walter, 2, 104, i, xxvi.
Corbett, Abraham, 204, 205, 376, li, lii, xcvi.
  Thomas, 371, xcv.
Corson, Samuel, 268, lxvii.
  Zebulon, 63, xvi.
Corliss, Ann, 299, lxxiv.
  Deborah, 299, lxxiv.
  George, 299, lxxiv,
  Hannah, 299, lxxiv.
  Huldah, 299, lxxiv.
  James, 299, lxxiv.
  Joanna, 299, lxxiv.
  John, 299, lxxiv.
  Mary, 299, lxxiv.
  Martha, 299, lxxiv.
  Sarah, 299, lxxiv.
Cotton, John, 184, xlvi.
  Mr., 27, 308, vii, lxxvii.
  Meriel, 395.
  Seaborn, 184, xlvi.
Courson, Samuel, 346, 347, lxxxvii.
Coventry, Jonan, 375, xcvi.
Covring, John, 96, xxv.
Cowan, James W., 10, iii.
  Mrs. Dr., 288, lxxii.
Cox, Betsey, 264, lxvi.
Coy, Goodman, 309, lxxvii.
  John, 310, lxxvii.
Cram, Pamelia, 107, lxxvii.
Cranfield, Edward, 20, 217, 284, v, lv, lxxi.
Crawlee, Thomas, 37, x.
Cressey, Thad. P., 100, xxvii.
Critchett, 59, xv.
Crockett, Andrew, 65, xvii.
  Joshua, 127, xxxii.
  Thomas, 368, xciii.
Cross, John, 20, 350, v, lxxxviii.
  Noah, 63, xvi.
Crosby, Oliver, 13, iv.
Cromwell, Ann, 398.
  Dorothy, 399.
  Elisha, 63, xvi.
  Eliphalet, 399.
  Elizabeth, 398.

Cromwell, Jeremiah, 59, xv.
  John, 59, 195, 398, 399, xv, xlix.
  Joshua, 399.
  Philip, 3, 59, 66, 69, 74, 95, 122, 133, 138, 141, 149, 162, 269, 355, 357, 362, 365, 375, i, xv, xvii, xviii, xix, xxv, xxxi, xxxiv, xxxv, xxxvi, xxxviii, xli, lxvii, xc, xci, xcii, xciii, xcvi.
  Rachel, 399.
  Samuel, 399.
Currier, Jacob, 14, iv.
Currin, Abigail, 279, lxix.
  Daniel, 418, 419.
  Jacob, 418, 419.
  Jacob M., 419.
  William, 419.
Curry, Mr. 306, lxxvi.
Curtis, John, 363, xcii.
Cushing, Alexis, 297, lxxiv.
  Asenith, 297, lxxiv.
  Augustus, 297, lxxiv.
  Caroline, 297, lxxiv.
  Charles, 297, lxxiv.
  Clarissa, 297, lxxiv.
  Daniel, 297, lxxiv.
  Deborah, 297, lxxiv.
  Eliza, 297, lxxiv.
  Elizabeth, 297, lxxiv.
  George W., 297, lxxiv.
  Hannah, 297, lxxiv.
  Jabez, 297, lxxiv.
  Jarvis, 297, lxxiv.
  John, 297, lxxiv.
  Jonathan, 297, lxxiv.
  Jonathan P., 297, lxxiv.
  Jonathan R., 297, lxxiv.
  Rev. Jonathan, 99, 102, 229, 250, 259, 267, 289, 296, 323, xxv, xxvi, lvii, lxii, lxiv, lxvi, lxxii, lxxiv, lxxxi.
  Josiah, 297, lxxiv.
  Louisa, 297, lxxiv.
  Lydia, 297, lxxiv.
  Mary, 297, lxxiv.
  Mary H., 297, lxxiv.
  Nathan, 297, lxxiv.
  Pamelia C., 297, lxxiv.
  Peter, 11, 296, 326, iii, lxxiv, lxxxii.
  Deacon Peter, 297, lxxiv.
  Robert H., 297, lxxiv.
  Samuel, 297, lxxiv.
  Samuel W., 297, lxxiv.
  Hon. Thomas, 296, lxxiv.

Cushing, Thomas H., 284, lxxi.
  Thomas, 297, lxxiv.
  William, 250, 297, lxii, lxxiv.
Cutt, Hannah, 226, lvii.
  Irsula, 278, lxix.
  John, 18, 69, 75, 97, 115, 141, 210, 215, 220, 373, 397, 411, 412, v, xviii, xix, xxvi, xxix, xxxvi, liii, liv, lv, xcvi, xcvii.
  President, 278, lxix.
  Richard, 68, 69, 75, 97, 115, xvii, xviii, xix, xxvi, xxix.
  Sarah, 186, xlvi.

Dalton, Mr., 29, viii.
  Samuel, 121, 190, xxxi, xlviii.
  Timothy, 38, 187, xlvii.
Dam(e), Abigail, 125, xxxii.
  Deacon John, 4, 24, 35, 66, 74, 96, 114, 133, 408, i, v, ix, xvii, xix, xxvi, xxix, xxxiv.
  John, 127, 132, 137, 141, 145, 160, 193, 259, 340, 349, 353, 357, 362, 365, 372, 378, 388, 401, xxxii, xxxiv, xxxv, xxxvi, xxxvii, xl, xlix, lxiv, lxxxv, lxxxviii, xc, xci, xcii, xciii, xcv, xcvii.
  Martha, 315, lxxix.
  Moses, 127, 193, xxxii, xlix.
  Pomfrett, 161, xli.
  Sarah, 315, lxxix.
  Theophilas, 100, 325, xxvii, lxxxii.
  William, 8, 63, 127, 164, 259, 315, ii, xvi, xl, xli, lxiv, lxix.
Danforth, Mr., 220, lvi.
Daniel, David, 58, 63, xv, xvi.
  Jacob, 63, xvii.
  John, 63, xvi.
  Jonathan, 63, xvi.
  Thomas, 117, xxx.
Daniels, David, 141, xxxvi.
  Joseph, 253, 260, lxiii, lxv.
  Maria, 107, lxxvi.
  Thomas, 210, 216, liii, liv.
Davidson, John, 131, xxxiii.
Davil, John, 363, xcii.
Davison, Major, 284, lxxi.
Davis, Abigail, 263, 305, lxv, lxxvi.
  Amos, 29, lxxiv.
  Ann, 29, lxxiv.
  Constance, 299, 406, lxxiv.
  Daniel, 299, 303, 305, lxxiv, lxxvi, lxxvii.
  David, 305, lxxvi.
  Deborah, 302, 305, lxxv, lxxvi.
  Ebenezer, 305, lxxvi.

Davis, Elisha, 305, lxxvi.
  Elizabeth, 253, 299, 304, lxiii, lxxiv, lxxvi.
  Ephraim, 298, 303, lxxiv, lxxvi.
  Esther, 299, 305, lxxiv, lxxvi.
  Gideon, 305, lxxvi.
  Hannah, 299, 300, 302, 303, lxxiv, lxxv, lxxvi.
  Jabez, 82, 150, 305, xxi, xxxviii, lxxvi.
  Col. James, 274, 303, 394, lxviii, lxxvi.
  James, 5, 10, 155, 159, 161, 194, 198, 298, 301, 305, 345, ii, iii, xxxix, xl, xli, xlix, l, lxxiv, lxxv, lxxvi, lxxxvii.
  James J., 317, lxxx.
  Jane, 300, 301, lxxiv, lxxv.
  Jemima, 300, 305, lxxv, lxxvi.
  Joanna, 298, lxxiv.
  Ens. John, 277, 339, 363, lxxvii, lxxxv, xcii.
  John, 3, 15, 49, 53, 58, 65, 74, 82, 121, 132, 140, 154, 158, 193, 205, 219, 238, 263, 274, 277, 298, 343, 356, 357, 372, 401, i, iv, xiii, xiv, xv, xvii, xix, xxi, xxxi, xxxiv, xxxvii, xxxix, xl, xlix, lii, lv, lix, lxv, lxviii, lxix, lxxiv, lxxxvi, xc, xci, xcv.
  Jonathan, 299, 305, lxxiv, lxxvi.
  Joseph, 161, 300, 301, 303, xli, lxxiv, lxxv, lxxvi.
  Josiah, 302, lxxv.
  Judith, 298, 301, 305, 317, lxxiv, lxxv, lxxvi, lxxx.
  Mary, 299, 302, 304, lxxiv, lxxv, lxxvi.
  Mary A., 317, lxxx.
  Mary E., 317, lxxx.
  Moses, 200, 274, 301, 303, 345, lxviii, lxxv, lxxxvii, lxxvi.
  Nathaniel, 63, 69, 87, 94, 115, 133, xvi, xviii, xxii, xxv, xxix, xxxiv.
  Philip, 179, xlv.
  Phebe, 305, lxxvi.
  Priscilla, 305, lxxvi.
  Paul, 59, xv.
  Richard, 78, xx.
  Samuel, 14, 63, 298, 303, 317, iv, xvi, lxxiv, lxxvi, lxxx.
  Sarah, 298, 302, lxxiv, lxxv.
  Stephen, 14, 253, 299, 305, iv, lxiii, lxxiv, lxxvi.
  Susanna, 299, 305, lxxiv, lxxvi.
  Thomas, 5, 11, 15, 237, 299, 303, 355, ii, iii, iv, lix, lxxiv, lxxvi, xc.
  William, 268, lxvii.
  William L., 317, lxxx.
Dean, John, 81, 274, 277, xxi, lxviii, lxix.
  Mrs. John, 275, lxviii.
Dearborn, Eliphalet, 180, xlv.
  Gen. Henry, 265, lxvi.
  Thomas, 380, xcvii.
Denbow, Salethiel, 58, 141, xv, xxxvi.
Denison, Annate, 117, xxx.
  Elizabeth, 117, 358, xxxi, xci.
  Edward, 117, xxx.
  Jachin, 117, xxx.
Denmark, Ann, 376, xcvi.
  Patrick, 376, xcvi.
Dennett, Ephraim, 307, lxxvi.
Demeritt, Deborah, 107, lxxvii.
  Ebenezer, 5, ii.
  Eli, 5, 59, 63, ii, xv, xvi.
  John, 63, 78, xvi, xx.
  Nathaniel, 79, xx.
  Samuel, 262, lxv.
  Solomon, 262, lxv.
  William, 63, xvi.
Dickenson, Thomas, 204, li.
Dimmock, Justin, 401.
Dislin, Agnes, 222, lvi.
Dodge, Betty, 323, lxxxi.
Dole, Aphia, 281, lxx.
  Richard, 382.
  Sarah, 281, lxx.
Dolhyrt, Christian, 382.
Dowty, Thomas, 145, 340, 363, 377, xxxvii, lxxxv, xcii, xcvii.
Doe, Francis, 251, lxii.
  John, 59, 160, xv, xl.
  Samson, 59, 157, xv, xl.
  Nathaniel, 250, lxii.
  Nicholas, 58, 114, 141, xv, xxix, xxxvi.
Dow, Henry, 188, xlvii.
  Jabez, 13, 112, iv, xxviii.
  John, 141, 303, xxxvi, lxxvi.
  Moses, 264, 303, lxvi, lxxvi.
  Neal, 266, lxvi.
  Nicholas, 140, 377, xxxvi, xcvi.
  Reuhamah, 303, lxxvi.
Downing, Denys, 372, xcv.
  Emanuel, 410, 425.
  John, 4, 128, 157, 161, 195, 198, i, ii, xxxiii, xl, xli, xlix, l.
  Richard, 127, 195, xxxii, xlix.
  Thomas, 3, i.
Downs, Ebenezer, 63, 268, 400, xvi, lxvii.
  Gershom, 258, lxiv.
  John, 63, xvi.
  Mary, 279, lxix.
  Samuel, 62, xvi.

Downs, Thomas, 61, 66, 74, 139, 160, 193, 198, 258, 362, 365, 378, 379, 408, 410, 411, xvi, xvii, xix, xxxv, xl, xlix, l, lxiv, xcii, xciii, xcvii.
  William, 61, xvi.
Dowse, Mary, 263, lxv.
Drake, Abraham, 403.
  S. G., the historian, 384.
Drew, Benjamin, 85, 276, xxii, lxix.
  Charles, 14, iv.
  Charlotte, 317, lxxx.
  Daniel, 318, lxxx.
  David L., 93, 105, 326, xxv, xxvii, lxxxii.
  Elizabeth, 58, 408, xv.
  Francis, 58, 63, 85, 141, 277, xv, xvi, xxii, xxxvi, lxix.
  John, 4, 85, 140, 276, i, xxii, xxxv, lxix.
  Jonathan, 308, lxxvii.
  Joseph, 12, 85, 349, iv, xxii.
  Martha A., 317, lxxx.
  Sarah, lxvii.
  Shadrach, lxxvii.
  Thomas, 58, 153, 196, 276, 408, xv, xxxix, xlix, lxix.
  William, 349, 354, 357, 363, 408, lxxxviii, xc, xci, xcii.
  William Plaisted, 10, iii.
Drummer, Mr., 306, lxxvi.
Dudley, Abigail, 250, lxii.
  Ann, 177, xlv.
  Elizabeth, 250, 259, lxii, lxiv.
  John, 178, xlv.
  Joseph, 126, 193, xxxii, xlix.
  Rev. Samuel, 40, 177, 192, 250, 259, 350, x, xlv, xlviii, lxii, lxiv, lxxxviii.
  Gov. Thomas, 164, 178, 259, xli, xlv, lxiv.
Duncan, Abraham, 12, iv.
Dunn, Hugh, 68, xvii.
  Samuel, 7, 14, 36, ii, iv, xxxiv.
Dunster, Thomas, 20, v.
Durell, Hon. Daniel M., 9, 13, 295, 296, iii, iv, lxxii.
  Mrs. E. H., 295, lxxiii.
  John Samuel, 14, 102, 288, iv, xxvi, lxxii.
  Philip, 59, 238, xv, lix.
Durgin, James, 51, 238, xv, lix.
  Truworthy, 78, xx.
  William, 141, 238, 377, 383, xxxvi, lix, xcvii.

Eaden, Robert, 223, lvi.
Eare, James, 145, xxxvii.
Earewin, Edward, 145, xxxvii.

Eaton, Theophilas, 373, 400, xcvi.
  Mary, 400.
Edgerly, John, 59, 84, 238, xv, xxii, lix.
  Joseph, 276, 277, lxix.
  Rebecca, 377, xcvii.
  Silas, 107, lxxvii.
  Thomas, 3, 10, 58, 72, 84, 96, 114, 132, 138, 148, 152, 219, 274, 276, 301, 378, 412, i, iii, xv, xviii, xxii, xxv, xxx, xxxv, xxxvi, xxxvii, xxxviii, lv, lxviii, lxix, lxxv, xcvii.
  Zachariah, 63, 84, 276, xvi, xxii, lxix.
Ela, Edna, 104, xxvii.
  Nathaniel W., 9, 14, 104, 109, iii, iv, xxvii, xxviii.
Eldredge, David, 252, lxiii.
  Joseph, 265, lxvi.
Eliot, Edward, 62, xvi.
  Robert, 311, lxxviii.
  Sarah, 311, lxxviii.
Elkins, Henry, 225, lvii.
Ellis, Edward, 61, xvi.
  John, 140, xxxv.
Emery, Anthony, 1, 2, 34, 348, 349, 353, 372, i, ix, lxxxvii, lxxxviii, xciii, xcv.
  Caleb, 261, lxv.
  Frances, 94, xxv.
  Moses, 109, xxviii.
  Nathaniel, 202, li.
  Tizzah, 266, lxvi.
Emerson, Eleanor, 305, lxxvi.
  Hannah, 305, lxxvi.
  Rev. John, 128, 307, xxxiii, lxxvi.
  John, 309, lxxviii.
  Mary, 307, 322, lxxvi, lxxxi.
  Moses, 79, xx.
  Samuel, 4, 15, 156, 161, 197, 237, 253, 268, ii, iv, xxxix, xli, l, lix, lxiii, lxvii.
  Solomon, 5, 11, 63, ii, iii, xvi.
Endicott, John, 203, li.
Epps, Daniel, 401.
Erwin, Edward, 340, lxxxv.
Estes, Anna, 326, lxxxii.
  Elijah, 6, 11, 391, ii, iii.
  Eliphalet, 99, xxvi.
  Israel, 99, xxvi.
  Joshua, 326, lxxxii.
  Mary, 326, 400, lxxxii.
  Matthew, 240, lx.
  Richard, 240, lx.
  William F., 10, iii.
Evans, Aaron, 295, lxxxii.

Evans, Abigail, 295, 406, lxxiii.
　Ann, 294, lxxiii.
　Benjamin, 12, 109, iii, xxviii.
　Daniel, 294, lxxiii.
　David, 294, lxxiii.
　Dorcas, 295, lxxiii.
　Edward, 155, 161, 253, 293, xxxix, xli, lxiii, lxxiii.
　Eleanor, 294, lxxiii.
　Eliza, 316, lxxix.
　Elizabeth, 293, 295, 406, lxxiii.
　Hannah, 294, 295, lxxiii.
　John, 2, 63, 132, 137, 151, 153, 293, 301, 410, i, xvi, xxxiv, xxxv, xxxviii, xxxix, lxxiii, lxxv.
　Jonathan, 293, 294, lxxiii.
　Joseph, 63, 107, 294, 316, 406, xvi, xxvii, lxxiii, lxxix.
　Lemuel, 294, lxxiii.
　Mercy, 294, lxxiii.
　Moses, 294, lxxiii.
　Mary, 109, 316, xxviii, lxxix.
　Rachel, 294, lxxiii.
　Rhoda, 316, lxxix.
　Robert, 63, 72, 109, 114, 140, 150, 153, 193, 243, 293, 345, 378, xvi, xviii, xxviii, xxxv, xxxviii, xxxix, lx, lxxiii, lxxxvii, xcvii.
　Sarah, 294, 315, lxxiii, lxxix.
　Samuel, 12, 316, iii, lxxix.
　Solomon, 295, lxxiii.
　Col. Stephen, 6, 12, 107, 109, 293, 294, 296, 329, 331, 406, ii, iii, xxvii, xxviii, lxxiv, lxxxiii.
　Tobias, 294, 295, lxxiii.
　Vesta, 406.
　William, 294, lxxiii.
　William E., 316, lxxix.
Eveleth, Abigail, 309, lxxviii.
　Isaac, 309, lxxviii.
　Sylvester, 309, lxxviii.
Eyare, Robert, 382.
　Thomas, 382.

Fabyan, Mr., 127, 128, xxxii, xxxiii.
Farrar, Hon. Timothy, 397.
Farnham, John, 180, xlv.
Farret, James, 385.
Farrington, Ebenezer, 14, iv.
Fayer, John, 55, xiv.
Faxon, Ebenezer, 14, iv.
Felker, Augustus A., 107, lxxvii.
　Benjamin F., 107, lxxvii.

Felker, Charles Francis, 107, lxxvii.
　Elizabeth, 107, lxxvii.
　Isaac G., 107, lxxvii.
　Capt. John, 107, lxxvii.
　John W., 107, lxxvii.
　Mary Susan, 107, lxxvii.
　Roxanna A., 107, lxxvii.
　Sarah Jane, 107, lxxvii,
　William Henry, 107, lxxvii,
Fellows, William, 228, lvii.
Fenner, E. W., 9, iii.
Ferall, John, 63, xvi.
Fernald, Renald, 44, 373, 409, xi, xcvi.
　Mrs. James E., 290, lxxii.
Field, Darby, 94, 352, 354, 372, xxv, lxxxviii, xc, xcv.
　Elizabeth, 391.
　"Goody," 349, lxxxviii.
　Joseph, 58, 141, 218, 344, 356, 357, 363, 409, xv, xxxvi, lv, lxxxvi, xc, xci, xcii.
　Mary, 380, xcvii.
　William, 187, xlvii.
　Zachariah, 3, 58, 137, 152, 153, 218, 408, i, xv, xxxv, xxxviii, xxxix, lv.
Fifield, Benjamin, 380, xcvii.
　Nancy, 107, lxxvii.1
Fisk, Dr. John, 235, lviii.
　Leftenant, 212, liv.
　Rev. Mr., 128, xxxiii.
Fitch, Rev. Jabez, 184, xlvi.
Folger, Peter, 130, 281, xxxiii, lxx.
Follett, John, 20, v.
　Nicholas, 138, 141, 145, 352, xxxv, xxxvi, xxxvii, xcv.
　Philip, 138, xxxv.
　William, 38, 68, 114, 141, 146, 164, 174, 202, 337, 344, 345, 350, 354, 357, 363, 377, x, xvii, xxx, xxxvi, xxxvii, xli, xliv, li, lxxxv, lxxxvi, lxxxvii, lxxxviii, xc, xci, xcii, xcvii.
Folsom, Abraham, 284, lxxi.
　Betsey, 180, xlv.
　George P., 10, iii.
　Isaac, 107, lxxvii.
　John, 89, xxiv.
　Josiah, 99, xxvi.
　Thomas, 104, xxvii.
Ford, Horace K., 107, lxxvii.
Foster, John, 116, 150, xxx, xxxviii.
Fost, John, 381.
Foss, Abigail, 260, lxv.
　David Tenney, 12, iv.
　Ephraim, 419.

Foss, John, 144, 260, 381, xxxvi, lxv, lxxvii.
    Jonathan, 260, lxv.
    Joseph, 260, lxv.
    Lois, 260, lxv.
    Nancy, 107, lxxvii.
    Samuel, 260, 263, lxv.
    Sarah, 260, lxv.
Footman, Thomas, 2, 36, 49, 72, 74, 101, 103, 145, 338, 349, 354, 357, 362, i, ix, xiii, xviii, xix, xxvi, xxvii, xxxvii, lxxxv, lxxxviii, xc, xci, xcii.
Fowler, Morris, 63, xvi.
Fox, George, 166, xlii.
    Rev. Jabez, 358, xci.
Foye, James, 63, xvi.
    John, 63, xvi.
    Lydia, 107, lxxvii.
    Ruth, 107, lxxvii.
    Stephen, 107, lxxvii.
Fletcher, Rev. Mr., 39, 56, 338, 392, x, xiv, lxxxv.
Flagg, Dr. Jonathan, 422.
    Rufus, 14, 288, iv, lxxii.
    William, 19, iii.
Floyd, Captain, 88, 272, 303, xxiii, lxviii, lxxv.
Franklin, Jonathan, 335, lxxxiv.
Freeman, Asa, 10, 15, 106, 287, iii, iv, xxvii, lxxi.
    Chandler, 310, lxxviii.
Friar, Nathaniel, 98, xxvi.
French, Peter, 78, xx.
Frye, William, 14, iv.
Fryer, Mr., 215, liv.
Fontenac, Count de, 270, 272, lxvii.
    Governor, 279, lxix.
Frost, Captain, 208, 212, 213, lii, liv.
    Charles, 207, lii.
    Nicholas, 45, xii.
    George, 79, 89, xx, xxiv.
    Major, 277, lxix.
    Margaret, 232, lviii.
    John, 72, 132, 133, 193, xviii, xxxiv, xlix.
    William, 4, 161, 197, 236, i, xli, l, lix.
Furber, Abigail, 388.
    Deborah, 388.
    Elizabeth, 374, 388, xcvi.
    Fabyan, 388.
    Jerusha, 388.
    Jethro, 156, 387, xxxix.
    Levi, 388.
    Mary, 388.
    Nehemiah, 388.
    Peirce, 308, lxxvii.

Furber, Richard, 308, lxxvii.
    Sarah, 356, 388, xc.
    Thomas, 372, xcv.
    William, 2, 8, 10, 20, 33, 41, 45, 48, 54, 63, 67, 72, 74, 95, 114, 122, 127, 140, 147, 150, 155, 157, 171, 190, 193, 202, 219, 336, 337, 348, 349, 353, 357, 362, 365, 371, 374, 375, 387, 388, 390, 410, 411, i, ii, iii, v, ix, xi, xii, xiv, xvii, xviii, xix, xxv, xxx, xxxi, xxxiii, xxxv, xxxvii, xxxviii, xxxix, xl, xliii, xlviii, xlix, li, lv, lxxxiv, lxxxv, lxxxvii, lxxxviii, xc, xci, xcii, xciii, xcv, xcvi.
Furbush, Sarah, 260, lxv.
    William, 364, xcii.
Ffursam, Thomas, 37, 55, 352, x, xiv, lxxxviii.

Gage, Betsey, 323, 325, lxxxi, lxxxii.
    Colonel John, 323, 413, lxxxi.
    Eliza, 323, 327, lxxxi, lxxxii.
    Capt. John, 101, 314, 323, 325, 329, 331, xxvi, lxxix, lxxxi, lxxxii, lxxxiii.
    John, 5, 11, 127, 294, 325, 347, 401, 418, ii, iii, xxxii, lxxiii, lxxxii, lxxxvii.
    Jonathan, 104, 105, 323, 418, xxvii, lxxxi.
    Joseph, 9, 313, 320, 321, 327, 419, iii, lxxix, lxxx, lxxxi, lxxxii.
    Mary Wingate, 419.
    Moses, 325, 418, lxxxii.
    Nancy, 9, 313, 320, 321, 327, iii, lxxix, lxxx, lxxxi, lxxxii.
    Sarah, 418.
Gardner, Ann, 131, 284, xxxiii, lxxi.
    George, 130, xxxiii.
    Isaac, 378, xcvii.
    James, 130, xxxiii.
    John, 284, lxxi.
    Lydia, 285, lxxi.
    Mary, 131, 285, xxxiii, lxxi.
    Nathaniel, 375, 378, xcvi, xcvii.
    Richard, 130, xxxiii.
    Thomas, 257, lxiv.
Garland, Dodivar, 63, xvi.
    Ebenezer, 61, 62, xvi.
    Hannah, 263, lxv.
    Jabez, 63, 194, xvi, xlix.
    James, 86, xxii.
    Mary, 263, lxv.
    Peter, 20, v.
    Richard, 125, lxii.
Gaskin, Deliverance, 319, lxxx.
Gattingsby, John, 378, xciii.
Gayer, Damaris, 130, 281, 289, xxxiii, lxx, lxxii.

Gayer, Dorcas, 130, xxxiii.
    William, 130, 281, xxxiii, lxx.
Gee, Ralph, 373, xcvi.
Gerrish, Family, 226, lvii.
    Abigail, 311, 312, lxxviii.
    Alphonzo, 14, 313, 418, iv, lxxix.
    Andrew, 312, lxxviii.
    Anna, 227, 311, lvii, lxxviii.
    Benjamin, 311, 312, lxxviii.
    Dorothy, 312, lxxviii.
    Eleanor, 312, lxxviii.
    Elizabeth, 225, 311, 312, lvii, lxxviii.
    Eunice, 312, lxxviii.
    James, 312, lxxviii.
    Jane, 512, lxxviii.
    John, 3, 8, 10, 116, 132, 138, 142, 148, 149, 153, 157, 194, 219, 225, 248, 301, 311, 312, 409, 418, i, ii, iii, xxx, xxxiv, xxxv, xxxvi, xxxvii, xxxviii, xxxix, xl, xlix, lv, lvii, lxi, lxxv, lxxviii.
    Jonathan, 311, 312, lxxviii.
    Joseph, 153, 225, 311, 312, xxxix, lvii, lxxviii.
    Rev. Joseph, 225, lvii.
    Judith, 311, lxxviii.
    Lydia, 311, 312, lxxviii.
    Mary, 311, 312, lxxviii.
    Martha, 312, lxxviii.
    Moses, 311, lxxviii.
    Nanny, 312, lxxviii.
    Nathaniel, 226, 310, lvii, lxxviii.
    Paul, 2, 8, 63, 225, 238, 253, 267, 310, 312, i, ii, xvi, lvii, lix, lxiii, lxvi, lxxviii.
    Richard, 226, 310, lvii, lxxviii.
    Capt. Samuel, 244, 310, 312, 321, lxi, lxxviii, lxxxi.
    Samuel, 109, 311, 312, 313, 418, xxviii, lxxviii.
    Sarah, 243, 248, lx, lxi.
    Thomas, 312, lxxviii.
    Col. Timothy, 346, lxxxviii.
    Capt. Timothy, 294, lxxiii.
    Timothy, 8, 196, 198, 226, 236, 310, ii, xlix, l, lvii, lix, lxxviii.
    Toby, 312, lxxviii.
    Capt. William, 310, lxxviii.
    William, 225, 311, lvii, lxxviii.
Gibbons, Ambrose, 1, 2, 34, 35, 40, 202, 348, 349, 352, 353, 366, 368, 380, 383, i, ix, x, li, lxxxvii, lxxxviii, xc, xciii, xcv.
    Capt. Edward, 425.
    Richard, 380, 385, xcv.
Giddings, Colonel, 261, lxv.
Giles, Mark, 140, 194, 410, xxxv, xlix.

Gild, Ephraim, 299, lxxiv.
    James, 299, lxxiv.
    Samuel, 299, lxxiv.
    Sarah, 299, lxxiv.
Gill, Dr., 335, lxxxiv.
Gilman, Arthur, 178, xlv.
    Bartholomew, 395.
    Bridget, 264, lxvi.
    Elizabeth, 395.
    Eliphalet, 286, lxxi.
    Col. John, 284, 286, lxxi.
    John, 48, 80, 131, 216, 371, 390, 405, xii, xxi, xxxiii, liv, xcv.
    John Philips, 12, 418, iii.
    John Taylor, 395.
    Joseph, 395.
    Joanna, 131, xxxiii.
    Josiah, 286, 395, lxxi.
    Nicholas, 395.
    Sarah, 395.
    Tristram, 395.
    Col. Samuel, 179, 266, 395, xlv, lxvi.
Gilmore, James, 88, xxiv.
    Joanna, 88, xxiv.
Glidden, Sarah, 89, xxiv.
Goddard, Benjamin, 80, 371, xxi, xcv.
    John, 3, 31, 38, 47, 53, 58, 63, 69, 76, 77, 80, 140, 174, 191, 343, 348, 349, 351, 354, 356, 357, 363, 367, 369, 371, 372, 374, i, viii, x, xii, xiv, xv, xvii, xviii, xix, xx, xxi, xxxvi, xliv, xlviii, lxxxvi, lxxxvii, lxxxviii, xc, xci, xcii, xciii, xcv, xcvi.
    Welthea, 371, xcv.
Godfrey, William, 187, xlvii.
Goldsmith, Thomas, 287, lxxi.
Goldweir, George, 362, 382, xcii.
Goodwin, Daniel, 62, xvi.
    Jeremiah, 14, v.
    Richard, 62, xvi.
Gookin, Dorothy, 286, lxxviii.
    Major, 211, 214, liii, liv.
    Nathaniel, 286, lxxi.
Gorges, Ferdinand, 16, 190, 368, iv, xlviii, xciii.
    Thomas, 26, vii.
Goss, Cyrus, 10, iii.
Gould, Mr., 136, xxxiv.
Gove, Edward, 217, 218, lv.
Grafton, Thomas, 245, lxi.
Grant, Captain, 384.
    Daniel, 261, lxv.
    Francis, 261, lxv.

Grant, James, 261, 355, 357, 363, 364, lxv, xc, xci, xcii.
   Mary, 306, lxxvi.
   Peter, 364, xcii.
   Samuel, 261, lxv.
Graves, John, 363, xcii.
Gray, James, 316, lxxix.
   Rev. Robert, 100, xxvi.
Greeley, Peter, 242, lx.
   Philip, 382.
Green, Ezra, 12, 13, 103, 287, iii, iv, xxvi, lxxi.
   Hon. Henry, 379, xcvii.
   James, 142, xxxvi.
   Thomas, 363, xcii.
   Walter C., 14, iv.
Greenleaf, Capt. Edmund, 280, lxx.
   Capt. Stephen, 248, lxi.
Greenough, Daniel, 307, lxxvi.
   Mr., 306, lxxvi.
Greenoway, Mary, 309, lxxviii.
   Ursula, 309, lxxviii.
Grevill, Robert, 23, vi.
Griffin, James, 79, xx.
   John, 78, 79, xx.
   William E., 65, xvii.
Grover, Nathaniel, 349, lxxx.
Gyles, Elizabeth, 37, x.
   Matthew, 36, 349, 352, 354, 357, 363, 375, ix, lxxxviii, xc, xci, xcii, xcv.
Gullison, Elihu, 142, xxxvi.
Guppy, James, 61, 113, 346, 347, xvi, xxix, lxxxvii.
   Joseph D., 14, iv.

Hackett, Peter, 316, lxxix.
   William, 355, 357, 363, 364, xc, xci, xcii.
Hall, Aaron, 264, lxvi.
   Abigail, 258, 260, 261, 263, 264, 266, lxiv, lxv, lxvi.
   Abraham, 264, lxvi.
   Andrew, 260, 264, 265, lxv, lxvi.
   Anna, 260, 264, 265, lxv, lxvi.
   Amos, 264, lxvi.
   Augusta, 265, lxvi.
   Rev. Avery, 231, lvii.
   Benjamin, 63, 258, 260, 264, 265, xvi, lxiv, lxv, lxvi.
   Bethshua, 264, lxvi.
   Betsey, 262, 265, lxv, lxvi.
   Calete, 261, 266, lxv, lxvi.
   Charity, 263, 264, lxvi.
   Charles E., 266, lxvi.
   Comfort, 265, lxvi.
Hall, Col. Daniel, 318, lxxx.
   Daniel, 263, 264, 265, lxvi.
   Deborah, 260, 263, lxv.
   Dorcas, 264, lxvi.
   Dorothy, 260, 264, 265, lxv, lxvi.
   Dudley, 261, 265, 266, lxv, lxvi.
   Edmund, 264, lxvi.
   Edward, 89, 259, 261, 394, xxiv, lxiv, lxv.
   Elijah, 262, 264, lxvi.
   Elisha, 262, lxv.
   Elias, 264, lxvi.
   Eleanor, 263, lxv.
   Elizabeth, 224, 256, 261, 265, lvii, lxiv, lxv, lxvi.
   Enoch, 264, lxvi.
   Ebenezer, 260, 262, 264, lxv, lxvi.
   Ephraim, 265, lxvi.
   Esther, 262, 265, lxv, lxvi.
   Experience, 265, lxvi.
   Fred C., 318, lxxx.
   Francis, 260, 265, lxv, lxvi.
   Grace, 264, 267, lxiv, lxvi.
   George, 264, lxvi.
   Greenfield, 265, lxvi.
   Gilman, 318, lxxx.
   Hannah, 262, 264, 265, lxvi.
   Hanson, 265, lxvi.
   Hatevil, 259, 260, 264, lxiv, lxv, lxvi.
   Hezekiah, 264, lxvi.
   Huldah, 258, lxiv.
   Henry, 264, lxvi.
   Isaac, 260, 262, 264, lxv.
   Israel, 263, 264, lxvi.
   Ira, 264, lxvi.
   Jacob, 263, lxv.
   Jane, 263, 264, lxvi.
   James N., 62, 258, 264, 265, xvi, lxiv, lxvi.
   Jeremiah, 264, lxvi.
   Joanna, 262, lxv.
   Job, 264, lxvi.
   Jedediah, 260, 263, lxv.
   Joel, 264, lxvi.
   Jonathan, 258, 263, 264, lxiv, lxvi.
   Johnson, 265, lxvi.
   Joshua, 266, lxvi.
   Joshua E., 266, lxvi.
   Joseph, 150, 219, 224, 237, 256, 261, 266, 367, xxxviii, lv, lvii, lix, lxiv, lxvi.
   Deacon John, 2, 3, 20, 35, 41, 47, 49, 52, 65, 66, 69, 71, 74, 114, 150, 160, 340, 341, 343, 344, 355, 356, 362, 364, i, v, ix, xi, xii, xiii, xvii, xviii, xix, xxix, xxxviii, xl, lxxxv, lxxxvi, xc, xcii.

Hall, Sergt. John, 8, 69, 75, 140, 356, 365, 412, ii, xviii, xix, xxxv, xc, xciii.
Leftenant John, 46, 49, 51, 58, 63, 145, 219, 339, 340, 356, 364, xii, xiii, xiv, xvii, xxxvii, lviii, lxxxv, xc, xciii.
John, 62, 85, 114, 120, 132, 137, 140, 193, 218, 223, 255, 257, 261, 264, 282, 336, 345, 349, 354, 356, 357, 365, 373, 375, 409, xvi, xxii, xxix, xxxi, xxxiv, xxxv, xlix, lv, lvii, lxiv, lxv, lxvi, lxx, lxxxiv, lxxxvii, lxxxviii, xc, xci, xciii, xcvi.
Jemima, 89, 261, xxiv, lxv.
Josiah, 259, 261, 264, lxiv, lxvi.
Joseph, 375, 376, xcvi.
Hon. Joshua Gilman, 264, 266, lxvi.
Kingsley, 71, 178, 258, 261, 265, 266, xviii, xlv, lxiv, lxv, lxvi.
Keziah, 262, 263, lxv.
Love, 261, 263, 264, 265, lxv, lxvi.
Lois, 262, 263, 265, lxv, lxvi.
Lot, 265, lxv.
Lucy, 262, 264, lxvi.
Mary Esther, 318, lxxx.
Mary, 178, 258, 261, 265, 266, 376, xlv, lxiv, lxv, lxvi, xcvi.
Margaret, 264, lxvi.
Mercy, 259, 261, 264, lxiv, lxv.
Mirriam, 265, lxvi.
Mirribah, 265, lxvi.
Moses, 263, 264, lxvi.
Miltimore, 265, lxvi.
Nathaniel, 15, 257, iv, lxiv.
Neal, 265, lxvi.
Noah, 265, lxvi.
Nathan, 264, lxvi.
Nicholas, 260, 265, lxv, lxvi.
Obediah, 259, lxiv.
Olive, 265, lxvi.
Osney, 265, lxvi.
Paul, 260, 261, 265, lxiv, lxv, lxvi.
Patience, 262, 265, lxv, lxvi.
Peace, 265, lxvi.
Peter, 264, lxvi.
Polly, 264, lxvi.
Rachel, 264, lxvi.
Ralph, 2. 54, 62, 63, 66, 85, 145, 156, 178, 257, 260, 263, 266, 340, 343, 409, 411, 412, i, xiv, xvi, xvii, xviii, xxii, xxxvii, xxxix, xlv, lxiv, lxv, lxvi, lxxxv, lxxxvi.
Rebecca, 265, lxvi.
Reuben, 260, lxv.
Robert, 264, lxvi.
Hall, Ruth, 262, 264, lxv, lxvi.
Samuel, 62, 258, 259, 261, 264, 265, 373, xvi, lxiv, lxv, lxvi, xcvi.
Sarah, 224, 258, 264, 265, 266, li, lxiv, lxvi.
Sally, 263, lxv.
Shadrach, 264, lxvi.
Silas, 260, 262, 265, lxv, lxvi.
Silome, 264, lxvi.
Simon, 264, lxvi.
Solomon, 260, 263, 265, lxv, lxvi.
Sobriety, 260, 263, lxv.
Stephen, 262, lxv.
Submit, 264, lxvi.
Thomas, 258, 266, lxiv, lxvi.
Timothy, 264, lxvi.
Tizzah, 266, lxvi.
Trial, 264, lxvi.
William, 260, 262, 264, 265, lxv, lxvi.
Winslow, 264, lxvi.
Winthrop, 263, lxv.
Hale, Calvin, 10, iii.
Elizabeth, 320, lxxx.
Hon. John Parker, 9, 10, 14, 101, 396, iii, iv, xxvi.
Martha Susan, 320, lxxx.
Matthew, 320, lxxx.
Mary B., 233, lviii.
Hon. Parker, 396.
Robert, 285, lxxi.
Samuel, 106, xxvii.
Stephen, 233, lviii.
Thomas Wright, 320, lxxx.
Hon. William, 7, 9, 14, 15, 106, 109, 321, 414, ii, iii, iv, xxvii, xxviii, lxxxi.
Hallowell, Henry, 377, xcvii.
Ham, Aaron, 251, lxii.
Betsey C., 253, lxiii.
Charles, 10, iii.
Daniel, 12, ii.
Ephraim, 5, 13, 325, ii, iv, lxxxii.
James, 233, lviii.
John, 2, 137, 142, 150, 161, 236, 245, 323, 326, i, xxxv, xxxvi, xxxviii, xli, lix, lxi, lxxxi, lxxxii.
Joseph, 286, 291, lxxi, lxxii.
Moses, 323, 325, lxxxi, lxxxii.
Nancy, 323, lxxxi.
Nathaniel, 102, 251, 319, xxvi, lxii, lxxx.
Lydia, 326, lxxxii.
Samuel, 14, 323, 325, 326, iv, lxxxi, lxxxii.
Sarah, 319, lxxx.
Hammett, Capt. Joseph, 271, lxviii.

Hammett, Thomas, 140, xxxv.
Hamilton, Hannah, 310, lxxviii.
Hamlin, Walcott, 289, lxxii.
Hance, John, 341, 355, 356, 363, 377, lxxxvi, xc, xcii, xcvii.
Hannaford, Oliver, 107, lxxvii.
Hanson, Abraham, 105, xxvii.
  Betty, 323, 326, lxxxi, lxxxii.
  Benjamin, 100, 250, 325, xxvii, lxii, lxxxii.
  Caleb, 400.
  Catherine, 295, lxxiii.
  David, 100, xxvii.
  Daniel, 63, 400, xvi.
  Dominicus, 2, 105, 251, i, xxvii, lxii.
  Ebenezer, 7, 400, ii.
  Elizabeth, 105, 294, 400, xxvii, lxxiii.
  Ephraim, 2, 6, 105, 345, i, ii, xxvii, lxxxvi.
  Hannah, 105, 297, 323, 326, 400, xxvii, lxxiv, lxxxi, lxxxii.
  Humphrey, 105, 251, 326, xxvii, lxii, lxxxii.
  Isaac, 410, 412.
  Joanna, 323, lxxxi.
  John, 195, 289, 399, 400, xli, lxxii.
  John Burnham, 2, 6, 12, 105, 297, 323, 326, 331, i, ii, iii, xxvii, lxxiv, lxxxi, lxxxii, lxxxiii.
  Joseph, 2, 5, 11, 15, 106, 197, 314, 347, i, ii, iii, iv, xxvii, l, lxxix, lxxxvii.
  Keziah, 265, lxvi.
  Jonathan, 14, 27, 99, 100, 136, iv, xxvi, xxxiv.
  Judith, 314, lxxix.
  Isaac, 63, 293, 346, xvi, lxxiii, lxxxvii.
  Israel, 233, lviii.
  Moses, 100, xxvii.
  Mary, 38, 174, x, xliv.
  Mehitable, 325, lxxxii.
  Nathan, 63, xvi.
  Peggy, 105, xxvii.
  Rebecca, 327, lxxxii.
  Richard, 111, xxviii.
  Samuel, 10, 252, 294, 399, iii, lxii, lxxiii.
  Sarah, 400.
  Solomon, 6, ii.
  Susan, 323, lxxxi.
  Stephen, 100, xxvii.
  Tobias, 4, 5, 105, 115, 160, 162, 314, 378, i, ii, xxvii, xxx, xl, xli, lxxix, xcvii.
  Thomas, 65, 69, 105, 115, 140, 157, 162, 243, 378, 399, xvii, xviii, xxvii, xxx, xxxv, xl, xli, lx, xcvii.
  William, 63, xvi.
Harris, John, 259, lxiv.
  Nicholas, 141, 152, xxxvi, xxxviii.

Harrison, John, 157, xl.
  Nicholas, 3, 155, i, xxxix.
Hartford, Nicholas, 2, 4, 5, 8, 11, 237, 238, 255, 267, 269, i, ii, iii, lix, lxiii, lxvi, lxvii.
  Simon, 14, iv.
Hastings, Elizabeth, 304, lxxvi.
  Esther, 304, lxxvi.
  George, 304, lxxvi.
  John, 304, lxxvi.
  Katherine, 304, lxxvi.
  Robert, 304, lxxvi.
Hatch, Mr., 165, xlii.
Hathorn, Capt. William, 174, 176, 208, 359, xliv, liii, xci.
Haven, Elizabeth, 397.
  Rev. Dr., 397.
Hayden, Ebenezer, 377, xcvii.
Hayes, Albert, 108, lxxvii.
  Angelina, 108, lxxvii.
  Charles, 233, lviii.
  Daniel, 6, ii.
  Ichabod, 11, 316, iii, lxxix.
  George L., 108, lxxvii.
  Hannah, 316, lxxix.
  Capt. John, 158, 330, xl, lxxxiii.
  Jonathan, 297, lxxiv.
  Mary J., 108, lxxvii.
  Nancy, 297, lxxiv.
  Norman P., 108, lxxiv.
  Orville H., 108, lxxvii.
  Paul, Esq., 108, lxxvii.
  Ralph, 316, lxxix.
  Richard, 251, lxii.
  Samuel, 123, 320, 354, xxxi, lxxx, xc.
  Susanna, 103, xxvi.
  Tamson, 107, 297, lxxiv, lxxvii.
  Watson, 108, lxxvii.
Haynes, Samuel, 20, 350, 352, v, lxxxviii.
  Thomas, 140, xxxv.
Heard, Abigail, 392.
  Benjamin, 63, 116, 140, xvi, xxx, xxxv.
  Experience, 279, lxix.
  Elizabeth, 243, lx.
  Eben, 62, xvi.
  Jane, 285, 286, lxxi.
  Hannah, 80, xxi.
  James, 196, xlix.
  John, 20, 46, 65, 66, 70, 94, 114, 140, 154, 193, 218, 230, 341, 348, 355, 363, 364, 372, 375, 378, 392, 395, v, xii, xvii, xviii, xxv, xxix, xxxv, xxxix, xlix, lv, lvii, lxxxvi, lxxxvii, xc, xcii, xcv, xcvi, xcvii.
  Joseph, 237, 238, lix.

Heard, Nathaniel, 4, i.
  Samuel, 3, 6, i, ii.
  Tristram, 4, 63, 156, 157, 161, 195, 236, 254, i, xvi, xxxix, xl, xli, xlix, lix, lxiii.
Heath, William, 1, 2, i.
Hemmingway, John, 223, lvi.
Henrietta, Maria, Queen of England, 76, xix.
Hertel, Indian chief, 270, lxvii.
Hesling, Arthur, 192, xlviii.
Hethersey, Robert, 352, 354, lxxxviii, xc.
Hewitt, Mr., 192, xlviii.
Henderson, Abby, 316, lxxix.
  Alfred, 316, lxxix.
  Benjamin, 165, xlii.
  Betsey, 165, xlii.
  Daniel, 6, 9, ii, iii.
  Hiram, 316, lxxix.
  Howard, 6, 8, 165, ii, xlii.
  Capt. Howard, 413.
  Lydia, 316, lxxix.
  Richard, 316, lxxix.
  Richmond, 165, xlii.
  Stephen, 165, xlii.
  Uriah, 316, lxxix.
  Warren, 316, lxxix.
  William, 142, 366, xxxvi, xcii.
Hicks, Elizabeth, 303, lxxvi.
  Joseph, 63, xvi.
  Martha, 307, lxxvi.
  Sarah, 303, lxxvi.
Hickman, Elder Nicholas, 353, xc.
  Major Thomas, 220, lvi.
Hill, Caroline G., 31, viii.
  Elizabeth, 107, lxxvii.
  Isaac, 12, iii.
  Joseph, 4, i.
  John, 58, 70, 132, 123, 134, 137, 140, 142, 150, 173, 219, 349, 350, 353, 356, 363, xv, xviii, xxxiv, xxxv, xxxvi, xxxviii, xliv, lv, lxxxviii, xc, xcii.
  Nathaniel, 3, 4, 59, 79, 97, 125, 155, 194, 218, 388, 389, i, xv, xx, xxvi, xxxi, xxxix, xlix, lv.
  Samuel, 219, lv.
  Mrs. Valentine, 95, 97, xxv, xxvi.
  Valentine, 2, 8, 35, 40, 41, 46, 47, 54, 70, 97, 146, 191, 282, 301, 337, 338, 343, 348, 349, 356, 357, 363, 371, 373, 380, 389, 391, i, ii, ix, x, xi, xii, xiv, xviii, xxvi, xxxvii, xlviii, lxx, lxxv, lxxxv, lxxxvi, lxxxvii, lxxxviii, xc, xci, xcii, xcv, xcvi, xcvii.
Hill, William, 63, 140, 237, 238, xvi, xxxv, lix.
Hilton, Abigail, 180, xlv.
  Ann, 178, 179, 259, xlv, lxiv.
  Andrew, 180, xlv.
  Andrew, Jr., 180, xlv.
  Benjamin, 179, xlv.
  Bridget, 178, xlv.
  Captain, 272, lxviii.
  Clarissa, 179, xlv.
  Charles, 177, xlv.
  Dudley, 179, 259, 261, 265, xlv, lxiv, lxv, lxvi.
  Deborah, 178, xlv.
  Edward, 16, 19, 26, 27, 32, 48, 65, 66, 69, 90, 91, 161, 164, 176, 177, 179, 182, 191, 200, 259, 261, 351, 364, 382, 383, 390, 423, 424, iv, v, vii, viii, xii, xvii, xviii, xxiv, xli, xliv, xlv, xlviii, l, lxiv, lxv, lxxxviii, xcii.
  Elizabeth, 178, 180, xlv.
  Eliza, 180, xlv.
  Francis J., 180, lxv.
  George, 179, xlv.
  Hannah, 178, xlv.
  Ichabod, 179, xlv.
  Israel, 178, xlv.
  John F., 180, xlv.
  Joseph, 178, 180, xlv.
  Col. Joseph, 179, xlv.
  Judith, 178, xlv.
  John 91, 180, 352, 355, 356, 362, 363, 372, 379, xxiv, xlv, lxxxviii, xc, xcii, xcv.
  Jonathan, 91, 178, 364, xxiv, xlv, xcii.
  Martha, 180, xlv,
  Martha Ann, 180, xlv.
  Martha W., 180, xlv.
  Mary, 178, 179, 259, xlv, lxiv.
  Mary Ann, 180, xlv.
  Mary Jane, 180, xlv.
  Nathaniel, 179, xlv.
  Richard, 177, 178, 179, xlv.
  Sally, 180, xlv.
  Samuel, 177, 179, xlv.
  Sobriety, 178, xlv.
  Susan, 179, 180, xlv.
  Susanna, 179, xlv.
  Theodore, 178, 179, xlv.
  Thomas, 180, xlv.
  William, 1, 2, 16, 47, 65, 90, 91, 144, 176, 177, 179, 188, 339, 350, 383, 423, i, iv, xii, xvii, xxiv, xxxvi, xliv, xlv, xlvii, lxxxv, lxxxviii.
  Winthrop, 178, 179, 180, xlv.
Hoag, Enoch, 100, xxvii.

Hoag, Mary, 253, lxiii.
Hobbs, Henry, 69, 96, 142, 355, 357, 362, 365, xviii, xxvi, xxxvi, xc, xci, xcii, xciii.
   James, 61, xvi.
   John, 380, xcvii.
   Morris, 61, 238, xvi, lix.
   Sarah, 380, xcvii.
Hobson, John, 118, xxx.
   Humphrey, 118, xxx.
   William, 118, xxx.
Hodgdon, Shadrach, 5, 9, 327, ii, iii, lxxxii.
   Alexander, 127, xxxii.
   Caleb, 9, 13, 253, 329, 331, iii, iv, lxiii, lxxxiii.
   Hannah, 108, lxxvii.
   Israel, 400.
   Moses, 13, 103, 288, iv, xxvi, lxxii.
   Peter, 12, iii.
   Priscilla, 253, lxiii.
   Samuel, 400.
   Tamson, 316, lxxix.
   William, 288, lxxii.
Hodge, Samuel, 91, lxxii.
Hoitt, Eliza, 108, lxxvii.
Holland, Edward, 375, xcvi.
Holmes, Anna, 289, lxxii.
   Ephraim, 263, lxv.
   Thomas, 142, 271, xxxvi, lxviii.
Hook, Florence, 281, lxx.
Hooton, Elizabeth, 173, xliv.
Hopehood, Indian Chief, 271, 272, lxviii.
Horn, Abigail, 252, lxiii.
   Benjamin, 252, lxiii.
   Charity 252, lxiii.
   Daniel, 14, iv.
   Elizabeth, 381.
   John, 11, 230, iii, lvii.
   Isaac, 232, lvii.
   Lydia, 253, lxiii.
   Mary, 230, lvii,
   Moses, 110, xxviii.
   Mrs., 230, lvii.
   Nathaniel, 6, 418, ii.
   Oliver P., 235, lviii.
   Oliver S., 7, 10, ii, iii.
   Paul, 252, lxiii.
   Sarah, 400.
   Capt. William, 320, 376, lxxx, xcvi.
   William, 109, 140, 218, 230, 243, 365, 381, xxviii, xxxv, lv, lvii, lx, xciii.
Howard, Daniel, 165, xlii.
   Harriet, 108, lxxvii.
   Love, 165, xlii.

Howard, Mary A., 108, lxxvii.
   Samuel, 7, 15, ii, iv.
Howe, Moses, 11, iii.
Howell, Risse 349, 356, 357, 363, lxxxviii, xc, xci, xcii.
   Stephen, 142, xxxvi.
Hoyt, John, 160, 197, xl, l.
   Lydia, 307, lxxvi.
   William, 49, 127, 194, 195, xxxii.
Hubbard, Colonel, 265, lxiv.
   Hannah, 397.
   Thomas, 145, 340, xxxvii, lxxxv.
   Richard, 145, 340, xxxvii, lxxxv.
Huckins, James, 3, 58, 63, 132, 133, 139, 154, 218, 262, 269, 274, 277, i, xv, xvi, xxxiv, xxxv, xxxix, lv, lxv, lxvii, lxviii, lxix.
   John, 63, 382, xvi.
   Robert, 4, 20, 81, 159, 195, 350, i, v, xxi, xl, xlix, lxxxviii.
   Sarah, 262, lxv.
Hudson, Mr., 127, xxxii.
Hull, Rev. Benjamin, 395.
   Benjamin, 245, 363, lxi, xcii.
   Captain, 359, xci.
   Elizabeth, 395.
   Naomi, 411.
   Reuben, 412.
   Rev. Parson, 173, xliv.
Humphrey, Thomas, 65, 67, 138, 147, 363, 377, xvii, xxxv, xxxviii, xcii, xcvii.
Hunking, Elizabeth, 307, lxxvi.
   Capt. John, 306, lxxvi.
   John, 96, 211, 212, 412, xxvi, liv.
   Capt. Mark, 108, lxxvii.
   Mark, 302, lxxv.
   Martha, 108, lxxvii.
Hunt, Bartholomew, 20, v.
   Robert, 222, lvi.
Huntington, William, 186, xlvii.
Huntress, George, 127, xxxii.
   Jonathan, 319, lxxx.
   Samuel, 127, 197, xxxii, l.
Hurd, Anna, 316, lxxix.
   Eliza B., 233, lviii.
   George, 308, lxx.
   Hon. Ezekiel, 7, 14, 233, ii, iv, lviii.
   John, 232, 356, lviii, xc.
   Mary B., 233, lviii.
Hurkeness, Robert, 348, lxxxvii.
Huss, John, 82, xxi.
Hussey, Christopher, 216, lv.
   Daniel, 7, 10, ii, iii.

Hussey, Joseph, 61, 62, xvi, lxxvii.
   Robert, 363, xcii.
   Richard, 293, 346, lxxiii, lxxvii, lxxxvii.
   William, 11, 12, iii.
Hutchins, John, 381.
   Joseph, 381.
Hyde, Asenath, 297, lxxiv.
   Jacob, 297, lxxiv.
Hynck, Francis, 141, xxxvi.

Jackson, Elizabeth, 137, xxxv,
   Frank, 137, xxxv.
   James, 363, xcii.
   Jane, 250, lxii.
   John, 137, xxxv.
   Joseph, 63, xvi.
   Patrick, 145, xxxvii.
   Margery, 312, lxxviii.
   Walker, 140, xxxvi.
   Walter, 58, 72, 250, 340, v, xviii, lxii, lxxxv, xcii.
   William, 59, 157, 161, 238, 363, xv, xl, xli, lix.
Jaffrey, George, 128, 307, xxxiii, lxxvi.
Jameison, Patrick, 58, 68, 145, 340, 363, 373, 378, xv, xviii, xxxvii, lxxxv, xcii, xcvi, xcvii.
James, Francis, 261, lxv.
   Kinsley, 261, lxv.
Jenness, Abigail, 286, 288, 291, lxxi, lxxii.
   Hon. Benning Wentworth, 319, lxxx.
   John S., 20, v.
   Nathaniel, 10, 93, iii, xxiv.
   Solomon, 6, ii.
Jennings, Richard, 286, lxxi.
Jenkins, Ann, 264, lxvi.
   Elijah, 12, iv.
   Fred, 79, xx.
   Joseph, 59, 195, 197, 237, 238, xv, xlix, l, lix.
   Robert, 357, 363, xci, xcii.
   Ruth, 319, lxxx.
   Stephen, 237, lix.
Jenks, Simon, 424.
Jethro, Peter, 211, liii.
Jewett, Mary, 89, xxiv.
   Deacon, 118, xxx.
   Thomas, 12, iv.
Johnson, Charity, 263, lxv.
   Darius, T., 10, iii.
   Edward, 58, xv.
   James, 55, xiv.
   John, 177, xlv.

Johnson, Mary, 299, lxxiv.
   Thomas, 36, 41, 53, 97, 343, 349, 352, 354, 357, 363, 372, 389, ix, xi, xiv, lxxxvi, lxxxviii, xc, xci, xcii, xcv.
Jones, Eleanor, 392.
   Elizabeth, 374, xcvi.
   Jonathan, 259, lxiv.
   Joseph, 4, 59, 160, 161, 232, 253, i, xv, xl, xli, lix, lxiii.
   Jenkins, 218, 392, 411, lv.
   John Paul, 103, xxvi.
   Lydia, 308, lxxvii,
   Major, 81, xxi.
   Mary, 89, 279, 392, xxiv, lxix.
   Robert, 66, 355, 356, 362, 364, 391, xvii, xc, xcii.
   Samuel, 61, 62, 74, 268, xvi, xix, lxvii.
   Capt. Stephen, 276, lxix.
   Stephen, 3, 4, 5, 8, 15, 58, 59, 79, 97, 121, 140, 159, 161, 165, 193, 198, 255, 388, 391, i ii, iv, xv, xx, xxvi, xxxi, xxxvi, xl, xli, xlii, xlix, l, lxiii.
   Sir William, 215, liv.
   William, 20, 36, 56, 61, 268, 363, 364, 391, 392, v, ix, xiv, xvi, lxvii, xcii.
Jose, Richard, 178, 226, xlv, lvii.
Joselyn, Mr., 368, 370, xciii, xcv.
Junkins, Robert, 356, xc.

Kaise, Elizabeth, 242, lx.
   Samuel, 128, xxxiii.
Kaket, William, 115, xxx.
Kankamagus, Indian Chief, 220, 221, lvi.
Keazer, Hannah, 301, lxxv.
   John, 303, lxxv.
   Sarah, 252, lxiii.
Keene, William, 378, xcvii.
Kelley, Ebenezer, 260, lxv.
   John, 291, 310, lxxii, lxxviii.
Kellow, Augusta A., 317, lxxx.
Kembrick, Louise L., 317, lxxx.
Kent, Oliver, 377, xcvii.
   Oliver, 349, 352, 354, 356, 357, 363, 377, lxxxviii, xc, xci, xcii, xcvii.
Key, John, 355, xc.
Kidd, James, 25, 48, 355, 356, 365, 409, vii, xii, xc, xciii.
Kidder, Stephen, 368, xciii.
Kielle, John, 6, 9, 11, 13, 178, 179, 329, ii, iii, iv, xlv, lxxxiii.
Kimball, Elizabeth, 366, xciii.
   Ephraim, 11, iii.

Kimball, Ezra, 230, 356, lvii, xciii.
  Mr., 364, xcii.
  Paul, 13, iv.
  Samuel, 6, 9, ii, iii.
  Thomas, 47, 366, 378, 379, 380, xii, xciii, xcvii.
King, Philip, 98, xxvi.
  Thomas, 382.
Kingman, Olive, 308, lxxvii.
Kingsley, James, 178, xlv.
Kirk, Henry, 95, 96, xxv.
Kittredge, Doctor, 106, xxvii.
  George, 14, iv.
  Jacob, 9, iii.
  John, 7, ii.
  Thomas W., 7, 9, ii, iii.
Kneil, Charles, 368, xciii.
Knight, Capt. John, 161, 162, iv.
  Deborah, 396.
  John, 4, 128, 152, 160, 194, 195, 197, i, xxxiii, xxxviii, xl, xlix, l.
  Joseph, 153, xxxix.
  Nathan, 127, xxxii.
  Richard, 364, xcii.
  Roger, 368, xciii.
Knollys, Rev. Hanserd, 20, 27, 28, 30, 35, 73, 129, 182, 331, 332, 384, 385, v, vii, viii, ix, xix, xxxiii, xlvi, lxxxiii.

Ladd, Elizabeth, 261, lxv.
  Eliphalet, 12, 101, iv, xxvi.
  Nathaniel, 178, 261, xlv, lxv.
  Samuel, 13, iv.
Lahan, Henry, 20, v.
  Richard, 20, v.
Lake, Thomas, 191, 375, 378, 410, xlviii, xcvi, xcvii.
Lamos, Abigail, 137, xxxv.
  Hannah, 93, xxiv.
  Nathaniel, 14, 158, iv, xl.
Lane, Deacon Edmund J., 7, 10, 101, 120, ii, iii, xxvi, xxxi.
  Hannah, 119, xxx.
  Job, 118, 356, xxx, xci.
Langdon, Abigail, 265, lxvi.
  Elizabeth, 265, lxvi.
  John, 78, 265, xx, lxvi.
  Mary, 265, lxvi.
  Martha, 265, lxvi.
  Sarah, 307, lxxvi.
  Theophilas, 265, lxvi.
  Thomas, 265, lxvi.
  Tobias, 305, lxxvi.

Langdon, Woodbury, 265, lxvi.
Langstaff, Henry, 2, 3, 55, 205, 219, 376, i, xiv, lii, lv, xcvi.
Lankster, Henry, 41, 65, 66, 68, 71, 75, 115, 116, 122, 125, 340, 341, 348, 349, 352, 354, 356, 357, 362, 365, xi, xvii, xviii, xix, xxx, xxxi, xxxii, lxxxv, lxxxvi, lxxxvii, lxxxviii, xc, xci, xcii, xciii.
  John, 71, 179, 140, 150, xviii, xxxv, xxxviii.
Langley, Daniel, 180, xlv.
  Maria, lxxvii.
  Mary A., 317, lxxx.
  James, 199, l.
  Lydia, 279, lxix.
  Samuel, 179, xlv.
Larkham, Rev. Thomas, 385, 425.
Larkin, David, 139, 140, xxxv.
  Thomas, 20, 29, 30, 31, 35, 73, 190, 191, 350, 367, 371, v, viii, ix, xix, xlviii, lxxxviii, xciii, xcv.
Laud, Archbishop of England, 19, 25, 385, 424, v, vii.
Lawson, Christopher, 367, xciii.
Layn, David, lxxvii.
  Edmund, lxxvii.
  John, lxxvii.
  Mary Susan, lxxvii.
  Samuel, lxxvii.
Lear, Tobias, 261, lxv.
Leathers, Abel, 63, xvi.
  Edward, 58, 59, 84. 138, 140, 274, 277, 378, xv, xxii, xxxv, lxviii, lxix, xcvii.
  William, 84, xxii.
Leavitt, Samuel, 379, xcvii.
Lebrock, John, 62, xvi.
Lee, Abraham, 242, lx.
  Mrs. Abraham, 243, lx.
Legat, John, 379, xcvii.
Leighton, Abigail, 260, lxv.
  Andrew, 260, lxv.
  Daniel, 260, lxv.
  David, 260, lxv.
  Elizabeth, 260, lxv.
  Ezekiel, 257, lxiv.
  George, 93, 260, xxv, lxv.
  Hannah, 260, 264, lxv.
  Hatevil, 260, lxv.
  James, lxxvii.
  John, 160, 161, 162, 195, xl, xli, xlix.
  Joseph, 260, lxv.
  Jedidiah, 260, lxv.
  Lydia, 260, lxv.

Leighton, Mary, 310, lxxviii.
    Paul, 260, lxv.
    Peletiah, 260, lxv.
    Robert, 260, lxv.
    Sarah, 260, lxv.
    Seth, 307, lxxvi.
    Silas, 260, lxv.
    Susanna, 260, lxv.
    Stephen, 260, lxv.
    Thomas, 1, 2, 20, 34, 35, 66, 68, 69, 71, 75, 114, 124, 128, 137, 140, 145, 146, 150, 193, 202, 257, 340, 349, 350, 351, 354, 355, 356, 361, 362, 364 408, 409, i, v, ix, xvii, xviii, xix, xxix, xxxi, xxxiii, xxxv, xxxvii, xxxix, xlix, li, lxiv, lxxxv, lxxxviii, xc, xcii.
Lemon, Mary, 399.
Leveridge, Rev. William, 24, 384, vi.
Lewis, Philip, 41, 55, 96, 97, 98, 164, 219, 336, 349, 372, 409, xi, xiv, xxvi, xli, lv, lxxxiv, lxxxviii, xcv.
    Maria, 77.
Libbey, Daniel, 63, xvi.
    Isaac, 231, 232, 294, 347, 366, lvii, lxxiii, lxxxvii, xciii.
    John, 366, xciii.
    Richard, 366, xciii.
    Samuel, 232, 366, lviii, xciii.
    Sarah, 308, 366, lxxvii, xciii.
Lidall, John, 176, xliv.
Light, Dorothy, 188, xlvii.
    Hannah, 261, lxv.
    John, 261, 265, lxv, lxvi.
    Mary, 261, 265, lxv.
    Tizzah, 261, lxv.
Lindsay, John, 102, xxvi.
Lippincott, Bartholomew, 363, xcii.
Lisson, Nicholas, 402, 403, 404.
Locke, Eleanor, 89, xxiv.
    Jonathan, 7, 141, 419, ii, iv.
    Mary, 88, 308, xxiv, lxxvii.
Long, Abigail, 242, lx,
Lord, Ann, 105, 314, lxxvii, lxxix.
    Gershom, 10, xxvii.
    Hannah, 261, lxv,
    Margaret, 106, xxvii.
    Robert, 261, lxv.
Lore, Robert, 61, xvi.
Lougee, Sarah, lxxvii.
Love, John, 354, xc.
    William, 363, xcii.
Lovring, Mr., 71, 94, 193, 355, 357, 363, 365, viii, xxv, xlix, xc, xci, xcii, xciii.

Low, Dr. Nathaniel, 10, 101, 311, iii, xxvi, lxxviii.
Lowden, Anthony, 279, lxix.
Ludias, David, 377, xcvii.
    Mrs., 375, xcvi.
Lummack, Nathaniel, 141, xxxvi.
Lundall, Thomas, 340, lxxxv.
Lunt, Daniel, 242, lx.
Lyford, Theophilus, 261, lxv.
    Thomas, 261, lxv.

Macy, Thomas, 29, 280, xxxiii, lxx.
Madokawando, Indian Chief, 212, liii.
Magoun, Henry, 344, 345, 355, 357, lxxxvi, lxxxvii, xc, xci.
Main, Rev. Amos, 323, lxxxi.
    Lydia, 323, lxxxi.
Maltahouse, Indian Sagamore, 213, liv.
Maltby, Jane, 317, lxxx.
Mann, John, 13, 101, 399, iv, xxvi.
Maramsquad, Indian Chief, 220, lvi.
March, Henry, 59, xv.
    Jonas C., 14, ix.
Mardy, Nathaniel, 290, lxxii.
Marshall, Betty, 101, xxvi.
    John, 101, xxvi.
Marston, John, 179, xlv.
    Winthrop, 288, lxxii.
Martyn, John, 3, 67, 69, 71, 75, 92, 245, 246, 343, 349, 352, 354, 356, 357, 363, i, xvii, xviii, xix, xxiv, lxi, lxxxvi, lxxxviii, xc, xci, xcii.
    Mary, 307, lxxvii,
    Noah, 10, iii.
    Richard, 69, 117, 210, 216, 270, 272, xiii, xxx, liii, lv, lxvii, lxviii.
Mason, Elizabeth, 92, xxiv.
    John, 16, 61, 62, 141, 215, 368, 369, 370, 373, 424, iv, xvi, xxxvi, liv, xciii, xcv, xcvi.
    Joseph, 373, xcvi.
    Mrs., 370, xcv.
    Thomas, 124, xxxi.
    True, 308, lxxvii.
    Robert, 215, 217, 218, liv, lv.
Mathes, Benjamin, 78, xx.
    Francis, 5, 8, 12, 59, 254, 267, 268, 269, i, ii, iii, xv, lxiii, lxvi, lxvii.
    Mr., 349, lxxx.
    Mrs., 354, xc.
    Phebe, 303, lxxvi.
    Valentine, 79, xx.
Mathews, Benjamin, 58, 116, 122, 141, 150, 363, xv, xxx, xxxi, xxxvi, xxxviii, xcii.

Mathews, Francis, 76, 77, 79, 80, 91, 372, xix, xx, xxi, xxiv, xcv.
   Mrs., 352, 356, 357, lxxxviii, xc, xci.
   Walter, 58, 114, xv, xxix.
Mathewson, George, 10, iii.
Mattoon, Richard, 178, xlv.
Mather, Rev. Cotton, 76, 184, 229, xix, xlvi lvii.
Maverick, Samuel, 204, li.
   Antipas, 404.
Maud, Rev. Daniel, 32, 33, 42, 72, 117, 129, 184, 392, viii, ix, xi, xix, xxx, xxxiii, xlvi.
Mazet, John, 63, xvi.
McCauslin, Hannah, 297, lxxiv.
Meader, John, 4, 59, 66, 70, 82, 94, 122, 140, 157, 219, 276, 301, 302, 355, 357, 363, 384, 409, i, xv, xvii, xviii, xxi, xxv, xxxi, xxxvi, xl, lv, lxix, lxxv, xc, xci, xcii.
   Joseph, 3, 4, 59, 155, 160, 301, i, xv, xxxix, xl, lxxv.
   Nathaniel, 59, xv.
   Timothy, 79, xx.
Meddelton, James, 145, 340, 375, xxxvii, lxxxv, xcvi.
Medellman, James, 363, xcii.
Megunaway, Indians, 213, liv.
Mellen, 12, 103, iv, xx.
Merry, James, 145, xxxvii.
Mesandowit, Indian Chief, 220, 221, lv.
Meserve, Andrew, 262, lxv.
   Curtis Coe, 263, lxv.
   Colonel, 326, lxxxii.
   Clement, 6, 13, 127, ii, iv, xxxii.
   Daniel, 63, 345, xvi, lxxxvii.
   Ebenezer, 88, xxiv.
   Mary, 263, lxv.
   Isaac H., 263, lxv.
Michamore, John, 142, xxxvi.
Michiel, John, 137, 150, xxxv, xxxviii.
   Thomas, 378, xcvii.
Micklethayte, Nathalie, 373, 391, xcvi.
Migill, John, 139, 141, xxxv, xxxvi.
Millard, Jane, 176, xliv.
Milliken Hannah, 252, 253, lxiii.
Miller, Joseph, 367, 371, 374, xciii, xcv, xcvi.
   Thomas, 63, xvi.
Millett, Abigail, 310, lxxviii.
   Asa, 310, lxxviii.
   Benjamin, 310, lxxviii.
   Betsey, 310, lxxviii.
   David, 310, lxxviii.
   Elizabeth, 165, xlii.
   Eunice, 310, lxxviii.

Millett, Hannah, 165, xlii.
   John, 164, 310, xli, lxxviii.
   Lydia, 89, 165, xxiv, xlii.
   Mary, 310, lxxviii.
   Parsons, 310, lxxviii.
   Solomon, 310, lxxviii.
   Susan, 165, xlii.
   Thomas, 5, 8, 11, 89, 310, ii, iii, xxiv, lxxviii.
   Zebulon, 310, lxxviii.
Mills, Samuel, 407.
Mimmey, Abraham, 62, xvi.
Mogg, Indian Chief, 212, liii.
Mohawk Indians, 214, liv.
Mohermite, Indian Sagamore, 400.
Moody, John, 261, lxv.
   Rev. Joshua, 184, 284, xlvi, lxxi.
   Joshua, 120, xxx.
   Mary, 261, lxv.
   Silas, 10, iii.
Mooney, Hercules, 63, xvi.
Moore, Jacob B., 285, lxxi.
Montgomery, David K., 308, lxxvii.
   David M., 308, lxxvii.
   John Swain, 308, lxxvii.
Mordantt, Benjamin, 322, lxxxi.
   Margaret, 322, lxxxi.
   Mary, 322, lxxxi.
Morgan, Richard, 365, xciii.
Morrill, Anna, 261, lxv.
   Asa, 263, lxv.
   Joanna, 263, lxv.
   Joseph, 10, 233, iii, lviii.
   Prudence, 263, lxv.
   Rhoda, 263, lxv.
Morris, Thomas, 141, xxxvi.
Morse, Kitty, 323, 325, lxxxi, lxxxii.
   Sarah, 325, lxxxii.
Morton, William, 335, lxxxiv.
Moses, Timothy, 63, xvi.
Moulton, Henry, 177, xlv.
   James P., 10, iii.
   Jonathan, 109, xxviii.
   William, 188, xlvii.
Machamug, Peter, Indian Chief, 214, liv.
Murry, Abigail, 317, lxxx.
   James, 340, 366, lxxxv, xciii.
Mussey, James, 195, xlix.

Nanny, Robert, 20, 354, v, xc.
Narragansett Indians, 212, liv.
Nash, Isaac, 349, 355, 356, 362, lxxxviii, xc, xcii.
Nason, Benjamin, 142, xxxvi.
   John, 142, xxxvi.

Nason, Richard, 45, 127, 142, 355, 410, xii, xxxii, xxxvi, xc.
Natick Indians, 212, liv.
Neal, Capt. Francis, 24, vi.
   Herbert, 89, xxiv.
   John, 266, lxvi.
   Marjory, 262, lxv.
   Moses L., 13, 14, iv.
   Sarah, 89, xxiv.
Newgrove, John, 348, 409, lxxxvii.
Newhouse, Thomas, 176, xliv.
Newmarch, Joseph, 346, lxxxvii.
Nichols, Randall, 380, xcvii.
Nicols, Governor, 183, xlvi.
   Richard, 204, li.
Noble, Stephen, 78, xx.
Nock, Drisco, 63, xvi.
   Henry, 59, 62, 159, xv, xvi, xl.
   James, 63, 238, 314, xvi, lix, lxxix.
   Jonathan, 62, xvi.
   Nathaniel, 62, xvi.
   Samuel, 62, xvi.
   Silvanus, 61, 142, 156, 163, 238, xvi, xxxvi, xxxix, xli, lix.
   Thomas, 61, 66, 70, 94, 199, 355, 356, 362, 364, 365, 372, 395, 411, xvi, xviii, xxii, xxv, xlix, xc, xcii, xciii, xcv.
   Zachariah, 61, xvi.
Norton, Francis, 370, xcv.
   John, 319, lxxx.
Noyes, Judith, 285, lxxi.
Nute, Abraham, 140, 157, 410, xxxv, xl.
   Clarissa, 308, lxxvii.
   James, 2, 4, 20, 37, 38, 66, 68, 132, 133, 134, 137, 139, 140, 151, 164, 174, 202, 238, 267, 268, 269, 340, 348, 349, 352, 353, 356, 362, 363, 364, 378, 409, 410, i, v, x, xvii, xxxiv, xxxv, xxxviii, xli, li, lix, lxvi, lxvii, lxxxv, lxxxvii, lxxxviii, xc, xcii, xcvii.
   Sarah, 410.
Nutt, James, 355, 362, 363, 364, xc, xcii.
Nutter Family, 122 et seq., xxxi.
Nutter, Abigail, 92, 124, 125, 126, xxiv, xxxi, xxxii.
   Annie, 123, 395, xxxi.
   Anthony (Antony), 3, 8, 37, 41, 53, 67, 70, 74, 75, 76, 95, 96, 114, 115, 116, 117, 122, 123, 124, 132, 133, 139, 140, 142, 150, 219, 341, 349, 354, 356, 357, 362, 365, 376, 377, i, ii, x, xi, xiv, xvii, xviii, xxv, xxx, xxxi, xxxiv, xxxv, xxxvi, xxxviii, lv, lxxxvi, lxxxviii, xc, xci, xcii, xciii, xcvi, xcvii.
   Dorothy, 126, xxxii.
   Eleanor, 125, 319, xxxii, lxxx.
   Elizabeth, 125, 409, xxxii.
   Elder Hatevil, 2, 3, 10, 34, 66, 68, 70, 71, 74, 75, 92, 96, 120, 140, 145, 146, 256, 310, 348, 349, 356, 362, 364, 365, 408, 409, i, iii, ix, xvii, xviii, xix, xxiv, xxv, xxxi, xxxv, xxxvii, lxiv, lxxxv, lxxxvii, lxxxviii, xc, xcii, xciii.
   Hatevil, 122, 125, 126, 160, 173, 190, 198, 200, 223, 350, 352, 353, 371, 374, 376, 377, 378, 379, 405, 412, xxxi, xxxii, xl, xliv, xlviii, xlix, l, lvi, lxxxviii, xc, xcv, xcvi, xcvii.
   Hannah, 126, xxxii.
   Henry, 125, 126, 161, xxxii, xli.
   James, 125, xxxii.
   Joseph, 125, xxxii.
   John, 123, 125, 126, 127, 157, 377, xxxi, xxxii, xl, xcvii.
   Joshua, 125, xxxii.
   Mary, 124, 126, 408, xxxi, xxxii.
   Matthias, 125, xxxii.
   Nathaniel, 125, 375, xxxii, xcvi.
   Oliver, 125, xxxii.
   Samuel, 125, xxxii.
   Sarah, 125, 375, xxxii, xcvi.
   Valentine, 125, xxxii.
Odiorne, John B. H., 9, 324, 417, iii, lxxxi.
Oer, James, 363, 389, xcii.
Oliver, Joanna, 310, lxxviii.
   John, 311, lxxviii.
   Richard, 379, xcvii.
Otis, A. H., 10, 95, 115, iii, xxv, xxix.
   Christine, 243, 251, 279, 400, lx, lxii, lxix.
   Grizel, 279, lxix.
   Hannah, 243, lx.
   Hon. Job, 308, lxxvii.
   John, 279, lxix.
   Mary, 400.
   Nathaniel, 242, 243, lx.
   Nicholas, 279, lxix.
   Richard, 3, 53, 54, 68, 72, 75, 140, 142, 202, 242, 243, 263, 279, 340, 341, 343, 355, 357, 363, 364, 376, 379, 411, i, xiv, xvii, xviii, xix, xxxv, xxxvi, li, lx, lxv, lxix, lxxxv, lxxxvi, xc, xci, xcii, xcvi, xcvii.
   Rose, 135, 279, 308, xxxiv, lxix, lxxvii.
   Sarah, 308, lxxvii.
   Stephen, 242, 243, 279, 308, lx, lxix, lxxvii.
   Susan, 308, lxxvii.
One-Eyed John, Indian Chief, 211, liii.

Ordway, Ann, 376, xcvi.
   James, 353, 376, xc, xcvi.
Osborne, Daniel, 7, 100, ii, xxvii.
   Marble, 100, xxvii.
   William, 296, lxxiv.

Pacheco, Moses, 412.
Packer, Thomas, 224, 256, 277, lvii, lxiv, lxix.
Paddy, William, 373, xcvi.
Page, Carter, 298, lxxiv.
   Deborah, 380, xcvii.
   Francis, 188, xlvii.
   John, 299, lxxiv.
   Lucy, 299, lxxiv.
   Mary J., 308, lxxvii.
   Mehitable, 390, xcvii.
   Rev. Robert, 398.
   Robert, 188, 399, xlvii, xcvii.
   Samuel, 88, 380, xxiii, xcvii.
   Shuah, 380, xcvii.
   Taylor, 230, 231, lvii.
   Thomas, 188, xlvii.
   Theodate Drake, 396.
Park, William, 58, xv.
Parker, Elizabeth, 396.
   John, 396.
   Rev. Mr., 297, lxxiv.
   Rachel, 297, lxxiv.
   Richard G., 396.
   Bishop Samuel, 396.
   Hon. William, 396.
   William, 242, 267, lx, lxvi.
Parkinson, William, 58, 114, 141, 377, xv, xxix, xxxvi, xcvii.
Parnell, John, 114, xxix.
Paquamehood, John, 376, xcvi.
Palmer, Barnabas, 261, lxv.
   Christopher, 177, 188, xlv, xlvii.
   Stephen P., 230, lvii.
   William, 14, iv.
Parmelee, Horace, 13, iv.
Parsons, George, 379, xcvii.
   Jaffrey, 380, xcvii.
   Sarah, 88, xxiii.
   William, 88, xxiii.
   Deacon William, 310, lxxviii.
Partridge, William, 152, xxxviii.
   John, 409.
   Mary, 409.
   Nehemiah, 409.
Patten, Stephen, 6, 7, ii.
Passaconaway, Indian Chief, 186, 220, xlvii, lvi.

Patterson, Edward, 53, 355, 356, 362, 363, 378, 390, xiv, xc, xcii, xcvii.
Paul, Ivory, 10, iii.
   Moses, 14, 15, iv.
   Capt. Moses, 327, lxxxii.
   Nathaniel, 7, ii.
Paxton, Capt., 306, lxxvi.
Payne, Thomas, 153, 219, 245, 283, 365, 376, 411, xxxix, lv, lxi, lxx, xciii, xcvi.
   William, 40, 140, 350, 382, 416, 419, x, xxxv, lxxxviii.
   Elizabeth, 304, lxxvi.
Peacock, Samuel, 377, xcvii.
Pearson, David, 14, iv.
Pearl, Benjamin, 315, lxxix.
Peaslee, Amos, 326, lxxxii.
   James, 300, lxxv.
   John, 326, lxxxii.
   Joseph T., 10, iii.
   Nicholas, 6, 7, 326, ii, lxxxii.
   Robert, 323, 325, lxxxi, lxxxii.
   Samuel, 326, lxxxii.
   Sylvester, 326, lxxxii.
   William, 323, lxxxi.
Peavey, Abel, 127, xxxii.
   Edward, 127, xxxii.
   Joseph, 61, xvi.
Peirce, Andrew, 2, 6, 7, 9, 10, 14, 103, 112, i, ii, iii, iv, xxvi, xxviii.
   Col. Andrew, 324, lxxxi.
   Betty, 323, lxxxi.
   Deacon Benjamin, 6, 61, 104, 112, 323, 324, ii, xvi, xxvii, xxix, lxxxi.
   Daniel, 11, iii.
   David, 7, iii.
   Joseph, 228, 323, lvii, lxxxi.
   Joseph A., 112, xxviii.
   Tamson, 308, lxxvii.
Pendexter, George, 13, 14, iv.
   Lydia, 320, lxxx.
Pendleton, Arion, 375, xcvi.
   Byan, 374, 408, xcvi.
   Captain, 68, 69, 71, 337, xvii, xviii, lxxxv.
   James, 96, xxvi.
Pepperell, Sir William, 397.
Percival, Richard, 190, xlviii.
Perkins, Ann Louise, 252, lxiii.
   Asa, 14, iv.
   Daniel, 12, iv.
   Daniel Libbey, 252, lxiii.
   Eri, 7, 9, ii, iii.
   Harriet Ella, 252, lxiii.

Perkins, Isabella, 252, lxiii.
   Jeremy, 101, 250, 252, xxvi, lxiii.
   John, Esq., 308, lxxvii.
   Joseph, 279, lxix.
   Joshua, 11, iii.
   Lemuel, 63, xvi.
   Lydia A., 252, lxiii.
   Nathaniel, 63, xvi.
   Sarah E., 252, lxiii.
   Thomas, 115, 116, 132, 133, 138, 140, xxx, xxxiv, xxxv.
   William, 99, 116, 141, 309, 382, xxvi, xxx, xxxvi, lxxviii.
Permet, Lasserres, 365, xciii.
Persons, John, 279, lxix.
   Ruth, 279, lxix.
Peterborough (Eng.), Bishop of, 30, viii.
Peters, Andrew, 127, xxxii.
   Hugh, 29, 385, viii.
Peter Ephraim, Indian Chief, 214, liv.
Pequaket Indians, 220, lvi.
Peverly, Temperance, 319, lxxx.
Philbrick, James, 92, 188, xxiv, xlvii.
   Thomas, 187, xlvii.
Philips, John, 20, 367, v, xciii.
   Samuel, 118, xxx.
Philip, King, the Indian Chief, 208, lii.
Philpot, Richard, 63, xvi.
Phips, Sir William, 250, 278, lxii, lxix.
Pickering, Betsey, 233, lviii.
Pierpont, Ann, 178, xlv.
   Benjamin, 178, xlv.
   Ebenezer, 178, xlv.
   John, 178, xlv.
   William, 178, xlv.
Pierson, Abel, 396.
   Deborah, 397.
Pike, Alfred W., 97, xxvi.
   Hannah, 185, xlvi.
   Rev. James, 185, xlvi.
   Rev. John, 10, 157, 161, 183, 185, 194, 361, xxviii, xl, xli, xlvi, xlix, xci.
   Joshua, 13, 185, iv, xlvi.
   Joseph, 185, xlvi.
   Mercy, 185, xlvi.
   Nathaniel, 185, xlvi.
   Major Robert, 66, 68, 69, 70, 71, 97, 115, 121, 183, 185, 202, 210, 245, 246, 247, 269, 277, xvii, xviii, xix, xxvi, xxx, xxxi, xlvi, li, liii, lxi, lxvii, lxix.
   Sarah, 186, xlvii.
   Solomon, 185, xlvi.

Pike, William, 178, 357, xlv, xci.
Pindar, John, 59, 159, xv, xl.
Pinkham Family, 134 et seq., xxxiv.
Pinkham, Amos, 86, 135, 195, xxii, xxxiv, xlix.
   Benjamin, 135, xxxiv.
   Betty, 399.
   Daniel, 7, 14, 136, ii, iv, xxxiv.
   Edward, 136, xxxiv.
   Elijah, 135, 136, xxxiv.
   Elizabeth, 135, 136, 258, xxxiv, lxiv.
   Enoch, 136, xxxiv.
   Hannah, 135, 136, xxxiv.
   J. Burley, 137, xxxv.
   James, 88, 135, 136, xxiii, xxxiv.
   Jellian, 38, 174, x, xliv.
   Jeremiah, 136, xxxiv.
   John, 12, 14, 135, 136, 279, 408, iv, xxxiv, xxxv, lxix.
   Jonathan, 136, xxxiv.
   Joseph, 135, xxxiv.
   Lois, 136, xxxiv.
   Mary, 136, xxxiv.
   Nathaniel, 137, xxxv.
   Nicholas, 136, 137, xxxiv, xxxv.
   Otis, 135, 136, xxxiv.
   Paul, 12, 136, iii, xxxiv.
   Phebe, 136, 137, xxxiv, xxxv.
   Rebecca, 136, xxxiv.
   Richard, 20, 35, 73, 135, 136, 140, 141, 161, 258, 350, 379, 408, v, ix, xix, xxxiv, xxxv, xxxvi, xli, lxiv, lxxxviii, xcvii.
   Rose, 135, 136, xxxiv.
   Samuel, 136, 137, xxxiv, xxxv.
   Sarah, 136, xxxiv.
   Solomon, 135, xxxiv.
   Stephen, 63, xvi.
   Thomas, 135, 378, xxxiv, xcvii.
   Tristram, 135, xxxiv.
   Wesley, 136, xxxiv.
Piper, Francis, 261, lxv.
   George, 2, 14, 322, i, iv, lxxxi.
Pitman, Derry, 63, xvi.
   Elizabeth, 308, lxxxvii.
   Ezekiel, 81, 274, 276, xxi, lxviii, lxix.
   Francis, 59, xv.
   John, 139, xxxv.
   Nathan, 160, 161, xl, xli.
   William, 58, 138, 141, 355, 356, 357, 363, xv, xxxv, xxxvi, xc, xci, xcii.
   Zachariah, 63, xvi.
Plaisted, Roger, 207, lii.
   William, 270, lxviii.

Plantagenets, 21, vi.
Plumer, Daniel, 61, 415, xvi.
   Francis, 65, xvii.
   George W., 319, lxxx.
   John, 233, lviii.
Point, Thomas, 352, lxxxviii.
Pomeroy, Richard, 127, xxxii.
Pomfrett, William, 1, 2, 20, 34, 35, 47, 65, 66, 68, 70, 71, 75, 95, 96, 97, 98, 115, 137, 140, 146, 149, 198, 202, 336, 338, 343, 350, 351, 353, 355, 356, 362, 364, 365, 371, 372, 375, 376, 378, i, v, ix, xii, xviii, xix, xxv, xxvi, xxix, xxxv, xxxvii, xxxviii, xlix, li, lxxxiv, lxxxv, lxxxvi, lxxxviii, xc, xcii, xciii, xcv, xcvi, xcvii.
Poor, John, 375, xcvi.
Pope, Barnard, 58, xv.
Pray, Moses, 65, xvii.
   William, 55, xiv.
Preble, Obediah, 279, lxix.
Prentiss, Rev. Caleb, 232, lviii.
   Hon. John, 396.
Preston, George, 168, 169, 173, xlii, xliii, xliv.
Prout, Ebenezer, 246, lxii.
Purinton, Amos, 264, lxvi.
   Emily Jane, 264, lxvi.
   George, 264, lxvi.
   Harriet, 264, lxvi.
   Jacob K., 102, 136, xxvi, xxxiv.
   James M., 264, lxvi.
   Lavina, 264, lxvi.
   Mary Ann, 264, lxvi.
   Mary E., 136, xxxiv.
   Robert, 264, lxvi.
   Sarah A., 136, xxxiv.
   Simon, 264, lxvi.
   William, 264, lxvi.
   Winslow Hall, 264, lxvi.
Pyle, Mary, 232, lviii.
   William, 355, 381, xc.
Pynchon, John, 58, xv.

Quakers, 22, 38, 74, 91, 123, 168, 170, 172, 203, vi, x, xix, xxiv, xxxi, xlii, xliii, li.
Quimby, George W., 233, lviii.
Quincy, Edmund, 359, xci.
   Elizabeth, 230, lvii.
   Joanna, 359, xci.
   Josiah, 230, lvii.
   Judith, 359, xci.
Quint, George, 15, iv.
Quint, John, 127, xxxii.
   Rev. Alonzo Hall, 16, 18, 28, 86, 97, 116, 122, 142, 146, 290, 325, iv, v, vii, xxii, xxvii, xxx, xxxi, xxxvi, xxxvii, lxxii.
Ragg, Jeffrey, 352, lxxxviii.
Rale, Sebastian, 184, xlvi.
Randall, Capt. Benjamin, 324, lxxxi.
   Elder Benjamin, 241, 263, 324, lx, lxv, lxxxi.
   Daniel, 102, xxvi.
   Elisha, 63, xvi.
   James, 242, 412, lx.
   Mary, 242, lx.
   Mary S., 263, lxv.
   Richard, 162, 195, xli, xlix.
   Samuel, 61, 62, xvi.
   William, 58, xv.
Rand, Leonard S., 7, ii.
   John, 412.
   Samuel, 240, 279, lx, lxix.
Randolph, Edward, 215, liv.
Rane, John, 150, 396, xxxviii.
Ranlett, Charles, 206, 265, lii, lxv.
Raven, Catherine, 222, lvi.
Rawson, Edward, 33, 58, 190, 191, 350, 410, ix, xv, xlviii, lxxxviii.
   Jonathan, 13, 215, 320, iv, liv, lxxx.
Raymond, Hatter, 317, lxxx.
Reade, Michael, 12, 14, 109, 110, 116, 407, 415, iii, iv, xxviii, xxx.
Redford, William, 279, lxix.
Redman, John, 367, 376, xciii, xcvi.
Remick, James, 100, xxvii.
   John, 101, xxvi.
Reyner, Abigail, 118, 119, 358, 361, xxx, xci
   Anna, 358, xci.
   Dorothy, 118, 158, xxx, xci.
   Edward, 358, xci.
   Elizabeth, 118, 119, 358, xxx, xci.
   Frances, 120, 410, xxxi.
   Hannah, 118, 358, xxx, xci.
   Humphrey, 118, xxx.
   Jachin, 117, 119, 358, xxx, xci.
   Joseph, 118, 358, xxx, xci.
   Judith, 118, 119, xxxv.
   Mercy, 118, xxx.
   Rev. John, Sr., 48, 49, 50, 52, 53, 56, 68, 69, 74, 116, 117, 168, 169, 170, 173, 193, 202, 230, 341, 343, 358, 361, 366, 376, 377, 379, 392, xii, xiii, xiv, xvii, xviii, xix, xxx, xlii, xliii, xliv, xlviii, li, lvii, lxxxvi, xci, xciii, xcvi, xcvii.

Reyner, Rev. John, Jr., 118, 119, 120, 123, 137, 143,
    150, 258, xxx, xxxi, xxxv, xxxvi, xxxviii,
    lxiv.
  Wigglesworth, 118, xxx.
Reynolds, Capt. Benjamin Oliver, 252, lxiii.
  Cecilia Amanda, 252, lxiii.
  John, 335, lxxxiv.
  Juliette, 252, lxiii.
  Olive L., 252, lxiii.
Rice, Bridget, 224, lvii.
  Rev. Dr. J. H., 298, lxxiv.
Rich, Ichabod, 139, xxxv.
  Richard, 92, 140, 412, xxiv, xxxv.
  Sarah, 412.
Ricord, Mary, 409.
Richards, John, 197, l.
Richardson, James, 2, 14, i, iv.
  Joseph, 63, xvi.
  John, 386.
Ridley, Mary, 399.
Ricker, Ephraim, 62, xvi.
  George, 61, 62, 137, 160, 268, xvi, xxxv, xl,
    lxvii.
  Hannah, 392.
  Israel, 233, lviii.
  John, 62, 197, xvi, l.
  Judith, 279, lxix.
  Maturin, 61, 62, xvi.
  Nicholas, 315, xcvii.
  Samuel, 416.
  William, 416.
Riley, John, 7, 9, 99, ii, iii, xxvi.
Riggs, Virginia, 407.
Rines, Joseph, 63, xvi.
Risley, William, 94, 363, xxv, xcii.
Robins, Rev. Dr., 237, lix.
Robertson, Timothy, 255, 345, lxiii, lxxxvii.
Roby, Thomas, 240, lx.
Rooks, Richard, 257, 258, lxiv, lxvii.
Roberts, Abigail, 92, 93, 94, xxv.
  Amasa, 2, 93, i, xxv.
  Ann, 92, 366, xxiv, xciii.
  Alexander, 94, xxv.
  Andretta, 93, xxv.
  Aaron, 6, 92, ii, xxiv.
  Alonzo, 7, 92, ii, xxiv.
  Betty, 94, 323, xxv, lxxxi.
  Benjamin, 63, 93, xvi, xxv.
  Daniel, 92, xxiv.
  David, 92, 93, 136, xxv, xxxiv.
  Deborah, 94, xxv.
  Dorothy, 152, xxxviii.
  Ebenezer, 62, 93, 94, xvi, xxv.

Roberts, Elizabeth, 92, 93, 94, 258, 326, xxiv
    xxv, lxiv, lxxxii.
  Ephraim, 93, 94, xxv.
  Emily, 93, xxv.
  Ensign, 326, lxxxii.
  Francis, 63, 92, xvi, xxv.
  Hall, 266, lxvi.
  Hatevil, 63, 92, 93, 163, 255, xvi, xxiv, xxv,
    xli, lxiii.
  Hester, 92, xxiv.
  Hannah, 93, 94, xxv.
  Hanson, 10, 74, 75, 93, 96, 104, 135, iii, xix,
    xxiv, xxv, xxvi, xxxiv.
  James, 93, 326, xxv, lxxxii.
  Joshua, 61, 63, 93, xvi, xxv.
  Joseph, 6, 71, 92, 93, 94, 161, 236, 346, ii, xviii,
    xxiv, xxv, xli, xlix, lxxxvii.
  John, 3, 61, 63, 65, 68, 70, 71, 72, 91, 92, 93, 94,
    114, 115, 124, 132, 133, 134, 140, 142, 148, 171,
    193, 205, 219, 231, 255, 257, 258, 343, 349, 354,
    355, 356, 362, 364, 374, 375, 376, 377, 379, 412,
    i, xvi, xvii, xviii, xxiv, xxv, xxx, xxxi,
    xxxiv, xxxv, xxxvi, xxxvii, xliii, xlix,
    lii, lv, lvii, lxiii, lxiv, lxxxvi, lxxxviii,
    xc, xcii, xcvi, xcvii.
  Jerry, 93, xxv.
  Love, 63, 94, 198, xvi, xxv, l.
  Loyd, 325, lxxxii.
  Lydia, 93, 94, xxv.
  Mr., 353, 356, 357, 363, 377, xc, xci, xcii, xcvii.
  Mary, 93, 94, 377, xxv, xcvii.
  Miriam, 92, xxv.
  Moses, 93, xxv.
  Nathaniel, 92, 93, 196, xxiv, xxv, xlix.
  Nicholas, 93, xxiv.
  Phebe, 94, xxv.
  Paul, 92, xxv.
  Sarah, 92, xxiv.
  Stephen, 93, xxiv.
  Thomas, 3, 4, 18, 19, 20, 28, 38, 66, 69, 90, 91, 92,
    115, 122, 124, 137, 139, 140, 156, 160, 161, 171,
    173, 174, 176, 195, 218, 219, 236, 238, 254, 269,
    349, 350, 356, 357, 362, 364, 365, 375, 377, 378,
    379, 408, 412, 425, i, v, vii, x, xvii, xviii,
    xxiv, xxix, xxxi, xxxv, xxxix, xl, xli,
    xliii, xliv, xlix, lv, lix, lxiii, lxviii,
    lxxxviii, xc, xci, xcii, xciii, xcvi, xcvii.
  Timothy, 231, 293, 346, 347, li, lxxiii, lxxxvii.
  William, 36, 38, 53, 54, 75, 93, 115, 154, 174, 207,
    343, 349, 352, 354, 356, 357, 363, 377, ix, x,
    xiv, xix, xxv, xxx, xxxix, xliv, lii,
    lxxxvi, lxxxviii, xc, xci, xcii, xcvii.
Robinson, Abednego, 12, iii.

Robinson, Christopher, 178, 261, xlv, lxv.
   "Goodman," 206, lii.
   John Paul, 327, lxxxii.
   Paul, 327, lxxxii.
   Stephen, 72, 374, xviii, xcvi.
   Timothy, 4, 14, 156, 237, 238, i, iii, xxxix, lix.
Rogers, Constable, 37, x.
   Elizabeth, 105, xxvii.
   Richard, 350, lxxxviii.
   Robert, 9, iii.
Root, Rev. Daniel, 72, xix.
Rollins (Rawlings), Abigail, 308, lxxvii.
   Augusta, 308, lxxvii.
   Elizabeth, 126, xxxii.
   Ichabod, 61, xvi.
   James, 37, 127, 267, 311, 348, 349, 352, 354, 356, 357, 362, 365, 372, 373, 375, x, xxxii, lxiv, lxxviii, lxxxvii, lxxxviii, xc, xci, xcii, xciii, xcv, xcvi.
   John, 127, 197, 311, xxxii, l, lxxviii.
   Jeremiah, 61, xvi.
   Joseph, 127, 154, xxxii, xl.
   Lorenzo, 233, lviii.
   Moses, 308, lxxvii.
   Samuel, 127, xxxii.
   William Wentworth, 65, xvii.
   William, 233, lviii.
Rowe, Edward, 127, xxxii.
   James S., 14, iv.
   John, 63, xvi.
   Richard, 75, 150, 193, 365, xix, xxxviii, xlix, xciii.
   Thomas, 127, xxxiv.
Royall, Bailey, 310, lxxviii.
   Teague, 58, 141, 378, xv, xxxvi, xcvii.
Rundlett, Homer, 266, lxvi.
Rush, Dr. Benjamin, 321, lxxxi.
Rust, Anna, 226, lvii.
   Henry, 228, lviii.
Russell, Benjamin, 228, lviii.
   Eleazer, 227, 228, lvii.
   Eleanor, 227, lvii.
   Henry, 228, lviii.
   Margaret, 226, 228, lviii.
   Philip, 377, xcvii.
   Richard, 372, 375, xcv, xcvi.

Sage, John, 401.
Saltonstall, Richard, 192, 227, 228, 299, xlviii, lviii, lxxiv.
Sanborn, John, 382.
Sanders, Mary, 263, lxv.
Sanders, Hannah, 263, lxv.
   John, 263, 382, lxv.
   Joseph, 142, 243, 365, 375, 378, xxxvi, lx, xciii, xcvi, xcvii.
Sargent, Daniel, 297, lxxiv.
   William, 375, xcvi.
Savage, Hon. James, 18, 383, 424, v.
Saward, Esther, 279, lxix.
   Mary, 279, lxix.
Sawyer, Edward, 252, lxiii.
   Elizabeth, 395.
   Emma, 265, lxvi.
   Hosea, 13, iv.
   Jacob, 6, ii.
   Mary Elizabeth, 252, lxiii.
   Charles Walter, 252, lxiii.
   Moses, 11, 103, iii, xxvi.
   Ruth Ann, 252, lxiii.
   Stephen, 6, ii.
   Thomas E., 7, 10, 14, 252, ii, iii, iv, lxviii.
   Walter, 6, 9, ii, iii.
Say, Lord, 17, 192, v, xlviii.
Scales, John, 1, 16, 18, 20, 32, 76, 112, 176, 221, 233, 239, 290, 295, 316, i, iv, v, viii, xix, xxviii, xliv, lvi, lviii, lx, lxxii, lxxiii, lxxix.
Scammell, Alexander, 78, 79, 80, xx, xxi.
Scammon, Anna, 225, lvii.
   Nicholas, 190, 191, xlviii.
   Richard, 142, 223, xxxvi, lvi.
   Sarah, 105, xxvii.
Shackford, Abigail Burnham, 320, lxxx.
   Caroline, 320, lxxx.
   Charles Harrison, 320, lxxx.
   Eliza, 320, lxxx.
   George, 320, lxxx.
   John, 307, 320, lxxvi, lxxx.
   Lucy, 320, lxxx.
   Mary, 320, lxxx.
   Martha Susan, 320, lxxx.
   Onslow, 320, lxxx.
   Samuel, 307, 319, 320, lxxvi, lxxx.
   William, 116, 127, 150, xxx, xxxii, xxxviii.
Shannon, Captain, 109, xx.
   Richard, 110, xxviii.
   Thomas, 12, 110, 407, iii, xxviii.
   Capt. Thomas, 416.
Shapleigh, Elisha, 233, lviii.
   Major, 96, 169, 171, 215, xxvi, xliii, liv.
   Nicholas, 45, 191, 211, xi, xlviii, liii.
Shaw, Grace, 305, lxxvi.
Small, Benjamin, 78, xx.
   Edward, 81, 154, xxi, xxxix.

Small, Francis, 352, lxxxviii.
　Isaac, 78, xx.
Smallcorn, Betsey, 262, lxv.
Smart, Elizabeth, 279, lxix.
　Robert, 47, 382, 383, xii.
　John, 64, 382, xvi.
Sparhawk, Nathaniel, 397.
Smay, Barthy, 350, lxxxviii.
Sprague, Grace, 264, lxvi.
　Tera, 63, xvi.
Stackpole, Douglas, 323, lxxxi.
　James, 63, xvi.
　Jeremiah, 326, lxxxii.
　Joshua, 326, lxxxii.
　Lucy, 251, 326, lxii, lxxxii.
　Dr. Paul A., 104, 251, xxvi, lxii.
　Philip, 61, 62, xvi.
　Samuel, 104, 251, 323, xxvi, lxii, lxxxi.
　Sarah, 261, lxv.
　Thomas, 2, i.
　William, 63, xvi.
Stanton, Benjamin, 61, 62, 233, xvi, lviii.
　Tamson, 308, lxxxvii.
Starbuck, Family, 128, *et seq.*, xxxii.
　Abigail, 130, 131, 284, xxxiii, lxxi.
　Barnabus, 130, xxxiii.
　Dorcas, 130, 281, xxxiii, lxx.
　Elder Edward, 1, 2, 30, 34, 35, 36, 37, 39, 40, 45, 74, 128, 130, 164, 191, 202, 223, 280, 284, 288, 348, 350, 352, 353, 355, 357, 362, 364, 372, 376, 410, i, viii, ix, x, xii, xix, xxxiii, xli, xlviii, lvi, lxx, lxxi, lxxii, lxxxvii, lxxxviii, xc, xci, xcii, xcv, xcvi.
　Elizabeth, 130, xxxiii.
　Eunice, 130, xxxiii.
　Hepsibah, 130, xxxiii.
　Jethro, 130, xxxiii.
　Katherine, 130, 372, xxxiii, xcv.
　Nathaniel, 130, 281, 355, 357, 362, 364, 376, xxxiii, lxx, xc, xci, xcii, xcvi.
　Priscilla, 130, xxxiii.
　Sarah, 130, xxxiii.
Starr, Edward, 20, v.
Swaddon, Philip, 20, v.
Swain, Eliakim, 285, lxxi.
　Francis, 378, xcvii.
　Mary, 308, lxxvii.
　Richard, 381.
Swansbury, Mr., 20, v.
Swarton, 279, lxix.
Swasey, Asa, 14, iv.
Seabrook, Thomas, 377, xcvii.

Sealey, Capt. John, 373, xcvi.
Seavey, Olive, 252, lxiii.
　Stephen, 142, xxxvi.
　William, 373, xcvi.
Sebundowitt, Indian Chief, 249, lxi.
Seeley, Mr., 352, lxxxviii.
Sever, Nicholas, 194, 296, xlix, lxxiv.
Severance, Mary, 280, lxx.
Sewall, Samuel, 359, xci.
Sheaf, Jacob, 89, xxiv.
　Mehitable, 89, xxiv.
　Olive Ringe, 407.
　Sarah, 242, lx.
Sherburn, Capt. John, 319, lxxx.
　Henry, 72, 96, 370, viii, xxvi, xcv.
　Samuel, 269, 277, 370, lxviii, lxix, xcv.
Sherman, Rev. Mr., 296, lxxiv.
Shepard, Joanna, 232, lvii.
　Rebecca, 105, xxvii.
　William, 123, xxxi.
Sheffield, Ichabod, 362, xcii.
　William, 355, 357, 362, 365, xc, xci, xcii, xciii.
Skepp, John, 335, lxxxiv.
Sleeper, Benjamin, 286, lxxi.
Spencer, Thomas, 78, 191, 369, xx, xlviii, xcv.
Stearns, Col. William, 369, xcv.
Steed, Robert, 335, lxxxiv.
Steel, David, 7, ii.
Stevens, Dionis, 280, lxx.
　Joseph, 79, xx.
　Moses, 61, xvi.
　Nathaniel, 140, 380, 410, 411, xxxv, xcvii.
　Thomas, 62, xvi.
　William, 6, iii.
Stevenson, Bartholomew, 345, lxxxvii.
　Margaret, 80, xxi.
　Thomas, 53, 80, 219, 343, 345, 349, 354, 356, 357, 363, 387, xiv, xxi, lv, lxxxvi, lxxxvii, lxxxviii, xc, xci, xcii.
Sias, Joseph, 64, xvi.
Simons, Martha W., 371, xcv.
　Samuel, 32, viii.
Sims, Anna, 126, xxxii.
Sinclair, Mary, 178, xlv.
Sise, Edward, 12, 14, iv.
Scriven, John, 66, 74, 94, 122, xvi, xix, xxv, xxxi.
Stickney, Jeremiah, 419.
Skipper, Jane, 371, 387, xcv.
Smith Family, 87, xxii, *et seq.*
　Alfred, 90, xxiv.
　Andrew, 89, xxiv.

Smith, Ballard, 76, 79, 81, 82, 84, 91, xix, xx, xxi, xxiv.
Bartholomew, 20, v.
Benjamin, 79, 88, 89, 261, xx, xxiii, xxiv, lxv.
Comfort, 89, xxiv.
Dr. Cheney, 101, xxvi.
Daniel, 63, 89, 406, xvi, xxiv.
Ebenezer, 86, 89, 90, xxii, xxiv.
Edward, 89, 258, xxiv, lxiv.
Elizabeth, 88, 89, 256, 322, xxiii, xxiv, lxiv, lxxxi.
George, 2, 35, 36, 87, 191, 223, 351, 353, 355, 372, 374, i, ix, xxii, xlviii, lvi, lxxxviii, xc, xcv, xcvi.
Gilman, 89, xxiv.
Hannah, 88, 89, 285, 286, xxiii, xxiv, lxxi.
Henry, 90, xxiv,
Hilton, 89, xxiv.
Ichabod, 89, xxiv.
Israel, 89, xxiv.
James, 38, 58, 87, 88, 116, 140, 142, 174, 302, 325, 378, 406, x, xv, xxii, xxiii, xxx, xxxvi, xliv, lxxv, lxxxii, xcii.
Jacob, 89, xxiv.
Jarvis, 322, lxxxi.
Dr. Jefferson, 109, xxviii.
Jeremiah, 88, 89, xxiii, xxiv.
John, 4, 16, 58, 59, 79, 85, 87, 88, 89, 165, 197, 237, 238, 254, 255, 267, 268, 276, 318, i, iv, xv, xx, xxii, xxiii, xxiv, xlii, l, lix, lxiii, lxvi, lxix, lxxx.
Joseph, 4, 10, 13, 88, 89, 115, 122, 140, 154, 155, 161, 162, 195, 313, 321, 322, i, iii, iv, xxiii, xxiv, xxx, xxxi, xxxvi, xxxix, xli, xlix, lxxix, lxxxi.
Love, 89, xxiv.
Lydia, 89, xxiv.
Margaret, 89, xxiv
Mary, 88, 89, 303, 406, xxiii, xxiv, lxxv.
Nicholas, 380, xcvii.
Patience, 88, xxiii.
Robert, 88, xxiv.
Samuel, 4, 88, 89, 198, 302, ii, xxiii, xxiv, l, lxxv.
Sarah, 88, 301, 303, 318, xxiii, lxxv, lxxx.
Sarah Fisher, 322, lxxxi.
Susanna, 89, xxiv.
Temperance, 88, xxiii.
Thomas, 89, xxiv.
Thomas Westbrook, 406.
Valentine, 81, 89, 266, 280, xxi, xxiv, lxvi, lxx.

Smith, William, 322, 365, lxxxi, xciii.
Winthrop, 89, xxiv.
Squire, Elizabeth, 279, lxix.
Stiles, John, 263, lxv.
Stileman, Elias, 72, 75, 97, 115, 120, 202, 376, 377, xviii, xix, xxvi, xxix, xxxi, li, xcvi, xcvii.
Stinson, Joseph 58, 141, xv, xxxvi.
Soule, Charles Emery, 2, 120, i, xxxi.
Somerby, Henry, 280, lxx.
H. G., 223, lvi.
Judith, 28, lxx.
Southworth, Capt. Thomas, 358, xci.
Scott, Mary, 233, lvii.
Scottow, Captain, 215, liv.
Short, H. S., 279, lxix.
Sloper, Richard, 96, 97, 355, 357, 362, xxvi, xc, xci, xcii.
Stockman, Joseph, 186, xlvii.
Stokes, Isaac, 138, 140, 141, 343, 364, xxxv, xxxvi, lxxxvi, xcii.
Stone, Experience, 265, lxvi.
Mr., 308, lxxvii,
Mary Ann, 320, lxxx.
Samuel, 292, lxxxii.
Story, Charles, 128, xxxiii.
William, 20, 123, 130, 145, 338, 349, 350, 352, 353, 355, 356, 362, 366, 375, 389, v, xxxi, xxxiii, xxxvii, lxxxv, lxxxviii, xc, xcii, xciii, xcvi.
Shute, Governor, 393.
Stoughton, Israel, 32, 364, viii, xcii.
Sullivan, Ebenezer, 78, xx.
James, 265, lxvi.
John, 63, 78, 79, xvi, xx.
Scruton, George, 263, lxv.
Lydia, 263, lxv.
Stephen, 14, iv.
Thomas, 372, xcv.
Syll, Capt. Joseph, 208, 209, 359, liii, xci.
Symonds, John, 132, 133, xxxiv.
William, 401, 403, 404, 405.
Samuel, 364, 400, 401, 402, 403, 404, 405, xcii.
Harlackenden, 401, 402.

Tasker, John, 6, 63, 83, 275, 294, 347, ii, xvi, xxi, lxviii, lxxiii, lxxxvii.
Paul, 308, lxxvii.
William, 59, 140, 218, 277, xv, xxxv, lv, lxix.
Tapley, John, 14, iv.
Taprell, Alice, 240, lx.
Priscilla, 240, lx.

Taprell, Robert, 224, 374, lvii, xcvi.
Taylor, James, 12, 179, iii, xlv.
Teare, Thomas, 140, xxxv.
Tebbets (or Tibbits), Abigail, 136, xxxiv.
  Adeline, 252, lxiii.
  Anna, 93, xxv.
  Charles Wesley, 239, lx.
  Ebenezer, 104, 110, xxvii, xxviii.
  Elsa, 93, xxv.
  Ephraim, 136, xxxiv.
  Elizabeth, 93, xxv.
  Ezekiel, 93, xxv.
  Hannah, 93, xxv.
  Henry, 63, 146, 162, 193, 238, 349, 350, 352, 353, 355, 356, 362, 364, 367, 372, xvi, xxxvii, xli, xlix, lix lxxxviii, xc, xcii, xciii, xcv.
  Ichabod, 13, 61, iv, xvi.
  Jeremiah, 66, 71, 94, 133, 174, 193, 257, 355, 356, 362, 364, 373, xvii, xviii, xxv, xxxiv, xliv, xlix, lxiv, xc, xcii, xcvi.
  John, 13, 61, 92, 103, 233, 268, iv, xvi, xxv, xxvi, lviii, lxvii.
  Capt. John, 112, 414, xxix.
  Joseph, 160, 238, 262, xl, lix, lxv.
  Judith, 268, lxvi.
  Lucy, 93, xxv.
  Mary, 93, xxv.
  Moses, 61, 62, 93, xvi, xxv.
  Nathaniel, 109, xxviii.
  Phebe, 136, xxxiv.
  Philip, 93, xxv.
  Polly, 110, xxviii.
  Reuben, 311, lxxviii.
  Samuel, 4, 8, 15, 114, 157, 161, 162, 180, 195, 198, 239, 253, i, ii, iv, xxvii, xl, xli, xlvi, xlix, l, lix, lxiii.
  Thomas, 2, 3, 4, 61, 62, 135, 152, 156, 157, 159, 162, 194, 199, 236, 254, 268, 344, 345, i, xvi, xxxiv, xxxviii, xxxix, xl, xli, xlix, l, lix, lxiii, lxvii, lxxxvi, lxxxvii.
  William, 308, lxxvii.
Tedder, Stephen, 20, v.
Tenney, Rev. Samuel, 285, lxxi.
Tredick, John, 7, ii.
  Thomas, 365, xciii.
Timson, Joseph, 346, lxxxvii.
Tinge, William, 32, viii.
Titcomb, Col. Benjamin, 6, 13, 98, 331, ii, iv, xxvi, lxxxiii.
  John, 11, 326, iii, lxxxii.
  Sarah, 326, lxxxii.
  Sally, 323, lxxxi.
Titcomb, Wilder, 323, lxxxi.
  William, 13, 61, iv, xvi.
Thines, Elizabeth, 85, 409, xxii.
  George, 85, xxii.
  Joseph, 85, xxii.
  Thomas, 85, xxii.
Thing, Bartholomew, 285, 395, lxxi.
  Benjamin, 285, lxxi.
  Jonathan, 404.
  Mary, 395.
  Samuel, 178, xlv.
Trickey, Francis, 354, xc.
  Henry, 349, lxxxviii.
  Isaac, 142, xxxvi.
  John, 127, xxxii.
  Sarah, 305, lxxvi.
  Thomas, 55, 71, 127, 305, 352, 355, 356, 357, 362, xiv, xviii, xxxii, lxxvi, lxxxviii, xc, xci, xcii.
Trimmings, Oliver, 55, xiv.
Tripe, Nancy, 319, lxxx.
  Richard, 9, 104, 106, 414, iii, xxvii, xxxiv.
  Silvanus, 165, xiii.
Tomkins, Mark, 169, xliii.
  Mary, 168, 169, 170, 172, 173, xlii, xliii, xliv.
Toppan, Stephen, 7, ii.
Torr, Andrew, 6, 9, 331, ii, iii, lxxxiii.
  Benjamin, 13, iv.
  Benedictus, 197, l.
Townsend, Jonas D., 7, 10, ii, iii.
Toxus, Indian Chief, 278, lxix.
Tozier, Richard, 207, 365, lii, xciii.
Thomas, Elisha, 100, xxvii.
  James, 58, 59, 80, 371, xv, xxii, xcv.
  John, 198, l.
Thompson, Charles, 136, xxxiv.
  David, 16, 176, iv, xliv.
  Ebenezer, 78, 79, xx.
  Col. Ebenezer, 177, xlv.
  John, 60, xv.
  Jonathan, 5, ii.
  Lucien, 15, iv.
  Robert, 383.
  Samuel, 127, xxxii.
  Thomas, 253, lxiii.
  William, 356, 362, 365, 411, xc, xcii, xciii.
  Rev. William A., 401.
Twombly, Abigail, 316, lxxix.
  Aaron, 316, lxxix.
  Andrew, 316, lxxix.
  Benjamin, 61, 62, 294, 314, 315, 316, 317, xvi, xxiii, lxxix.

Twombly, Charles A., 317, lxxix.
  Charles E., 317, lxxix.
  Daniel, 315, 316, lxxix.
  David, 315, lxxix.
  Elizabeth, 314, 316, 378, lxxix, xcvii.
  Esther, 314, lxxix.
  Ezekiel, 77, xx.
  Frank H., 314, lxxix,
  George E., 318, lxxix.
  George W., 317, lxxix.
  George W. K., 317, lxxix.
  Gilman Hall, 317, lxxix.
  Hannah, 314, 316, 317, lxxix.
  Harry L., 318, lxxix.
  Helen F., 317, lxxix.
  Herbert A., 317, lxxix.
  Hope, 314, lxxix.
  Hurd, 316, 317, lxxix.
  Hurd W., 317, lxxix.
  Ira, 316, lxxix.
  Isaac, 63, 314, xvi, lxxix.
  James T., 317, lxxvii.
  Jacob, 316, lxxix.
  Jeremiah, 316, lxxix.
  John, 231, 314, 315, 316, 317, lvii, lxxix.
  John C., 317, lxxix.
  John Herbert, 317, 318, lxxix.
  Jonathan, 314, lxxix.
  Joseph, 63, 314, xvi, lxxix.
  Kate, 314, lxxix.
  Lavinia, 317, 318, lxxix.
  Mary, 314, 316, 317, lxxix.
  Mary J., 316, lxxix.
  Martha, 315, lxxix.
  Martha J., 317, lxxix.
  Mehitable, 316, lxxix.
  Moses, 316, lxxix.
  Nathaniel, 316, 317, lxxix.
  Nathaniel A., 317, lxxix.
  Peter, 316, lxxix.
  Phebe, 316, lxxix.
  Polly, 316, lxxix.
  Rachel, 314, 316, lxxix.
  Ralph, 13, 70, 140, 355, 356, 362, 364, 374, 378, 412, iv, xviii, xxxv, xc, xcii, xcvi, xcvii.
  Rebecca, 315, lxxix.
  Roscoe, 318, lxxix.
  Sarah, 314, 315, 316, lxxix.
  Sarah A., 317, lxxix.
  Sarah C., 317, lxxix.
  Sally, 317, lxxix.
  Samuel, 316, lxxix.

Twombly, Smith, 316, lxxix.
  Susan, 316, lxxix.
  Tamsin, 233, 315, lviii, lxxix.
  Timothy, 314, lxxix.
  Walter J., 317, lxxix.
  William, 11, 63, 103, 231, 314, 316, iii, xvi, xxvi, lvii, lxxix.
  William K., 316, lxxix.
  William Henry Harrison, 317, lxxix.
Tuck, Amos, 382.
  Robert, 187, 382, xlvii.
  William, 382.
Tucker, John, 262, 279, lxv, lxix.
  Mary, 365, lxxvi.
Tufts, Dr. Asa Alvord, 13, 108, 120, 287, 289, iv, xxvii, xxxi, lxxi, lxxii.
  Dr. Charles Augustus, 2, 15, 31, i, iv, viii.
Turck, John, 352, lxxxviii.
Turner, Thomas, 94, 144, 339, xxv, xxxvi, lxxxv.
Tuttle, Anna, 297, lxxiv.
  David, 13, iv.
  Eunice, 136, xxxiv.
  James, 7, 136, iii, xxxiv.
  John, 1, 2, 3, 8, 66, 132, 137, 140, 148, 151, 155, 156, 157, 160, 161, 162, 194, 196, 198, 199, 236, 238, 255, 258, 349, 352, 353, 356, 362, 364, 365, 372, 387, i, ii, xvii, xxxiv, xxxv, xxxvii, xxxviii, xxxix, xl, xli, xlix, l, lix, lxiv, lxxxviii, xc, xcii, xciii, xcv.
  Judge John, 371, xcv.
  Joseph, 7, 13, 136, ii, iv, xxxiv.
  Lavinia, 317, lxxx.
  Otis, 92, xxv.
  Sarah, 308, lxxvii.
  Thomas, 6, 11, 12, ii, iii.
  Tobias, 6, 7, 9, 13, ii, iii, iv.
  William, 12, iv.
Thury, M., 274, lxviii.
True, Capt. Henry, 185, xlvii.
Truworthy, Elizabeth, 240, lx.
  James, 177, xlv.

Ukquackussennum, Thomas, Indian Chief, 220, lvi.
Ugroufe, John, 20, 350, v, lxxxviii.
Underhill, Capt. John, 19, 20, 21, 26, 27, 29, 30, 91, 180, 384, 400, iv, vii, viii, xxiv, xlv.
Usher, Eleazer, 176, xliv.
  John, 58, 153, 278, xv, xxxix, lxix.
Upham, Gen. Timothy, 397.

Varney, Andrew, 7, 13, 92, ii, iv, xxiv.
  Anna, 323, lxxxi.

Varney, Benjamin, 61, xvi.
  Bridget, 380, xcvii.
  Eben, 113, xxix.
  Ebenezer, 315, 400, lxxix.
  Elijah, 92, xxv.
  Eunice, 93, xxv.
  Ezekiel, 6, ii.
  George, 365, xciii.
  Humphrey, 38, 66, 130, 140, 174, 341, 365, x, xvii, xxxiii, xxxv, xliv, lxxxvi, xciii.
  Isaac, 13, 92, iv, xxv.
  James B., 7, 13, ii, iv.
  Joseph, 11, 63, iii, xvi.
  Jesse, 14, iv.
  Joshua, 93, 223, xxv, lxxxi.
  Moses, 11, 323, 326, iii, lxxxi, lxxxii.
  Peter, 162, 195, 197, xli, xlix, l.
  Rachel, 380, xcvii.
  Reuben, 14, iv.
  Ruth, 326, lxxxii.
  Shubael, 10, iii.
  Stephen, 11, iii.
  Susan, 323, lxxxi.
  Thomas, 92, 345, 380, xxv, lxxxvi, xcvii.
  William, 380, xcvii.
Vaughan, Eleanor, 226, lvii.
  Eliza, 227, lvii.
  Ezekiel, 251, lxii.
  William, 210, 216, 245, 246, 247, 270, 272, liii, lv, lxi, lxviii.
Veza, Mr., 99, xxiv.
Vickery, John, 62, xvi.
  Neal, 63, xvi.
Villieu, Sicurde, 274, lxvii.
Vines, Henry, 59, xv.

Wadleigh, Elijah, 7, 10, ii, iii.
  George, 10, iii.
  Harlackenden, 403.
  Jonathan, 178, xlv.
  Robert, 95, 115, 122, 402, 403, 404, 405, xxv, xxx, xxxi.
Wahwa, Indian Chief, 270, lxviii.
Wakeham, Edward, 59, xv.
Walderne, Alexander, 114, 222, 224, xxix, lvi.
  Alice, 232, lvi.
  Anna, 225, 372, lviii, xcv.
  Christopher, 224, lvi.
  Edward, 222, lvi.
  Eleanor, 222, lvi.
  Eleazer, 225, lvii.
  Elizabeth, 222, 224, 225, 310, lvii, lxxviii.

Walderne, Esther, 225, lvii.
  Foulke, 222, lvi.
  George, 222, 224, lvi.
  Humphrey, 222, lvi.
  Isaac, 366, xciii.
  John, 222, 223, lvi.
  Margaret, 222, lvi.
  Margery, 222, lvi.
  Maria, 225, lvii.
  Mary, 224, lvii.
  Paul, 225, lvii.
  Prudence, 223, 224, lvii.
  Major Richard, 1, 2, 3, 4, 8, 10, 18, 20, 24, 31, 35, 36, 40, 41, 42, 48, 50, 54, 58, 65, 66, 67, 68, 69, 70, 71, 72, 74, 76, 94, 96, 97, 114, 120, 122, 128, 131, 137, 140, 141, 142, 146, 148, 149, 150, 153, 156, 157, 161, 170, 173, 174, 177, 189, 191, 200, 210, i, ii, iii, v, vi, viii, ix, x, xi, xii, xiii, xiv, xv, xvii, xviii, xix, xxv, xxvi, xxix, xxxi, xxxii, xxxiii, xxxv, xxxvi, xxxvii, xxxviii, xxxix, xl, xli, xliii, xliv, xlv, xlviii, l, liii.
  Major Richard, 215, 216, 217, 218, 221, 222, 224, 225, 288, 293, 310, 336, 337, 338, 342, 343, 350, 356, 359, 360, 362, 365, 366, 367, 372, 573, 374, 375, 376, 408, 410, 413, 415, 425, lv, lvi, lvii, lxiv, lxxii, lxxiii, lxxviii, lxxxiv, lxxxv, lxxxvi, lxxxviii, xc, xci, xcii, xciii, xcv, xcvi.
  Robert, 222, lvi.
  Rose, 222, lvi.
  Samuel, 224, lvi.
  Susan, 222, lvi.
  Thomas, 222, lvi.
  Timothy, 225, 375, lvii, xcvi.
  William, 2, 17, 18, 20, 22, 31, 164, 190, 193, 200, 222, 224, 256, 348, 352, 366, i, v, vi, viii, xli, xlviii, xlix lvi, lxiv, lxxxvii, lxxxviii, xciii.
Waldron, Abigail, 228, 230, 406, lviii, lxix.
  Mrs. Adelaide Cilley, 234, lxix.
  Anna, 228, 230, 407, lviii, lxix.
  Betsey, 231, lvii.
  Bridget, 231, lvii.
  Charles, 323, 325, 406, 407, 416, lxxxi, lxxxii.
  Daniel, 110, 205, 287, 406, 407, 416, 418, 419, xxviii, lvii, lxxi.
  Ebenezer, 231, lvii.
  Rev. Edmund, 407.
  Edmund, Quincy Sheaf, 234, lviii.
  Eleanor, 323, 325, 406, lxxxi, lxxxii.
  Eliza, 233, lviii.

Waldron, Elizabeth, 228, 230, 233, 406, lviii, lxix.
  Ephraim, 231, lvii.
  George, 106, 140, 228, 230, 405, 416, xxvii, xxxv, lviii, lxix.
  George P., 233, lviii.
  Hannah, 231, 233, lvii, lviii.
  James, 231, 233, lvii, lviii.
  Jeremiah, 232, lviii.
  Joanna, 233, lviii.
  Job, 14, 233, iv, lviii.
  John, 6, 9, 12, 13, 14, 160, 195, 230, 233, 234, 238, 322, 366, ii, iii, iv, xl, xlix, lvii, lviii, lix, lxxxiii, xciii.
  Col. John, 232, lviii.
  Jonathan, 407.
  Joseph, 231, 233, lvii, lviii.
  Margaret, 228, lvii.
  Mary, 231, 233, 407, lvii, lviii.
  Mary Constance, 407.
  Mehitable, 231, 233, lvii, lviii.
  Moses, 233, lviii.
  Nathaniel Sheaf, 407.
  Olive, 233, lviii.
  Polly, 106, 107, xxvii.
  Richard, 10, 12, 60, 62, 111, 160, 186, 227, 228, 230, 231, 233, 234, 236, 237, 267, 326, 406, 407, 416, iii, xv, xvi, xxviii, xl, xlvii, lvii, lviii, lxix, lxvi, lxxxii.
  Col. Richard, 278, 283, lxix, lxx.
  Richard Russell, 407.
  Samuel, 228, 231, 233, 406, 407, lviii.
  Sarah, 231, 232, lviii.
  Susan, 233, lviii.
  Hon. Thomas Westbrook, 2, 5, 8, 11, 12, 106, 107, 110, 111, 228, 234, 318, 323, 324, 405, 406, 407, 416, i, ii, iii, xxvii, xxviii, lviii, lix, lxxx, lxxxi.
  Wells, 10, iii.
  William, 227, 228, 230, 406, lvii, lviii.
  William H., 233, lviii.
Walker, Anna, 319, lxxx.
  Ansel, 319, lxxx.
  Clara, 319, lxxx.
  Ebenezer, 319, lxxx.
  Edward, 319, lxxx.
  Elizabeth, 306, 319, lxxvi, lxxx.
  Gideon, 319, lxxx.
  John S., 319, lxxx.
  Lucy, 319, lxxx.
  Mark, 6, 319, 406, ii, lxxx.
  Mary, 319, lxxx.
  Martha, 319, lxxx.
  Walker, Nancy, 319, lxxx.
  Sarah, 125, xxxii.
  Seth, 319, lxxx.
  Seth S., 88, 318, xxiii, lxxx.
Wall, Elizabeth, 380, xcvii.
  Hannah, 380, xcvii.
  James, 191, 200, 354, 367, 380, 391, xlviii, l, xc, xciii, xcvii.
  Mary, 380, xcvii.
  Sarah, 380, xcvii.
Wallingford, Thomas, 5, 8, 11, 268, ii, iii, xlvii.
Walton, Abigail, 241, lx.
  Alice, 240, lx.
  Benjamin, 241, 242, lx.
  Dorcas, 240, lx.
  Elizabeth, 241, lx.
  Francis, 242, lx.
  George, 35, 36, 240, 241, 348, 351, 372, 377, 382, ix, lx, lxxxvii, lxxxviii, xcv, xcvii.
  Martha, 240, lx.
  Mary, 240, 241, lx.
  Samuel, 240, lx.
  Sarah, 241, lx.
  Shadrach, 240, 241, 381, lx.
Wardel, Eliakim, 171, xliii.
Warren, Benjamin, 63, xvi.
  John, 381, 382.
Washington, Gen. George, 261, lxv.
Waters, Herbert, 259, lxiv.
Wharton, Edward, 168, 173, 174, 176, xlii, xliii.
Waterhouse, Jeremiah, 308, lxxvii.
  Margaret, 308, lxxvii.
  Richard, 308, lxxvii.
  Dr. William, 308, lxxvii.
Watkins, Thomas, 412.
Watson, Family, 250 et seq., lxii.
  Alice, 253, lxiii.
  Ahimaaz, 12, iv.
  Andrew, 252, lxiii.
  Benjamin, 13, 105, 251, 252, 253, 323, iv, xxvii, lxii, lxiii, lxxxi.
  Betsey, 233, lviii.
  Christian, 252, lxiii.
  Daniel, 250, 297, lxii, lxxiv.
  David, 11, 238, 250, 251, 252, 297, iii, lix, lxii, lxxiv.
  Dudley, 6, 102, 233, 250, 251, ii, xxvi, lviii, lxii.
  Lieut. Dudley, 413.
  Eleazer H., 252, lxiii.
  Elizabeth, 251, 252, 253, lxii.
  Esther, 252, lxiii.
  Frederick, 251, lxii.

Watson, George, 102, xxvi.
  Hannah, 102, 251, 252, xxvi, lxii.
  Horace, 253, lxiii.
  Isaac, 104, 105, 250, 251, 252, 253, xxvii, lxiii.
  Capt. Isaac, 322, lxxxi.
  James, 252, 326, lxiii, lxxxii.
  Joanna, 105, 251, 326, xxvii, lxii, lxxxii.
  John, 251, lxii.
  John Adams, 252, lxiii.
  Jonathan, 140, 250, 253, xxxv, lxii, lxiii.
  Joseph, 251, 252, lxi.
  Keziah, 251, lxii.
  Lewis, 252, lxiii.
  Lilian, 110, xxviii.
  Lucy, 251, 253, lxii, lxiii.
  Lydia, 251, 252, 253, 319, lxii, lxxx.
  Mary, 250, 251, 297, lxii, lxxiv.
  Mercy, 250, lxii.
  Nancy, 253, lxiii.
  Otis, 252, lxiii.
  Richard, 245, 247, lxi, lxii.
  Robert, 58, 140, 250, 274, 277, xv, xxxvi, lxii, lxviii, lxix.
  Samuel, 99, 245, 250, 253, xxvi, lxi, lxii, lxiii.
  Sarah, 250, 251, 252, lxiii.
  Sarah Hanson, 252, lxiii.
  Seth, 105, 251, 252, xxvii, lxii.
  Sophia, 252, lxiii.
  Thomas, 140, 251, 252, xxxv, lxii.
  Varney, 291, lxxii.
  William, 103, 250, 251, 323, 326, xxvi, lxii, lxxxi, lxxxii.
  Winthrop, 233, 250, 251, lviii, lxii.
Weare, Nathaniel, 219, lv.
Webb, George, 35, 36, 349, 350, 351, 353, ix, lxxxviii, xciii.
Webber, George, 20, v.
Webster, John, 408.
Wedon, George, 364, xcii.
Weeks, Joshua, 179, 261, 266, xlv, lxv, lxvi.
  Josiah, 261, 266, lxv, lxvi.
  Margaret, 89, xxiv.
  Martha, 179, xlv.
  Nathaniel, 261, 266, lxv, lxvi.
Welch, Mary, 135, xxxiv.
  Ralph, 140, xxxv.
Wenerton, Thomas, 370, xcv.
Wencoll, Capt. John, 72, 121, 202, 270, xviii, xxxi, li, lxviii.
Wendell, Daniel H., 10, iii.
  Isaac, 419.
  William, 232, lviii.

Wentworth, Benjamin, 4, 61, 62, 157, 197, 237, 238, 255, 267, i, xvi, xl, l, lix, lxiv, lxvi.
  Benning, 138, xxxv.
  Ebenezer, 61, 62, 293, 346, 347, xvi, lxxiii, lxxxvii.
  Elizabeth, 411.
  Ephraim, 156, xxxix.
  Ezekiel, 4, 15, 62, 140, 155, 157, 159, 161, 163, 194, i, iv, xvi, xxxv, xxxix, xl, xli, xlix.
  George Thomas, 2, 15, i, iv.
  Gershom, 140, 142, 231, 293, 346, 366, xxxv, xxxvi, lvii, lxxiii, lxxxvii, xciii.
  Job, 329, lxxxiii.
  Col. John, 165, 311, xlii, lxxviii.
  John, 5, 9, 12, 62, 63, 116, 162, 197, 242, 261, 295, 296, 329, ii, iii, xvi, xxx, xli, l, lx, lxv, lxxiii, lxxiv, lxxxiii.
  John B., 65, xii.
  Jonathan, 106, xxvii.
  Joseph, 61, xvi.
  Mark, 63, xvi.
  Paul, 4, 5, 8, 11, 61, 106, 236, 237, i, ii, iii, xvi, xxvii, lix.
  Richard, 61, 70, xvi, xviii.
  Capt. Samuel, 313, 347, 365, 378, lxxix, lxxxvii, xciii, xcvii.
  Samuel, 6, 62, 115, 116, 411, ii, xvi, xxx.
  Thomas, 62, xvi.
  William, 115, 122, 154, 193, 242, xxx, xxxi, xxxix, xlix, lx.
  Elder William, 1, 2, 10, 25, 41, 44, 46, 49, 53, 54, 62, 65, 67, 68, 74, 75, 114, 141, 331, 343, 349, 357, 362, 363, 373, 411, i, iii, vii, xi, xii, xiii, xiv, xvi, xvii, xix, xxix, xxxvi, lxxv, lxxxvi, lxxxviii, xci, xcii, xcvi.
Wesley, Philip, 354, xc.
West, Edward, 240, lx.
  John, 240, lx.
Westbrook, Elizabeth, 228, lviii.
  Thomas, 228, lviii.
Weymouth, Benjamin, 195, xlix.
  Edward, 173, xliv.
  Samuel, 63, xvi.
Wheeler, Dr. James H., 324, lxxxi.
  John B., 103, xxvi.
  John, 9, 160, iii, xl.
  John H., 101, 293, xxvi, lxxiii.
  Mrs. John H., 231, lvii.
Wheelwright, Rev. Mr., 75, 181, 186, xix, xlv, xlvii.
Wiggin (or Wiggan or Wiggins), Andrew, 164, 365, 409, xli, xciii.

Wiggin, Benjamin, 9, 10, 14, 288, iii, iv, lxxii.
  Chase, 179, xlv.
  John H., 10, 70, iii, xviii.
  Nathaniel, 7, 10, 14, ii, iii, iv.
  Thomas, 174, 176, 367, 409, 411, xliv, xciii.
  Capt. Thomas, 17, 19, 24, 26, 27, 39, 40, 41, 42, 46, 71, 76, 90, 123, 124. 187, 191, 200, 223, 348, 355, 357, 362, 364, 373, 384, 423, v, vi, vii, x, xi, xii, xviii, xix, xxiv, xxxi, xlvii, xlviii, l, lvi, lxxxvii, xc, xci, xcii, xcvi.
  William B., 7, 10, 111, 225, ii, iii, xxviii, lvii.
Wigglesworth, Dr. Samuel, 79, 106, xx, xxvii.
Wilcox, John, 257, lxiv.
Willand, Paul, 11, iii.
Willey, Benjamin, 63, xvi.
  Elizabeth, 260, 262, 279, lxv, lxxxix.
  Frances, 260, lxv.
  Hannah, 316, lxxix.
  John, 59, 81, 157, 195, 254, 276, xv, xxi, xl, xlix, lxiii, lxix.
  Judy, 279, lxix.
  Margaret, 373, xcvi.
  Robert, 63, xvi.
  Samuel, 141, xxxvi.
  Stephen, 141, 377, xxxvi, xcvi.
  Thomas, 58, 59, 63, 75, 116, 140, 145, 162, 349, 352, 354, 356, 357, 363, 373, 376, xv, xvi, xix, xxx, xxxvi, xxxvii, xli, lxxxviii, xc, xci, xcii, xcvi, xcvii.
Willoughby, Governor, 226, lvii.
Williams, Francis, 29, 32, 364, viii, xcii.
  Henry, 80, xxi.
  John, 9, 14, 59, 77, 80, 101, 155, 197, 238, 356, 419, iii, iv, xv, xx, xxi, xxvi, xxxix, l, lix, xc.
  Jonathan, 77, xx.
  Matthew, 58, 144, 356, 357, 363, xv, xxxvi, xc, xci, xcii.
  William, 38, 59, 69, 76, 77, 80, 88, 94, 114, 138, 141, 144, 174, 338, 341, 343, 344, 357, 363, 370, 372, 377, x, xv, xviii, xix, xx, xxi, xxiii, xxv, xxix, xxxv, xxxvi, xliv, lxxxv, lxxxvi, xci, xcii, xcv, xcvii.
Wilson, Ann, 178, xlv.
  David, 10, iii.
  Elizabeth, 264, lxvi.
  Humphrey, 187, xlvii.
  Rev. John, 285, lxxi.
  Sally, 396.
Windiet, John, 142, 219, xxxvi, lv.
Wingate, Aaron, 11, iii.
  Hannah, 308, lxxvii.

Wingate, Joshua, 6, 9, 12, 329, ii, iii, lxxxiii.
  Col. Joshua, 331, lxxxiii.
  John, 3, 5, 6, 8, 11, 123, 132, 133, 137, 138, 139, 142, 152, 153, 195, 218, 343, 408, i, ii, iii, xxxi, xxxiv, xxxv, xxxvi, xxxviii, xxxix, xlix, lv, lxxxvi.
  Moses, 6, 9, 345, ii, iii, lxxxvi.
  Oliver, 375, xcvi.
  Sarah, 325, lxxxii.
  Susan, 407.
Winn, Polly, 232, lviii.
  Timothy, 233, lviii.
Winnington, Sir Francis, 215, liv.
Winslow, Lorana, 264, lxvi.
  Mr., 40, 350, x, lxxxviii.
  Ruth, 264, lxvi.
Winkley, Abby D., 308, lxxvii.
  Abby V., 308, lxxvii.
  Abial, 308, lxxvii.
  Alonzo, 308, lxxvii.
  Ann, 308, lxxvii.
  Asa, 308, lxxvii.
  Benjamin, 308, lxxvii.
  Benjamin F., 308, lxxvii.
  Clarissa, 308, lxxvii.
  Charlotte, 308, lxxvii.
  Cynthia K., 308, lxxvii.
  Daniel, 308, lxxvii.
  Daniel S., 308, lxxvii.
  Darius, 308, lxxvii.
  Col. David, 308, lxxvii.
  David B., 308, lxxvii.
  Dennis, 308, lxxvii.
  Dorcas, 307, lxxvii.
  Dorothy, 307, lxxvii.
  Eben P., 308, lxxvii.
  Elizabeth, 305, 307, lxxvii.
  Emerson, 307, lxxvii.
  Enoch, 308, lxxvii.
  Esther, 307, 308, lxxvii.
  Francis, 307, 308, lxxvii.
  Francis J., 308, lxxvii.
  George, 307, lxxvii.
  Henry, 307, lxxvii.
  James, 308, lxxvii.
  Jefferson, 308, lxxvii.
  Jeremiah, 308, lxxvii.
  Joanna, 308, lxxvii.
  Job Otis, 307, lxxvii.
  John, 307, lxxvi.
  Dea. John, 308, lxxvii.
  John F., 308, lxxvii.

Winkley, John Hunking, 307, lxxvii.
   Joseph, 307, lxxvi, lxxvii.
   Martha, 307, 308, lxxvi, lxxvii.
   Martha M., 308, lxxvii.
   Mary, 307, lxxvi.
   Mary G., 307, lxxvii.
   Mary S., 308, lxxvii.
   Mark Hunking, 308, lxxvii.
   Mehitable, 307, lxxvii.
   Nicholas, 305, 306, lxxvi.
   Otis, 308, lxxvii.
   Paul, 308, lxxvii.
   Paul T., 307, lxxvii.
   Samuel, Esq., 305, 306, lxxvi, lxxvii.
   Sarah, 307, lxxvii.
   Sarah L., 307, lxxvii.
   Sarah M., 307, lxxvii.
   Thomas, 305, lxxvi.
   Viola, 307, lxxvii.
   William, 305, 306, lxxvi, lxxvii.
   William P., 308, lxxvii.
Winthrop, Dudley, 178, xlv.
   Jane, 178, xlv.
   Gov. John, 385, 424.
   John, 178, 180, 191, 259, xlv, xlviii, lxiv.
   Joseph, 178, xlv.
   Mary, 178, xlv.
Wise, Mr., 184, xlvi.
   Nathaniel, 355, xc.
Wistill, John V., 350, lxxxviii.
Wiswall, Capt., 272, lxviii.
Witham, William, 127, xxxii.
Whidden, Michael, 103, 228, xxvi, lvii.
   Samuel, 409.
Whipple, B. F., 308, lxxvii.
Whitcomb, Eliza, 308, lxxvii.
White, Amos, Esq., 287, 320, 420, lxxi, lxxx.
   Hon. John Hubbard, 7, 9, 103, 112, 120, 321, ii, iii, xxvi, xxviii, xxxi, lxxxi.
   Nathaniel, 288, lxxii.
   Sarah, 279, lxix.
   Timothy, 320, 321, 323, lxxx, lxxxi.
   William, 299, lxxiv.
Whitehouse, Elizabeth, 93, xxv.
   George L., 14, iv.
   James, 101, xxvi.
   Pomfret, 164, xli.
   Richard, 252, lxiii.
   Thomas, 71, 72, 93, 142, 157, 194, xviii, xxv, xxxvi, xl, xlix.
Whittemore, William H., 358, xci.

Whiting, Mr., 192, xlviii.
   William, 17, 366, v, xciii.
Wright, Thomas, 14, iv.
Wonolanset, Indian Chief, 211, 222, liii, lvi.
Wood, John, 5, 11, ii, iii.
Woodbridge, Abra, 316, lxxix.
Woodbury, Mary, 261, lxv.
   Nathaniel, 285, lxxi.
Woodman, Capt. John, 3, 8, 10, 58, 67, 70, 75, 94, 96, 122, 132, 137, 139, 141, 142, 149, 152, 153, 155, 159, 193, 219, 277, 338, 356, 357, 363, 371, 374, 378, i, ii, iii, xv, xvii, xviii, xix, xxv, xxxi, xxxiv, xxxv, xxxvi, xxxviii, xxxix, xl, xlix, lv, lxix, lxxxv, xc, xci, xcii, xcv, xcvi, xcvii.
   Charles, 10, 14, iii, iv.
   Jonathan, 4, 79, 156, 160, i, xx, xxxix, xl.
   Nathan, 277, lxix.
Woodward, Eunice, 396.
Wooster, Mr., 395.
Wyatt, Samuel, 14, iv.
Wyer, Eleazer, 62, xvi.
Wyllys, Mr., 192, xlviii.
Wyman, Zebuhick, 192, xlviii.

Yeaton, Philip, 61, xvi.
York, Benjamin, 40, 383, xxxvi.
   Elizabeth, 374, xcvi.
   John, 116, 140, xxx, xxxvi.
   Richard, 53, 58, 69, 114, 190, 343, 349, 352, 353, 356, 357, 363, 374, xiv, xv, xviii, xxix, xlviii, lxxxvi, lxxxviii, xc, xci, xcii, xcvi.
   Samuel, 263, lxv.
Young, Betty, 101, xxvi.
   Edward L., 318, lxxx.
   Esther S., 318, lxxx.
   Hannah, 136, xxxiv.
   Isaac, 2, 11, 291, i, iii, lxxii.
   James, 5, 6, 11, 63, ii, iii, xvi.
   Hon. Jacob D., 317, lxxx.
   John, 136, xxxiv.
   Rev. J. K., 90, xxiv.
   Jonathan, 288, lxxii.
   Lewis H., 317, lxxx.
   Lilian L., 318, lxxx.
   Mary V., 308, lxxvii.
   Nathanel, 9, iii.
   Roland, 279, lxix.
   Solomon, 319, lxxx.
   Thomas, 12, 142, 198, 330, iii, xxxvi, l, lxxxiii.

INDEX OF PLACES.

INDEX OF PLACES.

Agamenticus, 26, vii.
Alden House, 112, xxviii.
American House, 109, 110, xxviii.
Atkinson House, 113, xxix.

Bay Colony, 26, vii.
Beck's Slip, at Dover Neck, 238, lix.
Boston, Mass., 24, 29, 30, 32, vi, viii.
Bunhill Fields, Eng., 335, lxxxiv.
Burial Ground of Major Richard Walderne, 225, lvii.
Bloody Point, Newington, 24, 55, 56, 300, vi, xiv, xxvi.
Black Point, 212, liv.
Blind Will's Neck, 214, liv.
Breakfast Hill, 279, lxix.
Bristol, England, 16, 17, iv.
Broken Wharf, 30, viii.

Calves' Pasture on Dover Neck, 344, 365, lxxxvi, xciii.
Cambridge, Eng., 30, viii.
Campron River, 34, ix.
Cape Cod, 16, iv.
Carkwell, Eng., 30, viii.
Cocheco, at Dover, in 1780, 23, 24, 98, vi, xxvi.
Cockermouth, Eng., 31, viii.
Coffin field, Division of, 288, lxxii.
Coffin House, 112, xxviii.
Cripple Gate, Eng., 335, lxxxiv.

Digby, Nova Scotia, 235, lviii.
Dorchester, Mass., 16, vi.
Dover Garrisons, 219, lv.
Dover Hotel, 104, 112, xxvii, xxix.
Dover Neck, 18, 22, 24, 39, v, vi, x.
Dover Point, 17, 18, 23, 176, v, vi, xliv.
Dover Village, "Cocheco," in 1780, 98, xxvi.
Dover, when first so named, 385.
Durham, 25, vii.
Durham Point, 76, xix.
Durell House, 113, xxix.
Drew Garrison, 113, xxix.
Drew House, 113, xxix.

Ela's Tavern, 108, xxvii.
Evans House (Col. Stephen), 113, xxix.
Exeter, 16, 21, 28, iv, vi, vii.

First Church in Dover, 19, 72, v, xix.
First Meeting-house at Dover Neck, 41, 73, xi, xix.
Freeman House, 112, xxix.

Garrisons at Cocheco in Dover in 1689, 242, lx.
Garrison Hill, 74, xix.
Great Bay, 33, 40, 55, ix, x, xiv.
Great St. Helens, Eng., 30, viii.

Great Tower Hill, Eng., 30, viii.
Green House, Dr. Ezra's, 112, xxviii.
Guppy House, 113, xxix.

Ham House, 113, xxix.
Hampton Church, 19, 24, 29, v, vi, viii.
Hathaway House, 130, xxxix.
Historic Houses in Dover, 1898, 112, xxviii.
Hogsty Cove, Great Bay, 56, xiv.
Huntington, Long Island, N. Y., 24, vi.
Indigo Hill, 25, vii.

Ipswich, Mass., 32, viii.
Isles of Shoals, 36, 385, ix.
Island Falls, 401.

Kennebunk, 212, liv.
Kittery, 45, xii.
Kittredge House, 98, xxvi.

Lamprill River, 41, 50, xi, xiv.
Lee, Parish, 25, 64, vii, xvi.
Little Harbor, 16, 19, v, vi.
Liquor Law, first in Dover, 37, x.
London, Eng., 28, vii.
Lynn, Mass., 31, viii.

Mason Hall, 6, iv.

Nantucket, 129, xxxiii.
Newichawannick, 45, 56, 357, xii, xiv, xciii.
Newington Parish, 60, 126, xv, xxxii.

New Plymouth, 16, iv.
Newton, Long Island, N. Y., 24, vi.
Northam, 17, 31, 56, 385, v, viii, xiv.
Ox Pasture at Dover Neck, 41, 66, 336, xi, xvii, lxxxiv.
Oyster River, 25, 39, 53, 56, 57, 76, 81, 85, 273, 365, vii, x, xiv, xv, xix, xxi, xxii, lxviii, xciii.
Oyster River, first settlement of, 392.
Oyster River People, petitions to General Court, 57, 58, xv.
Packer's Falls, 78, xx.
Palmer House, 112, xxviii.
Pascataqua, to what the name is applied, 24, 32, vi, viii.
Pendexter House, 112, xxix.
Pine Hill Cemetery, 100, xxvii.
Pine Hill Schoolhouse, 100, xxvii.
Portsmouth, 22, vi.
Plymouth, Mass., 16, 116, iv, xxx.
Prices of commodities before 1700, 140, 151, 337, xxxv, xxxviii, lxxxv.

Quamphegan, 25, 41, vii, xi.

Reyner, Rev. John's house, 117, xxx.
Rocky Point, 54, xiv.
Rollinsford, 25, 64, vii, xvi.
Salem, 25, 29, 32, vii, viii.

Salmon Falls, Village, Indian battle, 270, lxvii.
Sandwich, 24, vi.
Sandy Point, or Beach, 66, xvii.
Sham fight with Indians at Cocheco in Dover, 1675, 208, v.
Swamscott, 21, vi.
Strawberry Bank, 21, 29, 33, 55, 56, vi, viii, ix, xiv.
St. Alban's Cove, 25, 162, vii, xli.
St. Mary Axe, 30, viii.
Spencer's Garrison, 271, lxviii.
Streets at Dover Neck, in the 17th Century, 163, xli.
Site of Parson Reyner's House on Dover Neck, 117, xxx.
Sligo, 25, vii.
Sligo Garrison, 163, xli.
Somersetshire, Eng., 24, vi.
Somersworth Parish, 25, 61, 62, viii, xvi.

Tannery at Dover Neck, 163, xli.
Tavistock, Eng., 31, viii,

Wadleigh's Falls, 400.
Warwickshire, Eng., 23, vi.
Wecannacohunt, 17, v.
Wecohamet, 17, v.

Yarmouth, Eng., 25, vii.

MISCELLANEOUS.

MISCELLANEOUS.

Agreement between Dover [Neck and Oyster River, 49, xiii.
Agreement between Dover and Exeter, 64, xv.
Alewives, law for catching and disposing of, 33, ix.
Ancestors of Major Richard Walderne, 221, lvi.
Arms and supplies at Newichawannock in 1634, 369, xcv.

Boston News-Letter, extracts from, 386.
Bell for the meeting-house at Dover Neck, 51, xiii.
Bell tower for meeting-house at Dover Neck, 69, xviii.
Brewery at Dover Neck, 147, 163, xxxvii, xli.
Bridges in Dover, 161, 196, 413, xli, xlix.
Boundaries of Dover, 40, 54, 60, 266, x, xiv, xv, xxxii.
Bounty for wolves, 71, xviii.
Biographical sketches, Aunt Nabby Belknap, 420.
    Mr. Thomas Broughton, 360, xci.
    Blind Will, Indian Chief, 213, lii.
    Hon. Peter Coffin, 280, lxx.
    Admiral Sir Isaac Coffin, 289, lxxii.
    Aunt Deborah Coffin, 289, lxxii.
    Canonicus, Indian Chief, 211, 359, liii, xci.
    Rev. Jonathan Cushing, 296, lxxiv.
    Col. James Davis, 303, lxxvi.
    Col. Stephen Evans, 293, lxxiii.
    Capt. Samuel Gerrish, 312, lxxviii.
    Sarah Gerrish, 312, lxxviii.
    Ambrose Gibbons, 370, xcv.
    John Goddard, 371, xcv.
    Mr. Edward Hilton, 176, xliv.
    Mr. William Hilton, 176, xliv.
    Col. Winthrop Hilton, 178, xlv.
    Howard Henderson, 165, xlii.
    Hon. John Langdon.
    Rev. Daniel Maud, 386.
    Capt. Thomas Millett, 309, lxxviii.
    Mr. Thomas Millett, 164, xli.
    Rev. John Pike, 183, xlv.

Mr. William Pomfrett, 164, xli.
Philip of Pokanoket, Indian Chief, 206, lii.
Rev. John Reyner, Sr., 358, xci.
Rev. John Reyner, Jr., 143, 359, xxxvi, xci.
Capt. John Underhill, 180, xlv.
Major Richard Walderne, 199, l.
Col. John Waldron, 232, lviii.
Capt. Thomas Wiggin, 163, xli.
Hon. Amos White, 321, lxxx.
Mr. Timothy White, 323, lxxx.
Mark Walker, 318, lxxx.

Canal at Newmarket, the first proposed in New England, 389.
Characteristics of the Combination of 1640, 20, v.
Coffin Lands, location of, 287, lxxi.
Combination of 1640, 17, 19, v.
Commission of Capt. Peter Coffin, 291, lxxii.
County Court of Dover and Portsmouth, 67, xvii.
County of old Norfolk, Mass., 202, li.
Court Records, 37, x.
Church Records, by Rev. Jeremy Belknap, 29, viii.
Cocheco River and Falls, 412.
Cocheco Mill Privilege, 415.
Church at Oyster River, 388.

Dates of Events in Dover History, 383.
Deeds to or from Dover men, taken from the registry at Exeter, 375, 408, xcvi.
Dover and its Boundaries, 54, 63, xiv, xvi.
Dover in the Revolution, 327, lxxxii.
Drum, when used to call the people to meeting on the Sabbath, 35, ix.

Early Ministers of Dover, 25, vi.
Early Settlements in Dover, 16, 90, vi, xxiv.
Expedition Against the Indians in Maine, 212, liv.

Fight between Capt. Wiggin and Governor Barefoot, 124, xxxi.
Fines for not attending church, 34, 174, x, xliv.

Fines for not attending town-meeting, 141, xxxvi.
First Parish in Dover, 19, v.
First Church in Boston, 386.
First Rulers in Dover, 19, v.
First Liquor Law in New Hampshire, 37, x.
First Settlement at Oyster River, 392.
First Minister at Oyster River, 56, xiv.
Fox Point attacked by the Indians, 272, lxviii.

Great St. Helens, Eng., 30, viii.
Great Tower Hill, Eng., 30, viii.

Indian Battle at Wheelwright's pond, in Lee, 273, lxviii.
Indian Wars, 205, 208, 269, 271, lii, lxviii.

Land Grants in Dover, 350, lxxxviii.

Meeting House at Oyster River, 392.
Meeting House at Dover Neck, 24, 51, vi, xiii.
Minister's House at Oyster River, 338, lxxxv.
Madbury, 24, 25, 64, vi, vii, xvi.
Map of Dover, down to 1713, 65, xvii.
Mason's lawsuits with the early settlers, 219, lv.
Massacre at Cochecho in June, 1689, 242, lx.
Massacre at Oyster River in 1694, 273, lxviii.
Massacre at Salmon Falls, 270, lxvii.
Moderators in Dover town-meetings, 10, iii.

Newspapers of Dover, 101, xxvi.
Natick Indians, 212, liv.
New Government, 1679, for New Hampshire, 216, lv.
Narraganset Indians, 212, liv.
News from Boston papers, 386, 388, 391, 392, 395, 398.

Orders given to the deputy by town-meeting for guiding him in the Massachusetts General Court, 52, 72, 96, 144, xiii, xviii, xxvi, xxxvii.
Orthography of the name Cocheco, 108, xxvii.
Odiorne's' Point, 16, iv.
Order for holding courts for Dover and Portsmouth, 364, xcii.
Organization of church at Oyster River, 393.

Penobscot, 16, iv.
"Pide Cow," Ambrose Gibbon's ship, 369, xcv.
Pequot War, 19, v.
Penobscot Indians, 211, liii.
Penacook Indians, 211, liii.

Pascataqua River, 21, vi.
Pew in First Parish church, belonging to Col. Stephen Evans, 295, lxxiii.
Prudential Men, their service, 55, xiv.
Petition, in 1695, to the General Court asking to have Oyster River made a separate town from Dover, 57, 58, xv.
Puritans, 28, 68, vii, xvii.

Reade (Michael) house, 113, xxix.
Representatives (list of), from 1650 to 1854, 8, ii.
Roads in Dover; from Bloody Point to Hampton, 116, xxx.
Roads in Dover; from Fresh Creek to Quamphegan, 163, iv.

Salary of Ministers at Dover Neck, 53, xiv.
Salem, 25, 29, 32, vii, viii.
Salt Works in Dover, 17, v.
Sawmills in Dover, 34, 200, ix, l.
Selectmen of Dover, list of, from 1650 to 1854.
Site of Parson Raynor's house at Dover Neck.
Sligo, 25, vii.
Sligo Garrison, 163, xli.
Stocks for Punishing Offenders at Dover Neck, 38, x.
Schoolmasters at Dover Neck, 42, 49, 50, 144, 338, xi, xiii, xxxvi, lxxxv.
Streets on Dover Neck in the Seventeenth Century, 163, xli.
St. John's M. E. church, 111, xxviii.

Town Records, 31, 33, 39, 41, 45, 50, 53, 65, 69, 75, 94, 114, 120, 131, 140, 141, 145, 151, 156, 160, 195, 198, 235, 253, 267, 336, 339, 345, 349, 355, 363, viii, ix, x, xi, xii, xiii, xiv, xvii, xviii, xix, xxv, xxix, xxxi, xxxiii, xxxv, xxxvi, xxxvii, xxxviii, xxxix, xl, xlix, l, lix, lxiii, lxvi, lxxxiv, lxxxv, lxxxvii, lxxxviii, xc, xcii.
Town clerks of Dover from 1650 to 1864, 2, ii.
Taxpayers in Dover in 1648, 351, lxxxviii.
 in 1650, 349, lxxxviii.
 in 1657, 355, xc.
 in 1659, 354, xc.
 in 1675, 140, xxxvi.
Trials of Mason's land claims, 218, lv.

Union of Dover with Massachusetts, 18, v.
Unitarians, 28, vii.

Weirsmen, 33, ix.
Whipping post at Dover Neck, 33, 163, ix, xli.
Will of Benjamin Twombly, 315, lxxix.

Will of Rev. Daniel Maud, 43, xi.
    Rev. John Reyner, Sr., 118, xxx.
    Col. James Davis, 304, lxxvi.
    Ens. John Davis, Sr., 300, lxxv.
    William Twombly, 315, lxxix.
    John Twombly, 315, lxxix.
    Tristram Coffin, 290, lxxii.
    Richard Gerrish, 310, lxxxviii.
    Samuel Winkley, Esq., 305, lxxvi.
    Major Richard Walderne, 226, lxvii.

Will of Eliphalet Coffin, 285, lxxi.
    George Walton, 241, lx.
    Shadrach Walton, 242, lx.
    Thomas Westbrook Waldron, 406.
Wheelwright's Pond, battle with the Indians at, 273, lxviii.
Waldron Cemetery, 111, xxviii.
    Garrison, 111, xxviii.
    Mansion, 110, 113, xxviii, xxix.
    Mills, 225, lvii.

www.ingramcontent.com/pod-product-compliance
Lightning Source LLC
Chambersburg PA
CBHW050132240426
43673CB00043B/1644